Contemporary

Issues in

Edited

a

HOUGHTON MIFFLIN COMPAN

Cost Accounting

A Discipline in Transition

Second Edition

HECTOR R. ANTON, *University of California*

PETER A. FIRMIN, *Tulane University*

BOSTON *New York · Atlanta · Geneva, Ill. · Dallas · Palo Alto*

To our wives — still

LOIS AND JEAN,

respectively

Preface to the Second Edition

The theme of the first edition of this book — that cost accounting is a "discipline in transition" — proves to have been well founded. The second edition rests solidly on the first. Cost and managerial accounting continue to be in transition, a state which, in itself, implies a base. The preface to the first edition is still relevant and, for that reason, is retained. Many articles are retained. Many others, which, in timely fashion, served their purpose, have been dropped. Twelve new articles have been added.

In the last half-dozen years, three major trends have accelerated: (1) mathematical analysis and its use in management problems, (2) the application of behavioral science to cost and managerial accounting, and (3) the extension of cost analysis techniques to governmental and not-for-profit organizations.

All three trends permeate the current literature. The American Accounting Association is offering intensive seminars for faculty members in both quantitative methods and behavioral science applications to accounting. Planned Programming Budgeting (PPB) and other cost and management procedures are being extended — from the Department of Defense to the entire federal government. Also, these procedures have been incorporated in, for instance, hospitals, transit systems, and state regulatory agencies. Although not a panacea, they add immensely to more efficient planning and control.

It is difficult today to isolate innovative articles. For that reason, the first edition's part on *Challenges to Future Cost Accounting* has been discontinued. Instead, articles which might embody such a part are to be found under more substantive headings. Examples of these are Onsi's "A Transfer Pricing System Based on Opportunity Cost," Livingstone's "Input-Output Analysis for Cost Accounting, Planning and Control," the American Accounting Association's "Report of the Committee on Managerial Decision Models."

Overall, the part organization of the second edition is at one with the newer thinking about approaches to cost and managerial accounting. Part

One, *Cost and Managerial Accounting: A Perspective,* takes a broad view of the several conceptual and research fields. It offers articles dealing with basis concepts, decision models, behavioral implications, empirical approaches, and planned programming budgeting. These articles enable the reader to obtain an insight into practical as well as theoretical problems; simultaneously they set the stage for many of the succeeding articles. Parts Two through Seven are grouped into two major areas — *Cost Planning, Decision, and Control* and *Motivation, Performance, and Evaluation.* The first area includes *Forecasting and Budgeting, Capital Budgeting,* and *Cost-Volume-Profit Analysis;* the second, *Standards and Variance Analysis, Responsibility Accounting and Direct Costing,* and *Decentralization, Internal Transfer Pricing,* and *Cost Allocation.* These categories afford a continuity with the first edition and, at the same time, a congruence with the new cost accounting texts' order of presentation.

The editors again offer their appreciation to the authors of the various articles, and to the publishers whose kind permission to reprint have made the book possible. Many professors including J. H. Brasseaux of Louisiana State University, New Orleans, D. T. de Coster of the University of Washington, Nicholas Dopuch of the University of Chicago, William Ferrara of Pennsylvania State University, Yuji Ijiri of Carnegie-Mellon University, and Gordon Shillinglaw of Columbia University have provided valuable "feedback" on the first edition. A special note of appreciation is due to Miss Joanne Sterbenz, a student at Tulane University, who read the entire first edition and much of the recent literature and offered valuable insight from the student point of view. Tulane students David R. Meek and Timothy C. Ackley also participated in that process. Mrs. Geri Barnes assisted with the assembling of the manuscript. Once again, of course, the editors of this volume assume sole responsibility for any oversights or errors in the book.

Hector R. Anton

UNIVERSITY OF CALIFORNIA, BERKELEY

Peter A. Firmin

TULANE UNIVERSITY

Preface to the First Edition

Accounting's purpose is to communicate information about economic events — past, present, and future — to persons who will use the information to plan and control activities, and to choose among alternative courses of action.

Cost accounting is especially capable of serving this purpose, for the scope of its concepts and methodology does not *need* to be fettered by the superstructure of "generally accepted" accounting principles, customs, and traditions that constrain financial accounting.

The first part of this century witnessed the development of such important cost accounting concepts as job and process costing, overhead allocation, cost-volume-profit analysis, standard costs, and variance analysis. Cost information, although developed within structures oriented to the needs of financial accounting, was nonetheless an important tool for analysis. Yet, for many years cost accounting literature seemed to emphasize the procedural aspects of generating cost data, and the discussion was concerned with the relationship of cost data to financial accounting information. Rarely was the *full* potential of cost information for analytical purposes explored.

Two factors may account for this phenomenon. Conditioned by the financial accounting model, concepts of cost which were inconsistent with "generally accepted accounting principles" did not readily reach maturity. More importantly, cost accounting analysis made only infrequent use of operational mathematical tools. As a result, cost analyses were relatively unsophisticated, and cost behavior models often were gross oversimplifications of reality.

In recent years, significant and near-revolutionary changes have taken place in the field of cost accounting. Cost accountants have become aware of the potential generality of cost data and of its validity in a multitude of managerial contexts. "Managerial accounting" and "cost accounting" have become synonyms, and are so used here. Even institutional professional organizations have explicitly recognized this phenomenon. In 1958, the

National Association of Cost Accountants became the National Association of Accountants, and in 1965, the Institute of Cost and Works Accountants (United Kingdom) changed the name of its journal from *The Cost Accountant* to *Management Accounting.*

Even more significantly, managerial accountants have become aware of the power of mathematical analysis and of its applicability to many of management's accounting problems.

In most professional disciplines, acceptance of new concepts and tools comes at a tortuously slow pace. New concepts and tools must be tested and proven. Especially in a practical discipline like managerial accounting, usefulness and payoff must be demonstrated. In addition, many shun the tedious learning process which is involved.

This book, then, is a reflection of a discipline in transition. The material chosen for reproduction here has been selected exclusively from the periodical literature because the time lag between the generation of an idea and its publication usually is less in this medium than in others. Furthermore, important concepts discussed in the periodical literature often escape the student's attention.

Traditional as well as newer concepts and methods have been presented, and articles have been selected which mirror the spectrum of evolutionary changes currently taking place in the discipline. Thus the reader will find that this book is compatible with and complementary to both traditional and newer cost accounting textbooks. The sections on *Concepts and Methods of Cost Accounting* and *Controls in Cost Accounting* may be assigned along with basic reading in similar sections of any good text in fundamentals of cost accounting, either to complement or reinforce the text material. Advanced-level students in cost accounting, on the other hand, will find that many of the articles contain refreshing points of view and are noteworthy.

The sections in this book dealing with *Budgets and Forecasting* and *Capital Budgeting and Rate of Return* reflect newer ideas and concepts in managerial accounting. In these sections, the role of accounting in decision-making is emphasized. All of the concepts included are proven by application and are to be found in successful current usage. The controversial issues in capital budgeting and measurement of rate of return have been accorded special attention.

The last section in this book — *Challenges to Future Cost Accounting* — has been reserved for the untried and the experimental techniques and concepts. Here are the evidences of current research and the promise of the future. Particular emphasis has been given to the relationship between operations research and managerial accounting. Many have argued that "Operations Research" developed as a recognized discipline only because a vacuum existed which accountants should have filled, but did not. If managerial accounting rises to the challenge, these articles should excite the student's imagination and provide some insight into the future development of our discipline.

The editors would like to express appreciation to the authors and publishers whose kind permissions to reprint have made this book possible, to graduate students Il Sung Kang, Thomas Hannon, and Clyde Deaux for verifying citations and proofreading, and to Mrs. Pamela H. Jendrek, Mrs. William L. Nash, and Mrs. Charlotte A. Firmin for typing and assembling the manuscript. The editors assume sole responsibility for oversights and errors.

Hector R. Anton

UNIVERSITY OF CALIFORNIA, BERKELEY

Peter A. Firmin

TULANE UNIVERSITY

Contents

PART THREE

Cost Planning, Decision, and Control: Capital Budgeting 176

PART FOUR

Cost Planning, Decision, and Control: Cost-Volume-Profit Analysis 258

PART FIVE

Motivation, Performance, and Evaluation: Standards and Variance Analysis 346

PART SIX

Motivation, Performance, and Evaluation: Responsibility Accounting and Direct Costing   405

PART SEVEN

Motivation, Performance, and Evaluation: Decentralization, Internal Transfer Pricing, and Cost Allocation   458

Contributors

AMERICAN ACCOUNTING ASSOCIATION
COMMITTEE ON MANAGERIAL DECISION MODELS
MEMBERS: CHARLES T. HORNGREN, CHAIRMAN, *Stanford University*
HECTOR R. ANTON, *University of California*
HAROLD BIERMAN, JR., *Cornell University*
EUGENE H. BROOKS, JR., *University of North Carolina*
PETER A. FIRMIN, *Tulane University*
ELLSWORTH MORSE, JR., *U.S. General Accounting Office*
THOMAS H. WILLIAMS, *University of Texas*
ZENON ZANNETOS, *Massachusetts Institute of Technology*

GILBERT AMERMAN
East Orange, New Jersey

GEORGE J. BENSTON
University of Rochester

JACOB G. BIRNBERG
University of Pittsburgh

VICTOR H. BROWN
Touche Ross & Co., New York

ABRAHAM CHARNES
Northwestern University

W. W. COOPER
Carnegie-Mellon University

JOEL DEMSKI
Stanford University

CARL T. DEVINE
Florida State University

NICHOLAS DOPUCH
University of Chicago

JAMES L. GIBSON
University of Kentucky

HOWARD C. GREER
Formerly, Kingan & Company

DAVID B. HERTZ
McKinsey & Co., Inc. New York

CHARLES T. HORNGREN
Stanford University

YUJI IJIRI
Carnegie-Mellon University

V. BRUCE IRVINE
University of Saskatchewan

ROBERT K. JAEDICKE
Stanford University

EUGENE KACZKA
University of Massachusetts

MAURICE KILBRIDGE
Agency for International Development

ROBERT A. KNAPP
General Electric, Johnson City, New York

FERDINAND K. LEVY
Rice University

JOHN L. LIVINGSTONE
Ohio State University

CARL L. MOORE
Lehigh University

THOMAS A. MORRISON
University of Massachusetts

E. W. NETTEN
Price, Waterhouse & Co., Vancouver, B.C.

DAVID NOVICK
The RAND Corporation

xv

MOHAMED ONSI
Syracuse University

JOHN R. E. PARKER
Riddell, Stead, Graham & Hutchinson, Montreal

ALFRED RAPPAPORT
Northwestern University

JAMES H. RUSHTON
Eli Lilly and Company, Indianapolis

GORDON SHILLINGLAW
Columbia University

DAVID SOLOMONS
University of Pennsylvania

GERALD L. THOMPSON
Carnegie-Mellon University

DOUGLAS VICKERS
University of Pennsylvania

H. MARTIN WEINGARTNER
University of Rochester

JEROME D. WIEST
Rice University

JAMES D. WILLSON
Tidewater Oil Co., Los Angeles

STEPHEN A. ZEFF
Tulane University

PART ONE

Cost and Managerial Accounting:

A Perspective

C ost accounting, like accounting in general, is a dynamic, evolving discipline. Although cost accounting deals to a considerable extent with the accumulation and allocation of factory costs and product for inventory valuation and income determination, it encompasses many other areas. These areas include cost control, pricing, internal pricing, budgeting, and various decision-oriented problem areas. Traditionally, cost accounting has been at the nexus of accounting and engineering, and it continues to be so as both fields expand into operations research and other types of operational analyses. Part One gives us a broad perspective, from a variety of viewpoints — from the pragmatic-conceptual, analytical model-oriented, behavioral, empirical, and program budgeting viewpoints.

Horngren outlines the scope, content, and method of management accounting. Carefully and clearly, he delineates between financial accounting and accounting for "internal reporting for managers for planning, controlling current operations . . [and] for making special decisions and formulating long-range plans." He develops a clear understanding of objectives and an excellent pattern of informational requirements. While stressing management accounting, the Horngren article and others in this section are equally applicable to not-for-profit organizations. Indeed, cost and management accounting increasingly are being recognized as of great relevance to hospitals, governmental and other fiduciary organizations. Horngren also foresees many later developments — decision analysis, divisional reporting problems, and flexible organizational systems.

The interaction of various decision models with accounting and information systems is developed in the Report of the Committee on Managerial Decision Models of the American Accounting Association. Many of the concepts of advanced contemporary thought are concisely stated. The usefulness of operations research models within a managerial accounting framework is evaluated. The Committee attacks the problem of making relevant

1

the American Accounting Association's 1966 Statement to cost and managerial accounting. Finally, the reader is treated to an expression of "futuristic" thinking relative to analytical models and their impact on accounting thinking and relative to their influence on information requirements. Many of the articles in the book fit within the pattern developed by the Committee's report.

One of the major developments in accounting has been the long overdue recognition of the major impact of behavioral sciences on accounting. This impact has been reflected in extensive literature in the area of motivation and organizational behavior, and the concomitant influence between these. Benston gives a good survey of the literature, and additionally relates the concept of motivation to budgets and organizational structure. As one of the earlier articles on behavior and accounting, his is a useful introduction to the area.

An empirical study of the uses of accounting in the decision-making process is given by Gibson. This practical, yet scholarly, article delineates the factors which affect the role of accounting in decision-making and the factors which create diversity of practice. Couched in a small-firm framework — based on the experience of forty-four companies — the observations can be generalized even to large firms. Many of the factors considered — ability of the firm to react, availability of information about viable alternatives, and so forth — are important to any firm's budget process.

Part One is concluded by a look at planning and control through program budgeting. Program budgeting has been used extensively in long-run planning and resource allocation in the federal government and other large-scale organizations. It focuses on making explicit the organization's goals and on relating the organization's resources, programs, and activities to these. Cost-benefit analysis and other technical tools are used extensively. Novick's article clearly demonstrates the dimensions of program budgeting, without being overly-technical and narrow. He demonstrates that systems analysis through program budgeting is equally effective in profit-making businesses and in governments. This further reinforces the generality of the management decision-making process and the analytical activity surrounding estimated costs and expected benefits of alternative program decisions. Although not as fashionable as it used to be in the Department of Defense, program budgeting is used increasingly in universities, state and federal governmental agencies, and business enterprises.

1   *The scope and content of financial accounting is well known. In this article the author defines the scope of managerial accounting and contrasts it with financial accounting. The objectives of management accounting and the types of information requirements are clearly outlined.*

The main purposes are given as routine reporting of financial data or "score-keeping"; routine reporting to management for planning and control or "attention-directing"; and special reporting to management for non-recurring decisions or "problem-solving." Any guide to management accounting must pay major attention to relevancy of information and its timeliness. Accuracy, while important, may be non-relevant. Future accounting information systems' needs are clearly outlined including structuring, cost-behavior rules, and responsibility accounting.

Choosing Accounting Practices for Reporting to Management*

Charles T. Horngren†

Objectives of Management Accounting

MANAGEMENT ACCOUNTING — ITS DISTINCTIVE PURPOSES

The accounting system is the major formal information system in almost every organization. An effective accounting system provides information for three broad purposes: (1) external reporting to stockholders, government,

* From NAA Bulletin, *Vol. XLIV, No. 1 (September, 1962), pp. 3–15. Reprinted by permission of the publisher.*

† I am indebted to the members of the Workshop in Accounting Research, Institute of Professional Accountancy, Graduate School of Business, University of Chicago — especially Professors Sidney Davidson, David Green, Jr., Richard Lindhe, and George H. Sorter — for constructive criticism.

and other outside parties, (2) internal reporting to managers for planning and controlling current operations, and (3) internal reporting to managers for making special decisions and formulating long-range plans.

Management (internal parties) and external parties share an interest in all three important purposes, but the emphasis of financial accounting and management accounting differs. Financial accounting has been mainly concerned with the first purpose and has traditionally been oriented toward the historical, stewardship aspects of external reporting. The distinguishing feature of management accounting is its emphasis on the second and third purposes.

The job of serving both internal and external demands can be an imposing one. Conventional accounting systems have tended to grow primarily in response to external forces. Management accounting, on the other hand, attempts to implement a more balanced, multi-goaled perspective. The widespread problem that management accountants must face has been aptly described as follows:

> Very few people in business have had the opportunity to reflect on the way in which the accounting model developed, particularly on how an instrument well adapted to detect fraud and measure tax liability has gradually been used as a general information source. Having become accustomed to information presented in this form, business people have adapted their concepts and patterns of thought and communication to it rather than adapting the information to the job or person. When one suggests the reverse process, as now seems not only logical but well within economic limits, he must expect a real reluctance to abandon a pattern of behavior that has a long history of working apparently quite well.[1]

A management accounting planning and control system should be designed to spur and help executives in searching for and selecting short-run and long-run goals, formulating plans for attaining those goals, implementing plans, appraising performance and pin-pointing deviations from plans, investigating reasons for deviations, reselecting goals, etc. Management accounting is concerned with accumulating, classifying, and interpreting costs and other information that induce and aid individual executives in fulfilling organizational objectives as revealed explicitly or implicitly by top management.

TYPES OF INFORMATION SUPPLIED BY MANAGEMENT ACCOUNTING

What information should the management accountant supply? The types of information needed have been neatly described by Simon *et al.* as a result

---

[1] William R. Fair, "The Next Step in Management Controls," in Donald G. Malcom and Alan J. Rowe, (ed.), *Management Control Systems* (New York: John Wiley & Sons, Inc., 1960), pp. 229–230.

of their study of seven large companies with geographically dispersed operations. The approach of the Simon research team would probably be fruitful in any company:

> By observation of the actual decision-making process, specific types of data needs were identified at particular organizational levels — the vice presidential level, the level of the factory manager, and the level of the factory head, for example — each involving quite distinct problems of communication for the accounting department.[2]

The research team found that three types of information, each serving a different purpose, often at various management levels, raise and help answer three basic questions:

1. Score-card questions: "Am I doing well or badly?"
2. Attention-directing questions: "What problems should I look into?"
3. Problem-solving questions: "Of the several ways of doing the job, which is the best?"

Score-card and attention-directing uses of data are closely related. The same data may serve a score-card function for a foreman and an attention-directing function for his superior. For example, many accounting systems provide performance reports through which actual results are compared to predetermined budgets or standards. Such a performance report often helps answer score-card questions and attention-directing questions simultaneously. Furthermore, the "actual results" collected can help fulfill not only control purposes but also the traditional needs of financial accounting. The answering of score-card questions, which mainly involves collection, classification, and reporting, is the task that has predominated in the day-to-day effort of the accounting function.

Problem-solving data may be used to help in special nonrecurring decisions and long-range planning. Examples include make-or-buy, equipment replacement, adding or dropping products, etc. These decisions often require expert advice from specialists such as industrial engineers, budgetary accountants, statisticians, and others.

MANAGEMENT ACCOUNTING AND THE OVERALL INFORMATION SYSTEM

These three uses of data may be related to the broad purposes of the accounting system. The business information system of the future should be a single, multi-purpose system with a highly-selective reporting scheme. It will

---

[2] H. A. Simon, *Administrative Behavior* (2nd ed.; New York: The Macmillan Company, 1957), p. 20. For the complete study see H. A. Simon, H. Guetzkow, G. Kozmetsky, and G. Tyndall, *Centralization vs. Decentralization in Organizing the Controller's Department* (New York: Controllership Foundation, Inc. 1954). This perceptive study is much broader than its title implies.

be tightly integrated and will serve three main purposes: (1) routine reporting on financial results, oriented primarily for external parties (score-keeping); (2) routine reporting to management, primarily for planning and controlling current operations (score-keeping and attention-directing); and (3) special reporting to management, primarily for long-range planning and nonrecurring decisions (problem-solving). Although such a system can probably be designed in a self-contained, integrated manner to serve routine purposes simultaneously, its special decision function will always entail much data that will not lie within the system.

USES OF DATA AND ORGANIZATION OF THE ACCOUNTANT'S WORK

The Simon study also emphasized that ideally the management accountant's staff should have its three distinct functions manned by full-time accountants: (1) score-keepers, who compile routine data and keep the information system running smoothly; (2) attention-directors, who attempt to understand operating management's viewpoint most fully and who spotlight, interpret, and explain those operating areas that are most in need of attention; and (3) problem-solvers, who search for alternatives, study the probable consequences, and help management follow an objective approach to special decisions.

If one accountant bears responsibility for more than one of these three functions, his energies are prone to be directed to (1), then to (2), and finally to (3). If this occurs, his two foremost values, as far as management is concerned, are likely to be dissipated.[3]

Guides to Selection of Management Accounting Practices

RELEVANT INFORMATION — THE BASIC NEED

The National Association of Accountants' Research Planning Committee has stated: "Guides are needed by the management accountant to aid him in selecting practices from among the many alternatives. These guides provide assurance that practices chosen will yield data *relevant to the recipient's purposes.*" [Emphasis supplied.] Any guide, therefore, must be concerned with the concept of relevancy, because the assembly and interpretation of relevant data is the management accountant's fundamental task.

Relevant data may be defined broadly as that data which will lead to an optimum decision. The distinction between *relevancy* and *accuracy* should be kept in mind. Ideally management accounting data should be relevant (valid, pertinent) and accurate (precise). However, figures can be precise but irrelevant, or imprecise but relevant. But relevancy is basic to manage-

---

[3] Simon, *et al.*, *op. cit.*, p. 5.

ment accounting. Although accuracy is always desirable and often extremely important, it is really a subobjective in any conceptual approach to gathering data for planning and control.

Some executives have implied that many accountants have a twisted orientation regarding accuracy and relevancy. That is, many accountants are preoccupied with accuracy and are little concerned with relevancy. This is a reflection of the product costing and income determination goal of industrial accounting that so often overrides other important goals. What may be accurate with respect to the product costing goal may be entirely irrelevant with respect to management decisions. For example, scrupulous determinations of bases for overhead allocation may yield seemingly "accurate" results for product costing purposes but may be wholly misleading for planning and control purposes. Reverence for accuracy, while admirable, may narrow the horizons and usefulness of the industrial accountant.

Now we shall examine the meaning of relevancy as it bears on the two broad purposes of management accounting.

OBJECTIVE OF PLANNING AND CONTROLLING OPERATIONS

THE KEY QUESTIONS

The directing of attention, the providing of clues, the raising of pertinent questions, the inducing of desired behavior — these are the principal tasks of accounting for planning and controlling operations. The accountant's role here includes score-keeping and attention-directing.

Some guides to management accounting practice in this area have been described profusely in the accounting literature. For example, it has become almost self-evident that appropriate budgets and standards have wide usefulness in the execution of the accountant's attention-directing function. Much of the literature on standard costs[4] gives the impression that they are always based on sound engineering studies and rigorous specifications. Although this approach is often useful, it should be stressed that less scientific standards provide a forceful way of presenting information in order to stimulate corrective action. An accounting system is effective when it automatically calls management's attention to the areas that most sorely need investigation. Accuracy of standards, while desirable, is not as basic to successful management accounting as the more fundamental notion — that of the relevancy of using some predetermined targets as a means of implementing management by exception.

Another example of an obvious guide is the frequent need to sacrifice precision for promptness in reporting. The need for timely data is so acute

[4] Consider the definition by the 1951 Committee on Cost Concepts, American Accounting Association, *The Accounting Review*, (April, 1952), p. 177, "Standard costs are *scientifically* predetermined costs." (Emphasis supplied.)

in many cases that it should be fulfilled promptly in a flash report, even if the wanted data ordinarily are only part of a more complete formal report. Thus, an effective management accounting system is designed to supply reports on a highly selective basis; relevancy often overrides accuracy in these score-keeping and attention-directing areas. That is, highly accurate but stale data are irrelevant, because they have no bearing on the decisions then facing the recipient.

This notion of relevancy provides the cornerstone in constructing guides for the purpose of planning and controlling current operations. The logical questions to be asked are:

1. What are the objectives of the organization as a whole?
2. Who are the executives who are expected to seek such objectives? What are their spheres of responsibility?
3. What data can be provided to help them toward making individual decisions that will harmonize with and spur them toward overall company objectives?

Assuming that the answers to question (1) are available,[5] we turn to the questions under (2).

TAILORING THE SYSTEM TO THE ORGANIZATION —
RESPONSIBILITY ACCOUNTING

Our initial guide is as follows: *Focus the basic design of the accounting system upon the responsibility centers of individual managers.* The accounting system must cohesively reflect the plans and actions of all responsibility centers in the organization — from the smallest to the biggest. This basic idea is being implemented on a wide scale in the form of so-called *responsibility accounting, profitability accounting,* or *activity accounting* systems.[6]

Ideally, particular revenues and costs would be recorded and automatically traced to the one individual in the organization who shoulders primary responsibility for the item. He is in the best position to evaluate and to influence a situation. For example:

The sales department requests a rush production. The plant scheduler argues that it will disrupt his production and cost a substantial though not clearly

[5] Profitability is generally regarded as the prime objective. A discussion of organizational objectives, such as profitability, growth, power, or social service, is beyond the scope of this paper. See Wm. Travers Jerome III, *Executive Control — The Catalyst* (New York: John Wiley & Sons, Inc., 1961), Chapters 4 and 14.

[6] Martin N. Kellogg, "Fundamentals of Responsibility Accounting," *N.A.A. Bulletin* (April, 1962), pp. 5–16. John A. Higgins, "Responsibility Accounting," *The Arthur Andersen Chronicle* (April, 1952). The term *activity accounting* is used by Eric Kohler and may be used interchangeably with *responsibility accounting.* See Kohler, *A Dictionary for Accountants* (2nd ed.; New York: Prentice-Hall, Inc., 1957), pp. 22–23.

determined amount of money. The answer coming from sales is: "Do you want to take the responsibility of losing the X Company as a customer?" Of course the production scheduler does not want to take such a responsibility, and he gives up, but not before a heavy exchange of arguments and the accumulation of a substantial backlog of ill feeling.

Analysis of the payroll in the assembly department, determining the costs involved in getting out rush orders, eliminated the cause of the argument. Henceforth, any rush order was accepted with a smile by the production scheduler, who made sure that the extra cost would be duly recorded and charged to the sales department — "no questions asked." As a result, the tension created by rush orders disappeared completely; and, somehow, the number of rush orders requested by the sales department was reduced to an insignificant level.[7]

Practically, the diffusion of control throughout the organization complicates the task of collecting relevant data by responsibility centers.[8] The organizational networks, the communication patterns, and the decision-making processes are complex — far too complex to yield either pat answers or *the* ideal management accounting system.[9]

HARMONY OF OBJECTIVES

Our next guide is: *Study and delineate individual manager needs in relation to his sphere of responsibility and the objectives of the organization as a whole.*

This sweeping guide has many subguides in the area of planning and controlling current operations. We have already seen that the individual manager requires score-card and attention-directing data. But what data are relevant? To be relevant, the data should impel the manager toward decisions that will harmonize with top management objectives. It follows that the management accountant must evaluate the influence of the accounting system on the motivations of individuals. The example of rush orders cited above shows how the accounting system can affect management behavior.

The trouble here is that conflicts arise between individual goals and top management goals. We all know of instances where a manager's attempt to "look good" on a performance report resulted in action detrimental to the best interest of the organization as a whole. Examples include tinkering with

[7] Raymond Villers, "Control and Freedom in a Decentralized Company," *Harvard Business Review*, Vol. XXXII, No. 2, p. 95.

[8] One of the major difficulties here is that the organization structure itself is often only vaguely understood. Problems of organization are discussed in many management texts. See Pfiffner and Sherwood, *Administrative Organization* (Englewood Cliffs, N. J.: Prentice-Hall, Inc., 1960); March and Simon, *Organizations* (New York: John Wiley & Sons, 1958).

[9] Any thorough study of an information system is likely to disclose points of strength and weakness in the organization. No management accounting system by itself can cure basic weaknesses in executive talent or organization structure. However, it can pinpoint areas that demand attention.

scrap and usage reports, encouraging false timekeeping on the part of sub-ordinates, reducing costs by lowering quality or by causing higher costs in other departments and, in general, doing "a little monkey business to come out right."

These examples do not necessarily imply nefarious behavior on the part of the individual manager. Often it is merely a matter of faulty cost analysis that is engendered by the accounting system. For example, the use of *net* assets as an investment base for judging managerial efficiency may encourage incorrect decisions by divisional management. If assets are replaced or scrapped before they are fully depreciated, the division may have to show a loss. Even though such a loss is irrelevant to replacement decisions (except for its impact on the timing of future income tax outlays), it does affect the division's immediate profit and could wrongly influence the division man-ager's decision.[10]

The successful use of budgets, standards, and various other measuring sticks is largely dependent on their value as motivating devices — as mech-anisms that will influence managers and subordinates to act in accordance with the desires of top management. For example, different types of moti-vation may result when maintenance costs are charged to a responsibility center on the basis of (1) a rate per maintenance labor hour, (2) a rate per job, or (3) a single amount per month.[11] Anthony has commented on the motivational approach as follows:

> The usefulness of such a motivational approach becomes apparent when the concepts are applied to a practical control problem. Without such an approach, one can easily become immersed in pointless arguments on such matters as whether rent should be allocated on the basis of square footage or cubic footage. There is no sound way of settling such disputes. With the notion of motivation, the problem comes into clear focus. What cost constructions are most likely to induce people to take the action that management desires? Answering this question in a specific situation is difficult. . . .[12]

Although the views on these matters are far from settled,[13] most accoun-tants and executives probably would agree with the following summary observations on costs for motivation:

[10] For an interesting discussion of how division managers' interests can conflict with the interests of the company as a whole, see John Dearden, "Problem in Decentralized Profit Responsibility," *Harvard Business Review* (May-June, 1960), pp. 79–86.

[11] Report of the 1955 Committee on Cost Concepts, American Accounting Association, *The Accounting Review* (April, 1956), p. 189. Also see Norton M. Bedford, "Cost Account-ing as a Motivation Technique," *N.A.(C.)A. Bulletin* (June, 1957), pp. 1250–1257.

[12] Robert N. Anthony, "Cost Concepts for Control," *Accounting Review* (April, 1957), p. 234. Anthony has suggested that a control technique can be judged in two ways: by the *direction* and by the *strength* of its motivation. See his *Management Accounting* (rev. ed.; Homewood, Ill.: Richard D. Irwin, Inc., 1960), p. 317.

[13] For a provocative view, see Andrew Stedry, *Budget Control and Cost Behavior* (Engle-wood Cliffs, N. J.: Prentice-Hall, Inc., 1960).

Interview results show that a particular figure does not operate as a norm, in either a score-card or attention-directing sense, simply because the controller's department calls it a standard. It operates as a norm only to the extent that the executives and supervisors, whose activity it measures, accept it as a fair and attainable yardstick of their performance. Generally, operating executives were inclined to accept a standard to the extent that they were satisfied that the data were *accurately recorded*, that the standard level was *reasonably attainable*, and the variables it measured were *controllable* by them.[14]

The above quotation centers on three guides that are basic to the management accountant's work in this area:

1. Score-keeping data should be *accurate*.
2. Budgets or standards should be *understood* and *accepted* as reasonably attainable goals.
3. The items used to judge performance must be *controllable* by the recipient.

IMPORTANCE OF ACCURACY: THE SCORE-KEEPING FUNCTION

The success of the score-keeping function in management accounting depends heavily on accuracy. Earlier we saw that relevancy and accuracy were both important but that accuracy was a subobjective in any conceptual approach to management accounting. This in no way meant that accuracy was unimportant. An accounting system will not mean much to management if the score-keeping function is haphazard. This problem of having source documents reflect physical realities is immense and pervasive.

For example, Scharff[15] had a study made of the accuracy of time reporting in the shops of a large steel and alloy plate fabricator. Each workman reported his own time. The findings revealed that the time reported against any job could vary as much as 15 or 20 percent from actual time without this circumstance being detected by the foreman's checking of time cards at the end of the day or by other checks, such as comparing estimated with actual hours, etc. The two most glaring sources of error were, first, inadvertently charging time to the wrong job and, second, willfully charging time to the wrong job when it was obvious that a given job was running over the estimated hours. In all, some twenty-five sources of error were identified. Scharff believes that the average accountant should be more sensitive to possible errors, more aware of the futility of trying to get time reported accurately in small increments, and more conscious of the natural tendency of individuals to report their activities so as to minimize their individual bother and maximize their personal showing.

[14] Simon, *et al.*, *op. cit.*, p. 29.
[15] Sam E. Scharff, "The Industrial Engineer and the Cost Accountant," *N.A.A. Bulletin* (March, 1961), pp. 17–18.

UNDERSTANDING THE ACCEPTANCE OF GOALS: THE ATTENTION-DIRECTING OR INTERPRETATIVE FUNCTION

Score-keeping is essential for cost accumulation, but attention-directing is the key to augmenting management's appreciation of the accounting function. The accountant's "staff" role includes being an attention-director (interpreter and analyst) and a score-keeper (cost accumulation and reporter — a policeman of sorts). However, these two roles often clash. Therefore, as mentioned earlier, the accounting department should divorce attention-directing from score-keeping. Otherwise, the day-to-day routine, the unending deadlines, and the insidious pressures of cost accumulation will shunt attention-directing (with the accompanying frequent contacts between accountants and operating people) into the background and, most likely, into oblivion.

The attention-directing roles (for example, explaining variances) should be occupied by capable, experienced accountants who, at least to some degree, can talk the line manager's language. Indeed, the attention-directors are the individuals who will largely establish the status of the controller's department in the company. Close, direct, active contacts between accountants and operating managers strengthen understanding and acceptability of the standards, budgets, and reports that are the measuring devices of performance.[16]

CONTROLLABILITY OF ITEMS: THE IMPORTANCE OF COST BEHAVIOR PATTERNS

Management accountants are increasingly aware of the desirability of distinguishing between controllable and uncontrollable items on a performance report. From the viewpoint of planning and controlling operations, little is accomplished by mixing controllable and uncontrollable items in the same report; in fact the indiscriminate listing of such costs often leads to confusion and discouragement on the part of the departmental manager. Again, the motivational impact should provide the guide here. For example, some top managements assign central research costs and facilities to divisions, not because the resulting divisional rates of return can be defended but because the division manager's resentment sparks an interest in central research activities. On the other hand, many accountants confine performance reports to controllable items only.

This fundamental idea that individuals should be charged only with costs subject to their control is conceptually appealing. Practically, however, there is still much to be learned about interpreting and using the following guides:

[16] Simon *et al.*, *op. cit.*, pp. 45–56.

There are few, if any, elements of cost that are the sole responsibility of one person. Some guides in deciding the appropriate costs to be charged to a person (responsibility center) are as follows:

a. If the person has authority over both the acquisition and the use of the services, he should be charged with the cost of such services.

b. If the person can significantly influence the amount of cost through his own action, he may be charged with such costs.

c. Even if the person cannot significantly influence the amount of cost through his own action, he may be charged with those elements with which the management desires him to be concerned, so that he will help to influence those who are responsible.[17]

OBJECTIVE OF LONG-RANGE PLANNING AND SPECIAL DECISIONS

NEED FOR A GENERAL APPROACH

Management accounting has a clear need for a general approach to accounting for special decision-making purposes. Existing literature and practice are characterized by diversity of general approaches and by disjointed efforts to meet very specific needs. Managerial economists, operations researchers, and statistical decision theorists perhaps have made more progress than accountants in attempting to formulate general quantitative approaches to special decisions. The rise of operations research as a distinct field may indicate that not enough practicing accountants have responded to the management need for aid in tackling these business problems.

The area of long-range planning and special decisions offers very imposing problems for executives. Management accountants need to keep abreast of the growing body of knowledge and standards concerning the decision-making process. For example, the general superiority of discounted cash flow approaches in capital budgeting decisions is being increasingly acknowledged.[18] The correct application of relevant cost analysis, discounted cash flow techniques, and possibly statistical probability theory will help management toward intelligent decision-making. All of these techniques can easily be deemed to fall within the province of the management accountant's problem-solving function.

At the same time, the need for a team approach to these decisions is well recognized. The effective management accountant knows when to call upon

---

[17] Report of 1955 Committee on Cost Concepts, *op. cit.*, p. 189.
[18] N.A.A. Research Report No. 35, *Return on Capital as a Guide to Managerial Decisions* (New York: National Association of Accountants, 1959).

appropriate specialists such as mathematicians, statisticians, industrial engineers, and others.[19]

There are two joint guides for the accountant in this area: (1) an awareness of what constitutes relevant data for special decisions and (2) a recognition of the conflicts existing between certain accounting concepts and purposes.

RELEVANT DATA FOR SPECIAL DECISIONS

The isolation and measurement of *relevant* revenue and cost factors are by far the most challenging chores in the area of special decisions. Business decision-making entails choosing between alternative courses of action. The alternative actions take place in the future, whether it be five seconds or many years ahead; hence, the decision will be influenced by the expected results under the various alternatives. The financial ingredients of the forecast must necessarily be based on expected future data. Consequently, to be relevant for these purposes, all data must be expected future data.

But *all* future data are not necessarily relevant to a given decision; only those data that will be *different* under alternatives are relevant. For example, relevant costs for special decisions are those *future* costs that will be *different* under available alternatives. The key question in determining relevancy is, "What difference will it make?"

For example, assume that a company is thinking of rearranging its plant facilities. Accounting records show that past direct labor costs were $2.00 per unit. No wage rate changes are expected, but the rearrangement is expected to reduce direct labor usage by 25 percent. Direct material costs of $6.00 per unit will not change under either alternative. An analysis follows:

	Relevant Costs per Unit	
	Do Not Rearrange	Rearrange
Direct labor	$2.00	$1.50

The cost comparison above is one of *expected future costs* that will *differ* under alternatives. The $2.00 direct labor charge may be the same as in the past, and the past records may have been extremely helpful in preparing the $2.00 forecast. The trouble is that most accountants and managers view the $2.00 past cost as the future cost. But the crucial point is that the $2.00 is an expected future cost, not a past cost. *Historical costs in themselves are*

---

[19] Although the electronic computer has enlarged the accountant's opportunities, it has also accelerated a challenge — the threat of other quantitative specialists. The management accountant should view accounting broadly and learn how allied disciplines pertain to his job. Otherwise, the management scientists, the statisticians, and the operations researchers may nibble away at his job and gradually devour it — leaving for the accountants only the routine duty of score-keeping for income statements and balance sheets.

irrelevant though they may be the best available basis for estimating future costs.

The direct material costs of $6.00 per unit are expected future costs, not historical costs. Yet these future costs are irrelevant because they will not differ under alternatives. There may be no harm in preparing a comparative analysis that includes both the relevant direct labor cost forecast and the irrelevant direct material cost forecast:

	Cost Comparison per Unit	
	Do Not Rearrange	*Rearrange*
Direct material	$6.00	$6.00
Direct labor	2.00	1.50

However, note that we can safely ignore the direct material cost, because it is not an element of difference between the alternatives. The point is that irrelevant costs may be included in cost comparisons for decisions, provided that they are included properly and do not mislead the decision-maker. A corollary point is that concentrating solely on relevant costs may eliminate cluttersome irrelevancies and may sharpen both the accountant's and the manager's thinking regarding costs for decision-making.

In summary, Exhibit 1 shows that relevant costs for decisions are expected future costs, that will differ under alternatives. Historical costs, while helpful in predicting relevant costs, are always irrelevant costs *per se.*

EXHIBIT 1

	Past Costs		*Expected Future Costs*	
	(often used as a guide for prediction)		*Do Not Rearrange*	*Rearrange*
Direct material	$6.00		$6.00*	$6.00*
			Second line of demarcation	
Direct labor	2.00		2.00	1.50

First line
of
demarcation in a conceptual
approach to distinction between
"relevant" and "irrelevant"

* Although these are expected future costs, they are irrelevant because they are the same for both alternatives. Thus, the second line of demarcation is drawn between those costs that are the same for the alternatives under consideration and those that differ; *only* the latter are relevant costs *as defined here.*

The basic approach to relevant cost analysis provides a common thread among all special decisions. The accountant or executive who develops an understanding of the concept of relevancy has taken a giant stride toward being able to analyze properly the quantitative aspects of any special decision, whether it be make or buy, the special order, buy or rent, equipment replacement, and so forth.

Note, too, that the area of special decisions again demonstrates the contrast between relevancy and accuracy. For example, the conventional ledgers amass data that are, in varying degrees, considered accurate or at least objectively determinable. Yet in long-range planning and special decisions, all the key data employed are necessarily expected future data. No general ledger system yet devised can possibly produce such data *per se*. Admittedly, much historical ("accurate") data may be helpful in predicting the appropriate future (relevant) data. But, in exercising his problem-solving function, the management accountant looks at the future first. He then selects the forecasting procedure that seems best under the circumstances.

Here we see that management accounting's scope is not limited by whatever accounting system design is used for routine data compilation, no matter how impressive and responsive the system may be. The problems of management accounting are too broad and too deep to be jammed into a single systems design, even if it is attuned to multi-purpose uses.

Conflict of Concepts and Purposes

Heavy spending on capital assets since World War II has been accompanied by a hearty interest on the part of economists, financial analysts, and accountants in management approaches to these capital budgeting decisions. Space does not permit an expanded discussion of the technical issues here.

Much of the uproar has arisen because conventional accounting practices have not been aimed at the needs of the specific decision-making process. Regarding the relative merits of capital budgeting techniques, N.A.A. Research Report No. 35 rightly favors the discounted cash flow technique. The discounted cash flow method is more objective because its answer is not directly influenced by decisions as to depreciation methods, capitalization versus expense decisions, and conservatism. Erratic flows of revenue and expenses over a project's life are directly considered under discounted cash flow but are "averaged" under the financial statement (conventional) method. "The financial statement method utilizes concepts of capital and income which were originally designed for the quite different purpose of accounting for periodic income and financial position."[20]

[20] *Ibid.*, p. 64.

COST BEHAVIOR AND OVERALL REPORTING

The need for knowledge of cost behavior patterns pervades all functions of management accounting. For example, we have already seen the need for distinguishing between controllable and uncontrollable costs. In addition, so-called *breakeven analysis* cannot be conducted effectively without assurance that the cost-volume-profit relationships depicted are valid and reasonably accurate. So, while he recognizes the importance of cost accounting for compiling costs of product, the management accountant is also concerned with a host of other cost concepts. He realizes that no single cost concept is pertinent for all purposes. He has what may be called a *relevant costing* viewpoint.

Accounting reports should be designed to highlight the relevant data approach that has been supported here. For example, as a minimum, the income statement should be designed to facilitate its possible use for many purposes, not just one. As Exhibit 2 demonstrates, the income statement for management use should no longer aim at producing one income figure. Modern needs have made a singular concept of income obsolete.

The model income statement focuses on the appropriate data for overall appraisals of current performance. Also, special decisions such as pricing, dropping or adding products, advertising and promoting specific products, and selecting distribution channels are more likely to be based on relevant information. The conventional income statement often fails to distinguish between fixed and variable costs; controllable and uncontrollable costs; and joint (common) and separable costs. These distinctions are vital for judging performance and for various marketing, manufacturing, and financial decisions.

Examples of how different figures in Exhibit 2 may be relevant for various purposes follow (numbers refer to those at left of exhibit):

1. Contribution margin: This is particularly helpful in selecting which products to push and in quickly estimating the changes in profits that will ensue from fluctuations in volume or product mix.[21]
2. Performance margin: This version of income is probably most appropriate for judging performance by division managers or product managers. It is superior to the contribution margin for this purpose because these managers can influence certain fixed costs, which are sometimes called *programmed* or *managed* costs. (Note that while certain programmed costs, such as salesmen's salaries, may be easily traced to divisions, they may not be directly traceable to products.)
3. Segment margin: This is computed after deducting the directly identifiable fixed costs that are generally considered uncontrollable in the

[21] For a number of examples of the usefulness of the contribution margin see N.A.A. Research Report 37, *Current Application of Direct Costing*, 1961.

short run. Although this figure may be helpful as a crude indicator of long-run segment profitability, it should ordinarily not influence appraisals of current performance.

4. Net income before income taxes: This may sometimes be a helpful gauge of the long-run earning power of a whole company. However, the attempt to refine this ultimate measure by breaking it into segments (and still have the whole equal the sum of the parts) seldom can yield meaningful results. Here again, we see where relevancy is a more fundamental concept than accuracy. It is difficult to see how segment performance can be judged on the basis of net income after deductions for a "fair" share of general company costs over which the segment manager exerts no influence. Examples of such costs would be central research and central administrative costs. Despite the example of allocation to Divisions A and B, unless the general company costs are clearly separable, the usefulness of such allocation is questionable.

Responsibility for Selecting Management Accounting Practices

An enlightened chief management accountant, working with top management and qualified internal or external consultants, should bear primary responsibility for selecting company management accounting practices. He should tap all resources, including the industry trade associations, the professional accounting bodies, outside auditors, government agencies, friends in the industry, and the growing literature on management and management accounting.

The biggest danger here is probably the temptation to superimpose a sample management accounting system on a company without making a tough-minded appraisal of the underlying needs of the organization and its individual executives.

Despite the obvious need for the tailor-making of management accounting systems, outside groups have an opportunity to propel the progress of management accounting. There is a continuing need for research and education, such as that conducted by the N.A.A., to describe current practices that are effective for specified purposes. Most important, there is a burgeoning mass of fundamental knowledge that should be conveyed by the N.A.A., other associations, and educational institutions if management accounting is to thrive.[22]

---

[22] Critics of conventional education in accountancy basically maintain that too much effort is given to preparing scorekeepers and not enough to educating attention-directors and problem-solvers. See Herbert F. Taggart, "Cost Accounting Versus Cost Bookkeeping," *Accounting Review* (April, 1951), pp. 141–151.

		Company Breakdown into Two Divisions		Possible Breakdown of Division B Only				
	Company as a Whole	Division A	Division B	Not Allocated	Product 1	Product 2	Product 3	Product 4
Net sales	1,500	500	1,000	0	300	200	100	400
Variable manufacturing cost of sales	780	200	580	0	120	155	45	260
Manufacturing contribution margin	720	300	420	0	180	45	55	140
Variable selling and administrative costs	220	100	120	0	60	15	25	20
1. Contribution margin	500	200	300	0	120(40%)	30(15%)	30(30%)	120(30%)
Fixed expenses directly identifiable with divisions:								
Programmed** fixed costs (certain advertising, sales promotion, engineering, research, management consulting, and supervision costs)	190	110	80	45***	10	6	4	15
2. Performance margin	310	90	220	(45)	110	24	26	105
Other fixed costs (generally uncontrollable, such as depreciation, property taxes, insurance, and perhaps the division manager's salary)	70	20	50	20	3	15	4	8
3. Segment margin	240	70	170	(65)	107	9	22	97
Joint fixed costs (not clearly or practically allocable to any segment except by some questionable allocation base)	135	45	90	(no allocations attempted beyond Divisions A and B)				
4. Net income before income taxes	105	25	80					

* There are two different types of segments illustrated here: *divisions* and *products*. A *segment* is any line of activity or subdivision of the business for which separate determination of costs and sales is wanted. Examples might be divisions, products, customers, plants, territories, and so forth.
** Programmed costs are those relatively fixed costs arising from policy decisions of management; they may have no particular relation to any base of activity. These are controllable at least when they are planned.
*** Only those costs clearly identifiable with particular products within a division should be allocated.

Conclusion

An understanding of the overall purposes and functions of the accounting system is basic to choosing effective accounting practices for reporting to management. The business information system of the future should be a multi-purpose system with a highly selective reporting scheme. It will be highly integrated and will serve three main purposes: (1) routine reporting on financial results, oriented primarily for external parties (score-keeping); (2) routine reporting to management, primarily for planning and controlling current operations (score-keeping and attention-directing); and (3) special reporting to management, primarily for long-range planning and non-recurring decisions (problem-solving).

Any guide to management accounting must aim at supplying relevant information — the basic need. Relevant data may be defined broadly as that data which will lead to an optimum decision, a decision that will best aid individuals toward overall organizational objectives.

With regard to the objective of planning and controlling operations, some of the more important guides center about responsibility accounting, accounting techniques for motivation in harmony with organizational goals, accurate score-keeping, full-fledged attention-directing, and careful classifying of controllable items.

With regard to long-range planning and special decisions, there is an evident need for a general, future-oriented approach that de-emphasizes historical revenues and costs, and there is a need for recognizing the conflict between the purposes and methods of conventional accounting and management accounting.

The accounting reports themselves should be structured to highlight relevant data. The need for knowledge of cost behavior patterns pervades all functions of management accounting. Reports at various management levels should distinguish between controllable and uncontrollable costs, variable and fixed costs, and joint (common) and separable costs.

The chief management accountant, working with top management and qualified internal or external consultants, should bear primary responsibility for the selection of company management accounting practices. In order to execute this responsibility, he needs to keep abreast of the growing body of fundamental knowledge in management accounting. Moreover, he must see that his staff receives training and experience in attention-directing and problem-solving as well as score-keeping, if the role of management accounting is to flourish in the organizations of tomorrow.

2 *The charge of this committee is to review standard managerial decision models for the purpose of making recommendations regarding the preparation and reporting of accounting information needed to implement the models, with reference to the standards for accounting information suggested in the American Accounting Association Statement of Basic Accounting Theory. This document is a tentative statement along the long road to a full understanding of how accounting and decision models should fit together. The report advocates a modern interpretation of accounting — one that responds to the broad needs for managerial information. It concentrates on how accounting systems may best identify, measure, record, and then report the results of decisions that must be made.*

Report of Committee
on Managerial
Decision Models*

*American Accounting Association
Committee on Managerial Decision Models†*

Some soothsayers, including even a few accountants, have predicted that management accounting, as we know it, will vanish by the end of the century. Accountants will be strictly data collectors, scorekeepers in the most mundane sense. According to these merchants of gloom, a new breed of information specialists will take over the accountant's existing attention-directing and problem-solving functions as a part of their very broad duties.

* *From* The Accounting Review, *Vol. XLIV, No. 1 (Supplement, 1969), pp. 42–76 excerpted. Reprinted by permission of the editor.*

† Membership: Charles T. Horngren, Chairman, Stanford University; Hector R. Anton, University of California; Harold Bierman, Jr., Cornell University; Eugene H. Brooks, Jr., University of North Carolina; Peter A. Firmin, Tulane University; Ellsworth Morse, Jr., U.S. General Accounting Office; Thomas H. Williams, University of Texas; Zenon Zannetos, Massachusetts Institute of Technology.

The likelihood of such an event is directly dependent on how accountants view their role as providers of information to management. This report advocates a modern interpretation of accounting that responds to the broad needs for management information.

The accountant must obtain the necessary qualifications for playing a larger rather than a smaller role in information systems. Many accountants are distressed by the prospective narrowing of their work as operations researchers and similar specialists obtain some control over information systems. However, if accountants are to maintain or increase their position, they must understand where decision models relate to the planning and controlling functions.

We have decided to concentrate on how accounting systems may best identify, measure, record, and report the relevant data needed to implement decision models and then report the results of the decisions that are made. Too often, decision model information is considered as being separate and distinct from management accounting information; each set of information may be accumulated and used without ever being viewed as interlocking sub-parts of a cohesive over-all information system. This is undesirable and wasteful. Our major objective is to fuse the two, to link the best concepts and practices in management accounting with the power of the decision models now available . . .

I. General Overview

A. THE NATURE OF DECISION MODELS

Accountants continually work with accounting systems and financial reports, which are financial models of company operations. Models are useful because they provide a conceptual representation of realities, enabling the decision maker to anticipate and measure the effects of alternative actions. In this section, we briefly discuss the general characteristics of decision models.

A *model* is a depiction of the relationships among the recognized factors in a particular situation; it emphasizes the key interrelationships and frequently omits some unimportant factors. Models have many forms and purposes: they may be descriptive or predictive; mathematical, physical or verbal; dynamic or static, and so on.

Decision making is choosing among alternatives; it occurs as managers conduct their planning and controlling functions. A decision model is one which, in effect, performs management's planning and control functions — but only to the extent that management delegates when the model is constructed and implemented. For example, management may decide that inventory levels should be regulated by a system based on a decision model that specifies when to order, how much to order, how much safety stock to carry, and so forth. From that point on, the system can fully perform the delegated inventory planning and control functions unless management explicitly intervenes.

Of course, a mathematical decision model may indicate a choice which is rejected by management because of more dominant legal, sociological, psychological, political, and other considerations not included in the specific model. In such instances, the output of the mathematical model is only one input into a more complicated decision model which includes qualitative as well as quantitative dimensions.

The outputs of many decision models are often used as the relevant inputs to higher-level decision making. The Department of Defense provides an example. Simulation or capital budgeting or other models may present evaluations of a vast array of alternatives. These evaluations are considered along with other factors not contained in the specific models before a final decision is made.

In mathematical decision models, the following steps are usually taken:

1. Specify an organizational objective which can be expressed quantitatively. This objective can take many forms. For brevity, we shall assume in this report that the objective is either to maximize profit or minimize cost. Other objectives are also possible, singly or in combination (for example, maximize market share, employee satisfaction or, in the case of governmental services, output).

2. Identify and describe the mathematical relationships between the relevant variables which affect the profit (cost or other objective). These variables are of two types: environmental and decision variables. The decision variables are subject to control of the decision maker, while environmental variables are not.

3. Perform the necessary mathematical operations, using the values identified in (2). The solution consists of finding the combination of values for the decision variables that maximizes profit (or minimizes cost), given the values for the environmental variables.

In almost every case, the objective to be maximized by the model is only one of several objective criteria important to the organization. In a business organization, for example, the goal of organizational survival usually may be regarded for practical purposes as a distinct constraint. In such a situation, any maximization of one objective must be carried out subject to constraints or the introduction of penalties. In addition, the optimal solution provided by the model should be regarded as merely one of a large family of optima which might result from varying the constraints. An over-all optimum would be possible where the constraints could be fully specified and the objectives fully described; however, in practice, we can only approach such a result.

To illustrate, consider a linear programming problem with a profit maximization objective subject to a constraint on supervisory time available. The solution provided by the model may be optimal if supervisory time is considered completely fixed, while in fact more supervisory time could be made available by having supervisors work overtime. In such a case, the maximum possible profit could vary with the amount of supervisory time regarded as available, and it would be logical to fix the time constraint by comparing the profit per incremental hour with the costs of obtaining the time. The principal difficulty would be that the cost of the policy described probably should include a reduction in "employee morale" because of more overtime. The question then becomes how much employee morale (a function of overtime hours) we are willing to trade for dollar profits.

The judicious use of decision models supplements intuition and implicit guides with explicit assumptions and criteria. If the decision can be depicted by a mathematical model, and if the model builder captures within his model the critical factors bearing on the decision, the resulting model is likely to lead to decisions that are more consistent with a firm's objectives.

Mathematical model building is sometimes criticized because the process of abstraction may drastically simplify the problem and overlook significant underlying factors or difficulties. Such a danger exists. Nevertheless, numerous examples of successful applications can be cited. Consider the widespread use of linear programming in scheduling production, blending raw materials, and selecting shipping routes. The test of success is not whether mathematical models are the perfect answers to the manager's needs, but whether such models provide better answers than would have been achieved via alternative techniques. (Of course, the relative costs and benefits of using various techniques are also important.)

The vastness and complexity of the entire management process preclude a complete takeover of management by mathematical decision models. Still, mathematical decision models are being increasingly used for planning and controlling operating activities. Examples include inventory control, transportation, and production scheduling models. This more widespread use of mathematical models has also prompted attempts to program parts of the management process formerly considered unprogrammable. To "program" means to describe a process in explicit step-by-step detail so that pre-determined rules can govern day-to-day performance. In a sense, the design and implementation of mathematical models require this transformation of unprogrammed activities into programmed activities. This suggests a close relationship between accounting and mathematical models because the more highly programmed the activity, the more essential it is for an accounting system to provide the needed information (see *Statement,* p. 47). To the extent that the models relieve the manager of his programmable tasks, he can concentrate on more complex management models at a higher level.

B. BEHAVIORAL FACTORS AND DECISION MODELS

The most widely used decision models are rooted in the tools and assumptions of economics. Their implementation, however, is apt to be affected by behavioral complications which sometimes are so complex that the original economic decision models must be drastically altered before they are used. Although we are aware of the cardinal importance of these behavioral considerations, we can do little here beyond underscoring the need for more research and stressing that an overwhelming amount of research on decision models and accounting is based on the flimsy assumption that the user is an economic man. The latter assumption is often necessary for productive analysis that supplies normative answers *which must then either be implemented or modified in light of attempts at implementation.*

Implementation is frequently a behavioral problem. Economic analysis, then, is not wrong or undesirable; it is simply incomplete. In his role as a supplier of information, the accountant must be concerned with both the economic decision models and their implementation as an entire package.

The trouble at this point is that our knowledge of behavioral effects is too fragmented. The information produced by decision models and accounting systems is supposed to "exert influence or have the potential for exerting influence on the designated actions" (*Statement,* p. 9). Little systematic evidence is available concerning the complex effects of decision models and accounting information on user behavior. Instead, the relationship is either overlooked or it is described by over-simplified assertions. Too often, the assertions or generalizations seem to be valid in one organization but not in another, usually because they are not based on any rigorously compiled evidence that permits *prediction* rather than *explanation.*

Because accounting information is aimed at users (external users as well as internal), hardly any major accounting issue can be resolved without making some assumptions about behavior. We need more evidence to find out which assumptions are valid. Behavioral considerations need intensive research of a fundamental kind. For example, the *Statement* assertion that "accounting information could usefully be expressed in probabilistic terms" (p. 55) contains the implicit assumption that the user will be more likely to make "better" decisions with probabilistic rather than with deterministic information. Certainly a more complete decision model may be specified using probabilities, but do users deal with probabilities in a consistent, "rational" way, as every good "economic man" should? The information specialist should know the answers to such questions before giving unqualified support to any particular timing, summarization, format, or configuration of information.

The increasing use of mathematical decision models has some intriguing behavioral ramifications. Dehumanization of specific planning and controlling functions occurs when mathematical models and computers are used.

Therefore, at least for the specific activities being analyzed, the human problem disappears as activities are finely programmed and computerized. But there are still many behavioral problems. How does the use of more rules and models affect the organization as a whole and the managers who determine the inputs to the models?

C. RELATIONSHIPS OF THE STATEMENT STANDARDS TO INFORMATION FOR DECISION MODELS

1. The Standard of Relevance. Relevance is clearly the dominant standard. Relevant information is that which bears upon or is useful to "the action it is designed to facilitate or the result it is desired to produce" (p. 9). For management planning, relevant costs (and relevant revenues) are those expected future costs (and revenues) which will be *different* for one or more of the alternatives under consideration. Information about these relevant costs and revenues has value only if it may change a decision from what it would have been had the information not been received.

Historical costs may be the basis for predicting expected future costs, but the latter are the necessary inputs to the relevant cost and decision models. This point is demonstrated in Exhibit 1 . . .

EXHIBIT 1

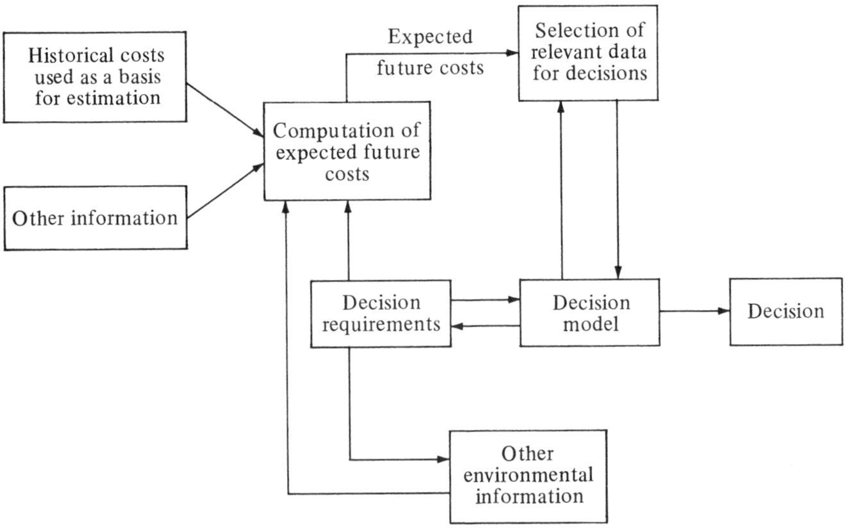

Relevant and irrelevant data are often intermingled; ordinarily, they should be sharply distinguished. Irrelevant information may do damage by contributing to confusion, error, and inefficiency, particularly if the irrelevance is not detected.

The "other information" flowing into the decision model box in Exhibit 1 includes all behavioral and social considerations. The relevant economic cost is not the only concern of management. Psychological and public policy considerations also frequently affect the actual decision.

The concept of cost as the forgoing of a benefit (the opportunity cost concept) is implicit in decision models. This view differs from the traditional idea that considers sacrifice as a "using up" or expiration of historical cost. The increased use of model-related, future-oriented opportunity costs may liberalize accountants' attitudes regarding the appropriate uses of alternatives to historical cost.

Although the standard of relevance is indisputably fundamental in spanning the gaps between accounting and decision models, it represents only the conceptual beginning. That is, the standard of relevance must be used to find answers to the questions of what inputs belong in the models and how the inputs should be measured. But that does not get us very far when we consider the overwhelming practical problems of preparing and reporting accounting information for implementing decision models. For example, in particular instances we may know that opportunity costs are relevant, but we may not know how to obtain reliable measurements of such costs. Furthermore, even if such measurements are possible, the accountant usually does not have a practical cost-and-value-of-information model which assures him that the potential benefits from making such measurements will exceed their costs.

2. The Standard of Verifiability. Verifiability aims at protecting the user from arbitrary subjective judgments by those who generate the data. The standard of verifiability must be regarded as important but less crucial for internal reporting purposes than for external reporting. Internal users are more often concerned with expected future data rather than historical data. Also, because managers usually are familiar with the underlying events, they are often in a better position to judge the validity of the accounting information . . .

Verifiability has long been regarded as more important for control and evaluation than for planning. The increasing use of decision models employing future costs and benefits will increase the importance of verifiability in the planning phases of internal accounting. Management audits, which stress the use of correct decision-making procedures by management, will focus on both planning and controlling. For this reason, evidence must be accumulated not only on day-to-day control activities, but on the procedures used for various planning decisions, and the relevance and accuracy of data employed. As aspects of planning and control become increasingly programmed, the information used therein may have to be sufficiently verifiable to allow qualified individuals (or machines) to develop essentially similar measures or conclusions from an examination of the same evidence . . .

Despite its desirability, verifiability must be traded for relevance in many instances. For example, it may be relatively easy to estimate the out-of-pocket costs of a research project that has resulted in a new product. Such costs may be verifiable but are irrelevant if a manager is seeking to estimate the value of the research project. The value would depend on estimates of future revenues and costs, items that may be impossible to verify objectively at the instant of the decision . . .

Quantitative decision models have in some cases provided the means for obtaining relevant information with increased verifiability. A linear programming model, for example, may display opportunity costs and may specify the range of outputs and inputs over which those costs are relevant . . .

3. The Standard of Freedom from Bias. It is difficult to relate clearly the standard of freedom from bias to information for decision models. Two kinds of bias are identified (but not defined). "Statistical" bias is said to result from the use of inappropriate techniques of measurement; "personal" bias apparently encompasses conscious manipulation of information for personal gain. In fact, however, deliberate manipulation of information might be implemented by selecting "statistically" biased measures . . .

Bias, although used in many contexts, is generally defined as the amount of the displacement from some "true value". As used in the field of statistics, for instance, bias generally represents the amount of difference between the expected value of some estimate (statistic) obtained by sampling and the true value of the parameter in the universe being estimated. In everyday usage, a biased opinion is one which can be expected to differ in a systematic manner (in a particular direction) from the typical or "average" opinion on the subject regarding the "true value".

Because bias is defined as a difference from some true value, it is not possible to deal in an operational manner with that concept without first specifying what the true value is or how it can be derived. One type of bias in accounting information can be usefully defined as the difference between the expected value of measurements produced by some set of measurement rules (such as absorption inventory costing) and the corresponding measurement of those values which would produce optimal decisions when introduced into a user's decision model (perhaps, in a particular case, direct costing). Because this difference is a result of the measurement rules employed, we will call it *measurement system bias.*

Obviously, when accounting bias is defined in terms of users' decision models, bias has no operational meaning until the decision models are specified. Also, a particular measurement or type of measurement may be unbiased for certain users or uses and biased for others . . .

On the other hand, in many instances deliberate bias may be beneficial if it is not personal. Deliberate impersonal bias would arise where the consensus of informed opinion would favor the insertion of bias. Management may report historical and predictive information in such a way as to motivate desired action in users. Setting of sales forecasts and various cost targets (standards or budgets) may be conditioned by their motivational impact. Standard costs, for example, might properly be set at a level which represents a biased estimate of actually attainable costs. Choice of methods for displaying historical information also may be guided by motivational considerations.

The distinction between the insertion of bias in information for motivating and in information about actual performance is subtle but important. Deliberate bias, in the context of information for motivating, may properly relate to the specification of *content* of input data. For example, should the budget be tight or loose? In the context of reporting actual performance, however, such bias will usually relate to selection of *procedures* for reporting and display . . .

Unavoidable personal bias exists almost universally because the accountant must make subjective judgments of a professional nature. In some instances, management may not prescribe formats for displaying either historical or predictive information. Managers may not even stipulate the information they need for their own decision models. In such cases, the accountant, as the expert in measurement, must often present information which in *his* judgment is proper input for the decision model or operation in question. In such cases, the introduction of personal bias in the information system may be unavoidable because our knowledge of optimal decision techniques is insufficient. This is why proper documentation for verification is necessary . . .

In summary, accounting, as a measurement process, attempts to reach unbiased estimates of particular values (even though bias may be deliberately introduced later). Unbiased estimates, in turn, require objective procedures based upon clearly defined inputs to known decision models. Bias can be substantially reduced where subjective judgments can be eliminated from the information process. The use of standard decision models has great potential in this area.

In order to develop accounting information which is relatively free of bias, therefore, it will be necessary to move further in the direction of tying accounting to quantifiable decision models.

4. The Standard of Quantifiability. We are unsure whether quantifiability is a standard in the same sense as the other standards. A particular item of information is either quantifiable, or it is not. Accounting information is often regarded as quantitative by definition. Under this view, the standard of quantifiability may be regarded as redundant — as not being subject to the same trade-offs that are frequently made among relevance, verifiability, and freedom from bias.

However, if we think of information in general, quantifiability can be viewed as a standard that may be traded off against other standards. Accounting is not necessarily confined to reporting quantitative information. For example, the concept of full disclosure in annual reports stipulates that non-quantitative information be included in financial statements where required to make them not misleading.

Moreover, quantifiability can be a misleading standard to the extent that it may contribute to the tendency for accountants and managers to weigh the quantifiable, less relevant item more heavily than the nonquantifiable, more relevant item. This is particularly graphic where short-range objectives dominate because they are easily measurable and because they may fit snugly into an over-all system. The tendency to over-emphasize short-run profits is an example . . .

In short, qualitative information may be relevant, and quantitative information may be irrelevant, or at least less useful.

The point is that accountants should seek to quantify as much important information as seems feasible. Quantification can systematically capture information that may otherwise be overlooked. This is a desirable strength of accounting, as long as such quantification does not distract from other information that may be more important but less precise . . .

5. The Standard of Economic Feasibility. As every manager and accountant knows, there are often heavy costs associated with the improvement of information systems. The potential benefits must exceed these costs if a prospective change in a system is to be justified on economic grounds . . . Economic feasibility must be a part of the trade-offs among relevance, freedom from bias, and verifiability. Economic feasibility may be measured by using cost and value of information models, the least developed but most universally important models for making decisions about the design of information systems . . .

D. General Implications of Decision Models for Accounting Systems and Accountants

1. The Accountant's Role and the Need for Integrated Information Systems. Many types of information[1] are required by decision models. What types of information should be considered as falling within the domain of accounting? There are no clear-cut answers to this difficult question, but we choose to view accounting information and accounting systems broadly as encompassing all economic data bearing on the affairs of a given entity . . .

The objective of the internal accountant has always been to generate useful information for management. As the usefulness of quantitative decision models becomes more widely understood by managers, the demand

[1] "Information" and "data" have a variety of meanings in both the technical and popular literature. Information is often conceived of as that subset of data which is useful for a particular purpose. A rigorous distinction in this terminology is not necessary for our purposes.

for information as model inputs will grow. Such a demand can be satisfied in many ways. For example, separate data-gathering systems can exist for each model. However, proliferation of systems would probably be wasteful because of the likely duplication of effort. Organizations and management can generally gain by combining the conventional accounting system and the other data-gathering functions necessary for decision models. Therefore, the accounting system should be designed to insure ready accessibility to the information required by the models as well as to present types of accounting information.

A major disadvantage of multiple information systems is the likelihood of "overlap". Different data libraries and different basic assumptions may produce different and sometimes contradictory information bearing on the same decision, leading to confusion and possibly to the use of irrelevant data. The various techniques used for capital budgeting are an example, particularly where discounted cash flow approaches are used for subsequent evaluation of performance. (See Section II for an elaboration.)

A contrasting disadvantage of multiple systems is the problem of "information gaps". None of the competing systems may provide the total information needed. If a company is considering hiring additional salesmen, for example, the market research group may supply the necessary estimates of incremental revenues, while the accounting system may supply out-of-pocket costs of hiring new salesmen. However, no accurate estimate of the incremental costs of selecting, training, and supervising additional salesmen may be available from either source . . .

Accountants, because of their experience and skills in systematic data gathering, should be able to provide needed information efficiently and economically. However, to do so, the accountant must be familiar with the assumptions of the mathematical decision models. If the accountant does not possess such understanding, there is a serious danger that the model builders will obtain erroneous or irrelevant data. The need for accountants to obtain adequate understanding of decision models is critical, not only for the future role of the accountant in organizations, but also for the increased success of managers and quantitative specialists who build and utilize the models . . .

2. The Raw Material of the Information System: The Data Library. A problem which has long been of primary concern to accountants is that of identifying and measuring costs and benefits with sufficient verifiability (or objectivity) to insure the reliability of the information process. Historical exchange-based data have been favored because these are frequently single-valued and generally are easily verified. Such emphasis may work within limited objectives, but its scope is far too narrow for an over-all information system.

Accounting information deals with economic events and their effects on an entity. Accounting has traditionally focused on explicit transactions.

The accountant has scrutinized many events, has selected certain kinds of formal recording, and has labeled these as accounting transactions. Accounting in the future probably will have to broaden the kinds of events which are recorded to satisfy an increasing variety of objectives. Accounting information probably should incorporate some events or transactions not now recorded. It should be multi-dimensional, encompassing both the past and projections of the future . . .

Data generated by the routine operations of the organization usually can be collected relatively quickly and inexpensively. In contrast, the generation of special or nonroutine data often requires extensive planning and considerable additional expense. For these reasons, accounting systems have often been unable to supply needed but nonroutine information. Users frequently have had to transform the available information to their particular uses as best they could, or gather information in clumsy, error-prone ways, or go without crucial information.

New, less expensive data gathering, storage, and accessibility capabilities of computers will enhance the feasibility of having a system that essentially contains a library of raw data in as elementary, unstructured but well-defined form as possible, properly indexed for subsequent retrieval and stored so as to facilitate a wide variety of manipulation, classification, and aggregation. Such data may include many events which have not been traditionally recorded . . .

3. Internal vs. External Data. Decision models, to be effective, often must use information originating outside the organization. External information must be systematically obtained to supply the inputs for operation of the model. The pricing strategies of competitors, for example, might be considered important in competitive bidding and in determining the demand factor for use in an inventory model. To incorporate such a factor in the model, it would probably be necessary to monitor the selling prices of competitive products for a period of time to ascertain the functional relationships between these prices and the demand for products.

Accountants should be aware of the trend toward the greater use of external data. Decision models may need such information as industry output trends; regional production and sales by product classifications; relationships of sales to disposable income, population trends, or birth and death rates; competitor or industry advertising costs, research costs, or other measures. They should be prepared to incorporate such data in the accounting system wherever feasible and desirable . . .

Unless the collection of external data is incorporated as a routine part of information gathering, it tends to be neglected. No manager seems to miss anything, but at the same time many opportunities are not exploited because nobody has observed a shift in the environmental parameters soon enough for action.

4. The Problem of Uncertainty. Many quantitative decision models must deal in some manner with the problem of uncertainty. Control models must allow for the effects of random variations and measurement errors, while planning models are faced with the additional difficulty of accurate forecasting where the consequences of over- and under-estimation often differ. The traditional accounting attitude often regards past events as facts leading to unique measures of economic activities. The increased use of decision models may spur a statistical approach which regards each estimation as having a range of possible values . . .

To provide information for planning models, the accounting system should be structured to obtain useful information from unusual events. A shortage of raw material caused by highly unusual weather conditions, for example, might allow new understanding of certain cost relationships by producing observations of a low area of the production curve. This might result in substantial alterations of routine input data for planning models.

Planning techniques involving models typically deal with uncertainty either through the use of expected values (explicitly weighing possible outcomes by their probabilities of occurrence), or through sensitivity analysis (in which the values of possible alternative outcomes are compared). In either case, it is helpful to have reliable estimates of the probabilities of future states. Such information is often very difficult to obtain, but the organization of the accounting system so as to give information about the past can be of great help in assigning probabilities. For example, accounting systems frequently collect and report data on sales activities by season, month, or even day-of-week. Many organizations routinely use daily cash flow and cash position reports. Such information can be used to establish historical frequency distribution of sales and cash flow data which can be helpful in assigning probabilities to these types of events.

A central problem in using decision models for control is the effect of random events. Here again, the design of the accounting system may play an important part. The systematic use of supplementary measures (often related to externally generated data) can go far toward reducing the limitations of conventional data . . .

5. Incremental Measures and Problems of Classifying Information. Almost all data-gathering processes involve some degree of aggregation. The economics of information accumulation usually necessitates a level of aggregation that results in a considerable loss of detail and information potential. As a result, accounting information typically specifies average relationships over specified segments of some variable (such as time), whereas usually the optimization criteria of managerial decision models logically require incremental data. The supplying of average and incremental measures is a key need in adapting accounting systems to decision models; a data library should be able to provide both types of information. Classifications of accounts should be expanded to incorporate other characteristics, particularly those which help to identify cost behavior patterns.

E. SUMMARY AND CONCLUSION

Mathematical decision models will probably be used increasingly in all types of organizations. These models require the routine collection and analysis of data not previously processed. The accounting system should provide the information required by the models to the greatest extent feasible because the maintenance of separate information systems is likely to be uneconomic, and because accountants are well suited for the task. A fundamental reorientation of the accounting system will be required if accountants are to continue as major suppliers of information for planning and controlling.

Decision models are typically based on the assumption that their users are economic men. But the implementation of decision models is heavily affected by behavioral considerations. As a supplier of information, the accountant must be concerned with both the models themselves and their implementation. No practical plans for linking decision models and accounting can afford to ignore these behavioral complexities.

The standard of relevance provides the conceptual first step to coordinating accounting and decision models and to determining the appropriate inputs and how to measure them. As a practical matter, various perceptions of and trade-offs between the standards of quantifiability, relevance, verifiability, freedom from bias, and economic feasibility will determine the shape of the information systems.

As the specific models described in Section II illustrate, the data must encompass both the historical and the predictive. They must facilitate incremental analysis and projection, include non-monetary items, embrace external factors, include interval estimates and probability distributions, and range over several levels of aggregation. Such diverse needs, coupled with modern computer technology, point toward the information system of the future as being based on a data library containing raw data in a very elementary form codified for subsequent retrieval, manipulation, classification, and aggregation.

But capturing masses of raw data is not the only job of the accountant. He must necessarily examine how his classifications, aggregations and reports influence the validity of the models and the ultimate decision-making process. Accountants have often classified cost by object of expenditure, by function, and by cost behavior patterns. Now decision models will generate their own unique needs which must be transformed by the accountant into new classification systems.

We have focused largely on the types of data needed to facilitate the use of decision models. Future research must necessarily pursue this avenue further. However, there are two other major areas that also deserve the attention of researchers in accounting. The first area was mentioned earlier: the need to consider the behavioral implications of implementing the models. The second area, which is perhaps a facet of the first, is the need to base performance evaluation (control standards) on the planning models used.

As mathematical decision models become more widely utilized, accountants and managers will be confronted with some serious problems in co-ordinating the models and the accounting reports that are commonly used for evaluating management performance. That is, planning and control decisions will be made using concepts of incremental costs, cash flows, and opportunity costs. Unless subsequent performance reports are prepared on a consistent basis, the manager may be inclined to make decisions which will bolster his performance as monitored by the conventional accounting model. This may often lead to dysfunctional decision making. A primary example is capital budgeting, where the manager's decision may be more heavily affected by how his present and near-future income statements will appear than by the long-run merits of the decision as shown by a discounted cash flow model. Another example is inventory control. The heaviest cost of carrying inventory is usually the cost of funds invested, which is often an imputed cost. Unless performance reports recognize such a cost, managers will be confronted by an evaluation system which is inconsistent with the decision model.

A major challenge for the accountant is to devise a system for reporting performance that will be consistent with the models used to make decisions. This will mean modifying the traditional accrual full-cost statements based on historical transactions. Sometimes, as in capital budgeting, the performance report may be based on cash flows and may impute opportunity costs. In other instances, as in linear programming, the performance report must be geared to a "contribution to profit" basis accompanied by a limited amount of cost allocations. In any case, the scope and flexibility of the accountant must widen if accounting is to strengthen its aid to management.

In many organizations within the past fifteen years, the posture of accounting systems has shifted from a basic orientation toward external users to a primary orientation toward internal users. For example, consider the rise of responsibility accounting, market-based transfer prices, contribution margin reporting, and profit centers. This trend will probably accelerate and bring with it a de-emphasis of the conventional accounting model geared toward external reporting. The latter should be a sub-set of the accounting system. The overall product should be a tightly-knit system that feeds the best available decision models and supports them via performance reports consistent with the models. But this progress cannot occur without a major commitment by management to use available technology and by researchers to investigate such difficult problems — problems that have both economic and behavioral implications.

II. Specific Decision Models

A. Cost and Value of Accounting Information Models

A rational decision-maker must determine which information to collect. He should obtain information where the expected value of the incremental information exceeds its expected cost. The cost and value of information models are the most general in the sense that their objective is often to decide whether some other model (such as capital budgeting or inventory models) is economically feasible. That is, the cost and value of information models answer the question of whether the value of the additional information generated by the other specific models exceeds its costs. Frequently, value depends on the use to be made of the information as input to other models.

Certain fundamental cost-benefit relationships in the information processing function may be established. For a given state of the art of information generation, greater precision, reliability, frequency, or timeliness of information normally can be achieved only by incurring greater costs. Whether data are collected to serve the requirements of a capital budgeting model, an inventory control model, or some other specific managerial model does not alter this fundamental relationship.

Problems of measurement currently limit the implementation of general models of value and cost of accounting information. Nevertheless, such models aid our understanding and perspective regarding the economic feasibility of many decision models.

1. Cost Models. "Cost of Information" refers to the cost of generating a specific information set which can be identified with a particular output requirement, such as a specific decision or planning model or an environmental requirement for information such as those imposed by the legal or tax authorities. Within this framework, many decisions must be made about the information generating process . . .

When management has defined a set of information reporting requirements and the related data needs, it must identify the cost of the information-generating process. Typically, the following natural elements of cost will be incurred:

1. Amounts paid for personal service, including professional fees and administrative salaries paid in connection with system design and installation, and clerical, administrative, and maintenance salaries or wages paid in connection with system operation.
2. Costs of equipment rental or usage represented by rental payments or by economic depreciation and interest.
3. Cost of supplies purchased to facilitate clerical or maintenance operations.

4. Power and other utilities.

Generally, the unit prices of the cost factors enumerated above may be treated as environmental variables.

In many cases, the output of a cost of information model will serve as input to another model such as a pricing model. If management wishes to determine the cost of generating information so that it may choose among alternative courses of action, the short-run incremental costs of generating the information will be one relevant input. Even in such situations, however, determining the cost of information will require decisions regarding alternative uses of the fixed resources.[2]

Some cost elements which may not be easily measured should nevertheless be considered. For example, the installation of a new electronic data processing system usually causes upheaval and disruption of routine, changes in employee morale, obsolescence of employee skills, changes in organization structure, and other phenomena. Management functions may be drastically revised, and some routine management functions may be replaced by programs in the data processing system. These and other similar changes will result in costs that should be included. Typical overhead allocation processes may not attribute the costs of such changes to the cost of generating information.

Similarly, the cost of retraining employees whose skills need updating because of new data processing systems should be considered an incremental cost of generating information. In some cases the investment in training necessitated by the installation of a new data processing system will increase the worth of the employee and result in a benefit that exceeds the cost of the training program.

2. Value Models. Value of information may be conceptualized in terms of incremental expected profit or benefit which will result from the information. We will assume that the expected value of information is the maximum amount which a rational decision-maker would be willing to pay for additional information. The after-the-fact value is not the relevant measure in deciding whether the information should have been obtained.

Some information must be gathered because the failure to do so brings such heavy costs that the decision is obvious. For example, the penalties for not filing tax returns and other reports to governmental agencies usually cause managers to place a very high value on the information needed for compliance.

Despite the difficulties of quantifying the expected value of information, we should frequently attempt to compare the expected cost of additional information with its expected value. However, because the comparison is

---

[2] Sometimes a priority of needs must be established where information is needed for several different functions.

imprecise, and the process of comparison does have a cost, it may not be an improvement over the intuitive decision-process used by most managers.

We have restricted our discussion of the value of information to concepts of expected monetary value. However, an actual decision may depend on the way decision makers incorporate attitudes toward risk and the value of non-monetary benefits. The decision maker's perceptions about the relevance of information for specific decisions will influence the information that is generated and displayed and, in turn, the data that are collected.

Value of information also depends on its timeliness. We have stated that managers should seek information as long as the perceived incremental value of the information exceeds its expected incremental cost. But management may be forced to make a decision on the basis of less information than it would like, simply because there is insufficient time to acquire additional information before the decision must be made.

It is necessary for information to be received by the manager quickly to facilitate planning or controlling . . .

III. Inventory Models

Inventory management problems exist because of the need for acquiring and storing resources, often of a substantial magnitude, in order to meet expected future demands. An inventory model abstracts the behavior of such a system in order to provide a basis for decisions regarding the optimal level and pattern of investment in inventories. In most instances, an inventory model identifies the timing and size of inventory orders and provides a solution which will minimize the costs associated with administering the inventory.

SUMMARY OF REQUIRED INFORMATION

Four basic categories of information are required in order to implement the inventory model. These categories are:

1. Determination of decision variables
2. Measurement of environmental variables
3. Determination of cost components
4. Structure of operational relationships.

The decision variables most commonly considered in an inventory model are the order quantity and the reorder point. Although the amount of safety stock to be carried is sometimes considered a relevant decision variable, this is redundant in the general model; determination of the optimal reorder level provides a basis for servicing demand during the lead time. However, in the modified, practical approach suggested later, determination of a satisfactory safety stock level will become an explicit decision variable. Other decision variables should be incorporated in the model depending upon the individual circumstance. For example, the supply source would also become a relevant decision variable when different suppliers offer different unit prices, quantity discounts and/or different lead times.

The principal environmental variables include unit purchase costs of inventory, demand rate, and order lead time. In order to achieve some reasonable correspondence with reality, each of these three variables should reflect, implicitly or explicitly, the appropriate underlying probability distribution. It is particularly important to recognize the probabilistic nature of demand in many cases. Other environmental variables may include restrictions imposed by the supplier (e.g., minimum order size).

The major independent *cost components* are carrying costs, ordering costs, shortage costs, and overstock costs . . .

Operational relationships describe the assumptions about the interacting influences among the decision variables, the environmental variables and cost components. These assumptions preferably should be based upon empirical observations. However, for purposes of initiating the analysis, intuitive assumptions may be useful . . .

ELEMENTS OF COST COMPONENTS

The following costs are explicitly considered in this model.

Carrying costs include both out-of-pocket costs and opportunity costs associated with the function of physically maintaining, or holding, a stock of goods. The major costs normally identifiable with this function are insurance, taxes, and storage. The principal opportunity cost normally included in this classification is the imputed interest on funds directly invested in inventory as measured by the rate of return that may be gained through the best alternative use of such funds . . .

Ordering costs consist of requisition costs, purchase order or setup costs, and receiving costs. Opportunity costs for this class include the imputed interest on funds expended and may also include the value of the best alternative uses of equipment and personnel utilized in ordering and receiving.

Shortage costs are those incurred when the demand rate exceeds the sales rate. Again, these costs can be classified as out-of-pocket costs and opportunity costs. Out-of-pocket costs result from special orders (expediting costs, special freight costs, etc.). Opportunity costs include both the immediate effect of the loss of sales (lost profits) and the future impact of the present out-of-stock condition (adverse customer good-will).

Overstock costs are incurred when the demand rate is less than the expected sales rate. These costs include spoilage, (including price concessions, replacement price decreases, and costs of special promotions in order to reduce overstocks), and interest on funds invested in special promotion . . .

Carrying cost and ordering cost are relevant cost components under any environmental conditions — certainty or uncertainty. On the other hand, shortage cost and overstock cost exist only under the condition of uncertainty.

MEASUREMENT OF ORDERING AND CARRYING COSTS

Identification of the cost components is only the first step toward providing the required input data for the inventory model. Measurement procedures must then be formulated and implemented.

The basic approach to the measurement problem is incremental analysis; that is, we are concerned with those costs that will be directly affected by the inventory decision, or decisions . . .

The basic form of the operational relationship to be minimized for each of the products under analysis may be summarized as follows:

Total relevant inventory cost = (Incremental carrying cost per dollar of average inventory × average inventory in dollars) + (incremental ordering costs per order × number of orders).

The essential notion in this formulation is that of "incremental cost", as measured by the change in total cost given a change in policy (order quantity or reorder point).

A. Short-Run Analysis. Measurement of incremental carrying costs involves the determination of the functional relationship between the amount of inventory and total carrying costs for the product(s) under consideration within the relevant time-frame. Estimates of out-of-pocket carrying costs may be based on past expenditures for taxes, insurance, and storage. Opportunity costs are usually more difficult to measure. Subjective judgment, tempered by empirical observation, is often the best measurement basis available . . .

Relevant ordering costs may be estimated in a similar manner, where the basic cost relationship is specified in terms of ordering cost and total orders placed.

B. Long-Run Analysis. Measurement of average cost elements implies that the scope of the model includes long-run, multi-product policy considerations. The focus is on the incremental cost of units over time. Measurement of average carrying costs per dollar of inventory may be estimated . . .

The relevant time period for determining the inclusion or exclusion of costs is somewhat amorphous. Generally, it should be coexistent with the effect of decisions. Thus, warehousing salaries might provide an example of a cost which would be excluded under a short-run approach and included under a long-run approach, as the longer time period associated with the more comprehensive policy decision enables an adjustment of the size of the work force.

Average ordering costs per order is determined by calculating a similar ratio . . .

Regression analysis may be applied to determine the relationship between the total costs and each of the two relevant independent variables (total inventories and total orders placed) . . . Whatever method is selected, however, an estimate of future cost behavior is desired, and appropriate adjustments for known or expected changes in the cost behavior pattern should be made to the historical data. To be relevant, the cost must be affected by the decision whatever the time dimension . . .

A solution derived from the inventory model in the multi-product, long-run case may indicate the present facilities and personnel are inadequate to implement the inventory levels and/or purchasing procedures provided by the model output. We then have an investment decision combined with inventory decisions.

SHORTAGE AND OVERSTOCK COSTS

. . . Under conditions of uncertainty shortage costs and overstock costs are relevant and are often substantial. The problem then becomes the measurement of those costs and the functional relationship between them and the demand and sales rates . . .

The amount of inventory held under conditions of uncertainty should be adjusted upward (essentially a larger order size and reorder point) to reduce the effects of shortages, and adjusted downward (both the order quantity and the reorder point) to reduce the effects of overstocks. The inverse behavior pattern implicit in this analysis prevents the formulation of a decision rule which minimizes the effects of these two costs on total costs. Accordingly, a practical solution divides the inventory items into two basic classes: (1) those items predominantly subject to shortage costs (staple items); and (2) those items predominantly subject to overstock costs (fashion items and items highly subject to physical deterioration). Then, some measure, or measures, of operating effectiveness — such as service level, percentage of spoilage or obsolescence, etc. — can be defined for each class . . .

The complexity of the analysis increases when overstock costs are a significant factor. However, there is evidence that many inventory management problems are primarily subject to the shortage cost element. The measure of operating effectiveness might, for example, be defined in terms of the probability of stockouts. Then, the costs of holding given quantities of safety stock may be compared with the corresponding probabilities of stockouts occurring . . .

SOURCES OF DATA INPUTS

Most of the monetary out-of-pocket costs discussed in the preceding sections can be obtained, directly or indirectly, from existing accounting records. In those instances where the accounting records are maintained in a highly summarized form, the information still can usually be extracted — although less efficiently — from the source documents underlying these summary classifications . . . The primary source of the principal opportunity cost data is usually a management decision as to the appropriate rate of return on current (or desired) investment opportunities. Where opportunity costs are involved in shortage, or out-of-stock costs, the suggested approach essentially permits a derived measure of the cost implicitly contained in the management choice from an array of cost-benefit alternatives.

Although the necessary cost information is generally available somewhere in the accounting system, it is not easily extracted from a conventional system . . .

There is, of course, the additional problem of securing the data inputs for the highly important environmental variables, such as demand forecasts. Those data often are independent of the accounting system per se. This separation may further block the timely provision of accurate data, and should also be considered in any redesign of an accounting information system oriented to the needs of managerial decision models . . .

IV. Queuing Models

STRUCTURAL SIMILARITY WITH INVENTORY MODELS

A system providing a supply of service facilities in order to satisfy random arrivals demanding these services may be generally described as a queuing system. For example, a drive-in bank must provide booths (service facilities) in order to process customers (demand) as they arrive . . . Facilities are merely an inventory of services; the queuing model is a special case of the inventory model. Many of the concepts in the section on inventory models are also applicable to queuing models.

Depending upon the number and type of service facilities established, a certain quantity of units will, at any time, be waiting in a line (queue) for access to these services; conversely, at other times, these service facilities will be idle. It should be apparent that an increase in the number of service facilities will decrease the average number of units in the queue. However, there are costs associated with the provision of each additional service facility which must be weighed against the corresponding reduction in costs incurred when units reside in the queue. The basic management problem is, therefore, the determination of the optimal number of service facilities which will minimize the sum of these costs.[3]

SUMMARY OF REQUIRED INFORMATION

The four basic categories of information required for inventory models are equally applicable to queuing models . . .

SOURCES OF DATA INPUTS

Data inputs for queuing models may be extracted from the conventional accounting system. Because this information again generally resides in payroll records, material consumption cost records, equipment schedules, etc., the problems discussed in the section on inventory models relating to the availability and access time to this information are also comparable.

Certain differences should be noted, however. There are not as many individual cost elements in queuing models, and fewer of these elements are subject to questions of joint benefits. The primary joint cost problem is in the measurement of standby facility costs, where personnel are often moved from other functions as required. The service facility operating cost and standby facility cost, if appropriately defined in the basic accounting records, may usually be determined with a higher degree of accuracy than the corresponding carrying and ordering costs in the inventory model.

On the other hand, the required information for the basic environment variables (rate of demand for the services provided and the service rate of each service facility) generally poses a more significant problem than is encountered in the inventory model . . .

V. Capital Budgeting Models

There are many different methods of making capital budgeting decisions, and the information requirements are somewhat dependent on the method chosen. In this section we discuss the requirements for implementing the present value method of evaluating investments, the method being used by an increasing number of organizations.

The present value model incorporates the objectives of maximizing the present monetary value of internal investments, where that present value is

---

[3] There are many illustrations of queuing models in the literature. For example, see Miller and Starr, *Executive Decisions and Operations Research* (Englewood Cliffs, N.J., Prentice-Hall, Inc., 1969), pp. 193–97. A simpler illustration is included in Roy and MacNeill, *Horizons for a Profession* (New York: AICPA, 1967), pp. 278–79.

the sum of all expected cash flows associated with the investments, discounted to the present. Non-monetary objectives are not explicitly included in the model.

Management must decide whether to invest. The most important environment variables are the potential cash flows and the structure of interest rates confronting the organization.

The information requirements of capital budgeting decisions may be associated with:

1. The evaluation leading to a decision as to whether the asset should be acquired.
2. The accumulation of costs identified with the asset as it is acquired or constructed.
3. The evaluation of the performance of the investment after it begins operations.

1. THE DECISION TO ACQUIRE

The first step in the decision process is the identification of the decision variables: the feasible investment alternatives. Accounting information can play an important role by identifying the areas and types of investment which are presently producing high returns. Search in these areas is likely to produce more profitable investment opportunities.

After potential investments are identified, their net present value must be computed[4] . . .

Future cash flows from operations are primary inputs into the present value calculations. The accounting system cannot supply directly the necessary information but in many situations it can assist in the estimation process . . .

The amount of each type of cost associated with the investment should be determined for different levels of production. Some costs will not change as production changes; other costs will increase directly as production increases. These characteristics must be defined before we can compute the cash flows of a period. Because prices of factors of production differ if there is a new location, the manager might want the accounting system to supply the physical units of inputs as well as the dollar amounts necessary to achieve the different levels of production. Essentially, he would be utilizing the information storage capability of the accounting system at this stage of the investment process.

The decision-maker does not ordinarily need to know the average full cost per unit of product over a period of time, because such cost includes

---

[4] The choice of the discount factor is a complex question. Suggestions range from the use of a default-free interest rate to a weighted-average cost of capital. The crucial question is whether the discount factor used to compute present value equivalents should include an adjustment for risk.

depreciation and overhead allocations such as central office and corporate advertising expenses. These would be irrelevant inputs to the investment decision model, though this information might be of interest in other contexts.

Investment decisions are generally incremental to the overall operation of the organization. This means that the manager wants to know the incremental costs associated with the decision rather than the average costs. The average costs may be affected by factor inputs that are not affected by the decision and therefore should not affect the decision . . .

There are three additional inputs that are vital to the capital budgeting model: current disposal value of old assets, estimated disposal value of new assets, and expected useful life of new assets or projects. Accounting data cannot ordinarily provide direct help on any of these except to the extent that historical data can aid in formulating predictions. For example, managers may estimate a useful life on new equipment to be 20 years. But accounting records for similar equipment or projects may reveal that the useful life has been 10 or 12 years. Such information, along with the use of sensitivity analysis, can be of sizable help in judging the merits of capital budgeting proposals.

2. ACCUMULATION OF COSTS

When the investment is accepted and the acquisition occurs, the accountant records the investment costs as they are incurred. There is a need to control the costs incurred and to see that the project undertaken is the same as the one approved, and that the actual costs do not differ significantly from the budgeted costs. If material differences do occur, they must be explored. Here the accounting system is acting as an accumulator of information and then reporting the results of economic activity in the form of a comparison of actual and budgeted costs . . .

The cost of the capital tied up during a construction period is sometimes considered in practice to be a cost of the investment if the funds have been obtained using debt type securities. For managerial purposes (at a minimum), the principle of opportunity cost applies and the cost of the funds committed to the project should be considered to be a cost of the project, regardless of the source of the capital.

3. EVALUATION OF PERFORMANCE

The third phase of an investment project is its actual operation, and here the accounting system should be designed, where possible, to report the information necessary for evaluation of the project's performance. In situations where the investment is a small component of a larger interrelated operation, it may be difficult to evaluate the performance in terms of revenues and expenses (or in terms of net cash flows), because of the jointness of the expenses and revenues with those of other activities. A large amount of accounting effort is directed to the problem of measuring the effectiveness of the utilization of assets, and this effort may be viewed as the evaluation of the performance of an investment. Measurements of income and return on investment are extensions of the investment decision; they are relevant to the decision process because the anticipated post-investment accounting measures of performance may influence whether that investment is undertaken.

The use of traditional accrual accounting methods for evaluating performance is a critical roadblock to the implementation of present value models. Clearly, there is an inconsistency between citing present value models as being superior for capital budgeting decisions and then using entirely different concepts for tallying performance. As long as such practices persist, managers will often be tempted to make decisions which may be non-optimal under the present value criterion but optimal, at least over short or intermediate spans of time, under conventional accounting methods of evaluating operating performance . . .

If discounted cash flow approaches to decision making are being used by the firm, it is both possible and desirable that the accounting for the investment (or equivalently the accounting for assets) be consistent with the information that went into the investment's evaluation . . .

In sum, the implementation of discounted cash flow models will be facilitated if a practical means for the follow-up of decisions is devised. Among the major alternatives are:

1. Evaluating all major decisions and a sample of minor decisions by recording results on the same cash-flow basis used to make the original decision.
2. Using discounted cash-flow approaches to the decision but simultaneously preparing an accounting rate of return analysis which will be used as the basis for evaluating results.
3. Adopting depreciation and amortization patterns that more closely fit those patterns implicit in discounted cash-flow models . . .

3 *The motivation of employees to accomplish the goals of an organization has been one of management's main problems. The literature relevant to motivation is surveyed both in organization theory and the behavioral sciences areas — with the finding that the organizational structure best suited to motivation is the decentralized form. Accounting systems are examined in the light of this finding. And weight is given to responsibility accounting as preferable to budgets and standards for effective motivation. Accounting reports are seen as being in part negative contributors to motivation, although positive factors predominate. An informal structure of goals is found to be important, as is participatory budgeting.*

The Role of the Firm's Accounting System for Motivation*

George J. Benston†

Introduction

Motivating employees to work for the goals of the firm has long been one of management's most important and vexing problems. The search for methods that motivate effectively, that induce the employee to work harder

* From The Accounting Review, *Vol. XXXVIII, No. 2 (April, 1963), pp. 347–354. Reprinted by permission of the editor.*

† Grateful acknowledgement is due the members of the Workshop in Accounting Research of the Institute of Professional Accountancy at the University of Chicago for their helpful (though often devastating) criticism, and especially to Professor Charles Horngren for his encouragement and aid. Regrettably, they cannot be held responsible for errors in fact or opinion.

for the firm's goals, led to experimentation with a wide diversity of devices.[1] In recent years, several writers emphasized that the firm's accounting system has a direct influence on the motivation of managers.[2] This paper (a) surveys the available findings of research done in the behavioral sciences and organization theory as they bear on motivation and (b) critically examines the accounting system and reports in the light of such findings.

Part I surveys the literature related to motivation and organizational structure and concludes that the decentralized[3] form of organization provides the conditions in which effective motivation can occur. In the light of Part I and other evidence, the accounting system and reports are critically evaluated in Part II. The major conclusions of Part II are that:

1. The empirical research reinforces and justifies the recent emphasis on the virtues of responsibility accounting. Responsibility accounting provides an effective overall aid to decentralization and, hence, while indirect and not as dramatic as some proposed direct uses (such as "proper" budgets or standards), perhaps is more important for effective motivation.

2. The evidence does not support the unqualified use of accounting reports as direct motivating factors. Indeed, there is evidence that the direct use of budgets can lead to a reduction in effective motivation. Nevertheless, there are positive aspects to the direct use of accounting reports.

[1] See M. S. Viteles, *Motivation and Morale in Industry*, New York: W. W. Norton and Co., 1953.

[2] C. Argyris, *The Impact of Budgets on People*, New York: The Controllership Foundation, 1952.

"Tentative Statement on Cost Accounting Concepts Underlying Reports for Management Purposes," *The Accounting Review*, 1956, Vol. 31, p. 188.

R. Anthony, "Cost Concepts for Control," *The Accounting Review*, 1957, Vol. 32, pp. 229–234.

N. Bedford, "Cost Accounting as a Motivation Technique," N.A.C.A. Bulletin, 1957, pp. 1250–1257.

A. Stedry, *Budget Control and Cost Behavior*, Englewood Cliffs, N.J.: Prentice-Hall, 1960.

[3] Decentralization, as used in this paper and in organization theory generally, refers to the vesting of authority and responsibility in the department manager or supervisor for the day-to-day conduct of departmental operations. The department in question need not be physically or organizationally separate from the rest of firm. The title "department manager" and the organizational grouping "department," then, signify any supervisory position and work group for which authority and responsibility over specific tasks are delegated and for which accounting reports are prepared. With this system of organization, the department manager is given the authority to operate his department and supervise his employees as he would do if he were an individual entrepreneur.

I. Motivation and Organizational Structure

The motivation of employees may be attempted by the use of a very large variety of techniques, applied in a number of ways. Among these techniques are direct wage incentives, participation schemes, goal setting, and morale boosters. These may be offered directly to the employee by the firm in a centralized fashion (by the personnel department, for example), or indirectly, by the department head in a decentralized firm.[4] Since even a cursory examination of the literature on motivation leads to the realization that the specific techniques of motivation are of almost infinite variety, this paper will concentrate on the problem of application. Indeed, the survey of the literature presented below led the writer to conclude that the organizational structure of the firm is very important for the successful application of motivation techniques, especially with respect to the ordinary worker.[5] The influence of organizational structure on motivation, then, is examined below.

Decentralization and Centralization

The organizational structure of decentralization is one in which managers and employees are in direct and continuous contact. This face-to-face relationship facilitates the manager's perception of the needs and goals of his workers. With the authority given him by decentralization, the manager can provide those specific rewards and penalties that are effective for motivating individual workers and groups. Thus, he is in a good position to persuade them to accept the goals of the firm as their own (or as not opposed to their goals) and work to achieve these ends.

In contrast, centralization and large size make perception of the workers' needs difficult. Communication between the decision makers and those who carry out their decisions becomes complicated and subject to more interference ("noise").[6] And, as a study of ten voluntary associations revealed, ordinary members become more passive and disassociated from the central purposes of the organization and leaders become further removed from the activities they plan.[7]

[4] In a small firm, these two procedures of application may merge, since the central decision maker is in direct contact with the employees.

[5] The motivation of managers and other executives similarly is affected by organizational structure. However, since published findings that dealt with the motivation of executives specifically could not be found, the major emphasis in this paper is on the motivation of the ordinary worker.

[6] T. M. Whitin, "On the Span of Central Direction," *Naval Research Logistics Quarterly,* 1954, Vol. 1, p. 27.

[7] F. S. Chapin and J. E. Tsouderos, "Formalization Observed in Ten Voluntary Associations: Concepts, Morphology, Process," *Social Forces,* 1955, Vol. 33, pp. 306–309.

In addition, research at Sears, Roebuck and Co. revealed that organizational size alone unquestionably is one of the most important factors in determining the quality of employee relationships: "the smaller the unit, the higher the morale and vice versa."[8] And, a study of two British motor-car factories demonstrated that the size factor affects productivity directly. Significant (though low) correlations were found between output and size, the smaller work groups showing consistently larger output in each factory.[9]

However, the existence of small groups, per se, is not a sufficient condition for motivation. Workers may feel a greater sense of belonging if they work in smaller, more cohesive groups, but they will not necessarily be motivated toward fulfilling the goals of the organization. Some writers, notably Argyris (who has done extensive research at Yale's Labor and Management Center) believe that it is inevitable that the ordinary worker fight the organization. He writes that the organization characterized by ". . . task specialization, unity of direction, chain of command, and span of control . . . may create frustration, conflict and failure for the employee. He may react by regressing, decreasing his efficiency, and creating informal systems against management."[10]

This tendency for informal organizations to be created has been explored extensively.[11] Selznick, for example, writes that "In every organization, the goals of the organization are modified (abandoned, deflected, or elaborated) by processes within it. The process of modification is effected through the informal structure."[12] After reviewing several empirical studies, he concludes that "the day-to-day behavior of the group becomes centered around specific problems and proximate goals which have primarily an internal relevance. Then, since these activities come to consume an increasing proportion of the time and thoughts of the participants, they are — from the point of view of actual behavior — *substituted* for the professed goals."[13]

The Motivation of Small Groups

There also is ample evidence that these informal groups can work to increase or decrease productivity, depending on whether or not the workers

---

[8] J. C. Worthy, "Organization Structure and Employee Morale," *American Sociological Review,* 1950, Vol. 15, p. 173.

[9] R. Marriott, "Size of Working Group and Output," *Occupational Psychology,* 1949, Vol. 23, p. 56.

[10] C. Argyris, "The Individual and Organization: Some Problems of Mutual Adjustment," *Administrative Science Quarterly,* 1957, Vol. 2, p. 1.

[11] For example see C. I. Barnard, *The Functions of the Executive,* Cambridge, Mass.: Harvard University Press, 1938; J. A. March and H. A. Simon, *Organizations,* New York: John Wiley and Sons, 1958; P. Selznick, "An Approach to a Theory of Organization," *American Sociological Review,* 1943, Vol. 8, pp. 47–54; and H. A. Simon, *Administrative Behavior,* New York: The Macmillan Co., 1947.

[12] *Ibid.,* p. 47.

[13] *Ibid.,* p. 48. (Emphasis appears in the original.)

perceive that the organization's goals are not contrary to theirs.[14] Two types of procedures have been proposed to cope with this problem. One, the direct approach, involves an immediate attempt by top management to influence the worker through direct wage incentive plans, company-wide incentive plans, and group discussions. The other, the indirect approach, gives primary responsibility and authority to the department manager to motivate his workers effectively.

The direct approach is often effective but it is also difficult to administer successfully. Direct incentive plans are not feasible generally unless a homogeneous product is produced under repetitive conditions.[15] Also, attempts to promote individual increases in productivity usually are disruptive and detrimental to efficiency where the employees' tasks are interrelated.[16] Company-wide incentive plans have had a spotty record of success.[17] They seem to work best where there is a long history of trust between labor and management or an unusual person as chief executive of the company.[18] However, efforts to impose company-wide incentive plans in other situations have been generally unsuccessful. Group discussions also do not appear to be reliable. A famous experiment conducted in an American plant on the effect of group discussions on productivity and worker acceptance of change produced negative results when replicated in Norway.[19]

The indirect approach makes the informal group's goals synonymous with the organization's goal through effective company leadership of the informal group. The firm then can take advantage of the demonstrated positive relationship between group goals and productivity (cited above).[20] Also, this approach does not rule out the use of direct techniques when and where they are deemed feasible.

[14] For example see L. Berkowitz, "Group Standards, Cohesiveness and Productivity," *Human Relations,* 1954, Vol. 7, pp. 509–19; D. Cartwright and A. Zander, "Group Pressures and Group Standards," in *Group Dynamics,* Second Edition, D. Cartwright and A. Zander, eds., Evanston, Illinois: Row, Peterson and Co., 1960, pp. 165–188; S. Schachter, N. Ellertson, D. McBride, and D. Gregory, "An Experimental Study of Cohesiveness and Productivity," *Human Relations,* 1951, Vol. 4, pp. 229–38, and W. F. Whyte and others, *Money and Motivation,* New York: Harper, 1955.

[15] W. B. Wolf, *Wage Incentives as a Management Tool,* New York: Columbia University Press, 1957.

[16] P. M. Blau, *The Dynamics of Bureaucracy,* Chicago: University of Chicago Press, 1955, Chapter IV; M. Deutch, "The Effects of Cooperation and Competition Upon Group Process," in *Group Dynamics,* Second Edition, *op. cit.* footnote 14, pp. 414–48; and E. J. Thomas, "Effects of Facilitative Role Interdependence on Group Functioning," *Human Relations,* 1957, Vol. 10, pp. 347–66.

[17] J. N. Scanlon, "Profit Sharing: Three Case Studies," *Industrial and Labor Relations Review,* 1948, Vol. 2, pp. 58–75.

[18] See J. F. Lincoln, *Lincoln's Incentive System,* New York: McGraw-Hill, 1946.

[19] L. Coch and J. R. P. French, Jr., "Overcoming Resistance to Change," *Human Relations,* 1948, Vol. 1, pp. 512–32; and J. R. P. French, Jr., J. Israel and D. As, "An Experiment on Participation in a Norwegian Factory," *Human Relations,* 1960, Vol. 30, pp. 3–19.

[20] See footnote 14.

The Role of the Department Manager

The indirect approach can be effected most readily in the decentralized firm. The department manager, who is likely to understand and accept the firm's goals,[21] can be assigned the task of leading the informal group. In assigning the department manager this role, the departmentalized firm can take advantage of the probability that the informal grouping of workers will follow the formal department organization. Task specialization and frequent interaction provide this cohesiveness.[22]

It is very important that the organization-oriented manager assume the leadership role, for when he abdicates or is incapable in his role as leader, an informal leader arises.[23] Without a management-oriented leader, the drives of workers for satisfaction are often channeled into nonproductive or destructive practices.[24] This behavior is to be expected, since the effort necessary for high production rarely is satisfying in itself. Indeed, many empirical investigations have shown that there seldom is positive, but occasionally negative, correlation between productivity and job satisfaction.[25]

The factors that are likely to make the department manager an effective leader also are a product of decentralization. Bass, who considers much of the literature on leadership, concludes that the effective supervisor satisfies the needs of his subordinates.[26] Since these needs are diverse, any number of leadership styles have been found to work in a variety of situations. Thus, the organizational structure must allow the manager the freedom and authority to reward his workers. Freedom is necessary so that the manager can adapt his methods to the particular needs of his group. And, the employees will respond to the demands of the manager only if he has enough influence to make the employees' behavior pay off in terms of actual benefits.[27]

---

[21] Research that examined the motivation of managers, as distinct from production workers, could not be found. However, managers are in more direct and continual contact with the firm's policy makers than are ordinary workers. Hence, they are likely to assume the goals of top-management (see evidence cited in footnotes 14 and 22). Also, top management can exercise control over the performance and possibly the motivation of department managers through budgets and accounting reports of performance (as discussed below).

[22] J. M. Jackson, "Reference Group Processes in a Formal Organization," *Sociometry,* 1959, Vol. 22, pp. 307–327. Also reprinted in *Group Dynamics,* Second Edition, *op. cit.,* footnote 14.

[23] R. L. Kahn and D. Katz, "Leadership Practices in Relation to Productivity and Morale," in *Group Dynamics,* Second Edition, *op. cit.,* footnote 14, pp. 554–70.

[24] W. F. Whyte and others, *op. cit.,* footnote 14.

[25] A. H. Brayfield and W. H. Crockett, "Employee Attitudes and Employee Performance," *Psychological Bulletin,* 1955, Vol. 52, pp. 396–424; and R. L. Kahn and N. C. Morse, "The Relationship of Productivity to Morale," *Journal of Social Issues,* 1951, Vol. 7, pp. 8–17.

[26] B. M. Bass, *Leadership, Psychology, and Organizational Behavior,* New York: Harper and Bros., 1960. The bibliography of this work includes 1155 items.

[27] D. C. Petz, "Influence: A Key to Effective Leadership in the First Line Supervisor," *Personnel,* 1952, Vol. 29. A similar conclusion is reached by Fiedler for

Decentralization also is effective in encouraging the manager to use a style of leadership that promotes effective motivation. It was found in several empirical studies that the fewer the restraints put upon a group (within limits), the more it produced.[28] Kahn and Katz have done extensive research on this aspect of motivation. They find that "Apparently, close supervision can interfere with the gratification of some strongly felt needs."[29] They go on to observe that "There is a great deal of evidence that this factor of closeness of supervision, which is very important, is by no means determined at the first level of supervision. . . . The style of supervision which is characteristic of first-level supervisors reflects in considerable degree the organizational climate which exists at higher levels in the management hierarchy."[30] Thus decentralization, which is characterized by the autonomy of action given the department manager by top management, serves both to allow the managers the necessary freedom and authority needed for motivation and to encourage them to supervise their workers effectively.

II. Accounting Systems and Motivation

Decentralization, which provides the motivational advantages described above, is aided by the firm's accounting system. In fact, many students of decentralization agree with E. F. L. Brech's conclusion (in a review of British experience with decentralization):

> By whatever arrangements and procedures, decentralization necessitates provision for the periodic review of performance and progress and the expression of approval.[31]

This need is met by the firm's accounting system. Top management can afford to give authority to the department manager, since it can control the basic activities of the department with the help of accounting reports of performance. Furthermore, accounting reports and budgets may serve as reliable means of communication, wherein top management can inform the manager of the goals of the firm that it expects him to fulfill.

---

military and sports groups. He concludes that ". . . leadership traits can become operative in influencing group productivity only when the leader has considerable power in the group." (F. E. Fiedler, "The Leader's Psychological Distance and Group Effectiveness," in *Group Dynamics*, Second Edition, *op. cit.*, footnote 14, p. 605). Kahn and Katz also reach this conclusion (*op. cit.*, footnote 22, p. 561), as do W. S. High, R. D. Wilson, and A. Comrey, "Factors Influencing Organizational Effectiveness VIII," *Personnel Psychology*, 1955, Vol. 8, p. 368.

[28] R. M. Stogdill, *Individual Behavior and Group Achievement*, New York: Oxford University Press, 1959, p. 272.

[29] R. L. Kahn and D. Katz, *op. cit.*, footnote 22, p. 560.

[30] *Ibid.*, p. 560.

[31] E. F. L. Brech, "The Balance Between Centralization and Decentralization in Managerial Control," *British Management Review*, 1954, Vol. 12, p. 195.

Responsibility Accounting

More specifically, the findings surveyed above reinforce the recent emphasis on responsibility accounting. In making the smallest areas of responsibility the fundamental building blocks of the accounting system, accountants facilitate effective motivation. With a system of responsibility accounting, top management can afford to widen its span of control and allow operating decisions to be made on a decentralized basis. Correlatively, assigning costs to the individual managers who have control over their incurrence is a factor in encouraging these managers to exercise effectively their authority to motivate their supervisees. The managers' performance in this regard is measured by the accounting reports, which are likely to be an incentive for the effective motivation of the managers.

Budgets and Motivation

Indeed, several writers have proposed that accounting reports be used as a direct factor for effective motivation. The most extensive examination of the use of budgets as a tool for motivation was made by Stedry, who measured the effect of various budgets on an individual's level of aspiration as a method of determining the differences in motivation on these budgets.[32] His experiment, in which the subjects attempted to solve problems for which they received budgets and were rewarded for achievement, resulted in the following determinations:

> The experimental results indicate that an "implicit" budget (where the subject is not told what goal he must attain) produced the best performance, closely followed by a "medium" budget and a "high" budget. The "low" budget, which was the only one which satisfied the criterion of "attainable but not too loose," resulted in performance significantly lower than the other budget groups.
> However, there is a strong interaction effect between budgets and the aspiration level determination grouping. The group of "high" budget subjects who received their budgets prior to setting their aspiration levels performed better than any other group, whereas the "high" budget group who set their aspirations before receiving the budget were the lowest performers of any group.[33]

After presenting arguments to the effect that firms probably do not operate at optimal efficiency, Stedry concludes that ". . . it seems at least reasonable to suppose that it is a proper task of budgetary control to be concerned with strategies for constant improvement in performance."[34] He

---

[32] *Op. cit.,* footnote 2.
[33] *Ibid.,* pp. 89–90.
[34] *Ibid.,* p. 147.

implies that the budget should be used to motivate department managers. The function of the budget would be to raise the manager's level of aspiration and thereby increase his level of performance, rather than to inform him of top management's goals and decisions.

Stedry briefly notes, but does not really consider, the effects of accounting reports on the setting of aspiration levels. His experiment was deliberately designed so that the subjects would not have knowledge of their performance.[35] The budget then became their primary point of reference.[36] But would this happen where the managers had knowledge of their previous performance to compare with the budget that is supposed to motivate them to new productive heights?

It is likely that department managers can make a fairly accurate estimate of their performance. The experience of time study engineers can be noted, since the setting of a rate for a particular job is analogous to the setting of a budget for a department. In both situations the attempt is made to motivate the worker to produce more by setting high standards. But, as many articles, texts, and case studies attest, the worker almost always can gauge his performance. The worker generally will fight a "tight" rate by refusing to produce efficiently, because of his fear that the "carrot" will always be pushed ahead every time he attempts to overtake it.[37] There is no reason to expect department managers to be less perceptive than factory workers.

In an actual situation, the department manager probably would compare his estimate of his performance with the budget to see how well he did. This means that the manager would have knowledge of his success or failure. Several experimenters have examined the effect of this knowledge on aspiration levels. Levin, Dembro, Festinger, and Sears, in an often quoted review and analysis of the literature to 1944 conclude that ". . . generally the level of aspiration will be raised and lowered respectively as performance (attainment) reaches or does not reach the level of aspiration."[38]

The effects of success and failure are difficult problems for the would-be budget manipulator. Stedry's findings indicate that a high budget (one technically impossible of attainment) produced the best performance where

---

[35] *Ibid.*, p. 71.

[36] *Ibid.*, p. 82.

[37] See W. F. Whyte and others, *op. cit.*, footnote 14, Chapter 3, "Setting the Rate," for a delightful description of this practice.

[38] K. Levin, T. Dembro, L. Festinger, and P. Sears, "Level of Aspiration," in *Personality and the Behavioral Disorders,* Vol. I., J. McV. Hunt, ed., New York: Ronald Press, 1944, p. 337. A comprehensive test of the hypothesis stated by Levin, *et al.,* which confirmed it, was made by I. L. Child and J. W. M. Whiting, "Determinants of Level of Aspiration: Evidence from Everyday Life," *Journal of Abnormal and Social Psychology,* 1949, Vol. 44, p. 314. Similar results are reported by I. M. Steisel and B. D. Cohen, "Effects of Two Degrees of Failure on Level of Aspiration in Performance," *Journal of Abnormal and Social Psychology,* 1951, Vol. 46, pp. 78–82.

the subject received it before setting his level of aspiration. The attainable low budget produced the worst results. But in working conditions, assuming knowledge, the high budget probably will result in failure for the deparment manager and, consequently, in lowering his level of aspiration (motivation) and performance.[39] The budget manipulator, then, must either give the manager false reports about his performance or attempt to set the budget just enough above the manager's perception of his performance to encourage him.

The first alternative, false reports, is a potentially dangerous procedure and is likely to be quite expensive. Performance reports would have to be secretly prepared. This would make accounting data on the department's actual operations (needed for economic decisions) difficult to obtain, since the department manager could not be consulted. Also, this procedure must be based on the assumption that the manager will believe a cost report, even if it conflicts with his own estimates. The validity of this assumption is denied in a study by Simon, Guetzkow, Kozmetsky and Tyndall:

> Interview results show that a particular figure does not operate as a norm, in either a score-card or attention-directing sense, simply because the controller's department calls it a standard. It operates as a norm only to the extent that the executives and supervisors, whose activity it measures, accept it as a fair and attainable yardstick of their performance. Generally, operating executives were inclined to accept a standard to the extent that they were satisfied that the data were *accurately recorded,* that the standard level was *reasonably attainable,* and that the variables it measured were *controllable* by them.[40]

The second alternative open to the budget manipulator is rather difficult to effect. The manager's level of aspiration must be measured, and *his* perception of his performance level must be estimated. However, measurement of an individual's aspiration level is not a well-developed science. Some fairly successful, though crude, procedures for measuring level of aspiration have been developed. Unfortunately, they depend on the subject's verbal response to questions about the goal explicitly to be undertaken, such as the score expected (not hoped for) in a dart-throwing contest.[41] The usefulness of this technique for a work situation is limited, since the employee has an incentive to state a false, low goal and thus avoid failure. A more precise measure has been developed by Siegel,[42]

[39] This may have happened even in Stedry's experiment, since he found that the poorest performance occurred where the subjects determined their aspiration levels before they were given the high budget.

[40] H. A. Simon, H. Guetzkow, G. Kozmetsky, and G. Tyndall, *Centralization vs. Decentralization in Organizing the Controllers Department,* New York: The Controllership Foundation, 1954, p. 29. (Emphasis appears in the original.)

[41] K. Levin, T. Dembro, L. Festinger, and P. Sears, *op. cit.,* footnote 38.

[42] S. Siegel, "Level of Aspiration and Decision Making," *Psychological Review,* 1957, Vol. 64, pp. 253–63.

but the technique itself restricts it to highly artificial conditions. Thus, it is doubtful that the use of budgets for motivation can be effective except in carefully selected situations.

The direct influence of the budget on motivation may be more effective than is indicated above if the budget is a participation budget, rather than an imposed budget of the type used by Stedry. In a forthcoming article, Becker and Green present evidence and arguments to show that participation in budget-making in conjunction with the comparison and reviewing process may lead to increased cohesiveness and goal acceptance by the participants.[43] If this goal acceptance is at a higher level than previous goals, the aspiration level of the participants has been raised and should lead to increased production.[44]

Accounting Reports of Performance and Motivation

Budgets are not the only accounting reports that may be used for motivation. Accounting reports of performance also have a direct effect on motivation by giving the department manager knowledge of his performance. Most of the published experiments on this subject consider the effects of knowledge on the learning or performance of physical tasks. However, the general findings reported ought to be relevant to the effect of accounting information on the manager's performance. Ammons surveyed most of the literature in this area (to 1956) and reached the following generalizations that seem applicable to the present problem:[45]

> Knowledge of performance affects rate of learning and level reached by learning.
> *Knowledge of performance affects motivation.* The most common effects of knowledge of performance is to increase motivation.
> The more specific the knowledge of performance, the more rapid improvement and the higher the level of performance.
> The longer the delay in giving knowledge of performance, the less effect the given performance has.
> When knowledge of performance is decreased, performance drops.

However, overemphasis of departmental cost reports may have undesirable effects, since accounting data often does not measure fulfillment of

[43] S. Becker and D. Green, Jr., "Budgeting and Employee Behavior," *The Journal of Business,* 1962, Vol. 35, pp. 392–402.

[44] For a fuller treatment of this subject see the Becker and Green paper, in which is discussed the conditions under which cohesiveness, goal acceptance, and productivity can be lowered as well as increased.

[45] R. B. Ammons, "Effects of Knowledge of Performance: A Survey and Tentative Theoretical Information," *Journal of General Psychology,* 1956, Vol. 54, pp. 283–290. (Emphasis appears in the original.)

the firm's goals. Ammons notes that "It is very important to keep in mind *what* the subject is motivated to do when knowledge of performance increases his motivation. Often he is motivated to score higher, not necessarily to learn the task faster and better. He may then resort to taking advantage of weaknesses in the apparatus, learning habits which are of no value or actually lead to poorer performance when he later attempts to learn a similar task."[46] Overemphasis of accounting reports has been found to result from this behavior.[47] Where the reports became the sole criteria for evaluating performance, managers resorted to such anti-productive techniques as delayed maintenance, bickering over cost allocations, and even falsification of inventories. Thus, recognition of the positive motivational aspects of accounting reports should not lead to the conclusion that they can be used without limits. Indeed, the history of the search for "the key to motivation" indicates that people's needs are too diverse and changeable to be satisfied by any single device or mechanically applied procedure.

Conclusion

Decentralization contributes to effective motivation. The firm's accounting system facilitates decentralization and hence has an indirect but important impact on motivation. The direct use of accounting reports, such as budgets, for motivation can result in reduced performance, if the budget is imposed on the department manager. However, a participation budget may be effective in increasing motivation. Also, accounting reports of activities aid motivation by giving the manager knowledge of his performance.

In short, the accounting system facilitates decentralization, which is conducive to effective motivation. Furthermore, the careful use of accounting reports can directly contribute toward effective motivation by expressing goals and by supplying knowledge of performance.

---

[46] *Ibid.,* p. 280.
[47] See C. Argyris, *op. cit.,* footnote 10; P. W. Cook, Jr., "Decentralization and the Transfer Price Problem," *Journal of Business,* 1955, Vol. 27, p. 87; and V. F. Ridgeway, "Dysfunctional Consequences of Performance Measurements," *Administrative Science Quarterly,* 1956, Vol. 1, pp. 240–47.

4 Research on management's use of accounting information in decision-making is reported in this article
based on experience from forty-four small companies. The research encompassed the use of accounting data which was found to be used
(1) primarily to recognize the need for a decision, and (2) for comparing
alternative actions.

Detailed analysis of factors influencing the first point is given including:
(1) the ability of the firm to react, (2) availability of information about
viable variables, (3) ability of management to use data, (4) size of the
management hierarchy, (5) trade customs, and (6) external information.
Naturally, variations were found on all these points depending on type
and size of firm.

Variations on the theme of importance of accounting data for alternative
choice decisions depended on: (1) reduction of uncertainty, (2) competition, (3) perceived accuracy, (4) cost identification, (5) diversity of product lines, (6) timeliness of the decision, and (7) relative importance of
non-accounting information. The author concludes by citing some implications for practice of his theme of "point control" using marginal
income analysis, direct costing, and merchandise management accounting.

Accounting in the
Decision-Making Process:
Some Empirical Evidence*

James L. Gibson

This paper reports some of the findings of intensive research on management's use of accounting in decision-making.[1] The core of the research is 44
case studies of decision making in small firms. In recent years, the issue of

* From The Accounting Review, Vol. XXXVIII, No. 3 (July, 1963), pp. 492–500. Reprinted by permission of the editor.

[1] The complete findings are reported in J. L. Gibson and W. W. Haynes, Accounting in
Small Business Decisions (Lexington, Kentucky: University of Kentucky Press, 1963).

accounting in decision making has received considerable attention, but there is a dearth of large scale empirical evidence to suggest how managers actually use accounting data. Accordingly, the objectives of this research were: (1) to describe how managers use accounting data in decision-making, (2) to evaluate the consistency of accounting data with the logic of economic analysis, and (3) to prescribe the role of accounting data in decision making. Because of space limitations, the descriptive element will be emphasized here.

The case studies indicate that management uses accounting data as a means of recognizing the need for a decision and for comparing alternative courses of action. The remainder of this paper discusses those factors which influence the extent of management's use of accounting data in each of the two phases and concludes with suggestions for a general framework of thought concerning managerial accounting.

Accounting Data as Stimuli in Decision-Making

Factors which influence the role of accounting in stimulating the decision-making process are: (1) the ability of the firm to react quickly to changing circumstances, (2) the availability of information in the accounts on variables which the firm considers important, (3) the capability of the firm's management to organize and use accounting data, (4) the size of the firm, especially as measured by the number of tiers of management, (5) the customs of the industry in which the firm is situated, and (6) the availability of information on key variables from sources external to the firm. These factors are discussed and illustrated from practice in this section.

THE REACTION OF FIRMS TO CHANGING CONDITIONS

Retailers stress accounting ratios, averages, and comparative data as means of detecting weaknesses in the operations; this emphasis on accounting data is due, in part, to their ability to react quickly to changing circumstances. Retailers can revise merchandise lines and prices as the data report changes in demand and costs; the tactics used by retailers in reaction to the recognized changes include markdowns, close-out sales, loss leaders, intensified selling efforts, etc. The reaction of the retailer is limited only by the type of merchandise traditionally carried by the store (a men's clothing store cannot add women's clothing unless the firm is prepared to make a major change in operations), and the firm's long-range consideration of maintaining a particular "image" (a store with a reputation for quality merchandise cannot add "seconds" or "factory rejects" to its line). But, within limits, the typical retailer has considerable flexibility in reacting to changing conditions.

Printing firms can react less quickly and with less latitude than retailers; their flexibility is reduced by the fixity of the plant layout and the type of equipment. Within a range of possibilities, printing firms can shift from one type of work to another, but the fixed facilities are the limiting factors. A second constraint on printing firms' flexibility is that they are discontinuous producers. They do not produce a product for consumption by a large number of consumers; on the contrary, printers must wait for each consumer to place his order and reveal his demand. All of which means that printers do not have flexibility in production planning and scheduling. As a result of this inflexibility, most printing firms do not collect a great amount of accounting data for comparative purposes. Large and medium-size firms with multi-level management make comparative analyses when internal financial statements are available; such analyses are made in conjunction with issues involving financial policy, sources of revenue, and cost control, rather than day-to-day operating decisions. Some firms attempt to control the accuracy of estimating by comparing actual costs with estimated costs; however, they do not revise their pricing practices immediately when discrepancies are noted.

Small manufacturing firms, at least as represented in this research, find their reaction time reduced by the nature of fixed facilities. Concrete product manufacturers cannot shift resources easily, particularly because production is determined by the number and type of molds that the firm has on hand. Once committed to a scale of output and a particular complement of products, the manufacturing firm cannot revise production easily. These firms do not make systematic ratio analysis of their statements, but they may be stimulated to some kinds of corrective action as a result of the annual income figure.

At the extreme of inflexibility are nurserymen whose problem is apparent: The firms must allocate a fixed amount of land to a variety of plants with varying growing periods. Once a planting season commences, the nurserymen are committed to the product line; they cannot adjust the product mix to take advantage of shifts in demand for the individual plants. As the growing season progresses, nurserymen clear out slow-moving plants by price reductions and, in this respect, nurserymen have some flexibility. The decision to lower prices is not accompanied by an analysis of financial data, since the firm need only observe the plants that remain in the ground.

THE AVAILABILITY OF ACCEPTABLE ACCOUNTING DATA

Acceptable information on relevant variables must be available in the accounts before a firm will use accounting data systematically. Managers of retail stores believe the average markup to be the key variable and they can easily calculate it: 1 − Merchandise Cost/Sales. Retailers can readily find the relevant data, cost of merchandise and sales revenue, in the accounts. As demand or cost change, the effect on markup is easily determined and retailers can react quickly to restore the required relationship. On the other hand, printers desire information on the hourly costs of individual processes in the firm, but hourly costs are not easily calculated at a given point in time. The hourly cost is determined by the rate of output and total costs, and these factors are not easily calculated even with the most refined accounting system. As an alternative to internally developed hourly cost data, many printers rely on regionally published selling rates for pricing decisions. Printers can calculate the incremental cost of production with some accuracy since it consists primarily of materials costs, but they usually ignore incremental costs because of their alleged inconsistency with long-run objectives of the firm. Future demand is an important variable in printing as in retailing, but one on which accounting data give little information. Production scheduling, the allocation of machines to jobs, is dependent upon estimates of future orders; accounting data provide only "after-the-fact" information, whereas optimum production scheduling requires data about the future.

Small manufacturers in this study operate without any kind of budgets or standard costs. Some information might be obtained if they did employ such devices; however, the firms are not greatly concerned with costs since, for the most part, they are fixed (with the exception of materials). The principal concerns of the manufacturers are that they maintain production at a high level and that they allocate the fixed facilities to secure optimum use. To control output, the manufacturer requires some index of capacity utilization but accounting does not readily provide such an index. Total-sales is an indicator of volume, but it reveals nothing about the allocation of fixed resources. The same desire for optimum allocation of fixed facilities is noted in nurseries; the firms must allocate the land so that the over-all return is maximized, but, as in manufacturing, accounting data cannot indicate whether the firm has achieved an optimum allocation of land. Accounting data are relatively unimportant as control measures in both small manufacturers and nurseries, although the firms do note the level of cash and income at times and take some corrective action.

THE CAPABILITY OF MANAGEMENT

This factor refers to managements' talent (1) in recognizing the variables that are most important in determining the profitability of the firm, and (2) in recognizing the extent to which accounting data are relevant as sources of information on these variables. The industry classification breaks down as a vehicle for presenting this argument since the more knowledgeable managers do not operate retail stores while the less enlightened are situated in nurseries. On the contrary, it is the nurseryman's credit that they do not attempt to calculate individual plant costs, a calculation which would be most nebulous and arbitrary. Ratio analysis and comparison of accounting measurements require a great deal of skill and understanding of accounting principles; such requirements limit their universal usage. Analyses of financial data, if used incorrectly, can lead to wrong inferences and costly misinterpretations of the problem at hand. The case studies indicate that some managers are capable of using the analyses when relevant and rejecting the analyses when irrelevant. The studies also indicate that less capable managers either do not use the analyses or frequently use them incorrectly.

THE SIZE OF THE FIRM

As a small firm grows in size, management becomes less involved with the actual operations of the firm. In a small firm, the manager not only makes decisions, but also puts the decisions into effect; in larger stores, the manager makes the decisions, but subordinates put his decisions into operation. In retailing, department-store managers collect and use more accounting data than their counterparts in smaller retail outlets. In printing firms, the larger multi-management firms rely more heavily on the accounting system for control reports than the smaller single-management firms. This characteristic also holds for manufacturers. In nurseries, however, there appears to be little difference in the extent to which large firms accumulate accounting data for decision-making purposes as compared to the smaller firms. Large nurseries accumulate information on certain revenue and cost categories, due to tax and creditor requirements, but there is no evidence that the more complete accounting data exert a stronger influence on decision-making in larger firms than in smaller nurseries. In general, however, managers that are removed from the scene of day-to-day operations accumulate accounting data designed to point up areas requiring their attention.

CUSTOMS OF THE INDUSTRY AND AVAILABLE EXTERNAL DATA

Retailers are accustomed to emphasizing average markups and retail trade associations provide a great deal of comparative data. However, underlying these considerations are the facts that information on markup is easily calculated and retailers are able to react quickly to changes in the environment. Printers, by custom, emphasize hourly costs and believe them to be the true indicators of printing firms' product — "time." Printers also receive information on regional hourly costs with which they can compare their own costs. The evidence on industry customs and available outside information is less conclusive in manufacturing and nurseries. Manufacturing is a broad area and the case studies cover only a small segment. Nurseries receive information from other sources; e.g., one nursery compares its price schedule with those of firms in neighboring areas, but the exact relationship between price revisions and the outside data is not well defined. No doubt many firms, regardless of industry type, have certain customary relationships that they desire to maintain; one laundry and dry cleaning firm required that the ratio of wages to sales be maintained at $33\frac{1}{3}$ per cent. In firms which have these "customs," accounting data are used if the data are relevant in measuring the required relationships.

Accounting Data in the Choice Among Alternatives

Not all firms use accounting data in analyzing the relative profitability of alternative courses of action; there are definite factors underlying this observed diversity of practice. These factors are: (1) the extent to which accounting data reduce some of the uncertainties of a decision, (2) the relative importance of demand and competition, (3) the degree of accuracy that managements attach to accounting data, (4) the ease by which costs are identifiable with products, segments, processes, etc., (5) the extent to which a firm has diversified its product line, (6) the urgency of the decision, (7) the time dimension of the decision, i.e., the relative importance of long-run and short-run variables, (8) the availability of relevant information on alternatives from sources other than the accounts, and (9) the importance of opportunity costs and other considerations not measured by accounting data.

The Extent to Which Accounting Data Reduce Uncertainty

A situation of uncertainty exists when the outcome of a decision is not fully known. For some decisions, it is possible for management to reduce the uncertainty by gathering information on the possible future states of nature and the possible outcomes. To the extent that accounting data convey relevant information on these states and outcomes, and thus reduce uncertainty, they are important in a decision. For example, retailers use past sales data as the first approximation of future demand in merchandising decisions involving items that they have previously stocked; if the items have not previously been stocked in the store, the firm must search for information other than that in the accounting system. On the cost side, a concrete-product manufacturer prepared a cost analysis of a new product involving the same production characteristics as the existing products from internal accounting records. However, a second concrete-product manufacturer had to get cost data from external sources because the new product involved none of the production characteristics with which the firm had experience. Thus, in the first case, accounting data reduced some of the uncertainty about future costs, but, in the second case, accounting data were of little help.

In some decisions, the degree of uncertainty is so high and relevant information is so scarce and costly, that firms will use accounting data simply because they are available, tangible, and a means of circumventing uncertainty. The sale of a printing firm's assets, for example, was based on book value, even though the parties involved recognized that the value was not realistic. And we observed that printers are not completely satisfied with accounting measurements of unit costs, but such measurements are tangible and allow the firm to include a "solid" figure in the pricing analysis. No doubt, many firms use accounting data because they desire an expedient way to make decisions in the face of overwhelming circumstances.

THE RELATIVE IMPORTANCE OF DEMAND AND OF COMPETITION

The relationship between demand and competition and the importance of accounting data is complex. There is some evidence that firms facing little competition and inelastic demand stress accounting information on costs, particularly full costs, rather than demand in pricing and product-line decisions. This emphasis on costs is contrary to the theoretical model of monopoly pricing which indicates that prices will be quite flexible and adaptable to changes in demand. But there are a number of reasons which explain why small firms in monopoly positions do not adjust prices on the basis of elasticities of demand. As examples, a concrete-products manufacturer prices on the basis of full cost plus a fixed markup because of his concern for maintaining his reputation as a "fair" businessman in the community, his concern for the possible entry of a new firm, and his satisfaction with the standard of living that he presently enjoys; a furniture manufacturer rations scarce capacity by requiring that all jobs cover prime costs plus a markup; a building-materials manufacturer has a monopoly position on many contracts, but the firm requires the price to cover only the full cost plus a predetermined markup because it is more concerned with stable long-run revenues than with maximizing short-run profits.

The case studies suggest that pricing decisions of firms located in competitive markets rest less heavily on accounting data than do similar decisions of firms in monopoly markets. But the evidence is not conclusive. Printing firms in highly competitive markets attempt to use full costs as the basis for pricing decisions; their objective is to reduce price competition in the market through the adoption by all firms of a common pricing method. However, as positive pieces of evidence, two firms, a concrete-products manufacturer and a readi-mix concrete producer, in highly competitive markets, completely ignored internal cost data in pricing decisions; they had to adapt completely to a change in demand or stop production. Thus, and in general, accounting data are less important in the decisions of firms in competitive markets than in the decisions of firms in monopoly positions.

THE DEGREE OF ACCURACY THAT MANAGEMENT ATTACHES
TO ACCOUNTING DATA

The issue here is not the actual accuracy of accounting measurements but the extent to which management believes that the data are accurate. At the time printers calculate unit costs, they consider them to be quite accurate; however, as time passes, their confidence in the measurements wanes, especially as actual production deviates from estimated output. Nurserymen have little confidence in measurements of the cost of a single plant; such calculations would include a host of arbitrary allocations of labor (a common cost in nurseries) and overheads. On the other hand, a concrete-products manufacturer believes that the accounting data, full-cost, are quite accurate calculations of average total cost even though the figure includes an arbitrary allocation basis (overhead is charged at 10 per cent of direct labor and materials, a basis suggested at a trade convention).

THE EASE WITH WHICH COSTS ARE IDENTIFIABLE WITH PRODUCTS, PROCESSES, ETC.

In some firms common costs are such a large part of the total cost that any measurement of unit costs would be meaningless. Retailing and the nursery firms included in this study do not attempt to calculate unit costs, nor do their decisions reflect any consideration of unit costs. The problem of common costs is no less crucial in printing, but in this industry a common denominator, i.e., an index of production, has been developed which reduces the problem of common costs to an extent. The common denominator is time spent on an individual job; the problem of allocating common costs remains, but it is not as great as it would be if the job were the focus of attention.

THE EXTENT OF PRODUCT DIVERSIFICATION

The number of decisions that a firm must make in a specified period of time will obviously influence the extent to which management will give full attention to the analysis of each individual decision; the extent to which a firm diversifies its product line is an important determinant of the multiplicity of decisions that management must make. Printers must quote a price on a number of different jobs during a day or week; should they evaluate all the possible sources of information on costs, demand elasticities, and competitors' reactions, decisions might never be made. To expedite the pricing decision, a routine is established by which the printer estimates only the time required by the job. The pricing and merchandise-evaluation decisions of retailers are also numerous, but merchandise cost is a convenient beginning in setting prices. On the other hand, the manufacturer of a single product, such as readi-mix concrete, has no such multitude of decisions. The initial price reflects not only costs, but the firm's estimate of market conditions and the duration of the construction season. The more numerous similar decisions are, the more the firm relies on the accounting system as a source of data.

THE URGENCY OF THE NEED FOR THE DECISION

The more urgent the need for a decision, the more emphasis the firm places on accounting data. This proposition is borne out by the practice of printers who often must quote a price immediately to a customer. The accounting data provide a routine by which the firm can quote the price quickly. But not all prices of printers must be quoted as quickly; if, for example, the firm is invited to submit a bid on an especially large job, management gives more attention to such factors as production scheduling and the possible bids of competitors for the same job. A refractory manager was considering the possible replacement of a large scoop shovel and, because the present shovel would last a while longer, considered many sources of data other than accounting. Nurserymen must make price decisions a year in advance, and they also rely on nonaccounting data in these decisions. Other evidence from the case studies supports the conclusion that managers who must make a decision rapidly rely on accounting data if such are available.

THE TIME DIMENSION OF THE DECISION

Accounting data play a more important role in decisions of a short-run nature than in decisions entailing long-run repercussions. Printers and retailers must make pricing decisions based on provisional cost data; i.e., if the facts of the supporting analysis are not borne out, the firms can make adjustments in subsequent pricing decisions, without encountering long-run difficulties. A laundry and dry cleaning firm manager based his analysis of whether to continue the shirt-laundry segment for the duration of the summer on accounting data; the data reflected short-run costs and revenues, the manager's major concerns. A readi-mix concrete producer, however, maintained accounting data on individual truck costs, but did not use the data in truck-replacement decisions because this action required estimates of future costs, demand, and financial restrictions. And two concrete-product manufacturers based product-diversification decisions on information from suppliers and customers relevant to long-run demand and market conditions. Accounting data can reflect only costs and revenues pertaining to the existing production scheme; any decision which proposes to change this scheme must be analyzed on the basis of nonaccounting information.

THE AVAILABILITY OF EXTERNAL INFORMATION

Firms which find that external sources can supply relevant information for decision-making do not rely so heavily on the accounting system. As an example, one small retailer does not keep records of merchandise purchases because he knows that suppliers can give him this information; he bases merchandise buying decisions on the suppliers' information. Other examples include retailers who rely on "estimated profitability" studies prepared by suppliers of a possible new merchandise line and printers who base pricing decisions on hourly cost information published by trade associations. These external sources may be taken without question by the firms, or they may be evaluated in terms of the firm's own experience. If the external information is relevant and less costly than accounting data, the firm will have little cause to expend money for internally developed data.

THE IMPORTANCE OF OPPORTUNITY COSTS

Accounting methods cannot measure opportunity costs; accounting data refer to past sacrifices, whereas opportunity costs are future sacrifices. Yet, in some instances, accounting data are estimates of opportunity costs. For example, if a multi-product firm is producing at capacity, the full cost of each product may be an indication of the contribution an alternative product-mix can make with the same utilization of resources. A case in point is the practice of a special-order furniture manufacturer who prices all orders at direct cost plus a 90 per cent markup. The firm operates at capacity with a continual stream of new business presenting itself; by pricing all orders at cost-plus the firm rations its scarce resources. Similarly, printing firms which have all the work they can handle allocate resources by requiring that each job cover full cost plus the profit margin.

In most instances, however, accounting data are incapable of measuring opportunity costs. The decisions of an automobile tire firm to open a new retail outlet, for example, required that a salesman and principal executive be transferred to the new outlet. Such a move would have involved a sacrifice of sales at the present location and a strain on the over-all management capabilities. The accounting data were not useful in analyzing the particular sacrifices involved. Another illustration is provided by the decision of a television repairman involving a truck replacement. The cost, i.e., the sacrifice, of keeping the truck one more year was the interest on the salvage value for the year plus the loss in salvage value during the year. The depreciation on the books was computed on a straight-line basis and thus provided no indication of the real loss in economic value. We also interviewed the manager of a printing firm who, when analyzing the true value of the business, recognized the information in the balance sheet was of little value. Whenever opportunity costs are extremely important in the analysis of a decision, accounting data play a small role in the analysis.

To summarize these factors which underlie the use of accounting in various decisions of a number of firms, we note that the role of accounting is a function of: (1) the characteristics of the industry (relative importance of demand and competition and the availability of external sources of information), (2) the characteristics of the firm (importance of common costs, the considered accuracy of accounting data, and the extent of product diversification), and (3) the characteristics of the decision (the degree of uncertainty, the urgency of the decision, the time dimensions of the proposed actions, and the importance of opportunity costs).

IMPLICATIONS FOR PRACTICE

The concept which should guide the firm in the accumulation of accounting data for the purpose of stimulating decisions is strategic point control. Only information on critical, or limiting, points is necessary for optimum control of the firm's operations. To illustrate a misuse of this concept, some retailers accumulate a great deal of information on ratios, averages, etc., but only a small part of the information is ever put to use. Two outcomes of this practice of "over-information" are apparent: (1) Financial resources are misallocated, and (2) the critical factors are apt to be obscured. Instead of accumulating a mass of data, the retailer needs to identify strategic points, establish standards for their measurement, and accumulate accounting data relevant to them.

Strategic points should be factors on which accounting data can develop accurate measurements and to which the firm can react quickly when deviations appear between the standard and the actual state of the factor. There are factors for which accounting data cannot develop measurements, e.g., customer goodwill, market conditions, and demand. An important part of the model is the firm's recognition of the limitations of accounting data in this respect.

Accounting methods which develop data for use in analyzing the relative merits of alternative courses of action must be based on certain provisions: (1) The accounting data must be consistent with the logic of economic analysis. (2) The firm must distinguish carefully between the kinds of decisions that can be analyzed with the help of accounting data and those for which the accounting data are irrelevant.

The logic of marginalism precludes the use of any method that entails allocation of fixed costs. Or, to state the requirement positively, marginalism requires that only those costs which will change as the result of a decision be included in the analysis. Thus, many decisions involve an increase or decrease in the firm's output and, as a result, an increase or decrease in variable costs. Fixed costs do not change and the allocation of such costs serves only to discourage the proper use of marginal analysis. Yet, there are instances when the firm requires some measure of capacity utilization built into the product costs. There are also instances in which firms, particularly printing firms, have found that full-cost estimates are acceptable in the market as a basis for pricing decisions. Cost allocations are not necessarily inconsistent with economic analysis. But whenever the firm allocates costs, its objective should be to allocate true economic costs, rather than accounting costs.

Accounting principles serve an important function in maintaining consistency and objectivity in financial reporting, but for decision-making such principles are irrelevant. Each firm is guided by different goals and objectives; each decision involves different variables and parameters. There can be no universally acceptable set of standards except as dictated by marginalism. Economic costs must be incorporated in any method which develops data for decision-making; but to the extent that accounting data are a practical measurement of economic costs, using them may not result in a great loss of precision.

Marginal income analysis, direct costing, and merchandise management accounting are methods designed for use in selected decisions; the methods are not applicable in every decision a firm encounters. The design of decision-making accounting methods must be preceded by a careful study of the firm's operations to determine which decisions can be programmed, i.e., what decisions are sufficiently repetitive to allow management to formulate a general solution to the problem whenever it presents itself. Once determined, the firm can develop accounting data which indicate the occurrence of the general problem and which provide a basis for its solution.

Management's use of accounting data which reflect marginalism and economic costs in decision-making is discouraged by (1) management's ignorance of economic analysis and (2) the cost of accounting information. Accounting systems are costly; no doubt many firms would misallocate financial resources should they adopt all the refinements of routinized accounting methods. On the other hand, in an uncertain business world in which information is at a premium, accounting data are a relatively cheap form of information.

5 *"Program budgeting is designed to strengthen an organization's capability to do long-range planning and to provide
a systematic method for resolving major resource allocation issues.
The planning-programming-budgeting (PPB) process focuses on the
basic function of management, which is to use the organization's
available resources in ways that will be most effective in meeting its
goals. It establishes and makes explicit the relationships among the
organization's objectives, its programs and activities, and the resource implications of projected programs. Perhaps most important
is the analytical activity, which contributes directly to management
decision making by providing analyses of the consequences, in terms
of estimated costs and expected benefits, of possible alternative
program decisions."*

Long-Range Planning
Through Program
Budgeting*

David Novick

A plan for an organization, whether a government agency or a business
firm, prescribes actions to be taken and activities to be carried on to advance the organization's perceived objectives. Plans vary widely in substance and form according to the nature of the organization, the scope of
the plan, and the time-frame to which it applies. However, one element

* From Business Horizons, *Vol. XII, No. 1 (February, 1969), pp. 59–65. Copyright 1969 by the Foundation for the School of Business at Indiana University.
Reprinted by permission.*

is universal in the planning of any organization that produces goods or services: at some point, the plan must deal with the question, "How shall the organization make use of its available resources?" This — the resource allocation question — is fundamental, because in every sphere of the organization's activity the amount of resources sets limits to what can be accomplished.

The strategic and most comprehensive form of planning is long-range planning of the organization's total program. In business, such planning may embrace the full set of product lines and productive functions of a diversified corporation. In government, it may encompass the programs of an entire department or ministry or, perhaps, the development of a "five-year plan" for an entire jurisdiction. This article deals with a system for organizing the long-range planning function and for helping managers to reach the key resource allocation decisions that confront them in this context.

For more than twenty-five years I have been developing a management tool — program budgeting — which is designed to strengthen an organization's capability to do long-range planning and to provide a systematic method for resolving major resource allocation issues.[1] Program budgeting — or the planning-programming-budgeting systems abbreviated to PPB — focuses on the basic function of management, which is to use the organization's available resources in the way that will be most effective in meeting its goals. Basically, the PPB system contributes to the planning process in two ways.

First, it establishes and makes explicit the relationships or linkages among the organization's objectives, its programs and activities, the resource implications of those activities, and their financial expression in a budget. In so doing, it provides much of the information needed for rational planning in an easily usable form. *Second,* PPB contributes directly to management decision making by providing analyses of the consequences, in terms of estimated costs and expected benefits, of possible program decisions.

This may sound like a broad charter, but it should be borne in mind that PPB does not do a number of important things. As it is discussed here, PPB is an instrument for over-all planning that utilizes existing systems for directing and controlling operations and therefore does not necessitate change in either the existing organization or methods of administration. In addition, PPB is specifically designed for long-range planning and budgeting; it is not primarily a tool for conducting the annual budgeting-accounting cycle, although next year's budget must be included in its purview, and accounting supplies part of the reports. Last, although PPB stresses the use of quantitative analytical methods and, in some cases, a rather extensive use of modern computer technology, it does not attempt

---

[1] "Introduction," in David Novick, ed., *Program Budgeting: Program Analysis and the Federal Budget* (2nd ed.; Cambridge, Mass.: Harvard University Press, 1967).

to quantify every part of the problem or to computerize the decision-making process.[2]

PPB has been in operation for seven years in the U.S. Department of Defense, and, since 1965, efforts have been under way to extend the system to other departments and agencies. Many state and local governments have applied PPB methods to their own planning problems, and similar methods are in use in major business firms. Nevertheless, in some organizations the adoption of PPB has caused apprehension and insecurity, largely as the result of a misunderstanding of what PPB is and does. People assume program budgeting is revolutionary and complex. When in operation and understood, the real content comes through; it is revolutionary but simple and based on common sense.

The Program Budget Concept

The PPB system is constructed on a few basic concepts related to objectives, programs, resources, cost, effectiveness, and benefits.

Objectives are the organization's aims or purposes, which, collectively, define its raison d'etre. They may be stated initially in broad and relatively abstract terms, as, for example, when we say that the objective of a defense program is to provide national security or the objectives of education are to provide good citizens and productive participants in the economy. However, objectives at this level are too remote from the organization's specific activities to be useful for formulating or evaluating programs to be operational; they must be translated into lower-level objectives that can be stated in concrete terms.

Programs are the sets of activities undertaken to accomplish objectives.[3] A program generally has an identifiable end product. (Some programs may be undertaken in support of others; if so, they have identifiable intermediate products.) Several programs may be associated with an objective, in which case they may be identified with distinct subobjectives or with complementary, but distinguishable, means for accomplishing the objective.

Resources are the goods and services consumed by program activities. They may be thought of as the inputs required to produce each program's end product. Program cost is the monetary value of resources identified with a program.

Effectiveness is a measure of the degree to which programs accomplish their objectives. It is related to benefit, which is a measure of the utility to be derived from each program.

Program budgeting for an organization begins with an effort to identify and define objectives, and group the organization's activities into programs

[2] David Novick, *The Role of Quantitative Analysis and the Computer in Program Budgeting,* The RAND Corporation, P-3716, October, 1967.

[3] M. Anshen, D. Novick, and W. C. Truppner, *Wartime Production Controls* (New York: Columbia University Press, 1949), pp. 109–11.

that can be related to each objective. This is the revolutionary aspect, since it requires grouping by end product rather than by administrative organization or by function. This method allows us to look at *what* we produce — output — in addition to *how* we produce or what inputs we consume. The program budget itself presents resources and costs categorized according to the program or end product to which they apply. This contrasts with traditional budgets found in most organizations that assemble costs by type of resource input (line item) and by organizational or functional categories. The point of this restructuring of budget information is that it aids planning by focusing attention on competition for resources among programs and on the effectiveness of resource use within programs. The entire process by which objectives are identified, programs are defined and quantitatively described, and the budget is recast into a program budget format is called the structural phase of planning-programming-budgeting.

Often, both in government and in business, responsibility for the work required to accomplish a coherent set of objectives is divided among a number of organizations. In the government, for example, programs with objectives for health and education are each fragmented among a dozen bureaus and independent agencies. The activities of each one are sometimes complementary, sometimes contradictory, or in conflict with those of the others. As a result, there is no over-all coordination of the resource allocation decisions relevant to program objectives. One of the strengths of program budgeting is that it cuts across organizational boundaries, drawing together the information needed by decision makers without regard to divisions in operating authority among jurisdictions. The advantage for planning is obvious: a program can be examined as a whole, contradictions are more likely to be recognized, and a context is supplied for consideration of changes that would alter or cut across existing agency lines.

One product of the structural phase is a conversion matrix or "crosswalk" from the budget in program terms to the traditional or functional budget, which treats of organizations like departments and sections in categories such as wages and salaries, supplies, equipment, and the like. Through the crosswalk we are able to translate ongoing methods of recordkeeping and reporting into data for program planning; we are also able to translate program decisions into existing methods for directing, authorizing, controlling, recording, and reporting operations. If existing management methods in any of these areas are inadequate or unsatisfactory, they should be upgraded and improved whether or not the organization has a PPB system. In any case, the program budget must derive information and relationships from existing management records and practices, and must rely on them for the implementation of the programs.

The long-range planner encounters problems of choice at several levels. At the highest level, the different programs and objectives compete for their shares of the organization's total resources or total budget. For example, in a government Transportation Ministry, programs for international transportation, domestic intercity transportation, and local transportation compete with each other. In a business firm, competition for investment funds may involve different product lines, different research and development projects, and so forth. At a lower level, the problem of choice focuses on decisions among alternative ways of carrying out a program. For instance, in connection with the Transportation Ministry's program of domestic intercity transportation, choices have to be made among alternative transport modes — railway, automobile, and air transport — or among alternative combinations of modes.

In program budgeting, the appproach to this problem is to apply analysis wherever it is possible, so that decision makers will be able to make the final judgments with as much objective information as can be assembled. Thus, a planning-programming-budgeting system subsumes a systems analysis capability with which the resource and cost implications of program alternatives and their expected "outputs" or accomplishments may be estimated, examined, and compared. (When a systems analysis capability does not exist or is inadequate, it should be created or upgraded since analysis is perhaps the most important part of PPB.) A wide range of techniques is employed in these program analyses, including statistical analysis; modeling, gaming, and simulation; operations analysis; and econometric techniques. Systems analysis examines both the resource/cost side and the benefit/effectiveness side of program consequences.

An important aspect of systems analysis in connection with program planning is that it often goes far beyond the decision problem as initially given. Program analysis is not confined to examination of predetermined alternatives; development of new and better alternatives is part of the process. It is likely that analysis of possibilities A, B, and C will lead to the invention of alternatives D and E, which may be preferable (more cost/effective) to the original candidates. Therefore, the analytical aspect of PPB cannot be viewed merely as the application of a collection of well-defined analytical techniques to a problem. The process is much more flexible and subtle, and calls for creativity by the analyst and interaction between the analyst and the decision maker during the decision process.

Other Important Features

Some other features of the PPB system will convey a fuller impression of the context in which these principles are applied. First, since program decisions that we make today often have implications that extend far into the future, and since program costs may be incurred and benefits enjoyed many years after a decision is made, meaningful planning requires a *long-time horizon*. Generally, the program budget itself and the associated program analyses cover at least a five-year period and, where appropriate, should extend ten, fifteen, or more years into the future.

Planning, not forecasting, is the purpose of the PPB system. Our aim is to examine the cost and benefit implications for the future of relevant alternative courses of action. The program budget, which conveys a projection of existing programs and a display of decisions already made, provides a base line and serves as a frame of reference for specification and analysis of alternatives. It should not be thought of as a static extrapolation of a program.

Comparability rather than accuracy is the main consideration in our analysis of program cost and benefits. Because of intrinsic uncertainties in long-range planning, absolute accuracy is not attainable. The relevant criterion for analyses is consistency in treatment of different alternatives; this must be accompanied by explicit treatment of uncertainties, including tests of the sensitivity of analytical results to variations in circumstances. Excessive concentration on absolute accuracy is likely to be self-defeating since it would tend to overwhelm the work with detail and make this kind of planning impracticable. In addition, aggregate, not detailed, data must generally be used in cost and benefit estimation. Examination of many alternatives is costly or impossible, so we must focus on variables that have important impacts on program consequences.

Several points may be made about the cost concepts that enter into program analysis. *Full costing* of programs and program alternatives is required if we are to achieve consistency in our estimates. Programs often have indirect cost implications that are difficult to trace; important interdependencies may exist between "direct" and "support" programs or among direct programs themselves (for example, joint cost situations). In order to sort out the full cost implications of alternatives, it is often necessary to have a cost model or its equivalent that is capable of translating the total program of the organization into resource and cost implications. The cost figures that will actually be compared with benefit estimates are incremental costs associated with specific program decisions, but these must be derived by comparing the full costs of either another program alternative or a base case.

Resources and costs are generally divided into three categories, corresponding to differences in the time pattern by which they are incurred and in the duration of their contribution to benefits. Research and development costs are the one-time outlays to create new capability, for example, studies of new products, services, or technologies, or of new methods for accomplishing programs. Investment costs are the nonrecurring outlays required to install new capability, for example, construction of plants or facilities, purchase of equipment, or training of personnel for participation in new programs. Annual operating costs are the recurring costs required either to operate new capability to be installed or existing capability to be maintained. Each of these elements of cost enters into the full cost of a program. All three are projected on a year-by-year basis and summed for each program and for the total program of the organization. Capital and operating cost implications of programs are looked at together, not separately as is the traditional practice.

A planning-programming-budgeting system provides for communication between analysts and decision makers and between analysts, operating organizations, and decision makers at different organizational levels. Some specific documentary forms have been developed to facilitate this exchange of information. For example, *program memoranda* provide the communication between the analysts within a program area and the analytical staff that services the decision-making group. In these paper studies the program group lays out the issues it identifies in the program area, the alternatives it recommends, and the pros and cons for its recommendations, as well as the data, analysis, and arguments for the possibilities it has rejected.

The top-side analytical group reanalyzes the program memorandum and writes its memorandum in response. The reply may accept the recommendations for the same, different, or modified reasons; determine issues that have not been raised; suggest alternative program packages that have not been considered; or modify alternatives that were examined. After as much study, analysis, and reanalysis as time permits, the top staff, with concurrence or objection from the program manager, drafts the final program memorandum covering all issues and all alternatives for consideration by the decision maker.

Special studies require more time and/or study resources than are available during the program memorandum period as scheduled. These areas are assigned for completion in the near future in order of importance and will frequently (not always) cut across areas handled by two or more program managers. For reasons of time or specialized knowledge, parts or all of these studies may be contracted out.

Program change is another administrative step calling for analysis and study. Program budgeting aims at a continuing, fluid management process. This means setting up a "base case" or set of decisions taken now, which are revised and updated as required. When change is or appears to be in order, the proposed change is considered in a total resource, over-all time context, just as though it was a program memorandum in the original deliberations. Ideally, this would mean only one over-all program budget exercise. Changes would be made as required and the revised total plan would become the new base case, which would be used for the crosswalk from the program budget into the immediate changes in the budget as well as next year's organizational and functional operating budgets.

Introducing PPB

Two possible courses of action are open for the introduction of program budgeting. One is to set up a study group to examine the government's or company's objectives, develop a program structure tailored to those objectives, recommend alternative organization and administration schemes, examine the organization's analytical capabilities, and recommend education, training, and hiring policies to be followed in developing the analysis capacity required for program budgeting. (Reassignment, upgrading, and so on would obviously be included.) This approach would aim at an operation to start eighteen months to two years in the future.

The other course of action starts with the assumption that program budgeting is the thing to do and to get on with it. This would mean taking some great leaps to put it in use in a current planning and budget cycle, and to learn in the process the answers the study group would otherwise have provided. This procedure is described in the following steps.

1. Set up a program structure that uses major activities or lines of business as final product programs, taking major government agency-wide or company-wide activities like electronic data processing (EDP), and calling them major support programs and putting everything else, like research, planning, and executives, into a general support program category. This may or may not be the right program basis. Probably, it is not. However, it will fit existing practice and is a satisfactory starting point for developing improvements.

2. Have several final product programs and major support programs made the subject of program memoranda to be completed in six to eight weeks. Use the existing analytic capability. The development of program memoranda and the other communication materials of the program budget relies heavily on analysis. Therefore, if the analytic organization is either understaffed or inadequate, immediate steps should be taken to expand and upgrade.

3. Designate the individual or individuals to complete the program structure in order to accomodate all activities to the three major areas identified in step 1 above. These studies should be completed in eight to ten weeks.

4. Designate the individual or individuals to develop a first-cut study on alternatives available for organization and administration of program budgeting in the government unit or the business organization.

5. Agree on program identification, possible program manager, organization and administration, schedule of steps to be taken, and dates.

6. Get executive approval and move on.

One of the major advantages of this approach is that from the outset we get the required interaction between the operating, analytical, and decision-making parts of the organization; this interaction is essential to the development of an effective program budgeting system. Time is saved and more intimate knowledge of the content of the administrative procedure is developed by both analytical and operating personnel.

Relationship Described

The relationship between program and budget and planning, programming, and budgeting merits more complete description. It is rather commonplace in the literature on budgeting for business to say, "The budget is the financial expression of a plan." Many people apply the same definition for government. Nonetheless, we are all familiar with the budget that was developed without a plan (particularly a long-range plan). In fact, it is probably fair to say that in most budgets any planning is a projection of the status quo with increments added on the basis of the most current experience. A statement made by Roswell Gilpatric, when he was Deputy Secretary of Defense in 1961, typifies one of these situations: "In the past, the Defense Department has often developed its force structure by starting with a budget and sending it off in search of a program."[4] On the other hand there are elaborate plans made by either government or business that never get beyond top level approval — that is, are never budgeted.

Planning is the production of a range of meaningful potential courses of action through a systematic consideration of alternatives. In the short range, it deals with a limited number of alternatives because past actions have already locked in the available paths. However, for the long range (the major emphasis of program budgeting) the planning activity attempts to examine as many alternative courses of action as appear to be feasible and to project the future course of the organization against these in cost-benefit terms. Since the objective is not to make specific decisions but rather to turn up likely possibilities, the work is done in a general and highly aggregative form.

Programming is the more detailed determination of the manpower, equipment, and facilities necessary for accomplishing a program-feasibility testing in terms of specific resources and time. The program and its elements used in the planning process in highly aggregative terms are moved down the scale to more detailed terms (as detailed as is appropriate) required for determining the feasibility of the possibilities. Even here, for most cost elements, we are at a level of aggregation above that required for the detailed determinations involved in next year's budget. That budget is the translation of program cost elements into the specific funding and time requirements identified in traditional terms such as object class, function, and organization.

How do we distinguish the program budget from the traditional next-year's budget? PPB is the development and preparation of a budget in a planning context, that is, with information about what is in store for the future. The planning context puts it in contrast to the short-range fiscal

---

[4] Roswell L. Gilpatric, "Defense — How Much Will It Cost?" *California Management Review,* V (Fall, 1962), p. 53.

management and expenditure control objectives that categorize the traditional approach. This new method allows for major shifts among purposes for which resources are to be used, ranging from changes in funding levels to the introduction of completely new activities.

Under the program budget, annual allotments to administrative organizations allow them to take the next step along a path thoughtfully set by policy makers at all levels. Probably more important, the direction of the path and the distance to be covered in the next year will have been established after considering a number of possible futures.

Supplemental
Readings
to Part One

Hector R. Anton, "Activity Analysis of the Firm: A Theoretical Approach to Accounting (Systems) Development," *The Journal of Business Economics,* Vol. IV, (1961), pp. 290–305.

Accounting needs to design more general theoretical systems to satisfy the information requirements of managerial decision-making. Accountants also must not lose sight of the interdependency between the information structure and organizational behavior.

John A. Beckett, "A Study of the Principles of Allocating Costs," *The Accounting Review,* Vol. XXVI, No. 3 (July, 1951), pp. 327–333.

Rules for applying, allocating, and prorating costs are described, in the context of various intended uses of the data, e.g., profit measurement and general control, cost planning and control, pricing, and evaluation of alternative actions.

Norton M. Bedford, "The Nature of Business Costs, General Concepts," *The Accounting Review,* Vol. XXXII, No. 1 (January, 1957), pp. 8–14.

Basic cost concepts are described, and specific attention is given to the behavior of cost and its measurement. This article serves as an introduction to broad conceptual problems and a means of approaching them.

Jacob G. Birnberg and Raghu Nath, "Implications of Behavioral Science for Managerial Accounting," *The Accounting Review,* Vol. XLII, No. 3 (July, 1967), pp. 468–479.

Relevant literature and fruitful areas for further research are discussed.

R. Lee Brummet, Eric G. Flamholtz, and William C. Pyle, "Human Resource Measurement — A Challenge for Accountants," *The Accounting Review,* Vol. XLIII, No. 2 (April, 1968), pp. 217–224.

Complexities of human resource measurement, and its relevance to managerial decisions are discussed.

William J. Bruns, Jr., "Accounting Information and Decision-Making: Some Behavioral Aspects," *The Accounting Review,* Vol. XLIII, No. 3 (July, 1968), pp. 469–480.

A model identifies factors which determine when accounting data affect decisions.

Edwin H. Caplan, "Behavioral Assumptions of Management Accounting," *The Accounting Review,* Vol. XLI, No. 3 (July, 1966), pp. 496–509.

Behavioral assumptions associated with "traditional" management accounting are postulated.

Edwin H. Caplan, "Behavioral Assumptions of Management Accounting — Report of a Field Study," *The Accounting Review*, Vol. XLIII, No. 2 (April, 1968), pp. 342–362.

Two models concerning management accountants' views of human behavior are described.

Edwin H. Caplan, "Management Accounting and the Behavioral Sciences," *Management Accounting*, Vol. 50, No. 10 (June, 1969), pp. 41–45.

Behavioral implications of various aspects of management accounting are presented.

Howard M. Carlisle, "Cost Accounting for Advanced Technology Programs," *The Accounting Review*, Vol. XLI, No. 1 (January, 1966), pp. 115–120.

Guidelines for the use of cost accounting in research programs are provided.

A. Charnes and W. W. Cooper, "Some Network Characterizations for Mathematical Programming and Accounting Approaches to Planning and Control," *The Accounting Review*, Vol. XLII, No. 1 (January, 1967), pp. 24–52.

Some of the ways in which accounting and mathematical programming might be related are explored.

Neil Churchill, "Linear Algebra and Cost Allocations: Some Examples," *The Accounting Review*, Vol. 39, No. 4 (October, 1964), pp. 894–904.

Linear algebra is applied to a problem of reciprocal cost allocation.

James C. Cohrs, "The Accountant's Responsibility for Effective Management Control," *Management Controls*, Vol. 12, No. 2 (February, 1965), pp. 32–37.

The role of the accounting system in helping management exercise control is examined.

Bertram A. Colbert, "The Management Information System," *The Price Waterhouse Review*, Vol. 12, No. 1 (Spring, 1967), pp. 4–14.

The "what", "when", and "how" of vital management information needs: an overview.

John W. Coughlan, "Industrial Accounting," *The Accounting Review*, Vol. XXXIX, No. 3 (July, 1959), pp. 415–428.

Financial and industrial accounting are contrasted. To avoid periodic allocations and elaborate cost distributions, attention is centered on *project* time rather than "realization". Advantages of industrial accounting approaches are emphasized.

Joe J. Cramer, Jr. and Thomas Iwand, "Financial Reporting for Conglomerates: An Economic Analysis," *California Management Review*, Vol. XI, No. 3 (Spring, 1969), pp. 25–33.

Proposed SEC regulations on conglomerate reporting, including a discussion of joint costs, are examined.

C. William Devaney, "Examples of Program Budgeting for Non-Profit Administrative Decisions," *The Price Waterhouse Review*, Vol. 13, No. 2 (Summer, 1968), pp. 44–53.

Illustrations of Planning — Program — Budgeting Systems for nonprofit groups are given.

Franz Edelman, "Accounting and Operations Research — Example of a Problem in Marketing Channels", *NAA Bulletin,* Vol. XLI, No. 6 (February, 1960), pp. 27–36.

Acknowledging the role of accounting as the primary information system for planning and controlling, a case is used to illustrate how a blend of OR and accounting can remedy accounting deficiencies.

John E. Field, "Toward a Multi-Level, Multi-Goal Information System," *The Accounting Review,* Vol. XLIV, No. 3 (July, 1969), pp. 593–599.

Accounting must be designed to facilitate control of a multi-level, multi-goal organization structure.

Gerald A. Feltham, "The Value of Information," *The Accounting Review,* Vol. XLIII, No. 4 (October, 1968), pp. 684–696.

A model for determining the net value of a change in the information system is described.

Saul Gellerman, "Behavioral Strategies," *California Management Review,* Vol. XII, No. 2 (Winter, 1969), pp. 45–51.

Comparison is made of "traditional" cost control strategy with one which encourages increased productivity.

Charles H. Griffin, "Multiple Products Costing in Petroleum Refining," *The Journal of Accountancy,* Vol. 105, No. 3 (March, 1958), pp. 46–52.

The problem dealing with joint costs is discussed in the context of petroleum refining. Suggestions for generalization of the methodology are given.

E. Reece Harrill, "Cost Accounting and Control — In Government," *Management Controls,* Vol. 15, No. 12 (December, 1968), pp. 265–269.

The use of cost accounting in all phases of government accounting is explained.

Charles J. Hitch, "Program Budgeting," *Datamation,* Vol. 13, No. 9 (September, 1967), pp. 37–40.

Risks and opportunities in expanding program budgeting to non-military areas are explored.

Charles T. Horngren, "Motivation and Coordination in Management Control Systems," *Management Accounting,* Vol. 48, No. 9 (May, 1967), pp. 3–7.

Do budgets and responsibility accounting foster departmental orientation at the expense of total organizational orientation?

Yuji Ijiri, Robert K. Jaedicke, and Kenneth E. Knight, "The Effects of Accounting Alternatives on Management Decisions," *Research in Accounting Measurement,* (Chicago: American Accounting Association, 1966), pp. 186–199.

Conditions under which alternative accounting methods affect management decisions are explained.

Howard G. Johnson, "Key Item Control," *The Price Waterhouse Review,* Vol. 11, No. 3 (Autumn, 1966), pp. 26–32.

Managerial effectiveness can be increased through control of "key items".

Rene P. Manes, "Comment on Matrix Theory and Cost Allocations," *The Accounting Review,* Vol. XL, No. 3 (July, 1965), pp. 640–643.

Another view on the use of matrices for cost allocation is presented.

Robert K. Mautz and K. Fred Skousen, "Common Cost Allocation in Diversified Companies," *Financial Executive,* Vol. 36, No. 6 (June, 1968), pp. 15–25.

Various approaches to the resolution of the problem of common cost allocation in diversified enterprises are presented.

T. W. McRae, "Opportunity and Incremental Cost: An Attempt to Define in Systems Terms," *The Accounting Review,* Vol. XLV, No. 2 (April, 1970), pp. 315–321.

A comparison is made of "traditional" concepts of opportunity and incremental costs with a "systems" approach to the concepts.

Alfred Rappaport, "Sensitivity Analysis in Decision Making," *The Accounting Review,* Vol. XLII, No. 3 (July, 1967), pp. 441–456.

Sensitivity analysis can improve the basis for decision making: an illustration.

Kenneth R. Rickey, "Control Cost Accounting," *Management Accounting,* Vol. 51, No. 10 (April, 1970), pp. 9–13.

Control cost accounting is based on the theory that all costs are created by people.

L. S. Rosen and R. E. Schneck, "Some Behavioral Consequences of Accounting Measurement Systems," *Cost and Management,* Vol. 41, No. 9 (October, 1967), pp. 6–16.

Behavioral weaknesses of accounting measurement systems, and what to do about them, are reviewed.

Robert M. Trueblood, "Operations Research — A Challenge to Accounting," *The Journal of Accountancy,* Vol. 109, No. 5 (May, 1960), pp. 47–51.

Methods of operations research, implemented by computer, can help cost accountants and enhance the value of accounting information.

Additional Bibliography to Part One

American Marketing Association, "The Values and Uses of Distribution Costs," *Journal of Marketing,* Vol. 21 (April, 1957), pp. 395–400.

Robert N. Anthony, "Cost Concepts for Control," *The Accounting Review,* Vol. XXXII, No. 2 (April, 1957), pp. 229–234.

————, "Framework for Analysis," *Management Services,* Vol. 1, No. 1 (March-April, 1964), pp. 18–24.

Dirck Barhydt, Robert H. Clement, Dan W. Lufkin, A. Jones Yorke, "Planning Concepts in the Tentative Statement of Cost Concepts," *The Accounting Review,* Vol. XXXII, No. 4 (October, 1957), pp. 593–597.

William J. Baumol and Charles H. Sevin, "Marketing Costs and Mathematical Programming," *Harvard Business Review,* Vol. 35, No. 5 (September-October, 1957), pp. 52–60.

Norton M. Bedford, "Cost Accounting as a Motivation Technique," *NA(C)A Bulletin,* Vol. XXXVIII, No. 10 (June, 1957), pp. 1250–1257.

E. J. Broster, "The Concept and Practice of Marginal Costing," *The Accountant,* Vol. 150, No. 4652, pp. 179–183, and No. 4653, pp. 227–230. (February 15 and 22, 1964).

R. Lee Brummet, "Overhead Costing: The Costing of Manufactured Products," *Michigan Business Studies,* Vol. 13, No. 2 (1957).

A. Charnes, W. W. Cooper and M. H. Miller, "Application of L-P to Financial Budgeting and the Costing of Funds," *The Journal of Business,* Vol. XXXII, No. 1 (January, 1959), pp. 20–46.

Neil Churchill, "Another Look at Accounting for Idle Capacity," *NAA Bulletin,* Vol. XXXIX, No. 5 (January, 1958), pp. 83–87.

C. West Churchman and Russell L. Ackoff, "Operational Accounting and Operations Research," *The Journal of Accountancy,* Vol. 99, No. 2 (February, 1955), pp. 33–39.

Paul Crossman, "Functions of the Cost Accountant in Cost Control," *The Accounting Review,* Vol. XXVIII, No. 1 (January, 1953), pp. 25–31.

Lewis R. Crum, "Role of Cost Accounting in Cost Control," *The Accounting Review,* Vol. XXVIII, No. 3 (July, 1953), pp. 363–372.

H. Justin Davidson and Robert M. Trueblood, "Accounting for Decision-Making," *The Accounting Review,* Vol. XXXVI, No. 4 (October, 1961), pp. 577–582.

Sidney Davison, "Old Wine into New Bottles," *The Accounting Review,* Vol. XXXVIII, No. 2 (April, 1963), pp. 278–284.

John Dearden, "Monthly Unit Costs — Are They Still Significant?" *NAA Bulletin,* Vol. XLII, No. 7 (March, 1961), pp. 83–91.

Thomas S. Dudick, "Common Errors in Costing," *The Controller,* Vol. XXIX, No. 6 (June, 1961), pp. 280–284.

James S. Earley and Willard T. Carleton, "Budgeting and the Theory of the Firm," *The Journal of Industrial Economics,* Vol. X, No. 3 (July, 1962), pp. 165–173.

Wilford J. Eiteman and Glen E. Guthrie, "The Shape of the Average Cost Curve," *The American Economic Review,* Vol. XLII, No. 5 (December, 1952), pp. 832–838.

Mordecai Ezekial and Kathryn H. Wylie, "Cost Functions for the Steel Industry," *Journal of the American Statistical Association,* Vol. 36, No. 213 (March, 1941), pp. 91–99.

A. R. Ferguson, "Empirical Determination of a Multidimensional Marginal Cost Function," *Econometrica,* Vol. 18, No. 3 (July, 1950), pp. 217–235.

William L. Ferrara, "Overhead Costs and Income Measurement," *The Accounting Review,* Vol. XXXVI, No. 1 (January, 1961), pp. 63–70.

————, "Relevant Costing — Two Points of View," *The Accounting Review,* Vol. XXXVIII, No. 4 (October, 1963), pp. 719–722.

————, "What Managerial Functions Does Accounting Serve?" *Financial Executive,* Vol. XXXII, No. 7 (July, 1964), pp. 27–33.

George W. Frank, "Combined Costing Procedures at Work," *NAA Bulletin,* Vol. XLIII, No. 10 (June, 1962), pp. 15–24.

Harold E. Gannon, Jr., "Methods of Measuring and Controlling Distribution Costs," *NA(C)A Bulletin,* Vol. XXXVI, No. 7 (March, 1955), pp. 931–939.

Melvyn Greene and Richard J. Cornwell, A.C.A., "Added Value — An Important Factor in Financial Control," *The Accountant,* Vol. 150, No. 4660 (April 11, 1964), pp. 431–433.

Leonard W. Hein, "J. Lee Nicholson: Pioneer Cost Accountant," *The Accounting Review,* Vol. XXXIV, No. 1 (January, 1959), pp. 106–111.

J. Hugh Jackson, "A Quarter Century of Cost Accounting Progress," *NA(C)A Bulletin,* Vol. XXVIII, No. 19 (June, 1947), pp. 1201–1209.

Robert K. Jaedicke, "Marketing Cost Analysis — A Reply," *NAA Bulletin,* Vol. XLIII, No. 11 (July, 1962), pp. 57–61.

E. W. Kelley, "Marketing Cost Analysis — The Accountant's Most Neglected Opportunity," *NAA Bulletin,* Vol. XLI, No. 11 (July, 1960), pp. 11–21.

————, "Marketing Needs Cost Control," *The Controller,* Vol. XXI, No. 5 (May, 1953), pp. 219–222.

Walter Kennon, "Fixed Cost and Product Mix Control by Activity Analysis," *NA(C)A Bulletin,* Vol. XXXVII, No. 3 (November, 1955), pp. 319–334.

Philip Kreger, "Better Accounting for Fixed Expenses in a Seasonal Business," *NAA Bulletin,* Vol. XXXIX, No. 8 (April, 1958), pp. 65–70.

Eugene Ladin, "The Role of the Accountant in Operation Analysis," *The Accounting Review,* Vol. XXXVII, No. 2 (April, 1962), pp. 289–294.

Theodore Lang, "Concepts of Cost, Past and Present," *NA(C)A Bulletin,* Vol. XXVIII, No. 22 (July 15, 1947), pp. 1337–1390.

Gerald H. Lawson, "Joint Cost Analysis as an Aid to Management — A Further Note," *The Accounting Review,* Vol. XXXII, No. 3 (July, 1957), pp. 431–433.

Arthur N. Lorig, "Joint Cost Analysis as an Aid to Management," *The Accounting Review,* Vol. XXX, No. 4 (October, 1955), pp. 634–637.

————, "Replying to 'A Further Note' on Joint Cost Analysis," *The Accounting Review,* Vol. XXXIII, No. 1 (January, 1958), pp. 35–36.

W. F. Luttrell, "Some Problems of Inter-Plant Cost Comparisons," *Accounting Research,* Vol. 5, No. 2 (April, 1954), pp. 107–120.

Roger S. Makepeace, "Time-Based Distribution of Selling and General Costs," *NA(C)A Bulletin,* Vol. XXXVIII, No. 1 (September, 1956), pp. 40–55.

H. B. Malmgren, "What Conclusions Can Be Drawn from Empirical Cost Data?" *The Journal of Industrial Economics,* Vol. VII, No. 2 (March, 1959), pp. 136–144.

Rene Pierre Manes, "Using Computers to Improve Distribution of Service Costs," *The Journal of Accountancy,* Vol. 115, No. 3 (March, 1963), pp. 57–60.

R. P. Manes and Vernon L. Smith, "Economic Joint Cost Theory and Accounting Practice," *The Accounting Review,* Vol. XL, No. 1 (January, 1965), pp. 31–35.

Brian A. Maynard, "Productivity in the Office," *Accountancy,* Vol. LXXIV, No. 842 (October, 1963), pp. 866–874.

Robert K. McLain, "The Pool Method of Setting Overhead Rates," *NAA Bulletin,* Vol. XLI, No. 5 (January, 1960), pp. 75–83.

Martin Mellman, "Cost Analysis for the Marketing Function," *The New York Certified Public Accountant,* Vol. XXXII, Nos. 5 and 6 (May and June, 1962), pp. 327–333; 395.

————, "Marketing Cost Analysis — Its Relationship to Factory Costing Methods," *NAA Bulletin,* Vol. XLIII, No. 5 (January, 1962), pp. 25–33.

M. J. Mepham, "Concepts of Cost," *The Accountant,* Vol. 150, No. 4648 (January 18, 1964), pp. 61–64.

Frank H. Mossman, "Distribution Costs, Where Are They?" *The Controller,* Vol. XXX, No. 5 (May, 1962), pp. 302 ff.

Osamu Nisizawa, "Inventory Cost Allocation Practices and Concepts," *NAA Bulletin,* Vol. XLI, No. 4 (December, 1959), pp. 81–93.

Harold E. Paddock, "Production Waste — Its Nature and Its Accounting," *The Accounting Review,* Vol. XXXIII, No. 1 (January, 1958), pp. 50–55.

Claude M. Papion, "Operations Research and Inventory Control," *The Canadian Chartered Accountant,* Vol. 82, No. 6 (June, 1963), pp. 427–432.

Carlton D. Randleman, "Achieving Benefits of Practical and Average Capacity in Burden Accounting," *NA(C)A Bulletin,* Vol. XXXVIII, No. 3 (November, 1956), pp. 376–383.

Donald L. Raun, "Accounting for Decisions," *The Accounting Review,* Vol. XXXVI, No. 3 (July, 1961), pp. 460–471.

Nicholas St. Peter, "New Concepts of Information for Management Decisions — In Production," *NAA Bulletin,* Vol. XL, No. 12 (August, 1959), pp. 3–10.

Hadley P. Schaefer, "The Distribution Cost Problem," *The Accounting Review,* Vol. XXXIII, No. 4 (October, 1958), pp. 625–631.

Sam E. Schraff, "The Industrial Engineer and the Cost Accountant," *NAA Bulletin,* Vol. XLII, No. 7 (March, 1961), pp. 13–24.

Charles F. Schlatter, "Fixed Expense," *The Accounting Review,* Vol. XX, No. 2 (April, 1945), pp. 156–163.

Anthony D. Scott, "Notes on User Cost," *The Economic Journal,* Vol. 63, No. 2 (June, 1953), pp. 369–384.

D. R. Scott, "Accounting Principles and Cost Accounting," *The Journal of Accountancy,* Vol. 67, No. 2 (February, 1939), pp. 70–76.

Wilson T. Seney, "Accounting — A Tool for Managers," *NA(C)A Bulletin,* Vol. XXXVI, No. 7 (March, 1955), pp. 891–903.

R. D. S. Shrimpton, "Service to Management," *Accountancy,* Vol. LXIV, No. 834 (February, 1963), pp. 129–138.

Sidney I. Simon, "Cost Accounting and the Law," *The Accounting Review,* Vol. XXXIX, No. 4 (October, 1964), pp. 884–889.

Marion H. Simpsen, "The Fallacies and Postulates of Accounting," *NAA Bulletin,* Vol. XXXIX, No. 6 (February, 1958), pp. 37–44.

David Solomons, "Uniform Cost Accounting: A Survey," *Economica Internazionale,* Vol. 17, Nos. 3–4 (August and November, 1950), pp. 237–273 and 386–400.

George H. Sorter and Charles T. Horngren, "Asset Recognition and Economic Attributes — The Relevant Costing Approach," *The Accounting Review,* Vol. XXXVII, No. 3 (July, 1962), pp. 391–399.

Leland G. Spencer, "Integrating Control and Allocation of Service Section Expense," *NAA Bulletin,* Vol. XLI, No. 5 (January, 1960), pp. 63–74.

Lambert H. Spronck, "Today's Costing Methods and Their Objectives," *The New York Certified Public Accountant,* Vol. XXVI, No. 5 (May, 1956), pp. 285–294.

Hans Staehle, "The Measurement of Statistical Cost Functions: Appraisal of Recent Developments," *The American Economic Review,* Vol. XXXII, No. 3 (June, 1942), pp. 321–333.

George J. Staubus, "Direct, Relevant or Absorption Costing?" *The Accounting Review,* Vol. XXXVIII, No. 1 (January, 1963), pp. 64–74.

G. F. Thirlby, "The Subjective Theory of Value and Accounting Cost," *Economica Internazionale,* Vol. 13, No. 1 (February, 1946), pp. 32–49.

Robert M. Trueblood, "Accounting and New Management Attitudes," *The Journal of Accountancy,* Vol. 106, No. 4 (October, 1958), pp. 37–42.

Jerrold G. Van Cise, "The Robinson-Patman Act and the Accountant," *The New York Certified Public Accountant,* Vol. XXVIII, No. 5 (May, 1958), pp. 351–362.

William J. Vatter, "Control Function of the Accountant As an Indispensable Part of Management," *The Journal of Accountancy,* Vol. 93, No. 6 (June, 1952), pp. 705–710.

Edward L. Wallace, "Some Comments on the Statement of Planning Costs," *The Accounting Review,* Vol. XXXII, No. 3 (July, 1957), pp. 448–466.

Robert H. Watson, "Two-Variate Analysis," *The Accounting Review,* Vol. XXXV, No. 1 (January, 1960), pp. 96–99.

Thomas H. Williams and Charles H. Griffin, "Matrix Theory and Cost Allocation," *The Accounting Review,* Vol. XXXIX, No. 3 (July, 1964), pp. 671–678.

J. P. Wilson, "Integral Accounting," *The Accountant,* Vol. 148, No. 4604 (March 16, 1963), pp. 308–312.

PART TWO

Cost Planning, Decision, and Control:
Forecasting and Budgeting

$\mathbf{A}$ first decision problem of accounting measurement is the selection of the object (or property of an object) to be measured. Prerequisite to this decision is a definition of organizational goals or objectives against which performance is to be evaluated. As predictive measurements, budgets and forecasts provide the standards for subsequent evaluation and control of organizational performance. In their practical application, many factors condition both the selection of measurement objects and the use of the measurements.

The first article in Part Two studies a major objective of business organizations — to maximize return on investment through sound pricing procedure. Pricing practice is seen as a coordinated effort of the cost accountant, industrial engineer, economist, statistician, and "marketeer." Forecasting future product costs and target prices for planned return on investment are central — as are market estimates, attainment, and promotion. Together with elasticity of demand and sales and cost trends, these are used to derive the price proposal. Rushton gives a detailed, step-by-step procedure for using the forecasts and the resulting price proposal. He eschews both cost- push and price-pull as being too simplistic; his program takes both views into account. His article also touches in a sound manner on other aspects of pricing. It is conclusive that adequate pricing forecasts are crucial for budgets that help to maximize long-run return on investment.

Budgets and forecasts should be as accurate and reliable as possible, subject to the constraint, of course, that the cost of achieving given levels of accuracy and reliability should not exceed the value of the incremental information yielded by the process. Some reasonable levels of accuracy and reliability are necessary, obviously, if budget and forecast data are to be useful as standards and predictors of performance. To achieve proper

90

levels of accuracy and reliability, Knapp advocates the use of correlation analysis in the forecasting and budgeting process. He argues further that the resultant increased precision in the budgeting process would increase management's sensitivity to problems of control.

Budgeting and forecasting include many specialized tools. Kilbridge has developed a mathematical model for industrial learning costs, emphasizing the fact that knowledge of the structure of the learning curve is important to the budgeting process. Increasingly, learning curves have been used in helping to set up realistic standards in situations requiring relatively large set-up costs or unique, but repetitive, operations — such as construction work. Standards employing learning characteristics can become useful in worker motivation and in the setting up of more realistic budgets. These in turn become better planning and control devices.

Irvine explores in a thorough and scholarly fashion the impact of budgeting on people. The article is especially valuable because it deals with both the good and the bad consequences of budgeting — depending on the way it is applied in various types of organizations. Irvine draws heavily on sociological and psychological studies of men and organizations in addition to the relevant accounting literature. He relates this literature to a carefully developed analytical study of budget systems.

CPM (Critical Path Method and PERT (Program Evaluation and Review Technique) were developed first as project scheduling techniques; later as more generalized scheduling and budgetary tools. Experience of many industries and governmental units, particularly the Department of Defense, has validated these procedures. Levy, Thompson, and Wiest introduce the Critical Path Method as a technique of scheduling and budgeting. They extend this discussion to the closely related PERT methods and related cost analysis. The article presents an excellent review of CPM and gives insight into PERT.

6 *Pricing on the basis of cost has long been a debatable practice, but the cost-plus formula abounds in practice. In this article emphasis is placed on pricing to maximize return on investment through a sound pricing policy.*

The author abjures a simple, single, criterion approach to pricing. In his analysis for price development he takes into account various factors such as profit goals, future product costs, target prices for given returns, competitive prices, market estimates, elasticity of demand, sales trends, and possible customer reaction to suggested price. A concise discussion of each of these points is given, then they are integrated in a price-development summary procedure that permits effective treatment of each factor.

Pricing to Maximize
Return on Investment*

James H. Rushton

Why is it that many businessmen dote on profit margin — percentage of profit on sales — yet when the same men trade in securities they ask, "What's the yield — the return on my investment?"

True, in business, adequate profit margins are necessary for stability and growth, but it is the ultimate return which encourages or discourages investment in corporate securities, and without investment there can be no business.

What is return on investment? The spontaneous answer is, the percentage of dollar profits to capital invested or capital employed. But more important, what produces return? There are two important factors: (1) profit margin and (2) turnover of investment which when put together in proper proportion produce return as follows:

- Profit margin multiplied by turnover of investment equals return on investment.

* From The Controller, *Vol. XXIII, No. 3 (March, 1955), pp. 107–112, 132–133.* Reprinted by permission of the publisher.*

Both factors, turnover and margin, are equally important. A percentage change in either of the factors has a corresponding effect on the return on investment, for example:

- A 20% profit margin multiplied by one turnover equals 20% return on investment.
- A 10% profit margin multiplied by two turnovers equals the same (20%) return on investment.

For purposes of this article profit margin is considered to be the result of dividing dollar operating profit by sales. Turnover of investment is the result of sales divided by the gross operating investment. Although the foregoing may be elementary, it is stressed because return on investment is the foundation of business enterprise, and therefore a business practice — particularly a pricing practice — should have one fundamental economic goal: To maximize long-range return on investment.

Right off the bat some may say, "From an economic standpoint your goal is sound, but sociologically speaking that kind of thinking breeds socialism." No, the sociology of pricing has not been overlooked — it is all wrapped up in the two words, "long range." Anything that is sociologically unsound is usually economically unsound over the long run. For example, the "all-the-market-will-bear" pricer might maximize his profits temporarily, but in so doing he likely prices himself out of the market, or so limits the demand that sales and profit disappear in the long run.

First, A Sound Pricing Policy

Although highly important, space does not permit the belaboring of the point that until a company has established a sound pricing policy to which management is agreed there is little hope of developing an effective pricing practice. It is well that the policy be evaluated periodically by comparison with a set of criteria compiled for the purpose. With these obvious comments, we will assume a sound pricing policy and get right on with pricing practice to which this article is dedicated.

A Practical Pricing Practice

Most of the pricing theorists and practitioners differ on the theories of pricing, but most recommend what Dr. Joel Dean of Columbia University describes as the "research approach to pricing." Likewise, most authorities agree that pricing is a complex subject and is not a one-man or one-activity job. Rather it needs the coordination of the cost accountant, industrial engineer, economist, statistician, and marketeer. Also, most agree that the job is, let us say, about one-third computation and two-thirds judgment. Nevertheless, the one-third computation is an essential aid to management in applying the two-thirds judgment.

Economic Analysis — A Panoramic View

How often has the executive asked: "Why don't we have some means of interpreting this maze of data which come across my desk in such a manner that I can reach a decision easily and timely?" What really is being asked for is a method by which he can take a "panoramic view" of all factors operating, pinpoint those most influencing the situation, and with this "one-third computation," apply the "two-thirds judgment" in reaching a decision. It seems logical that there is a place in almost any size organization for a data interpretation activity or program which, for purposes of this article, will be referred to as "Economic Analysis for Price Development."

Figure 1 contains an outline of an eight-step program of economic analysis for pricing and repricing of consumer products in a multi-product manufacturing company. This is not a program of cost-plus, or market-will-bear, or rule-of-thumb pricing; rather, it is one wherein all factors operating in our price economy can be evaluated for each product in a relatively simple and expeditious manner. As can be seen from Figure 1, the factors operating encompass costs, competitive prices, market, elasticity of demand, competitor and customer reactions, as well as other economic considerations.

FIGURE 1

Economic Analysis for Price Development

Objective: To Maximize Long-range Return on Investment

1. Master profit plan.
2. "Future" product costs specifically developed for pricing.
3. Target prices aimed at planned return on investment.
4. Competitive and companion-product prices.
5. Market estimates, market attainment, and promotion.
6. Elasticity of demand — sales, cost, and price trends.
7. Customers' and competitors' reactions.
8. The price proposal.

A hypothetical product, which will be identified as P-421, is used to illustrate this program. Let us assume that it is an established consumer product, made in production center "P," and is a part of product line "C," a homogeneous group of items with the same or similar utility. Examples might be a television tube, a screwdriver, an antibiotic tablet, or the like. Let us proceed to bring together all the factors operating for the purpose of evaluating the present price in determining whether or not our return on investment can be improved by repricing the product.

To see where we are headed, let us first take a quick glance at the end result, the Price Development Summary on P-421, illustrated in Figure 2. This is our "panoramic view" of all or most of the factors which make for a sound

FIGURE 2

Price Development Summary

Product Line: C Production Center: P Product #421

	Price	Sales		Direct Profit		Est. Net Profit (Before Tax)		% Product-Line Sales
		Units	$	$	%	$	%	
Present	$3.10	300	$930	$510	55%	$210	23%	20%
Proposed	2.65	366	970	510	53	210	22	21
% Change	−15%	+22%	+4%					

Unit Cost and Target Price			Company		Competitive Prices		Mkt. Attainment	Promotion Rating	Companion Products
	Con-version	Total Direct				Trend			
			Own	$3.10		0	10%	B	P-422
Present Cost	$0.75	$1.40	A	2.55		—	16	A	P-598
Future Cost	.65	1.25	B	2.50		—	17	C	P-621
Mark-on	100%	160%	C	1.90		0	3	D	
Target Price	$0.65	$2.00						Units	
$2.65			Market Estimate					3000	
			Attainment Goal			15%		450	

Sales, Cost and Price Trends			Customers' and Competitors' Reactions
Unit	(1950–51)	+15%	Demand appears relatively elastic. Cos. "A" and "B" are not likely to reduce price further. Co. "C's" product not fully comparable in quality and potency.
Sales	(1952–53)	−12%	
Direct	(1950–52)	–0–	
Cost	(1953)	−11%	
Price	(1950–53)	–0–	
ACTION: Proposed price adopted Effective: 3–54			Comments:

price. Reference will be made to this chart from time to time. Of interest now is the present price, $3.10 per unit, and the new price being proposed, $2.65, a 15% reduction. The why and the wherefore of this proposal is developed in the following by discussing each step of the economic analysis in the order shown — not necessarily in the order of importance.

1. A MASTER PROFIT PLAN

There should not be disagreement on Step No. 1 that any program needs an economic goal — not just a sales quota or a profit budget, but a plan aimed at achieving an adequate return on investment. Figure 3 illustrates a hypothetical plan aimed at 20% return in production center "P". A 20% return may be wishful thinking in any industry today, but it should not be unrealistic when we consider that it is before federal income tax and measured on "gross operating investment," which as defined in this instance is the actual capital employed in producing operating profit.

The oversimplified breakdown of income and expense in Figure 3 is given solely to illustrate pricing techniques described later. In segregating income and expense between "direct cost" and "direct profit," the author does not advocate the "direct costing" method of accounting but does wish to say that the method has much to recommend it from an economic and statistical planning standpoint.

Total direct costs (sometimes referred to as variable, marginal, or product costs) are used instead of cost of goods sold because, first, knowledge is desired of all costs, not only manufacturing but also of administrative, selling, etc., which can be conveniently identified with selling a given amount of sales.

Secondly, we should know the direct profit, the excess of selling price over direct cost (or marginal profit, or contribution profit, as some call it), because it represents the out-and-out real profit of a company after break-even volume has been obtained. Why combine fixed costs and profit before tax under direct profit? Because there is little, if any, change in rate of direct profit or direct profit per unit regardless of the level of production — not considering cost, price and capacity changes. At the unit-product level all

FIGURE 3

Profit Plan

Goal: 20% Profit (Before Tax) Return on Gross Investment

Income and Expense		
Sales		$1,000
Direct Cost:		
Material	$300	
Conversion	200	500
Direct Profit:		
Fixed Cost Absorption	$250	
Profit (Before Tax)	250	$ 500

Gross Investment		Direct Profit
Current Assets	$ 750	$300
Fixed Assets	500	200
Total	$1,250	$500

$$\boxed{\begin{array}{c} \text{Direct Profit} \\ \text{Margin} \\ \dfrac{\$500}{\$1,000} = 50\% \end{array}} \times \boxed{\begin{array}{c} \text{Turnover of} \\ \text{Investment} \\ \dfrac{\$1,000}{\$1,250} = 80\% \end{array}} = \boxed{\begin{array}{c} \text{Direct Profit} \\ \text{Return on} \\ \text{Investment} \\ 40\% \end{array}}$$

that occurs is a switch between the two components, namely, fixed cost absorption and real profits. Therefore, it is not enough to say that $250 will be earned in this instance to achieve 20% return on gross operating investment of $1,250, but rather that the $250 profit plus $250 fixed cost must be earned to achieve the 20%.

With these points in mind we can come back to the return on investment equation, redefine it as above and put in the hypothetical figures, namely:

- 50% direct profit margin multiplied by 80% turnover of investment equals a 40% direct profit return on investment, which must be earned to achieve our 20% pre-tax profit return on total investment.

(See bottom of Figure 3.)

2. "FUTURE" PRODUCT COSTS

Most pricing theorists are taboo on the "cost plus" approach to pricing but most agree that a firm needs to have a thorough understanding of its unit-product costs — if not to guide its pricing — at least to have a rational estimate of the profitability of the product.

Costs for valuation of inventories and profit determination are primarily historical; whereas, the costs needed for pricing are future costs planned, analyzed, and interpreted specifically for that purpose. By "future costs" is meant the latest information on prevailing *trends* in material, warehousing, and shipping costs, labor rates, engineered standards, yields, etc.

Furthermore, such unit costs will not give maximum benefit until the direct and fixed portions are segregated. Management needs to know not only the profitableness of the product but also whether the product can be competitively priced in the industry and still contribute sufficiently to direct profits to justify keeping it in the price list; also, management needs to be prepared to move the price along with technological improvements toward that point of optimum profit, namely, where marginal revenue equals marginal cost.

In brief, it can be said that when we step back from the trees and look at the woods what is needed for pricing are dynamic future costs compiled in a manner to give:

1. Direct cost of each product, both manufacturing and nonmanufacturing, and
2. Fixed costs by production center, division, or whole plant, whichever of the three, or combination of the three, is most realistic to the product line in light of industry conditions.

A realistic unit cost analysis for pricing and planning is illustrated in the upper left-hand section of Figure 4.

By placing emphasis on realistic cost data, it is not meant to give them importance out of proportion to their usefulness. Unit costs are merely a signpost to the profit status of the product and, as we will see, to the return on investment in the product. Too frequently in multi-product pricing, full dependence is placed on the cost percentage on sales or its complement gross margin. As said at the outset profit margin is just one of the factors in the return on investment equation. This leads to the third step, "target prices."

3. TARGET PRICES

If the objective is to maximize return on investment, should not each product be priced so that it will contribute to the planned dollar return? True, other factors which will be discussed later may require the pricing of some products at a higher or lower rate of return than others, but certainly there should be an optimum starting point.

Some might say, "Your theory is fine for planning company-wide return, but how can the investment applicable to each product be determined in a multi-product plant?" This is desirable but it is not absolutely necessary because of accounting principles which make the income and expense statement and the statement of financial condition interrelated — one produces the other.

Financially a business enterprise represents a flow of funds. Funds are converted into assets; these assets are reconverted into more funds through sales; and in turn these funds are converted into more assets, and so on. Certain assets turn over more rapidly than others; consequently, if the funds used for manufacturing costs can be identified with the assets which produce them, the unit costs themselves can be made to reflect investment, and thereby

FIGURE 4

Target Price — Product P-421

Est. Future Cost Per Unit:		Direct Profit Mark-on	
Material	$0.60		
Conversion	.65	× 100% =	$0.65
Total Direct Cost	1.25	× 160% =	2.00
Direct Profit	1.40		
Target Price	$2.65		$2.65

Direct Profit Per Unit			
Standard Capacity =	80%	90%	100%
Fixed Cost Absorption	$1.10	$1.00	$ .90
Profit (Before Tax)	.30	.40	.50
Direct Profit	$1.40	$1.40	$1.40
Profit (Before Tax) Margin	11%	15%	19%

an adequate return can be computed for each product or, at least, for a group of products produced by the same assets.

Out of these theorems comes an idea which, for identification, will be called "The Return on Investment Theory of Pricing." The idea was sparked by a manuscript presented by H. T. McAnly, CPA (see related reading). In brief, Mr. McAnly stated:

> In determining the portion of gross margin sufficient to absorb general selling expense and provide a reasonable profit, consideration should be given to the turnover of working capital in relation to sales and the turnover of investment in physical properties in relation to the value or hours of conversion cost produced.

The explanation of this theory may appear complicated; nevertheless, in application once the basic figures are compiled it is relatively simple to apply. This is the logical place to discuss the theory, but it is well to be forewarned not to allow the computation of the target price to overshadow the other equally important factors listed on the program. It is just one point in the economic analysis.

For an insight into the theory, the hypothetical product P-421 will be used for illustration. First, turn to the master profit plan of production center "P" (Figure 3). The basic return-on-investment equation is now to be put into play at the product level to produce the desired 40% direct-profit return. The job is to fill in the other elements of the equation.

The gross investment is split between two major components, current assets and fixed assets, because the turnover of the two vary, and therefore one component may need more margin than the other. It follows from the foregoing that the turnover of each component must be known. Working capital, or gross current assets, as has been used here, supplies the money for manufacturing; so it is logical to earn the current asset portion on total direct cost. Since physical properties are used for converting materials into finished products, it stands to reason that its portion should be earned on conversion costs. The elements used, although different from those used by Mr. McAnly, do not alter the principles. Furthermore, the various elements will differ between industries and even companies within industries. Consequently, it is advisable to determine through statistical measures what costs correlate with what assets and furthermore to ascertain whether the correlation is typical of the industry — a very important point.

Let us assume that for the purpose of this illustration our contentions have been tested and validated that conversion costs and fixed assets correlate and is found typical and that the turnover is projected at 40% per year. Also that total direct cost and current assets correlate, and that the turnover is projected at $66\frac{2}{3}\%$ per year.

We are now ready to complete the return on investment equation at the product level. Figure 5 repeats the equation as it appeared on the profit plan at production center level. At the product level, since the desired direct-profit return is given, and turnover must necessarily be based on costs instead of sales value, the equation is turned around to read:

• Direct profit return, divided by turnover at cost, equals the direct profit mark-on necessary to earn the desired return.

Inserting the turnover figures assumed above, it is found that a 100% mark-on must be added to conversion costs and 60% must be added to total direct costs of each product to earn 40% direct-profit return. (See Figure 5.)

FIGURE 5

Return on Investment Pricing

	Direct		Turnover of		Direct Profit
IF	Profit	$\times$	Investment	$=$	Return on
	Margin		(Sales)		Investment
	50%		80%		40%

	Direct Profit		Turnover of		Direct
THEN	Return on	$\div$	Investment	$=$	Profit
	Investment		(Cost)		Mark-on

Production Center P

Return on:						On
Fixed Assets	40%	$\div$	40%	$=$	100%	Conversion Cost
						On Total
Current Assets	40%	$\div$	$66\frac{2}{3}\%$	$=$	60%	Direct Cost

Returning to the estimated future costs of P-421 (Figure 4) we can apply these mark-ons to arrive at a target price of $2.65 per unit. This consists of 65¢ direct profit on conversion, and 75¢ on total direct cost which when added to cost equals $2.00. The sum of the two, $2.65, is the computed target price. (The 100% added to the 60% mark-on automatically adds in the total cost of $1.25.)

It can be seen that what actually happens is the application of 60% on material costs and 160% on conversion. An inherent characteristic of this theory which causes conversion to yield the lion's share of direct profit is supported by another economic concept termed the "conversion cost theory of value" which holds that profits earned are commensurate with the effort and risk required to convert raw material into finished product.

This is a plausible reason why profit margins of some industries and some companies are greater than others. It is not true in all cases, but it is manifested emphatically in the smaller margins of the retailer and wholesaler who primarily distribute versus the larger margin of the manufacturer who assumes the risk and expends the effort of distribution plus research and production. When turnover is applied to margin the returns on investment of all three are relatively comparable.

Although the conversion theory is inherent in the return on investment theory, the two are not identical. The conversion theory holds that profits are earned on conversion alone; whereas the return theory attempts to indicate what the price should be to yield a reasonable return on the capital used in producing, selling, and distributing the product. There are other methods of computing target prices, but the feature of this one is that it aims at the very goal of business enterprise — return on investment.

4. COMPETITIVE AND COMPANION-PRODUCT PRICES

The $2.65 target price should by no means be considered the final price; in fact the real job of economic analysis starts with the target price. The fourth step (see Figure 1) is to investigate competitive and companion-product prices.

It is said that in our price economy, "Competition sets the selling price." If that is accepted, then it is obvious that a firm needs to know all there is to know about its competitors' prices and pricing practices. If the criteria set forth at the outset is to be met, it is not enough to know the competitive prices after they have been set, but rather the competitors' actions should be anticipated, thus allowing for action before the market is stolen.

A difficult job? Yes! However, experience has shown that the comparison of target with current competitive prices frequently leads to evidences of what competitors' actions might be. If one's current price overprices target, it would be timely to study the possibility of industry price reductions. On the other hand, if the opposite is true, perhaps the industry is waiting for a leader to increase the price and thereby help preserve an adequate return.

Furthermore, comparison of the target price with competitive prices and the investigation of differences may lead to cost improvements that otherwise would not be disclosed. Obviously, one's competitors are also in business to make an adequate return, and if they can underprice the computed target price there must be a reason — and it might not be solely price-cutting, which frequently catches the blame.

The hypothetical product, P-421, illustrates the first of the foregoing situations. The present price is $3.10 while the target price is $2.65. Competition has already reduced its price: "A" offers it for $2.55; "B" for $2.50; and "C" for $1.90. The questions here are: How can "C" do it? Is "C" a factor in the market? This will take further analysis which is discussed later.

A further consideration is the price of similar items in the company's own line commonly called "companion products." In this instance, it was found that products P-422, P-598 and P-621 should be priced in relation to P-421 and therefore all four should be reviewed concurrently. (See Figure 2.)

Being up to the minute is essential not only on the competitors' published prices but also on the net prices resulting from special deals and contractual arrangements. One should guard against placing too much dependence on occasional reports from the field, for chances are they may be the abnormal situations and far from typical. It may be found beneficial and necessary to employ outside research agencies to keep up to date on typical industry prices.

5. MARKET ESTIMATES, MARKET ATTAINMENT AND PROMOTION

The fifth step, the determination of the product's market potential and where it stands in the market, is of such importance that it could well come at the start.

An important measure of the success of a company or of a product is its dollar-sales and dollar-profits attainment in a given market. A product might have a million dollar sales volume yet be doing poorly if that represents an insignificant share of the market; yet $10,000 might be a whale of a job in another market, providing it is yielding an adequate return on investment.

The demand for almost every economic good follows some statistical curve. For example, drug sales taken as a whole are known to correlate with national disposable income through the application of certain statistical formulas. The Department of Commerce through the Bureau of Census, Office of Business Economics, Tariff Commission, and other bureaus, has done a noteworthy job in providing basic market statistics for industry. Great strides are now being made by commercial market research houses in projecting market potentials at the industry level, at the product-line and even in some instances at the individual-product level. Then it is up to the firm's own market research staff to interpret the data and tailor them to its own uses.

Degree of promotion is also a meaningful consideration in pricing, for it can materially affect the potential attainment of the competitor as well as of one's own firm.

In case of product P-421 (see Figure 2) market research showed that the potential annual market is 3,000 units. Of this our "own" company was getting just 10%; competitor "A" 16%; competitor "B" 17%; and competitor "C" just 3%. The promotion survey rated company "A" 's promotion as the best; our "own" company as second; company "B" as third; and company "C" last. Evidently "C" with its $1.90 price is not a major factor. All these are considerations in the final setting of the price.

There are now outside services available for determining market attainment at the product level, and for estimating certain advertising and promotion on given product lines. In going into this important phase, there are two important considerations:

1. The cost of the services in relation to the potential profits to be gained, and
2. Selection of the research methods and the firm which will do the job to the best advantage.

6. ELASTICITY OF DEMAND

If elasticity of demand is determinable, much of the analysis could be focused that way. It would merely be a matter of drawing a demand curve, superimposing marginal revenue and cost curves, and aiming the price at the point where the two approach or equate. In some industries elasticity of demand is determinable. In others, statisticians have found the development of elasticity to give unrealistic results.

In the absence of elasticity of demand, use of sales, cost, and price trends are found helpful. Figure 6 gives an illustration of the sales trend of product P-421. The trend lines can be drawn by statistical methods, but frequently trends of this type of data can be drawn by sight. In this instance, it was found that P-421 had a 15% favorable annual trend through the years 1950 and 1951, but then it appeared to turn downward at approximately 12% annually during the next two years. As soon as this downturn is noticed, it is time to investigate "Why?"

FIGURE 6

Sales Trend — Product P-421

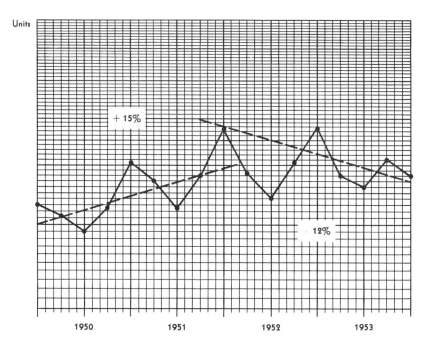

It is also a good idea to plot cost trends and price trends. The important point here is that trend is the thing, and not month-to-month, or year-to-year comparison. Such allows "creeping paralysis" to set in, and by the time the unfavorable trend is detected, it is sometimes too late to take remedial action. In all these economic and statistical analyses a word of caution is needed. With the emphasis being placed today on statistical sampling and operational research, there are some who believe that management's problems can be solved through statistical techniques alone. Statistical techniques are not tools for amateurs. None are any better than the ability and judgment of the men who apply them. It is well to beware of accepting sampling data at face value without testing their validity and reasonableness. In our company our marketing research people command company-wide respect not only because of their statistical adeptness, but more so because of their ability to use sound judgment in interpreting the data into appropriate action.

7. Customers' and Competitors' Reactions

With the statistical data compiled we are now ready to begin Step 7 — the panoramic viewing for the purpose of proposing a price. To start this process it is necessary to engage in reflective thinking on some of the more intangible aspects, namely, customers' and competitors' reactions. What will competitors do if the price is this or that? One means of projection is to take a look at what the tendency was in the past. Next, what will the consumer be willing to pay? There is usually a price limit to which a customer will go depending on the utility of the product. Whether the product is bought on habit or impulse may likewise influence the price.

8. The Price Proposal

Now comes the *modus operandi* of the economic analysis program. All the data discussed — the "one-third computation" — has now been collected and is ready for the application of the "two-thirds judgment" to propose the final price to management. In this particular instance, as is shown in Figure 2, Price Development Summary, the target price of $2.65 is proposed. This is very likely an exception to the general rule, but in this instance no other data indicated the contrary.

This product was previously a patented item; the patent had expired; the sales trend, as we have shown, turned down; the cost trend is down. Companies "A" and "B" had dropped their prices and were getting 16% and 17% of the market. Company "C" is not considered a factor because of its attainment and its promotion rating, even in light of its low price; furthermore its product is deemed inferior. The demand appeared relatively elastic to price if the declining sales trend is a good criterion. It was conjectured that companies "A" and "B" are not likely to reduce their prices further.

In view of present attainment of competition, let us say that a goal is set at 15% of the market potential or 450 units. To break even at present direct profit of $510, only 366 units are needed at the target price. Net profit at break-even is likely to be the same or even higher because of better fixed cost absorption. Consequently, if the attainment goal of 15% can be reached, the direct profits on the excess of 450 over 366 units will be out-and-out real profit. The target price is only ten cents higher than the highest competitive price, and it is felt that the firm can differentiate its product sufficiently to overcome that small price difference. Accordingly the proposed $2.65 price is accepted.

Pricing New Products

The foregoing has principally dealt with repricing of established products. What about pricing new products? The principles are the same and the application of the economic analysis program is similar. New products call for a slightly different outlook and some other considerations.

Since there is no past for the particular product, forecasting of the future may call for more intuitive and ingenious means. History of similar products may be found helpful. "Test marketing," that is, testing the acceptance of the product in a selected area has much to recommend it. This involves the whole scheme of product introduction and is too involved to be discussed as a part of this subject.

Two important alternatives facing management on new product pricing, especially patented or controlled items, are (1) set the initial prices high enough to skim the cream of demand, or (2) start with low prices aimed at full market penetration and discouraging competition. A sound decision can only come from a complete weighing of all the factors involved. If competition is likely to be active regardless of the approach, then it is advisable to attempt the first alternative in order that research or engineering costs and initial promotional costs may be absorbed as quickly as possible. If, on the other hand, significantly lower costs are forecasted through increased volume, then it would be well to adopt low prices at the outset, again for the purpose of equating marginal revenue and marginal costs and thereby maximizing profits in the long run.

As in any kind of pricing, pricing new products is not a matter of applying a formula and saying, "That's that!" As in repricing, it calls for a process of building up an integrated picture by estimating the economic factors of investment, costs, market, promotion, and elasticity; then, by engaging in reflective thinking, apply sound judgment in deciding among the various alternatives offered.

The process does not end here, for new-product conditions change rapidly. The economic analysis must be constantly projected forward to keep the price abreast of current and foreseeable conditions.

Conclusion

The foregoing program is not represented as a panacea for all pricing problems. Nonetheless the mere fact of being able to take a "panoramic view" of an integrated picture leads to effective pricing which is a vital step toward maximizing long-range return on investment.

7 *The use of correlation analysis as a tool for fore-*
casting, budgeting, and measurement of operating
elements is advocated. Statistical analysis offers more accurate forecasts,
capacity to predict limits of acceptable error, and the isolation of causes
of forecast error. The budget man is thus alerted to the need for a revision
of forecast, or additional or more stringent controls if random influences
and errors persist.

Examples are given of actual experience with the method as well as
valuable insight into the requirements for good correlations. Poor corre-
lations experienced are also explained with some notion of the inherent
problem. Three statistical appendices explain the details of the methods
used and their properties.

Forecasting and Measuring With Correlation Analysis*

Robert A. Knapp

Correlation analysis has been described as one of the most powerful tools available for business analysis, planning, and forecasting. It is in general use by econometricians, operations researchers and management consultants; however, there is too little evidence of its day-to-day use as a tool for fore-casting, or for budgeting and measuring the operating elements, the assets and the liabilities of business.

Since our business operates almost 100 per cent within the defense market, we are faced with market vagaries that prompted us to approach our appli-cation of this technique from the inside out, building experience on the

* *From* Financial Executive, *Vol. XXXI, No. 5 (May, 1963), pp. 13–19. Reprinted by permission of the publisher.*

simpler, more stable relationships rather than jumping right into international politics.

Our plan has been to investigate successive business elements on the basis of need and ability to discern logically the pertinent causal relationships. Our goal is to synthesize as complete a network of reliable predicting equations as possible, excluding certain program-type elements, such as, rearrangement expense, maintenance, plant and equipment expenditures, and certain tax and other accruals which, in our case, and usually, are better handled by other methods. This network will provide the basis for mechanized programs of forecasting, budgeting and measurement of performance that will be more accurate, more realistic and more perceptive, respectively, than any based on less sophisticated techniques. These attributes derive from three distinctive features of correlation analysis:

1. Individual (e.g., monthly) errors are minimized and offset one another to the maximum extent, leading to a minimum total period (e.g., year) error.

2. Statistical by-products provide the capacity to predict limits of acceptable error, or variance, both monthly and year-to-date and thus signal the need for second looks.

3. Through the predicting equation, causes for forecast error, or budget variance, can be quantitatively identified.

Correlation analysis may be indicated whenever accuracy of forecast, planning of budget, or measurement of performance need improvement. Its contribution depends on the analyst's ability to distinguish the logical complex of relationships, and on the stability and durability of these relationships in each case. So there are cases in which correlation analysis may not be considered applicable in spite of the need. However, in the many applicable cases correlation analysis provides a sensitivity to more causal factors, and a flexibility to more business situations than any of the more common methods such as experience ratios, pure extrapolation, or seat-of-pants evaluation of a mental or written list of pertinent conditions.

Table 1 provides a sample of our experience with correlation analysis as compared to other methods previously in use, or concurrently in use.

The first two lines of Column A depict performance in predicting the average investment in the largest of our asset and liability accounts respectively. Since these accounts were budgeted with predicting equations derived through correlation analysis, no parallel forecast is available for comparison.

In Column B a comparison is made with the 1961 budget and the previous two years' budget experience.

Line four provides an example of an application to an interim overhead rate revision wherein the same analysis used for line three is updated to include the latest available experience, and the accuracy of the resulting predicting equation compared to a forecast employing a combination of extrapolation and judgment. In addition to eliminating 28 per cent of the error in

TABLE 1

			A	B		
				Experienced % Error Using Other Methods		
Forecasts With Correlation Analysis				*Previous Two Years*		
Item Forecasted	*Source Period of Data Correlated*	*Year Forecasted*	*% Error*	*1961*	*Least*	*Average*
Customers Receivables	Oct. 58–Oct. 60	1961	2.5	NA	23.2	41.9
Accounts Payable	Jan. 58–Oct. 60	1961	9.0	NA	16.9	27.2
Gross IME	Nov. 58–Oct. 60	1961	5.4	10.7	9.7	17.8
Gross IME	Nov. 58–Aug. 61	1961	1.6	2.3	NA	NA

the forecast actually used, this updating and prediction were accomplished in considerably less time.

Correlation analysis does not, of course, supplant an investigative procedure whereby the forecaster looks through the eyes of the people responsible for the area of operations to be forecast. Only through such a process can impending developments without historical precedent be factored into any prediction. Correlation analysis does provide the most concise expression of the historical interrelationships of the selected variables that can be derived. It offers no guarantee that the relationships will hold. But, used in combination with knowledge of operating plans and judgment of future business conditions, it can eliminate a large percentage of the error inherent in other forecasting methods.

As would be expected, month-by-month accuracy for any given item is not so great as the total year accuracy shown in Table 1. Vagaries in the occurrence and timing of events, which tend to balance out over a 12-month period, accentuate shorter-term fluctuations. A unique feature of correlation analysis, supplied by the measures of the predicting equation's capabilities, allows the forecaster to predict the amount of error that is likely to result from these short-term random influences. Errors in excess of expected signal the introduction into the business picture of unprecedented and unforeseen factors. The forecaster, or budget man, is thus alerted to the need for a second look which may suggest: (1) a revision in the forecast, or the budget itself, if the changing influences promise to be continuing and pronounced, and/or (2) that additional or more stringent controls may be required to modify the effect of these new, or more pronounced, influences.

It is also characteristic of the predicting equation derived through correlation analysis, as discussed more fully in Appendices A and B, that it will minimize the sum of the forecast errors[1] by month (or whatever the time increment of the data may be).

The closer the forecast period resembles the period from which the data correlated were obtained, the more completely will the errors offset, so that total-year error approaches 0 as a parameter. This is not an exclusive feature since, as illustrated in Appendix A, more than one approximation of the relationship between variables can be made that will minimize the sum of the errors. However, as discussed therein, there is only one such approximation that will at the same time minimize the individual (monthly) errors. This is what distinguishes correlation analysis from less sophisticated methods.

To illustrate the unique capabilities claimed for correlation analysis in the preceding two paragraphs, we forecasted our 1961 average investment in Customers Receivables (excluding retention which was handled separately) within 2.5 per cent. This represents a 90 per cent improvement over the lowest error realized in the previous two years. The measures of this predicting equation's capabilities indicated a monthly error not to exceed 14.5 per cent eight months out of twelve. Actual errors ranged from −18 per cent to +17 per cent, with errors less than 14.5 per cent eight months out of twelve. Because there were some slight differences during 1961 in the way in which the account balance responded to the chosen independent variables and random influences, these monthly errors did not balance out to 0 (as we should hardly ever expect they would in a dynamic business environment). However, total-year error was reduced substantially, and to a satisfactorily low amount. This is to be expected in the application of correlation analysis to business element prediction where relatively stable accounting procedures and business practices lend a degree of durability to historical interactions, and where, with a large amount of control centered within the business, relatively dependable plans can be considered in the analysis. In other words, we are dealing with the greater assurances inherent in a microeconomic application of correlation analysis as opposed to a macroeconomic application requiring the prediction of such things as national defense expenditures by weapon system, number of housing starts, or national employment levels.

The ±14.5 per cent in the above illustration was the approximate equivalent of one standard error of estimate. As the year progressed, had one of the monthly errors exceeded two standard errors of estimate (29 per cent) which would be expected only five times out of one hundred, or had the monthly errors not demonstrated an offsetting year to date pattern within calculable converging limits, a change in the basic relationships among the variables, or the influence of a new variable might have been indicated, and

---

[1] This is an extrapolation of the characteristic of minimizing the sum of the + and − deviations of the values of the dependent variable (element to be forecasted) estimated through the equation from the respective actual values correlated. The degree of accuracy of the statement varies with (1) the representativeness and size of the historical sample analyzed; (2) errors in the historical values not discovered and corrected in the processes of accumulation and adjustment of the data; (3) any significant dissimilarity between the sample and a normal distribution.

a re-analysis required. While neither of these eventualities are likely with the variables involved in this case, there is always a possibility that a change in environmental or accounting structure will distort historical relationships, and introduce substantial errors in a predicting equation. In contrast to less sophisticated techniques, correlation analysis provides the analytical perception needed to provide early warning of such developments.

Forecasting, budgeting and measuring with correlation analysis is a developmental process. It can be used effectively for long-range forecasting, where more popular methods leave the most to be desired, at an earlier stage of development than it can for forecasting, budgeting and measuring by month because it takes less refined correlations to promise total year accuracies well above previous standards. The farther into the future the forecast is carried, the less confidence can be placed in the endurance of historical patterns, or the continuing appropriateness of judgment adjustments. But this is a failing of all forecasting methods, and there is no reason to believe that correlation analysis does not maintain its lead over less sophisticated methods throughout the forecast period. In fact, there are numerous examples at the macroeconomic level, at least, of very satisfactory durability of correlation derived predicting equations.

The application to forecasting budgeting and measuring by month, for the year ahead, is more exacting. Here, the results form the basis for a much larger percentage of irreversible decisions that will affect the immediate economic future of the business. The greater stringency of the demands on the method employed actually enhances the attractiveness of correlation analysis. At the same time, it dictates that higher degrees of correlation be obtained since we are, in this case, concerned with monthly accuracy, and more critical total-year accuracies. This requirement multiplies the problem of adjustment of the data correlated, the significance of which is discussed more fully in Appendix C. Adjustment of raw data is the most time-consuming phase in correlation analysis. Parts of an element to be forecast or budgeted may have to be segregated, seasonal adjustments made, and the parts correlated with their respectively appropriate independent variables. While some adjustment is required for good correlations in any case, the finer adjustments required to make a good correlation better demand a thorough insight into the interactions of the variables and their seasonal behavior, which must sometimes be supplemented with trial and error.

Once a significant correlation is obtained, the judgment as to whether or not it is good enough will depend upon the experienced accuracy with other methods, the standard for accuracy that has been set, and the time available for further refinement.

Table 2 presents a sample of correlations, including the best and the weakest, that we have accepted for use for 1962.

Obviously, we are not satisfied with explanations of monthly error as incomplete as that for Accounts Payable. We are, nevertheless, employing predicting equations in such cases for both budgeting and forecasting because of the expected total-year accuracy.

TABLE 2

Element To Be Forecasted	Maximum % of Expected Error Two Out of Three Times			Independent Variables	% of Variation Explained by Independent Variables	Source Period of Data Correlated
	Monthly	*Quar-terly*	*Total Year*			
Customer Receivables	9	—	→ 0	Three classes of sales and a working-day index	78	Jan. '59–Sept. '61
Contributed Value	7	—	→ 0	Sales by product line (five)	88	Jan. '58–Oct. '61
Plant Labor Cost	3	—	→ 0	Employment and hour-ly/total employment index	98	Jan. '58–Sept. '61
Accounts Payable	25	—	→ 0	Cost of operations input, direct material input, and a working-day index	58	Jan. '58–Sept. '61
Sundry Creditors	—	3	→ 0	Plant labor cost	69	1st Q '60–3rd Q '61
Gross IME	—	—	0.7	Direct and applied labor base and direct material input	97	12 mos. ended Oct. '59–12 mos. ended Nov. '61

NOTE: → 0 = approaching 0: From our experience we expect these total-year errors to range from 0.5 per cent to 10 per cent in line with the spread of expected monthly errors.

The contribution of correlation analysis to measurement of performance is supplied by the mathematical expressions of the relationship between variables included in the predicting equation. Forecasts or budgets can be reappraised through this media in the light of actual developments (analysis of variance). Causes for error, or variance, can thus be quantitatively identified so that we are supplied with a statistical tool for apprising responsible individuals of the approximate amount of variance attributable to their performance versus the amount attributable to factors beyond their control.

Referring to our 1961 Customers Receivables experience again, the greatest monthly variance (18 per cent) occurred in July. Reappraisal through the predicting equation (substituting actual values of the independent variables) indicated that three percentage points of the 18 were caused by a higher-than-budgeted proportion of fixed-price sales, a much lower proportion of cost-recovery sales subject to interim billing, plus a slightly higher-than-budgeted total sales volume. With business volume and mix eliminated, we logically look to our collection performance for the explanation of the remaining 15 per cent. Our aged analysis of customers receivables showed an increase over the year-to-date average in receivables over 30 days old amounting to 15 per cent of the total account balance, thus accounting for the rest of the variation. In this case, the deterioration in collection performance could be attributed to an externally caused reaction in the month following the end of our customer's fiscal year and the effect of our vacation shutdown. The full combined effect of these two influences had not been experienced during the period from which the data correlated were obtained, and the seasonal adjustment was consequently inadequate.

Initiating a program of correlation analysis requires a working knowledge of, and cautious respect for, statistical tools combined with a solid financial background. Because of the need for extensive historical data, and the analysis and adjustment that is required before the actual correlation can be productive, significant results are at first slow in evolving. However, as the chain of predicting equations grows, results begin to snowball. Established correlations can be updated in a matter of minutes on the smallest computers and new predictions made in a fraction of the time required for re-analysis by more common methods, and with much greater confidence in the results. Given the predicting equations, substantial portions of the work of forecasting and budgeting can be readily mechanized, leaving more time for analysis, and making substantial last-minute revisions possible that could not otherwise be contemplated. Although at least a small computer must be occasionally available for any broad-scale program, isolated problem areas can be economically analyzed with a standard desk calculator.

Correlation analysis is more expensive than the more commonly employed methods of forecasting, budgeting and measuring, but it can more than pay for itself by providing the base for more astute planning, pricing and control of performance — in short, more profitable decision-making.

Bibliography

Spencer, Milton H. and Louis Siegelman, *Managerial Economics*, Richard D. Irwin, Inc., 1959.

Waugh, Albert E., *Elements of Statistical Methods*, Third Edition, McGraw-Hill, 1952.

Ezekiel, Mordecai and Karl A. Fox, *Methods of Correlation and Regression Analysis*, Third Edition, McGraw-Hill, 1959.

Croxton, Frederick E. and Dudley J. Cowden, *Applied General Statistics*, First Edition, Prentice-Hall, 1939.

Kenney, J. F. and E. S. Keeping, *Mathematics of Statistics*, Third Edition, D. Van Nostrand Co., Inc., 1957.

Appendix A

CORRELATION ANALYSIS

The purpose of correlation analysis is to derive a mathematical equation which best discloses the nature of the relationship that exists between a business element to be predicted (dependent variable) and one or more causal factors (independent variables). This mathematical equation is known by various names of which: (1) "predicting equation" probably best describes its role in forecasting and part of its role in budgeting, when the primary objective is the value of the dependent variable calculated by substitution of estimated or actual values of the independent variable(s) in the equation, and (2) "regression equation" most closely defines its role in the measurement of performance when the primary objective is to determine the amount and nature of variance attributable to variations in the independent variable(s). However, since the two objectives are usually intertwined, particularly in budget application, we have selected the single term "predicting equation" for this report.

The derivation of the predicting equation amounts to weighting the separate causal factors according to their individual importance in their effect upon the element to be forecast. This is accomplished most commonly by correlating historical data chosen from a period judged to be representative of the future period for which a forecast, budget and subsequent measurement of performance is desired. As discussed more fully in Appendix C, the data may require adjustment to obtain satisfactory representativeness.

This correlation process (least squares method) characteristically provides the equation of the line (simple linear correlation) that comes closest to all of the actual values used in the analysis. Unless the correlation is perfect, this line will fall below some actual values and above others. But the sum of all these + and − deviations will always equal 0, and if we square these deviations and add them together, this sum of the squares will always be less than it would be from any other line. The significance of the latter characteristic applies especially to the time segment of the data correlated and can be illustrated as in Figure 1.

FIGURE 1

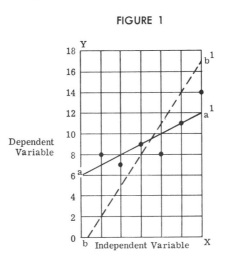

In Figure 1, the sum of the + or − deviations from either regression line equals 0. But the squared deviations are at a minimum from line aa^1 $((+1)^2 + (-1)^2 + (0)^2 + (-2)^2 + (0)^2 + (+2)^2 = 10)$. The sum of the squared deviations from $bb^1 = (+6)^2 + (+2)^2 + (+1)^2 + (-3)^2 + (-3)^2 + (-3)^2 = 68$. If we view this figure as a picture of a six-month historical period with the dots representing actual observations, line aa^1 representing the equation derived by correlation analysis and bb^1 representing another approximation of the relationship between the dependent and independent variables, we can see that either line will estimate the total or average value for the dependent variable for the six-month period as a whole with no error, since the $+$ and $-$ deviation cancel out. However, it is obvious that individual month's accuracy is substantially greater using the line (equation) derived by the least squares method.

It should also be apparent that should the future period for which a forecast of the dependent variable is to be made require an extrapolation of the line beyond the range of independent variable values included in the historical period, the bb^1 line (or equation representing it), or for that matter any other line but aa^1, will introduce a bias in the total or average future period prediction, in addition to failing to minimize the individual month's errors.

Although a simple linear correlation has been used to illustrate these characteristics of the least squares method, the comments apply to multiple linear and simple and multiple curvilinear correlation as well. There is a wide choice of curve types in simple (single independent variable) correlation and of combination of curve types in multiple correlation (two or more independent variables). It is difficult to conceptually present more than two independent variable correlations, but some of the one and two independent variable relationships that we have found applicable are presented in Figure 2 with their respective equations in general form.

The expeditious selection of appropriate curve type or combination of curve types is contingent upon logic and a knowledge of the business element interactions. Various methods of curve fitting are available to supplement the process.

The purpose of the preceding description has been to emphasize that (1) a wide variety of predicting equations are available to fit any logically synthesized correlation problem; (2) whether the equation is linear or curvilinear, simple or multiple, the two characteristics of offsetting individual deviations and minimized sum of the squared deviations, so valuable to the application of correlation analysis to forecasting, budgeting and measuring, are retained.

While the predicting equation is the vehicle with which we forecast, budget and quantitatively analyze variance, at least two statistics describing the capabilities of the predicting equation should be mentioned.

Correlation analysis provides the Coefficient of Determination (R^2), measuring the percentage of variation in the dependent variable explained by the independent variable(s) and the Standard Error of Estimate (S_y) which gives an idea in absolute terms of the dependability of estimates provided by the predicting equation.

The coefficient of determination helps to evaluate (1) the wisdom of the particular selection of independent variables; (2) the effectiveness of the elimination, by adjustment of the original data, of periodic fluctuations and/or elements of the variables that should logically be analyzed separately; (3) the appropriateness of the selected curve-type.

FIGURE 2

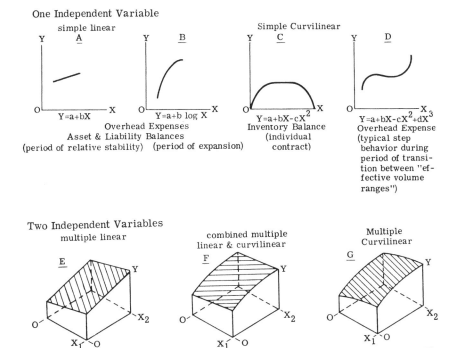

The standard error of estimate states the maximum amount of error that should be expected in two out of three estimates and allows the calculation of other maximum amounts of error to be expected with different probabilities. Thus forecasts can be made and decisions based upon them weighing the decision against measurable risk of being wrong.

We have attempted in this Appendix to convey a utility-oriented, as opposed to a mechanically oriented, feel for correlation analysis. In keeping with this goal we have used only the most essential statistical terms to avoid the clutter of definition.

Appendix B

ACCURACY OF FORECAST AND THE PRACTICAL
SELECTION OF INDEPENDENT VARIABLES

The probable forecasting error, S_1, of a predicting equation derived through correlation analysis (least squares method) is a function of (1) the standard deviation, σ (relative dispersion, or observed magnitude of variation about the arithmetic mean) of the dependent variable (element to be forecast), (2) the coefficient of determination, R^2 (amount of variation that is explained or accounted for by the independent variables), (3) the number of observations, N_1 (number of months, years, etc., of data included in the analysis[2]), and (4) the number and probable forecasting accuracy of the independent variables (forecasting bases).

The specific mathematical relationship[3] predetermines that the greater the historical variability (or instability) of the element to be forecast, the greater will be the forecasting error with a given ability to explain the variation. In establishing an acceptable maximum error, it follows that a higher standard for your ability to explain variation, R^2, will be required for a relatively unstable business element than for a relatively stable one. As a practical consideration, the standard set for forecasting accuracy may have to be lowered, remembering that an unstable element is also more difficult to forecast by other methods. Comparison of a forecast using a predicting equation with seemingly unacceptable probable accuracy to the experienced accuracy of forecasts by other methods often indicates marked improvement in forecasting ability.

The measures of forecasting ability derived through correlation analysis describe this ability in terms of the time increment of the data correlated. Thus correlation of monthly data provides measures of your ability to predict by month. The ability to forecast and budget by month are important goals. Much of their importance, however, attaches to the forecast or budget for the year in the form of supplying patterns for attainment.

With accuracy for the year the primary goal, it becomes extremely significant that predicting equations derived through correlation analysis characteristically minimize the sum of the forecast errors. Monthly errors will largely offset so that the cumulative error for the year will approximate zero given a business and accounting climate that is approximately described within the period analyzed[4] and subject to the bias of error in forecasting bases.

The job of minimizing the bias from errors in predicting the forecasting bases (independent variables) can be accomplished by practical selection of

---

[2] See Appendix C

[3] $S_1 = \sigma\sqrt{1 - R^2}$

[4] See comments in Appendix C.

variables. The independent variables chosen on the basis of logic and knowledge of business element interaction must be evaluated not only in terms of the amount of variation in the dependent variable that they explain but also (1) in terms of their own individual stabilities, the amount of their separate variabilities that can be explained, and so the probable errors in forecasting them; (2) the significance of these probable errors, or the relative bias that may be transmitted to the forecast of the dependent variable through the predicting equation[5]; and (3) the combination of variables that will supply the greatest potential offsetting error capability.

Consideration (1) above is a repetition of the same problem discussed previously in connection with the dependent variable.

Consideration (2) involves expressing the transmitted error as a percentage of the average magnitude of the element to be forecast. Such a comparison is essential to the evaluation of the predicting equation. Without this knowledge it is possible to be grossly misled in the use of a predicting equation described by acceptable statistics, i.e., satisfactorily low forecast error, an equation which includes independent variables with satisfactorily low forecast error for the purpose of forecasting these bases, the absolute amount of which, however, as transmitted to the dependent variable forecast imputes entirely unacceptable inaccuracy.

Possible solutions to this problem include:

1. Appropriate adjustment of the offending independent variable(s) to exclude elements causing the greatest variability (provided these can be forecast with acceptable accuracy, and provided their exclusion does not destroy the effective correlation to the dependent variable).

2. Substituting a second choice forecast base, one whose indicated forecasting error in relation to itself is not so good, and one which may not explain so much of the variation in the dependent variable, but whose indicated forecasting error related to the size of the dependent variable is enough smaller to more than compensate.

On the other hand, independent variables which might significantly improve the ability to explain variations in the dependent variable may be avoided because of relatively less ability to predict them when, in fact, their relatively high indicated forecasting errors as judged in relation to their own average size may, in transmission through the predicting equation and comparison with the average size of the dependent variable, prove to be insignificant.

Consideration (3), the selection of the optimum combination of independent variables, we have attacked as a problem of $\pm$ signs of coefficients

---

[5] Which may be expressed as relative forecast error through the expression

b_i = predicting equation coefficient of the independent variable

S_i = standard forecast error of the independent variable

$b_i \dfrac{S_i}{\overline{X_1}}$ = arithmetic average of the dependent variable

i = numerical designation of the independent variable $(1, 2, \ldots, n)$

in the predicting equation and positive, negative, or no interaction of the independent variables within business operations. Proper construction and evaluation of the predicting equation must allow for or take advantage of the imputed influence from (1) complementary independent variables; (2) independent variables that substitute for one another within the operations of the business; and (3) independent variables that show little or no tendency to vary either positively or negatively with changes in another.

Error in forecasting complementary independent variables will be additive in transmission through the predicting equation if the signs of their coefficients are both, or all, the same, since we should expect an increase in any one above the forecast to be accompanied by an increase in the other(s). In contrast, if the signs of their coefficients in the predicting equation are opposite, there will be an offsetting influence in transmission.

With independent variables that tend to vary in opposite directions, we can expect our forecast of one to be low if the other(s) is (are) high. Given like signs of their coefficients, the errors will tend to offset in the forecast of the dependent variable. Unlike signs in this case will, of course, cause the errors to be additive.

Whether errors transmitted from independent variables that are, for practical purposes, independent of each other will be additive or offsetting, generally speaking, is unpredictable. However, the use of such variables, given the choice, promises greater ability to explain variations in the dependent variable since correlation between or among independent variables tends to reduce this ability.

There is probably never complete freedom of choice in the combination of independent variables. The problem is to exploit the limited selection available so that the optimum combination of the least number of variables can be constructed. Given a limited number of observations, the fewer the variables the greater the dependability of the statistics, the less time will be consumed both in arriving at and using the predicting equation, and the simpler will be the analysis of variance and its interpretation to management.

Appendix C

DEPENDABILITY AND THE NUMBER AND ADJUSTMENT OF OBSERVATIONS

The dependability of a predicting equation derived through correlation analysis is a function of the number of observations and the number of independent variables.[6] Generally speaking, the greater the number of independent variables used, the greater will be the number of observations required (e.g., months of data).

---

[6] Actually the number of constants in the predicting equation which includes one for each independent variable plus one, commonly expressed in general forms as "a", representing the Y intercept, or value of the dependent variable when the value(s) of the independent variable(s) is (are) equal to zero.

Because of the predominance of complicated interrelationships in the operations of a business, requiring multiple correlation for satisfactory analysis, the number of observations becomes a critical quantity. For this reason, the shortest period for which the data are recorded should be used whenever periodic variation can be removed by appropriate averaging (e.g., converting monthly data to average weekly or average daily), and/or accounted for by the inclusion of an appropriate time variable (e.g., number of weeks or number of working days in the fiscal month).

With data subject to quarterly cycles, such as some liability accounts, which can be acceptably forecast with few variables and, therefore, the number of observations is less critical, we have found it expedient to correlate quarterly totals and estimate monthly balances as percentages of the quarterly totals, or to correlate contemporary months of each quarter separately rather than search for the sometimes very illusive time variable. Either approach, of course, cuts the number of observations by 75 per cent.

Where a 12-month cycle is predominant and cannot otherwise be adjusted for, moving 12-month totals or averages will supplement the number of observations effectively. By this means three fiscal years of data can be made to yield 25 observations, four years — 37 observations, etc. However, averaging creates the problem of adjusting for bias in the predicting equation and extends the time required for both deriving, and forecasting with, the predicting equation.

Proper adjustment of the data to be correlated is a prime prerequisite to obtaining acceptable correlation statistics. Program-type portions of the element for which a predicting equation is desired must be removed for separate treatment, as, for example, rearrangement and factory and equipment development from manufacturing overhead. Any other significant portions that do not logically vary with the independent variables selected for the total element or vary in a different manner (along a different type curve) must also be removed as, for example, retention dollars from customers receivables and assessments from manufacturing overhead. Changes in accounting practice must be either adjusted for by indexing, or the account removed and handled separately, as, for example, depreciation from manufacturing overhead due to the change from straight line to sum of the digits.

Basically, appropriate adjustment requires the recognition of the segments of operating elements which are homogeneous from an accounting standpoint but heterogeneous for correlation purposes, separating these segments for individual analysis, indexing the segments appropriately, and removing the irrelevant periodic fluctuations.

A thorough knowledge of the financial interactions and accounting practices of the business is essential in this phase of the application of correlation analysis to forecasting, budgeting and measuring. Without it correlation analysis will be sterile. On the other hand, without correlation analysis, forecasting, budgeting and measuring cannot provide its maximum contribution to management decision-making.

8 *This paper presents a framework for the mathematical analysis of operator learning cost with special reference to assembly groups. Learning has the limited meaning of skill acquisition as measured by increased productivity. Learning cost is formulated as a function of the length of task to be learned, other variables being fixed. Three components of learning cost are distinguished and analyzed separately. The total learning cost model is the sum of the three component models.†*

A Model for Industrial Learning Costs*

Maurice Kilbridge

Perhaps the major economy associated with the extensive division of labor in industry results from the ease and rapidity with which short tasks can be learned.[1] As work is subdivided and deskilled the rate at which operators learn their tasks increases sharply and the learning costs associated with employee turnover and product or model changes decline. There is a point, of course, at which, although learning costs may continue to decline, other economic and psychological factors inhibit further division. This paper will not be concerned with establishing that point, or what these other factors might be. It will treat only the relationship between length of work task and learning costs.

The need is widely felt in industry for a system of formulating the task length-learning cost function. Not only is it an important consideration in determining the optimum division of work, but the learning curves involved

* *From* Management Science, *Vol. 8, No. 4 (July, 1962), pp. 516–527. Reprinted by permission of the editor.*
† Adapted from editor's summary in *Management Science.*
[1] Learning as used in this paper has the limited meaning of skill aquisition as measured by increased productivity.

in the formulation have many operational uses. These include employee training and evaluation [5, 7], standard cost analysis and decisions on optimum production runs [2], and aid in personnel assignment [3]. Although of considerable interest in themselves, these applications of learning analysis are outside the scope of this paper.

The premier industrial example of minute work division is the progressive assembly line. The total assembly job is divided and assigned in approximately equal shares to the stations on the line. As the product progresses down the line each operator adds to it his share of the work. This is the situation chosen in which to study the task-length and learning-cost relationship. In this context "learning" becomes "group learning," since all operators on the line must progress at the same rate. The method of analysis will be seen, however, to be sufficiently general for adaptation to other industrial learning situations.

The cost of learning will depend, of course, on other factors in addition to the length of task, but in this analysis only task length is considered. All other factors are held fixed. Also, the nature of the assembly work and the volume of the production run are assumed known and wage rates are held constant and uniform for the assembly group. This can be done without loss of generality and will be seen to closely approximate the typical short-run industrial situation. The problem then is to establish the general relationship between task length as the independent variable and learning cost as the dependent variable. This paper establishes the relationship and provides a framework within which specific cost studies can be made.

Empirical Data Used

Data were gathered over a period of about one and one-half years in two large Chicago companies in the consumer electronics industry. The tasks chosen for study were conveyor assembly of television chassis. The number of operators on the individual lines studied ranged from 15 to 155. The length of assembly task ranged from .15 minutes to 6.0 minutes, averaging about one minute. In total about forty operating lines involving about 1860 employees were included in the study.

Variables in Group Learning

Some of the factors, other than task length, that influence group learning cost are:

1. *Group size.* As the group size increases, that is, as the line gets longer, the range of learning capacities of the operators on the line also increases. Since the line can progress no faster than the slowest operator, the time it takes the group to reach a given pace will be influenced by group size.

2. *General level of skill and experience of the group.* Groups in which the level of skill and aptitude for the work are high, and which have considerable experience in the type of assembly involved, will reach a given pace more quickly than a less skilled or less experienced group.
3. *Complexity of the work.* The degree of complexity of the assembly work may vary from product to product. The more complex the work the longer it takes a group to reach a given pace.
4. *The degree of change the work presents from previous work.* It is sometimes necessary to consider partial learning, or relearning. This applies to situations in which the same or a similar assembly was partially or completely learned in the past. The time for relearning varies with the time lapse between similar production runs and the pace attained on the previous run.
5. *Worker motivation.* Wage incentives and other forms of motivation greatly influence the speed with which a line reaches full production.
6. *Extraneous influences.* These take the form of supervisory pressure, worker-initiated restrictions, and production-schedule restrictions.

At any instant, when, in a given company, the choice of assembly task length for a product is being made, the above factors, with the exception of group size, are largely fixed by the realities of the situation. A work force with a given level of general skill and experience is already employed. The assembly product is designed and ready for production. Past learning is an unalterable factor. And, unless a conscious attempt is made to change them, motivational and extraneous influences will remain generally invariant. Only group size and task length are freely and commonly adjusted. These are seen, however, to be covariants. For a given amount of total assembly work on a product, the choice of individual task length determines the number of assemblers required on the line. Group size, therefore, need not be considered independently; it is implicit in relationships involving task length.

In the empirical studies on which this paper is based, work situations were sought in which the above factors were fixed in approximately the same degree so that comparable task length-learning cost relationships were isolated. The resulting empirical information led to the formulation of three working hypotheses.

Three Task Length Components of Learning Cost

The following hypotheses are presented in the context of the consumer electronics industry and data drawn therefrom are used to support and illustrate them. Each hypothesis pertains to a different component of learning cost. These are later shown to be additive, resulting in a general relationship between task length and total learning cost that has predictive value. In summary, these hypotheses state that task length influences learning cost in three ways, through:

1. the pace ultimately attainable,
2. the initial learning time, and
3. the recurring learning cost.

TASK LENGTH AS A DETERMINANT OF ULTIMATE PACE ATTAINABLE (HYPOTHESIS 1)

Empirical data indicate that the work pace a group of assemblers can achieve is a function of, among other things, the length of their tasks. In the case of line assembly the task length is the same[2] for all operators and is equal to the rate at which product comes off the line. When the line is operating at 100 per cent efficiency, or standard pace, the time the product spends at each work station is called "standard cycle time." This time is equal to the task length. In practice, when the assembly group has reached its ultimate, or fastest pace, the rate of production is faster than the standard rate and the corresponding "actual cycle time" is faster than the standard cycle time.

"Standard," as used in "standard cycle time" and "standard pace," means the normal output requirement of the line as determined by the system of work measurement in use in the particular company. The absolute measure of these standards does not matter in this analysis so long as the system on which they are based has internal consistency.

Hypothesis 1 states that: *The work pace ultimately attainable for a given kind of work on an assembly line is a function of the length of task. The function is such that ultimate pace is slowest for very short and very long tasks and fastest for tasks of intermediate length.*

When the task length is very short a simple and restricted motion pattern is repeated continuously. Observations indicate that this induces cramping and excessive muscle fatigue which inhibit the worker's ability to maintain a uniformly fast pace. The reaction is known in industry and is commonly called "short-task fatigue." As the task length increases and the motion pattern becomes more diversified simple muscle fatigue declines. Beyond a point, however, a countervailing influence tends to reduce the pace attainable. Forgetting, fumbling, loss of motor skill and rechecking time increase, resulting in a slowing of pace called "long-task delay."

A task of intermediate length avoids the penalties of both extremes. The operator can develop a touch system, constant unchanging rhythm, and a smooth continuous work pattern that is not too restricted and yet well defined, resulting in a high level of speed and skill.

It is generally thought, although the fact has not been well demonstrated, that if this ideal task were incorporated as part of a larger job, while being, in itself, done in exactly the same way with the same motions, it would be

---

[2] This is only approximately true, since in practice it is seldom possible to divide the work exactly evenly between operators. The amount of idle time caused by the lack of balance or the unequal division of work averages about four per cent of total assembly time for the companies studied.

done at a slower pace. It is assumed that there would be a hangover of momentum from previous motions, retroactive inhibitions, disruption of rhythm, fumbling, decision time, and perhaps adjusting and repairing of poor quality.

What is being discussed here is not the same as initial learning, which as a function of task length is treated later in this paper. The gist of the above is that, even after the job is learned as well as it ever will be learned and the rate of production has leveled off, there will be, for a given kind of work, a difference in the level of pace ultimately achieved depending upon the length of task. This means that if, for example, for a given kind of work, on a one minute task the work group could ultimately reach, say, 145 per cent of a predetermined time standard, then on a three minute task the same group could ultimately reach only, say, 125 per cent of a predetermined standard. Or conversely, on a one-tenth of a minute task, the group may be able to reach only, say, 130 per cent of a predetermined standard.

This difference in attainable pace is measurable and consistent in the companies studied because of their practice of setting production standards using systems of predetermined standard times. Each fundamental motion of a given kind and degree has an invariant predetermined time value and these are assumed to be additive without respect to the size of the total task. When these fundamental motion times are absolute, irrespective of the length of the task of which they are a part, variations in achievable pace bear a functional relationship to task length.

Figure 1 shows the pace attainable as a function of task length for TV chassis assembly in the companies studied. It suggests that, other things being equal, the highest work pace attainable is for tasks of from $\frac{1}{3}$ minutes to about $1\frac{1}{2}$ minutes. This would be the range of optimum assembly task lengths, if only the factor of attainable pace were considered.

The actual cycle time, a, at any point in time, is usually different from the standard cycle time, c. The minimum actual cycle time attainable, $a_{\min}$, corresponds to the optimum[3] task length, l. If $p(l)$ is the pace attainable for task

FIGURE 1

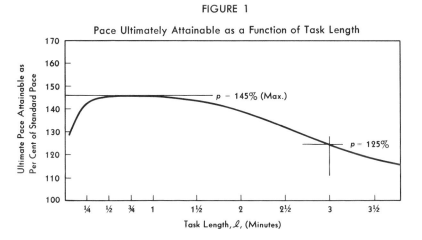

Pace Ultimately Attainable as a Function of Task Length

length l (expressed in minutes), then the corresponding actual cycle time ultimately attainable is

$$a_u = \frac{100}{p(l)} \, l.$$

The difference between the actual cycle time attainable and the minimum actual cycle time attainable is the time-cost per unit, per station, of suboptimization in the choice of task length. It is

$$a_u - a_{\min} = \left(\frac{100}{p(l)} - \frac{100}{p(\hat{l})} \right) l$$

where $p(l)$ and $p(\hat{l})$ are taken directly from a curve of the type shown in Figure 1.

If $\sum$ is the total work content of the assembly job in minutes, and w is the hourly wage rate, then the extra unit labor cost of assembly, C_1 due to the difference in pace attainable is given by

(1)
$$C_1 = nw \left[\frac{100}{p(l)} - \frac{100}{p(\hat{l})} \right] \frac{l}{60}$$

where $n = \left[\dfrac{\sum}{l} \right]$ is the number of operators necessary to staff the line.[4]

TASK LENGTH AND INITIAL LEARNING TIME (HYPOTHESIS 2)

Initial learning refers to the time required for a group of assembly workers to reach the pace they ultimately attain. More precisely, it is the time for a group of assembly operators to learn to do, at ultimate pace, a specific new task which belongs to the general class of tasks in which they are experienced. It is the practice effect only and does not apply to the training of unskilled workers.

Before initial learning can begin, a unit of product must be in front of each operator. A common instruction method starts a new product at the beginning of the line. The instructor moves down the line and instructs each operator in turn. He continues until the line is filled with product and all operators are instructed. The initial learning time is the period of skill acquisition starting with the end of this new-product instruction and ending when the group reaches its ultimate or plateau pace.

---

[3] "Optimum" is used here in the limited sense of "optimum as pertains only to pace attainable."

[4] The bracket around $\dfrac{\sum}{l}$ indicates that the number enclosed in the bracket is the least integer greater than or equal to $\dfrac{\sum}{l}$. Under unusual circumstances it may be necessary for the number of operators on the line to exceed this least integer. For a discussion of this case see reference [4].

The rate of initial learning depends on the six factors mentioned at the beginning of this paper as well as on the length of task.[5] This analysis, however, directly concerns only the length of task. For a given kind of work it naturally takes a group more time to learn a long task than a short one. There are two reasons for this: (1) The longer task contains more to be learned, and (2) The longer task is repeated less often in a given time interval and thus the learning opportunity is less, in this interval, than for a shorter task. To neutralize this second factor so that learning time can be analyzed with respect to task length only, the following analysis is based on the number of repetitions of the cycle rather than the length of learning time.

Hypothesis 2 states that: *Other things being equal, for a given kind of work, the initial learning time is a function of task length. This function is of the form* $y = ax^b$.

Industrial learning curves, for both individual and group learning, are typically power functions [1, 3, 6]. Learning data gathered in this study in the consumer electronics industry are consistent with this form of curve. Figure 2 shows typical learning curves for seven task lengths ranging from $\frac{1}{2}$ minute to $3\frac{1}{2}$ minutes. For any given number of repetitions the attained pace is seen to be higher for short task jobs than for long task ones. Thus, for example, after 1,000 repetitions of a $2\frac{1}{2}$ minute task the pace attained is about 88% of standard pace, while for a $1\frac{1}{2}$ minute task it is about 102% of standard.

The upper boundary of the curves of Figure 2 is the curve of pace ultimately attainable from Figure 1. When the group reaches the highest pace achievable the learning curve becomes horizontal. Each of the curves of Figure 2 could therefore be extended horizontally to the right to show that work pace had reached a plateau.

Figure 2 is a one-parameter family of curves which, although discrete (the number of repetitions must be an integer), are shown as continuous. If f is the attained pace, expressed as per cent of standard pace, the parameter, l, is the task length, and r is the repetitions of the assembly cycle, then

$$f = f(r, l).$$

The actual production time per unit of product for the $(r + 1)^{st}$ unit to pass any given station is (from Figure 2)

$$t(r + 1) = \frac{l}{f(r, l)}.$$

[5] The factor of group size (see discussion under "Variables in Group Learning") is contained in this analysis implicitly. The empirical curves of Figure 2 are all for TV chassis of about 90 minutes of total work content. The choice of individual task length, therefore, immediately determined the number of operators required, eliminating this as an independent variable. Given a fixed total task, such curves will account for both individual task length and group size. Empirical learning curves for a given kind of industrial work will typically be of this kind.

FIGURE 2

Family of Learning Curves Showing Pace Attained after Various Repetitions of the Operating Cycle. ($\sum = 90$ Minutes)

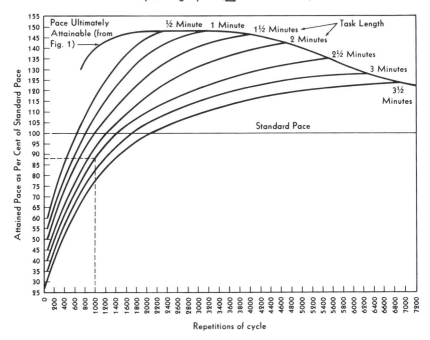

Thus, for example, using Figure 2, on an operation with a task length of $2\frac{1}{2}$ minutes, 1,000 repetitions have been performed at a given station. What is the actual production time required at this station for the $1,001^{st}$ unit? The learning curve for a $2\frac{1}{2}$ minute task crosses the 1,000 repetitions axis at a point equivalent to 88% of standard pace (see broken line). Thus, the time required for the $1,001^{st}$ unit at the given station is $2.5/.88 = 2.84$ minutes.

The total production time, T, required at any station to process a given number of units, N is

$$T(N) = t(1) + t(2) + \cdots + t(N) = \sum_{r=0}^{N-1} t(r+1) = l \sum_{r=0}^{N-1} \frac{1}{f(r, l)}.$$

Let r_a be the least number of repetitions for which the ultimate pace is attained for a given task length, l. Then

$$f(r_a, l) = p(l).$$

(This is the pace attainable discussed under Hypothesis 1.) And

$$t(r_a + 1) = \frac{l}{f(r_a, l)} = \frac{l}{p(l)}.$$

The time lost through initial learning, at any station, in producing N units is given by

$$L(N) = T(N) - N \cdot t(r_a + 1) = l\left[\sum_{r=0}^{N-1} \frac{1}{f(r, l)} - \frac{N}{p(l)}\right].$$

In producing $r_a + 1$ units the time lost is

$$L(r_a + 1) = T(r_a + 1) - (r_a + 1) \cdot t(r_a + 1) = l\left[\sum_{r=0}^{r_a} \frac{1}{f(r, l)} - \frac{r_a + 1}{p(l)}\right].$$

Since r_a is a function of l, $L(r_a + 1)$ is a function of l only.

If M is the number of units in the production run, n is the number of operators, and w is the hourly wage rate, the average unit cost of initial learning for the entire line is

(2)
$$C_2 = nw \frac{L(l)}{M}$$

$$= nw \frac{l}{M}\left[\sum_{r=0}^{r_a} \frac{1}{f(r, l)} - \frac{r_a + 1}{p(l)}\right],$$

where the values of $p(l)$ and $f(r, l)$ are taken from curves such as shown in Figures 1 and 2 respectively.

RECURRING LEARNING COST (HYPOTHESIS 3)

The learning process described above is a continuing one. Because of employee turnover and transfers learning costs continue, even after the line has reached ultimate pace. When replacement workers are added to the line the company sustains a learning cost. Either the entire line slows to the pace of the replacement worker, or a special operator is put with the replacement worker at his station. In the latter case, which is the customary solution, the two workers together meet the pace of the line until the replacement worker is able to keep up alone. The analysis here is based on the assumption that a special operator is added and the line does not slow down. The recurring learning cost is therefore the wages of special operators while assisting replacement operators to reach the pace of the line. It is a function of the task length and the points in the production run at which replacements are made.

Recurring learning is analyzed with reference to Figure 2 which shows group curves of initial learning for various task lengths. A replacement operator learns as an individual until he overtakes the pace of the group. Both the individual learning curve and the group learning curve for the particular task length are therefore involved in the analysis. To develop a statement of recurring learning it is thus necessary to express analytically the time it takes the average replacement operator to overtake the group pace, considering the pace of the group when he starts and the respective group and individual learning curves.

Figure 3 shows typical group and individual learning curves for a three minute task length. The group curve is taken from Figure 2. A distribution of individual learning curves, shown above the group one, represents the learning curves of potential replacement operators. They are assumed to be drawn from the same class of operators as the group who originally staff the line. Since the group learns at the pace of its slowest operator, the lowest curve in the distribution of individual curves coincides with the group curve. The highest individual curve is that of the fastest learner among the replacement operators. If a normal distribution of replacement operators is assumed, the modal curve will represent the learning pattern of the average replacement operator. In theory, this curve will always rise steeper and go higher than the group curve. That is, the average individual learns more quickly than the group and is capable of higher ultimate pace.

In practice, however, it is not possible for the pace of the individual to exceed that of the group, because he cannot work faster than the speed of the line. Thus, the individual learning curves of replacement operators do not cross the group curve, but upon intersecting it they become identical with it as the pace of the individual conforms to that of the group.

FIGURE 3

Group Learning Curve and Distribution of Individual Learning Curves for a Three Minute Task Length

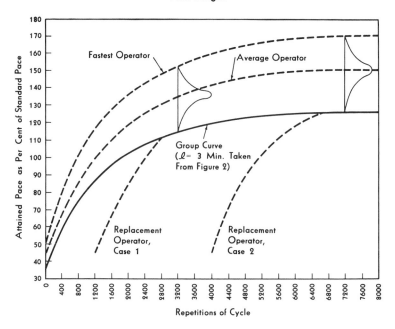

Figure 3 shows learning curves for an average replacement operator drawn at two points of learning progress of the group. The curve of Case 1 represents the situation in which the replacement operator starts early in the production run and overtakes the group before they have reached ultimate pace. Case 2 shows the curve of a later replacement in which the individual operator overtakes the group after ultimate pace has been reached. This takes longer than Case 1 and the learning cost is higher. This is reasonable since it is obviously a greater loss to the company if an operator who has completed the learning process and reached ultimate pace leaves the line than if a less skilled operator leaves.

The curves of Cases 1 and 2 are the same curve, in truncated form, as the modal individual curve drawn above the group curve. The modal curve is simply placed so as to have its origin at the number of repetitions of the cycle at which the replacement operator starts.

The learning cost of replacing an assembly-line worker is the wages of the special operator who assists the replacement worker until he reaches the line pace. This is the time it takes the replacement operator to overtake the group multiplied by the special operator's wage rate. Without loss of generality it can be assumed that the wage rate of the special operator is the same as that of the group. The average individual replacement cost multiplied by the frequency of replacement, or turnover for a given time period yields the recurring learning cost for that period.

If the replacement operator starts work on the line at the Ith (initial) repetition, and overtakes the pace of the line at the Fth (final) repetition, the time required for him to do this is that required for the line to process the units from I. to F. From the previous section this time is

$$T(r_{F-I}) = t(I) + t(I + 1) + \cdots + t(F) = \sum_{r=I-1}^{F-1} t(r + 1)$$

$$= l \cdot \sum_{r=I-1}^{F-1} \frac{1}{f(r, l)}$$

where l is the task length. The cost to replace a single operator is then

$$l \cdot w \cdot \sum_{r=I-1}^{F-1} \frac{1}{f(r, l)}$$

where w is the hourly wage rate. If the annual turnover rate is λ (usually expressed as per cent), and n is the number of operators on the line, then $n\lambda$ operators will annually be replaced and the annual cost of recurring learning is

$$l \cdot w \sum_{r=I_1-1}^{F_1-1} \frac{1}{f(r, l)} + l \cdot w \sum_{r=I_2-1}^{F_2-1} \frac{1}{f(r, l)} + \cdots + l \cdot w \sum_{r=I_{n\lambda}-1}^{F_{n\lambda}-1} \frac{1}{f(r, l)}$$

$$= lw \sum_{I_1-1}^{F_1-1} \frac{1}{f(r,\,l)} + \sum_{I_2-1}^{F_2-1} \frac{1}{f(r,\,l)} + \cdots + \sum_{I_{n\lambda}-1}^{F_{n\lambda}-1} \frac{1}{f(r,\,l)}$$

$$= lw \sum_{j=1}^{n\lambda} \sum_{r=I-1}^{F_j-1} \frac{1}{f(r,\,l)}\,.$$

Using an annual production of Q units, gives a unit cost of recurring learning of

(3)
$$C_3 = \frac{lw}{Q} \sum_{j=1}^{n\lambda} \sum_{r=I-1}^{F_j-1} \frac{1}{f(r,\,l)}\,.$$

The double summation in (3) is necessary because each individual replacement operator has a potentially different learning time. This was illustrated for two cases in Figure 3. It can be seen from the figure that all replacements subsequent to that shown as Case 2 involve the same learning time. This represents the bulk of replacements on all lines except those having extremely long learning periods or very short production runs. In practice, therefore, it is usually sufficiently accurate to assume that the learning cost is the same for all replacement operators. The error involved in making this simplifying assumption will depend on the length of the learning period relative to the length of the production run. With this assumption (3) becomes

(3, a)
$$C_3 = \frac{1}{Q}\,\lambda n l w \sum_{r=I-1}^{F-1} \frac{1}{f(r,\,l)}\,.$$

Total Learning Cost

Equations (1), (2), and (3, a) present the three task-length components of learning cost per unit of product. Thus, the total unit learning cost, $C_4 = C_1 + C_2 + C_3$, for the assembly line is given by

(4)
$$C_4 = nw \left[\frac{1}{p(l)} - \frac{1}{p(\hat{l})} \right] \frac{5l}{3} + \frac{nlw}{M} \left[\sum_{r=0}^{r_a} \frac{1}{f(r,\,l)} - \frac{r_a+1}{p(l)} \right]$$

$$+ \frac{n\lambda l w}{Q} \left[\sum_{r=I-1}^{F-1} \frac{1}{f(r,\,l)} \right]$$

$$= nlw \left\{ \frac{5}{3} \left[\frac{1}{p(l)} - \frac{1}{p(\hat{l})} \right] + \frac{1}{M} \sum_{r=0}^{r_a} \frac{1}{f(r,\,l)} - \frac{r_a+1}{p(l)} \right.$$

$$\left. + \frac{\lambda}{Q} \sum_{r=I-1}^{F-1} \frac{1}{f(r,\,l)} \right\}.$$

Equation (4) summarizes Hypotheses 1, 2, and 3 in a mathematical framework. A study of actual learning costs within this framework would require empirical data adequate to draw curves similar to those of Figures 1 and 2. C_1 would follow directly from the curve value of $p(l)$.[6] C_2 would require either a graphical calculation of areas under the curves $f(r, l)$, or integration of the corresponding functions. C_3 would follow from C_2 after assumptions were made regarding the rate and timing of employee turnover.

References

Epstein, Bertram, *Immediate and Retention Effects of Interpolated Rest Periods in Learning Performance*, Columbia University Press, New York, 1949.

Jones, R. P., *The Evaluation of Learning Costs and Determination of Optimum Production Quantities*, Manufacturing Services Department, Raytheon Manufacturing Company, Waltham, Mass., 1958.

Kilbridge, M. D., "Predetermined Learning Curves for Clerical Operations," *The Journal of Industrial Engineering*, Vol. 10, No. 3, (May-June, 1959).

—— and L. Wester, "A Heuristic Method of Assembly Line Balancing," *Journal of Industrial Engineering*, (July-August, 1961), p. 293.

Knowles, A. R. and L. F. Bell, "Learning Curves Will Tell You Who's Worth Training and Who Isn't," *Factory*, Vol. 108, No. 6, (June, 1950), pp. 114-15.

Shephard, A. H. and D. Lewis, "Prior Learning as a Factor in Shaping Performance Curves," Government Printing Office, Library of Congress Publication, No. 101487, (U. S. Navy Technical Report SOC 938-1-4).

Smyth, R. C., "How to Figure Learning Time," *Factory*, Vol. 101, No. 3, (March, 1943), pp. 94-96.

[6] The empirical evidence in support of Hypothesis 1 is considerably weaker than that of Hypotheses 2 and 3. If the achievable-pace effect is not, or cannot be, isolated in a given company situation, it can be left out of the cost analysis without seriously affecting the total learning cost.

9 *"The budget can be a powerful tool for motivating people to achieve the organization's objectives or it can be a positive hindrance. This article analyzes the effects of budgeting on people and shows how it can lead to either bad or good consequences according to the way it is applied in various types of organization."*

Budgeting: Functional Analysis and Behavioral Implications*

V. Bruce Irvine

Many of those who have written about budgets have emphasized the problems resulting from typical budgeting systems. Little enthusiasm has been voiced for the practical effectiveness of budgets as a means of obtaining the optimal benefits of which such a device is capable.

A more positive approach might result from a consideration of the control and motivational effects of budgets on the behavior of people. But an analysis of the reactions of these people (supervisors, foremen, laborers) to control devices (such as budgets) has received little attention as a specific subject in the literature of the past decade. The studies reported have usually concentrated attention on improving the usefulness of budgets from a top management viewpoint and have de-emphasized the subordinate positions. Also, many of the studies have been conducted by behavioral scientists and have not been incorporated into accounting and management thought and teaching. Consequently, although accountants and management are aware that their actions have behavioral implications, they have not thoroughly understood what these are. The result is uncertainty, confusion and indecision when human problems do arise.

* From Cost and Management, *Vol. 44, No. 2 (March-April, 1970), pp. 6–16.* Reprinted by permission of the publisher.

The purpose of this article will be to make a functional analysis of budgeting towards the goal of maximizing long-run profits (considered to be the present value of the owner's net worth). An analysis of reactions of the employees on whom budgets are primarily exercised, rather than a purely management viewpoint analysis, will be used to develop basic propositions. Human behavioral aspects of budgets, therefore, become a very relevant factor in this approach. After investigation of why employees react as they do, the usefulness of budgets in view of such reactions and the implications of suggestions for making budgets more successful and acceptable can be considered within particular situations facing modern-day business.

Definitional and Technical Considerations

A functional analysis considers the various consequences of a particular activity and determines whether or not these consequences aid in the achievement of the organization's objective. According to Merton,[1] the consequences of an activity are functional if they increase the ability of a given system to achieve a desired goal. A consequence is dysfunctional if it hinders the achievement of the goal. Consequences of an activity may also be classified as manifest (recognized and intended by the participants in the system) or latent (neither intended nor recognized). Decisions based only on manifest consequences may often be incorrect because of latent consequences.

A budget is a device intended to provide greater effectiveness in achieving organizational efficiency. To be effective, however, the functional aspects must outweigh the dysfunctional aspects. Whether or not this will be true will depend upon many factors which will be discussed and summarized in a model of the elements of budgeting.

First, it is necessary to understand what a budget is. Although formal definitions of a budget exist, a definition is not always the most relevant aspect of understanding a concept.

Amitai Etzioni distinguishes between two types of models in organizational analysis.[2] The survival system consists of activities which, if fulfilled, allow a system to exist. Budgets are not part of such a system. Organizations in the past have functioned and in the future will function

---

[1] Merton, R., "A Paradigm for Functional Analysis in Sociology" in *Sociological Theory: A Book of Readings* by L. Coser and B. Rosenberg, New York, Macmillan, 1957, pp. 458–467.

[2] Etzioni, Amitai, "Two Approaches to Organizational Analysis: A Critique and a Suggestion" in Bobbs-Merrill Reprint Series in the Social Sciences 8–80. Reprinted by permission of *Administrative Science Quarterly*, Vol. 5 (Sept. 1960), pp. 257–278.

without the help of budgets. Budgets can be classified within an effectiveness system. These "define a pattern of interactions among the elements of the system which would make it more effective in the service of a given goal."[3]

A budget, as a formal set of figures written on a piece of paper, is in itself merely a quantified plan for future activities. However, when budgets are used for control, planning and motivation, they become instruments which cause functional and dysfunctional consequences both manifest and latent which determine how successful the tool will be.

Budgets mean different things to different people according to their different points of view. Accountants see them from the preparation aspect, managers from the implementation aspect, and behavioral scientists from the human implication aspects. All of these viewpoints must be melded together if budgets are to obtain the best functional results.

There are many types of budgets. The major purpose for having budgets, the type of organization using a budget, the personalities of people handling the budget, the personal characteristics of people subject to budget direction, the leadership style of the organization, and the method of preparing a budget are all factors accounting for budget type and style.

The technical procedures involved in the preparation and use of budget figures are similar for most organizations. People make estimates (standards) of what they expect should reflect future events. These estimates are then compared to what actually happened and the differences (variances) are studied.

The Functional Aspects of Budget Systems

In what specific way do budgets make management action more efficient and effective in maximizing the present value of the owners' worth?

Basically, a budget system enables management more effectively to plan, coordinate, control and evaluate the activities of the business. These are functional, manifest consequences in terms of their desirability.

Planning means establishing objectives in advance so that members of the organization will have specific, activity-directed goals to guide their actions. Budgets are quantitative plans for action. As such, they force management to examine the available resources and to determine how these can be used efficiently.

The point that budgets require this clarification and concrete quantification of ideas is not usually recognized directly by budgeting people as a benefit. As such, it could be considered functional and latent.

The planning aspect of budgeting has other latent functions. Planning requires that the plans be communicated to those involved in carrying them

[3] Ibid., p. 272.

out. Communication is enhanced by distributing the budget to those responsible for various parts of it.

A budget makes lower level managers more aware of where they fit into an organization. Their budget indicates what is expected of them and that they have a goal towards which their activities are to be directed.

With a budget, junior (new) members of an organization have a better idea of where the company is going and are made to feel that the business is concerned about their future. This can affect both their own future plans and the company's recruitment policy and turnover problems.

When a person is given an objective, he is more likely to feel that he is part of the organization and that the upper echelons are interested in his work. Conversely, top management is likely to become more interested in, and aware of, the activities of lower level employees.

These latent, functional consequences of budgets create interest and, possibly, enthusiasm which increases morale and could result in greater efficiency and initiative.

Planning of departmental activities must be coordinated so that bottlenecks do not occur and interdepartmental strife can be limited. A budget system can assist in this coordination. By basing organizational activity on the limiting factor (such as sales, production, working capital), a comprehensive budget coordinating all of the firm's activities can be approved by top management and the controller. Such a budget permits these people to bring together their overall knowledge of the firm's abilities and limitations. By using budgets to coordinate activities, the organization is more likely to operate at an optimal level, given the constraints on its resources.

The control consequences are among the more important aspects of budgeting. Because a budget plan exists, decisions are not merely spontaneous reactions to stimuli in an environment of unclarified goals. The budget provides relevant information to a decision maker at the time he must choose between alternatives. Therefore, a budget implicitly incorporates control at the point of the decision. However, provision for taking advantage of unforeseen situations should certainly be allowed even though a budget is violated.

A second type of control can be derived from budgets. A comparison of actual with budgeted performance after decisions have been made reveals to management the performance of the organization as a whole and of the individual responsible members.

A comparison merely reveals discrepancies. The action which is taken as a result of variances is in the hands of management. But the investigation of why there are variances, whether or not they are controllable, and the resulting control procedures is stimulated by the budgeting process. The result is the discovery of methods to save costs, improvement in the firm's efficiency, and better future planning.

Control of both types is important to top management because its cannot maintain personal contact with those in the lower management ranks.

Devices such as budgets, employment contracts, job descriptions and rules are therefore necessary to direct subordinate behavior. In general, control is based on the assumption that individuals are motivated by their own security needs to fulfil the plans and obey the rules. To the extent that this is true, the benefits to be derived from the control aspects of budgeting can be deemed functional and manifest.

These benefits could be obtained only in the ideal situation where budgets work as they are intended to work. The theoretical benefits make budgets very appealing devices, but the practical problems of implementing and using them greatly affect their usefulness. Most of the problems arise from the difficulty of convincing people to accept and use a budget. Mechanical problems also exist. These difficulties create many possibilities for dysfunctional consequences to occur with the result that some functional consequences become difficult, if not impossible, to attain.

Dysfunctional Aspects of Budget Systems

Any system which involves motivation and control of individuals has dysfunctional aspects, simply because human behavior cannot be predicted or controlled with certainty. Frequently, activities by management to obtain desired functional results will actually lead to dysfunctional consequences. Management must understand why such a reversal can occur so that existing problems can be solved or an environment created which prevents problems arising.

This section will indicate how results of a budget system can be dysfunctional in nature. The basic approach will be to analyze the deterrents to achieving particular functional results. Within a particular organization, the dysfunctional aspects must be considered in relation to the functional aspects in order to evaluate the worthiness of a budget system. Obviously, if the dysfunctional consequences of an action outweigh the functional aspects, management should delete the activity. Because each business is unique, no attempt can be made to state that certain activities will be dysfunctional or functional in every situation.

Because factors which can lead to dysfunctional consequences are complex, each will be analyzed separately although it is realized they are usually inter-related.

A. The Term "Budget"

The first dysfunctional consequence of a budget system results from the name itself. Traditionally, budgets have carried a negative connotation for many:

". . . some of the words historically associated with the term budget are: imposed, dictated by the top, authorized. And what are the original purposes of control — to reduce, to eliminate, to increase productivity, to secure

conformance, to assure compliance, to inform about deviation. An historical meaning of budget is to husband resources — to be niggardly, tight, Scrooge-like."[4]

If attitudes expressing such beliefs are not eliminated at the start, the budget will never get off the ground. One method of eliminating this problem is to refrain from calling the activity "budgeting."

B. Organizational Arrangements of Authority and Responsibility

If a budget system is to be used to control and evaluate personnel, the persons involved must possess responsibility and authority over what is being assigned to them. Consequently a large and/or decentralized organization would probably have a greater potential use for budgeting than would a small, highly centralized business.

Centralized organizations may simply use budgets to plan and co-ordinate future activities. Because responsibility, control and authority rest with the top executives in such a business, any attempt to reward, punish or hold lower level employees responsible for variances would achieve nothing beneficial and would probably cause resentment. Any negative feelings on the part of those who follow directives in carrying out operations would likely lead to less than optimal achievement of organizational objectives. Therefore, even though budgets can be used to improve planning and coordination, assignment of control responsibilities where there is no power to carry out those responsibilities could easily create dysfunctional, latent consequences.

On the other hand, over-emphasis on departmentalization can also have dysfunctional, latent effects:

> *"Budget records, as administered, foster a narrow viewpoint on the part of the user. The budget records serve as a constant reminder that the important aspect to consider is one's own department and not one's own plant."*[5]

Over-emphasis on one's own department can lead to considerable cost in man hours, money and interpersonal relations when responsibility for variances, particularly large ones, is being determined. The result is a weakening of cooperation and coordination between departments.

C. Role-Conflict Aspects of Budgeting

Status differences, or more accurately role-conflict between staff and line personnel, are an important source of dysfunctional consequences. The

---

[4] Green, Jr., David, "Budgeting and Accounting: The Inseparable Siamese Twins," *Budgeting,* Nov. 1965, p. 11.

[5] Argyris, Chris, *The Impact of Budgets on People,* Ithaca, N.Y. Prepared for the Controllership Foundation, Inc. at Cornell University, 1952, p. 23.

problems created affect budget usefulness directly and also indirectly through their effect on communication, motivation and participation. The basic difficulties arise because of differences in the way budget staff people and line personnel understand the budgeting system and each other.

From Figure 1,[6] it can be seen how important budgets and the budget staff are in the supervisors' or foremen's working world. Ninety-nine per cent of the supervisors and foremen questioned in four companies stated that the budget department was either first or second in importance of impact on the performance of their activity.

FIGURE 1

Responses to the request "Name the departments affecting your actions most" asked of supervisors and foremen individually in four firms.

	Most Affect	2nd Most Affect	Total
Production Control	55%		
Budget Department	45%	54%	99%

From the supervisors' and foremen's follow-up comments, it was readily apparent that the budget department's influence was not only significant, it was usually considered troublesome as well. Why should this be so? Some suggested reasons are:

1. Line employees see budgets as providing results only and not the reasons for those results. Any explanations of variances by the financial staff, such as failure to meet expected production or inadequate use of materials, prove grossly insufficient. Causes behind these explanations still have to be determined before the supervisors and foremen could consider budget reports as being useful to them or presenting a fair appraisal of their activities to top management.

2. Budgets are seen as emphasizing past performance and as a device for predicting the future. Supervisors and foremen are basically concerned with the present and with handling immediate problems. Budget figures would often be ignored in order to solve present difficulties.

3. Supervisors and foremen apparently see budgets as being too rigid. In some cases, budget standards have not been changed for two or three years. Even if they now met such a budget, they often would not be performing efficiently. Budget people would then adjust the budget. In such cases,

---

[6] The source of this figure and study is Argyris, C., op. cit., a summary of comments and statements, pp. 10–12.

those working under a budget would not really know what was expected of them until after they had submitted their cost reports and had received a control report.

4. Supervisors and foremen would also resent the opposite treatment of constantly changing a budget in the belief that increased efficiency would result. Such a procedure would lead them to believe, and often justly so, that budgets were unrealistically set. Budget men would be seen as individuals who could never be satisfied as they would raise the budget if a person made or came close to his previous budget. This would only result in frustration for the supervisor or foreman. The feeling that the company executives did not believe in the supervisor's own desire to do a good job could easily be implied when budgets are continually changing.

5. Thoughts about budgets are further aggravated when foremen and supervisors receive budget reports on their performance in a complicated format with an analysis that is incomprehensible to them. Supervisors felt that the job of budget people was to be critical and that the use of jargon and specialized formats enabled them to justify their criticism of others without too much debate.

Whether or not these criticisms are logical and rational is not important. The point is that such feelings can and do exist. If the budget is regarded as merely emphasizing history, being too rigid, unrealistic, unattainable and unclear and if budget people are seen as over-concerned with figures, unconcerned with line problems and cut off by a language of their own, there can be no doubt that the effectiveness of a budget system would deteriorate.

The problems are compounded if the budget personnel's attitude is unconducive to overcoming these opinions. Budget people should see their jobs as examining, analyzing and looking for new ways to improve plant efficiency. They should also think of a budget as an objective that should fairly challenge factory personnel. Since it cannot be assumed that line personnel subscribe to or even recognize these ideas, the ideas should be impressed upon them directly through adequate budget introduction and education. Moreover, the effective use of budgets cannot be forced upon supervisors and foremen; it must be accepted by them. This can only be accomplished if budget people try to work constructively with line people as compatriots rather than commanders. This accord is usually very difficult to bring about. Often budget people will not even attempt it or simply give up on it because of lack of success. They conclude, correctly or incorrectly, that the line personnel's unsatisfactory use of budgets is due to their lack of education, understanding and interest.

Given this unwillingness to buck line opposition by the budget personnel and the line's viewpoint of budgeting as a hindrance to their performance, a classic role-conflict is created. The optimal benefits possible from budgeting cannot be obtained in such an environment.

Argyris also determined how foremen and supervisors felt the potential dysfunctional results of budgeting could be overcome. Suggestions dealt mainly with improving the outlook of budget men. According to the line personnel, budgeting people should be taught that budgets are merely opinions, not the "be-all and end-all." They should also be taught, it was felt, that line employees are not inherently lazy, that budget men should learn to look at a problem from another's point of view, and that they are not superior to supervisory people. Also suggested were the use of timely and understandable reports to foremen and supervisors, the practice of conferring with people who have variances so that the budget report indicates the real cause to top management, and the setting of realistic budgets.

The problems arising are not, however, entirely the fault of the budget staff. Supervisors and foremen must put more effort into understanding the budget figures, they must not be continually suspicious of budgets, and they should use budgets in performing their duties. Most important, they should alter their outlook toward budgeting. Budgets must be realistic and fair, but also foremen and supervisors should realize that the budget is designed to help them achieve the standards management expects of them.

How can these requirements be achieved? An educational program involving foremen, supervisors, middle and upper management, and budget personnel could help to clarify the different viewpoints and promote understanding of each other's objectives and difficulties. Such a program should precede the introduction of a budgeting system and continue after the system has been introduced.

D. BUDGETS AND NON-MANAGEMENT PEOPLE

The involvement of laborers (non-management personnel) in the budgeting process presents both functional and dysfunctional possibilities. Often, front-line supervisors who have a budget to meet do not use it as a device to spur their subordinates. According to the comments reported by Argyris, they fear that workers would look upon such action unfavorably and that no benefit would be received.

The proposition that workers would not respond to budgetary pressures is challenged by W. F. Whyte:

> *"How do workers see budgets? They often recognize that management people are worried about costs, but with the foremen afraid to put the cost situation to them, they remain uninvolved in the struggle."*[7]

Since workers generally have not been directly involved in budgetary systems, the question of whether or not such involvement would be functional is unresolved.

---

[7] Whyte, W. F., *Men at Work,* Richard D. Irwin, Inc. and The Dorsey Press, Inc., Homewood, Ill., 1961, p. 495.

E. MOTIVATIONAL ASPECTS OF BUDGETING

The most controversial area of budgeting concerns its motivational implications. The budget makes available information for comparison of expected with actual performance. When such an evaluation of performance is known to result in rewards and punishments, people are expected to be motivated to do their best. Let us examine this assumption and its possible functional or dysfunctional consequences.

Argyris states that budgets are principal instruments for creating pressure which motivates individuals.[8] Budgets can also be seen as creating more pressure than they actually do. This "pressure illusion" is due to the fact that the budget is a concrete, quantitative instrument and managers and supervisors, feeling pressure from more abstract sources, place the blame for it on the concrete budget.

Factors directly related to budget pressures are budget "pep" talks (A), red circles around poor showings (B), production and sales drives using budgets (C), threats of reprimand (D), and feelings of failure if budgets are not met (E). These can all be considered as functional and manifest in terms of their motivational intent.

There are, however, counteracting effects which can be dysfunctional and latent in terms of budget effectiveness. These factors include informal agreements among managers and/or supervisors (V), fear of loss of job if efficiency increases but cannot be maintained (W), union agreements against speedups (X), performance abilities of individual employees (Y), and abilities of work teams as a whole (Z).

Equilibrium is attained when:

$$A + B + C + D + E = V + W + X + Y + Z$$

Management, by increasing one or more of the components on the left hand side of the relationship or by adding additional ones, can increase productivity. This increase is matched by an increase in tension, uneasiness, resentment and suspicion on the part of the employees. This pressure increase is absorbed by joining groups which are strongly cohesive against top management and budget people. Again equilibrium is attained but each time pressures are increased by top management, they must become more intense as resistance is higher.

When and if management feels that the pressures are detrimental to the organization, it may attempt to reduce the causes on the left hand side of the equation. This does not result in decreased anti-management feeling because the groups have developed into relatively permanent social units and the individuals feel the pressures may occur again. Therefore, in the long

[8] Op. cit., Argyris.

run, increasing pressures may be very dysfunctional because of these latent features.

The rational way for management to approach this problem would be to concentrate its activities on reducing the forces that decrease efficiency rather than on increasing the factors that tend to increase efficiency.

Other dysfunctional ways of relieving motivational pressure could easily exist:

1. Interdepartmental strife could occur. A manager, supervisor or foreman could try to blame the variances on someone else. This would result in concentrated effort by individuals to promote only the cause of their own departments. The personal rivalries thus caused and the lack of cooperation among departments could mean decreased efficiency for the company in achieving its overall goals.
2. Another type of strife develops when the line employees blame the staff employees for their predicaments and absolve themselves of the responsibility for the variances. Budget people become scapegoats for problems and salesmen are blamed for incorrect predictions or orders that make the production process unstable.
3. An individual may internalize the personal pressure he feels. By not outwardly showing his problems, he would build up tension within himself. Eventually, frustration would develop and he would perform less efficiently in the long run.
4. If internal means of relieving pressure are used, manipulation of activities may result. Reporting sizable variances when one knows he will be over his budget may allow him to shift his costs so that he will easily make his budget in the next period. Saving easy jobs until just before the end of a budget period may enable a person to achieve the stipulated goal.

The point is that, in the short run, increasing motivational pressure through budgets may be functional but, in the long run, it may also be very dysfunctional.

Andrew C. Stedry postulates additional concepts concerning motivation through budgeting.[9] Through experiment, Stedry developed the findings shown in Figure 2.

The level of costs for which a person will strive (aspired costs) will be conceived by the individual in relation to past experience, confidence in his personal skills, expectation of future difficulties, and his feelings about the budget costs. Aspired and budget costs do not necessarily (or usually) coincide. The aspired costs are what the individual sets for himself. The budget costs are set by top management. When actual costs are compared

[9] Stedry, Andrew C., *Budget Control and Cost Behavior*, Englewood Cliffs, N.J., Prentice-Hall, Inc., 1960.

FIGURE 2

Simplified Model of Stedry's Motivational
Relationships Involving Aspirations

Start	Budget Costs	Aspired Costs	Previous Actual Costs

| If Encouragement | Budget Costs ← | New Aspired Costs ← | Start Actual Costs |

| If Discouraged | Budget Costs | | New Aspired Costs ———→ | Start Actual Costs |

| If Failure | | Quit or a change in the system such as a lowering of the budget | |

to these two costs, the reaction of the employees depends on the discrepancies involved:

1. Other things being equal, aspiration levels will move relative to the actual costs depending on the degree of discrepancy.

2. A person will be encouraged if the discrepancy between actual costs and aspired costs is not greater than an amount known as the discouragement point. Aspirations would be set higher on the next period of performance measurement.

3. A person will be discouraged if the discrepancy is greater than the discouragement point but less than a failure point. In this case, aspirations would move downward.

4. If the discrepancy is greater than the failure point, the system would cease to exist or a new one would be needed. Otherwise the individual concerned would resign.

Stedry concludes that management should set high, unattainable budgets to motivate individuals to achieve the greatest efficiency. "Unattainable" would have to mean that the discrepancy between aspired costs, formulated after the high budget was presented, and actual costs could not exceed the discouragement point. Such a policy would mean that individuals receiving separate budgets would be manipulated in accordance with the variances in the size of their discouragement points.

This may sound all right in theory but in practice the reactions of employees could make this a dangerous proposition for long-run efficiency. If individuals found out that they were the subjects of outright manipulation, they could become rebellious and ignore future budgets whether they were fair or not. Other management control devices would probably be considered with unwarranted suspicion. Moreover, how is management going to determine the aspiration level and discouragement point of each individual, a necessary requirement for setting "personal" budgets? The use of individual budget standards would also have to be kept confidential. Otherwise, the resentment that employees would feel might lead them to resist all budgeting attempts and even to leave the organization.

Stedry's study suggests that participation in budget preparation is not as beneficial as having management set the budget. He points out, however, that participation may be desirable where low budgets are given as managers, supervisors and foremen would likely feel that they are capable of achieving greater efficiency and would say so.

Stedry's study is limited in that long-run results were not extensively examined. Also, the nature of his "laboratory" data leads to serious questions as to whether "real business world" conditions were reproduced.[10] However, his research on the reactions of lower level management to budgets does help to explain the behavior of these people. The study also indicates how management can improve a budgeting process where budgets are being ignored or causing personnel problems, because it shows why situations exist.

Another consequence of budgetary motivation which has received little emphasis involves "a fear of failure" on the part of the individual. The failure to meet a budget or at least come close to it when it is accepted and fairly determined and when other members of a person's reference group are successful, represents a potential loss of status both within the group and the organization. A person's self-concept is also deflated in such circumstances.

The fear of such a loss may be a stronger motivating factor for a person to achieve his budget than any of the other pressures mentioned. "Fear of failure" then is a very powerful functional consequence of budgeting systems and, quite likely, is latent.

One of the major benefits of budgeting is motivation, explicitly incorporated in the use of standards. Budgets should reflect a goal which people can strive towards and achieve. To provide maximum motivation for employees, management should judge failure to achieve an objective in the context of the situation causing failure and not merely in terms of a figure circled in red. All members of the organization must be aware of this basic principle.

---

[10] Becker, Selwyn and Green, Jr., David, "Budgeting and Employee Behavior" in *Journal of Business,* Vol. 35 (1962). These are among the authors who debate the practical application of Stedry's conclusions.

F. PARTICIPATION IN BUDGETING

In a participatory system of budgeting, preparation of budget schedules would start at the lower levels of the hierarchy and move upward. As it moved upward, various people would make additional suggestions and some eliminations until the schedules reached the controller and top management. These people would analyze it and see that it was a coordinated plan in accordance with organizational goals before final approval would be given. Movement up and down the hierarchy could be made if drastic changes were necessary. By reciprocal communications, people would know why changes were justified and could constructively criticize them if they desired.

Behavioral scientists and accountants generally believe that such a system would be an improvement on imposed budgets. The functional, manifest results claimed for this system are:

1. It would have a healthful effect on interest, initiative, morale and enthusiasm.
2. It would result in a better plan because the knowledge of many individuals is combined.
3. It would make all levels of management more aware of how their particular functions fit into the total operational picture.
4. It would increase interdepartmental cooperation.
5. As a result of their direct involvement in the planning function, it would make junior management more aware of the future with respect to objectives, problems and other considerations.

It is possible to achieve these benefits through successful participation. There are, however, factors that have a significant impact on whether or not participation can lead to successful results.

One essential requirement is that participation be legitimate. If participation is allowed but top management continually changes the budgeted figures resulting from participation, legitimate participation does not exist. This might better be described as a form of "pseudo-participation." The supposed "participants" would likely resent such a policy and the consequences would be dysfunctional. This is borne out by the studies of V. H. Vroom who found that productivity was higher when participation was viewed as legitimate, but lower when it was viewed as not legitimate.[11]

Other factors limiting the usefulness of budget participation are:

1. Personality differences of managers as reflected in their leadership style are important. Aggressive managers can put forth their demands more

---

[11] Stedry, Andrew C., "Budgeting and Employee Behavior: A Reply" in *The Journal of Business,* Vol. 37 (April 1964), p. 198.

strongly than meek ones. Subordinates would view the latter as not looking out for their interests and antagonism between subordinates and their superiors, and managers themselves, could easily develop.

2. An autocratic, centralized organization would have little use for a participation policy whereas a democratic, decentralized organization would likely benefit from, and almost require, a participation policy.

3. Those allowed participation rights must be positively oriented towards the objectives of the firm. Only if the group is cohesive in thought and desire toward and understands the plan can participation policy be functional.

4. The cultural setting of an organization and the background of employees should be considered. People in rural areas or with a rural background are more inclined to accept assigned tasks. In such an atmosphere, a participation policy would probably meet with little response.

Studies have been carried out showing that participation in any situation is not necessarily useful for increasing efficiency.[12] Other studies have reported that when a non-participative group became participative and was compared with an existing non-participative or participative group, the former never caught up in terms of performance with the latter two groups. These studies imply that the introduction of a participation policy for a formerly non-participative group would not likely lead to increased efficiency and may even result in decreased efficiency. If this conclusion is accepted, a group should be endowed with the right to participate only when the group is created or the budget system is being implemented and not after either has previously been directed through decisions made by superiors.

The most severe criticism offered against participation is that the increased morale which supposedly results does not necessarily result in increased efficiency. Is high morale a cause of increased efficiency or is greater efficiency a cause of high morale, or is there some intervening variable which must be present if a true causal relationship is to exist? Group cohesiveness seems to be the most significant of possible variables that have been examined although other variables are obviously involved. Figure 3 shows postulated relationships that could develop using group cohesiveness with regard to subordinate thoughts toward management.

As those participating in a budget (foremen and up) would be management-oriented, at least to some extent, they would probably have a positive approach to management activities and objectives. The previous discussion

---

[12] See Stedry, ibid., p. 196; also Morse, Nancy and Reimer, E., "The Experimental Change of a Major Organizational Variable" in *Journal of Abnormal and Social Psychology*, Vol. LII (1956), pp. 120–129; and French, Jr., J. R. P., Kay, E. and Meyer, H. H., *A Study of Threat and Participation in a Performance Appraisal Situation*, New York, General Electric Co., 1962.

FIGURE 3
Participation and Budgets

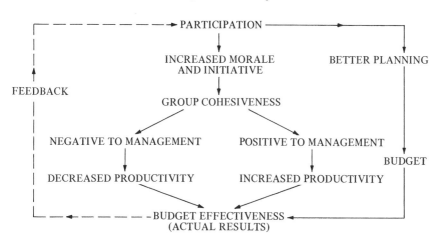

on role-conflict situations shows, however, that negative attitudes towards budgeting are quite possible.

If the group is anti-management or anti-budget, a participation policy would be of little use. Supervisors may even propose ridiculously low standards and upper management would be forced to revise them. Pseudo-participation would exist and likely result in the increase of negative attitudes toward management or budgeting.

If the atmosphere is favorable for allowing participation, group cohesiveness toward management and budgeting should be maintained and enhanced if possible. Group discussions led by an able management man to inform *and* listen to supervisors, foremen and other management people could probably aid in implementing the budget. By listening to and taking action on suggestions made by the group, he would be able to indicate his and top management's sincerity in gaining successful participation in the budgeting system.

Undoubtedly, the evidence on the effectiveness of participation in budgeting is mixed. Supporters of participation readily admit that it is by no means a panacea for achieving the full motivational potential of the budget. The fact is that participation is not a segregated aspect of management but embraces several technical and behavioral concepts which make it more or less useful in different organizations. The organization's particular situation with regard to the development of these concepts must be recognized and thoughtfully considered when contemplating or evaluating a participation policy.

It should be noted that, even if productivity does not increase directly through participation, better planning and increased morale and initiative may, of themselves, justify such a policy.

G. COMMUNICATION ASPECTS OF BUDGETING

Researchers on control and motivation generally agree that information on planned and actual results should be communicated to the employee whose performance is being measured.

Nevertheless, many budget departments merely communicate the results to management with the result that the employee does not know how he has done until he is called up to discuss his performance report. Consequently, the individual may ignore the budget and perform without a guide, hoping for the best.

When results are communicated as rapidly as possible, an employee's mistakes can be associated with his recent actions and he is likely to learn more from the experience than if reports are received long after the action has been taken. This learning would likely result in improved performance on future budgets.

When reports given to management employees are timely, reasonably accurate and understandable, functional consequences are more likely to occur than if the opposite exists. Figure 4 summarizes the effect of the communication system on the behavior of line people.

FIGURE 4
The Importance of the Communication Factor
When Using Budgets to Control and Motivate Employees

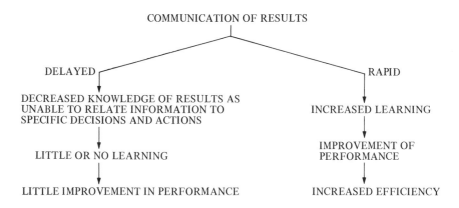

H. EMPLOYEE GROUP BEHAVIOR AND ITS EFFECTS ON BUDGETING

Peter Blau's study on the use of statistical measures in evaluating employee performance has implications for evaluating and understanding budgeting.[13] The study examined the effect of group cohesiveness, in the sense

[13] Blau, Peter M., "Cooperation and Competition in a Bureaucracy" in Bobbs-Merrill Reprint Series in the Social Sciences, S-28. Reprinted by the permission of *The American Journal of Sociology*, Vol. LIX, May 1964.

of willingness to cooperate among members, and the resulting productivity in different situations.

His findings showed that the group which cooperated was more productive than the group which did not cooperate but competed individually among themselves. He also discovered that highly competitive individuals in the latter group were more productive than any individual in the cooperative group. Blau's hypothesis was that a paradox existed:

> ". . . The resulting paradox is that competitiveness and productivity are inversely related for groups but directly related for individuals in the competitive group."[14]

In terms of the achievement of organizational objectives, the implication is that cooperative cohesiveness among group members assigned a particular task is most desirable. When this is achieved, cooperation will result in each member helping others in the group even though it may result in a decrease in the performance record of the assisting individual.

Applying this to budgeting, the suggestion is that individual performance should not be the ultimate objective in the eyes of top management or employees. Rewards and punishments should not be based entirely on an individual's performance as compared to the plan. The budget reports should be only one of many factors used for evaluation and superiors should recognize this fact. The result would be a decline in individual competition and greater cooperation towards the achievement of a goal. This environment could eliminate possible dysfunctional consequences. Group cohesiveness will be affected greatly by the leadership style of the group's superior. Whether he believes in rigidity or flexibility, whether he is authoritative or democratic, and the freedom granted him by the organizational structure and policies, will influence the way he controls his subordinates.

I. Mechanical Considerations of Budgeting

Dysfunctional consequences can arise from the mechanical aspects of budgeting.

Budgeting systems cost money to install and continue. These costs must always be considered in evaluating the worthiness of a system.

It must also be remembered that budgets are merely estimates or predictions. As such, they could be incorrect or inappropriate because of economic, technical and environmental changes. The estimating procedure itself may be inappropriate. If budgets are thought of as a goal rather than a means of reaching the goal, the emphasis on budgets cannot help but carry dysfunctional consequences, particularly when the estimates have been incorrectly computed.

[14] Ibid., p. 530.

A final mechanical problem involves the assignment of costs to the person deemed responsible for them. There is always a strong possibility that costs assigned to one person may have been caused by another. The subsequent bickering and ill-feeling would obviously be dysfunctional.

Budgets must be capable of flexibility. This is fundamentally the result of management attitudes and not inherent in the budget itself. Management must recognize that forced adherence to a plan could cause decisions to be made that are not in the long-run interest of the business. Unforeseen opportunities may arise which were not planned. A decision resulting in a significant, unfavorable variance on the short-range plan may be the best alternative in terms of long-range profitability. Failure to take advantage of such situations may result in adherence to the budget but also in dysfunctional consequences in terms of achieving the objectives of budgeting.

Alternatively, failure to adhere to budget figures when they are correct, merely to protect the individuals involved or their superiors, must also be avoided. Such an attitude would destroy one of the corner-stones of a successful budgeting system.

General Model of the Consequences of a Budgeting System

Figure 5 summarizes the factors which must be considered when determining the functional and dysfunctional consequences possible from a budgeting system.

The square immediately outside the BUDGET square indicates the potential benefits to be derived from a successful budgeting system. These benefits are functional to the more efficient achievement of an organization's goal of making profit. The next surrounding square indicates many of the factors which can aid or prevent the achievement of the desired benefits. The descriptive model is arranged so that the effects of various environmental circumstances and managerial policies (participation, motivational intentions, organization structure, etc.) can be immediately related to a particular benefit (planning). The square at the top of the diagram includes factors which are not specifically related to any one particular benefit but which have an important influence on the success or failure of the overall budget system.

The points mentioned in the peripheral square and the top square cannot be clearly identified as either functional or dysfunctional. The relationship of these points to the benefits of budgeting depends upon the particular circumstances.

Conclusion

The model which has been developed to point out the functional possibilities of budgeting and to identify the sources of possible dysfunctional

FIGURE 5
General Model of the Factors to Consider
When Determining the Functional and Dysfunctional Aspects
of Introducing and Using a Budgeting System

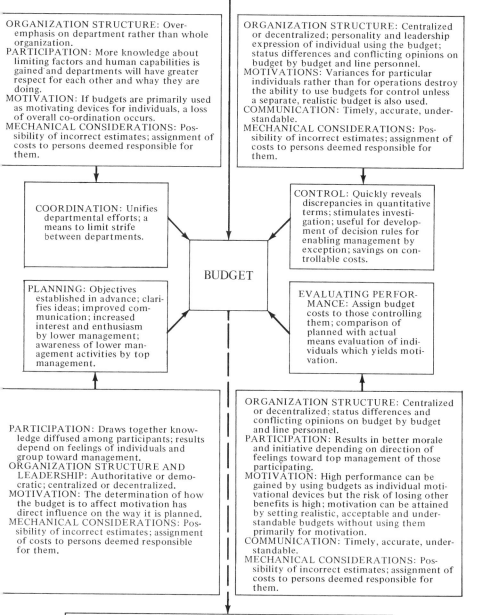

● Interpreted meaning of word "Budget"
● Personality and leadership expression of person subject to a budget or using a budget
● Role conflict involving line and budget staff personnel
● Involvement of workers
● Mechanical considerations: —monetary cost
 —Substitution of budget as goal rather than as means to a goal
 —Realistic standards

ORGANIZATION STRUCTURE: Over-emphasis on department rather than whole organization.
PARTICIPATION: More knowledge about limiting factors and human capabilities is gained and departments will have greater respect for each other and whay they are doing.
MOTIVATION: If budgets are primarily used as motivating devices for individuals, a loss of overall co-ordination occurs.
MECHANICAL CONSIDERATIONS: Possibility of incorrect estimates; assignment of costs to persons deemed responsible for them.

ORGANIZATION STRUCTURE: Centralized or decentralized; personality and leadership expression of individual using the budget; status differences and conflicting opinions on budget by budget and line personnel.
MOTIVATIONS: Variances for particular individuals rather than for operations destroy the ability to use budgets for control unless a separate, realistic budget is also used.
COMMUNICATION: Timely, accurate, under-standable.
MECHANICAL CONSIDERATIONS: Possibility of incorrect estimates; assignment of costs to persons deemed responsible for them.

COORDINATION: Unifies departmental efforts; a means to limit strife between departments.

CONTROL: Quickly reveals discrepancies in quantitative terms; stimulates investigation; useful for development of decision rules for enabling management by exception; savings on controllable costs.

BUDGET

PLANNING: Objectives established in advance; clarifies ideas; improved communication; increased interest and enthusiasm by lower management; awareness of lower management activities by top management.

EVALUATING PERFORMANCE: Assign budget costs to those controlling them; comparison of planned with actual means evaluation of individuals which yields motivation.

PARTICIPATION: Draws together knowledge diffused among participants; results depend on feelings of individuals and group toward management.
ORGANIZATION STRUCTURE AND LEADERSHIP: Authoritative or democratic; centralized or decentralized.
MOTIVATION: The determination of how the budget is to affect motivation has direct influence on the way it is planned.
MECHANICAL CONSIDERATIONS: Possibility of incorrect estimates; assignment of costs to persons deemed responsible for them.

ORGANIZATION STRUCTURE: Centralized or decentralized; status differences and conflicting opinions on budget by budget and line personnel.
PARTICIPATION: Results in better morale and initiative depending on direction of feelings toward top management of those participating.
MOTIVATION: High performance can be gained by using budgets as individual motivational devices but the risk of losing other benefits is high; motivation can be attained by setting realistic, acceptable and understandable budgets without using them primarily for motivation.
COMMUNICATION: Timely, accurate, under-standable.
MECHANICAL CONSIDERATIONS: Possibility of incorrect estimates; assignment of costs to persons deemed responsible for them.

Effectiveness in increasing organizational efficiency in achieving its goal of maximizing the present value of the owner's wealth consequences represents a summary of relevant findings and statements by behavioral scientists, accountants and managers.

Budgeting is only one type of control technique used by top management. Many of the propositions developed are equally applicable to other types of quantitatively-oriented control techniques.

The points developed in this paper should be considered by any organization using or contemplating the introduction of a budgeting process. The importance of each point will vary, however, according to the particular organization, its strategy, history, organizational structure, reasons for using the system, the personalities involved, the leadership style of individuals in responsible positions, the general attitudes of employees toward the organization and control devices, the cohesiveness of reference groups working on and with the budget, and the personal attitudes of employees regarding the justification of, and methods of achieving, organizational goals.

The major proposition suggested is that a budgeting system designed to accomplish the designated benefits is something more than a series of figures. Its origination, implementation, and degree of success are significantly related to the behaviorally-oriented problems that can easily arise. Management methods for solving these problems cannot be generalized into a specific set of rules. Definite rules can seldom cover the particular developments of unique situations. Therefore, only general aspects of budgeting systems with emphasis on behavioral topics have been considered.

The only absolute conclusion that can be proposed is that the human factors involved are generally more difficult to identify and deal with and more serious in nature than the development of quantifying and figure determination techniques. Accountants and managers must recognize this fact if they expect to perform their functions adequately.

10 *Critical Path Method, like PERT, is a decision-making tool which can find wide appreciation at all levels of management. Both (along with other similar techniques) are methods of determining which activities in a project or task are critical to the timely completion of the total project.*

CPM is most effective within the context of well-defined, ordered jobs or tasks which may be performed independently of each other. An obvious and early application — the construction industry — is illustrated in this painstaking and thorough introduction to the methodology of CPM.

One of the significant advantages of either PERT or CPM is that the user is required to give considerable attention to planning and scheduling, which yields a return which is independent of the PERT–CPM technique.

The ABCs of the Critical Path Method*

Ferdinand K. Levy, Gerald L. Thompson,
Jerome D. Wiest†

Recently added to the growing assortment of quantitative tools for business decision making is the Critical Path Method — a powerful but basically simple technique for analyzing, planning, and scheduling large, complex projects. In essence, the tool provides a means of determining (1) which jobs or activities, of the many that comprise a project, are "critical" in their

* *From* Harvard Business Review, *Vol. 41, No. 5 (September–October, 1963), pp. 98–108. Reprinted by permission of the publisher.*

† The preparation of this article was supported by the Office of Naval Research and the Bureau of Ships through grants to the Graduate School of Industrial Administration, Carnegie Institute of Technology. A different version of this material appears as Chapter 20 in *Industrial Scheduling*, edited by J. F. Muth and G. L. Thompson (Englewood Cliffs, New Jersey: Prentice-Hall, Inc., 1963). The job list and project graph for the house-building example were developed by Peter R. Winters.

effect on total project time, and (2) how best to schedule all jobs in the project in order to meet a target date at minimum cost. Widely diverse kinds of projects lend themselves to analysis by CPM, as is suggested in the following list of applications:

- The construction of a building (or a highway).
- Planning and launching a new product.
- A turnaround in an oil refinery (or other maintenance projects).
- Installing and debugging a computer system.
- Research and engineering design projects.
- Scheduling ship construction and repairs.
- The manufacture and assembly of a large generator (or other job-lot operations).
- Missile countdown procedures.

Each of these projects has several characteristics that are essential for analysis by CPM:

1. The project consists of a well-defined collection of jobs (or activities) which, when completed, mark the end of the project.
2. The jobs may be started and stopped independently of each other, within a given sequence. (This requirement eliminates continuous-flow process activities, such as oil refining, where "jobs" or operations necessarily follow one after another with essentially no slack.)
3. The jobs are ordered — that is, they must be performed in technological sequence. (For example, the foundation of a house must be constructed before the walls are erected.)

What Is the Method?

The concept of CPM is quite simple and may best be illustrated in terms of a project graph. The graph is not an essential part of CPM; computer programs have been written which permit necessary calculations to be made without reference to a graph. Nevertheless, the project graph is valuable as a means of depicting, visually and clearly, the complex of jobs in a project and their interrelations:

First of all, each job necessary for the completion of a project is listed with a unique identifying symbol (such as a letter or number), the time required to complete the job, and its immediate prerequisite jobs. For convenience in graphing, and as a check on certain kinds of data errors, the jobs may be arranged in "technological order," which means that no job appears on the list until all of its predecessors have been listed. Technological ordering is impossible if a cycle error exists in the job data (e.g., job *a* precedes *b*, *b* precedes *c*, and *c* precedes *a*).

Then each job is drawn on the graph as a circle, with its identifying symbol and time appearing within the circle. Sequence relationships are indicated by arrows connecting each circle (job) with its immediate successors, with the arrows pointing to the latter. For convenience, all circles with no predecessors are connected to a circle marked "Start"; likewise, all circles with no successors are connected to a circle marked "Finish." (The "Start" and "Finish" circles may be considered pseudo jobs of zero time length.)

Typically, the graph then depicts a number of different "arrow paths" from Start to Finish. The time required to traverse each path is the sum of the times associated with all jobs on the path. The critical path (or paths) is the longest path (in time) from Start to Finish; it indicates the minimum time necessary to complete the entire project.

This method of depicting a project graph differs in some respects from that used by James E. Kelley, Jr., and Morgan R. Walker, who, perhaps more than anyone else, were responsible for the initial development of CPM. (For an interesting account of its early history see their paper, "Critical-Path Planning and Scheduling."[1]) In the widely used Kelley-Walker form, a project graph is just the opposite of that described above: jobs are shown as arrows, and the arrows are connected by means of circles (or dots) that indicate sequence relationships. Thus all immediate predecessors of a given job connect to a circle at the tail of the job arrow, and all immediate successor jobs emanate from the circle at the head of the job arrow. In essence, then, a circle marks an event — the completion of all jobs leading into the circle. Since these jobs are the immediate prerequisites for all jobs leading out of the circle, they must all be completed before *any* of the succeeding jobs can begin.

In order to accurately portray all predecessor relationships, "dummy jobs" must often be added to the project graph in the Kelley-Walker form. The method described in this article avoids the necessity and complexity of dummy jobs, is easier to program for a computer, and also seems more straightforward in explanation and application.

In essence, the critical path is the bottleneck route. Only by finding ways to shorten jobs along the critical path can the over-all project time be reduced; the time required to perform noncritical jobs is irrelevant from the viewpoint of total project time. The frequent (and costly) practice of "crashing" *all* jobs in a project in order to reduce total project time is thus unnecessary. Typically, only about 10% of the jobs in large projects are critical. (This figure will naturally vary from project to project.) Of course, if some way is found to shorten one or more of the critical jobs, then not only will the whole project time be shortened but the critical path itself may shift and some previously noncritical jobs may become critical.

Example: Building a House

A simple and familiar example should help to clarify the notion of critical path scheduling and the process of constructing a graph. The project of

[1] *Proceedings of the Eastern Joint Computer Conference*, Boston, December 1–3, 1959; see also James E. Kelley, Jr., "Critical-Path Planning and Scheduling: Mathematical Basis," *Operations Research*, May–June, 1961, pp. 296–320.

building a house is readily analyzed by the CPM technique and is typical of a large class of similar applications. While a contractor might want a more detailed analysis, we will be satisfied here with the list of major jobs (together with the estimated time and the immediate predecessors for each job) shown in Exhibit 1.

In that exhibit, the column "immediate predecessors" determines the sequence relationships of the jobs and enables us to draw the project graph,

EXHIBIT 1

Sequence and Time Requirements of Jobs

JOB NO.	DESCRIPTION	IMMEDIATE PREDECESSORS	NORMAL TIME (DAYS)
a	START		0
b	EXCAVATE AND POUR FOOTERS	a	4
c	POUR CONCRETE FOUNDATION	b	2
d	ERECT WOODEN FRAME INCLUDING ROUGH ROOF	c	4
e	LAY BRICKWORK	d	6
f	INSTALL BASEMENT DRAINS AND PLUMBING	c	1
g	POUR BASEMENT FLOOR	f	2
h	INSTALL ROUGH PLUMBING	f	3
i	INSTALL ROUGH WIRING	d	2
j	INSTALL HEATING AND VENTILATING	d,g	4
k	FASTEN PLASTER BOARD AND PLASTER (INCLUDING DRYING)	i,j,h	10
l	LAY FINISH FLOORING	k	3
m	INSTALL KITCHEN FIXTURES	l	1
n	INSTALL FINISH PLUMBING	l	2
o	FINISH CARPENTRY	l	3
p	FINISH ROOFING AND FLASHING	e	2
q	FASTEN GUTTERS AND DOWNSPOUTS	p	1
r	LAY STORM DRAINS FOR RAIN WATER	c	1
s	SAND AND VARNISH FLOORING	o,t	2
t	PAINT	m,n	3
u	FINISH ELECTRICAL WORK	t	1
v	FINISH GRADING	q,r	2
w	POUR WALKS AND COMPLETE LANDSCAPING	v	5
x	FINISH	s,u,w	0

Exhibit 2. Here, in each circle the letter before the comma identifies the job and the number after the comma indicates the job time.

Following the rule that a "legal" path must always move in the direction of the arrows, we could enumerate 22 unique paths from Start to Finish,

EXHIBIT 2

Project Graph

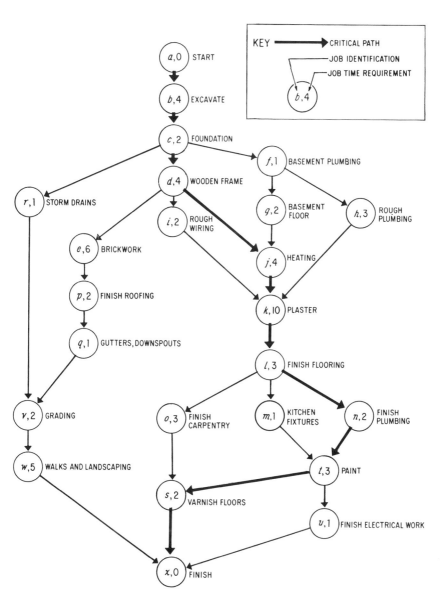

with associate times ranging from a minimum of 14 days (path *a-b-c-r-v-w-x*) to a maximum of 34 days (path *a-b-c-d-j-k-l-n-t-s-x*). The latter is the critical path; it determines the over-all project time and tells us which jobs are critical in their effect on this time. If the contractor wishes to complete the house in less than 34 days, it would be useless to shorten jobs not on the critical path. It may seem to him, for example, that the brickwork (*e*) delays progress, since work on a whole series of jobs (*p-q-v-w*) must wait until it is completed. But it would be fruitless to rush the completion of the brickwork, since it is not on the critical path and so is irrelevant in determining total project time.

SHORTENING THE CP

If the contractor were to use CPM techniques, he would examine the critical path for possible improvements. Perhaps he could assign more carpenters to job *d*, reducing it from four to two days. Then the critical path would change slightly, passing through jobs *f* and *g* instead of *d*. Notice that total project time would be reduced only one day, even though two days had been shaved off job *d*. Thus the contractor must watch for possible shifting of the critical path as he effects changes in critical jobs.

Shortening the critical path requires a consideration of both engineering problems and economic questions. Is it physically possible to shorten the time required by critical jobs (by assigning more men to the job, working overtime, using different equipment, and so on)? If so, would the costs of speedup be less than the savings resulting from the reduction in overall project time? CPM is a useful tool because it quickly focuses attention on those jobs that are critical to the project time, it provides an easy way to determine the effects of shortening various jobs in the project, and it enables the user to evaluate the costs of a "crash" program.

Two important applications of these features come to mind:

• Du Pont, a pioneer in the application of CPM to construction and maintenance projects, was concerned with the amount of downtime for maintenance at its Louisville works, which produces an intermediate product in the neoprene process. Analyzing the maintenance schedule by CPM, Du Pont engineers were able to cut downtime for maintenance from 125 to 93 hours. CPM pointed to further refinements that were expected to reduce total time to 78 hours. As a result, performance of the plant improved by about one million pounds in 1959, and the intermediate was no longer a bottleneck in the neoprene process.

PERT (i.e., Program Evaluation Review Technique), a technique closely related to the critical path method, is widely credited with helping to shorten by two years the time originally estimated for completion of the engineering and development program for the Navy's Polaris missile. By pinpointing the longest paths through the vast maze of jobs necessary for completion of the missile design, PERT enabled the program managers to concentrate their efforts on those activities that vitally affected total project time.[2]

Even with our small house-building project, however, the process of enumerating and measuring the length of every path through the maze of jobs is tedious. A simple method of finding the critical path and, at the same time, developing useful information about each job is described next.

Critical Path Algorithm

If the start time or date for the project is given (we denote it by S), then there exists for each job an earliest starting time (ES), which is the earliest possible time that a job can begin, if all its predecessors are also started at their ES. And if the time to complete the job is t, we can define, analogously, its earliest finish time (EF) to be ES + t.

There is a simple way of computing ES and EF times using the project graph. It proceeds as follows:

1. Mark the value of S to the left and to the right of Start.
2. Consider any new unmarked job *all of whose predecessors have been marked*, and mark to the left of the new job the *largest* number marked to the right of any of its *immediate* predecessors. This number is its early start time.
3. Add to this number the job time and mark the result (EF time) to the right of the job.
4. Continue until Finish has been reached, then stop.

Thus, at the conclusion of this calculation the ES time for each job will appear to the left of the circle which identifies it, and the EF time will appear to the right of the circle. The number which appears to the right of the last job, Finish, is the early finish time (F) for the entire project.

To illustrate these calculations let us consider the following simple production process:

An assembly is to be made from two parts, A and B. Both parts must be turned on the lathe, and B must be polished while A need not be. The list of jobs to be performed, together with the predecessors of each job and the time in minutes to perform each job, is given in Exhibit 3.

The project graph is shown in Exhibit 4. As previously, the letter identifying each job appears before the comma and its job time after the comma. Also shown on the graph are the ES and EF times for each job, assuming that the start time, S, is *zero*. The ES time appears to the left of the circle representing a job, and the EF time appears to the right of the circle. Note that F = 100. The reader may wish to duplicate the diagram without these times and carry out the calculations for himself as a check on his understanding of the computation process described above.

[2] See Robert W. Miller, "How to Plan and Control with PERT," *Harvard Business Review*, March–April, 1962, p. 93.

EXHIBIT 3

Data for Production Process

JOB NO.	DESCRIPTION	IMMEDIATE PREDECESSORS	NORMAL TIME (MINUTES)
a	START		0
b	GET MATERIALS FOR A	a	10
c	GET MATERIALS FOR B	a	20
d	TURN A ON LATHE	b,c	30
e	TURN B ON LATHE	b,c	20
f	POLISH B	e	40
g	ASSEMBLE A AND B	d,f	20
h	FINISH	g	0

EXHIBIT 4

Calculation of Early Start and Early Finish Times for Each Job

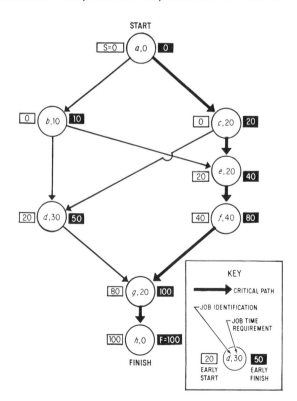

LATEST START AND FINISH TIMES

Suppose now that we have a target time (T) for completing the project. T may have been originally expressed as a calendar date, e.g., October 1 or February 15. When is the latest time that the project can be started and finished?

In order to be feasible it is clear that T must be greater (later) than or equal to F, the early finish time for the project. Assuming this is so, we can define the concept of late finish (LF), or the latest time that a job can be finished, without delaying the total project beyond its target time (T). Similarly, late start (LS) is defined to be LF − *t*, where *t* is the job time.

These numbers are determined for each job in a manner similar to the previous calculations except that we work from the end of the project to its beginning. We proceed as follows:

1. Mark the value of T to the right and left of Finish.
2. Consider any new unmarked job *all of whose successors have been marked*, and mark to the right of the new job the *smallest* LS time marked to the left of any of its immediate successors.

   The logic of this is hard to explain in a few words, although apparent enough by inspection. It helps to remember that the smallest LS time of the successors of a given job, if translated into calendar times, would be the latest finish time of that job.
3. Subtract from this number the job time and mark the result to the left of the job.
4. Continue until Start has been reached, then stop.

   At the conclusion of this calculation the LF time for a job will appear to the right of the circle which identifies it, and the LS time for the job will appear to the left of the circle. The number appearing to the right of Start is the latest time that the entire project can be started and still finish at the target time T.

In Exhibit 5 we carry out these calculations for the example of Exhibit 3. Here T = F = 100, and we separate early start and finish and late start and finish times by semicolons so that ES; LS appears to the left of the job and EF; LF to the right. Again the reader may wish to check these calculations for himself.

Concept of Slack

Examination of Exhibit 5 reveals that some jobs have their early start equal to late start, while others do not. The difference between a job's early start and its late start (or between early finish and late finish) is called total slack (TS). Total slack represents the maximum amount of time a job may be delayed beyond its early start without necessarily delaying the project completion time.

EXHIBIT 5

Calculation of Late Start and Late Finish Times for Each Job

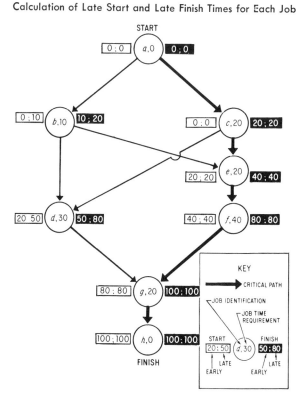

We earlier defined critical jobs as those on the longest path through the project. That is, critical jobs *directly* affect the total project time. We can now relate the critical path to the concept of slack.

FINDING THE CRITICAL PATH

If the target date (T) equals the early finish date for the whole project (F), then all critical jobs will have *zero* total slack. There will be at least one path going from Start to Finish that includes critical jobs only, i.e., the *critical path*.

If T is greater (later) than F, then the critical jobs will have total slack equal to T minus F. This is a minimum value; since the critical path includes only critical jobs, it includes those with the smallest TS. All noncritical jobs will have *greater* total slack.

In Exhibit 5, the critical path is shown by darkening the arrows connecting critical jobs. In this case there is just one critical path, and all critical jobs lie on it; however, in other cases there may be more than one critical path.

Note that T = F; thus the critical jobs have zero total slack. Job *b* has TS = 10, and job *d* has TS = 30; either or both of these jobs could be delayed by these amounts of time without delaying the project.

Another kind of slack is worth mentioning. Free slack (FS) is the amount a job can be delayed without delaying the early start of any other job. A job with positive total slack may or may not also have free slack, but the latter never exceeds the former. For purposes of computation, the free slack of a job is defined as the difference between the job's EF time and the *earliest* of the ES times of all its immediate successors. Thus, in Exhibit 5, job *b* has FS of 10, and job *d* has FS of 30. All other jobs have zero free slack.

SIGNIFICANCE OF SLACK

When a job has zero total slack, its scheduled start time is automatically fixed (that is, ES = LS); and to delay the calculated start time is to delay the whole project. Jobs with positive total slack, however, allow the scheduler some discretion in setting their start times. This flexibility can usefully be applied to smoothing work schedules. Peak loads that develop in a particular shop (or on a machine, or within an engineering design group, to cite other examples) may be relieved by shifting jobs on the peak days to their late starts. Slack allows this kind of juggling without affecting project time.[3]

Free slack can be used effectively at the operating level. For example, if a job has free slack, the foreman may be given some flexibility in deciding when to start the job. Even if he delays the start by an amount equal to (or less than) the free slack, the delay will not affect the start times or slack of succeeding jobs (which is not true of jobs that have no free slack). For an illustration of these notions, we return to our house-building example.

BACK TO THE CONTRACTOR

In Exhibit 6, we reproduce the diagram of house-building jobs, marking the ES and LS to the left, and the EF and LF to the right of each job (for example, "0;3" and "4;7" on either side of the *b*,4 circle). We assume that construction begins on day zero and must be completed by day 37. Total slack for each job is not marked, since it is evident as the difference between the pairs of numbers ES and LS or EF and LF. However, jobs that have positive free slack are so marked. There is one critical path, which is shown darkened in the diagram. All critical jobs on this path have total slack of three days.

[3] For a method for smoothing operations in a job shop, based on CPM and the use of slack, see F. K. Levy, G. L. Thompson, and J. D. Wiest, "Multi-ship, Multi-Shop Production Smoothing Algorithm," *Naval Logistics Research Quarterly*, March 9, 1962.

EXHIBIT 6
Project Graph with Start and Finish Times

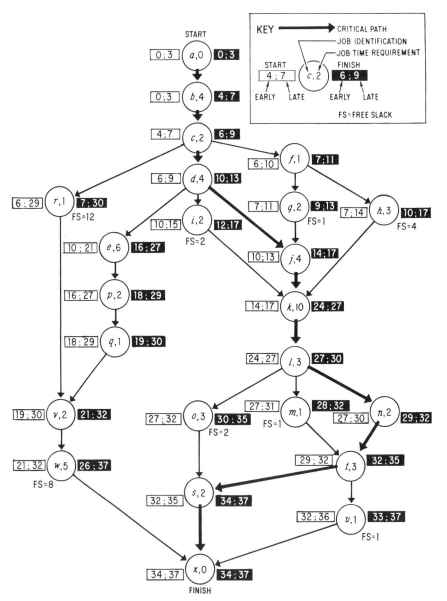

Several observations can be drawn immediately from the diagram:

1. The contractor could postpone starting the house three days and still complete it on schedule, barring unforeseen difficulties (see the difference between early and late times at the Finish). This would reduce the total slack of all jobs by three days, and hence reduce TS for critical jobs to zero.

2. Several jobs have free slack. Thus the contractor could delay the completion of *i* (rough wiring) by two days, *g* (the basement floor) by one day, *h* (rough plumbing) by four days, *r* (the storm drains) by 12 days, and so on — without affecting succeeding jobs.

3. The series of jobs *e* (brickwork), *p* (roofing), *q* (gutters), *v* (grading), and *w* (landscaping) have a comfortable amount of total slack (nine days). The contractor can use these and other slack jobs as "fill in" jobs for workers who become available when their skills are not needed for currently critical jobs. This is a simple application of work-load smoothing: juggling the jobs with slack in order to reduce peak demands for certain skilled workers or machines.

If the contractor were to effect changes in one or more of the critical jobs, by contrast, the calculations would have to be performed again. This he can easily do; but in large projects with complex sequence relationships, hand calculations are considerably more difficult and liable to error. Computer programs have been developed, however, for calculating ES, LS, EF, LF, TS, and FS for each job in a project, given the set of immediate prerequisites and the job times for each job.[4]

Handling Data Errors

Information concerning job times and predecessor relationships is gathered, typically, by shop foremen, scheduling clerks, or others closely associated with a project. It is conceivable that several kinds of errors may occur in such job data:

1. The estimated job times may be in error.

2. The predecessor relationship may contain cycles: e.g., job *a* is a predecessor for *b*, *b* is a predecessor for *c*, and *c* is a predecessor for *a*.

3. The list of prerequisites for a job may include more than the immediate prerequisites; e.g., job *a* is a predecessor of *b*, *b* is a predecessor of *c*, and *a* and *b* both are predecessors of *c*.

4. Some predecessor relationships may be overlooked.

5. Some predecessor relationships may be listed that are spurious.

How can management deal with these problems? We shall examine each briefly in turn.

---

[4] An algorithm on which one such computer program is based is discussed by F. K. Levy, G. L. Thompson, and J. D. Wiest, in Chapter 22, "Mathematical Basis of the Critical Path Method," *Industrial Scheduling*.

Job Times. An accurate estimate of total project time depends, of course, on accurate job-time data. CPM eliminates the necessity (and expense) of careful time studies for *all* jobs. Instead the following procedure can be used:
· Given rough time estimates, construct a CPM graph of the project.
· Then those jobs that are on the critical path (together with jobs that have very small total slack, indicating that they are nearly critical) can be more closely checked, their times re-estimated, and another CPM graph constructed with the refined data.
· If the critical path has changed to include jobs still having rough time estimates, then the process is repeated.

In many projects studied, it has been found that only a small fraction of jobs are critical; so it is likely that refined time studies will be needed for relatively few jobs in a project in order to arrive at a reasonably accurate estimate of the total project time. CPM thus can be used to reduce the problem of Type 1 errors at a small total cost.

Prerequisites. A computer algorithm has been developed to check for errors of Types 2 and 3 above. The algorithm (mentioned in footnote 4) systematically examines the set of prerequisites for each job and cancels from the set all but immediate predecessor jobs. When an error of Type 2 is present in the job data, the algorithm will signal a "cycle error" and print out the cycle in question.

Wrong or Missing Facts. Errors of Types 4 and 5 cannot be discovered by computer routines. Instead, manual checking (perhaps by a committee) is necessary to see that prerequisites are accurately reported.

Cost Calculations

The cost of carrying out a project can be readily calculated from the job data if the cost of doing each job is included in the data. If jobs are done by crews, and the speed with which the job is done depends on the crew size, then it is possible to shorten or lengthen the project time by adding or removing men from crews. Other means for compressing job times might also be found; but any speedup is likely to carry a price tag. Suppose that we assign to each job a "normal time" and a "crash time" and also calculate the associated costs necessary to carry the job in each time. If we want to shorten the project, we can assign some of the critical jobs to their crash time, and compute the corresponding direct cost. In this way it is possible to calculate the cost of completing the project in various total times, with the direct costs increasing as the over-all time decreases.

Added to direct costs are certain overhead expenses which are usually allocated on the basis of total project time. Fixed costs per project thus decrease as project time is shortened. In ordinary circumstances a combination of fixed and direct costs as a function of total project time would probably fall into the pattern shown in Exhibit 7. The minimum total cost (point A) would

EXHIBIT 7

Typical Cost Pattern

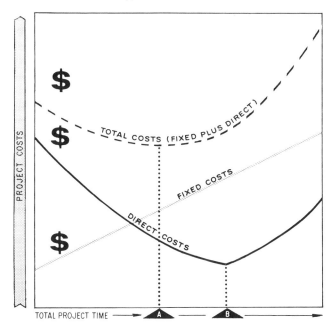

likely fall to the left of the minimum point on the direct cost curve (point B) indicating that the optimum project time is somewhat shorter than an analysis of direct costs only would indicate.

Other economic factors, of course, can be included in the analysis. For example, pricing might be brought in:

> A large chemical company starts to build a plant for producing a new chemical. After the construction schedule and completion date are established, an important potential customer indicates a willingness to pay a premium price for the new chemical if it can be made available earlier than scheduled. The chemical producer applies techniques of CPM to its construction schedule and calculates the additional costs associated with "crash" completion of jobs on the critical path. With a plot of costs correlated with total project time, the producer is able to select a new completion date such that the increased costs are met by the additional revenue offered by the customer.

New Developments

Because of their great potential for applications, both CPM and PERT have received intensive development in the past few years. This effort is sparked, in part, because of the Air Force (and other governmental agency) requirements that contractors use these methods in planning and monitoring their work. Here are some illustrations of progress made:

- One of the present authors (Wiest) has developed extensions of the workload smoothing algorithm. These extensions are the so-called SPAR (for Scheduling Program for Allocating Resources) programs for scheduling projects having limited resources.
- A contemporaneous development by C-E-I-R, Inc., has produced RAMPS (for Resource Allocation and Multi-Project Scheduling), which is similar but not identical.
- The most recent version of PERT, called PERT/COST, was developed by the armed services and various businesses for use on weapon-systems development projects contracted by the government. Essentially, PERT/COST adds the consideration of resource costs to the schedule produced by the PERT procedure. Indications of how smoothing can be accomplished are also made. Other recent versions are called PERT II, PERT III, PEP, PEPCO, and Super PERT.

Conclusion

For the manager of large projects, CPM is a powerful and flexible tool, indeed, for decision making:

- It is useful at various stages of project management, from initial planning or analyzing of alternative programs, to scheduling and controlling the jobs (activities) that comprise a project.
- It can be applied to a great variety of project types — from our house-building example to the vastly more complicated design project for the Polaris — and at various levels of planning — from scheduling jobs in a single shop, or shops in a plant, to scheduling plants within a corporation.
- In a simple and direct way it displays the interrelations in the complex of jobs that comprise a large project.
- It is easily explainable to the layman by means of the project graph. Data calculations for large projects, while tedious, are not difficult, and can readily be handled by a computer.
- It pinpoints attention to the small subset of jobs that are critical to project completion time, thus contributing to more accurate planning and more precise control.
- It enables the manager to quickly study the effects of "crash" programs and to anticipate potential bottlenecks that might result from shortening certain critical jobs.
- It leads to reasonable estimates of total project costs for various completion dates, which enable the manager to select an optimum schedule.

Because of the above characteristics of CPM — and especially its intuitive logic and graphic appeal — it is a decision-making tool which can find wide appreciation at all levels of management.[5] The project graph helps the foreman to understand the sequencing of jobs and the necessity of pushing those that are critical. For the manager concerned with day-to-day operations in all departments, CPM enables him to measure progress (or lack of it) against plans and to take appropriate action quickly when needed. And the underlying simplicity of CPM and its ability to focus attention on crucial problem areas of large projects make it an ideal tool for the top manager. On his shoulders falls the ultimate responsibility for over-all planning and coordination of such projects in the light of company-wide objectives.

[5] See A. Charnes and W. W. Cooper, "A Network Interpretation and a Directed Sub-Dual Algorithm for Critical Path Scheduling," *Journal of Industrial Engineering*, July–August 1962, pp. 213–219.

EDITORS' NOTE: PERT differs from CPM by requiring three time estimates for each project: most optimistic, most pessimistic, and most likely. These estimates are averaged, with appropriate weights $\left(\text{usually } \dfrac{P + 4L + 0}{6} \right)$ to derive the time estimate utilized by the PERT algorithm. Probability distributions for the various completion time expectations can also be generated, and appropriate measures of central tendency calculated.

Supplemental
Readings
to Part Two

Jacob G. Birnberg and Louis R. Pondy, "An Experimental Study of the Allocation of Financial Resources Within Small, Hierarchical Task Groups,"
Administrative Science Quarterly, Vol. 14, No. 2 (June, 1969), pp. 192–201.
Budgeting systems must be designed to counteract, or take advantage of,
the self-interested behavior of budget managers.

Hugh E. Bradley, "Setting and Controlling Budgets With Regression Analysis,"
Management Accounting, Vol. 51, No. 5 (November, 1969), pp. 31–34, 40.
An illustration of the use of regression analysis in budgeting is presented.

Eugene E. Comiskey, "Better Budgeting With Multiple Regression Analysis,"
Cost and Management, Vol. 41, No. 1 (January, 1967), pp. 14–17.
Improvements in cost budgeting or forecasting through multiple linear
regression are illustrated.

Don T. DeCoster, "PERT/Cost — The Challenge," *Management Services,*
Vol. 1, No. 2 (May-June, 1964), pp. 13–18.
A variation of flexible budgeting, PERT/Cost requires that accounting
systems be project-oriented. It also demands effective coordination of
all management personnel involved in projects.

Henry Gunders, "Better Profit Planning," *Management Accounting,* Vol. 46,
No. 12 (August, 1965), pp. 3–24.
Applications of operations research to all forms of budgeting are
illustrated.

Ernest I. Hanson, "The Budgetary Control Function," *The Accounting Review,*
Vol. XLI, No. 2 (April, 1966), pp. 239–243.
An expansion of conventional concepts of control is made to include
factors influencing employee response to the budget process.

Y. Ijiri, J. C. Kinard, and F. B. Putney, "An Integrated Evaluation System for
Budget Forecasting and Operating Performance With a Classified Budgeting
Bibliography," *Journal of Accounting Research,* Vol. 6, No. 1 (Spring, 1968),
pp. 1–28.
A system for budget evaluation is provided, with a comprehensive
bibliography of related materials.

Arie Y. Lewin and Michael Schiff, "The Impact of People on Budgets," *The
Accounting Review,* Vol. XLV, No. 2 (April, 1970), pp. 259–268.
The relationship between the controller and the controlled is explored in
the context of the budget process.

Arie Y. Lewin and Michael Schiff, "Where Traditional Budgeting Fails," *Financial Executive,* Vol. 36, No. 5 (May, 1968), pp. 51–62.

Behavioral implications of the occurrence of slack as an unintended result of the budget and control system are examined.

R. D. F. Morris, "Budgetary Control is Obsolete," *The Accountant,* Vol. 158, No. 4874 (May 18, 1968), pp. 654–656.

An explanation of why the use of budgets for control purposes is obsolete is presented.

Michael E. Wallace, "Behavioral Considerations in Budgeting," *Management Accounting,* Vol. 47, No. 12 (August, 1966), pp. 3–8.

Behavioral considerations in budgeting are studied.

Additional
Bibliography
to Part Two

William E. Arnstein, "The Fundamentals of Profit Planning," *The New York Certified Public Accountant*, Vol. XXXII, No. 5 (May, 1962), pp. 313–321.

Sterling K. Atkinson, "Short- and Long-Range Considerations in Cost Analyses," *NA(C)A Bulletin*, Vol. XXXVIII, No. 3 (November, 1956), pp. 343–352.

Ernest E. Bareuther and Bert E. Stromberg, "Budgeting Policy and Practice in a Decentralized Company," *NAA Bulletin*, Vol. XXXIX, No. 2 (October, 1957), pp. 31–44.

Dirck Barhydt, Robert H. Clement, Dan W. Lufkin, and A. Jones Yorke, "Planning Concept in the Tentative Statement of Cost Concepts," *The Accounting Review*, Vol. XXXII, No. 4 (October, 1957) pp. 593–597.

Ronald Brenneck, "Learning Curve Techniques for More Profitable Controls," *NAA Bulletin*, Vol. XL, No. 11 (July, 1959), pp. 59–69.

George B. Cleveland, "Building the Factory Expense Budget and Its Utilization," *NAA Bulletin*, Vol. XLIII, No. 1 (September, 1961), pp. 63–74.

E. Hay Davison, "Productivity and the Industrial Accountant," *The Accountant*, Vol. 149, No. 4641 (November 30, 1963), pp. 678–683.

John Dearden, "Budgeting and Accounting for R & D Costs," *Financial Executive*, Vol. XXXI, No. 12 (December, 1963), pp. 20 ff.

Henry C. Doofe, "The Profit Path as Seen Through the Budgetary Control Program," *NAA Bulletin*, Vol. XLI, No. 3 (November, 1959), pp. 47–58.

R. L. Dressel, "Input-Output Relationships as a Forecasting Tool," *NAA Bulletin*, Vol. XLIII, No. 10 (June, 1962), pp. 25–32.

James S. Earley, "Marginal Policies of Excellently Managed Companies," *The American Economic Review*, Vol. XLVI, No. 1 (March, 1956), pp. 44–70.

Granville R. Gargiulo, "Critical Path Methods," *NAA Bulletin*, Vol. XLVI, No. 5 (January, 1965), pp. 3–16.

Leon E. Hay, "Planning for Profits — How Some Executives Are Doing It," *The Accounting Review*, Vol. XXXV, No. 2 (April, 1960), pp. 233–237.

John R. Hennessy and E. I. Roberson, "Budget Preparation from the Bottom Up," *NAA Bulletin*, Vol. XXXVIII, No. 4 (December, 1956), pp. 508–519.

William A. Heuser, Jr. and B. E. Wynne, Jr., "CPM — An Effective Management Tool, — Part II," *Financial Executive*, Vol. XXXI, No. 8 (August, 1963) pp. 18 ff.

John V. James, "Management Planning of Capital Allocations to Business Activities," *NAA Bulletin*, Vol. XLIII, No. 1 (September, 1961), pp. 5–15.

174

Robert K. Jaedicke, "Accounting Data for Purposes of Control," *The Accounting Review*, Vol. XXXVII, No. 2 (April, 1962), pp. 181–188.

Raymond B. Jordan, "Learning How to Use the Learning Curve," *NAA Bulletin*, Vol. XXXIX, No. 5 (January, 1958), pp. 27–39.

John Jodka, "PERT — A Recent Control Concept," *NAA Bulletin*, Vol. XLIII, No. 5 (January, 1962), pp. 81–86.

John H. Kempster, "Economic Yardsticks in Management Reports," *NAA Bulletin*, Vol. XL, No. 1 (September, 1958), pp. 5–15.

Alexander C. Koren, "The Critical Path Method (CPM); A Planning and Control Procedure," *The New York Certified Public Accountant*, Vol. XXXIII, No. 10 (October, 1963), pp. 697–705.

P. F. Lorenz, "Accounting for Management Planning," *The Illinois CPA*, Vol. 22, No. 4 (Summer, 1960), pp. 18–29.

Richard Mattessich, "Budgeting Models and System Simulation," *The Accounting Review*, Vol. XXXVI, No. 3 (July, 1961), pp. 384–397.

Herbert T. McAnly, "Bringing the Budget to Bear on Operations," *NAA Bulletin*, Vol. XXXIX, No. 5 (January, 1958), pp. 41–49.

W. J. R. McEwan, "Productivity and Profits," *The Accountant*, Vol. 150, No. 4664 (May 9, 1964), pp. 587–590.

Kenneth S. Most, "Practical Problems in Measuring Productivity," *The Accountant*, Vol. 149, No. 4642 (December 7, 1963), pp. 714 ff.

Kenneth J. Murley, "Expected Cost — The Common Denominator," *The Controller*, Vol. XXVIII, No. 7 (July, 1960), pp. 307–312.

Dewey W. Neal, "Straight-Line Projections with the Learning Curve," *NAA Bulletin*, Vol. XLII, No. 10 (June, 1961), p. 62.

Maurice S. Newman, "The Essence of Budgetary Control," *Management Services*, Vol. 2, No. 1 (January–February, 1965), pp. 19–26.

William W. Richardson, "Significance of Company Forward Planning," *NAA Bulletin*, Vol. XLI, No. 5 (January, 1960), pp. 5–10.

Michael Shegda and Hyman Weinberg, "Costs for Inventory Control and Production Planning," *NAA Bulletin*, Vol. XLV, No. 11 (July, 1964), pp. 3–12.

D. Richard Smith, "Budgetary Planning and Control in a Steel Company," *NAA Bulletin*, Vol. XLIII, No. 6 (February, 1962), pp. 5–16.

Richard L. Smith, "Capital Expenditures — Control Today for Profit Tomorrow," *NAA Bulletin*, Vol. XXXIX, No. 3 (November, 1957), pp. 23–32.

Chester H. Sneider, "Setting Operating Goals and Measuring Achievements," *NAA Bulletin*, Vol. XXXIX, No. 11 (July, 1958), pp. 25–31.

Linden C. Speers, "Forward Planning the Planning and Control Tools," *NAA Bulletin*, Vol. XXXVIII, No. 9 (May, 1957), pp. 1123–1129.

Richard B. Troxel, "Variable Budgets Through Correlation Analysis: A Simplified Approach," *NAA Bulletin*, Vol. XLVI, No. 6 (February, 1965), pp. 48–55.

Ernest H. Weinwurm, "A Middle Ground Between Fixed and Flexible Budgeting," *NAA Bulletin*, Vol. XL, No. 1 (September, 1958), pp. 47–58.

Allen Weiss, "Budgeting — First Step in Cost Estimating," *Management Services*, Vol. 1, No. 4 (September–October, 1964), pp. 51–56.

PART THREE

Cost Planning, Decision, and Control:
Capital Budgeting

Although "rate of return" long has been an acceptable measure of organizational performance, it is of such importance in evaluating capital budgeting decisions that it is included in this section for both general and specific discussion. The decision problems of defining invested capital and cost, of measuring effect of price level fluctuations, and of establishing valid profit measurements which will enable the "rate of return" computation are not easy. The problem of evaluating alternative capital investment opportunities has received abundant discussion in the literature of accounting and allied disciplines, and the topic has been included in the newer texts in cost accounting and managerial accounting.

Attention given this problem in recent years is well deserved in view of the fact that capital expenditures by industry constitute an extremely significant proportion of our gross national product. The potential payoff from application of better analytical tools to the capital budgeting process is high. Concern of accountants with the problem of capital budgeting and with the emerging sophisticated techniques for its solution is symbolic of the direction of the profession's interest and potential.

In the first article, Brown considers the appropriateness of "rate of return" for evaluating capital budgeting decisions. He recognizes that rate of return is still a basic way of measuring the attractiveness of an investment, either past or present, and of choosing among alternative investments. Brown makes the point very well that rate of return is not the only tool, but on balance he concludes that it strongly recommends itself for application in evaluating capital investment proposals, and that it has substantial merits not possessed by alternative methods of assessing financial worth. In this connection, Brown examines the determinants of a proposal's financial worth: (1) its economic life, (2) the capital outlays required, and (3) the amount and timing of the revenues and costs resulting from its adoption.

176

He relates how the rate of return calculations explicitly consider all three. He also deals with the means of obtaining comparability between projects, cost of capital considerations, uncertainty, and implied future outlays and other administrative problems.

Evaluation of capital investment opportunities or of alternative choices usually involves estimating net cash or income flows for varying future periods. Risk and uncertainty are factors which must be considered carefully in the analysis. Hertz introduces the problem of risk and describes some rather sophisticated techniques for increasing reliability and accuracy of estimates under conditions of uncertainty. This article has induced others — such as Rappaport's, in which Rappaport studies the reasons for the continued popularity of the payback period method in spite of its theoretical shortcomings. Uncertainty of future cash flows and liquidity preferences of businessmen are given as the rationale. Rappaport then proposes an improvement on the payback period method that would take into account alternative opportunities and the time value of money.

Weingartner continues the payback period discussion in a scholarly and somewhat difficult paper. Trying to evaluate why businessmen continue to use payback, he considers the role of the concept as a criterion versus a payback constraint, payback as a break-even concept, and payback as a crude measure of the rate of resolution of uncertainty. Payback is seen to imply a form of break-even which makes no sense in a world of certainty, but can function like other rules of thumb to shorten the process of generating information and evaluating it. In another sense, payback is found to be primarily a constraint criterion rather than an optimizable one. The main consideration is that even though the payback concept is an oversimplification in each case, the problems which managers seek to attack through its use will not disappear simply by considering the payback period method not meaningful. It is necessary to face up to those problems, and to employ methods to solve them. Weingartner argues.

In Part Three's concluding paper, Moore presents a clever adaptation of the profit-volume graph for use in capital investment decisions based on discounted cash flows.

11

"As a quantitative profitability appraisal technique, rate of return has substantial merits not possessed by alternative methods [of evaluating capital investment proposals]."

Unless other assumptions are warranted, rate of return analysis implies that each project's expected cash flows will be reinvested indefinitely at the same return as that implied by the project itself. In dealing with unequal investments in conflicting projects, the incremental added investment method is suggested.

In judging the adequacy of expected rate of return, the future cost of capital may serve as a standard, but due weight must be given to the uncertainty inherent in the measurement.

Most practical applications involve not simple choices between two conflicting proposals, but selection of an optimum investment mix. Interdependencies and "system" characteristics of the mix may modify results of single project analyses.

Rate of Return: Some Comments on its Applicability in Capital Budgeting*

Victor H. Brown

An essential phase of a rational capital budgeting process concerns appraising the profitability potentials of recognized opportunities for capital investment. Typically, management must decide upon an effective rationing of capital among the numerous capital proposals recommended to it for adoption. Profitability considerations are manifestly important in such decisions.

Appraising profitability requires explicit forecasting of the three determinants of each proposal's financial worth: (1) the proposal's economic life;

* *From* The Accounting Review, *Vol. XXXVI, No. 1 (January, 1961), pp. 50–62. Reprinted by permission of the editor.*

(2) the capital outlay(s) required to adopt it; and (3) the amounts and timing of the revenues and costs resulting from its adoption. These capital outlays as well as revenues and costs should be estimated in terms of future, differential flows of cash or the equivalent.[1] Such forecasts alone, however, do not permit ready profitability evaluations and comparisons to be made. For this purpose, a direct measure or index of each proposal's projected profitability is needed. This paper comments upon the suitability of rate of return as such a measure and the extent to which rate of return analysis is applicable as a guide to sound capital investment decisions.

RATE OF RETURN DETERMINATION

While the notion of rate of return on investment is commonplace, the term is widely employed to describe a variety of historical and projected mathematical relationships between earnings and investment. In this paper, rate of return refers to that rate of interest which equates through time a project's anticipated cash flows with the initial capital outlay required to adopt it. A project's implied rate of return is thus that value of i which satisfies the equation:

$$P = \frac{S_1}{(1 + i)^1} + \frac{S_2}{(1 + i)^2} \cdots + \frac{S_n}{(1 + i)^n}$$

where

P = the project's required initial capital investment;

S = the project's cash throwoffs (i.e., net cash flows) in indicated future time periods (in any given time period S may have a positive or negative value);

and

n = the number of time periods in the project's economic life.

(If all values of S are equal, this formula reduces to $P = S_{a_{\overline{n}|i}}$; the common formula for the present worth of an annuity.) If cash throwoffs are estimated on an annual basis, the project's rate of return is an annual rate of compound interest.

It may be noted that annual cash flow estimates are satisfactory for most proposals, but shorter time periods may be more appropriate for certain projects contemplating significant intrayear cash flow irregularities.[2] (Such

---

[1] For a discussion of the cost and revenue constructions relevant for capital budgeting purposes, see American Accounting Association Committee on Cost Concepts and Standards, "Tentative Statement of Cost Concepts Underlying Reports for Management Purposes," *The Accounting Review* (April, 1956), pp. 182–93, and Edward L. Wallace, "Some Comments on the Statement of Planning Costs," *The Accounting Review* (July, 1957), pp. 448–66.

[2] A point to note is that the above formula presumes that each year's cash flow will obtain at the end of the year. If cash flows are projected on an annual basis but are expected at regular intrayear intervals (e.g., monthly collections of customer accounts), more refined formulas can be used to obtain more exact rate of return values. See, for example, Charles Christenson, "Construction of Present Value Tables for Use in Evaluating Capital Investment Opportunities," *The Accounting Review* (October, 1955), pp. 666–72.

irregularities may be expected, for example, from projects involving sales of products with highly seasonal sales patterns.) If shorter than annual periods are used, however, it is desirable to convert the resulting rates of return to annual effective rates for interpretive reasons. Executives are accustomed to thinking in terms of annual planning periods.

Rate of return determination explicitly considers all three determinants of a proposal's financial worth and ignores external considerations such as the cost of the capital required to adopt the proposal. Via the discounting procedure, the time value of money is taken into account. A proposal's expected profitability is expressed in a single figure representing the average annual rate of compound interest at which the project's initial investment is expected to be "recovered" through cash flow generation. These attributes suggest the possible applicability of rate of return analysis for capital budgeting purposes.

A Capital Budgeting Tool

Expressing profitability potentials in rate of return terms enables financial worth comparisons and rankings of capital proposals of all types to be made in a uniform and intelligible fashion. Comparative profitability evaluations are important in appraising conflicting, or mutually exclusive, proposals. A consistent system for ranking competing projects facilitates top management selection of a desirable mix of capital investments.

A comment on the above distinction between conflicting and competing projects is in order. Conflicting proposals are alternative to one another; the selection of one such project signals the rejection of all others. A company considering whether to make or buy a particular item, for example, is confronted with two conflicting proposals. Competing projects are those which are not mutually exclusive. While these projects collectively "compete" for available capital, a decision to adopt any individual competing proposal does not per se preclude the acceptance of others. A proposal to expand foreign operations and another to buy new accounting equipment for the home office, for example, are competing — the company may well decide to adopt both. A rigid dichotomy between conflicting and competing projects, of course, is impossible since many projects are partially substitutable for others. However, a practical distinction between the two types is useful for evaluation purposes.

Applied to assess the relative profitability of conflicting proposals, rate of return analysis can guide the selection from among them. As a common denominator of economic worth, rate of return permits ranking competing proposals in descending order of their expected profitability. This array gives management a systematic examination technique for evaluating known demands upon available capital. Conceptually, management can maximize corporate profits by selecting each ranked proposal with a rate of return exceeding the company's cost of capital.[3] As a practical matter, of course, such an automatic cutoff procedure is quite inappropriate; a high order of management judgment is required in selecting capital investments. However, rate of return analysis and knowledge of the firm's cost of capital can provide a rational basis for formulating these judgmental decisions.

Administratively, top management can employ rate of return as a screening device to shield it from a deluge of undesirable capital requests by supplying lower management levels with a minimum acceptable rate of return. This procedure tends to force explicit divisional recognition and forecasting of the relevant determinants of a proposal's economic worth as well as to assure company-wide uniformity in profitability appraisals. Knowledge that an objective profitability index is employed by top management in rationing capital can also prove beneficial to morale at subordinate management levels.

While the above merits of rate of return as a guide to budgeting capital are substantial, it is important both to recognize the complexities involved in effectively employing the analysis and to be aware of its limitations. These complexities and limitations can be examined in terms of both conceptual considerations with practical ramifications and administrative considerations.

Conceptual Considerations

THE REINVESTMENT ASSUMPTION

An assumption concerning the profitability of cash throwoff reinvestments is always made in rate of return evaluations. If no *explicit* contrary assumption is made, profitability conclusions drawn from rate of return comparisons are based upon the *implicit* assumption that each project's cash flows will be indefinitely reinvested at the same rate of return as that directly implied by the project itself.

For example, assume that adopting either Project A *or* Project B would require a $100,000 initial investment; and that Project A would generate a single $150,000 cash sum at the end of one year, while Project B would produce approximately $54,800 in cash annually for six years. A 50% annual rate of return is directly implied by each proposal. Which project is the more attractive, however, depends upon the rate(s) of return at which cash throwoffs can be reinvested. Project A would be the more attractive if all cash throwoffs were reinvested at greater than a 50% rate of return; conversely, it would be the less attractive if the reinvestment rate were less than 50%.[4]

---

[3] This statement is valid in principle only if, as will be discussed subsequently, appropriate assumptions concerning the profitability of cash flow reinvestments are made in determining the rates of return used to rank competing proposals.

[4] To illustrate, assume a 10% reinvestment rate. If Project A's $150,000 cash throwoff were reinvested at 10%, a capital sum of $241,650 would accumulate six years after the project's adoption [$150,000(1.10)^5]. If Project B's cash throwoffs were reinvested at 10%,

The inference that the proposals are equally profitable because each has a 50% implied rate of return is *absolutely* valid only if *indefinite* cash flow reinvestments at 50% rates of return are presumed. This inference, however, is *practically* valid if cash flow reinvestments are expected to earn 50% for fairly limited (as opposed to indefinite) future time periods. (Via the discounting procedure distant cash throwoffs and resulting reinvestments are weighted much less heavily than near ones.)

Recognizing the need for some assumption concerning the profitability of cash flow reinvestment is of particular practical importance in evaluating conflicting investment proposals. This is especially true if their economic lives and/or their cash flow time patterns are expected to differ significantly. Factors related to the financial outcome of alternative projects should be appraised on a comparable basis. Thus, for example, evaluations of conflicting projects with different anticipated life spans should be made for comparable time periods. This necessitates a consideration of the profitability of reinvestments of the shorter-lived project's cash throwoffs. While precision in forecasting reinvestment rates is admittedly impossible, management may, with varying degrees of confidence, wish to make explicit reinvestment rate assumptions different from that implicitly made in direct rate of return comparisons. For example, management may have definite expectations concerning the profitability of proposals that it believes are feasible for the near future. These expectations should be explicitly substituted for the implicit reinvestment rate assumption.

In evaluating ranked competing proposals, it is usually impossible, even with the best of forecasts, explicitly to estimate the profitability of cash flow reinvestments on an individual project basis. This is because cash flows available for reinvestment at any particular time are typically derived from numerous projects and constitute a homogeneous pool of capital at management's disposal; identification of specific segments of this pool with individual reinvestment proposals is possible on only an arbitrary basis. Thus, in appraising most competing opportunities the implicit reinvestment assumption appears to be the most reasonable one that can be made since, over time, a company appears most likely to maximize profits by continually

---

a capital sum of approximately \$422,800 would obtain six years after the project's adoption

$$\left[\$54,800\ \frac{(1.10)^6 - 1}{.10} \right].$$

Considering the two projects over a six year period and taking explicit account of the expected 10% reinvestment rate, one can determine Project A's implied rate of return to be approximately 15% [\$241,650 = \$100,000 $(1 + i)$; $i \cong 15\%$] and B's implied rate of return to be approximately 27% [\$422,800 = \$100,000 $(1 + i)^6$; $i \cong 27\%$]. Project B is thus more attractive.

Identical capital sums would accumulate at the end of six years only if the reinvestment rate were exactly 50%. But since accumulations would probably not be entirely available in liquid form at the end of six years, an assumption concerning *indefinite* cash flow reinvestment is theoretically necessary, as noted in the text.

selecting those proposals with the highest directly implied rates of return. This is a practical approach which is generally appropriate.[5]

In individual appraisals of particular competing proposals, however, the implicit reinvestment assumption may be inappropriate. For example, the feasibility of certain foreseeable future proposals may be contingent upon the adoption of certain present alternatives (e.g., a plan to construct a plant one year hence may require the present reservation of liquid capital). In such cases explicit account should be taken of the future proposal's profitability potential in determining a rate of return measure for the present alternative.

The point to note is that while management may deem the implicit reinvestment rate assumption satisfactory in many cases, other situations arise where this assumption is clearly unsatisfactory. In such situations, a more appropriate explicit assumption should be made and taken into account in rate of return determination.

UNEQUAL INITIAL INVESTMENTS

Implied rates of return are *directly* comparable only if they are computed for proposals requiring equal initial investments. Project A's 20% implied rate of return, for example, cannot directly be compared with the 26% rate implied by Project B if the projects require initial investments of $100,000 and $40,000 respectively. Which project is more profitable depends upon the rate of return that would be earned upon (or not have to be paid for the use of) the differential $60,000 that would be "available" if Project B were accepted. Only if this differential rate were exactly 16% would the two projects be equally profitable.[6] (And this is true if the implicit reinvestment assumption noted above is appropriate.)

This observation is of small consequence in appraising competing investment proposals since direct comparative evaluation of individual projects is not required. In evaluating conflicting projects, however, recognizing the inability to compare effectually rates of return computed for unequal investments is quite important. Conflicting proposals typically require unequal capital outlays and must be evaluated on comparable bases.

Rate of return analysis can be adapted satisfactorily to evaluate conflicting proposals by means of the "incremental added investment method." This procedure involves the following three steps:

---

[5] Theoretically, ranked appraisals of competing proposals could be avoided entirely by immediately attacking the ultimate problem of selecting desirable *combinations* of investment opportunities. That is, one might initially determine, on a quantitative basis, an optimum mix of present and future investment proposals. Practically, however, mix considerations must await initial evaluations of competing proposals on an individual basis.

[6] This is because 20% on Project A's $100,000 is equivalent to 26% on Project B's $40,000 *plus* 16% on the differential $60,000. Assuming all proposals to have infinite lives and to generate equal annual cash flows, $20,000 annual cash flows would result in either case. (20% × Project A's $100,000 = $20,000. 26% × Project B's $40,000 = $10,400; 16% × $60,000 = $9,600. $10,400 + $9,600 = $20,000.)

1. Determine the rate of return implied by the proposal requiring the smallest initial investment.
2. If this rate is equal to or greater than the relevant cost of capital,[7] compute the rate of return implied by the *incremental* capital needed to adopt the proposal requiring the next largest initial investment. If the resulting rate equals or exceeds the cost of capital, drop the first project from further consideration. Using the second project as a new standard, repeat this incremental approach until only one proposal remains. This is financially the most attractive project.
3. If the first rate of return computed in Step 1 is less than the cost of capital, reject the first project and determine the rate of return implied by the *total* investment needed to adopt the proposal requiring the next largest initial investment. If this rate at least equals the cost of capital, use this proposal as a standard and proceed as in Step 2; if this rate is less than the cost of capital, reject the proposal and compute the rate of return implied by the project requiring the next largest initial capital outlay. Repeat this process until either: (a) no conflicting proposal appears satisfactory: or (b) a single project emerges as the most desirable.

This adaptation of rate of return analysis is straightforward and can serve satisfactorily to evaluate conflicting investment opportunities. Care, however, is required in applying this procedure in individual situations. Three points are especially worthy of note. First, judicious selection of a relevant cost of capital measure is necessary. Second, careful and logical measurement of the differential cash flows expected from successive incremental investments is essential. This can be a somewhat complicated process involving initially a recognition of the appropriate alternatives to include within a set of conflicting proposals. (Frequently overlooked alternatives, for example, are the possibility of doing nothing at all and that of deferring the adoption of any particular proposal.) Third, some incremental investments (and, less frequently, some individual proposals) can have more than one directly implied rate of return. Appropriate *explicit* reinvestment assumptions must be made in developing usable rate of return measures in these instances.

Further comment on this last point is in order. An investment expected to produce cash flows of both positive and negative amounts can have more than one directly implied rate of return; the maximum number of implied rates is equal to the number of sign (i.e., positive or negative) changes in the net cash flows.[8] For example, Project C requires a $10,000 initial outlay (a

---

[7] Fundamentally, the relevant cost of capital is an "opportunity cost," indicating the higher of: (1) the return that could be earned upon this capital by commitment to the best alternative project; or (2) the firm's market cost of capital (the cost of obtaining and/or retaining funds for employment within the business as a whole).

[8] The point that proposals may have more than one implied rate of return is made and more fully discussed by James H. Lorie and Leonard J. Savage in their article, "Three Problems in Rationing Capital," *Journal of Business* (October, 1955), pp. 236–38. These authors also discuss the procedure outlined above for evaluating conflicting proposals (*Ibid.*, p. 239).

negative cash flow) and will produce three cash throwoffs as follows: Year 1, $60,000; Year 2, $-$110,000 (negative); and Year 3, $60,000. This project has three implied rates of return (0%, 100%, and 200%) — the maximum number possible since there are three reversals of cash flow signs. Manifestly, this illustrative proposal does not have three different valid indices of profitability.

Valid rate of return measures can be developed for projects with multiple directly implied rates of return by initially explicitly assuming appropriate reinvestment rates. To illustrate, the proposal cited above has a *unique* $4\frac{1}{2}\%$ rate of return if a 10% reinvestment rate is assumed [cash throwoffs amount to $11,400 in three years; $10,000 $(1 + i)^3 = \$11,400$; $i = 4\frac{1}{2}\%$]. With an assumed 50% reinvestment rate; the project has a unique 44% rate of return [a capital sum of $30,000 obtains from the cash throwoffs after three years; $10,000 $(1 + i)^3 = \$30,000$; $i = 44\%$]. These resultant rates of return are unique and are valid profitability indices.

Individual competing, as well as conflicting, proposals with multiple rates of return are relatively rare. Differential cash flows developed for incremental investments, however, may well assume peculiar shapes through time. If projected cash flows alternate between positive and negative amounts, care must be taken to assure the use of unique rate of return measures.

CASH BUDGETING AND COST OF CAPITAL CONSIDERATIONS

Rate of return analysis is designed for evaluating profitability. Since rates of return are based on initial investments, subsidiary account is also taken of the immediate cash outlays required by investment proposals. However, since rates of return measure only *average* cash flow relationships expected over time, the analysis must be supplemented by future cash availability considerations. Many projects require substantial capital outlays, both present and future, prior to their expected generation of net cash inflows. The developmental and promotional work necessary to introduce a new product line, for example, may require several years of cash outlays before positive cash throwoffs materialize. Management must not only appraise the rates of return implied by such proposals, but must also examine the present and future availability of the capital needed to execute the proposals satisfactorily. Failure to do so can lead to unfortunate results — conceivably bankruptcy — prior to the receipt of net cash inflows. Profitability analysis and cash budgeting must thus be interrelated processes.

As noted previously, a company's cost of capital must be determined if rate of return analysis (or any other discounting procedure) is to be employed

---

The points that proposals can conceivably have more than two directly implied rates of return and that the number of possible rates depends upon the number of sign reversals in the estimated cash flow stream are made by Jack Hirshleifer, *An Isoquant Approach to Investment Decision Problems* (Santa Monica: Rand Corporation, Report P-1158, August, 1957), p. 38.

effectively. It will be recalled that a measure of this cost is needed for at least three purposes: (1) to serve as a subordinate level screening rate; (2) to be used in assessing the relative profitability potentials of conflicting proposals; and (3) to serve as a logical cutoff point in top management selection of competing projects.

Determining cost of capital is an extremely complex problem, the dimensions of which can only be suggested here. Since capital budgeting, by definition, involves choosing future courses of action, it is a *future* cost of capital which is needed. But some value judgments concerning management's conception of the firm's principal objective(s) must be made initially to establish a viewpoint from which this cost can be measured. One might, for example, measure cost of capital differently if management's primary goal were viewed as maximization of corporate net worth than if maximization of returns to shareholders were considered management's prime objective. (Especially is such a divergence in measures possible with respect to the cost of equity capital.)[9] Other theoretical questions arise concerning precisely what a cost of capital measure should measure. For example, should the cost of capital indicate the cost of the company's "permanent" capital, or should it represent an average cost of capital obtained from all sources? And, presuming agreement concerning the company's objectives, what cost should be assigned to internally generated capital — to capital obtained externally?

Answers to the above questions are necessary to ascertain what a cost of capital measure should signify. Once agreement on this point is reached, a host of practical problems arise concerning how such a measure can be determined, or at least approximated. For present purposes, it is sufficient to observe that approximation of a company's cost of capital is a prerequisite to the logical use of rate of return analysis. (The word "approximation" is intentionally used since, as a practical matter, minor errors in estimating cost of capital may be inconsequential. For example, management may, uncertainties considered, require that certain types of proposals have rates of return considerably in excess of the company's cost of capital to justify their acceptance.)

UNCERTAINTY CONSIDERATIONS

Uncertainties attend the forecasts made of virtually every proposal's cash flows. These uncertainties stem from the lack of definite knowledge concerning the future behavior of the many factors, economic and with economic

[9] Contrast, for example, the measures of equity capital cost suggested by Myron J. Gordon and Eli Shapiro ("Capital Equipment Analysis: The Required Rate of Profit," *Management Science* (October, 1956), pp. 102–10) with that suggested by Ezra Solomon ("Measuring a Company's Cost of Capital," *Journal of Business* (October, 1955), pp. 240–52).

implications, bearing upon each proposal's financial outcome. While some of these factors, such as the future general level of economic activity, are of a "common" nature, since their projected behavior serves as a common planning premise in estimating numerous proposals' cash flows, other factors more uniquely influence the profitability of specific projects. The combinations of important factors affecting cash flow forecasts vary from project to project. Therefore, uncertainties must initially be appraised on an individual project basis.

A high degree of "experienced judgment" is needed in weighing uncertainty elements against profitability potentials. Efforts to incorporate uncertainty considerations into rate of return analysis are possible. For example, one may weigh estimates of initial investments and cash flows by probability factors before determining rates of return.[10] Such efforts, however, do not obviate the need for exercising judgment; they merely partially advance the time when it must be exercised. The aforementioned probability factors, for example, typically must be projected on a judgmental basis.

Certain data supplemental to rate of return analysis can assist management in formulating these necessary judgments. Information concerning the major planning premises assumed in forecasting cash flows is important. Explicit statement of the assumptions upon which cash flow estimates are based tends to assure management recognition of the major uncertainty elements present in each situation. Further, it may be useful to present management with a range of estimated rates of return for particular projects — the range limits constituting what are deemed to be probable forecasting error limits. Related to the notion of forecasting error limits is another potentially useful technique involving expressing the "permissible degrees of error" which may be inherent in forecasts of a project's cash inflows and/or outflows (or particular segments thereof) without signaling the project's undesirability. For example, it might be determined that a project's actual cash inflows could be less than its projected cash inflows by as much as 9% and the project would still meet management's minimum standard of acceptability. Given this 9% permissible degree of error, management can subjectively estimate the probability of an error of this magnitude being inherent in forecasts of the project's cash inflows. If it desired, management could further weigh its subjective probability judgments against mathematically determined indifference probabilities.[11]

Explicit consideration of the possible penalties resulting from various forecasting errors can also be useful in uncertainty appraisals. Maximum

---

[10] This sort of procedure is suggested by Powell Niland in his article, "Investing in Special Automatic Equipment," *Harvard Business Review* (November–December, 1957), pp. 73–82.

[11] See Edward G. Bennion, "Capital Budgeting and Game Theory," *Harvard Business Review* (November–December, 1956), pp. 115–23 for a discussion of the possible applicability of the indifference probability concept in managerial uncertainty evaluations.

possible loss computations, for example, enable management to assess what would happen to the company's cash position should a particular proposal's projected cash inflows fail to materialize. As a further example, data concerning the amount of initially invested capital which could be recouped in case of abrupt termination of a proposal's economic life are doubtless important in certain choices, such as the selection of general purpose rather than special purpose equipment.

Payoff computations can also convey significant information in evaluating uncertainties. Given two conflicting proposals with equal rates of return, management may prefer the one with the shorter payoff period because of greater confidence in cash flow estimates made for nearer future years.

Each of the quantitative techniques mentioned may possess certain usefulness in assessing the uncertainties surrounding particular proposals. None of them, however, eliminates the need for informed judgment.

THE INFINITE RATE PROBLEM

Rate of return analysis is particularly suited for evaluating proposals requiring initial investments of substantial size relative to expected net cash inflows. Some proposals, however, involve small *initial* capital outlays but commit the firm to substantial *future* outlays. Projects contemplating the rental of facilities and purchase-lease back arrangements exemplify proposals of this type. These projects may have exceedingly large implied rates of return; infinite rates are conceivable.

Ascribing practical meaning to very large or infinite rates of return is most difficult. To illustrate, suppose a firm is considering purchasing an existing business expected to produce $20,000 annual net cash flows. The present owner is asking $100,000 for his business, but, for personal tax reasons, wishes to be paid $10,000 annually for ten years, beginning one year hence. The project thus requires no initial investment; its implied rate of return is infinity — infinitely larger than its 20% rate of return if immediate payment of the purchase price were required. From the purchaser's viewpoint, paying the purchase price over time is more desirable than immediate payment, but it is not infinitely more so. In both cases, similar uncertainties exist concerning forecasts of the business' cash inflows while no uncertainty is present concerning the contractual need for paying the purchase price. It is difficult to give practical meaning to the project's infinite rate of return.

The infinite rate problem assumes minor importance in evaluating conflicting proposals; the incremental investment approach outlined previously can be meaningfully used in evaluating these projects whether or not one of them has an infinite rate of return. It is in appraising competing proposals that the problem becomes practically significant. All competing projects with infinite rates of return appear highly attractive. Yet, management may not wish to accept all of them because of their somewhat peculiar uncertainties — viz., uncertain net cash inflows and contractually required capital outlays.

In principle, rate of return analysis can be adapted to appraise certain of these sorts of competing proposals. A proposal's initial investment might be defined as not only the required immediate cash outlay but also the presently available capital that management would reserve to assure the requisite liquidity to meet the *future* cash outlay commitments caused by adopting the project. Reservations of present capital may be considered a prudent safeguard against the possibility that the proposal's estimated net cash inflows will not materialize. Practically, however, implementing this procedure is difficult except for projects requiring exceptionally large future capital outlays. For other projects it is next to impossible to estimate on an individual project basis amounts of present capital reserved for precautionary reasons.

The above procedure is only one way to treat the special uncertainty problems posed by projects with extremely large or infinite rates of return. Others may be more appropriate in particular cases. The point to be noted is that cash budgeting and uncertainty considerations are dominant in appraising these proposals — more important than the direct indications of rate of return analysis.

MIX EVALUATION

In evaluating and selecting investment proposals, management's objective is to select an optimum *mix* or *complex* of capital investments. As noted previously, practical considerations do not permit this objective to be assessed directly in evaluating investment opportunities. Rather, proposals must initially be appraised and tentatively selected on an individual project basis.

Rate of return rankings of competing proposals can facilitate evaluating various investment mixes. However, investment complexes selected only on the basis of individual project evaluations may be unsatisfactory for at least four reasons: (1) The distinction between conflicting and competing projects is not absolute. Thus, there may be interrelationships among decisions to accept particular competing proposals and the cash flow values projected for other competing proposals. These interrelationships, ignored in individual evaluations, may be quite important; (2) The initially indicated complex may require an excessive future drain on the company's cash resources; (3) The initial mix may require the firm to assume collectively unfavorable uncertainties; and (4) The aggregate mix may not lead the company in what management believes to be a desirable direction. The indicated mix may, for example, comprise replacement proposals entirely; management may consider other types of projects (e.g., product diversification projects) as equally essential to the company's future well-being. Therefore, appraisals of entire complexes of investment proposals are necessary.

A workable general quantitative solution to the problem of selecting an optimum mix of capital investments is presently unavailable, and in large measure evaluating possible investment mixes must be on a qualitative basis. However, two admittedly imprecise quantitative procedures can be useful for this purpose. First, a tentatively selected investment mix can be tested within the framework of the financial accounting model. Thus, management can assess the impact that integrating a complex of proposals into over-all corporate operations will have upon the company's financial statements, which, in part at least, measure over-all corporate success.

The second procedure involves top management stipulation of a desirable percentage apportionment of total capital investment among various categories of proposals. Both the scheme used to categorize projects and the percentage breakdown developed should reflect the factors which management deems important to the particular company's future. For example, the management of a chemical company, believing that new product development is of vital importance to continued corporate success, may decide that, say, 25% of all new capital investments should be in a research and development category. Qualitative judgment is required to implement this procedure, and unthinking adherence to the indicated percentage apportionments should not be demanded. Judiciously applied, however, the procedure can be useful not only in top management evaluations of investment mixes but also in stimulating lower management level searches for desirable investment opportunities.

Administrative Considerations

Attention has thus far centered upon the rate of return concept itself, the care which must be exercised in applying the concept, and the limitations upon the concept's applicability as an exclusive, or in some cases even a dominant, capital investment selection device. Administrative problems can also arise in introducing and using rate of return analysis as a primary profitability evaluation technique.

Educational and Personnel Considerations

To persons unfamiliar with the concepts and procedures involved, rate of return analysis initially appears unduly complex. Further, these persons may find the results of the analysis difficult to interpret meaningfully. Substantial persuasive and educational efforts may thus be necessary in introducing this analysis and in assuring its appropriate use.

It is relatively easy to convey to persons a superficial knowledge of the meaning of implied rate of return and its manner of computation. Indeed, computing rates of return can be a very simple process. Charts and tables, for example, can be developed for use by clerical personnel to compute rates of return implied by projects in the common case where uniform net cash inflows are expected.[12] Assuring that persons really *understand* rate of return analysis and its ramifications, however, is a more difficult educational problem.

Happily, it is not essential that *all* company personnel charged with evaluating investment proposals understand rate of return analysis *fully* to use it satisfactorily. Low level screening and evaluations of repetitive types of proposals, for example, can be effectively accomplished by means of fairly mechanistic applications of the analysis. (In these cases, of course, it is still necessary that relevant cash flows be estimated as accurately as possible.) However, it is important that the areas wherein mechanical use of rate of return analysis is permitted be strictly delimited. Otherwise, investment decisions based upon erroneous evaluations of financial worth are quite possible.

Personnel with a real understanding of the concepts and techniques involved are needed to define judiciously the types of proposals amenable to rote application of rate of return analysis as well as to analyze the financial attractiveness of non-routine types of investment projects. These individuals should also be able to present meaningfully the results of their analyses to the executives responsible for making investment decisions. Such personnel should possess analytical ability and should be conversant with company problems and administrative practices.

POTENTIAL CONTROL PROBLEMS

The top managements of some multi-division companies employ a variant of the rate of return concept in appraising divisional financial performance. Thus, divisional managers may be expected to strive for as high a ratio as possible between reported divisional earnings and the gross (or net) book value of the assets assigned to their divisions.

Two potential problem areas suggest themselves if rate of return is employed both as a control mechanism and as a profitability appraisal device. First, the definitions of rate of return commonly used to assess performance do not depict the rate of return concept discussed here as a measure of financial worth. The concept must be defined to suit the purpose for which it is intended. Secondly, the managers of more profitable divisions may be reluctant to recommend projects meeting a company-wide standard of acceptability if the adoption of these projects would lower divisional rates of return. Coping with this type of problem requires intelligent administration

---

[12] See, for example, Ray I. Reul, "Profitability Index for Investments," *Harvard Business Review* (July-August, 1957), pp. 116–32.

of the rate of return control mechanism as well as structuring controls supplemental to rate of return. (For example, a division may be expected not only to show a satisfactory rate of return but also to maintain its market position.)

POST-SELECTION EVALUATIONS

After capital investments are selected, it is desirable periodically to examine how closely projects' actual initial investments and subsequent cash flows correspond to their previously estimated amounts. This is useful for three reasons: (1) to assure integrity on the part of individuals charged with making forecasts; (2) to discern past legitimate forecasting errors so as possibly to improve future forecasts; and (3) to permit prompt revisions of financial plans on the basis of differences between expected and actual cash flows thus disclosed.

Assembling information relevant in making useful post-selection evaluations, however, requires efforts additional to those normally required in accumulating financial accounting data. Conversion of these latter data to a cash flow basis is necessary. Post-selection evaluations are further complicated by the fact that cash flows are projected in differential terms for profitability appraisal purposes. The accuracy of differential forecasts is somewhat difficult to verify even after a proposal has been executed.

Alternative Evaluation Techniques

The aforementioned limitations of rate of return as a capital investment selection criterion as well as the many considerations, conceptual and administrative, required in applying the concept effectively are important and deserve explicit recognition. Intelligently applied, however, rate of return analysis is a useful capital budgeting tool. This is apparent when the short-comings of alternative evaluation methods are considered.

PAYOFF

Payoff, defined as the length of time within which the summation of a proposal's net cash inflows are expected to equal (and thus "pay off") its required initial investment, is probably the most widely used capital investment selection criterion. The payoff concept is very easily understood and, as noted before, is an adjunct computation which can be useful in uncertainty appraisals. As a measure of financial worth, however, payoff has two egregious deficiencies: (1) the device ignores cash flows expected beyond a proposal's payoff period; and (2) payoff ignores possible cash flow time pattern irregularities expected within a project's payoff period.

RATE OF RETURN VARIANTS

Another popular evaluative device is "rate of return" defined as the ratio of a proposal's projected average annual (or first year) *earnings* to either: (1) the proposal's total required initial investment; or (2) the average amount of capital expected to be committed to the proposal. These "rates of return" are invalid as profitability measures for several reasons. First, the earnings estimates used typically differ from relevant cash flow forecasts. Depreciation expense, for example, typically is deducted in estimating earnings, but is irrelevant in cash flow forecasting (except as it affects income taxes which, of course, are relevant cash outlays). Secondly, because these measures ignore the time value of money, they are insensitive to variations in expected cash flow time patterns. Further, neither of these "rates of return" reliably approximates proposals' implied rates of return. Thus, neither is a reliable index for financial worth appraisals.

OTHER DISCOUNTING METHODS

A third group of profitability evaluation techniques comprises methods which, like rate of return, use the discounting process and require relevant forecasts of proposals' initial capital outlays and subsequent cash flows. Present worth and capitalized cost analyses are outstanding examples. These methods differ from rate of return analysis in that, prior to their application, management stipulation of each proposal's minimum acceptable rate of return is necessary.

These methods can provide theoretically satisfactory indications of profitability potentials. (Indeed, it has been shown that in theory, given a presently non-existent degree of knowledge concerning future capital costs, the straightforward present value rule is superior to the ordinary internal rate of return rule in appraising projects' financial worth.)[13] On administrative grounds, however, these methods appear to have two shortcomings *vis-à-vis* rate of return analysis. First, obtaining necessary *advance* executive agreement on each proposed investment's minimum acceptable rate of return (the interest rate at which expected cash flows should be discounted) is administratively difficult and certainly time consuming. Since uncertainties vary from project to project, this advance agreement would be necessary on virtually an individual project basis. Secondly, the interpretational problems posed by alternative discounting methods seem more difficult than those presented by rate of return.

To illustrate this second point, suppose that a proposed new machine costing $20,000, is expected to effect annual net cash operating cost savings of $6,000 during its estimated six year economic life. Assuming a 10%

[13] Jack Hirshleifer, *op. cit.*, pp. 30–44.

minimum attractive rate of return, present worth analysis can be applied as follows:

Differential present worth $= \$6,000_{a_{\overline{6}|}\cdot 10} - \$20,000 = \$1,775.$

Explaining to management why this positive differential present worth indicates the proposal's attractiveness may pose difficulties; it appears easier to explain that the proposal's implied rate of return (approximately 13%) exceeds the 10% minimum attractive rate. Meaningfully comparing this proposal's financial worth with that of competing projects is even more difficult in present value terms. These comparisons are possible by ranking proposals in descending order of their present worths *per dollar of initial investment*.[14] Rate of return rankings appear more understandable.

Conclusion

The rate of return concept strongly recommends itself for application in evaluating capital investment proposals. As a quantitative profitability appraisal technique, rate of return has substantial merits not possessed by alternative methods of assessing financial worth, which suggest the integration of the analysis into a comprehensive system for planning and controlling capital investments.

Rate of return, however, is not an appropriate exclusive, or in particular cases a prime, capital investment selection criterion. Rather, it is a useful tool, and as such should be used with full recognition of its shortcomings and limitations. Applied mechanistically, it can lead to unfortunate investment decisions (except where appropriate constraints have been imposed upon its mechanistic use). In common with many other analytical tools, its use will yield benefits only in proportion to the understanding with which it is applied.

[14] See Lorie and Savage, *op. cit.*, p. 231

12 *Rate of return calculations involve three estimates: (1) estimated outlay, (2) estimated cash inflows, and (3) economic life. Use of a simple "best estimate" analysis may obscure vital information about risk — a relevant factor in any capital budgeting decision. Risk is influenced both by the odds on various events occurring and by the magnitude of the rewards or penalties which are involved when they do occur.*

More accurate forecasts, empirical adjustments to estimates, "conservative" cutoff rates, three-level estimates, or selected probabilities are methods which have been used to deal with uncertainty. But rate of return analysis may be made even more sensitive to management's uncertainties about the key factors underlying the measurement. Four steps are suggested: (1) Determine the probability function for each of the significant factors, (2) Select — at random — sets of these factors according to the chances they have of turning up in the future, (3) Determine rate of return for each combination, (4) Determine probability distribution of rate of return, and base investment decisions on this distribution.

Risk Analysis in Capital Investment*

David B. Hertz

Of all the decisions that business executives must make, none is more challenging — and none has received more attention — than choosing among alternative capital investment opportunities. What makes this kind of decision so demanding, of course, is not the problem of projecting return on investment under any given set of assumptions. The difficulty is in the assumptions and in their impact. Each assumption involves its own degree — often a high degree — of uncertainty; and, taken together, these combined

* From Harvard Business Review, *Vol. 42, No. 1 (January–February, 1964), pp. 95–106.* Reprinted by permission of the publisher.

uncertainties can multiply into a total uncertainty of critical proportions. This is where the element of risk enters, and it is in the evaluation of risk that the executive has been able to get little help from currently available tools and techniques.

There is a way to help the executive sharpen his key capital investment decisions by providing him with a realistic measurement of the risks involved. Armed with this measurement, which evaluates for him the risk at each possible level of return, he is then in a position to measure more knowledgeably alternative courses of action against corporate objectives.

Need for New Concept

The evaluation of a capital investment project starts with the principle that the productivity of capital is measured by the rate of return we expect to receive over some future period. A dollar received next year is worth less to us than a dollar in hand today. Expenditures three years hence are less costly than expenditures of equal magnitude two years from now. For this reason we cannot calculate the rate of return realistically unless we take into account (a) when the sums involved in an investment are spent and (b) when the returns are received.

Comparing alternative investments is thus complicated by the fact that they usually differ not only in size but also in the length of time over which expenditures will have to be made and benefits returned.

It is these facts of investment life that long ago made apparent the shortcomings of approaches that simply averaged expenditures and benefits, or lumped them, as in the number-of-years-to-pay-out method. These shortcomings stimulated students of decision making to explore more precise methods for determining whether one investment would leave a company better off in the long run than would another course of action.

It is not surprising, then, that much effort has been applied to the development of ways to improve our ability to discriminate among investment alternatives. The focus of all of these investigations has been to sharpen the definition of the value of capital investments to the company. The controversy and furor that once came out in the business press over the most appropriate way of calculating these values has largely been resolved in favor of the discounted cash flow method as a reasonable means of measuring the rate of return that can be expected in the future from an investment made today.

Thus we have methods which, in general, are more or less elaborate mathematical formulas for comparing the outcomes of various investments and the combinations of the variables that will affect the investments.[1] As these

---

[1] See for example, Joel Dean, *Capital Budgeting* (New York, Columbia University Press, 1951); "Return on Capital as a Guide to Managerial Decisions," *National Association of Accountants Research Report No. 35*, December 1, 1959; and Bruce F. Young, "Overcoming Obstacles to Use of Discounted Cash Flow for Investment Shares," *NAA Bulletin*, March, 1963, p. 15.

techniques have progressed, the mathematics involved has become more and more precise, so that we can now calculate discounted returns to a fraction of a per cent. But the sophisticated businessman knows that behind these precise calculations are data which are not that precise. At best, the rate-of-return information he is provided with is based on an average of different opinions with varying reliabilities and different ranges of probability. When the expected returns on two investments are close, he is likely to be influenced by "intangibles" — a precarious pursuit at best. Even when the figures for two investments are quite far apart, and the choice seems clear, there lurks in the back of the businessman's mind memories of the Edsel and other ill-fated ventures.

In short, the decision-maker realizes that there is something more he ought to know, something in addition to the expected rate of return. He suspects that what is missing has to do with the nature of the data on which the expected rate of return is calculated, and with the way those data are processed. It has something to do with uncertainty, with possibilities and probabilities extending across a wide range of rewards and risks.

THE ACHILLES HEEL

The fatal weakness of past approaches thus has nothing to do with the mathematics of rate-of-return calculation. We have pushed along this path so far that the precision of our calculation is, if anything, somewhat illusory. The fact is that, no matter what mathematics is used, each of the variables entering into the calculation of rate of return is subject to a high level of uncertainty. For example:

> The useful life of a new piece of capital equipment is rarely known in advance with any degree of certainty. It may be affected by variations in obsolescence or deterioration, and relatively small changes in use life can lead to large changes in return. Yet an expected value for the life of the equipment — based on a great deal of data from which a single best possible forecast has been developed — is entered into the rate-of-return calculation. The same is done for the other factors that have a significant bearing on the decision at hand.

Let us look at how this works out in a simple case — one in which the odds appear to be all in favor of a particular decision:

> The executives of a food company must decide whether to launch a new packaged cereal. They have come to the conclusion that five factors are the determining variables: *advertising and promotion expense, total cereal market, share of market for this product, operating costs,* and *new capital investment.* On the basis of the "most likely" estimate for each of these variables the picture looks very bright — a healthy 30% return. This future, however, depends on

each of the "most likely" estimates coming true in the actual case. If each of these "educated guesses" has, for example, a 60% chance of being correct, there is only an 8% chance that *all five* will be correct (.60 × .60 × .60 × .60 × .60). So the "expected" return is actually dependent on a rather unlikely coincidence. The decision-maker needs to know a great deal more about the *other* values used to make each of the five estimates and about what he stands to gain or lose from various combinations of these values.

This simple example illustrates that the rate of return actually depends on a specific combination of values of a great many different variables. But only the expected levels of ranges (e.g., worst, average, best; or pessimistic, most likely, optimistic) of these variables are used in formal mathematical ways to provide the figures given to management. Thus, predicting a single most likely rate of return gives precise numbers that do not tell the whole story.

The "expected" rate of return represents only a few points on a continuous curve of possible combinations of future happenings. It is a bit like trying to predict the outcome in a dice game by saying that the most likely outcome is a "7." The description is incomplete because it does not tell us about all the other things that could happen. In Exhibit 1, for instance, we see the odds on throws of only two dice having six sides. Now suppose that each die has 100 sides and there are eight of them! This is a situation more comparable to business investment, where the company's market share might become any one of 100 different sizes and where there are eight different factors (pricing, promotion, and so on) that can affect the outcome.

Nor is this the only trouble. Our willingness to bet on a roll of the dice depends not only on the odds but also on the stakes. Since the probability of rolling a "7" is 1 in 6, we might be quite willing to risk a few dollars on that outcome at suitable odds. But would we be equally willing to wager $10,000 or $100,000 at those same odds, or even at better odds? In short,

EXHIBIT 1

Describing Uncertainty — A Throw of the Dice

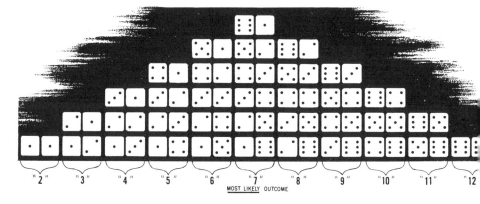

" 2 " " 3 " " 4 " " 5 " " 6 " " 7 " " 8 " " 9 " " 10 " " 11 " " 12 "

MOST LIKELY OUTCOME

risk is influenced both by the odds on various events occurring and by the magnitude of the rewards or penalties which are involved when they do occur. To illustrate again:

> Suppose that a company is considering an investment of $1 million. The "best estimate" of the probable return is $200,000 a year. It could well be that this estimate is the average of three possible returns — a 1-in-3 chance of getting no return at all, a 1-in-3 chance of getting $200,000 per year, a 1-in-3 chance of getting $400,000 per year. Suppose that getting no return at all would put the company out of business. Then, by accepting this proposal, management is taking a 1-in-3 chance of going bankrupt.
>
> If only the "best estimate" analysis is used, management might go ahead, however, unaware that it is taking a big chance. If all of the available information were examined, management might prefer an alternative proposal with a smaller, but more certain (i.e., less variable), expectation.

Such considerations have led almost all advocates of the use of modern capital-investment-index calculations to plead for a recognition of the elements of uncertainty. Perhaps Ross G. Walker sums up current thinking when he speaks of "the almost impenetrable mists of any forecast."[2]

How can the executive penetrate the mists of uncertainty that surround the choices among alternatives?

LIMITED IMPROVEMENTS

A number of efforts to cope with uncertainty have been successful up to a point, but all seem to fall short of the mark in one way or another:

1. *More accurate forecasts* — Reducing the error in estimates is a worthy objective. But no matter how many estimates of the future go into a capital investment decision, when all is said and done, the future is still the future. Therefore, however well we forecast, we are still left with the certain knowledge that we cannot eliminate all uncertainty.

2. *Empirical adjustments* — Adjusting the factors influencing the outcome of a decision is subject to serious difficulties. We would like to adjust them so as to cut down the likelihood that we will make a "bad" investment, but how can we do that without at the same time spoiling our chances to make a "good" one? And in any case, what is the basis for adjustment? We adjust, not for uncertainty, but for bias.

   For example, construction estimates are often exceeded. If a company's history of construction costs is that 90% of its estimates have been exceeded by 15%, then in a capital estimate there is every justification for increasing the value of this factor by 15%. This is a matter of improving the accuracy of the estimate.

---

[2] "The Judgment Factor in Investment Decisions," *Harvard Business Review* Vol. 39, No. 2 (March–April,1961), p. 99.

But suppose that new-product sales estimates have been exceeded by more than 75% in one-fourth of all historical cases, and have not reached 50% of the estimate in one-sixth of all such cases? Penalties for overestimating are very tangible, and so management is apt to reduce the sales estimate to "cover" the one case in six — thereby reducing the calculated rate of return. In doing so, it is possibly missing some of its best opportunities.

3. *Revising cutoff rates* — Selecting higher cutoff rates for protecting against uncertainty is attempting much the same thing. Management would like to have a possibility of return in proportion to the risk it takes. Where there is much uncertainty involved in the various estimates of sales, costs, prices, and so on, a high calculated return from the investment provides some incentive for taking the risk. This is, in fact, a perfectly sound position. The trouble is that the decision-maker still needs to know explicitly what risks he is taking — and what the odds are on achieving the expected return.

4. *Three-level estimates* — A start at spelling out risks is sometimes made by taking the high, medium, and low values of the estimated factors and calculating rates of return based on various combinations of the pessimistic, average, and optimistic estimates. These calculations give a picture of the range of possible results, but do not tell the executive whether the pessimistic result is more likely than the optimistic one — or, in fact, whether the average result is much more likely to occur than either of the extremes. So, although this is a step in the right direction, it still does not give a clear enough picture for comparing alternatives.

5. *Selected probabilities* — Various methods have been used to include the probabilities of specific factors in the return calculation. L. C. Grant discusses a program for forecasting discounted cash flow rates of return where the service life is subject to obsolescence and deterioration. He calculates the odds that the investment will terminate at any time after it is made depending on the probability distribution of the service-life factor. After calculating these factors for each year through maximum service life, he then determines an over-all expected rate of return.[3]

Edward G. Bennion suggests the use of game theory to take into account alternative market growth rates as they would determine rate of return for various alternatives. He uses the estimated probabilities that specific growth rates will occur to develop optimum strategies. Bennion points out:

Forecasting can result in a negative contribution to capital budget decisions unless it goes further than merely providing a single most probable prediction. . . . [With] an estimated probability coefficient for the forecast, plus knowledge of the payoffs for the company's alternative investments and calculation of indifference probabilities . . . the margin of error may be substantially reduced,

[3] "Monitoring Capital Investments," *Financial Executive*, April, 1963, p. 19.

and the businessman can tell just how far off his forecast may be before it leads him to a wrong decision.[4]

Note that both of these methods yield an expected return, each based on only one uncertain input factor — service life in the first case, market growth in the second. Both are helpful, and both tend to improve the clarity with which the executive can view investment alternatives. But neither sharpens up the range of "risk taken" or "return hoped for" sufficiently to help very much in the complex decisions of capital planning.

Sharpening the Picture

Since every one of the many factors that enter into the evaluation of a specific decision is subject to some uncertainty, the executive needs a helpful portrayal of the effects that the uncertainty surrounding each of the significant factors has on the returns he is likely to achieve. Therefore, the method we have developed at McKinsey & Company, Inc., combines the variabilities inherent in all the relevant factors. Our objective is to give a clear picture of the relative risk and the probable odds of coming out ahead or behind in the light of uncertain foreknowledge.

A simulation of the way these factors may combine as the future unfolds is the key to extracting the maximum information from the available forecasts. In fact, the approach is very simple, using a computer to do the necessary arithmetic. (Recently, a computer program to do this was suggested by S. W. Hess and H. A. Quigley for chemical process investments.[5])

To carry out the analysis, a company must follow three steps:

1. Estimate the range of values for each of the factors (e.g., range of selling price, sales growth rate, and so on) and within that range the likelihood of occurrence of each value.

2. Select at random from the distribution of values for each factor one particular value. Then combine the values for all of the factors and compute the rate of return (or present value) from that combination. For instance, the lowest in the range of prices might be combined with the highest in the range of growth rate and other factors. (The fact that the factors are dependent should be taken into account, as we shall see later.)

3. Do this over and over again to define and evaluate the odds of the occurrence of each possible rate of return. Since there are literally millions of possible combinations of values, we need to test the likelihood that various specific returns on the investment will occur. This is like

[4] "Capital Budgeting and Game Theory," *Harvard Business Review*, Vol. 34, No. 6 (November–December, 1956), p. 123.

[5] "Analysis of Risk in Investments Using Monte Carlo Techniques," *Chemical Engineering Symposium Series 42: Statistics and Numerical Methods in Chemical Engineering* (New York, American Institute of Chemical Engineering, 1963), p. 55.

finding out by recording the results of a great many throws what per cent of "7"s or other combinations we may expect in tossing dice. The result will be a listing of the rates of return we might achieve, ranging from a loss (if the factors go against us) to whatever maximum gain is possible with the estimates that have been made.

For each of these rates the chances that it may occur are determined. (Note that a specific return can usually be achieved through more than one combination of events. The more combinations for a given rate, the higher the chances of achieving it — as with "7"s in tossing dice.) The average expectation is the average of the values of all outcomes weighted by the chances of each occurring.

The variability of outcome values from the average is also determined. This is important since, all other factors being equal, management would presumably prefer lower variability for the same return if given the choice. This concept has already been applied to investment portfolios.[6]

When the expected return and variability of each of a series of investments have been determined, the same techniques may be used to examine the effectiveness of various combinations of them in meeting management objectives.

Practical Test

To see how this new approach works in practice, let us take the experience of a management that has already analyzed a specific investment proposal by conventional techniques. Taking the same investment schedule and the same expected values actually used, we can find what results the new method would produce and compare them with the results obtained when conventional methods were applied. As we shall see, the new picture of risks and returns is different from the old one. Yet the differences are attributable in no way to changes in the basic data — *only to the increased sensitivity of the method to management's uncertainties about the key factors.*

INVESTMENT PROPOSAL

In this case a medium-size industrial chemical producer is considering a $10-million extension to its processing plant. The estimated service life of the facility is 10 years; the engineers expect to be able to utilize 250,000 tons of processed material worth $510 per ton at an average processing cost of $435 per ton. Is this investment a good bet? In fact, what is the return that the company may expect? What are the risks? We need to make the best

[6] See Harry Markowitz, *Portfolio Selection, Efficient Diversification of Investments* (New York, John Wiley and Sons, 1959); Donald E. Farrar, *The Investment Decision Under Uncertainty* (Englewood Cliffs, New Jersey, Prentice-Hall, Inc., 1962); William F. Sharpe, "A Simplified Model for Portfolio Analysis," *Management Science*, January, 1963, p. 277.

and fullest use we can of all the market research and financial analyses that have been developed, so as to give management a clear picture of this project in an uncertain world.

The key input factors management has decided to use are:
1. Market size.
2. Selling prices.
3. Market growth rate.
4. Share of market (which results in physical sales volume).
5. Investment required.
6. Residual value of investment.
7. Operating costs.
8. Fixed costs.
9. Useful life of facilities.

These factors are typical of those in many company projects that must be analyzed and combined to obtain a measure of the attractiveness of a proposed capital facilities investment.

OBTAINING ESTIMATES

How do we make the recommended type of analysis of this proposal?

Our aim is to develop for each of the nine factors listed a frequency distribution or probability curve. The information we need includes the possible range of values for each factor, the average, and some ideas as to the likelihood that the various possible values will be reached. It has been our experience that for major capital proposals managements usually make a significant investment in time and funds to pinpoint information about each of the relevant factors. An objective analysis of the values to be assigned to each can, with little additional effort, yield a subjective probability distribution.

Specifically, it is necessary to probe and question each of the experts involved — to find out, for example, whether the estimated cost of production really can be said to be exactly a certain value or whether, as is more likely, it should be estimated to lie within a certain range of values. It is that range which is ignored in the analysis management usually makes. The range is relatively easy to determine; if a guess has to be made — as it often does — it is easier to guess with some accuracy a range rather than a specific single value. We have found from past experience at McKinsey & Company, Inc., that a series of meetings with management personnel to discuss such distributions is most helpful in getting at realistic answers to the a priori questions. (The term "realistic answers" implies all the information management does *not* have as well as all that it does have.)

The ranges are directly related to the degree of confidence that the estimator has in his estimate. Thus, certain estimates may be known to be quite accurate. They would be represented by probability distributions stating, for instance, that there is only 1 chance in 10 that the actual value will be different from the best estimate by more than 10%. Others may have as much as 100% ranges above and below the best estimate.

Thus, we treat the factor of selling price for the finished product by asking executives who are responsible for the original estimates these questions:

1. Given that $510 is the expected sales price, what is the probability that the price will exceed $550?
2. Is there any chance that the price will exceed $650?
3. How likely is it that the price will drop below $475?

Managements must ask similar questions for each of the other factors, until they can construct a curve for each. Experience shows that this is not as difficult as it might sound. Often information on the degree of variation in factors is readily available. For instance, historical information on variations in the price of a commodity is readily available. Similarly, management can estimate the variability of sales from industry sales records. Even for factors that have no history, such as operating costs for a new product, the person who makes the "average" estimate must have some idea of the degree of confidence he has in his prediction, and therefore he is usually only too glad to express his feelings. Likewise, the less confidence he has in his estimate, the greater will be the range of possible values that the variable will assume.

This last point is likely to trouble businessmen. Does it really make sense to seek estimates of variations? It cannot be emphasized too strongly that the less certainty there is in an "average" estimate, *the more important it is to consider the possible variation in that estimate.*

Further, an estimate of the variation possible in a factor, no matter how judgmental it may be, is always better than a simple "average" estimate, since it includes more information about what is known and what is not known. It is, in fact, this very *lack* of knowledge which may distinguish one investment possibility from another, so that for rational decision making it *must* be taken into account.

This lack of knowledge is in itself important information about the proposed investment. To throw any information away simply because it is highly uncertain is a serious error in analysis which the new approach is designed to correct.

COMPUTER RUNS

The next step in the proposed approach is to determine the returns that will result from random combinations of the factors involved. This requires realistic restrictions, such as not allowing the total market to vary more than some reasonable amount from year to year. Of course, any method of rating the return which is suitable to the company may be used at this point; in the actual case management preferred discounted cash flow for the reasons cited earlier, so that method is followed here.

A computer can be used to carry out the trials for the simulation method in very little time and at very little expense. Thus, for one trial actually made in this case, 3,600 discounted cash flow calculations, each based on a selection of the nine input factors, were run in two minutes at a cost of $15 for computer time. The resulting rate-of-return probabilities were read out immediately and graphed. The process is shown schematically in Exhibit 2.

DATA COMPARISONS

The nine input factors described earlier fall into three categories:
1. *Market analyses.* Included are market size, market growth rate, the firm's share of the market, and selling prices. For a given combination of these factors sales revenue may be determined.
2. *Investment cost analyses.* Being tied to the kinds of service-life and operating-cost characteristics expected, these are subject to various kinds of error and uncertainty; for instance, automation progress makes service life uncertain.
3. *Operating and fixed costs.* These also are subject to uncertainty, but are perhaps the easiest to estimate.

These categories are not independent, and for realistic results our approach allows the various factors to be tied together. Thus, if price determines the total market, we first select from a probability distribution the price for the specific computer run and then use for the total market a probability distribution that is logically related to the price selected.

We are now ready to compare the values obtained under the new approach with the values obtained under the old. This comparison is shown in Exhibit 3.

VALUABLE RESULTS

How do the results under the new and old approaches compare?

In this case, management had been informed, on the basis of the "one best estimate" approach, that the expected return was 25.2% before taxes. When we ran the new set of data through the computer program, however, we got an expected return of only 14.6% before taxes. This surprising difference not only is due to the fact that under the new approach we use a range of values; it also reflects the fact that we have weighted each value in the range by the chances of its occurrence.

Our new analysis thus may help management to avoid an unwise investment. In fact, the general result of carefully weighing the information and lack of information in the manner I have suggested is to indicate the true nature of otherwise seemingly satisfactory investment proposals. If this practice were followed by managements, much regretted over-capacity might be avoided.

EXHIBIT 2

Simulation for Investment Planning

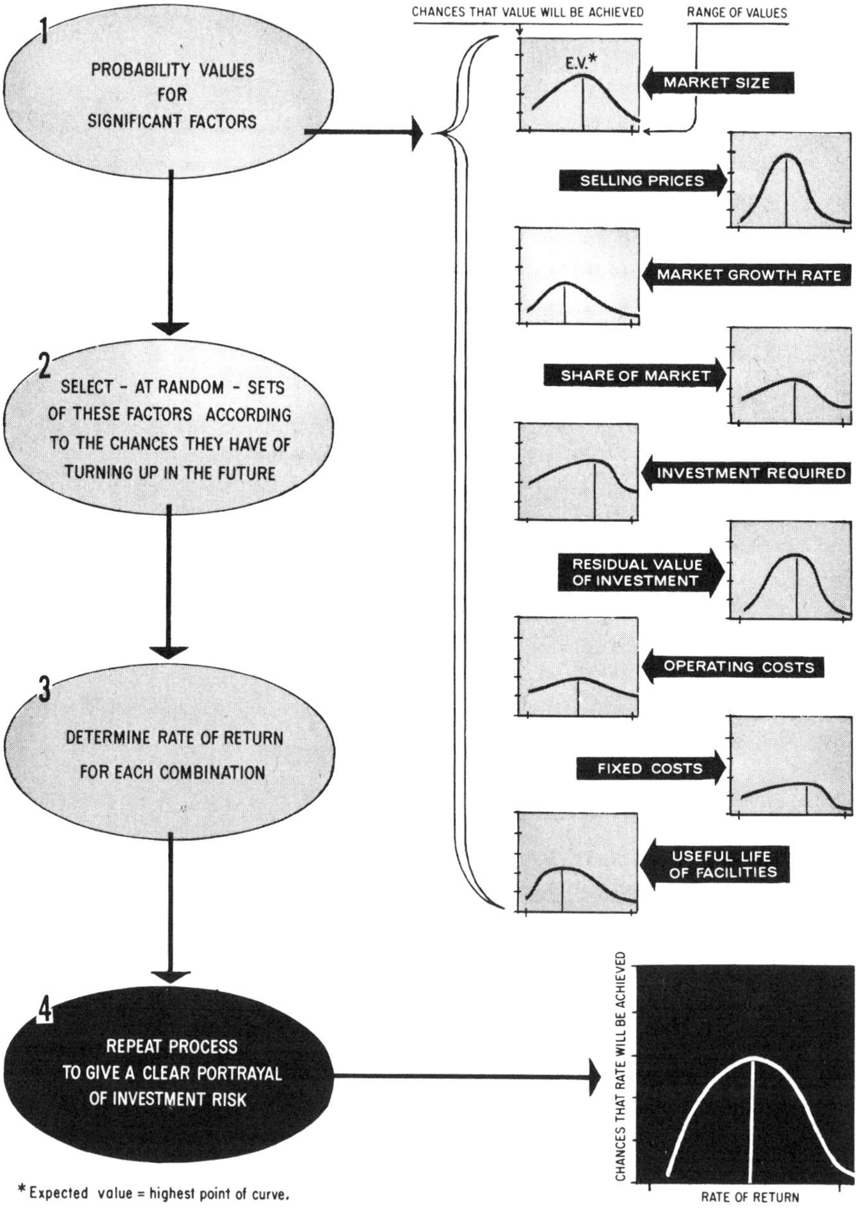

CHANCES THAT VALUE WILL BE ACHIEVED   RANGE OF VALUES

1 — PROBABILITY VALUES FOR SIGNIFICANT FACTORS

E.V.* — MARKET SIZE

SELLING PRICES

MARKET GROWTH RATE

2 — SELECT – AT RANDOM – SETS OF THESE FACTORS ACCORDING TO THE CHANCES THEY HAVE OF TURNING UP IN THE FUTURE

SHARE OF MARKET

INVESTMENT REQUIRED

RESIDUAL VALUE OF INVESTMENT

3 — DETERMINE RATE OF RETURN FOR EACH COMBINATION

OPERATING COSTS

FIXED COSTS

USEFUL LIFE OF FACILITIES

4 — REPEAT PROCESS TO GIVE A CLEAR PORTRAYAL OF INVESTMENT RISK

CHANCES THAT RATE WILL BE ACHIEVED

RATE OF RETURN

*Expected value = highest point of curve.

EXHIBIT 3

Comparison of Expected Values Under Old and New Approaches

	Conventional "Best Estimate" Approach	New Approach
MARKET ANALYSES		
1. *Market size*		
Expected value (in tons)	250,000	250,000
Range	—	100,000–340,000
2. *Selling prices*		
Expected value (in dollars/ton)	$510	$510
Range	—	$385–$575
3. *Market growth rate*		
Expected value	3%	3%
Range	—	0–6%
4. *Eventual share of market*		
Expected value	12%	12%
Range	—	3%–17%
INVESTMENT COST ANALYSES		
5. *Total investment required*		
Expected value (in millions)	$9.5	$9.5
Range	—	$7.0–$10.5
6. *Useful life of facilities*		
Expected value (in years)	10	10
Range	—	5–15
7. *Residual value (at 10 years)*		
Expected value (in millions)	$4.5	$4.5
Range	—	$3.5–$5.0
OTHER COSTS		
8. *Operating costs*		
Expected value (in dollars/ton)	$435	$435
Range	—	$370–$545
9. *Fixed costs*		
Expected value (in thousands)	$300	$300
Range	—	$250–$375

NOTE: Range figures in right-hand column represent approximately 1% to 99% probabilities. That is, there is only a 1 in a 100 chance that the value actually achieved will be respectively greater or less than the range.

The computer program developed to carry out the simulation allows for easy insertion of new variables. In fact, some programs have previously been suggested that take variability into account.[7] But most programs do not

[7] See Frederick S. Hillier, "The Derivation of Probabilistic Information for the Evaluation of Risky Investments," *Management Science*, April, 1963, p. 443.

allow for dependence relationships between the various input factors. Further, the program used here permits the choice of a value for price from one distribution, which value determines a particular probability distribution (from among several) that will be used to determine the value for sales volume. To show how this important technique works:

> Suppose we have a wheel, as in roulette, with the numbers from 0 to 15 representing one price for the product or material, the numbers 16 to 30 representing a second price, the numbers 31 to 45 a third price, and so on. For each of these segments we would have a different range of expected market volumes; e.g., $150,000–$200,000 for the first, $100,000–$150,000 for the second, $75,000–$100,000 for the third, and so forth. Now suppose that we spin the wheel and the ball falls in 37. This would mean that we pick a sales volume in the $75,000–$100,000 range. If the ball goes in 11, we have a different price and we turn to the $150,000–$200,000 range for a price.

Most significant, perhaps, is the fact that the program allows management to ascertain the sensitivity of the results to each or all of the input factors. Simply by running the program with changes in the distribution of an input factor, it is possible to determine the effect of added or changed information (or of the lack of information). It may turn out that fairly large changes in some factors do not significantly affect the outcomes. In this case, as a matter of fact, management was particularly concerned about the difficulty in estimating market growth. Running the program with variations in this factor quickly demonstrated to us that for average annual growths from 3% and 5% there was no significant difference in the expected outcome.

In addition, let us see what the implications are of the detailed knowledge the simulation method gives us. Under the method using single expected values, management arrives only at a hoped-for expectation of 25.2% after taxes (which, as we have seen, is wrong unless there is no variability in the

EXHIBIT 4

Anticipated Rates of Return Under Old and New Approaches

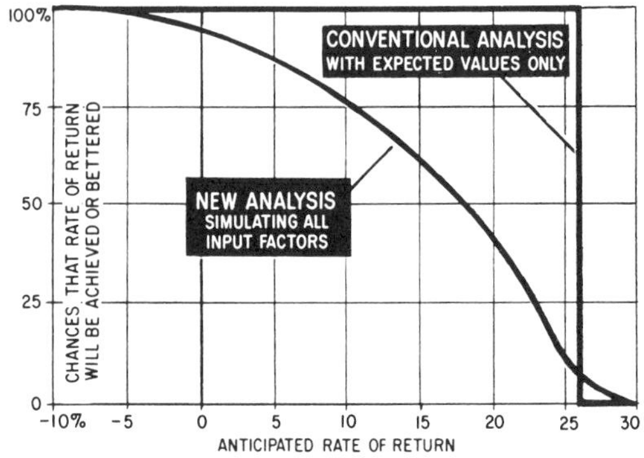

various input factors — a highly unlikely event). On the other hand, with the method we propose, the uncertainties are clearly portrayed:

Per cent return	Probability of achieving at least the return shown
0%	96.5%
5	80.6
10	75.2
15	53.8
20	43.0
25	12.6
30	0

This profile is shown in Exhibit 4. Note the contrast with the profile obtained under the conventional approach. This concept has been used also for evaluation of new product introductions, acquisitions of new businesses, and plant modernization.

Comparing Opportunities

From a decision-making point of view one of the most significant advantages of the new method of determining rate of return is that it allows

EXHIBIT 5

Comparison of Two Investment Opportunities

SELECTED STATISTICS	INVESTMENT A	INVESTMENT B
AMOUNT OF INVESTMENT	$10,000,000	$10,000,000
LIFE OF INVESTMENT (IN YEARS)	10	10
EXPECTED ANNUAL NET CASH INFLOW	$ 1,300,000	$ 1,400,000
VARIABILITY OF CASH INFLOW		
I CHANCE IN 50 OF BEING *GREATER* THAN	$ 1,700,000	$ 3,400,000
I CHANCE IN 50 OF BEING *LESS** THAN	$ 900,000	($600,000)
EXPECTED RETURN ON INVESTMENT	5.0%	6.8 %
VARIABILITY OF RETURN ON INVESTMENT		
I CHANCE IN 50 OF BEING *GREATER* THAN	7.0%	15.5 %
I CHANCE IN 50 OF BEING *LESS** THAN	3.0%	(4.0%)
RISK OF INVESTMENT		
CHANCES OF A LOSS	NEGLIGIBLE	I IN IO
EXPECTED SIZE OF LOSS		$ 200,000

management to discriminate between measures of (1) expected return based on weighted probabilities of all possible returns, (2) variability of return, and (3) risks.

To visualize this advantage, let us take an example which is based on another actual case but simplified for purposes of explanation. The example involves two investments under consideration, A and B.

When the investments are analyzed, the data tabulated and plotted in Exhibit 5 are obtained. We see that:

· Investment B has a higher expected return than Investment A.
· Investment B also has substantially more variability than Investment A. There is a good chance that Investment B will earn a return which is quite different from the expected return of 6.8%, possibly as high as 15% or as low as a loss of 5%. Investment A is not likely to vary greatly from the expected 5% return.
· Investment B involves far more risk than does Investment A. There is virtually no chance of incurring a loss on Investment A. However, there is 1 chance in 10 of losing money on Investment B. If such a loss occurs, its expected size is approximately $200,000.

Clearly, the new method of evaluating investments provides management with far more information on which to base a decision. Investment decisions made only on the basis of maximum expected return are not unequivocally the best decisions.

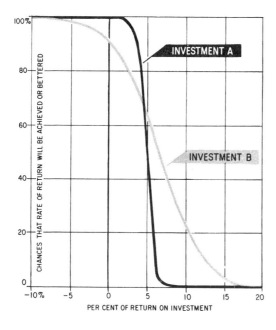

Conclusion

The question management faces in selecting capital investments is first and foremost: What information is needed to clarify the key differences among various alternatives? There is agreement as to the basic factors that should be considered — markets, prices, costs, and so on. And the way the future return on the investment should be calculated, if not agreed on, is at least limited to a few methods, any of which can be consistently used in a given company. If the input variables turn out as estimated, any of the methods customarily used to rate investments should provide satisfactory (if not necessarily maximum) returns.

In actual practice, however, the conventional methods do *not* work out satisfactorily. Why? The reason, as we have seen earlier in this article, and as every executive and economist knows, is that the estimates used in making the advance calculations are just that — estimates. More accurate estimates would be helpful, but at best the residual uncertainty can easily make a mockery of corporate hopes. Nevertheless, there is a solution. To collect realistic estimates for the key factors means to find out a great deal about them. Hence the kind of uncertainty that is involved in each estimate can be evaluated ahead of time. Using this knowledge of uncertainty, executives can maximize the value of the information for decision making.

The value of computer programs in developing clear portrayals of the uncertainty and risk surrounding alternative investments has been proved. Such programs can produce valuable information about the sensitivity of the possible outcomes to the variability of input factors and to the likelihood of achieving various possible rates of return. This information can be extremely important as a backup to management judgment. To have calculations of the odds on all possible outcomes lends some assurance to the decision-makers that the available information has been used with maximum efficiency.

This simulation approach has the inherent advantage of simplicity. It requires only an extension of the input estimates (to the best of our ability) in terms of probabilities. No projection should be pinpointed unless we are *certain* of it.

The discipline of thinking through the uncertainties of the problem will in itself help to ensure improvement in making investment choices. For to understand uncertainty and risk is to understand the key business problem — and the key business opportunity. Since the new approach can be applied on a continuing basis to each capital alternative as it comes up for consideration and progresses toward fruition, gradual progress may be expected in improving the estimation of the probabilities of variation.

Lastly, the courage to act boldly in the face of apparent uncertainty can be greatly bolstered by the clarity of portrayal of the risks and possible rewards. To achieve these lasting results requires only a slight effort beyond what most companies already exert in studying capital investments.

13 *Even though the payback period does not measure the profitability of proposed capital investments, it is still the favorite method of evaluating them in practice. After giving the limitations of the payback period method, the author discusses various reasons for its popularity, including difficulties in predicting cash flows for more than three to five years into the future, and the strong liquidity preferences of risk-conscious businessmen. An improved standard is then proposed.*

The Discounted
Payback Period*

Alfred Rappaport

One of the most striking disparities between theory and practice in management today lies in the field of capital budgeting. The literature of capital budgeting abounds with "sound" methods of measuring the economic value of proposed capital expenditures. Almost all of them are methods that give due consideration to the time value of money. Although the use of discounted cash flow techniques is increasing in American industry, it continues to be the exception rather than the rule.

Payback period remains the most popular method of evaluating capital projects. Despite almost unanimous agreement by the theorists that payback has little value in measuring profitability, it is the only financial measure used in capital expenditure evaluation in many companies.[1] Even

Reprinted by permission of Management Services *(July-August, 1965).* Copyright 1965 by the American Institute of CPAs.

[1] A number of recent studies show that payback period continues to be a widely used measure of acceptability for capital projects. A National Industrial Conference Board study of 346 manufacturing companies found payback period to be the most commonly employed financial measure for evaluating capital projects (Norman E. Pflomm, *Managing Capital Expenditures,* Business Policy Study No. 107, National Industrial Conference Board, Inc., New York, 1963, p. 42). Donald F. Istvan, in a study designed to ascertain how "big business" decides to invest in capital projects,

212

the large corporations that employ discounted cash flow analysis often retain payback period as an additional tool.

All this suggests that payback may have some real advantages in capital investment analysis. The purposes of this article are to analyze the reasons for its popularity and, assuming that this popularity will continue, to propose an improved concept of payback period, i.e., the discounted payback period.

Payback Shortcomings

The payback period measures the length of time it will take expected cash proceeds generated by an investment to equal the initial cash outlay required to make the investment. For example, if a new machine costs $75,000 and is expected to produce operating savings of $15,000 annually, it has a payback period of five years. If the expected cash flows vary from year to year, then PB is determined by adding the expected proceeds for each year until the sum equals the initial cash outlay. In any case, the shorter the PB the more desirable the project is assumed to be.

The principal objection to the payback period method is its failure to measure profitability. Simply measuring how long it will take to recover the initial investment outlay contributes little to gauging the earning power of a project. Because payback period analysis ignores differences in the timing of cash flows, it fails to recognize the difference between the present and the future value of money. Because it ignores all proceeds after the payback life, it does not allow for the possible advantages of a project with a longer economic life.

Using payback period as the sole criterion may well lead to an undue emphasis on liquidity at the expense of profitability. By way of illustration, consider two mutually exclusive projects, P_1 and P_2. Each requires an initial investment outlay of $100,000. P_1, with expected annual cash proceeds of $25,000 for the duration of its five-year economic life, has a payback period of four years. P_2 is expected to generate annual cash proceeds of $20,000 for ten years; hence, its payback period is five years. The payback period criterion points to the selection of P_1, but, in fact, whether one applies the

---

found that only 7 of 48 companies recognized the time value of money in their analyses. These 48 companies expended more than $8 billion for plant and equipment in 1959, almost 25 per cent of the aggregate $33 billion recorded by the Department of Commerce for that year (Donald F. Istvan, "The Economic Evaluation of Capital Expenditures," *The Journal of Business,* January, 1961, p. 45). Similar results were reported in James H. Miller's survey of 127 replying companies selected from the American Institute of Management's *Manual of Excellently Managed Companies* and *Fortune's* list of the 500 largest industrial companies. Only 38 of the 127 companies employed evaluation methods recognizing that a dollar received or disbursed in the future is not the value equivalent of a dollar received or disbursed today (James H. Miller, "A Glimpse at Practice in Calculating and Using Return on Investment," *N.A.A. Bulletin,* June, 1960, pp. 72–73).

unadjusted or the time-adjusted (discounted cash flow) rate of return criterion, P_2 is the more profitable investment. Even if we were to suggest that the economic life of P_1 is four years rather than five years, the payback period criterion would still favor P_1 despite the fact that P_1 would then yield no return or a negative return on a time value basis.

Reasons for Popularity

Why, then, does payback period continue to be so widely used as a measure of acceptability for capital projects? The following reasons appear to be the principal ones:

1. *It is easy to calculate.* This reduces the cost of the capital investment evaluation program.

2. *It is relatively easy to understand.* This advantage may be expected to decline in importance as executives gain familiarity with the so-called scientific approaches to decision making.

3. *Under certain conditions the payback reciprocal can serve as a reasonable approximation of a project's time-adjusted rate of return.* However, these conditions are so limited (projects must have relatively long economic lives — at least twice the payback period — and fairly stable earnings[2]) that use of the payback period reciprocal to measure project profitability should be highly selective. Probably its most advantageous application is as a means of quickly eliminating from consideration projects that obviously do not meet predetermined discounted profitability standards.

4. *Some businessmen believe that projecting cash flows more than a few years into the future involves too much uncertainty to incorporate in a useful measure of project acceptability.* As Neil W. Chamberlain explains, "The primary difficulty is that estimation of income receipts beyond a three- to five-year period strikes most managers as too problematical to be meaningful. Whether competing products will have ruled this one off the market, whether technological advances will have stripped this process of its present advantages, whether consumer tastes will sustain the present price structure, whether intensified competition will have shaved profit margins, whether a geographical shift in markets will undermine a present entrenched position — these and other unknowns make the procedure of giving specific values to such considerations not only speculative but a little foolish to many managements."[3]

---

[2] Myron J. Gordon, "The Payoff Period and the Rate of Profit," *Journal of Business,* October, 1955, pp. 253–260.

[3] Neil W. Chamberlain, *The Firm: Micro-Economic Planning and Action,* McGraw-Hill Book Company, New York, 1962, p. 270.

5. *Risk-conscious businessmen probably have stronger liquidity prefer-ences than economists generally acknowledge.* Strong liquidity preferences, like reluctance to engage in longer-term projections, find their basis in the uncertain nature of future outcomes. Uncertainty thus influences business-men to sacrifice some profitability in favor of projects that offer prospects of an early return of investment outlay. Payback period does emphasize the liquidity aspect of the investment decision. According to an executive of a major oil company, "With the passage of time, there are increasing possi-bilities of obsolescence in product design or equipment, of deviations from the original estimates of income and operating costs, and of changes in com-petitive conditions. Payout figures are useful measures of risk, because they show the length of time for which the original capital investment is exposed to these hazards."[4]

These last two reasons for payback period's popularity carry considerable weight. The businessman's necessary preoccupation with time risks and liquidity as well as with profitability indicates that some refinement of the payback period criterion may in fact serve a useful role in capital invest-ment decision making. However, even as an index of liquidity and time risk, the conventional calculation of the payback period has serious short-comings. As a means of overcoming these limitations, an alternative concept of payback period is proposed, namely, the discounted payback period.

Opportunity Investment Rate

The conventional payback period measures the length of time it will take to recover the absolute investment outlay. While such a measurement may have great intuitive significance to the capital investment decision maker, it neither considers the costs a company must incur to obtain and sustain capital nor the existence of alternative investment opportunities. In the language of capital budgeting, the conventional payback ignores the com-pany's "cost of capital."

In the context of capital budgeting, the cost of capital is generally re-garded as the minimum rate of return for accepting projects. Let us con-sider two distinct cost-of-capital rates — the borrowing rate and the lending rate. Horngren distinguishes between the two as follows: ". . . the 'borrow-ing' rate — the weighted-average rate that a company must pay for long-run capital. This is an indicator of the overall minimum return that the com-pany must earn if the stockholder's rate of return is going to be maintained. It is stockholder-oriented inasmuch as it is determined by market prices, which in turn are influenced by the investor's opportunities. The lending

[4] John G. McLean, "Measuring the Return on Capital — Relating Calculations to Uses," *N.A.A. Bulletin,* Sec. 3, September, 1960, p. 35.

rate is basically an opportunity-cost concept; it is the rate that can be earned on alternative investments having a like degree of risk. It is the investment rate, which varies with risk, that should be used for purposes of discounting future cash flow to the present. . . ."[5]

While these two rates are often used interchangeably in the literature, each serves a distinct purpose. The borrowing rate is properly employed in measuring the expected cost of new capital. The lending rate, on the other hand, is the appropriate rate for discounting future cash flows to the present. This is particularly true when the lending rate exceeds the borrowing rate. From a purely economic standpoint, a management would be hard pressed to justify the authorization of projects within the company when greater returns on "like-risk" equity investments outside the company are available. A company using the borrowing rate as the minimum return when the lending rate is significantly higher probably will find its shareholders shifting to the same higher-yielding equity investments whose rates of return the company should be using as a minimum standard for its own capital projects. The lending rate or, as it will be referred to hereafter, the "opportunity investment rate" is the appropriate rate for discounting cash flows.[6]

Discounted Payback Period

Let us now relate the "opportunity investment rate" notion to payback period measurement. The conventional payback period calculation clearly fails to consider a company's cost of capital. To contend that the conventionally measured payback date is the break-even date for a given project is

---

[5] Charles T. Horngren, *Cost Accounting — A Managerial Emphasis,* Prentice-Hall, Inc., Englewood Cliffs, N.J., 1962, p. 615. A more detailed discussion of the "borrowing rate" versus the "lending rate" may be found in Harry V. Roberts' "Current Problems in the Economics of Capital Budgeting" in Ezra Solomon's *The Management of Corporate Capital,* The Free Press of Glencoe, Illinois, 1959, pp. 198–202. For consideration of these rates under varying degrees of capital rationing see Harold Bierman, Jr., and Seymour Smidt, *The Capital Budgeting Decision,* The Macmillan Company, New York, 1960, pp. 162–170.

[6] A company may well employ several "opportunity investment rates" with increasing rates as the risks involved in investment projects increase. Multiple cutoff rates represent but one method of coping with risk and uncertainty. The application of probability concepts to capital budgeting calculations is surely one of the most significant developments of recent years. It is not feasible to discuss probability applications in this article. However, the discounted payback principle is susceptible to such applications. Indeed, as probability statements enhance the basis for projecting cash flows, discounted payback period calculations improve correspondingly. Those interested in the applicability of probability concepts to capital budgeting are referred to Edward G. Bennion, "Capital Budgeting and Game Theory," *Harvard Business Review,* November-December, 1956, pp. 115–123; Bierman and Smidt, *op. cit.,* Chapter 9; and David B. Hertz, "Risk Analysis in Capital Investment," *Harvard Business Review,* January-February, 1964, pp. 95–106.

tantamount to suggesting that capital is obtainable without cost. A more reasonable approach is suggested by the discounted payback period criterion.

The discounted payback period is the length of time it takes a project's incremental cash flows discounted at the "opportunity investment rate" to accumulate to investment outlay. Only at the end of this period is the breakeven claim one with economic substance, for this is the length of time it takes project proceeds (reinvested at the "opportunity investment rate") to accumulate to a sum equal to the investment outlay compounded at the "opportunity investment rate" over the same period. Then, and only then, has the project broken even with respect to alternative investment opportunities of like degree of risk. The technique of calculating discounted payback period and its significance as a measure of time risk and liquidity can be best demonstrated by means of an illustration.

Example

Consider a contemplated project with a required initial outlay of $100,-000 and forecasted incremental cash flows during its estimated seven years of economic life as follows: $20,000; $30,000; $50,000; $30,000; $20,000; $10,000; and $10,000, respectively. Within the framework of the conventional payback period calculation, the decision maker may well conclude that the initial investment will be recovered in three years and that at that point the firm has achieved a breakeven position. This is, of course, a grossly misleading notion, since it is based on the false premise that there are no alternative, productive uses for the invested capital.

Calculation

Assume that the company considering this project perceives its "opportunity investment rate" to be 15 per cent. Thus, for the project under consideration 15 per cent is the minimum acceptable rate of return and the relevant rate for discounting incremental cash flows. The discounted payback period calculation is presented in Exhibit 1. (See page 218.) Note that the discounted payback period for the project under consideration is five years, as contrasted with three years under the conventionally calculated payback period. Note also that at the end of three years the company will have recovered only 73 per cent of its original investment, not 100 per cent as suggested by the conventional payback calculation.

The discounted payback period may be viewed alternatively as the length of time it takes for a project's incremental cash flows reinvested at the "opportunity interest rate" to accumulate to a sum equal to the investment

EXHIBIT 1

Calculation of Discounted Payback Period and "Profitability Index"*

Period (year)	(1) Investment Outlay	(2) Incremental Cash Flow	(3) Present Value of $1 Discounted at 15%	(4) Present Value of Incremental Cash Flow $=(2)\times(3)$	(5) Cumulative Present Value of Incremental Cash Flow	(6) Percent Investment Recovery $=(5)\div(1)$
t_0	$100,000					
t_1		$20,000	$ .8696	$17,392	$ 17,392	17.39
t_2		30,000	.7561	22,683	40,075	40.08
t_3		50,000	.6575	32,875	72,950	72.95
t_4		30,000	.5718	17,154	90,104	90.10
t_5		20,000	.4972	9,944	100,048	100.05 Discounted Payback Date
t_6		10,000	.4323	4,323	104,371	104.37
t_7		10,000	.3759	3,759	108,130	108.13 Profit- ability Index

*Cash flows received at end of period

EXHIBIT 2

Comparison of Compounded Values of $100,000 Invested at "Opportunity Investment Rate" vs. Project's Incremental Cash Flows Reinvested at "Opportunity Investment Rate"*

Period	(1) Investment outlay	(2) Incremental Cash Flow	(3) $100,000 Invested in Project yielding 15%		(4) Incremental Cash Flows Reinvested at 15%
t_0	$100,000		$100,000		
t_1		$20,000	115,000		$ 20,000
t_2		30,000	132,250		53,000
t_3		50,000	152,087		110,950
t_4		30,000	174,900	⎧Discounted⎫	157,592
t_5		20,000	201,135	⎨ Payback ⎬	201,230
t_6		10,000	231,305	⎩ Date ⎭	241,415
t_7		10,000	266,000		287,627

* Cash flows received at end of period

outlay compounded at the same rate and over the same period. This approach to the discounted payback period calculation[7] is illustrated in Exhibit 2. Note that the compounded project cash flows (Column 4) do not begin to exceed the compounded initial investment (Column 3) until the end of the fifth year. At that point they are $201,230 and $201,135, respectively. Thus, we see that identical answers are gained from these two methods of calculating discounted payback period.

Advantages

The advantages of replacing the conventional payback measurement with the discounted payback period criterion are compelling. The principal ones are as follows:

1. Discounted payback period represents a significantly improved criterion for the measurement of project time risk, i.e., the length of time for which the original capital investment is exposed to economic hazards, because it recognizes the productivity of capital and consequently the time value of money.

[7] I am indebted to my colleague, Professor James T. Murphy of Tulane University, for suggesting this alternative approach to the discounted payback period calculation.

It is important to emphasize, however, that the discounted payback period is not a substitute for profitability measurements. Clearly, organizations that now employ only the conventional payback for evaluating investment acceptability can only stand to improve the basis for their decisions. Nevertheless, the proper role for the discounted payback period analysis is as a supplement to profitability measurements. In this case it might be used as a measure of relative time risk.

2. The discounted payback measurement allows management to compare the rate of a project's discounted (at "opportunity investment rate") cash flows with its own subjective time preferences for "accept or reject" decisions.

Assume, for example, that for a given class of investments management establishes 15 per cent as the minimum acceptable rate of return, i.e., 15 per cent is the "opportunity investment rate." In addition, management requires a discounted payback period not exceeding five years. Consider a given project that exceeds the minimum rate of return by only a marginal rate and has a discounted payback period of just under the maximum acceptable of five years. Management remains undecided regarding the desirability of investing in this project. The discounted payback data provide management with yet another criterion that may be useful in influencing the ultimate decision — "the discounted payback profile." Managerial time preferences may be represented by a minimum acceptable "discounted payback profile" illustrated in Exhibit 3. Note that in this example cumulative discounted cash flows are required to be at least 10%, 30%, 70%, 80%, and 100% of investment outlay at the end of each year, respectively. Note also in Exhibit 3 that the project illustrated in this paper has an acceptable 17%, 40%, 73%, 90%, and 100% "profile" (see Exhibit 1, Column 6, for the source of these percentages). It is acceptable because at the end of each year its cumulative capital recovery rate exceeds management's standard.

The "discounted payback profile" may also be a useful supplemental criterion for deciding between two or more mutually exclusive proposals. Consider, for example, two projects under consideration, only one of which can be undertaken. Each project is expected to attain the 15 per cent minimum acceptable rate of return and maximum five-year discounted payback standards. In fact, according to the best available forecasts, each project will better the minimum standards by comfortable but identical margins. Which project should be selected? The "discounted payback profile" criterion may be instrumental in resolving this question. The "profiles" for the hypothetical projects under consideration are as follows: Project A — 20%, 50%, 75%, 90%, 100%; Project B — 0%, 0%, 10%, 30%, 100%. While both projects have identical net present values and discounted payback periods, Project A can be expected to promote greater liquidity while reducing the magnitude of the time risk. Nonfinancial

EXHIBIT 3
"Discounted Payback Profile"
Standard versus Specific Project

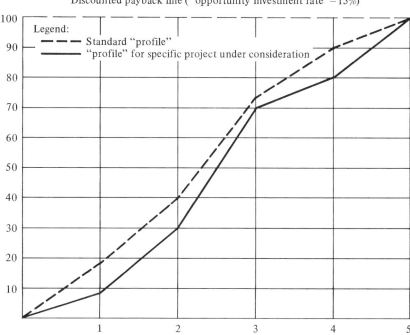

Discounted payback line ("opportunity investment rate"—15%)

Legend:
− − − − Standard "profile"
────── "profile" for specific project under consideration

Periods (years)

factors excluded, the selection of Project A in preference to Project B is indisputable.

The "discounted payback profile" is a simple yet effective means of dealing with the liquidity or time preference problem. The need for such a tool is clearly indicated in Chamberlain's succinct statement regarding the role of management time preferences in capital investment analysis, "A project which gives rise to small returns in the near future, building up very substantially in the more distant future, is discounted at the same objective rate as one which may return larger sums in the near term and virtually nothing later. If their present value is the same, or if their flows discount to the same rate, they are viewed as equally preferable. From the point of view of most businessmen, however, there would in fact be a clear-cut preference for the second investment, which yielded its cash returns more quickly. This is not because they fail out of ignorance to give adequate consideration to the future, but because their own subjective time preference — based on the uncertainty and riskiness of the future — leads them to that result. The economist may question their judgment, but only in the same way he might question consumer tastes. He would be on sounder ground in accepting their time preference and building it into his formulations."[8]

3. The discounted payback criterion is consistent with discounted cash flow profitability measurements, whereas the conventional payback is not. The two principal variations of the discounted cash flow method, discounted rate of return and present value, reflect the time value of money, as does the discounted payback period. Use of the conventional payback in conjunction with one of the discounted cash flow variations results in inconsistent criteria. The integration of these two criteria in a single investment decision is tantamount to denying while simultaneously upholding the time value of money.

4. Discounted payback can easily be integrated with discounted cash flow profitability measurements, particularly the present value approach. In brief, the present value method involves selecting a minimum acceptable rate of return, i.e., the "opportunity investment rate," and discounting both investment outlays and incremental cash flows to the present. If the present value of incremental cash flows exceeds the present value of investment outlays, then the project is rated as potentially acceptable. Under the present value approach some companies compute the "profitability index" for each project as a measure of relative profitability among competing projects. The "profitability index" is simply the ratio of the present value of incremental cash flows to the present value of the required investment outlay.[9]

The hypothetical project presented in Exhibit 1 makes the relationship between discounted payback and the present value approach very evident. In fact, the reader will now note that Exhibit 1 is actually an illustration of the present value approach and its logical by-product, the discounted payback period measurement. The first six figures in Column 6 represent intermediate measures of capital recovery and the final figure, 108.13, the project's "profitability index." The intermediate measurement at the end

---

[8] Chamberlain, *op. cit.,* pp. 274–275.

[9] The discounted rate of return and present value approaches may rank projects with unequal lives differently. This is explained by their differing assumptions regarding the rate of return on cash proceeds reinvested at the end of the shorter project's life. The present value approach assumes that cash proceeds can be reinvested at the discount rate. The discounted rate of return approach makes the implicit assumption that the reinvestment rate is equal to the rate indicated by the project itself. Solomon, *op. cit.,* p. 127, demonstrates that there will always be a consistent ranking of projects if explicit assumptions with respect to reinvestment rates for funds are made up to the terminal date of the longer-lived project. The "profitability index" must be used with great care since under certain circumstances it will yield project rankings that contradict rankings based on the excess present value approach. For an exposition of this problem see William Beranek, "A Note on the Equivalence of Certain Capital Budgeting Criteria," *The Accounting Review,* October, 1964, pp. 914–916.

of the fifth year, 100.05, indicates that at that point the project has broken even in the opportunity sense or that the discounted payback period for this project is just under five years. Companies currently employing the present value approach can calculate the discounted payback period as well as the "profile" with little or no extra effort, and consequently, can use all three criteria to produce a financial plan that balances profitability, liquidity, and time risk.

Organizations wishing to integrate their investment planning and cash forecasting activities may prefer the second method of calculating discounted payback as illustrated in Exhibit 2. In this case, the "profitability index" can be easily calculated from the data present. If Column 3 exceeds Column 4, the project yields less than the "opportunity investment rate" and is therefore unacceptable. If the project is acceptable, the excess of Column 4 terminal value ($287,627) over Column 3 terminal value ($266,000), discounted to the present at the "opportunity investment rate", will yield an amount equal to the excess of the present value of project cash flow over required investment outlay. This calculation is summarized in Exhibit 4. . . .

EXHIBIT 4
Profitability Index Calculation
(Alternative Method)

Terminal value of incremental cash flows reinvested at
"opportunity investment rate" (15%) $287,627

Terminal value of required investment amount ($100,000)
invested at "opportunity investment rate" (15%)   266,000
                                                                       $ 21,627

Present value of $1 to be received at the end of 7 years
and discounted at 15%   .3759

Excess present value $ 8,130

$$\text{"Profitability index"} = \frac{\text{Required investment} + \text{Excess present value}}{\text{Required investment}}$$

$$= \frac{100,000 + 8130}{100,000}$$

$$= 108.13$$

Summary

Despite the fact that the conventional payback criterion is not a measure of profitability, it remains the most commonly employed financial measure of project acceptability. Its popularity is mainly attributable to its simplicity, to the belief among some businessmen that it is futile to project cash flows beyond three or four years, and, finally, to the strong liquidity preferences of many businessmen.

Liquidity and time risk, as well as profitability, are important factors to be incorporated into investment decisions. The conventional payback, however, does not yield a meaningful, reliable measurement of time risk. Its failure can be traced to the fact that it ignores alternative investment opportunities of the firm and, consequently, the time value of money. This results in an underestimate of a project's time risk, i.e., the length of time for which the original capital investment is exposed to economic hazards.

The discounted payback criterion overcomes this basic failure and is a greatly improved measurement of project time risk. The calculation of the discounted payback period also yields a "profile" from which management can incorporate its subjective time preferences into investment decisions. Beyond its measurement virtues, the discounted payback period can be gained at bargain prices for it is an informational by-product of discounted cash flow profitability measurement. Because it is so demonstrably superior to the conventional payback criterion, I believe it should become a widely — and profitably — applied tool in capital investment analysis.

14

"*The Payback Period has been dismissed as mislead-ing and worthless by most writers on capital budget-ing at the same time that businessmen continue to utilize this con-cept. This paper seeks to identify the problems which businessmen try to solve by use of the payback period, so that better tools can be provided for solving these, since neither the present value nor the internal rate of return does so.*

In the course of the analysis the payback concept is considered in its role as a criterion versus a payback constraint, payback and liquidity of capital assets and the liquidity requirements of the firm, payback as a break-even concept, and payback as a crude measure of the rate of resolution of uncertainty. While payback is not advo-cated for capital investment decisions, the reasons for its popularity need to be understood before it is possible to develop superior alternatives."

Some New Views on the Payback Period and Capital Budgeting Decisions*

While academic writers have almost unanimously condemned use of the Payback Period in capital budgeting, it continues to be one of the most

* *From* Management Science, *Vol. 15, No. 12 (August, 1969), pp. B594–607. Reprinted by permission of the editor.*

† Motivation for this paper was provided by some stimulating discussions with W. W. Cooper whose agreement with what follows must not be assumed. Myron Gordon, Michael Jensen and Merton Miller made helpful comments on an earlier draft. It was presented as an Invited Paper at the TIMS/ORSA Meeting in San Francisco on May 2, 1968.

widely applied quantitative concepts in making investment decisions.[1] It must be conceded that the payback period, i.e., the time it is expected for an investment project to recoup its initial cost, is hardly a tool which can provide the decision maker with all the information he needs. As most text-books correctly point out, the time value of money via discounting of future cash flows never enters into its calculation. Nevertheless, a serious question must be raised and answered: why is the payback period so ubiquitously used, despite its universal critics? It may be the case that the problem which managers are seeking to solve by use of payback is not, in fact, handled by the tools many text-book writers espouse.

This paper seeks to provide a better understanding of the capital investment problem by carefully analyzing the payback concept. Given the complexity of the problem of capital investment decisions and our state of knowledge with respect to the economic, psychological and organizational bases for current practice, it must be admitted that what follows should more properly be labeled as a set of conjectures. Although the plausibility of the arguments will be supported wherever possible, the objective here is to widen the perspective within which much of the discussion of investment decision methods takes place. By following an encyclopedic approach in the paper, it should not be assumed that all or even most of the suggested rationales for the use of payback are operative at the same time, or within the same individuals, parts of the organization or even firms. Rather, it is suggested that all of them are considerations at one time or another, and that the variety of problems which the payback concept attacks helps to reinforce the appeal which businessmen profess for this measure of investment value.[2] In the course of the analysis which follows we shall discuss payback as a criterion versus payback as a constraint, liquidity of capital assets versus liquidity requirements of the firm, payback as a break-even concept and finally, payback and the resolution of uncertainty.

One point should be emphasized at the outset. *We shall not end by rehabilitating payback,* for more sophisticated and precise methods are available or can be developed to deal with the issues to be raised below. Hopefully, however, we shall have learned something about the nature of the investment problem and encouraged development of alternatives.

---

[1] See for example, [12]. For some views different to those presented here, see also [19], Chapter 9. It is also interesting to observe that numbers of companies which utilize sophisticated computer programs for the evaluation of capital investments have written payback into them in one form or another.

[2] The response which private circulation of this paper has generated so far, and it was surprisingly large, has been in the form of enthusiasm from businessmen, but much less agreement from academic colleagues. While opinion sampling cannot be used to establish the truth or falsehood of a set of arguments, the fairly clear-cut division between types of respondents here is particularly interesting in that the paper's contention is that the problem which businessmen face is generally oversimplified by academic writers. Should this paper persuade some of the academicians to broaden their view of the problem, I will regard it as having served its purpose.

One disclaimer seems appropriate at the outset. In seeking to analyze the capital investment decision within firms, one ought to include also a variety of aspects whose origin lies entirely within the organizational process of decision making. On the descriptive side, this would include preparation of the underlying data for a project, its review at higher levels, etc. These considerations will not be our concern here. Nevertheless, it would be useful to point out the immense difference between a single figure of merit which is attached to a proposed project for purposes of *communication* as opposed to use of that same figure as the *sole basis* for making the accept/reject decision. At various levels of the organization a hierarchy of different considerations is brought to bear on the problem, while other aspects are presumed to have been dealt with before a proposal has reached that stage.[3] The need to communicate explicit information between groups and levels is a function of the nature of the organization and its past. When a single figure of merit is cited as being "used" by a firm in its capital investment process, as for example, the Istvan study [12] reveals, care must be taken to distinguish its use as a communications device from its application as a decision criterion. While these remarks apply to all the common text-book criteria for capital budgeting decisions, they apply with special emphasis to the payback period.

Payback as a Criterion Versus Payback as a Constraint

Some writers, notably Gordon [10], have interpreted the payback period as an indirect though quick measure of return.[4] Given a uniform stream of receipts, the reciprocal of the payback period is the discounted cash-flow rate-of-return for a project of infinite life, or a good approximation to this rate for a long-lived project. Alternatively, using annuity tables one can translate the payback period directly into the correct rate of return given the project life, again if the inflows are uniform during this life.[5]

When the scale of the investment is itself a decision variable, the above interpretation of payback has also erroneously led to its advocacy as a criterion for optimization. We refer once more to investments of the "point-input, stream-output" type, and assume a perpetual stream of receipts whose level is a function of the amount of investment, exhibiting the usual property

---

[3] An example would be the use, explicit or implicit, of a discount rate in the *design* of a project, usually encompassed in what is called engineering economics, and the subsequent use of a different discount rate in the evaluation of the merit of that project.

[4] The conclusions of Gordon are arrived at more rigorously and also generalized by V. L. Smith in [19], pp. 220–224.

[5] The Present Value of an annuity of $1 per period for n periods at an interest rate r, is given by $V(r) = (1/r) [1 - (1 + r)^{-n}]$. To find the rate r one enters the annuity tables on the line for the correct number of years, n, and seeks the value of the project's outlay/annual inflow. The interest rate where this is found is the internal or discounted-cash-flow rate-of-return.

of decreasing returns to scale. Under these assumptions, the scale of investment which maximizes the internal rate of return also minimizes the payback period.[6] Unfortunately, maximization of the internal rate of return is not an appropriate criterion. As discussed already some time ago in the debate between Boulding and Samuelson ([5] and [18]), the scale must be decided upon by reference to economic variables external to the investment, viz., the interest rate. For present purposes this implies that the optimal scale is achieved by maximization of the net present value, and is given by the point at which the marginal rate of return equals the interest rate. This, in turn, is equivalent to the point at which the payback period is equal to the reciprocal of "the interest rate" or cost of capital.[7]

Before income taxes played an important role in investment decisions, one also could see a direct similarity between the payback period and the price/earnings ratio. Taking once more a uniform stream of receipts as the first approximation for an investment project, the ratio of cost to annual receipts, which is the payback period, is of the same form as the price to earnings per share multiple for common stock. Projecting earnings to be uniform for the foreseeable future, one may interpret P/E for a company's stock as a payback period, or, alternatively, the payback period may be regarded as the project's cost expressed as a multiple of earnings (receipts). Judgement as to whether specific numerical values associated with particular alternatives are "reasonable" or desirable is made in the same way, though obviously with different numerical standards.

Such use of payback as a figure of merit may describe business practice during the last century and perhaps the early decades of the present one. It is, however, difficult to believe that these plausible reasons plus a general cultural lag explain this tool's still-current popularity. Careful consideration of the effect of taxes and depreciation rules requires distinguishing between cash flows and the more general earnings concept represented in the firm's income statement.

It is not clear that payback is used as a direct figure of merit, i.e., that it is applied to choose that project among mutually exclusive alternatives which minimizes the payback period. It *is* often (and perhaps more properly) used as a constraint: no project may be accepted unless its payback period is shorter than some specified period of time.[8] Furthermore,

---

[6] See, for example, Lutz and Lutz [14]. So long as the internal rate of return is the payback reciprocal, maximization of the rate of return is equivalent to minimization of payback.

[7] See also [14], [19] and [24].

[8] Charnes, Cooper, Devoe and Learner [7] and Byrne, Charnes, Cooper, and Kortanek [6] emphasized this difference. It also follows from selection of the optimal scale of the investment. One can translate the criterion of maximizing the net present value into expanding the scale of the investment up to the point at which its marginal rate of return is equal to the interest rate, or until the payback period is below the reciprocal of the interest rate. In this fashion, payback is also more appropriately regarded as a constraint on the acceptability of an investment, rather than as a figure of merit to be optimized. See also Smith [19].

not all projects satisfying the payback constraint are automatically accepted. They must satisfy *additional* criteria as well.[9] The foremost among these, as the writer has pointed out elsewhere ([22] and [23]), concerns the interrelationships which exist between projects because of the use they make of resources that are of limited supply in the short run such as, especially, managerial manpower. Handling such problems formally requires sophisticated methods, as discussed in the references cited.

Assuming that the desirability of projects is judged on an individual project basis, perhaps by application of an appropriate discounted cash flow (DCF) measure, the question we wish to answer is, what does the payback period tell? To answer requires taking a step backward and glancing briefly at the framework of certainty within which the common DCF criteria are usually derived.

Under the assumption of certainty and perfect capital markets, the investor may be shown to be better off whenever he commits his funds to an undertaking which yields a positive net present value after allowance for all costs. The discount rate or rates which are applied to the venture's cash flows are also the market determined trade-offs between present and future consumption, which allows the investor to choose the timing of his consumption independently of the timing of his investment. Under conditions of uncertainty, the cash flows generated by the investment as well as all other claims the investor has on future benefits are subject to random fluctuations. The appropriate discount rates themselves are uncertain and these rates might be expected to change due not only to changes in market rates for risky investments, but also because the uncertainty of the cash flows of the particular investment most probably will change over its life. It is the latter notions that need to be unravelled to make sense out of the payback period.

There is one other item in the theoretical ancestry of DCF analyses which needs to be raised in these preliminaries. Basically, it is that capital goods of which economists traditionally speak are assumed to have a market value reasonably close to their depreciated cost, so that investment is essentially a reversible process.[10] Accordingly, at any time a firm finds

[9] Even when payback is cited as the sole quantitative concept applied to investment decisions, it does not follow that desirability is expressed in qualitative terms such as "strategic" value, while payback is utilized in the form of a constraint as just described. Reading of much of the literature would lead one to believe that investment decisions should always be made on the basis of some single figure of merit, such as the present value or the discounted cash flow rate of return. When the decision is placed into its organizational setting, it should become clear that no single number can answer all the questions which need to be raised concerning the commitment of the firm's resources. For additional reasons for rejecting a single number criterion see [25]. A referee for this paper has also pointed out that in optimizations involving multiple criteria any subset of them can be regarded as constraints.

[10] The definition of reversibility used here is that of Tobin ([21], Chapter 2, p. 8). "By the reversibility [as distinct from liquidity] of an asset is meant the value of the asset to its holder expressed as a percentage of its contemporaneous cost to a buyer. For a perfectly reversible asset, this percentage would be 100%, indicating that a seller could realize in cash all that it costs a buyer to acquire the asset."

changed conditions which indicate future profitability of some investments to be impaired, the firm is assumed to be able to sell the assets at prices which, while affected by these new conditions, nevertheless are not too far from original cost less allowance for wear and obsolescence. (Put in different terms, the return to capital called rent in such a situation is at most a minor component of the total return. While this model may hold for reasonably competitive industries, firms which make careful evaluations of their capital expenditures generally believe that they face falling demand curves, in which environment selecting the best level of output in the short run and capacity in the long run are among the most important managerial problems, along with choice of the best production function.)

If the investment implies potentially substantial returns to the combination of managerial or entrepreneurial skill in the form of marketing, production or other know-how; or, alternatively, if it requires substantial non-recoverable outlays such as for site preparation, etc., the "going concern value" of the assets of the project far exceeds their market value at all times of the project's existence. Such an investment does not fit the model of completely reversible investment implied, for example, in the writing of Fisher who derived the optimality of the yield or internal rate of return criterion for investment analysis.[11]

It is the case that common, though incomplete analysis of investment projects using the present value criterion is subject to the myopia problem. That is, a project usually has as one alternative its own postponement, with consequential changes in payoffs and costs. When measured from the present it is by no means always true that the highest discounted value is associated with the earliest starting date.[12] Application of the present value criterion here, viz., the selection of that project which has the highest net present value from among the set of mutually exclusive alternatives, would still be appropriate within this framework.

The imposition of constraints on capital expenditures invalidates the present value apparatus, as has been discussed in detail in [22] and especially in [2] and [25]. That is, when the expenditure of funds on capital projects has been limited to an amount not explicitly based on the investment opportunities, it is no longer true that the present value criterion satisfies a more basic objective of investment in terms of the investor's utility and consumption possibilities.[13] Here the myopic problem of constructing an investment

[11] See Irving Fisher [9]. Recent writers have brought out the importance of re-versibility assumption. See for example S. Marglin [16], and K. J. Arrow [1], and their discussion of the "Myopia Rule" for investment. It should be noted that reversibility and irreversibility are meaningful notions under certainty, being the result, primarily, of economies of scale or of less than perfect competition.

[12] For this reason the literature, as well as company practice, often refers to an "urgency rating" associated with projects.

[13] Of course, it need not be empirically true that firms *set* ceilings without regard to their opportunities for employing funds. It is nevertheless the case that once budgets have been set within a firm, those subject to the budget limitation are required to make choices among alternatives while staying within the expenditure ceiling.

project too early becomes more important in that the timing of expenditures and revenues requires internal valuation, e.g., in terms of the alternatives they open up and/or foreclose because of the capital constraints. In either of these instances the payback period contains information (in the form of a single number) regarding the timing of the inflows, which could be a warning against early commitment of funds if without its use the only choice evaluated is to accept the project now or not-at-all.

Payback and Liquidity

One consequence of insisting that each proposed investment have a short payback period is that, in some sense, the investments made are relatively "liquid."[14] Deferring more careful analysis of this statement for a moment, it would seem to imply that this early repayment of the invested funds is desirable in and of itself, specifically apart from the desirability measured by some DCF figure of merit. In the paper [6] referred to earlier, Byrne, et al, regard a low payback period as a way of minimizing "lost opportunity risk" so that the investor can assure himself of being restored to his initial position within a short span of time in order to be able to take advantage of additional, perhaps better investment possibilities that may come along.[15] Payback as utilized in the cited paper is applied as a constraint across all investment opportunities simultaneously, and not on a project-by-project basis, and also in a probabilistic way. Its advocacy and use there does represent a substantial departure from other recent writing.

This use of payback does raise some question about traditional project evaluation. For one thing, the investment opportunities which would have to be foregone were it not for the funds generated by the new projects, as implied there, are usually assumed to have been evaluated using an appropriate discounting rate or its equivalent. That is, if the cost of capital has been estimated, and the prospective investment yields a positive net present value after discounting at this rate, then, presumably, future investments offering a positive present value will still be available: they will yield more than they cost in terms of the combination of debt and equity capital and retained earnings which will be required to finance them. When this is not the case one might presume that either the cost of capital had changed *as a result* of making the investments, in which instance this change should have been anticipated and taken into account in the computation of present values currently. Alternatively, the particular liquidity requirement of

---

[14] Following the definitions of Tobin [21] once more, one would not want to characterize investments as liquid or illiquid. The question is not whether a long time is required to realize the value of the asset when it is for sale, but rather whether the asset yields its value in the form of product quickly or after some time.

[15] [6], p. 3.

Byrne, et al, implies that the concept of the cost of capital as the cost of foregone investment opportunities is not well defined.[16]

Put somewhat differently, the assumption of competitive capital markets, plus, perhaps the assumption that the expectations of the capital market regarding the firm's new investment are substantially the same as those of the managers of the firm itself, would guarantee that future opportunities must not be foregone for lack of funds. Additionally, growth by *internally* generated funds is by no means the only path for rapid growth. It would seem, therefore, that in this use of payback the motive of providing for the internal generation of funds from investments for future, as yet undetermined, additional investment is based more on an implicit or explicit spending limit than on an explicit limitation of risk. More directly, the usually designated speculative and/or precautionary motive of firms to hold liquid or near liquid funds[17] in order to seize upon unexpected opportunities is a *different* motive from that which requires each new investment separately to recover its original cost within a short time. Unless we assume that firms cannot plan for the generation of funds from operations generally, and from the investment program taken as a whole, we are forced to conclude that use of payback by Byrne, et al, is for purposes different from those related to an individual project payback constraint.

Payback as a Break-Even Concept

The payback period appears to be one of a common type of break-even notions frequently employed by businessmen. Generally, the break-even point is a point of indifference — with qualifications — beyond which an accounting profit is expected to be generated by the operation under analysis, and below which loss is expected. The qualifications come from use of accounting profit rather than some more meaningful economic measure which would attach a cost to the use of funds and to the application of managerial effort.

Once again, under certainty there is no significance to the break-even point. Under uncertainty, estimation of the break-even point serves to reduce the information search for resolving choices in allocation problems. The risk against which the profit potential is to be evaluated is the risk that the firm will not be "made whole again" as a result of undertaking some operation. The fact that this standard for comparison, the firm as it was before, is not the correct measure of foregone opportunities serves only to point out that the break-even measure is an oversimplification.[18]

---

[16] This question will be followed-up in a subsequent paper.

[17] See, for example, [8].

[18] Indeed, the break-even point may be primarily a tool for suboptimization by managers with asymmetric penalty functions between failing to act vs. failing by acting. See, for example, [15].

Indeed, some writers suggest that the payback period should be computed to include not only recovery of the original outlays, but also the foregone interest on the amount of capital committed to the project. Doing so would, to some degree, give expression to the requirement that under normal circumstances the firm would not stand still but would earn some "normal" rate of return. However, the essential differences between the ordinary cost-volume break-even point and the payback period as a break-even point must also be considered.

In the usual break-even analysis, the evaluation made implicitly concerns the chances that the firm would incur a loss as opposed to the chances that the particular undertaking would result in gains of varying amounts. Viewing the decision from the point of view of the decision maker, the asymmetry between payoffs and penalties can, to a first approximation, be represented

Success Failure

	Success	Failure
Accept	$+$	$-$
Reject	0	0

by a two-by-two payoff matrix which divides the world into two states, Success and Failure, and two actions, Accept the project and Reject it, as in the figure. Assuming that similar choices must be made with sufficient frequency so that *some* projects are likely to be accepted, the rejection of a particular one by the decision maker is probably neutral.

If degree of success is a refinement which plays a role secondary to the *counting* of successes in the evaluation of a manager's performance, his initial view of the decision as having two outcomes *for him* (in contrast to the outcomes for the firm) makes some sense. The question of interest then is the meaningful line of separation between Success and Failure.

The least ambiguous, even if not the most appropriate, dividing line, as already discussed, is whether the firm is ahead or not by doing the project.[19] It is not necessary to suggest that decision makers accept a minimax strategy with respect to such decisions. It is probably sufficient to say that unless the probability of "at least breaking even" is sufficient, the decision maker is likely to reject the project. Such a procedure appears to be a crude substitute for a computation which goes beyond merely the *expected* profit (in the statistical sense) to a consideration of some aspects of the *distribution* of outcomes and their consequences for the decision maker. In such a simplified short-cut procedure, the means of judging the distribution are

---

[19] It must be readily admitted that *ex post* it is seldom simple to prove that any single activity of a firm is "losing money."

combined with the measure itself. This is intended to take the place of a much more elaborate, if correct, two-step procedure in which the distribution is first generated, then evaluated.[20] The probability of failing to reach at least the break-even point (the area under the density of outcomes up to a zero accounting profit), is compared with the probability of making a profit (the area to the right of the break-even point).

By contrast, the payback period is a point in *time* at which the firm expects "to be made whole again" (except for foregone interest) after making an investment. When the life of the project's stream of revenues is subject to substantial uncertainty, the payback period focuses on the period of time over which the project is expected to generate a "profit." That is, assuming for simplicity that net revenues are constant through time and only the project's life is a random variable, the aggregate (undiscounted, i.e., accounting) profit is proportional to the life of the project after the payback period has elapsed. Prior to then the stream of net revenues has been used to offset the original cost.[21]

A measure of undiscounted profit is then the project life after the payback period, and the conditional probability distribution of the project's life, given that it has reached the payback period, becomes a measure of the distribution of project profitability. In the same sense as for break-even analyses in general, the decision maker then is presumed to weigh the probability that the project's life lasts longer than its payback period to make it worthwhile for him. For a given distribution of project lives, under the assumption of uniform flows, the longer the payback period the greater are the chances of incurring an accounting loss on the project. However, a short payback period would mean a higher probability of profit, and hence the project would be more attractive.

One additional observation seems still to be in order. The shorter the payback period, given the Net Present Value (or internal rate of return) of the project, the sooner its profitability would become known.[22] A manager

---

[20] On this see also the "Plumber's daughter" in the address by Ronald Howard [11].

[21] The proportionality is only approximate because of the depreciation expense deduction for reporting profit. The effect of taxes has also been ignored here. Project life, unfortunately, enters here in two distinct ways. Aside from the above remarks that profitability depends on the project's life (especially after payback), accounting profit depends also on the rate at which depreciation expense is charged against the project's revenues. Thus a longer anticipated life yields a higher initial profit, other things remaining equal, because depreciation expense will be lower. Indeed, the life of the project may be overestimated by the proposer not only to enchance its total profitability, but also to reduce the payback period on the accounting profit basis. A bias countering this one may arise in the selection of the shortest project or asset life which the tax authorities permit to improve the actual after-tax cash-flow profitability. Cash-flow payback, the usual concept, is less affected since depreciation enters only as a tax shield. (The above qualifications to the statement in the text were suggested by Sidney Davidson.)

[22] Given the net present value, a short payback period implies that early cash flows are expected to be high relative to later ones, and/or to the investment. Actually, of course, neither cash flows nor accounting profit will be easily attributable to a given project, and initial accounting profit may, in any case, be a loss due to heavy initial depreciation expense.

therefore could also reasonably expect that his wise decision would show up early enough for the rewards (e.g., in the form of a bonus or advancement) to be received when they will still do him some good, given his high personal rate of discount. If the forecast turns out, ex post, to have been too optimistic after a number of years have elapsed, the possibility for alibi in the form of higher future returns yet to come is not lost, a circumstance which makes risk and reward in this situation once more asymmetric for the manager.

Stability of the Payback Measure

An interesting observation regarding the payback period may also reinforce the basis for some of its appeal. This concerns its relative stability under random variation in the cash flows. Projection of cash flows is, at best, an imprecise art, and the ex post results are unlikely to have been included among the projections made in advance. The correctness of the decision will be somewhat more easily assessed after the fact, since the outcomes will have turned out to have been favorable or not when compared against alternatives thought to have been available. Hence the ex ante measure of project worth should be "robust", in analogous fashion to the concept as used by statisticians. The internal rate of return, for example, is quite sensitive to variation in the underlying cash flows, as was demonstrated numerically in [20]. By contrast if it is possible to generalize from results which use the simplifying assumptions analogous to those made earlier, the payback period appears to be relatively constant.

To illustrate, we assume that net revenue is normally distributed at each moment in time, with constant expectation and constant variance over time. Under these assumptions the probability distribution of the payback period can be obtained from the following expression:[23]

$$f(T) = \frac{I}{T} \frac{1}{(2\pi kT)^{\frac{1}{2}}} \exp\left[-(I - cT)^2/2kT\right]$$

where I is the initial investment, $c(t) = c$ is the uniform stream of net revenues, with variance $\sigma^2(t) = k$, and T is the payback period.

A few sample computations have been carried out using this formula, and the results are presented in the table . . . (on the following page). In the examples the amount invested, I, was assumed to be $10. The expected cash inflow, c, assumed to be received continuously, has an expected value of $4 per year, with three different values of the variance, k: 1, 2, and 5. The table gives six points on the right-tail cumulative distribution of payback periods for each of the three values of cash-flow variance, from the ten per cent point to the 95 per cent point.

---

[23] See [13], p. 1007.

Table of Payback Periods (in Years) Exceeded with Probability P,
for Three Values of Cash Flow Variance k, Given Investment 1 = 10,
Average Annual Cash Flow
c = 4

P	k		
	1	2	5
.05	3¼	3½	4¼
.10	3	3¼	3¾
.33	2¾ −	2¾ −	2¾
.50	2½	2½	2½
.67	2¼ +	2¼ −	2
.90	2	1¾	1½

The expected payback period of 2½ years appears for each of the values of k, the variance, in the row indicated by $P = 0.50$; i.e., fifty per cent of the time one would expect the mean value of $T = 2½$ years to be exceeded, while the other half of the time it would not be expected to be this high. Approximately one third of the time the payback period here would be as high as 2¾ years or higher, and this quantity is about the same for all three values of cash flow variance. Ten per cent of the time it would be as large as three years when the variance is one, 3¼ years when the variance is two, but 3¾ years when the variance is as high as five.

Payback and the Resolution of Uncertainty

In addition to the fact that the return on capital investment projects includes substantial rewards for good management of the project and related activities (economic rent), capital investments differ in the course of action afforded to those making the investment in contrast to the alternatives facing investors in other assets. To bring the differences into sharp relief it may be useful to compare "investments" or gambles at a roulette table, investments in bonds and stocks which are traded in a market, and capital investments.

Gambles on a roulette wheel have the characteristic that, once the wheel stops spinning the payoff has been determined and settlement is made. The outcome of subsequent spins is (presumed to be) independent of earlier outcomes. Also, the bettor's wealth has already been determined at the end of a spin, and in making his next bet he can take his new wealth position into account. Put more directly, the bets are made sequentially with the state of information the same at the beginning of each bet.

An investor purchasing marketable securities is essentially in the same position as the gambler at the roulette table. At any moment in time his decision to leave funds in an investment may be interpreted to be a reinvestment of the funds which the market value of his securities represents. The fact that the variability of outcomes is smaller for shorter intervals of time than for longer ones is unimportant here. The only significant discontinuities in this investment-disinvestment decision process are introduced by brokerage costs which are avoidable by leaving funds invested in the same securities. Another, though minor qualification, is that outcomes are not precisely known until the decision to liquidate the investment is actually carried out.[24] However, since a market price is quoted at all times, an investor knows his wealth position with only a small degree of uncertainty and can take this into account in making decisions with respect to the continued commitment of his funds. Additionally, the decision to make the commitment does not affect the outcome in a noticeable way. Given a reasonably broad market, an individual investor's decision to make a transaction does not affect the price of the security more than trivially. Thus it is not surprising that no one computes a payback period for, say, a bond, which is expected to generate a known income stream when held to maturity.

An extreme contrast with the preceding situations would be an investment in a space flight which is expected to last several years, and which is expected to bring back valuable objects from another planet. The space ship is presumed to be the first of its kind, and to be on a mission the scope of which had never before been attempted. It is assumed to be unable to communicate with the earth (or its outposts) during almost the entire duration of its voyage. Thus the outcome of the investment will not be known until some substantial time after the original commitment of funds, and little if any additional information is assumed to be generated in the interval to alter the subjective probabilities of the recovery of the space craft, or its success in bringing back the valuable cargo.

Under these rather extreme assumptions[25] the investor in this venture has tied up some of his capital for a potentially long time, with the interval to the time when the returns come in being itself a random variable. To analyze the investor's attitude to such an investment, we see that it can be broken down into two distinct components which, in turn, may be clarified by referring back to the roulette wheel.

First, suppose that the investor could place a bet today on one of two roulette wheels, the first being spun today, while the second is not spun until one year from today. If the odds were the same for the two wheels, a risk-averting bettor would prefer the first wheel to the second, assuming only that the availability of gambles next year is not expected to be curtailed or

---

[24] Even on securities listed on the New York Stock Exchange a stop-loss order becomes a market order when certain conditions are met, and the investor is not *guaranteed* a stipulated price.

[25] See also [3] for a related example.

yield less favorable odds. (It is important that in either case the bet is made today, and the chips are paid for today.) Reasons for preferring the present over the deferred payoff would include a) the bettor might not be alive next year, and his utility for a bequest may not be the same as his utility for consumption while alive; b) until the outcome is known, the bettor's wealth is uncertain and he cannot adjust to the preferred consumption based on his wealth *during* the year with the second wheel; and c) even if the gamble is for an objective in the distant future, e.g., retirement, by repeating similar gambles to the first wheel, the bettor can achieve the same expected payoff, but with a lower variance of payoff.[26] Selection of the second wheel would generally require more favorable odds.

Suppose now alternatively that the first wheel is still one which is spun today, but that a third wheel, physically identical to the second one, is not spun until some randomly selected time interval has passed, as might be determined by an auxiliary process. If the *expected* outcome of the auxiliary process, which determines the timing of the spin of the third wheel, were exactly one year, would the investor be indifferent between this deferred spin or the earlier one (the second wheel) for which the spin is slated to take place one year from now? Most likely not. Obviously, the nature of the auxiliary process would enter into the choice between the second and the third wheel.

The space venture resembles the third wheel here, since both the payoff and its timing are uncertain. The investor's consumption decisions until the return of the space craft are constrained in the following sense. The investor may be able to sell some or all of his shares in the venture, and, indeed, a market for them may exist. Prices for the shares may fluctuate in response to changes in expectations regarding the final outcome, its timing as well as its amount. For any given set of expectations regarding the amount of payoff, the elapse of time would presumably result in an increase in the price of the shares since the actual payoff is then closer.[27]

Alternative to selling his shares, the investor may prefer to borrow against them. While he could always lever himself generally, by pledging his other assets or earning power against a loan, the shares themselves do not lend themselves to bank borrowing in the form of the common demand note with the shares as collateral. From the nature of the probability distribution of outcomes facing the *lender,* the latter would find himself in a position with more than trivial risk. Of course, such a risk may fit the portfolio of some lenders, so that at some high enough rate of interest (contingent upon there being a payoff at all) the lender would advance

---

[26] These results are developed rigorously in a forthcoming paper.

[27] My colleague Myron Gordon steered me away from the incorrect conclusions implied by the results of Robichek and Myers in [17] which would be that the values of the shares, given constant expectations, would rise at the pure (i.e., riskless) rate of interest.

some or all of the required funds.[28] To make a loan attractive to both borrower and lender requires their utility functions to be of different shape, assuming that their expectations of the outcome are the same and the composition of their portfolios is otherwise similar. The size of the residual risk, however, precludes banks operating with the funds supplied by depositors from making loans of this type.[29]

In the preceding example the uncertainty arising from the delayed knowledge of the outcome is resolved all at once, at the end of the venture. The only time of relevance is the interval until the voyage is over. Capital investment projects of the ordinary kind represent a situation between the simple roulette wheel or security and the space venture with respect to the resolution of uncertainty. Cash flows are projected at the time the investment is first contemplated, and at least implicitly, the cash flows are considered to be subject to random deviation from their expected values. As time passes and some of the anticipated cash flows are realized, information is generated thereby as to the subsequent outcomes of the whole project. Each time such information is received, the "investor" may take any corrective managerial action he deems necessary to realize his expectations. For example, he may commit additional resources in the form of advertising, further product or process development, and especially assign additional or different managerial supervision to the project. More important, however, he is in a better position to make decisions with respect to his current consumption and with respect to other investment alternatives which present themselves. Thus the evolving information on the project's outcome is extremely valuable to him for making subsequent decisions.[30]

A natural scaling of the importance of the information content of the initial cash inflows might be the size of the original commitment of funds. In looking at the investment entirely *ex ante,* the rate at which the uncertainty devolving around the outcome is expected to be resolved may be measured, at least crudely, by the relation between the series of cumulated expected cash inflows and the amount of the investment. In terms of a standardized measure, the time interval required for the cumulated expected

[28] The detailed development of these arguments parallel fairly closely those contained in a forthcoming paper by Karl Borch [4] which came to my attention while this paper was being revised. They will therefore be omitted.

[29] An analogy would be the position of an individual expecting a potentially large legacy: The legator may change his will, he may outlive his heir (with a substitute heir and not the original heir's estate), or the legator may lose his fortune. In all these events the individual gets nothing or substantially less than expected. Based on these prospects, would a commercial bank lend him any funds? Clearly the bank's position would be different if the property were held in trust for him or for his estate.

[30] To the extent that motivations of potentially mobile managers differ from those of the firm, managers would choose projects for which the wisdom of their choices is *expected* to be revealed early, as was discussed before.

inflows exactly to equal the original investment is a measure of the rate at which the project's uncertainty is *expected* to be resolved. But this measure is precisely the Payback Period.

Conclusion

In this review of different ways in which the payback period can be interpreted, we have seen that only the first, the payback reciprocal as a measure of the rate of return of a project, had significance in the context of certainty. Even with this interpretation it is more appropriate to regard payback as a constraint which a project must satisfy than as a criterion which is to be optimized. The use of payback as a measure of the "liquidity" of an asset, essentially as the reciprocal of the capital turnover ratio, but computed separately for each proposed project, was found to be substantially different from a liquidity requirement for the firm as a whole.

Payback was seen to imply a form of break-even analysis, which makes no sense in a world of certainty, but which can function like many other "rules of thumb" to shortcut the process of generating information and then evaluating it. Thus it was shown that payback reduces the information search by focussing on that time at which the firm expects to "be made whole again" in some sense, and hence it allows the decision maker to judge whether the life of the project past the break-even point is sufficient to make the undertaking worthwhile. The fact that this break-even notion is both naive and incorrect does not alter the fact of its use in the absence of other simple measures which serve the same purpose. To this must be added the appeal of payback for the decision maker, rather than for his firm, in that it indicates how rapidly he can expect confirmation that he has made a good choice, and for which he can expect to benefit personally.

Finally, the paper discussed some of the inherent differences between financial investments and investments in capital projects by firms. While the choice of the investor in the former case revolves purely around the decision to withdraw the funds from an investment or to leave them, the situation is different with investments in physical assets. Not only is the market value of the assets substantially below the "going concern" value of the project at almost all times during the life of the project, but the range of alternatives available with respect to the project are quite different. Additional resources can be committed to alter the outcome of a project after it has been initiated, or less funds can be devoted to it than was originally contemplated. The randomness of both the size and timing of the outcomes themselves focus on the financial restrictions within which the firm is forced to operate. For both these reasons, information of a certain kind is extremely important to the decision maker. This is the rate at which he can expect the uncertainty devolving around a project to be resolved. While once more no single number can convey the necessary information, the payback period does provide some idea of the relevant data. As the detailed discussion above makes abundantly clear, the payback concept is an oversimplification in each case. However, the problems which managers seek to attack by its use will not disappear simply by arguing that payback is not meaningful. Rather, it is necessary to face up to these problems, and to employ methods which solve them.

References

1. Arrow, Kenneth J., "Optimal Capital Policy with Irreversible Investment," Stanford University Institute for Mathematical Studies in the Social Sciences, Technical Report No. 146, December 14, 1966.

2. Baumol, W. J., and Quandt, R. E., "Mathematical Programming and the Discount Rate Under Capital Rationing," *Economic Journal* (June 1965), pp. 317–329.

3. Boness, A. James, "A Pedagogic Note on the Cost of Capital," *Journal of Finance* (March 1964), pp. 99–106.

4. Borch, Karl, "Equilibrium, Optimum and Prejudices in Capital Markets," *Journal of Financial and Quantitative Analysis* (forthcoming).

5. Boulding, Kenneth, "The Theory of a Single Investment," *Quarterly Journal of Economics* (May 1935), pp. 475–494.

6. Byrne, R., Charnes, A., Cooper, W. W., and Kortanek, K., "A Chance Constrained Approach to Capital Budgeting with Portfolio Type Payback and Liquidity Constraints," *Journal of Financial and Quantitative Analysis* (December 1967), pp. 339–364.

7. Charnes, A., Cooper, W. W., Devoe, J. K., and Learner, D. B., "DEMON: Decision Mapping via Optimum Go-No-Go Networks," *Management Science,* Vol. 12, No. 11 (July 1966), pp. 865–887.

8. Duesenberry, James S., "The Portfolio Approach to the Demand for Money and other Assets," *Review of Economics and Statistics,* Vol. 45, Supplement (February 1963).

9. Fisher, Irving, *The Theory of Interest,* Reprints of Economic Classics, Augustus Kelly, New York, 1961.

10. Gordon, Myron J., "The Payoff Period and the Rate of Profit," *Journal of Business* (October 1955), pp. 253–261.

11. Howard, Ronald, "The Practicality Gap," *Management Science,* Vol. 14, No. 7 (March 1968), pp. 503–507.

12. Istvan, Donald F., *Capital-Expenditure Decisions: How They Are Made,* Bureau of Business Research, Indiana University, Bloomington, Ind. 1961.

13. Keilson, Julian, "The First Passage Time Density for Homogeneous Skip-Free Walks on the Continuium," *Annals of Mathematical Statistics,* (September 1963), pp. 1003–1011.

14. Lutz, F. and Lutz, V., *The Theory of Investment of the Firm*, Princeton University Press, Princeton, N.J., 1951.

15. Mansefield, E. and Wein, H., "A Study of Decision-Making Within the Firm", *Quarterly Journal of Economics* (November 1958), pp. 515–536.

16. Marglin, Steven, *Approaches to Dynamic Investment Planning*, North-Holland, Amsterdam, 1963.

17. Robichek, A. and Myers, S., "Risk Adjusted Discount Rates", *Journal of Finance* (December 1966), pp. 727–730.

18. Samuelson, Paul A., "Some Aspects of the Pure Theory of Capital," *Quarterly Journal of Economics* (May 1936), pp. 469–496.

19. Smith, Vernon L., *Investment and Production*, Harvard University Press, Cambridge, Mass., 1961.

20. Solomon, Martin B., Jr., "Uncertainty and Its Effects on Capital Investment Analysis," *Management Science*, Vol. 12, No. 8, (April 1966), pp. B334–339.

21. Tobin, James, Unpublished (but widely circulated) manuscript, 1959, Chapter 2.

22. Weingartner, H. Martin, *Mathematical Programming and the Analysis of Capital Budgeting Problems*, Prentice-Hall, Inc., Englewood Cliffs, N.J., 1963, reissued by Markham Publishing Company, Chicago, 1967.

23. ———, "Capital Budgeting of Interrelated Projects," *Management Science*, Vol. 12, No. 7 (March 1966), pp. 485–516, reprinted in the Markham edition of [22].

24. ———, "Equipment Replacement Analysis: A Note on the Optimum Investment Period," *Industrial Management Review*, (Fall 1965), pp. 47–51.

25. ———, "Criteria for Programming Investment Project Selection," *Journal of Industrial Economics*, Vol. 15, No. 1 (November 1966), pp. 65–76, reprinted in the Markham edition of [22].

15

A clever adaptation of the familiar profit-volume graph is used in capital investment planning based on discounted cash flows. It is seen as especially useful in relatively complex situations.

Dual break-even points may be determined; one equating the net discounted cash flows with the cost of capital, the other with the internal rate of return. Possibilities are indicated for analyzing alternatives, reinvestments, and cost of capital problems.

The Concept of the P/V Graph Applied to Capital Investment Planning*

Carl L. Moore

The profit-volume graph is a familiar device used in profit planning to show profits or losses which can be expected when various quantities of a product are sold at given prices and costs. See Exhibit 1 for a typical graph. The graph reveals at a glance that 2,000 units of a product must be sold if the company is to break even, and that when 5,000 units are sold the company should earn a profit of $3,000. This form of presentation is easy to understand and for that reason is superior to a series of tabulations which would give the same information.

The general concepts which are employed in break-even analysis and in the preparation of the profit-volume graph (P/V graph) can also be applied in capital investment analysis. It should be understood, of course, that the investment under consideration is expected to produce returns and is not

* *From* The Accounting Review, *Vol. XXXVII, No. 4 (October, 1962), pp. 721–729. Reprinted by permission of the editor.*

EXHIBIT 1

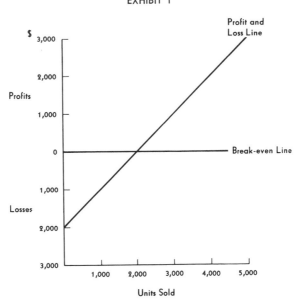

intended to be a prestige type of investment. In capital investment planning, there are also break-even points or limits to be observed. These limits will stand out in a graph which, like the P/V graph, will serve as a medium to convey information. Perhaps, some of the apparent difficulties in investment planning will appear to be less formidable. More attention can then be focused on the more difficult problem of collecting reliable data and refining the estimates.

The Capital Investment Graph

The net discounted cash flows expected from an investment can be measured like profits or losses on a P/V graph. Negative net discounted cash flows can be shown below a break-even line, and positive net discounted cash flows can be shown above this line. Discount rates will be shown on the X-axis in place of sales revenue or quantity of units sold.

The anticipated cash flows are discounted at various rates and are plotted on the graph. The net investment is a negative cash flow and when discounted is deducted from the discounted cash returns. The result is the net positive or net negative discounted cash flow to be depicted on the graph. The total investment will often be made in the present and will be on a present value basis with no calculation being necessary. However, if an investment is to be made on an installment basis, then the future amounts to be invested will have to be discounted to a present value.

The capital investment graph is illustrated in Exhibit 2 by assuming that an investment of $10,000 is to be made in the expectation that $2,000 will be received at the end of each of the next 10 years. The present value of the annual $2,000 returns at a discount rate of 15 per cent is $10,038. The internal rate of return is slightly more than 15 per cent, $10,038 being slightly larger than the $10,000 investment. At a 5 per cent discount rate, the present value of the $2,000 returns would be $15,444. The net positive discounted cash flow after deducting the investment of $10,000 would be $5,444. On a graph, the net cash flows at various discount rates would be shown as charted in Exhibit 2.

EXHIBIT 2

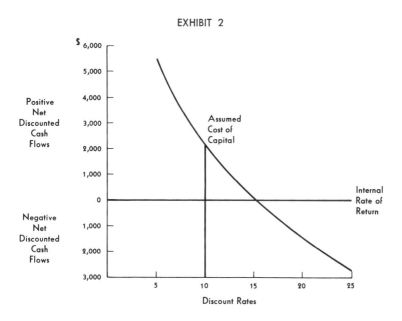

	5%	10%	15%	20%	25%
Discounted returns..........	$15,444	$12,290	$10,038	$ 8,384	$ 7,142
Investment...............	10,000	10,000	10,000	10,000	10,000
Net positive or (negative) cash flows...............	$ 5,444	$ 2,290	$ 38	($ 1,616)	($ 2,858)

As a general rule, it is stated that an investment should be made if it appears that it will earn a return which is greater than the cost of capital. In the illustration given, the investment should be made if the cost of capital is no more than 15 per cent. If the cost is higher, the investment should be rejected. A vertical break-even line can be drawn on the graph at the cost of capital which in this case is assumed at a rate of 10 per cent.

On the capital investment graph there are *two* break-even points. The zero line or the internal rate of return line is the most obvious limit. An investment is certainly not acceptable if it cannot produce positive net discounted cash flows anywhere along the line. A vertical line representing the cost of capital is the second break-even point. An investment is acceptable if the net discounted cash flows are positive at the point of intersection with the cost of capital line. If the present value line for the investment crosses the cost of capital line at its intersection with the zero line, there is no advantage in investment. At this point, the internal rate of return on the investment is equal to the cost of capital. The investment is marginal.

Investment Alternatives

For any given investment situation, there may be several alternatives. Each alternative may be able to produce a return which is greater than the cost of capital, yet only one can be chosen to fulfill the requirement. For example, a new machine may be needed. Various equipment manufacturers are able to furnish a machine of this type, but only one machine will be purchased. The problem is to select the best machine from among those which are available.

Assume that three investment alternatives each costing $20,000 are to be evaluated and that only one alternative can be selected. Estimates show that each alternative will probably yield equal annual cash returns over the next 10 years as follows:

Alternative 1...........	$3,200
Alternative 2..........	4,000
Alternative 3..........	5,000

A decision can be reached quite easily here. With no difference in the amount to be invested, it is clear that Alternative 3 should be chosen if it appears that it will return more than the cost of capital. On Exhibit 3 the present value line for Alternative 3 lies above the other lines at all discount rates and crosses the internal rate of return line to the right of the other present value lines.

Cash returns from business investments are not normally received in lump sums at the end of each year. Most likely the returns will be realized throughout each year in the course of business operation. As a practical matter, however, annual discount rates may be used in investment planning. All investment alternatives will be on the same basis. It will not be necessary to use a monthly rate unless it can be demonstrated that there will be a difference between the alternatives with respect to the shape of the returns within the year.

The most significant section of the capital investment graph is the upper left-hand portion bounded by the horizontal rate of return line and the vertical cost of capital line. Favorable results are shown on the graph to the left of the cost of capital line and above the internal rate of return line. The present value of the net cash returns decreases as the discount rates are increased. The P/V graph, in contrast, measures more favorable results to the right. Larger profits or smaller losses are shown as the quantities to be sold are increased on the horizontal scale.

Alternative 1 yields less than the cost of capital, crossing over the internal rate of return line to the left of its intersection with the cost of capital line. Alternative 3 produces the largest net discounted cash flow at the cost of capital. The graph (Exhibit 3) clearly shows that Alternative 1 does not

EXHIBIT 3

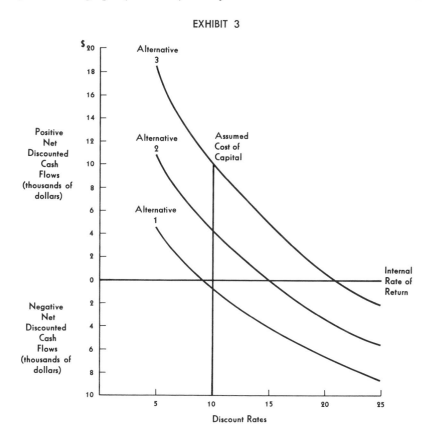

Net Discounted Cash Flows					
Rates	*5%*	*10%*	*15%*	*20%*	*25%*
Alternative 1....	$ 4,710	($ 336)	($3,939)	($6,586)	($8,573)
Alternative 2....	10,888	4,580	76	(3,232)	(5,716)
Alternative 3....	18,610	10,725	5,095	960	(2,145)

meet the break-even requirement and that Alternative 3 is the best choice because it produces the best discounted return when capital costs 10 percent. Many investment situations may be just as simple as the one illustrated. The curved lines representing the net discounted cash flows will not cross each other at any point. The alternative with the best internal rate of return will also give the greatest returns when the returns are discounted at the cost of capital. This general pattern will prevail if the amount to be invested in each alternative is the same and if each alternative is expected to produce uniform annual returns.

In some investment situations, however, the lines will cross, and it will not be easy to make a selection. In fact, analysis may be quite complicated. The amount to be invested may not all be invested at one point in time. Also, the cash returns may be received in varying amounts over the years.

The Reinvestment Problem

The average investor may look upon an investment as being a direct outlay of dollars for a property which he hopes will produce a return in excess of his dollar outlay. In choosing between alternatives, however, the investor must consider the opportunity cost attached to the selection of one alternative over another. The alternative chosen will be expected in the long run to produce returns which are at least as great as those which can be obtained from the alternatives rejected, the risk factor being equal. This selection process involves an evaluation of the time periods over which the investments must be made and the *probable rate or rates of return* which can be earned during those periods.

More immediate cash returns are ordinarily favored over later returns particularly if it appears that these returns can be reinvested at higher rates or at rates which are approximately equal to current rates. On the other hand, more immediate cash returns may be sacrificed for later returns if it is believed that the rate which can be earned during the intervening period will be lower.

This same type of problem faces the individual investor. If bonds are presently yielding 4.75 per cent, he may prefer a relatively long-term investment if he believes that the rate will soon drop to perhaps 3.75 per cent and remain at less than 4.75 per cent during the period of his investment. Conversely, he may expect interest rates to rise to perhaps 5.75 per cent in which case he will want a relatively short-term investment at 4.75 per cent so that he can reinvest at the higher rate.

The rate of return as it stands at any particular time is not the only factor to be considered. Some estimate should be made of future rates. It may be possible to get the best rate of return which can be earned upon current investments, yet lose out by reinvesting the returns at a very low rate. The objective is to maximize the return on investment over the long run, and this cannot always be accomplished by selecting an investment which yields the best rate of return at the present time.[1]

In the illustration given below, three investment alternatives each costing $15,000 are estimated to produce annual cash flows over the next five years as follows:

Years	Alternatives		
	1	2	3
1	$10,000	$5,000	$ 2,000
2	8,000	5,000	2,000
3	3,000	5,000	5,000
4	1,000	5,000	10,000
5	1,000	5,000	10,000

Only one investment alternative can be selected.

Alternative 1 produces large early returns in contrast to Alternative 3 which produces large returns in the later years. If Alternative 3 is accepted over Alternative 1, the investor must sacrifice an $8,000 return in Year 1 and a $6,000 return in Year 2 for an additional return of $2,000 in Year 3 and an additional return of $9,000 in each of the last two years. In total, $14,000 is sacrificed over the first two years to get $20,000 in the last three years. Is the sacrifice justified? The answer to this question depends upon the rate of return which can be expected in the *future* from the reinvestment of the cash returns.

Although Alternative 1 yields net discounted cash flows at a rate of between 25 and 30 per cent as compared with approximately 20 per cent for the other two alternatives, it will be a less desirable investment than Alternative 3 if future cash flows can only be invested at a rate of 10 per cent. Alternative 1, however, will be the best investment if the rate is estimated at 12 per cent or more.

Alternative 3 is revealed on Exhibit 4 as the best investment when a 10 per cent rate of return is expected. In short, Alternative 3 will give the firm a greater cash return than the other alternatives if the cash flows are reinvested at 10 per cent. The chart reduces future cash flows to present values by the use of a discount rate. A less sophisticated approach can be used if desired. Absolute dollar returns can be compounded at 10 per cent. At the end of 5 years, Alternative 3 will produce returns of $32,640 from a $15,000 investment at an interest rate of 10 per cent. The return from Alternative 1 at the same interest rate will only amount to $31,019. In capital investment studies,

[1] See Bierman, Harold, and Smidt, Seymour, *The Capital Budgeting Decision*, The Macmillan Company, New York, 1960, pp. 37–40 for further treatment of the reinvestment problem.

EXHIBIT 4

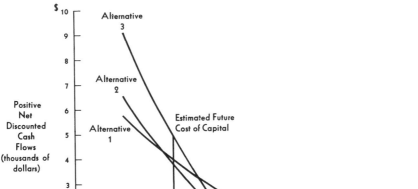

	Net Discounted Cash Flows					
Rates	*5%*	*10%*	*15%*	*20%*	*25%*	*30%*
Alternative 1........	$5,975	$4,255	$2,791	$1,503	$ 394	($ 590)
Alternative 2........	6,650	3,955	1,760	(45)	(1,555)	(2,820)
Alternative 3........	9,108	5,265	2,232	(211)	(2,180)	(3,813)

however, comparison is generally made on the basis of values adjusted to the present time.

The capital investment graph clearly shows the discounted cash flows which can be expected, the discounted rate of return from each alternative, and the alternative which should be accepted. The capital investment graph, like the P/V graph, is only as good as the data used in its preparation. As a form of presentation, both graphs serve a useful purpose. Various assumptions can be plotted on a graph and visualized. For example, the cost of future capital may be estimated at different rates and inserted on the graph.

The Cost of Capital

One of the most troublesome features of investment planning is the determination of the cost of capital.[2] The problem is further complicated by the reinvestment situation where the *future* cost of capital must be estimated. The cost of capital cannot be narrowly defined as being the cost of obtaining new capital. In decisional analysis, the cost of capital includes the sacrifice of giving up other investment opportunities. Should stockholders, for example, forego dividends which can be reinvested so that the corporation can use the funds for investment?[3]

The cost of capital in the future cannot be determined precisely, of course, but a range of rates may be predicted. Data drawn from past experience will serve as a guide along with other factors. By statistical method, it may be possible to assign probabilities to the range of rates which can be expected.

The break-even line on the graph for the cost of capital will then be a broad band or a zone rather than a definite line. In the illustration just given, a band could be drawn for a future cost of capital estimated to fall within a range of from 8 to 12 per cent. The upper left-hand section of the graph would then appear as shown in Exhibit 5.

Within the range Alternative 3 is still superior. The gap between Alternatives 1 and 3 narrows as the rate increases, and at the upper limit of 12 per cent, there is very little difference between the two.

A range of four per cent may be too wide to be of much help in some situations. The band or zone can perhaps be reduced to a zone of rates which are most probable. Some percentage of error in prediction will have to be accepted in return for the advantage of a narrow cost of capital band.

Suppose that there is a 90 per cent probability that the rate will fall between 9 and 10 per cent in the illustration used. This knowledge reinforces the decision in favor of Alternative 3.

On the other hand, assume that the range of rates extended from 10 to 14 per cent. A decision would be more difficult. Alternative 3 produces a lower net discounted cash flow than Alternative 1 at any rate greater than 12 per cent. Further analysis may show that there is 90 per cent certainty that the rate will lie between 12 and 13 per cent in which case Alternative 1 would be favored.

Summary

A graph similar in concept to the conventional P/V graph can be used in capital investment planning and can be especially useful in the analysis of

---

[2] See Solomon, Ezra, *The Management of Corporate Capital*, The Free Press of Glencoe, Illinois, 1959, pp. 128–140.
[3] See Bierman, Harold and Smidt, Seymour, *The Capital Budgeting Decision*, The Macmillan Company, New York, 1960, pp. 142–146.

EXHIBIT 5

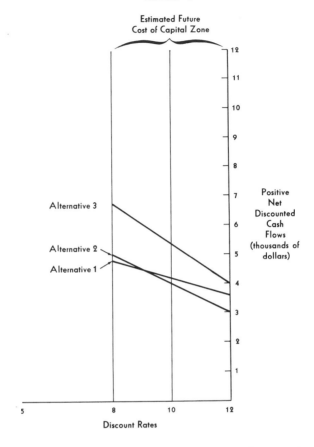

relatively complex investment situations. The net discounted cash flow line for the most profitable investment candidate crosses the expected cost of capital line or zone at the highest point. In a large number of investment situations, this line will also cross the internal rate of return line at the highest discount rate and will be above all other discounted cash flow lines at all points. There are also investment situations in which the discounted cash flow lines for the various alternatives will cross. The line for the most profitable alternative does not necessarily lie to the right of the other lines when it crosses over the internal rate of return line. It will, however, be the highest line when it crosses the expected cost of capital line or zone.

The future cost of capital cannot be determined exactly, but it may be possible to predict the cost within reasonable limits. This line of limitation on the graph is then not a fine line but is instead a fairly wide band or zone. Although the P/V graph is not the primary subject of discussion here, it may be mentioned in passing that data portrayed on that graph will also fall into zones rather than precise lines.

The use of a broad band or zone for the cost of capital may seem to add to the difficulties in making a selection. Actually there is greater assurance that the cost of capital will fall within established limits than there is that the cost of capital will be at any given point. The band can be reduced in width by assigning probabilities to the rates. In making the reduction, there is some probability that the actual rate will be above or below the limits. Agreement will have to be reached with respect to the degree of allowable error. If there is still difficulty in choosing one alternative over another because of lines crossing within the zone, then it may be a matter of indifference as to which alternative is selected. Assuming that the discounted cash flow lines do not run together in the expected cost of capital band, it should be possible to select the best alternative with more confidence than would be the case if the expected cost of capital were represented by a line.

Supplemental
Readings
to Part Three

Andrew Berczi and Jose Ventura, "A Proposal of Risk Analysis," *The Canadian Chartered Accountant,* Vol. 95, No. 2 (August, 1969), pp. 88–93.
A reconciliation of internal rate of return and net present value concepts, allowing for the risk factor, is presented.

John A. Denholm, "Investment By Simulation," *The Journal of Management Studies,* Vol. 6, No. 2 (May, 1969), pp. 167–180.
A model relating various investment decisions to present and future firm position is presented.

C. G. Edge, "Capital Budgeting: Principles and Projection," *Financial Executive,* Vol. 33, No. 9 (September, 1965), pp. 50–59.
Six basic principles of capital budgeting are presented.

R. Fraser and M. S. Henderson, "Uncertainty in Capital Budgeting — The Simulation Approach," *Cost and Management,* Vol. 44, No. 2 (March-April, 1970), pp. 47–50.
The advantages of simulation over probabilistic models for capital budgeting under uncertainty are presented.

Myron J. Gordon, "The Payoff Period and the Rate of Profit," *Journal of Business,* Vol. XXVIII, No. 4 (October, 1955), pp. 253–260.
The relative merits of alternative capital investment formulas — payoff period, average investment, and Terborgh — are argued and evaluated.

R. S. Gynther, "Using Return on Capital for Management Control," *Accountancy,* Vol. LXXLV, No. 841 and 843 (September, November, 1963), pp. 768–775; 971–976.
The need for implementing concepts of direct costing and responsibility accounting for measuring divisional performance is stressed. Special attention is paid to the effect of financial leases and price level movements on return on investment.

Timothy P. Haidinger, "The Case for Continuous Discounting," *Management Accounting,* Vol. 49, No. 6 (February, 1968), pp. 57–61.
The extent to which error is introduced into present value computations as a result of using discrete discounting is considered.

Miles Kennedy, "Risk in Capital Budgeting: An Interactive Sensitivity Approach," *Industrial Management Review,* Vol. 9, No. 3 (Spring, 1968), pp. 121–140.
A unified analysis encompassing Monte Carlo simulation, sensitivity analysis, and user-controlled intuitive explorations is presented.

Ivan J. Kilpatrick, "A Problem of Disinvestment," *The Canadian Chartered Accountant,* Vol. 94, No. 4 (April, 1969), pp. 235–238.

Seldom considered facets of capital budgeting — "provide capital to a subsidiary, or sell the subsidiary?" is presented.

Bernard J. Kravitz and Robert J. Monteverde, "An O. R. Approach to Capital Budgeting," *Management Controls,* Vol. 16, No. 3 (March, 1969), pp. 67–69.

Operations research approaches to capital budgeting are considered.

Eugene M. Lerner and Alfred Rappaport, "Limit DCF in Capital Budgeting," *Harvard Business Review,* Vol. 46, No. 5 (September-October, 1968), pp. 133–139.

A Discounted Cash Flow approach employing a constrained present value approach is presented.

A. J. Merrett, "Investment in Replacement: The Optimal Replacement Method," *The Journal of Management Studies,* Vol. 2, No. 2 (May, 1965), pp. 153–166.

Methods for optimizing the replacement decision are presented.

Roy C. Satchell, "Fallacies in Capital Investment Decisions," *Financial Executive,* Vol. 34, No. 8 (August, 1966), pp. 36–42.

Failure to distinguish between financing aspects and economic evaluation aspects of capital investment decisions is a fallacy in theory and practice.

James C. Van Horne, "The Analysis of Uncertainty Resolution in Capital Budgeting for New Products," *Management Science,* Vol. 15, No. 8 (April, 1969), pp. B-376–B-386.

A capital-budgeting framework is used to develop a method for resolving uncertainty in new product decisions.

H. Martin Weingartner, "Capital Budgeting of Interrelated Projects: Survey and Synthesis," *Management Science,* Vol. 12, No. 7 (March, 1966), pp. 485–516.

A survey of techniques available to handle project interrelationships is presented.

F. K. Wright, "Investment Criteria and the Cost of Capital," *The Journal of Management Studies,* Vol. 4, No. 3 (October, 1967), pp. 253–269.

A statement of useful investment criteria for producing approximate solutions to the optimizing problem is given.

Additional
Bibliography
to Part Three

Robert N. Anthony, "Some Fallacies in Figuring Return on Investment," *NAA Bulletin*, Vol. XLII, No. 4 (December, 1960), pp. 5–13.

Morton Backer, "Additional Considerations in Return on Investment Analysis," *NAA Bulletin*, Vol. XLIII, No. 5 (January, 1962), pp. 57–62.

D. Phillip Beaudry, Jr., "Can You Afford That Asset?" *NA(C)A Bulletin*, Vol. XXXV, No. 11 (July, 1954), pp. 1383–1405.

William Beranek, "A Note on the Equivalence of Certain Capital Budgeting Criteria," *The Accounting Review*, Vol. XXXIX, No. 4 (October, 1964), pp. 914–916.

Henry L. Clayton, "How to Handle Product Evaluation Procedure," *NAA Bulletin*, Vol. XLII, No. 6 (February, 1961), pp. 55–61.

John W. Coughlan, "Accounting and Capital Budgeting," *The Business Quarterly*, Vol. XXVII, No. 4 (Winter, 1962), pp. 39–48.

———, "Contrast Between Financial-Statement and Discounted-Cost-Flow Methods of Comparing Projects," *NAA Bulletin*, Vol. XLI, No. 10 (June, 1960), pp. 5–17.

H. Justin Davidson and Robert M. Trueblood, "Accounting for Decision-Making," *The Accounting Review*, Vol. XXXVI, No. 4 (October, 1961), pp. 577–582.

C. F. Day, " 'Shadow Prices' for Evaluating Alternative Uses of Available Capacity," *NAA Bulletin*, Vol. XL, No. 9 (May, 1959), pp. 67–76.

Herbert E. Dougall, "Payback As an Aid in Capital Budgeting," *The Controller*, Vol. XXIX, No. 2 (February, 1961), pp. 67–72.

Robert B. Grant, "Mathematically Influenced Decision-Making," *NAA Bulletin*, Vol. XLII, No. 5 (January, 1961), pp. 33–44.

John C. Gregory, "Capital Expenditure Evaluation by Direct Discounting," *The Accounting Review*, Vol. XXXVII, No. 2 (April, 1962), pp. 308–314.

James C. Hetrick, "Mathematical Models in Capital Budgeting," *Harvard Business Review*, Vol. 39, No. 1 (January-February, 1961), pp. 49–64.

Robert K. Jaedicke, "Rate of Return Verification by Follow-up Reporting on a Project Basis," *NAA Bulletin*, Vol. XLI, No. 10 (June, 1960), pp. 59–64.

———, "Some Notes on Product Combination Decisions," *The Accounting Review*, Vol. XXXIII, No. 4 (October, 1958), pp. 596–601.

Herbert W. Johnson, "Measuring the Earning Power of Investment — A Comparison of Methods," *NAA Bulletin*, Vol. XLIII, No. 5 (January, 1962), pp. 37–55.

Walter Kennon, "Fixed Cost and Product Mix by Activity Analysis," *NA(C)A Bulletin*, Vol. XXXVII, No. 3 (November, 1955), pp. 319–334.

William F. Kieser, "Product Cost Brought into Focus by Comparative Analysis," *NAA Bulletin*, Vol. XLII, No. 6 (February, 1961), pp. 73–79.

Gerald H. Lawson, "Capital Investment Criteria in Business," *The Accountant*, Vol. 148, Nos. 4608–4610 (April 13, 20 and 27, 1963), pp. 448–452, 491–496 and 544–547.

Gerald A. Pollack, "The Capital Budgeting Controversy: Present Value vs. Discounted Cash Flow Method," *NAA Bulletin*, Vol. XLIII, No. 3 (November, 1961), pp. 5–19.

John E. Rhodes, "How to Make Capital Controls Work," *NA(C)A Bulletin*, Vol. XXXVII, No. 1 (September, 1955), pp. 3–18.

Kenneth F. Schuba, "Make-or-Buy Decisions — Cost and Non-Cost Considerations," *NAA Bulletin*, Vol. XLI, No. 7 (March, 1960), pp. 53–66.

Gordon Shillinglaw, "Divisionalization, Decentralization and Return on Investment," *NAA Bulletin*, Vol. XLI, No. 4 (December, 1959), pp. 19–33.

Russell Taussig, "Information Requirements of Replacement Models," *Journal of Accounting Research*, Vol. 2, No. 1 (Spring, 1964), pp. 67–79.

H. K. Van Camp, "The Use of the Product Profit or Loss Budget for Marginal Sales Decisions," *NAA Bulletin*, Vol. XLII, No. 3 (November, 1960), pp. 5–16.

William J. Vatter, "Does the Rate of Return Measure Business Efficiency?" *NAA Bulletin*, Vol. XL, No. 5 (January, 1959), pp. 33–48.

C. W. Walton et al., "Company and Division Planning and Control," *NA(C)A Bulletin*, Vol. XXXVIII, No. 2 (October, 1956), Section 3, pp. 307–339.

Roger Wellington, "Capital Budgeting," *The Journal of Accountancy*, Vol. 115, No. 5 (May, 1963), pp. 46–53.

Arthur S. Wells, Jr., "Economic Analysis for Better Investment Decisions," *NAA Bulletin*, Vol. XL, No. 2 (October, 1958), pp. 5–14.

PART FOUR

Cost Planning, Decision, and Control:
Cost-Volume-Profit Analysis

Cost-volume-profit analysis is an exceedingly useful technique in helping to analyze basic relationships for business decisions. The technique, although useful, of course does not make the decisions. It does permit the evaluation of predictions based on cost-volume-profit assumptions, which relate cost and profit behavior to volume. Relationships are mainly considered to be linear within the normal operations of the firm for both cost and revenue relative to volume. Costs are normally represented by linear fixed and variable portions, while revenues are considered as being completely linearly variable with volume.

These projections may be determined historically, with projections made therefrom, taking expectations into account; or they may be made entirely from budget expectations. Various methods are used to define the rates — including geometric charts, free-hand correlations, and statistical correlations. Several unique methods of analysis and presentation have been developed and successively refined. These include break-even charts, profit graphs, and profit (P/V) charts.

The techniques themselves and their practical applications in various situations are fully explored by Willson. He develops at length the use of break-even analysis in forecasting, in control, and in special problem applications. (The last include plant expansion, changes in variable rates, changes in selling prices, and optimum mix.) Throughout, the discussion is clear and unambiguous, although some fairly complex situations are used.

Devine looks at the problem of effective reporting. In profit-volume analysis, which has as central criterion the probable behavior of costs in response to changes in volume, the main problem is defining the relevant costs. Devine discusses the need for reexamining the usual cost classifications with these considerations in mind. He argues that profit-volume relationships provide management with a simplified model in organizing its thinking; but that even this model really offers a family of relationships — with influences other than volume as parameters. Various approaches to profit-volume reporting are reviewed and evaluated, and suggestions are made for improvements in accumulating and allocating costs.

The close relationship between economics and accounting is often asserted. Vickers argues that a cleavage exists between economic concepts and the principles which managements appear to act on, and cites as a case in point break-even analysis, which ignores the economic theorems of cost and revenue. He recommends that industrial break-even charts be adapted and brought into closer conformity with economics, and that in turn economists devote attention to reinterpreting the analysis to clarify its true empirical significance. A key role in this effort is seen for the accountant.

Morrison and Kaczka continue the development of cost-volume-profit analysis beyond the extensions suggested by Vickers for curvi-linear, non-reversible cost and revenue functions. They address themselves to the practical problems involving changes in prices, cost, and quantities demanded. Criteria are devised for determining relevant factors and for ignoring irrelevant data. Finally, they carefully illustrate a *continuous* price-volume relationship that determines maximum profit points (even when linear break-even parameters are used) for all changes in selling price and volume.

To complete Part Four, Charnes, Cooper, and Ijiri explore applications of linear programming to break-even analysis. Of particular interest is their utilization of the linear programming algorithm in the budgeting process to generate opportunity cost data.

16

The typical company can find many useful ways of putting cost-volume-profit analysis to work. The author raises pertinent questions that may be asked by managements and offers methods to help answer them.

The basic break-even chart and its underlying assumptions are given, followed by more complex models. Forecasts are tested by means of a "standard profit structure" and illustrated by example. A profit-graph with standard and forecast is shown to highlight changes in cost structure.

A series of situations are postulated and solved to show the power of the method in alternative planning situations. Control is effected by means of a Break-even Sales Control Chart indicating cumulative sales volume and cumulative break-even sales volumes accumulating over time.

Practical Applications of Cost-Volume-Profit Analysis*

James D. Willson

The success of a top business executive today depends in large part on his ability to deal effectively with probable conditions of tomorrow. In such a task he needs knowledge of the economic characteristics or structure of the business he manages, which the accountant can provide him. The principal accounting official should constantly make available to the chief executive such information, in readily understandable reports, to enable him to evaluate the hazards and recognize the potentials in the various business alternatives available.

This entire field of "profit planning" has become associated with the break-even analysis, or the cost-volume-profit inter-relationship. We will not concern ourselves here with the usual preparation of such planning or control

* From NAA Bulletin, *Vol. XLI, No. 7 (March, 1960), pp. 5–18. Reprinted by permission of the publisher.*

devices as variable budgets or forecasts. It is assumed that the reader has a reasonable knowledge of the principles related to these areas of planning and control. Our starting point is in a more sophisticated area — the application of the break-even analysis and related data in profit planning techniques. Let us consider the forecast, for instance. What purpose does it serve? Is it satisfactory? How do we know? If your company is typical, there are many useful ways of putting cost-volume-profit analysis to work. Such a technique is not merely a means of determining at what point income equals outgo and the business "breaks even." The dynamic company of today wants more then to just break even. Profits or the expectation of profits must be in the picture, or the incentive under the free enterprise system is gone.

The significance of this type of thinking may be illustrated by some of the questions which management is prone to ask and which accounting executives should be ready to answer, or assist in development of the answer, by the use of break-even analysis:

1. Does the forecast represent a reasonable profit objective? (More particularly for this purpose, are costs and expenses in proper relationship to income?)
2. What will be the operating profit or loss at X sales volume?
3. What profit will result from a fifteen percent increase in sales volume?
4. What additional sales volume is necessary to produce X dollars of operating profit?
5. What additional sales volume is necessary to offset a ten percent reduction in selling price?
6. If the company can reduce fixed costs by X dollars and achieve a five percent reduction in material costs, what will be the effect on income?
7. What is the required sales volume to meet the additional fixed charges from the proposed plant expansion?
8. What sales volume is needed to provide for all costs in Territory Y?

Can you given an intelligent answer to intelligent questions of this nature as applied to your company? If you cannot, take heart. The techniques to develop answers to these questions are essentially quite simple.

Basic Assumptions in Cost-Volume-Profit Analysis

Before discussing some adaptations of the cost-volume-profit analysis to planning and control, a review of a few simple fundamentals might be helpful. The effectiveness of our application depends in large part on proper assumptions relating to costs and profits. The economic structure of a company may be portrayed in the more simple break-even chart to depict merely the profit or loss effect of an increase in volume of sales as related to a ratable increase in variable costs, with a sales income line, a fixed cost line, and a line of variable costs. It may also be portrayed in a more refined but complex presentation, as in Exhibit 1, setting forth the relationships to sales volume

EXHIBIT 1

The Presentation Company Profit Structure Chart
(Showing major segments of costs)

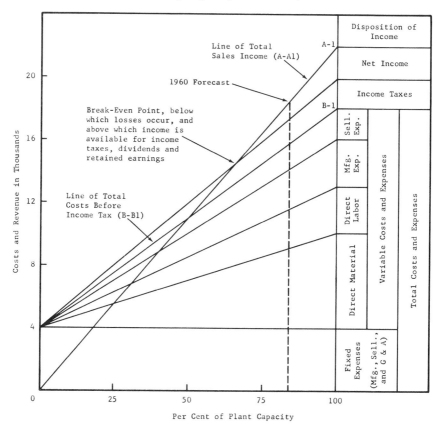

of various costs and expenses. Regardless of the degree of complexity of the analysis, the principal assumptions on which such a study is based are:

1. Unit selling prices will not change with volume.
2. Costs and expenses can be segregated with reasonable accuracy into their fixed and variable components.
3. Fixed or standby costs will remain constant in the aggregate within the limits of the study.
4. Variable costs will vary generally in a constant ratio, i.e., in direct proportion to volume.
5. Where several products are involved, the mix will remain constant.

When the proper cost segregations are known, income, costs, and the break-even point may be determined, with or without a chart. Whether or not it is decided to use the formalized chart in the determinations, the mathematical equation is:

$$\text{Break-even point} = \frac{\text{Aggregate fixed expense}}{1 - \dfrac{\text{Variable costs}}{\text{Sales}}}$$

The denominator, which is equal to the ratio of variable income to sales (marginal income ratio), represents that share of the sales dollar which is available to contribute to fixed costs and, if adequate, to income. It is a highly significant ratio. In analyzing economic behavior, this relationship becomes a much more useful concept than the break-even point itself.

Using Break-Even Analysis to Test the Forecast

For illustrative purposes, we will consider the Sample Company with an economic structure such as that shown in Exhibit 2. It is to be observed that not only have fixed and variable costs been segregated but also the variable costs for each major function or cost segment have been translated into their applicable percentages of the net sales dollar. This information can now be applied in an evaluation of the reasonableness of the forecast. Typically, a projection is compared with some past year, usually the immediately preceding year, to determine whether or not it appears satisfactory. Such a comparison has value. It may be a gauge as to the adequacy of the sales volume

EXHIBIT 2

The Sample Company

Profit Structure

		Variable Costs		
			%	
	Fixed		*Net*	
Description	*Costs*	*Total*	*Sales*	*Combined*
Net sales				$10,000,000
Costs and expenses:				
Direct material	$	$4,000,000	40.00%	
Direct labor		1,000,000	10.00	
Manufacturing expenses	500,000	1,000,000	10.00	
Selling expenses	400,000	100,000	1.00	
Research and development expenses	250,000	50,000	.50	
General and administrative expenses	150,000	50,000	.50	
	$1,300,000	$6,200,000	62.00%	7,500,000
Profit before income taxes				$ 2,500,000

and, in a general way, it may raise questions about cost or expense levels. However, such a comparison is not as sharp a tool as is available. Most of the time, the sales level and product mix in the forecast year will not be identical with that of the past year. Therefore, it may be difficult to measure more precisely the propriety of the costs and expenses in relationship to sales volume. To further complicate the problem, management, when looking at a higher sales volume and a net income which appears more favorable, tends to be less critical. In most instances, if net income expressed as a percent of sales is greater than the preceding year, the forecast is gleefully pronounced satisfactory.

Why not use a superior tool which permits a more effective evaluation of the volume factor? Once management has agreed upon a reasonable sales objective, a volume for the year under forecast, then it becomes practical to measure the proposed forecast against the break-even structure, i.e., to apply the break-even economic structure of the company to the projected sales volume. Essentially, we are saying that management should decide upon reasonable cost-profit-volume relationships and that this standard should be used as a measure of the forecast. The results of the application of the break-even factors, as shown in Exhibit 2, to a projected sales volume (standard profit structure) and the comparison of such results with the aggregate costs and expenses as set forth in an illustrative forecast, are shown in Exhibit 3. It is to be noted that percentage relationships are developed to aid in detecting out-of-line conditions. The exhibit portrays one of the basic considerations in the preparation of forecasts, i.e., that the company must not be allowed to develop or assume a less favorable cost structure. Hence, it is necessary to apply some overall tests quite distinct, for example, from individual departmental budget performance.

The greatest dollar increase and relative increase is in prime material costs. This 5 percent or $250,000 increase must be analyzed to determine whether the cost increase results from changes in product mix or from cost increases in any given product line. The initial break-even application has isolated this apparently excessive cost relationship. Now it should be analyzed in more depth and a decision made as to an acceptable plan. Perhaps the product mix is not the optimum believed to be attainable in the forecast year. Perhaps action can be taken on cost increases to reduce or eliminate them. The next largest relative increase, amounting to $60,000, is in direct labor. A similar analysis should be made to localize the cause and seek an improvement in the plan.

Next, manufacturing expenses have increased by 4 percent or $70,000. Departmental budgets should be reviewed to determine the areas of greatest increase and causes should be determined. Management must then decide what corrective action need be taken. If, for example, the increase is in maintenance expense, is it sound to defer projects? What is the best approach when considering the longer term interests of the business? Similar analyses should be made of the other expense areas. If expenses are under the standard, the accountant should ascertain that no omissions have been made erroneously.

It is to be observed that the break-even point has risen by 8.6 percent to $3,714,290. Perhaps a better way to state the case is that the forecast is based on a somewhat changed cost structure. This change may be shown graphically as in Exhibit 4. The solid lines indicate the acceptable cost-volume-profit structure and the dotted lines reveal the condition as planned in the forecast. Incidentally, any change in these relationships can be readily shown on the graph, whether they appear in sales, variable costs or fixed expense.

In poor economic weather, a reasonable margin of safety is necessary. Accordingly, in the Sample Company, if management agrees that the standard profit structure must be maintained, every element should be analyzed and

EXHIBIT 3

The Sample Company

Break-even Analysis of Forecast
Fiscal 1960

Description	Application of Standard Profit Structure	Tentative Forecast	Forecast Over (Under) Standard	
			Amount	%
Net sales	$12,500,000	$12,500,000		
Cost of sales:				
Direct material	$ 5,000,000	$ 5,250,000	$250,000	5.00%
Direct labor	1,250,000	1,310,000	60,000	4.80
Manufacturing expenses	1,750,000	1,820,000	70,000	4.00
Total	$ 8,000,000	$ 8,380,000	$380,000	4.75%
Gross margin	$ 4,500,000	$ 4,120,000	($380,000)	(8.44%)
Operating expenses:				
Selling	$ 525,000	$ 540,000	$ 15,000	2.86%
Research and development	312,500	310,000	(2,500)	(.80)
General and administrative	212,500	190,000	(22,500)	(10.59)
Total	$ 1,050,000	$ 1,040,000	($ 10,000)	(.95%)
Profit before taxes	$ 3,450,000	$ 3,080,000	$370,000	(10.72%)
Other data:				
Break-even point	$ 3,421,050	$ 3,714,290	$293,240	8.6%
Marginal income ratio	.38	.35		

EXHIBIT 4

The Sample Company Profit Graph

(Standard and Forecast)

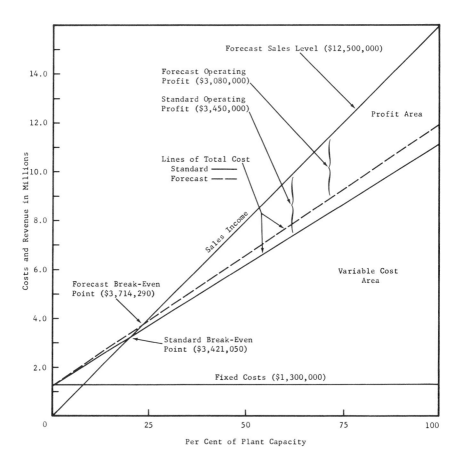

explored by the accountant so that the final business plan for the ensuing year retains the characteristics of this structure. As an alternative, once the most satisfactory cost-volume-profit relationship is determined, including the proper product mix, then the possibility of securing additional sales volume to offset cost increases is to be considered.

Other Uses of Cost-Volume-Profit Data

A knowledge of the economic structure of the business, together with the related analysis, can identify areas of cost increases and, as illustrated, permit an evaluation of the forecast. In addition, such information can provide answers to other typical questions. The value of the cost-volume-profit concept is inherently in the facility with which volume can be treated as a variable factor. Because of considerations relating to the market or to expansion, management many times desires information concerning the results of a contemplated action, such as what the operating profit would be at X dollars sales volume or what the effect on operating profit would be if X percentage increase in sales volume were realized, etc. The marginal income ratio and the related segregation of fixed expense simplify the solution of such problems.

Operating profit at any given sales volume — Using the Sample Company's profit structure, what would be the operating profit at an annual sales level of $13,000,000? The operating profit will be the marginal contribution (amount of sales income less all variable costs and expenses) less the fixed expense:

Contribution margin	= $13,000,000 × .38
	= $ 4,940,000
Less fixed expense	1,300,000
Equals operating profit of	$ 3,640,000

Effect on operating profit of a given percent increase in sales volume — In setting the sales objective each year or for several years, management typically likes to know the profit result at any number of sales levels expressed as amounts or percentages of increase. The answer may be determined easily from a reading of a cost-volume-profit graph as shown in Exhibit 4. This increased flexibility is a tremendous advantage of the chart approach. However, results from each requested percentage increase also can be individually calculated. If the present sales volume is $10,500,000, with our marginal income ratio of .38, the computation of a 15 percent increase in sales is as follows:

Sales increase = $10,500,000 × 15% = $1,575,000

At marginal income ratio of .38

Produces an increase in operating profit of $598,500

In such an instance, with no change in fixed expense, the operating profit is simply the sales increase multiplied by the marginal income ratio.

Sales volume required to produce X dollars of operating profit — In planning, management quite often decides that, for financial or other considerations, a given profit must be attained. The question then will naturally arise as to the sales volume necessary to produce it. In a calculation of this type, the desired operating profit becomes, in effect, the equivalent of fixed expense. If the desired operating profit of the Sample Company is $4,200,000, then the simple computation and result are as follows:

$$\text{Required sales volume} = \frac{\text{Fixed expense} + \text{Desired operating profit}}{\text{Marginal income ratio}}$$

$$= \frac{\$1,300,000 + \$4,200,000}{.38}$$

$$= \$14,173,700$$

Additional sales volume needed to offset a reduction in selling price — The sales department may insist that the present low sales volume is due to prices which are out of line with competition. It may advise a reduction of 10 percent in these prices. We will assume that the company has a sales volume of $10,500,000, with fixed expenses of $1,300,000, and a marginal income ratio of .38. With a 10 percent reduction in selling prices, what sales volume is needed just to maintain present operating results? Our initial step is to calculate the present operating income as follows:

Marginal income	= $10,500,000 × .38
	= $ 3,990,000
Deduct fixed expense	1,300,000
Present operating income	$ 2,690,000

Next, we must adjust to the changed marginal income ratio (or the variable cost ratio).

$$\begin{matrix}\text{Sales volume to} \\ \text{offset reduced} \\ \text{selling price}\end{matrix} = \frac{\text{Desired profit} + \text{Fixed expense}}{1 - \left(\dfrac{\text{Present variable cost ratio}}{1 - \text{Proposed \% reduction in selling price}}\right)}$$

$$= \frac{\$2,690,000 + \$1,300,000}{1 - \left(\dfrac{.62}{1 - .10}\right)} = \frac{\$3,990,000}{.3112} = \$12,821,000$$

The required sales volume of $12,821,000 represents an increase of about 22 percent over the present level. The ability to secure such an increase should be explored in terms of both sales potential and plant capacity.

Effect of changes in fixed expense and variable cost ratios — Since the objective of business management should be the earning of the maximum return on invested capital consistent with proper social objectives, there is often a continuous search for reduced costs. In the case of the Sample Company, assume that management, after some study, feels the "normal" or standard profit structure may be improved. As an example, it may be concluded that direct material costs may be reduced 10 percent through certain substitutions and that fixed expenses may be lowered by $250,000 annually. Then the question may be asked, "What would the probable operating profit be at a sales level of

$12,000,000 annually?" The answer could be calculated using the profit-structure shown in Exhibit 2:

The new variable cost ratio   = Present variable cost of material less
                             10% plus other variable costs
                       = (.40 less 10%) + .22 = .58

The new marginal income ratio = 1 − variable cost ratio = 1 − .58 = .42

Now operating results may be quickly determined as follows:

Marginal income   = Sales volume × marginal income ratio
                       = $12,000,000 × .42 = $5,040,000

The $5,040,000 marginal income less the revised fixed expense of $1,050,000 ($1,300,000 − $250,000) will produce a more favorable operating income of $3,990,000. If preferred, a more detailed comparison of the present operation and the $12,000,000 sales level may be made as follows:

	Present		*Higher Level*	
Description	*Amount*	*% Net Sales*	*Amount*	*% Net Sales*
Net Sales	$10,000,000	100.00	$12,000,000	100.00
Variable costs	6,200,000	62.00	6,960,000	58.00
Marginal income	$ 3,800,000	38.00	$ 5,040,000	42.00
Fixed expense	1,300,000	13.00	1,050,000	8.75
Operating income	$ 2,500,000	25.00	$ 3,990,000	33.25

Advisability of plant expansion — Sooner or later most progressive businesses are faced with a problem of plant expansion. This solution should not rest merely on available funds. Rather, management should have a full realization of the economic questions involved and here, again, cost-volume-profit analysis can be helpful. The chief executive might find break-even analysis valuable in providing information needed in a critical review of the proposed commitment, answering such points as:
1. Relative break-even points.
2. Sales volume required to earn the present level of profits.
3. Sales volume necessary to earn the same rate of profit on the proposed facility as on the existing one.
4. Maximum profit potential.
The development of these criteria is simply the application of the basic formula already discussed. There are simply more aspects to the problem and perhaps more sales attainment levels to consider before making an intelligent commitment of long-term funds.
Planning for adequate facilities preferably should take place sufficiently ahead of the date when the plant and equipment are needed for operations.

In our example, the Sample Company, the sales forecast is already at the $12,500,000 level. However, management is of the opinion that the full plant capacity of $15,000,000 will be required within the next eighteen months. Therefore, assume these facts, using the profit structure (Exhibit 2) of the company:

Maximum annual earnings of the company with present facilities:

Net Sales	$15,000,000
Costs and expenses:	
Variable (62% of net sales)	$ 9,300,000
Fixed	1,300,000
Total	$10,600,000
Income before taxes	$ 4,400,000
Federal income tax (50%)	2,200,000
Net income	$ 2,200,000
Annual fixed expense of new plant	$ 700,000
Desired annual income (net) on new investment	$ 140,000
Maximum sales volume of new plant	$ 8,600,000

On the basis of this information, these determinations can be made:

BREAK-EVEN POINTS

$$\text{Present facilities} \quad = \frac{\text{Fixed costs}}{\text{Marginal income ratio}} = \frac{\$1,300,000}{.38}$$

$$= \$3,421,050 \text{ sales volume.}$$

$$\text{Proposed facilities} = \frac{\text{Present} + \text{Additional fixed expense}}{\text{Marginal income ratio}}$$

$$= \frac{\$1,300,000 + \$700,000}{.38} = \$5,263,200 \text{ sales volume.}$$

SALES VOLUME REQUIRED

To earn existing income =

$$\frac{\text{Present fixed expense} + \text{Additional fixed expense} + \text{Existing income}}{\text{Marginal income ratio}}$$

$$= \frac{\$1,300,000 + \$700,000 + \$3,450,000}{.38} = \$14,340,000 \text{ sales volume.}$$

To earn a given return on investment =

$$\frac{\begin{array}{c}\text{Present fixed expense} + \text{Added fixed expense} + \text{Present return on}\\ \text{investment} + \text{Return (before taxes) on new investment}\end{array}}{\text{Marginal income ratio}}$$

$$= \frac{\$1,300,000 + \$700,000 + \$3,450,000 + \$280,000}{.38} = \frac{\$5,730,000}{.38}$$

$$= \$15,100,000 \text{ sales volume.}$$

MAXIMUM EARNINGS POTENTIAL WITH NEW PLANT

Net sales (capacity)		$23,600,000
Costs and expenses:		
Variable (62% of net sales)	$14,632,000	
Fixed or continuing expenses	2,000,000	16,632,000
Profit before income taxes		$ 6,968,000
Federal income taxes (50%)		3,484,000
Net income — potential		$ 3,484,000

These determinations may be summarized for management somewhat in this fashion:

Description	Present Facilities	Prospective Facilities	Increase
Annual break-even sales volume	$ 3,421,050	$ 5,263,200	$1,842,150
Annual sales volume to earn existing income	12,500,000	14,340,000	1,840,000
Annual sales volume to earn desired return on new facility	12,500,000	15,100,000	2,600,000
Maximum sales volume	15,000,000	23,600,000	8,600,000
Maximum profit potential	2,200,000	3,484,000	1,284,000

A prudent management will consider carefully its ability to secure and maintain, at the assumed prices, an additional sales volume of at least $2,600,000. Moreover, because of a very favorable marginal income ratio and the consequent relatively small increase in sales needed to provide an adequate return, further thought should be given to:
1. Possible or probable competitive action and the need for price changes to discourage competition.
2. The prospects of achieving a more substantial increase in sales to utilize the new facilities and realize more of the profit potential.

Uses of Cost-Volume-Profit Analysis for Part of the Business

Previous illustrations have dealt with the use of cost-volume-profit analysis for the business as a whole. Yet, the same approach may be applied to problems relative to individual product lines, territories, methods of sale, channels of distribution, or any particular segment of the business which is under scrutiny. In all of these decisions, the significant factors are the marginal income ratio and the fixed expense or cost. Where both direct and allocated costs are involved, several different break-even points may be determined. For example, suppose these conditions exist in a sales territory:

Direct and continuing territory selling expense	$310,000
Marginal income ratio	.25
Allocable share of home office (fixed) expense	$130,000

The sales volume required merely to cover the direct territorial fixed expense would be:

$$\frac{\text{Direct fixed expenses}}{\text{Marginal income ratio}} = \frac{\$310,000}{.25} = \$1,240,000 \text{ sales volume.}$$

The annual sales volume sufficient to cover the direct expenses and allocated home office fixed expense would be:

$$\frac{\text{Direct expense} + \text{allocated expense}}{\text{Marginal income ratio}} = \frac{\$310,000 + \$130,000}{.25}$$
$$= \$1,760,000 \text{ sales volume.}$$

EXHIBIT 5

The Graphic Company

Break-even Sales Control Chart

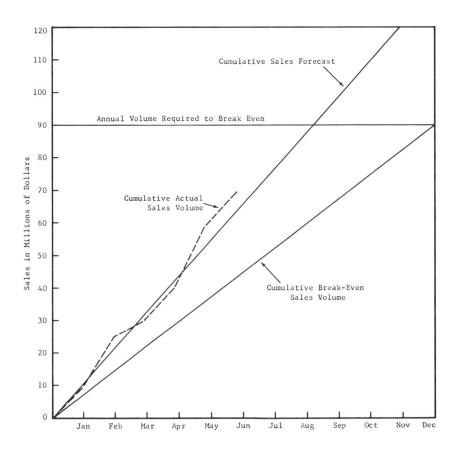

... And in Control

The preceding discussion has related principally to the planning phase of business, that is, to showing what must be done to achieve a given objective. Once the best plan has been selected and the goal has thus been defined, the same cost-volume-profit analysis can be used for control purposes. Charts may be helpful in such an approach. One such application is a sales control chart as shown in Exhibit 5. This chart shows three important factors cumulatively: actual sales volume, sales forecast, and sales volume required to break-even. Based on existing sales plans, the chart shows that eight months of sales are required just to meet all costs and expenses and that

EXHIBIT 6

The Illustrative Company

Break-even Control Chart
(monthly)

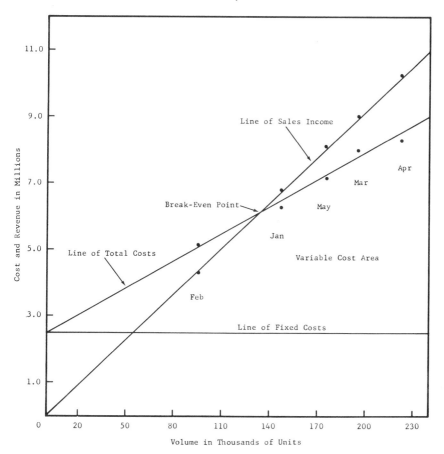

profits will be realized for the year only after the cumulative sales level has been attained.

Another chart designed to show progress — or lack of progress — in keeping with the acceptable cost-volume-profit structure is illustrated in Exhibit 6. In this application, monthly costs are charted against the corresponding sales level to detect out-of-line trends.

A Major Help in Answering Many Questions

The applications of the cost-volume-profit relationship, illustrated in this article, are suggestive only. Further refinements and modifications may be found necessary, desirable, and useful in your particular business. Moreover, as conditions change, the desired profit structure must be adjusted. Nevertheless, there are a great many questions that the cost-volume-profit relationship may help to answer. It is one facet of putting facts and figures to work for management, and it is one of the more interesting aspects of accounting for planning and control.

17 *The requirements for effective reporting are first de-veloped in this incisive article. These themselves are dependent on the objectives of the reporting and on the means of attaining the goals. Within this context, profit-volume reporting is discussed; first with respect to its uses, and then with respect to its limitations.*

Profit-volume reporting, whether in comparative alternative statement form, or in chart form, is seen to furnish a simplified framework that permits manipulation of the variables to predict behavior of the activity. Profit-volume analysis is seen as a family of relationships. The article concludes by giving suggestions for improving and expanding profit-volume reporting.

Boundaries and Potentials of Reporting on Profit-Volume Relationships*

In discussing a relatively small part of any information system, it is difficult to avoid the extremes of becoming excessively enthusiastic and eloquent concerning its unquestioned merits or becoming overly sophisticated and assuming that the matter is not worth discussing unless it accomplishes all objectives perfectly. Profit-volume analysis and reporting have suffered at both extremes, from friend and enemy, and it is only within the last decade or two that accountants and economists have seriously attempted to appraise

* From NAA Bulletin, *Vol. XLII, No. 5 (January, 1961), pp. 5–14. Reprinted by permission of the publisher.*

the concept, specify the pre-conditions for its usefulness and set forth guides for determining the limits of its effective range.[1]

The first part of this paper is devoted to a discussion of the requirements for effective reporting of any kind. Some of the limitations of profit-volume reporting are then outlined. The paper is concluded with some recommendations for improving and expanding the usefulness of reporting of this type.

Requirements for Effective Reporting

It should be evident that the purpose of reporting of any kind is to aid the accomplishment of worthy organizational objectives. The starting place for a discussion of reporting is, therefore, with the objectives to be attained and not, as is so often claimed, with the facts. In view of this popular misconception of the order of activity, it seems worthwhile to outline the necessary steps for an effective information gathering and reporting service. The following steps indicate the approximate order:

1. Identify the objectives of participating individuals and groups in the organizational structure.
2. Check these objectives for "worthiness" by the accepted ethical standards of the social structure. Also check the objectives for consistency with one another, and evaluate conflicting interests.
3. Discover and specify the *decisions* that are necessary to accomplish the accepted goals.
4. Determine the information necessary for reaching the decisions.
5. Identify the persons who make decisions, and correlate them with the specific decisions that must be made.
6. Determine the reaction patterns — behavioral responses — of each group of decision-makers. All do not think alike, evaluate alike or react alike.
7. Recognize the cost constraints that keep us from giving all the specifically tailored information that might be desired.
8. Appraise the possibility of "educating" the decision-makers. Do not overlook the possibility of persuading and training consumers of information to react in more convenient and acceptable ways.

---

[1] There is a strong temptation in discussions of this sort to devote most of the effort to historical aspects of the problem. This temptation is resisted here except for this bibliographical note. For a highly competent discussion see Joel Dean, "Cost Structures of Enterprises and Break-even Charts," *American Economic Review, Supplement*, Vol. 38, 1948. An enthusiastic and detailed discussion is found in Fred V. Gardner, *Profit Management and Control*, McGraw-Hill, New York, 1955, especially Section II, Chapters 12–27. R. L. Brummet treats the subject completely and introduces profit isolines in *Overhead Costing*, University of Michigan, Ann Arbor, 1957. Practically all modern textbooks and handbooks in the field consider profit-volume, fixed-variable, and break-even analysis in some detail. According to the *Encyclopaedia Britannica*, fixed-variable analysis is first credited to Dionysius Lardner (1850) and profit charting with flexible budgeting techniques to John Manger Fells (1903). Rautenstrauch and Knoeppel were early advocates of profit-volume planning, and each claimed to have introduced break-even charting.

9. Tailor the system. Decide what beliefs, judgments, estimates and prejudices should be collected and reported. (The traditional accountant who is addicted to the "facts" should reflect for a moment on the nature of depreciation, full capacity, management intent, etc.)

10. Correlate the data with decision levels, so that the reports will aid and not hinder organizational objectives.

Wide-Range Use of Profit-Volume Analysis

Most readers will be familiar with the purposes to which profit-volume relationships are applied and will realize that most attention is given to the probable behavior of cost in response to changes in volume. The general relationship that is pertinent to all costs is their relevance to the problems under consideration, and considerable effort might be saved by abandoning some current classifications and regrouping costs in terms of definite problems and types of problems. The fixed-variable division, for example, is not precisely defined, and care must be taken to emphasize that fixed costs are not necessarily fixed in the usual sense. In fact, many accountants now feel that the fixed-variable classification is so confused that it might well be abandoned. For line control it is convenient to think of fixed costs as those costs that are not controllable at the authority level under consideration. Unfortunately this usage has led some economists to make semi-nonsense assertions that variable costs are controllable and fixed costs are not. Some cost accountants have tried to remedy the situation by using sunk costs to indicate that the costs are not controllable at the level under consideration, but traditionally sunk costs have other connotations, and the suggestion does not seem to be a fruitful one.

In the minds of many businessmen, fixed costs are also mixed up with fixed charges. The latter term is usually related to fund requirements. Some are confused further by the fact that fixed costs differ widely, depending on whether the firm operates or shuts down. Shutdown costs are fixed in the ordinary, nontechnical sense, but they must be distinguished from fixed costs as used in cost accounting. The suggestion that costs be classified as inherently fixed, management fixed and accounting fixed may provide a useful framework but runs into the theoretical difficulties. It should be emphasized, however, that once definitions are accepted, accountants cannot change fixed costs to variable costs or vice versa by verbal manipulation.

It should be obvious that profit-volume relationships provide management with a simplified framework for organizing one's thinking on a number of problems. Certainly, budgeting, planning and predicting are improved by such a framework. It is probably easier to make "allowances" in the form of lump-sum amounts for many other influential variables and to focus attention on the influence of volume. Such a structure has the advantage inherent in many economic models by presenting opportunities for manipulating the variables in the model to help predict the possible behavior of the system. Influences other than volume may be treated as parameters, and it is therefore more accurate to consider profit-volume relationships as a family of relationships. Such a model has the effect of reminding management of other relevant variables and guarding against serious oversights. Considerable flexibility is available, for with slight modification the model may be adapted to product lines, territories, types of customer, size of order and a host of less familiar situations.

In our current concern with internal management decisions and our current emphasis on managerial accounting, we may sometimes forget that many external decision-making centers exist and influence the behavior of an organization. It goes without saying that investors, for example, are interested in a firm's reactions to business conditions and its vulnerability to declines in business activity. Profit-volume analysis in conjunction with income-elasticity studies may be extremely helpful in this area.

Workers and their leaders have a direct and personal interest in the expected behavior of enterprise profits in good and bad times. In addition, they are vitally interested in the possible effects of increased wage rates, changes in efficiency, drawn-out strikes, and pricing policies on the welfare of their employer. Without some form of profit-volume relation, the prediction of the effects of wage-rate changes is extremely difficult.

Governmental agencies sometimes wish to estimate income shifts from industry to industry and group to group when business conditions change. They may make use of some form of profit-volume analysis in appraising rate structures for public service concerns and in making monopoly investigations. Furthermore, they must sometimes estimate the need for and timing of new plant (capital) investments in various industries. Such estimates require prediction of capacity limits and the behavior of cost at and near such limits.

Various Approaches to Profit-Volume Reporting

The preferred model for profit-volume analysis appears as a functional relationship between costs and volume, and another between revenue and volume with other pertinent parameters such as setups, changeovers, quality-changes, product shifts, etc., specified and shown as preliminary modifications of the analysis. Such multifunctional relationships with other variables may not be beyond the comprehension of the typical businessman but they call for many refinements that we can consider here. Let us now turn to some relatively simple methods of presentation.

The oldest reporting procedure, and for many businessmen still the more easily understood, consists of a limited number of alternative income sheets that reflect different assumptions. The addition of a checklist for related parameters that require independent estimates as a supplement may make this approach extremely effective. The results are shown for a limited number of cases, and the method can be applied without the necessity for estimating the behavior of each variable over its whole range. For practical application, the projected income reports should be few and should be related to genuine alternatives that are, in fact, available to the organization. This type of presentation has the advantage of being in a familiar report form and the further advantage of requiring only a few estimates that are within the range of the firm's probable experience. Obviously, such an arrangement lacks the flexibility of a chart or a generalized relationship, and it does not stress the variable-fixed cleavage, unless the form of the income report is modified in that direction. It is, of course, possible that the typical profit-volume or break-even chart overemphasizes the importance of the volume-variability of costs and tends to hide or treat as relatively unimportant many of the other factors that should receive careful attention.

A series of contribution schedules can be used to supplement or replace the estimated income reports. These schedules tend to emphasize the separation of fixed and variable costs and thus are easily related to budgetary procedures. They are flexible in that they may be applied to territories, products, lines of products, channels of distribution, size of orders, or to any other base that might necessitate the incremental decisions. This approach has teaching merit, for it tends to emphasize that profit as it is usually calculated is the excess of contribution over the amount of fixed costs that some bookkeeper has decided to assign to the decision group. When variable costs are roughly equivalent to responsibility costs, this approach to profit-volume reporting is related to direct costing in the best sense, and may be expected to emphasize a classification that is relevant to practically all incremental decisions. P/V ratios are, of course, related to contribution schedules, although the results are usually expressed in percentage or in decimal form. Schedules and ratios need not use charts or graphs and thereby frighten the nonmathematical.

Reporting profit-volume relationships with the use of charts has some artistic appeal and may in some cases help gain acceptance for the concepts. Charts tend to emphasize relationships over large ranges of the variables and may be used effectively to highlight the regions of smooth relationships and the critical points or other discontinuities. Moreover, they have the advantage (or disadvantage) of practically forcing a reduction of the variables to meet the charting requirements. Unfortunately, they introduce problems of their own, such as scaling the variables and showing proportions in a useful manner.

The usual break-even or profit chart may be simplified by the use of profit lines instead of separate lines for revenues, variable and fixed costs. The resulting charts are then so simple that even the most nonquantitative mind can grasp them without difficulty. By making the charts only slightly more complicated, different price structures may be shown. The effect of the price-elasticity of demand is then indicated by the length of the price lines. Charts of this kind probably have more flexibility than is usually assumed. The effects of cost changes as the result of plant expansion or contraction, new wage agreements, changes in advertising appropriations, etc., may be shown easily. The shifting of break-even and profit points in response to shifts in costs and prices can be shown and emphasized quickly.

Some Additional Considerations

Before turning to some limitations of such devices as profit-volume analysis, it may be well to ask why costs are assigned, clustered or classified at all. It is probably true that if there were no uniformities, so that the relationship could not ever be expected to recur or could be expected to recur so rarely that no pattern could be determined or prediction made, then there would be no reason to classify and assign costs. Moreover, if every project is different and the bidding on each assumes that we begin with the facilities left over from previous jobs and that these facilities have no alternative uses, there is considerably less reason to assign "values" to the carry-over facilities and attempt to find total project cost. (At this point we are neglecting the problems of "fair" billing to different parties. It should be emphasized that this problem is an important one, even if an exact portrayal of "fair" is difficult.)

In a similar manner a horizon must be selected for determining variable (responsibility) costs. For certain decisions and for a clear view of certain relationships, it is convenient to disregard the entire complex of carry-over facilities and to consider them as free goods or as irrelevant for the decision at hand. In effect, we must tailor our cost information to the decision. In a transportation concern, for example, we may take as our starting point the assumption that the train is already scheduled and the further assumption that there is unused capacity. The resulting responsibility costs would then be extremely small and would consist of minor hauling costs. For another decision, it may be convenient to start with the assumption that all cars are loaded, and consider the incremental costs and revenues resulting from adding another car. In other instances, the decision involves an additional section or even another entire train. In each case the appropriate incremental cost is different. The point to be stressed here is that overall profit-volume charts and reporting tend to smooth out these discontinuities, and users must be cautioned about employing general, overall procedures to solve specific individual problems.

It appears, then, that an entire family of curves is necessary for a proper representation of relevant costs, and the prediction of profit behavior requires careful specification of the initial conditions. In some cases we may be able to make specific allowances for important irregularities or hope that they average out. If so, we may present a band of possibilities that spans the difference between the long-run picture and the curve that represents the most simple incremental conditions.

Limitations of Profit-Volume Projections

Many of the limitations of profit-volume projections are too simple to require extensive discussion. A generalized presentation is next to useless if materials costs fluctuate widely and are relatively important, or when the channel or product mix jumps around, or if advertising and sales pressure are changeable and important. This list could be extended almost indefinitely. Most readers are no doubt familiar with the usual difficulties that result from step functions and other discontinuities or from the economies of scale and overtime and shift premium. The disregard of cost control when business is good and the virtual compulsion for control when business is bad are discussed widely and are easily understood. It is usually feasible to include the additional cost of laxity at higher activity levels in the direct cost estimates or to make allowances in other ways.

A related discussion has arisen as to whether profit-volume models are dynamic or are examples of comparative statics. So far little progress has been made toward making these relationships dynamic, although some economists have made some faltering steps, using similar materials. We accountants have not worked with the dynamic aspects of the problem seriously, although we are aware that costs and revenues may be affected differently if changes are made at a rapid or more gradual rate. We are aware, too, that changes in costs sometimes depend on the amount of advance notice given to those with authority to adjust costs and revenues. To many, dynamic refinements in the model have not seemed to be worth the effort in view of the crudeness of some of our conventional assumptions, but it seems that the profession is now ready for a thorough study of the theory and methodology of such models.

Difficulties sometimes arise in the application of profit-volume analysis because the rate of production differs from the rate of shipments. A flurry of articles and discussions has followed the growing popularity of direct costing methods. Suppose, to illustrate, that a firm has fixed costs of $100,000 per year and makes a practice of recognizing idle-capacity losses as period costs. If this firm should manufacture nothing and sell at the rate of 100 percent capacity, the fixed costs metered to the income report would be $200,000. If, on the other hand, sales are zero and production is at the rate of 100 percent, the amount of fixed costs taken to income would be zero. Thus, a profit variation with limits of $200,000 could be induced by varying production and sales rates. The usual break-even or profit chart is based on the direct cost assumption or its equivalent assumption of equal production and sales.

The difficulty arises from the penchant of accountants for metering some fixed cost to income through the cost of goods sold channel, and the result is, of course, that a part of the fixed cost is matched with revenue as if it were in fact a variable cost. Furthermore, on the production side the fixed cost is transferred to inventory as if the cost were variable with production. Any discussion of the reporting of profit-volume predictions should make these peculiarities clear, and it is therefore usually desirable to supplement a schedule of differences in expected and actual performance with a reconciliation of fixed costs taken to revenue and fixed costs taken to or released from inventory. Some previous periods' costs and some current costs will be assigned to revenues through the current merchandise-sold route, and some current fixed costs will often be matched on a direct costing basis as an idleness loss. The reasoning is not changed if production is in an area designated as excess capacity.[2]

Improving Profit-Volume Reporting

We may now turn to some suggestions for improving the usefulness of profit-volume reporting. Perhaps the most immediate need for improvement is in the area of improved feedback. If goals are established and standards are available, the necessary feedback can be built around traditional variance analysis. Variations in planned costs on an individual basis may be analyzed in the usual budgetary manner with special attention to mix and price-concession variances and to the improvement of future estimates. The similarity of overall profit planning and profit-volume analysis to budgeting is obvious, and, when budgets are not in operation, it seems desirable to expand this kind of analysis to take advantage of budgetary techniques. It is perhaps natural that profit-volume analysis developed in the process of predicting behaviour but the order of development ought not to deter us from making full use of its possible control features.

Accountants have hardly begun to scratch the surface in the field of measuring and presenting confidence limits and the related field of delimiting the range over which the relationships have validity. We have been slow about reporting this type of information, because, unfortunately, we have been slow about bringing findings from other fields to bear on accounting problems. The techniques of statistics can yield measures of the extent to which a stated functional relationship could have predicted past changes. Some form of these statistical coefficients might be given as supplements of the usual profit-volume reports. Low coefficients suggest that other variables are at work and help initiate search to find what they are, how they work, and how their effects may be incorporated in the analysis. It is hardly necessary to remind accountants that such measures apply to past results and that it is always the future that is being estimated.

[2] While Jonathan N. Harris is usually considered to be the father of direct costing, the precedent for short-circuiting inventory with fixed costs has been well established from the beginning of cost accounting as we know it. Mr. Clark, controller of J. L. Hudson, and other merchandise accountants have been discussing the matter since the nineteen-twenties. Incidentally Clem N. Kohl demonstrated a thorough understanding of the problem in "What Is Wrong With Most Profit and Loss Statements?" *NA(C)A Bulletin*, July 1, 1937, pp. 1207–1219, about a year and a half after Mr. Harris' article, "What Did We Earn Last Month?" in the January 15, 1936 issue.

Accountants have been especially careless about explaining output limits, time horizons and initial conditions upon which and over which their predictions may have validity. Only recently a well-known professor of industrial management stated emphatically that he was not interested in fixed-incremental analysis because it had been his experience (largely in the printing business) that the incremental costs usually worked out to be long-run average costs, "when the smoke cleared away." Undoubtedly some businessmen do quote average costs as incremental costs — take the long-run view — and in many businesses costs not variable with volume are so unimportant that the substitution of long-run average costs for short-run incremental costs leads to no serious error. Thus, in some cases, a confusion of the initial conditions and the horizon may not lead to serious difficulty but, even so, there is no excuse for confusing them.

It is probable that in our zeal to simplify presentations and reports we have tried too hard to encourage the use of general-purpose summaries. In many situations the advantages of tailored reports are not great; we can use crude compromises and still reach effective decisions but, with advances in computer technology, we are now in a better position to submit more specific information. Where different initial conditions lead to widely different relationships (e.g., incremental passenger cost with unused car capacity as opposed to incremental cost with a full train), general compromises are not satisfactory, and the accountant is well-advised to make more specific reports and to encourage the user to take necessary time to understand the different situations clearly. Rarely is effort wasted when it is devoted to a better understanding of the relationships necessary for effective decisions. Certainly no businessman should be encouraged to believe that straight-line relationships between profit and volume over the usual range of activity can be extended indefinitely in spite of overtime, shift premium, material price, and wage increases.

Recently investment analysts have been interested in adding depreciation to reported profit and thereby estimating the net inflow of current funds from operations. The profit-volume kind of analysis can be easily adapted to this procedure in the form of a funds-volume analysis. Most variable costs require the outlay of current funds, with the result that a line or function to represent fund outlays should not be greatly different from the usual variable cost relation. The chief differences on the variable cost side are due to depreciation taken on an activity basis and to the fact that full costing usually treats depreciation in the cost-of-sales aggregate as variable and no immediate funds are required.

Clearly not all fixed costs require an outlay of current funds in a period, and care must be taken to separate those that require funds from those that do not. The presentation of fund charts offers no new problems. The "break-even" point will indicate the volume necessary for operations to provide enough funds to cover operating outlays. Additional lines may then be added to indicate requirements for bond interest, preferred dividends and regular common dividends. Other possibilities may suggest themselves.

18 *". . . in the large area of [operational] financial and economic decision-making . . . , the marriage of the economists' concepts and the principles on which managements appear to act . . . [seems] less [than] harmonious." Break-even analysis, which ignores the economists' theorems of cost and revenue behavior, is an example of one of the sharpest expressions of this cleavage of attitudes.*

Industrial break-even charts should be brought into closer conformity to economic theory, and they should be reinterpreted to clarify their true empirical significance.

". . . a key role should be played by the cost accountant, and the advanced techniques of cost accounting should be used as the bridge between theoretical concepts and real-world analysis at this point.

"Economic analysis should now take up new lines of development, based principally on quantitative studies under the auspices of firms and industrial groups."

On the Economics
of Break-Even*

Douglas Vickers

I

The practical analysis of business financial problems appears well suited to the use of the propositions and theorems of theoretical economics. But the interplay of empirical problems and the theories designed for their explanation has not yet proceeded to very great lengths. There has, of course, been a considerable progress in theoretical analysis in this area during the last three decades. And in more recent times attempts have been made to achieve more satisfying general theories of aspects of business behavior. The

* *From* The Accounting Review, *Vol. XXXV, No. 3, (July, 1960), pp. 405–412. Reprinted by permission of the editor.*

analysis of the criteria for investment decision in the corporate enterprise, the theory of optimum capital structure, and the relative costs of differing forms of capital financing are important instances of this progress. But in the large area of financial and economic decision-making within which the enterprise operates from day to day, the marriage of the economists' concepts and the principles on which managements appear to act has been less successful and less harmonious. The economists and the businessmen have examined similar problems with the aid of differing categories of thought. There has been too little communication of ideas between them.

The purpose of this paper is to draw attention to one of the sharpest expressions of this cleavage of attitudes, and to advance some tentative suggestions for improvements in both analysis and application. This relates to the use by business of a method of cost-volume-profit analysis, and of pricing and volume adjustments, which is referred to as break-even analysis and which, *prima facie*, ignores the economists' generalized theorems of cost and revenue behavior. Other important issues which call for a similar new attack will not be raised in this paper, but many potentially fruitful lines of development may be discovered in the literature referred to in the attached bibliographical note. Our principal conclusions in the matter of break-even analysis are threefold:

(a) The components of the break-even charts as used in industry are in need of reinterpretation to bring them more closely into line with some significant suggestions of economic theory, and, at the same time, to clarify their true empirical significance.

(b) In the new analysis and reinterpretation a key role should be played by the cost accountant, and the advanced techniques of cost accounting should be used as the bridge between theoretical concepts and real-world analysis at this point.

(c) Economic analysis should now take up new lines of development, based principally on quantitative studies under the auspices of firms and industrial groups.

In the course of the discussion, some of the traditional assumptions of economic theory which inhibit its empirical applicability will be indicated.

II

The key role of the accounting function can be highlighted by noting some recent developments within the business enterprise. The traditional role of the accountant as the recorder of costs, expenses, incomes, and profits has been broken down in many businesses into several more detailed functions. Firstly, new approaches have been made to the analysis and fragmentation of costs into such categories as fixed, semi-variable, and variable. Semi-variable costs have been separated more carefully into their fixed and variable components, and costs in general have been assigned more completely and in more detail to each of the various segments of the firm's operations. Developments in these respects have been most important for the refinement and the practical value of the break-even analysis. Details of alternative cost classifications need not be given at present, as the classifications themselves will change from one enterprise situation to another, and the basic dichotomy of fixed versus variable costs will be applied in as many different ways. One interesting refinement was suggested in this connection recently by K. J. Arkwright, writing in *The Australian Accountant*, December, 1958. He suggests the following sixfold categories: (a) unitary variable costs, which increase by one cost unit with each increase of one production unit; (b) non-unitary variable costs, which change by more or less than one cost unit with each unit change of production; (c) cost of reserve capacity necessarily incurred to cater for short-term fluctuations in the level of activity; (d) irregular independent costs which are completely irregular in amount and in frequency of occurrence, for example losses arising from inventory revaluations; (e) periodical independent costs which are periodical in occurrence but not predictable as to amount, for example additional factory heating expenses depending on the severity of the winter; (f) perfectly fixed costs, or costs of being in business and which could be eliminated only by winding up the firm. Whatever methods of classification are adopted, however, the thing of practical importance is the assignment of cost elements to the various segments of the firm's operations, and for this purpose a segment can be understood as a product, a process, or a market area, depending on the characteristics of the business.

The second development of the traditional accounting function has been the construction of revenue, production-cost, and profit budgets as a background for pricing studies. Central to this procedure is the summation of segmentized costs, that is the various cost elements assigned to segments of operations as referred to above, for purposes of balancing volume, price, and profit variations in each such segment and in the enterprise as a whole.

Thirdly, there remains the more traditional accounting function of the recording of income and outlay. Depending on the stage of development of the functions already referred to, this traditional task involves increasingly also the comparison of historic income and outlay data with the budgeted standards implicit in pricing studies. Finally, these several activities are frequently co-ordinated in the hands of a financial manager for the determination of budgeted and actual return on investment. This final economic and financial datum forms the basis of advice to the directors or owners of the business on policy changes and on expansion and new financing. To this last mentioned and co-ordinating function is frequently added the supervision of the internal cash flow of the business, the financing of short term cash requirements, and the more fundamental task of advising on the timing and techniques of long term capital financing.

The significance of this increasing sophistication of the traditional accounting function is that it points clearly to more general theorems of business behavior. Firstly, the principal focus of attention is now forward-looking and prospective, rather than concentrated on historical data alone, thus opening new applications of criteria of policy choice and action; and secondly, the bases for behavior which are thus established permit clear applications of the marginal balancing of costs and incomes. This occurs via the allocations of revenues and costs, and via the comparison of segment marginal revenues and relevant marginal costs. The kernel of these new and embryonic developments in the business firm is thus the emphasis on incremental values of revenues, costs, and profits, and on the additional returns realizable from changes in production volumes. It is in the light of these developments that the soundness, strength, and relevance of the break-even analysis will be examined.

III

The break-even chart has a long history, as indicated in the literature referred to in the bibliographical note. Throughout the 1930's, while economists were developing the theories of the firm on the assumption of curvilinear cost and revenue functions, as will be referred to briefly below, industrial consultants made large headway in an analysis of similar problems based explicitly on linearity assumptions. The break-even chart was a device of the industrialists, never at that time a tool of the economists. Perhaps the latter saw these charts, as Professor Machlup recently described them, as "nothing but glamorized multiplication tables." Joel Dean, on the other hand, has given the weight of his authority to the opinion that "break-even analysis . . . provides an important bridge between business behavior and the theory of the firm."

The typical break-even chart, as indicated in Figure 1, shows total dollar values on its vertical axis (total dollar values of revenues and expenses) and total quantities of output on its horizontal axis. Variations of the form may show on the *X* axis either output as a percentage of capacity, or total dollar values of sales. The last mentioned form is applicable for the analysis of the break-even situations of multi-product firms. The line *OZ* in Figure 1 indicates the total sales revenue derivable from varying levels of output on the assumption of a given market selling price. Variations in selling price will determine the possible slopes of this revenue line. The fixed costs of the enterprise are taken as *OA*, and the variable costs are described by the line *OV*, the angle of incidence of which depends on the established relationship of variable cost per unit of output produced. The total cost line *AB* (parallel to *OV*) represents the summation of fixed and variable costs and indicates, for example, that at output and sales of *OC*, total costs and total revenues will be equal at *CE*. *OC* will therefore represent the enterprise break-even

FIGURE 1

Break-even Chart

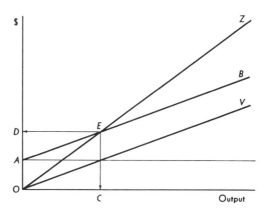

production level. If, as is useful in the case of multi-product analysis, the *X* axis is marked off in dollar values, the revenue line must take an angle of 45° and the unit selling price function is not implicit in the diagram. In other cases the unit selling price will determine the slope of the revenue line.

Before moving to consider the logical and empirical weaknesses of this popular device, a few of its principal implications can be noted. Firstly, the level of a single-product enterprise break-even point is dependent upon *both* the total revenue and the total cost characteristics. Given revenue possibilities, the level of production and sales at which an enterprise will break even will depend as much on the variable cost ratio as on the existing level of fixed charges. The level of *E* in Figure 1 will depend on the slope of *AB* as well as on the level of *A*. For the analysis of return on investment and for capital financing this has a threefold significance. Firstly, the percentage of capacity at which the firm breaks even is thus directly calculable, indicating, in other words, the level of production and sales beyond which the firm begins to penetrate what can be called its profit area, indicated by *ZEB* in Figure 1. Secondly, the relationship of forces so far envisaged determines the *rate* at which the firm penetrates its profit area after passing break-even point, or, alternatively, the rate at which losses mount up at levels of operation lower than this crucial point. Thirdly, the degree of possible fluctuations in operating incomes which are thus envisaged, depending on the severity of what can be called the firm's operational leverage, clearly contains implications for the desirable and possible structure of the firm's capitalization, thus giving rise to greater or lesser degrees of financial leverage. The manner in which this last mentioned feature affects the residual owners' or stockholders' position will not be considered at present.

In the second place, the shapes of these revenue and cost functions, while they ignore the arguments for curvi-linearity which economic theory adduces, probably do have a good deal of empirical justification, provided one important assumption is made in their use. This is the assumption that the extent of possible movements along the respective aggregate functions is limited to a fairly narrow range of output variation. In such a case, however, the break-even lines do *not* become relevant for management policy decisions throughout their entire length, but only within the distances representing possible marginal fluctuations from the level of production and sales at which the enterprise is currently operating. As soon as this is recognized, however, and as soon as it is seen that the break-even lines have empirical validity only within a narrow range of fluctuation from current output volume, the question arises whether the break-even diagram in this traditional form has any operationally significant meaning at all. For the break-even point itself, as drawn under these assumptions, has no meaning because the firm, in the normal course of events, will be endeavoring to operate *not* at break-even point, but at some volume level *above* break-even volume. The firm will, in other words normally endeavor to operate at a profit, which means, in terms of the traditional diagram as in Figure 1, somewhere in the profit area *ZEB*, or at some volume point higher than *OC*.

This does not mean that the break-even chart has no longer any potential usefulness, or that analysis of this kind can not be made to serve financial management objectives. But it does mean that a genuine reinterpretation of the break-even analysis is necessary, that a redefinition of its components and assumptions is called for, and that a recasting of the analysis should be made in terms of the assumptions which economic analysis has imported from its inspection of real-world enterprise situations. Before turning to the task of reinterpretation, it will be helpful to look briefly at the most relevant tools of theoretical economic analysis.

IV

Space does not permit an extended discussion of the economic theory of the firm. The literature referred to below, notably the works of Weintraub, Boulding, and Mrs. Robinson, set out the main points of the traditional theory. Some of the most relevant issues are summarized in Figure 2, in a form readily comparable with the break-even analysis in Figure 1.

Presented in this form, which depicts what may be called the break-even functions of the traditional theory, the total revenue and total cost functions, together with the assumption of given fixed costs, are directly analogous to the components of the business break-even analysis already examined. The analogue in the economists' tool kit is thus the *total* revenue and cost functions, and not the *average* functions in terms of which the behavior of the firm under varying competitive assumptions has frequently been analyzed.

It appears, therefore, that the functions of Figure 2, those of traditional economic theory, are formally similar to those of the break-even analysis in Figure 1. Only the shapes appear to differ. But this is not the whole of the contrast which has to be made, as will appear immediately below. A note on the shapes of the theoretical functions, however, is necessary at this point. Firstly, the total revenue function as drawn in this curvi-linear form depicts the fact that the enterprise is able to sell increasing quantities of output only at a diminishing selling price per unit, thus giving a total income which does not increase proportionally with output. This is the empirically valid assumption as to the market opportunities facing producers in conditions of what the economists refer to as imperfect or monopolistic competition. If conditions of perfect competition are assumed, on the other hand, indicating a situation in which an individual producer disposes of an undifferentiated product at a price set by the market, the total revenue curve will be linear through the origin in the manner of the total revenue function of Figure 1. This follows from the assumption that the individual producer's volume of the homogeneous commodity being supplied to the market by all producers is not sufficiently large to affect market price. The market price is therefore regarded by each producer as a parameter, or as a determinant of behavior which remains unchangeable for the length of time envisaged in his production policy decisions. Clearly, in the vast majority of non-agricultural, industrial enterprise situations this special case of perfect competition is not empirically significant. The literature cited examines fully the relevant and refined concepts of the elasticities of the functions and their sensitiveness to price and volume changes.

Equally important is the shape of the total cost function in Figure 2. The fixed cost component is taken as given in the same manner as in Figure 1. This simply indicates that a short period of time is being considered in which the capital equipment and fixed assets employed by the firm cannot be reduced or changed, and that output volume changes can be effected only by applying differing amounts of variable factors to the fixed factors already installed. In the very long run all factors are variable. In the short run some are fixed. The division between the two depends on the length of time under consideration.

The shape of the variable cost function, which again determines the shape of the total cost function, is the more significant component. This is determined by the so-called technological-economic "law of variable proportions," which states that as larger quantities of variable factors are applied to given fixed factors the resulting increase in total product, that is the marginal product, may increase for a short time but will ultimately diminish. Marginal costs per unit of output then rise rapidly. Instances of the practical reasons for this phenomenon will be familiar to industrial managers. Thus it is seen that by combining these assumptions as to the shapes of the total revenue and total cost functions, the pure theory of enterprise behavior is able to make the following definitional statements: (a) The slopes of the total cost and total revenue functions indicate respectively the marginal cost of production at any given output level, and the marginal revenue derivable from any given level of sales. (b) The equilibrium condition of the firm, that is the condition under which profits will be maximized, is that marginal cost should be equal to marginal revenue, which is the same as saying that the slopes of the total cost and revenue functions in Figure 2 should be equal. This condition is satisfied at some point such as output volume *OC*, at which the profit maximization is indicated by the maximum vertical distance between the cost and revenue functions. (c) The enterprise confronts, therefore, not one break-even point but two, indicated on Figure 2 at points *A* and *B*. Point *A* is analogous to the break-even point in Figure 1, and point *B* derives from the technological-economic laws of diminishing marginal productivity on the cost side and diminishing elasticity of demand on the revenue side.

Immediately, therefore, the economic theory goes one step further than the traditional break-even analysis, in specifying not only a *break-even* condition, but also an *equilibrium* condition. It specifies, in other words, the position *within* the profit area at which the firm should endeavor to operate. Break-even analysis, under its traditional assumptions of linearity, is able to say only that the break-even point should be passed, and it implies, what is logically and empirically untenable, that the profit area will keep on widening as production volume expands.

Can we say, then, that the cost accountants and financial managers should simply endeavor to redraw the break-even functions in such curvi-linear forms as the theory suggests, and that empirically relevant behavior lines will result, suitable to guide the management in financial decisions? It may not, unfortunately, be very meaningful to assume such a simple solution, or such a qualitative identity between the aggregate functions of theory and the empirically relevant cost and revenue curves. The curves of the theory, it is important to note, are severely static in form. They show a series of possible equilibrium positions based on the assumption of successively different, but *stable*, output rates, and they postulate smooth, continuous and *reversible* movements between alternative output positions. The curves, in other words, admit of analytical manipulations in describing comparative static

FIGURE 2

Enterprise Profit Maximization

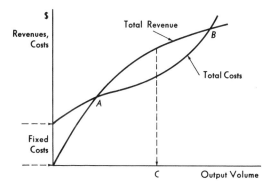

situations, and the shapes of the curves are in no sense envisaged as being alterable by the fact or degree of change.

If it is supposed that the break-even chart and the diagrams of theory *do* contain the same static assumptions, then clearly any number of alternative competitive assumptions and hypotheses can be examined and developed on the respective diagrams, for they then become in effect the very same thing. In such a case, however, we have stepped over from the field of hypothesizing about the conditions and behavior of industrial enterprises to imagining that we are actually *describing* enterprise situations. It is this gratuitous leap from hypothesis to imagined description that has invalidated much of the argument in this area.

V

Two important questions therefore arise at this point. Firstly, will the break-even lines, as applied to the analysis of practical problems, necessarily assume a linear form? And secondly, will a movement along the cost and revenue functions toward higher output levels be necessarily reversible? Logical and empirical reasons suggest that the developments envisaged would involve *irreversible* movements along *non-linear* functions, and it is in the clarification of these probabilities that the cost accountants and the economists can most fruitfully look for common ground.

Consider the aggregate revenue function first. Here the empirically valid economic assumption can be adduced that the elasticity of demand will diminish as producers lower price in order to increase sales, and that a curvi-linear total revenue function will result. But there exist, probably, ranges of output in which producers can sell varying amounts without any price change, and the curvi-linear total revenue function can in such a case be looked upon as made up of a series of short linear sections, the slope of each of which indicates a certain market selling price. The actual revenue function most significant for business policy decisions might then be regarded as the locus of the mid-points of such a succession of short linear sections, the revenue curve thus describing a movement-path as output moves through varying volume ranges. This may establish an empirically probable function as a basis for business decisions, but the probability and ambiguity it contains result principally from the fact that movements along the function in any direction as volume changes may not be reversible over time if volume should return to a previous level. There is no reason to believe that a rise in price following a fall in price would necessarily move the volume of market demand back to where it was before the fall. Market structures and patterns of demand might conceivably change.

On the cost side, the economists' empirically valid assumptions should again be invoked, and the phenomenon of diminishing marginal productivity can be expected to give a curvi-linear shape to the total cost function. Here again the function may be translated from the usual static form to a dynamic form in which the cost levels and cost components change as volume changes, and in which the achievable costs may not be reversible over time as output volume fluctuates. But at this point the accountants' fragmentation of costs can be intelligently employed to separate out, and allocate to the relevant segments of the enterprise, the fixed costs and the fixed elements of semi-variable costs referable to them, and to *define* a residuum of unitary variable costs in such a way as to give once again a series of short linear total cost sections as output changes. The total cost function can then be regarded as a movement-path, or locus of linear sections, analogous to the construction of the total revenue curve. But this, of course, implies fairly minute degrees of cost fragmentation and analysis. Fortunately, this is beginning to be done and gives promise of being carried further with the aid of standardized procedures in industry. Obviously, the degree of precision and sophistication which is called for or desired must depend on the size and character of the undertaking concerned.

But there remains again the question of reversibility. On the cost side the evidence for irreversibility rests mainly in two kinds of factors: firstly, changes in efficiency in the use of variable factors (wastes, methods of use, technology, etc.) can not easily be conceived to be reversible over movements between output ranges; and secondly, there is no necessary guarantee that all fixed elements of total costs which were added as output rose will be found by management to be regulatable or dispensable as output levels move again in the opposite direction. Whether the irreversibilities in the break-even cost and revenue functions would exert favorable or unfavorable effects on the level of the break-even point, or on the rapidity of penetration of the profit area, remains an issue for testing against empirical models.

Against the background of these arguments regarding the nature, shape, and reversibility of break-even cost and revenue functions, the familiar propositions depicted in Figure 1 call for reinterpretation. The analysis of industrial volume-profit experience and planning requires a more sensitive segmentized approach. Account should be taken of changes in the levels and shapes of the operative functions over as fine a variation of output ranges, or variations of intervals of time, as is administratively possible for budget and accounting purposes. It is not sufficient to argue, as is frequently done, that the case can be met by re-drawing the break-even chart of Figure 1 as often as budget changes are made, for this avoids the more fundamental issue of the nature and shape of the aggregate functions of Figure 1, and the extent of the output over which they have any empirical relevance or applicability.

It will be clear from the foregoing analysis that the conceptions which are here advanced of workable break-even models in industry have moved a good way from the naive and static models frequently relied upon in the firm itself, and which certainly have too frequently been used by the economist to caricature industry financial operations and management. The arguments which this paper has developed, however, set a program of research and development by the cost accountant, and suggest that economists now give their attention to examining the shape and stability of aggregate revenue and cost functions over time and over output ranges, applying their resources of statistical analysis to the reconstruction of empirical micro-functions and variables.

For the financial manager in industry the lesson of the analysis is that he cannot rely with the same degree of confidence on the more naive forms of his break-even charts. But the re-interpreted and reconstructed tools which are suggested to him by the economists and cost accountants should provide a firmer foundation for relevant policy decisions. This in no sense implies that the businessman should necessarily strive for the maximization of net revenue in the sense of the earlier static models of economic theory. But the indications of incremental costs applicable to production changes between or within, output ranges, such as is suggested by the analysis, should afford management clearer guidance as to the directions in which net incremental additions to income lie.

Bibliographical Note

The indispensable starting point for further theoretico-empirical work in this area is P. J. D. Wiles' *Price, Cost and Output* (Oxford, Blackwell, 1956). For the economic theory consult Sidney Weintraub, *Price Theory* (New York, Pitman, Revised edition, 1956), Joan Robinson, *The Economics of Imperfect Competition* (London, Macmillan, 1933) and Kenneth Boulding, *Economic Analysis* (New York, Harper, 3rd edition, 1955). For the development of break-even analysis in industry see Ned Chapin, "The Development of the Break-Even Chart: A Bibliographical Note" in *Journal of Business*, April 1955, and a comment on Chapin's article by Raymond Villers, *Journal of Business*, October 1955. A fairly complete exposition of break-even techniques from the industrial consultant's viewpoint appeared in Walter Rautenstrauch and Raymond Villers, *The Economics of Industrial Management* (New York, Funk and Wagnalls, 1949; 2nd Revised edition by Raymond Villers, 1957). See also the same authors' *Budgetary Control* (New York, Funk and Wagnalls, 1950.) Joel Dean's *Managerial Economics* (New York, Prentice-Hall, 1951) contains relevant sections. A critical attitude to the break-even analysis is taken by Fritz Machlup in *The Economics of Sellers' Competition* (Baltimore, Johns Hopkins, 1952).

Among the journal literature the following are important: Hans Brems, "A Discontinuous Cost Function," *American Economic Review*, Dec. 1952; Wilford J. Eiteman and Glenn E. Guthrie, "The Shape of the Average Cost Curve," *American Economic Review*, 1952; James S. Earley, "Recent Developments in Cost Accounting and the 'Marginal Analysis,' " *Journal of Political Economy*, June 1955; Sidney Robbins and Edward Foster, "Profit-planning and the Finance Function," *Journal of Finance*, Dec. 1957; K. J. Arkwright, "Marginal Costing: Reconciliation of Theory and Practice," *The Australian Accountant*, 1958; George Gibbs, "New Cost Accounting Concepts," *The Accounting Review*, Jan. 1958; Joel Dean, "Cost Structures of Enterprises and Break-even Charts," *American Economic Review Supplement*, May 1948.

19 *An extension is made to traditional breakeven analysis by the use of differential calculus to determine a formula and solution to the problem of volume changes which are related to price changes. The authors outline the defects of traditional cost-volume-profit analysis. Carefully, they trace the impact of changes in variable costs, changes in fixed costs, and they develop indifference points for prospective changes relative to original considerations. The authors are able to provide the businessman with tools that extend the use of cost-volume-profit analysis beyond only a few selected alternatives.*

A New Application of Calculus and Risk Analysis to Cost-Volume-Profit Changes*

Thomas A. Morrison and Eugene Kaczka

Differential calculus has recently been applied to some cost-volume-profit situations as an extension of breakeven analysis to find maximum profit levels when cost and/or revenue behavior is curvilinear.[1] However, there is another far more practical application that, for some unknown reason, has gone unrecognized up to now. It involves changes in selling prices and costs of changes in quality which result in changes in quantities demanded.

All companies consider the effect that changes in selling prices will have on the sales of their product. They are also laboring under a constant cost-push pressure to increase prices. Therefore, companies must forecast

* *From* The Accounting Review, *Vol. XLIV, No. 2 (April, 1969), pp. 330–343. Reprinted by permission of the editor.*
[1] Travis P. Goggans, "Break-even Analysis with Curvilinear Functions," THE ACCOUNTING REVIEW, (October 1965), pp. 867–871, and Horace R. Givens, "An Application of Curvilinear Break-even Analysis," THE ACCOUNTING REVIEW, (January 1966), pp. 141–143.

expected volume for the various changes in sales price. Then they must determine whether or not such changes will be profitable. Finally, the most profitable combination of changes should be selected.

Traditional Method

The traditional method of approaching these problems is to select several discrete changes in sales prices, forecast new levels of sales at these points, and select the most profitable alternative. All managerial accounting texts explain this method but go no further. A recent article used the typical illustration shown in Exhibit A.[2] The traditional approach makes the very substantial assumption that cost and demand functions are known. Since the data which are used in the analysis are in fact estimates, it is advisable to consider the accuracy of these estimates in making decisions. This article extends the usual approach by considering a continuum of price changes and incorporating risk in the analysis.

EXHIBIT A
Conventional Cost-Volume-Profit Analysis
Preliminary Budget for Period

Net Sales	$200,000
Variable Costs	170,000
Variable Margin	30,000
Specific Capacity Costs	17,500
Product contribution to common capacity costs and profit	$ 12,500

Detail: Units 40,000
    Unit rates: Selling price $5.00
        Variable costs 4.25
        Contribution .... .75

New Alternatives		Budget			
Price Increase		5%	10%	12.5%	15%
Unit Volume Reduction		10%	20%	30.0%	45%
Sales Price	$5.00	$5.25	$5.50	$5.63	$5.75
Variable Cost/unit	4.25	4.25	4.25	4.25	4.25
Variable Margin/unit	$.75	$1.00	$1.25	$1.38	$1.50
Sales Units	40,000	36,000	32,000	28,000	22,000
Variable Margin	$30,000	$36,000	$40,000	$38,640	$33,000

∴ Best solution = Increase sales price 10%

[2] I. Wayne Keller, "Controlling Contribution," *Management Accounting,* (June 1967), p. 23, 28. Similar illustrations used by Walter B. McFarland, *Concepts for Management Accounting,* (National Association of Accountants, 1966), p. 69, and Robert Beyer, *Profitability Accounting for Planning and Control,* (The Ronald Press Company, 1963) Chapter 7.

Defects of the Traditional Approach

Unfortunately, the traditional approach fails to make full use of the relationships given. Once the original contribution is given (original selling price minus original variable costs) as well as the expected change in the quantity demanded as determined by marketing analysis, a maximum profit can be determined for *any* change in price (not merely for 3 or 4 given alternatives) where some explicit or implicit functional relationship is assumed between price and volume.

Also, some misleading inferences might be made from the use of a few discrete alternatives. In the preceding example, the ratio of volume reduction to price increase went from 2:1

$$\left(\text{i.e., } \frac{10\%}{5\%}, \frac{20\%}{10\%}\right) \text{ to } 2.4:1 \left(\text{i.e., } \frac{30.0\%}{12.5\%}\right) \text{ to } 3:1 \left(\text{i.e., } \frac{45\%}{15\%}\right).$$

Since the alternate selected was the last point at which the ratio was 2:1, it might be inferred that as long as the volume change relative to price change remained in the ratio of 2:1, the company should continue to raise the price. This is not true. It will be shown that even if the ratio remained constant at 2:1, the profits would start to decline after a 17.5% price increase had been reached. This is caused by the fact that the contribution per unit changes in a curvilinear fashion even though the price-volume relationship is linear.

The Calculus Approach

The most important step is the development of a general formula which can be used for all changes in selling price and volume.[3]

The following notations will be used:

$a =$ constant intercept of Y axis
$b =$ constant slope of line
$OV =$ original volume in units
$OSP =$ original selling price per unit
$OVC =$ original variable cost per unit
$PCV =$ per cent change in volume
$PCP =$ per cent change in selling price
$OCP =$ original contribution as a per cent of selling price
$Z =$ variable margin divided by original revenue (original volume times original selling price)

[3] For explanatory purposes linear price-volume relationships are used over the relevant ranges. These may be assumed to be reasonable approximations of curvilinear relationships.

When a per cent increase of selling price is associated with a per cent decrease in volume, variable margin can be determined as follows:

(1.1)   Variable Margin $= [OV(1 - PCV)] \cdot [OSP(1 + PCP) - OVC]$

Since original volume (OV) and original selling price (OSP) are irrelevant, divide both sides by these:

(1.2) $Z = (1 - PCV) \cdot \left[(1 + PCP) - \dfrac{OVC}{OSP}\right]$

Since

$$OCP = 1 - \frac{OVC}{OSP},$$

then the general equation is:

(1.3) $Z = (1 - PCV)(OCP + PCP)$

Since OCP is a constant only PCV and PCP remain as variables. Finally, when PCV is expressed linearly in terms of PCP, only one independent variable is left as follows:

$$\text{since } PCV = a + bPCP$$
$$Z = [1 - (a + bPCP)](OCP + PCP)$$

This equation is identifiable as a parabola opening downward with its vertex a maximum, i.e., the second derivative is negative. The per cent price change at which the maximum occurs is determined by taking the first derivative and setting the resulting expression equal to zero and solving for PCP as follows:

$$Z = (1 - a)OCP + (1 - a)PCP - bPCP \cdot OCP - bPCP^2$$
$$\frac{dZ}{dPCP} = 0 + (1 - a) - bOCP - 2bPCP = 0$$

(1.4) $PCP = \dfrac{1 - a - bOCP}{2b}$

EXAMPLE

If in the above example the price-volume relationship can be assumed to remain constant 2:1 up to $PCP = 10\%$, 2.4:1 when PCP lies between 10% and 12.5% and 3:1 when PCP is greater than 12.5%, three different linear relationships could be plotted (Exhibit B). The maximum profit points (which are the same as the maximum variable margin points) for the three separate lines can be computed by taking the first derivative of

EXHIBIT B
Optimum for Price-Volume Change Relationships
(Solid line gives PCP PCV relationships within the relevant ranges)

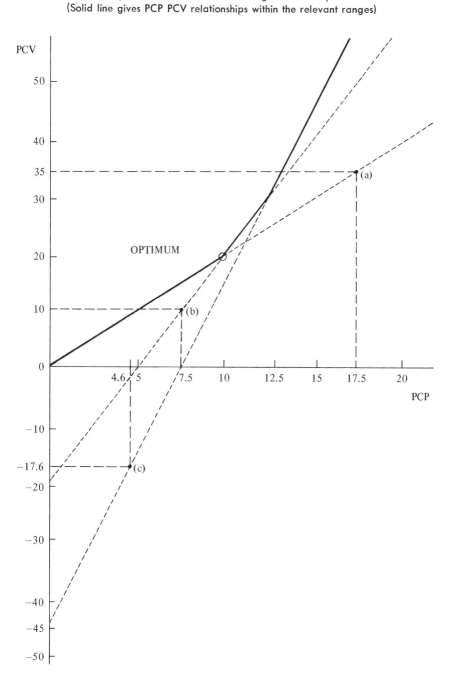

equation 1.3 after substituting the given relationships for PCV, or by using equation 1.4 directly as follows:

(a) When

$$PCV = 2PCP$$
$$a = 0$$
$$b = 2$$
$$OCP = \frac{.75}{5.00} = .15$$
$$\text{Maximum } PCP = \frac{1 - 0 - 2(.15)}{4}$$
$$PCP = .175 = 17.5\%$$

This is above the relevant range 0–10%.

Verification

PCP	17%	17.5%	18%
PCV	34%	35%	36%
New selling price	$5.35	$5.875	$5.90
New contribution	$1.60	$1.625	$1.65
New volume	26,400	26,000	25,600
New variable margin .	$42,240	$42,250	$42,240
		Max.	

(b) When

$$PCV = .2 + 4(PCP - .1)$$
$$PCV = -.2 + 4PCP$$
$$a = -.2$$
$$b = 4$$
$$OCP = .15$$
$$\text{Maximum } PCP = \frac{1 - (-.2) - 4(.15)}{8}$$
$$PCP = .075 = 7.5\%$$

This is below the relevant range 10%–12.5%.
This can be verified in a manner similar to (a).

(c) When

$$PCV = .3 + 6(PCP - .125)$$
$$PCV = -.45 + 6PCP$$
$$a = -.45$$
$$b = 6$$
$$OCP = .15$$
$$\text{Maximum } PCP = \frac{1 - (-.45) - 6(.15)}{12}$$
$$PCP = .046 = 4.6\%$$

This is below the relevant range 12.5% to ∞.
This can be verified in a manner similar to (a).

ANSWER TO EXAMPLE

The maximum profit point is located exactly at $PCP = 10\%$, since a movement in either direction from this point is away from the maximum profit points of (a) and (b) above. The answer can easily be demonstrated by taking points just above and below the maximum as follows:

PCP	9%	10%	11%
PCV	18%	20%	24%
New selling price	$5.45	$5.50	$5.55
New contribution	$1.20	$1.25	$1.30
New volume	32,800	32,000	30,400
New variable margin .	$39,360	$40,000	$39,520
		Max.	

The answer to this example is at a point of intersection. However, it should be emphasized that it is quite possible to have an optimum *not* falling at an intersection. If the relevant range in (a) had been from 0 to 20% (rather than from 0 to 10%) the maximum profit point would have been where $PCP = 17.5\%$ as computed in (a) above even though the intersection of the straight lines would have been at 20%.

The expressions developed up to this point have considered the typical product for which a downward sloping demand curve exists, but pertain only to that portion of the curve where prices are above the original (current) selling price. If we wish to consider decreasing the price, which for most products means an increase in volume, a slight modification is required in the general equation and its first derivative.

The basic variable margin expression (1.1) remains unchanged except for two signs as follows:

(2.1)   Variable Margin $= [OV(1 + PCV)] \cdot [OSP(1 - PCP) - OVC]$

(2.2) $$Z = (1 + PCV) \cdot \left[(1 - PCP) - \frac{OVC}{OSP} \right]$$

(2.3) $$Z = (1 + PCV)(OCP - PCP)$$

Substituting for *PCV* by use of the same identity $PCV = a + bPCP$, and then taking the first derivative, setting the resulting expression equal to zero and solving for *PCP*, the following result is obtained:

(2.4) $$PCP = \frac{bOCP - 1 - a}{2b}$$

The same result could have been obtained by merely using the general equation of (1.3) and using negative values for PCV and PCP (i.e., $PCV = -a - bPCP$, and $PCP = -PCP$).

EXAMPLE

If

$$PCV \text{ (increase)} = 10 \, PCP \text{ (decrease)},$$
$$a = 0$$
$$b = 10$$
$$OCP = .15$$
$$\text{Maximum } PCP = \frac{10(.15) - 1 - 0}{20}$$
$$PCP = .025 = 2.5\% \text{ (decrease)}$$
$$= -2.5\%$$

Verification

PCP	2%	2.5%	3%
PCV	20%	25%	30%
New selling price	$4.90	$4.875	$4.85
New contribution	$.65	$.625	$.60
New volume	48,000	50,000	52,000
New variable margin .	$31,200	$31,250	$31,200
		Max.	

Changes in Variable Costs

A company may decide that a change in the quality of its product requiring an increase or decrease in variable costs may be appropriate.

An increase in variable costs which improves quality may increase sales. The following new notations are necessary:

PCC = Per cent change in variable costs
$OVCP$ = Original variable cost per cent

(3.1) Variable Margin = $[OV(1 + PCV)] \cdot [OSP - OVC(1 + PCC)]$

(3.2) $$Z = (1 + PCV) \cdot \left(1 - \frac{OVC}{OSP} - \frac{OVC \cdot PCC}{OSP}\right)$$

(3.3) $$Z = (1 + PCV) \cdot (OCP - OVCP \cdot PCC)$$

The only variables are *PCV* and *PCC*. When *PCV* is expressed in terms of *PCC* a single variable equation remains and a maximum profit point can be found as follows:

if $PCV = a + bPCC$

$$Z = (1 + a + bPCC) \cdot (OCP - OVCP \cdot PCC)$$

$$Z = (1 + a)OCP - (1 + a) \cdot OVCP \cdot PCC + bOCP \cdot PCC - bOVCP \cdot PCC^2$$

$$\frac{dZ}{dPCC} = -(1 + a)OVCP + bOCP - 2bOVCP \cdot PCC = 0$$

$$PCC = \frac{bOCP - OVCP - aOVCP}{2bOVCP}$$

$$(3.4) \quad PCC = \frac{b\dfrac{OCP}{OVCP} - 1 - a}{2b}$$

Also, if poorer quality decreases sales, the following maximum can be determined:

$$(4.1) \quad PCC = \frac{1 - a - b\dfrac{OCP}{OVCP}}{2b}$$

The similarities between (3.4) and (2.4) and between (4.1) and (1.4) are due to the similarities in functional form describing the increase (or decrease) in volume associated with the decrease (or increase) in contribution.

Changes in Fixed Costs

A change in fixed costs does not lend itself to the above analysis. An infinite number of alternatives does not exist. If automation is being contemplated, a few machines may be considered resulting in only a few alternatives. Also, the contribution per cent does not vary directly with each incremental change in cost or selling price. There may be a reduction in variable costs when a machine is acquired, but any relationship between the reduction in variable costs and an increase in fixed costs is meaningful only at that one point. Furthermore, since with the acquisition of a new machine the fixed cost per period can vary according to the useful life and depreciation method selected, capital budgeting techniques using discounted cash flows are more meaningful for decisions among limited alternatives.

However, a portion of the analysis is pertinent when a change in fixed costs causes a change in variable costs. In the above formulas, a change in the original contribution per cent (OCP) would be made which would result in a different maximum point being attained.

Indifference Points and Risk

The usefulness of the determination of a maximum profit point hinges on the reliability of the changes in quantities demanded which have been assumed for different prices or quality improvements (cost changes). An important additional piece of information is the indifference point, i.e., the new volume level at which the company must operate in order to obtain the same total profit (or loss) as that obtained at the original volume level. Since this article assumes that there are an infinite number of possible volume levels, there are obviously an infinite number of indifference points.

In order to relate the indifference points to the volume and price changes when an increase in sales price causes a decrease in volume, the general equation (1.3) can again be used:

$$Z = (1 - PCV)(OCP + PCP)$$

The indifference point is by definition the point at which the changes in volume and price will result in the same profit. Assuming no change in fixed costs it would be where $Z = OCP$.

$$\therefore OCP = (1 - PCV)(OCP + PCP)$$

or

(5.1)
$$PCV = \frac{PCP}{OCP + PCP}$$

This profit indifference curve when plotted along with the original price-volume curve will result in portraying an "added profit" area expressed as a percentage relationship between price and volume changes (Exhibit C).[4]

The exact added profit in dollars can be computed easily as follows:

(5.2) $\quad$ Profit $= \dfrac{\text{Added Profit Vol. }\%}{\text{Indifference Vol. }\%} \times$ (increase in contribution $\times OV$)

EXAMPLE

When $PCP = 5\%$, indifference $PCV = 25\%$

---

[4] For a decrease in selling price requiring an increase in volume to arrive at the same profit point the equation would be:

$$PCV = \frac{PCP}{OCP - PCP}$$

EXHIBIT C
Introduction of Profit Indifference Curve (i.e. if price increases 10%
and volume decreases 40%, the profit remains $12,500 as in Exhibit A.)

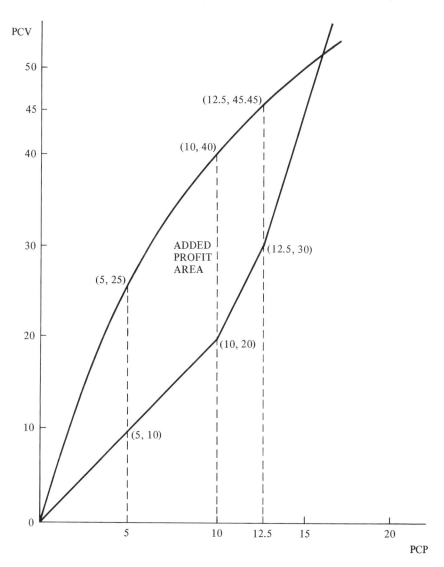

$$\text{Added profit} = \frac{15\%}{25\%} \times (.25 \times 40{,}000)$$
$$= \$6{,}000$$

The maximum profit point was previously found to be where $PCP = 10\%$. By use of the above equation (5.2) the maximum added profit can be computed.

When $PCP = 10\%$

Added Profit $= \dfrac{20\%}{40\%} \times (.50 \times 40{,}000)$

$= \$10{,}000$

Further confirmation that a maximum has been attained can be given by computing the added profit when $PCP = 9\%$ and $PCP = 11\%$.

When $PCP = 9\%$, Added profit $= \$9{,}360$.
When $PCP = 11\%$, Added profit $= \$9{,}520$.

Since both answers are less than $\$10{,}000$, 10% appears as a maximum.

In every decision-making situation, risk must be weighed. The preceding example employs an estimate of how volume changes as price changes. Certainly, before taking action one would like to know the accuracy of the estimate and the impact on profits that an error in this estimate will have. Whether the estimate was determined by classical statistical techniques or by subjective analysis, it is possible to ascertain the probability that a certain range of values about the estimate will contain the true value. More specifically, if the error in the estimate of the slope of the line is normally distributed with a mean of zero and a standard deviation equal to σ_b, it is possible to indicate in probabilistic terms a level of confidence that a range which is equal to the estimated slope plus or minus any number of standard deviations will contain the actual slope. For example, there is a 95% chance that the range defined by the estimate plus or minus 1.96 standard deviations will contain the value which will in fact be realized.

The information about the slope of the line can be used to determine the probability that the per cent change in volume which occurs when price is changed will lie within a specified range. This in turn is used to establish a range about the estimated profits at the specified probability level.

For the purpose of clarification, this approach will be applied to the previous example.

The following notation is used:

$\sigma_b =$ the standard deviation of the estimate of b
$Z\alpha =$ the number of standard deviations on each side of the mean which contain an area under the unit normal curve equal to the confidence level.

The confidence interval about the slope of the line for a specified α is thus

$$b \pm \sigma_b Z\alpha$$

which when substituted into the general linear expression for the per cent of volume change which results from a change in price yields

(5.3) $$PCV = a + (b \pm \sigma_b Z\alpha)PCP$$

If it is determined that $\sigma_b = .5$, the 95% confidence limits (i.e., $Z\alpha = -1.96$) about the change in volume are

$$PCV = a + (b \pm -.98)PCP$$

By substituting the values of a and b which are appropriate in the several ranges, Exhibit D can be generated. Notice that as the magnitude of the price change increases, the range of volume changes which may result in increases, and correspondingly the range of added profits increases. For a price change of 5% there is a 95% chance that added profits will fall between $7,960 and $4,040 while for a price change of 10% there is a 95% chance that the added profits will fall between $14,900 and $5,100.

In addition to this information, it is possible to summarize in a general form the probability that profits are less than, or equal to, the original profits for any price change. This can be obtained by performing algebraic manipulations on the difference between the expression for the upper limit on the per cent change in volume and the indifference volume, (equation 5.1 minus equation 5.3).

$$0 \geq \frac{PCP}{OCP + PCP} - [a + (b - \sigma_b Z\alpha)PCP].$$

The probability statement that results is

$$\text{Prob}\left[Z\alpha \leq \frac{a}{\sigma_b PCP} + \frac{b}{\sigma_b} - \frac{1}{\sigma_b(OCP + PCP)}\right] = \alpha$$

Substituting the values from the previous example at the point where maximum profits are realized

$$\text{Prob}\left[Z\alpha \leq 0 + \frac{2}{.5} - \frac{1}{.5(.15 + .10)}\right] = \alpha$$
$$\text{Prob}\,[Z\alpha \leq -4] = -\alpha$$
$$Z_{.000032} = -4$$
$$\therefore \alpha = .000032$$

indicates that the chance of attaining less than the original profit is thirty-two millionths.

The types of problems which would seem to be of greatest practical interest are those which bear resemblance to the example depicted in Exhibit D. (See page 308.) That is, situations where a change in price will result in an increase in expected profits. For the range of price changes (from the origin to point (a) on Exhibit D) which result in an increase in expected profits, some general statements can be made about the effects which changes in parameters and variables have on the probability that profits will be less than indifference profits.

Returning to the probability statement, one finds, as might be expected, that the probability of profits falling below the indifference level increases

EXHIBIT D

Introduction of Risk around Original Price-Volume Change Line

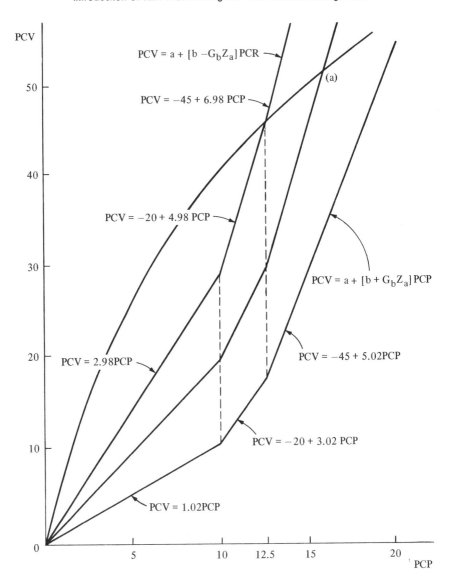

if a, σ_b, *PCP*, or b increases. To partially demonstrate this, a modification is made in the example problem. The estimates of the slopes and the intercepts are assumed to remain the same; however, the accuracy of the estimate of the slopes is lower for values of *PCP* greater than 5%. Specifically for *PCP* less than or equal to 5%, σ_b is .5, while for values of *PCP* greater than 5%, σ_b is 2.0. The price change at which maximum profits occur is unchanged, $PCP = 10\%$. However, from the probability statement

$$\text{Prob}\left[Z\alpha \leq \frac{2}{2} - \frac{1}{2(.15 + .10)}\right] = \alpha$$
$$\text{Prob}\,[Z\alpha \leq -1.0] = \alpha$$
$$Z_{.1587} = -1.0$$
$$\therefore \alpha = .1587$$

the chance of falling below the indifference profit is 15.87%. At $PCP = 5\%$,

$$\text{Prob}\,[Z\alpha \leq -6] = \alpha$$

indicates that the probability of obtaining less than the original profit is essentially zero. Given the probability information, the company may decide not to change prices to the point which would yield maximum profits, but may change to some point between $PCP = 5\%$ and $PCP = 10\%$. Management may be willing to accept lower profits rather than risk the possibility that profits will fall below the original value.

It is also possible to treat the situation where there exists uncertainty about the points A and B where a change takes place in the relationship of PCP to PCV. The dotted lines in Exhibit E (see page 310) indicate the 95% confidence limits about the change in volume which results when price is changed, $PCV = -.1 + 4PCP$. Thus, when $PCP = 10\%$, there is a 95% chance that added profits will lie between $100 and $9,900. Recall that when $PCP = 5\%$, the confidence limits on added profits are $4,040 and $7,960. Given the increased risk of small profits which occurs the company may now decide not to change prices to the point where $PCP = 10\%$ but to some other point.

The sagacity of their decision is further supported when one realizes that change in the relationship between price and volume also changes the maximum profit point. If the change in the relationship takes place at $PCP = 5\%$, as specified above the new optimum $PCP = 6.25\%$. Should it be possible to specify a probability distribution about the point where the relationship changes, one could determine the price change which would yield the greatest expected added profits.

Constraints and Opportunity Costs

Production of a product usually will be subject to various constraints such as limited raw materials, labor hours or machine hours. However, as soon as a constraint limits the company from attaining its maximum profit point a new alternative arises. How much should the company spend in order to eliminate the constraint? The lost profits (opportunity costs) should be weighed against the costs of eliminating the constraint.

EXHIBIT E
Introduction of Risk around Revised Price-Volume Change Line

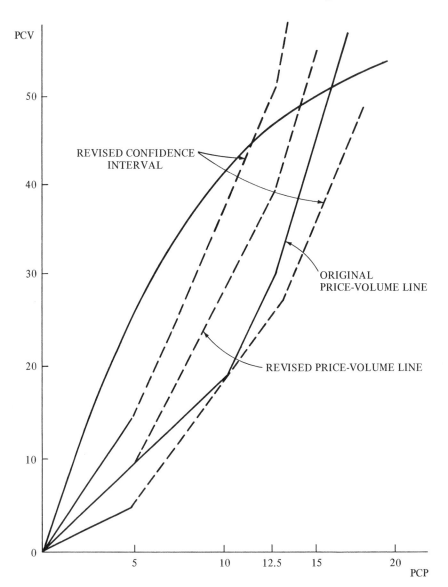

Exhibit F shows how a constraint would operate. Any constraint above $PCV = 20\%$ would not bother management since 20% is the maximum profit point. If the total number of machine hours available is 46,000 and it takes one machine hour to produce one unit, then the maximum volume possible is 46,000 units or $PCV = 16\%$ (i.e., $116\% \times 40,000$).

The previously determined maximum added profit is $10,000 where *PCP* = 10%. Added profits of $8,640 are attainable where *PCP* = 8%. The difference of $1,360 represents the opportunity cost of not being able to move to the maximum point. Management can now evaluate the costs of eliminating the constraint (new machine, purchase semi-finished goods from outsiders, operate longer hours, etc.) against the lost profits.

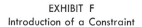

EXHIBIT F
Introduction of a Constraint

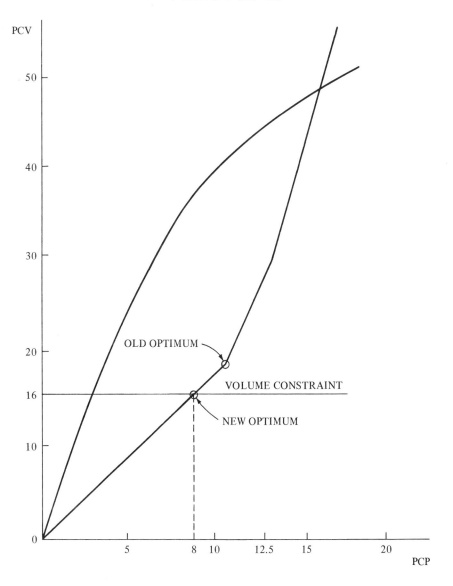

Comparison With Linear Programming

Any method that considers finding maximum profit points for products whose production is subject to linear constraints invites comparisons with linear programming techniques. The analysis discussed here is concerned with a single variable problem with a nonlinear objective function. If one is faced with a situation where the optimal price changes for several products are desired and a number of constraints exist, then it may be approached as a general constrained maxima problem using Lagrangian multipliers or nonlinear programming as dictated by the form of the problem.

Conclusions

Decision making involving projected profits of product lines has traditionally required the breakdown of costs into fixed and variable costs as well as a projection of demand when selling prices or product quality involving variable costs are changed. Unfortunately businessmen have made only limited use of such valuable information.

Cost-volume-profit analysis in the past has been seriously handicapped by its consideration of only a selected few possible alternatives. By the introduction of a continuous price-volume relationship maximum profit points can be found. Even in linear breakeven analysis, volume changes related to price changes result in a quadratic equation whose shape, when plotted, is in the form of a parabola with its rounded top at the price-volume point which gives the maximum profit (easily computed by differential calculus by finding the point at which the slope of the curve is zero).

When finding the selling price change which will result in the maximum profit, only the following need be considered:

(1) the original contribution per cent, (OCP),

(2) the per cent change in volume for each change in price, (b),

(3) and, only if the relationship changes, the point at which the change occurs and the Y axis intercept of the line expressing the new relationship (a).

When finding the variable cost change (quality change) which will result in the maximum profit only the addition of the following to the above three items need be considered:

(4) the original variable cost per cent, $(OVCP)$.

Much normally used but irrelevant data to the decision is disregarded, such as actual selling prices, actual volumes, actual variable costs or total profit at any point.

The analysis lends itself easily to further adaptations by using the simple general equation:

$$Z = (1 \mp PVC)(OCP \pm PCP)$$

(1) indifference points can be found for each change in price (or variable cost),
(2) an "added profit" area can be found from which total profit for any given price can be determined,
(3) risk can be introduced easily,
(4) constraints can be applied, optimal product mix can be found (although not done here),
(5) and even opportunity costs of not having adequate capacity to produce at the maximum profit point can be found.

2O *This paper explores some applications of linear programming . . . to breakeven analysis with special reference to ways in which accounting and mathematics might be joined to effect an extended and uniform approach to problems in financial and budgetary planning.*

". . . various physical (production) considerations [are joined] to the usual accounting rubrics of breakeven analyses . . . the notion of a 'spread sheet' [is introduced] . . . the relations between these approaches and the planning and projection of finished statements . . . [are] indicated."

One of the important observations of this article is the suggestion that the linear programming algorithm can be used to generate an "opportunity cost" income statement which management can use to evaluate alternatives.

A basic knowledge of linear programming concepts is helpful to an understanding of this article.

Breakeven Budgeting and Programming to Goals*

A. Charnes, W. W. Cooper, and Y. Ijiri†

Capitalism without double-entry bookkeeping is simply inconceivable. They hold together as form and matter. And one may indeed doubt whether capitalism has procured in double-entry bookkeeping a tool which activates its forces, or whether double-entry bookkeeping has first given rise to capitalism out of its own (rational and systematic) spirit. — Werner Sombart[1]

* From Journal of Accounting Research, *Vol. 1, No. 1 (Spring, 1963), pp. 16–43. Reprinted by permission of the publisher.*

† This paper was presented as part of a talk delivered to The University of Pittsburgh, Graduate School of Business, Institute in Applied Mathematics for Teachers of Business on March 9, 1962.

Part of the research underlying this paper was undertaken for the project *Temporal Planning and Management Decision under Risk and Uncertainty* at Northwestern University and part for the project *Planning and Control of Industrial Operations* at Carnegie Institute of Technology. Both projects are under contract with the U. S. Office of Naval Research. Reproduction of this paper in whole or in part is permitted for any purpose of the United States Government. Contract Nonr-1228(10), Project NR 047–021 and Contract Nonr-760(01), Project NR-047011.

[1] Werner Sombart, *Der moderne Kapitalismus* (Munchen und Leipzig: von Duncker und Humblot, 1922).

That the countries in which the science of bookkeeping made the most progress were always those in which most economic progress was being made can no doubt be explained as a mixture of cause and effect. — H. M. Robertson[2]

Introduction

This paper explores some applications of linear programming (referred to hereafter as L.P.) to breakeven analysis with special reference to ways in which accounting and mathematics might be joined to effect an extended and uniform approach to problems in financial and budgetary planning.

Accountants, economists and general students of business or finance are accustomed to the geometry and algebra of breakeven charts and, in fact, some time ago M. L. Pye showed how to effect further algebraic extensions to multiple product (mix) variations by means of simultaneous algebraic equations.[3] Because these ideas are already familiar, as is the separation of total costs into fixed and variable components,[4] there is no need to elaborate on either the general breakeven approach or the kinds of principles that apply when it is being implemented for ordinary accounting purposes.

Linear programming is relatively new, both as a branch of mathematics and as a tool for accounting. However, the mathematical techniques associated with L.P. have received widespread attention as well as some managerial applications under such names as "operations research," "management science," and the like. These, too, are now finding their way into accounting, where they have been considered as a possible alternative to the breakeven approach. Jaedicke [37], for example, has suggested that a L.P.[5] emphasis on optimizing objectives (e.g., maximum profit or minimum cost) may offer advantages over an analysis that centers on merely breaking even.

The pursuit of an optimum objective plays a prominent role in L.P. But this does not mean that *applications* are restricted to situations where optimization has been stated as an actual managerial objective. A variety of artifacts are available for use when other objectives are at issue and some of these same artifacts may be used to handle various kinds of *nonlinear*

---

[2] H. M. Robertson, *Aspects of the Rise of Economic Individualism* (Cambridge: University Press, 1935).

[3] See the item designated as [52] in the bibliography. See also [48].

[4] The *Encyclopaedia Britannica* credits Dionysius Lardner (1850) with being the first to make these distinctions and it also credits the ideas of profit charting and flexible budgeting to John Manger Fells (1903). W. Rautenstrach and R. Knoeppel are also mentioned as early advocates of profit-volume planning and breakeven charting. See also [64], p. 34 ff. and the references to C. A. Guilbault on pp. 59 ff. in [28].

[5] It is perhaps of interest to observe that the project graphs and PERT/PEP critical path scheduling techniques discussed in [39], can also be represented in terms of linear programming network models. This means, as will be shown later in this paper, that these new approaches to scheduling and control are immediately amenable to characterizations in terms of double entry principles. See, e.g., [8]. See also Chapter XVII in [9] for remarks on general relations between the Kirchhoff laws for networks and double-entry analyses and record keeping.

problems via mathematical models that are suitably arranged for applying any of the standard *linear* programming solution methods.[6]

These topics will be illustrated, at least in a simple way, by means of what is called a "goal programming model" in L.P. Comment will be interjected at various points to suggest how most of the objectives that have been discussed in the breakeven literature[7] can be achieved via suitable variations on this approach.

Linear programming methods have already demonstrated an ability to deal with very large management problems where many (hundreds and more) interacting variables have been involved. Furthermore, electronic computer codes have been prepared and are readily available whenever recourse to these kinds of facilities becomes necessary. It may therefore be desirable to show that L.P. can offer something more than a uniform approach to problems like mix-volume interactions, breakeven analyses, profit maximization and cost minimization. For this reason, various extensions will be essayed in the examples which are treated in this paper. First, the development will commence by joining various physical (production) considerations to the usual accounting rubrics of breakeven analyses. Second, extensions into the balance sheet accounts will be effected via the notion of a "spread sheet" or "articulation statement."[8] Finally, the relations between these approaches and the planning and projection of financial statements will be indicated.

There are still other possible developments and extensions that could be made by means of any contacts that can be established between accounting and L.P. and, only for illustration, we mention topics like the following, which have been treated by means of L.P.:[9] (1) determining transfer prices when multiple interdepartmental interactions should be taken into account; (2) obtaining statistical estimates that conform to prescribed organization arrangements and managerial policies; and (3) effecting optimum consolidations (e.g., on spread sheets) for the management decisions that are to be arranged.[10] Also of interest are the recent research reports pointed towards uses of L.P.[11] in (a) capital budgeting where complex congeries of interrelated investment decisions are involved and (b) costing or otherwise evaluating funds by reference to their alternative "best" uses for financing capital or operating expenditures, credit extensions to customers, borrowing and repayment, etc.

This very brief and incomplete summary (supplemented by the bibliography) is intended only to supply background material and a general

---

[6] *Vide*, e.g., [9].

[7] See the bibliography cited at the end of this article.

[8] *Vide*, E. L. Kohler [40] p. 389 for a definition and an accounting illustration of a spread sheet. See also Mattessich [47] and Richards [55].

[9] See [9], Chapters IX and X and Appendix E. See also [72].

[10] Cf. [51]. Mathematical approaches to consolidation and aggregation in other contexts may be found in [56] and [57] and [45.2].

[11] In [71] and [10].

perspective from which to judge the detailed developments that will now be undertaken.

A Breakeven Model with Production Constraints

In order to avoid recourse to abstract mathematical symbols, we shall follow the precedent of Jaedicke's article[12] and restrict the immediate presentation to a very simple numerical example that is easily graphed for further study and elucidation. Thus, let x_1 and x_2 represent the amounts of two different products that can be offered for sale under the labels "Product 1" and "Product 2," respectively. Suppose that the per unit contribution that each makes to profit and overhead is: $c_1 = \$1.00$ for Product 1, and $c_2 = \$.50$ for Product 2. Then, if the fixed cost per period is $2.50, the following expression can be solved for the values of x_1 and x_2 that achieve the required breakeven point:

(1) $$\$1x_1 + \$\tfrac{1}{2}x_2 = \$2.5.$$

Each possible pair which satisfies this expression, like $x_1 = 2$, $x_2 = 1$ or $x_1 = 1$, $x_2 = 3$, represents a different physical product mix that will contribute $2.50 over the variable cost of production and hence achieve the indicated breakeven level.

The equation represented in (1) is only one of several possible approaches to a breakeven analysis and, of course, a variety of refinements can be employed.[13] Since these are well known, a somewhat different course will be elected here. In particular, we shall utilize the data of Table 1 to show how certain "physical facts" of production may be studied in the context of a breakeven analysis.

The data of Table 1 are intended to have the following meanings. Each unit of Product 1 is supposed to require processing on two different machines: On Machine A this product requires 3 hours of processing time per unit and, on Machine B, 5 hours per unit. A completed unit of Product 2, on the other hand, can be secured from 2 hours of processing on Machine A. No processing is required (for this product) on Machine B and so a zero processing time (per unit) is entered in the cell where the Machine B row and the Product 2 column intersect.[14] Finally, the capacities available for each machine are shown in the right-hand column and positioned in the row where the relevant machine is designated. These are the rated capacities, of

---

[12] [37].

[13] See, for instance, the profit-graph breakeven chart in Kohler, [40] *op. cit.*, p. 65. For a discussion of possible managerial uses see Eastwood [22].

[14] Alternatively, this cell may be left blank, if desired, and this is the convention utilized in the immediately following mathematical expressions. E.g., the variable x_2 is omitted from the second expression in (2). See Charnes and Cooper, [9], Ch. I for further discussion of this and related examples.

course, stated in the hours that will be available during the period for which a breakeven analysis is being considered.

TABLE 1

Machine Processing Times and Capacities

	Machine processing times (hrs./unit)		Available machine capacities (hours)
	Product 1	*Product 2*	
Machine A.......	3	2	12
Machine B........	5	0	10

All of these operating "facts" are now given expression in the following inequalities:

$$(2) \qquad 3x_1 + 2x_2 \leq 12$$
$$5x_1 \qquad \leq 10,$$

which are intended to mean that any values (amounts of Product 1 and Product 2) can be assigned to x_1 and x_2, *provided* that such an assignment does not yield a number to the left of the "$\leq$" which exceeds the number positioned immediately to its right. The open side of the inequality symbol, "$\leq$," indicates the side that is allowed to be larger.

The meaning of these "$\leq$" symbols can be further elucidated in another connection. It is not meaningful in this context to assign negative quantities to either x_1 or x_2. This restriction to non-negative values is given mathematical form by means of the expressions $x_1 \geq 0$, $x_2 \geq 0$ or, more briefly, $x_1, x_2 \geq 0$. The latter is the so-called "non-negativity condition" of L.P. and its meaning is "neither x_1 nor x_2 can be less than zero." (I.e., $x_1 > 0$ or $x_1 = 0$ but never $x_1 < 0$, and the same applies for the numerical values that can be assigned to x_2.)

In preparation for the following sections, we now rewrite the expression (2) in the following equivalent set of equations:

$$3x_1 + 2x_2 + y_1 = 12$$
$$(3) \qquad 5x_1 \qquad + y_2 = 10$$
$$x_1, x_2, y_1, y_2 \geq 0.$$

In this form the variables y_1 and y_2 are technically referred to as "slack" — e.g., as distinguished from x_1 and x_2 which are referred to as "structural variables." Observe that the equivalence between (3) and (2) is achieved by constraining the slack variables y_1 and y_2 (along with the structural variables x_1 and x_2) to non-negative values only. Thus, a $y_1 > 0$ — i.e., a positive value for y_1 — corresponds to idle time programmed for Machine A and a $y_2 > 0$ represents idle time on Machine B. On the other hand, $y_2 = 0$

means no idle time on Machine B and similarly, $y_1 = 0$ means no idle time is being programmed on Machine A.

Goal Programming

A combination of all of the preceding constraints can now be arranged as follows:

(4)
$$\begin{aligned}
3x_1 + 2x_2 + y_1 &= 12 \\
5x_1 \qquad\qquad + y_2 &= 10 \\
x_1 + \tfrac{1}{2}x_2 &= 2.5 \\
x_1, x_2, y_1, y_2 &\geq 0
\end{aligned}$$

and any set of non-negative values that simultaneously satisfies all of these relations will provide (i) a breakeven volume and mix (cf. the third constraint) and (ii) a feasible machine load (cf. the first two constraints). Among the L.P. (optimization) approaches that can be used on such a problem is one called "goal programming." This approach is distinguished from others by virtue of the fact that at least one of the constraints is incorporated in the functional in such a manner that it becomes part of the objective (for maximization or minimization). This approach can also be employed to handle various kinds of nonlinearities and so it is the one that we shall elect.

In preparation for subsequent discussion, we therefore erect the following goal programming model for breakeven analysis:

$$\text{minimize } y_3^- + y_3^+$$

subject to:

(5)
$$\begin{aligned}
3x_1 + 2x_2 + y_1 &= 12 \\
5x_1 \qquad\qquad + y_2 &= 10 \\
x_1 + \tfrac{1}{2}x_2 \qquad\qquad + y_3^- - y_3^+ &= 2.5 \\
x_1, x_2, y_1, y_2, y_3^-, y_3^+ &\geq 0.
\end{aligned}$$

That is, the objective is to secure values for the variables which will (a) satisfy all of the constraints, including non-negativity, to which the variables have been subjected, and (b) make the sum $y_3^- + y_3^+$ a minimum.

To see what this involves, the function[15]

(6.1)
$$f(y_3^-, y_3^+) = y_3^- + y_3^+$$

and the third constraint — *viz.*,[16]

[15] The terms "function" and "functional" are used interchangeably throughout this article to mean that the function, "f," assumes a unique value (number) as soon as values for both of the variables y_3^+ and y_3^- are assigned. Thus, in this case the function "f" is $y_3^+ + y_3^-$.

[16] This is, of course, only a rewriting of the condition
$$x_1 + \tfrac{1}{2}x_2 + y_3^- - y_3^+ = 2.5.$$

(6.2) $y_3^- - y_3^+ = 2.5 - x_1 - \frac{1}{2}x_2$

are now sequestered for further examination. It is to be emphasized, again, that only non-negative values can be assigned to the variables. Thus, in any permissible case $y_3^- + y_3^+ \geq 0$ so that the function, $f(y_3^+, y_3^-)$, can never be negative. In fact, if the breakeven level can be achieved then the minimization process will drive the function to $y_3^- + y_3^+ = 0$ and neither a positive nor a negative deviation will occur for (6.2).

This last statement will now, perhaps, help to explain the plus and minus symbols that were assigned as distinguishing superscripts for both y_3 variables. If the values assigned to x_1 and x_2 give $x_1 + \frac{1}{2}x_2 > 2.5$, then the mathematical procedures (if they are to be meaningful) should arrange to give $y_3^- = 0$ and $-y_3^+ = 2.5 - x_1 - \frac{1}{2}x_2 < 0$. In short, it is intended that $y_3^+ > 0$ should represent a positive deviation above the breakeven level. Alternatively, if $x_1 + \frac{1}{2}x_2 < 2.5$ occurs, then the mathematics should arrange $y_3^+ = 0$ and $y_3^- = 2.5 - x_1 - \frac{1}{2}x_2 > 0$ so that a negative deviation (below the breakeven level) is thereby indicated. Since it is not meaningful to admit both a negative and a positive deviation simultaneously, the constraint (6.2) must never be allowed to utilize any nonzero *pairs* for the two variables in $y_3^- - y_3^+$, which are also available, at least in principle, when $2.5 - x_1 - \frac{1}{2}x_2 \neq 0$ occurs.[17]

A formal mathematical statement of the condition that at least one of y_3^+ and y_3^- must be zero is rendered by the quadratic (nonlinear) constraint:

(6.3) $y_3^+ \times y_3^- = 0,$

which can only be satisfied when at least one of y_3^+ and y_3^- is equal to zero. The standard solution procedures of L.P., on the other hand, *always* arrange to have at least one of the pair y_3^+ and y_3^- equal to zero. Hence these solution procedures may be applied to the model (5) with assurance that the nonlinear (quadratic) constraint (6.3) will also be satisfied. Moreover, and equally important, the optimizations are automatically arranged to ensure that $y_3^- > 0$ will occur only if this provides the least possible deviation from the supposed \$2.50 breakeven level whereas if the constraints of (5) and (6.3), together, jointly admit of a still smaller deviation from the other side then $y_3^- = 0$ and $y_3^+ > 0$ will occur. In this manner the constraint (6.2) is incorporated in the functional and, without any ambiguity whatsoever, the value of the function (6.1) provides a measure of the total dollar deviation by means of the expression $y_3^- + y_3^+ \geq 0$.

Alternate Optima and Product Mix Variations

The constraints of (5) admit of a solution with $y_3^+ + y_3^- = 0$ which is certainly minimal. Hence, the methods of L.P. will bring about such a solution in this case. These methods are also extended to other purposes as well.

---

[17] The symbol "$\neq$" means "not equal to."

For instance, they can be used to locate other programs (called alternate optima) which also minimize (6.1) with different values assigned to x_1, x_2, y_1 and y_2.

The data of this example have been arranged to bring this "alternate optima" aspect to the fore in order to show how product mix possibilities can be studied in a L.P. approach to breakeven analysis. Two such alternate optima, called "basic solutions," are, in fact, summarized in Table 2 by omitting all of the variables that have been assigned a value of zero.[18]

One reason for referring to these as "basic solutions" may be seen as follows. These two solutions are not the only ones that yield a product mix that gives $y_3^- + y_3^+ = 0$. But every product mix which will achieve the $2.50 breakeven level can be derived from suitable percentage combinations[19] of these two basic solutions. In particular, if "solution 1" is labelled "A" and "solution 2" is labelled "B" and if p is a fraction between zero and one then

$$(7) \qquad pA + (1 - p)B$$

is also an optimum for *any* $0 \leq p \leq 1$.

Chart 1 provides a graphic aid to understanding what is involved in the mathematical model (5) and the solutions of Table 2 and expression (7). Every point in the shaded region of Chart 1 assigns coordinate values to x_1 and x_2 which can be associated with y values that, together, satisfy all constraints in (5). Points above the line AB have values $y_3^+ > 0$ and points below this same line have values $y_3^- > 0$. Only points on the line from A to B give $y_3^- + y_3^+ = 0$. The first basic solution, with $x_2 = 5$, is shown at A and the second basic solution is shown at B (with $x_1 = 2, x_2 = 1$). Every point on the line segment between A and B can be obtained by choosing a suitable p. For instance, choosing $p = \frac{1}{4}$ gives $x_1 = 1\frac{1}{2}$, $x_2 = 2$, the coordinates at C, as can be seen by using the x_1 and x_2 values from solutions 1 and 2 to obtain:[20]

$$(8) \qquad \begin{aligned} x_1 &= \tfrac{1}{4} \times 0 + \tfrac{3}{4} \times 2 = 1\tfrac{1}{2} \\ x_2 &= \tfrac{1}{4} \times 5 + \tfrac{3}{4} \times 1 = 2 \end{aligned}$$

This is an alternate (derived)[21] breakeven program and every other possible breakeven program can also be derived from the basic solutions of Table 2 by simply choosing different $0 \leq p \leq 1$ and applying them to (7) in a wholly analogous manner. Thus, as this simple example shows, all possible product mix possibilities can be studied.

---

[18] E.g., column 1 of Table 2 shows the solution $x_1 = 0, x_2 = 5, y_1 = 2, y_2 = 10$ with, of course, $y_3^- + y_3^+ = 0$ so that no units of Product 1 and 5 units of Product 2 achieve the indicated breakeven level by assigning 2 hours of idle time on Machine A and 10 hours of idle time (all available capacity) on Machine B.

[19] Also called "convex combinations." *Vide* [9].

[20] The fraction $p = \frac{1}{4}$ (hence $1 - p = \frac{3}{4}$) is chosen to help in distinguishing between the two programs. Note that $p = \frac{1}{4}$ multiplies $x_1 = 0$ from solution 1 and $(1 - p) = \frac{3}{4}$ multiplies $x_1 = 2$ from solution 2. Similar remarks apply to the derivation of the x_2 coordinate for C from the previous x_2 values in A and B, respectively.

[21] I.e., it is derived from the preceding basic solutions at A and B.

CHART 1

Breakeven Points and Profit Possibilities

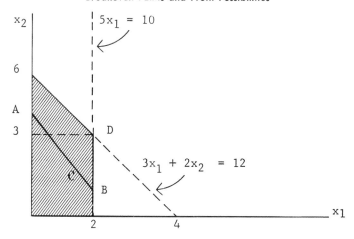

Further Extensions

It is possible, almost without pause, to extend the already achieved solution possibilities in order to explore still other topics that a breakeven analysis might suggest. Suppose, for instance, that it is desired to proceed from a breakeven analysis to a study of maximum profit possibilities. Simplifying the model (5) and reorienting the objective gives another (closely related) model which appears as follows:

$$\text{maximize } y_3^+$$

subject to:

(9)
$$
\begin{aligned}
3x_1 + 2x_2 + y_1 \quad\quad\quad &= 12 \\
5x_1 \quad\quad\quad + y_2 \quad\quad &= 10 \\
x_1 + \tfrac{1}{2}x_2 \quad\quad\quad - y_3^+ &= 2.5 \\
x_1, x_2, y_1, y_2, y_3^+ &\geq 0
\end{aligned}
$$

and the solution occurs, at point D, with $x_1 = 2$, $x_2 = 3$ so that $y_3^+ = \$1$ represents the maximum contribution (to profit) over and above the fixed costs of \$2.50. If, on the other hand, the fixed costs were at a still higher level such as, say \$4.50, then the model

$$\text{minimize } y_3^-$$

subject to:

(10)
$$
\begin{aligned}
3x_1 + 2x_2 + y_1 \quad\quad\quad &= 12 \\
5x_1 \quad\quad\quad + y_2 \quad\quad &= 10 \\
x_1 + \tfrac{1}{2}x_2 \quad\quad\quad + y_3^- &= 4.5 \\
x_1, x_2, y_1, y_2, y_3^- &\geq 0
\end{aligned}
$$

TABLE 2

Alternate Optima

Basic Solutions	
A Solution 1	*B* Solution 2
$x_2 = 5$	$x_1 = 2$
$y_1 = 2$	$x_2 = 1$
$y_2 = 10$	$y_1 = 4$

would also give $x_1 = 2$, $x_2 = 3$ while the $y_3^- = \$1$ would be a measure of the closest possibility that the constraints admit for covering all of the fixed costs — *viz.*, $y_3^- = \$4.50 - \$1 x_1 - \$\frac{1}{2} x_2 = \$1.00$ means that $x_1 = 2$, $x_2 = 3$, falls \$1.00 short of covering all fixed costs. But $y_3^- = \$1.00$ is minimal. Hence there is no other product mix which will do better (i.e., come closer) to covering all fixed costs.

The models (9) and (10) are only some of the possible variants of (5). Other variants will not be covered here, however, so that we may thereby gain space to examine other uses of L.P. To conclude this section we therefore only mention the following kinds of possibilities: First, when data are in doubt — e.g., on costs, prices, machine times, etc. — there are a variety of L.P. procedures[22] that can be brought into play in order to assess the program consequences that might attend possible errors in the data. Second, additional nonlinearities may also be dealt with by L.P. methods and among these may be numbered the kinds of accounting situations that are encountered when semi-fixed or semi-variable costs occur or when volume discounts and other arrangements enter in a way that can affect the profit-and-overhead contributions that are to be accommodated with different volumes and mixes.

Spread Sheet Analyses

An entrance into the next extension may be effected by means of the simplified spread sheet example exhibited in Table 3. The transactions are recorded as they have occurred for a company that is now being organized to lease the machine facilities portrayed in Table 1 at a fixed rental of \$2.50 per period. Preparatory to completing the leasing arrangements, a balance-sheet extension of the preceding breakeven analyses is desired.

In the spread sheet approach, every relevant account is assigned two positions, a row position and a column position. (1) It is positioned in the stub (row) to reflect the debits for any transaction where this account applies and (2) it is positioned in a column (caption) to reflect the credits for any transaction where this account applies.

---

[22] This includes the so-called parameterization procedures that are available on many of the extant computer codes.

TABLE 3

Spread Sheet

Debits \ Credits	C = Cash	G = Goods	R = Raw Materials	E = Net Worth	S = Sales	Totals
C = Cash				60		60
G = Goods	10					10
R = Raw Materials	10					10
E = Net Worth	10					10
S = Sales						0
Totals	30	0	0	60	0	90

Balance Sheet
End of Period One

Cash	$30	Net Worth	$50
Goods	10		
Materials	10		
Total	$50	Total	$50

With every relevant account being thus represented, the way a spread sheet gives effect to the "double-entry principle" is illustrated by the specimen transactions of Table 3.[23] The owners have opened the books of account by investing $60 in cash, a transaction which is reflected by means of the entry in row 1, which debits Cash in this amount and, simultaneously, credits Net Worth. Next, $10 is expended to acquire "Goods" which will become "Product 1" when suitably processed on Machines A and B. This number is the first entry in column 1 showing simultaneously a credit to Cash (the column caption) and a debit to Goods (the stub designation). An analogous entry is made for "Raw Materials," the raw material which

---

[23] The spread sheet approach (and other related working paper forms) suggests that it is not wholly adequate to assert that "A necessary prerequisite [of double entry] is that all transactions be recorded twice, once on the debit and once on the credit side." See deRoover [44.3], p. 114. In the early periods of accounting development, however, it seems to have been customary to emphasize this. See, e.g., [11], p. 107, where Paciolo is translated to say: "All entries posted in the book must be double; that is, if you make one creditor you must make one debtor."

Machine A can process into "Product 2." Finally, a withdrawal by the owners is recorded by the $10 figure that appears in the Cash column and the Net Worth row.

No sales have been undertaken pending completion of the leasing arrangements for the machines of Table 1. Hence the cells in the S ($=$ Sales) row and column remain vacant and the operating statement is void (or vacuous). A balance sheet can be readily prepared from these spread sheet data, however, and the one shown at the bottom of Table 3 is obtained by reference to the following considerations. Totaling any row gives the sum of all debits to the corresponding account. The total of all credits to this same account is secured by footing the appropriate column. The difference is then the net debit or credit balance in this account. For instance, row 1 yields a total of $60 in debits to Cash and column 1 yields a credit total of $30 to this same account. The net is a debit balance of $30 $=$ $60 $-$ $30 as shown by the figure reported for the Cash account in the balance sheet.

Evidently the other entries for the balance sheet, as exhibited, can be obtained in a precisely analogous manner. Indeed by further elaborations,[24] a spread sheet approach can be used to synthesize profit-and-loss statements, cost analyses and allocations, and other accounting reports, as wanted.[25] Although accruals and other non-cash items (credit sales and purchases) can also be accommodated in a spread sheet, this topic will not be pursued here. All transactions will be assumed to occur on a cash basis and no other expenses besides the lease rental and material costs will be incurred.[26]

Proceeding on these assumptions, the constraints for a simple instance of a spread-sheet-breakeven analysis will be elaborated, in steps, from the preceding examples. First the machine times and capacities are reproduced from (3) above:

$$(11.1) \qquad \begin{aligned} 12 &= 3x_1 + 2x_2 + y_1 \\ 10 &= 5x_1 \qquad\qquad\; + y_2. \end{aligned}$$

Then it is assumed that Product 1, when processed, sells for $2.50 $=$ $5/2 per unit while Product 2 brings in $1.75 $=$ $7/4 per unit. Because all transactions are in cash, this gives

$$(11.2) \qquad 0 = -\frac{5}{2} x_1 - \frac{7}{4} x_2 + x_{CS}$$

where x_{CS} means that the amount, x, is to be debited to C $=$ Cash and credited to S $=$ Sales.

---

[24] *Vide*, e.g., Kohler [40] or Richards [55] and Mattessich [46]. For a discussion of the closely related input-output approach to the national accounts see Chapter III in [9].

[25] Cf. Ijiri [35].

[26] A detailed treatment of payables, receivables, labor costs, etc. — for a firm operating in the (complex) Carnegie Tech Management Game business environment — may be found in the combined L.P. spread sheet approach used in [36].

The name-designating symbols which will be employed as subscripts are shown in the sideheadings and captions of Table 3. In every case the first letter of the subscript pair will refer to the debit entry and the second letter to the credit entry. Thus, if the unit purchase price of Goods = G is $1.50 = \$3/2$ and if the unit purchase price of Raw Materials = R is $1.25 = \$5/4$, then any transfer from inventory to Sales (= Profit and Loss) account gives

(11.3)
$$0 = \frac{3}{2} x_1 \quad - x_{SG}$$

$$0 = \quad \frac{5}{4} x_2 \quad - x_{SR}.$$

The immediate objective is to break even on all accounts so that we now impose the conditions

(11.4)
$$0 = x_{SG} \quad - x_{GC}$$

$$0 = \quad x_{SR} \quad - x_{RC}$$

to reflect the restoration to the Goods and Raw Materials inventories by means of cash purchases.[27]

Because these "breakeven conditions" give $x_{SG} = x_{GC}$ and $x_{SR} = x_{RC}$, we can next write

(11.5)
$$0 = -x_{CS} + x_{GC} + x_{RC} + x_{SE}$$

to indicate the residual entry (positive or negative)[28] which clears the net effects of these sales into E = Net Worth account. Then we impose the further breakeven condition

(11.6)
$$0 = -x_{SE} + x_{EC}$$

which is to be interpreted together with

(11.7)
$$-\frac{5}{2} = -x_{EC}$$

wherein x_{EC} is the amount ($5/2) to be debited to Net Worth and credited to Cash for the fixed rental of equipment.

A reason for the indicated choice of negative and positive signs on these variables will shortly be indicated. First, however, we collect all of the above constraints together:

[27] It is assumed that purchase prices do not change, but any such variations can be accommodated by rather obvious adjustments when this is not the case.
[28] That is, we do not restrict x_{SE} to non-negative values so that $x_{SE} > 0$ means a debit to Sales and a credit to Net Worth while $x_{SE} < 0$ means a credit to Sales (= Profit or Loss for period) and a debit to Net Worth. For further discussion, and other ways of handling this, see Chapter XVII in [9].

$$12 = \quad 3x_1 + 2x_2 + y_1$$
$$10 = \quad 5x_1 \qquad\qquad + y_2$$
$$0 = -\tfrac{5}{2}x_1 - \tfrac{7}{4}x_2 \qquad\quad + x_{CS}$$
$$0 = \quad \tfrac{3}{2}x_1 \qquad\qquad\qquad - x_{SG}$$
$$0 = \qquad\quad \tfrac{5}{4}x_2 \qquad\qquad\qquad - x_{SR}$$
(12)
$$0 = \qquad\qquad\qquad\qquad x_{SG} \qquad - x_{GC}$$
$$0 = \qquad\qquad\qquad\qquad\qquad x_{SR} \qquad\quad - x_{RC}$$
$$0 = \qquad\qquad\qquad\qquad - x_{CS} \qquad\quad + x_{GC} + x_{RC} + x_{SE}$$
$$0 = \qquad\qquad\qquad\qquad\qquad\qquad\qquad\qquad\quad - x_{SE} + x_{EC}$$
$$-\tfrac{5}{2} = \qquad\qquad\qquad\qquad\qquad\qquad\qquad\qquad\qquad\quad - x_{EC}$$

and then we impose the condition that all variables be restricted to non-negative values with the sole exception of x_{SE}.[29] Next we observe that the spread sheet variables always occur in exactly two constraints where, alternately, $+1$ or -1 appear as the coefficients of these variables. This means that the model is one of so-called incidence (or network) type[30] for which particularly efficient solution procedures can be, or have been, developed.[31]

The present article is not concerned with technical mathematical developments, and so we simply utilize these expressions in (12) to write down the network[32] shown in Chart 2. In order to interpret this network the following conventions should be accorded to its elements. Each account is assigned to a node. The links connecting these nodes represent routes for the possible transaction flows, when submitted to an accounting analysis, and the arrowheads are oriented in all cases towards the debit entry. The only exception is the link associated with x_{SE}, which has no arrowhead, because the flow can, in this case, be in either direction. Finally, the value — \$2.50 points outward from the Net Worth $= E$ node to show that this amount will flow out of the system (for rentals) during the period.

We can now close this section by noting that this network could be used as a guide for accounting simulation studies on either an analogue or digital computer. Alternatively a driving function, either for optimization or (controlled) simulation purposes can be achieved by stating an appropriate objective and function which would bring the model (12) into L.P. form.

[29] See preceding footnote. If optimization were the objective we could maximize x_{SE}, either gross or net of taxes, dividends, etc., and alter $-5/2 = -x_{EC}$ to $-5/2 \geq -x_{EC}$ and proceed to adjust the model so that it would also accommodate such other constraints (e.g., on working capital) as might be required. This means that the condition $x_{SE} \geq 0$ would be superfluous since the objective would then be to make it as large as possible and, *a fortiori*, positive whenever the constraints admit such a possibility. See [29] for such an application.

[30] See remarks in footnote,[5] *supra*. See also [45.1] for still another network characterization of double-entry accounting as reached from a different kind of mathematics.

[31] See the discussion of dyadic models and subdual methods in Chapter XV of [9]. For an illustration of the way subdual algorithms (solution methods) can be generated see the example of critical path scheduling in [8].

[32] More precisely this is only part of a total network which would have to be completed by showing an input as well as an output node.

CHART 2

Graph for an Accounting Network

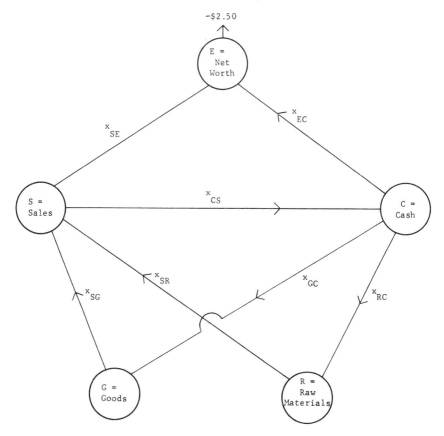

Preemptive Priorities and Breakeven Balance Sheets

Rather than repeating the previous analysis in order to extend it to the constraint system (12), we shall use a slight alteration in tactics and change the outflow at node E to $4.50 = $9/2$. The maximum net cash realization that this system will admit is still only $3.50. Cf. (12). Hence it is no longer possible to bring all accounts back up to their previous level in order, thereby, to break even on every balance sheet account.

Choices must be made under such circumstances and so it might seem natural to turn to some set of numerical weights that could reflect the relative preferences (degree of priority) which a management might want to accord to the various account balances that it would like to see maintained. This could be done whenever such a management is willing to supply the indicated weights. It is conceivable, however, that the indicated weights might not be forthcoming and, indeed, it is even conceivable that no set of numerical values will accurately reflect the wishes of some managements. Simply to illustrate the latter point, we will replace (11.7) by

$$(13.1) \qquad -\frac{9}{2} = -x_{EC}$$

so that there can be no solution (set of x and y values) which can simultaneously satisfy all of the other constraints, along with (13.1) — i.e., no solution is possible within the allowances imposed by non-negativity. Then we will replace (11.5) by

$$(13.2) \qquad 0 = -x_{CS} + x_{SG} + x_{SR} - y_{\overline{RC}} - y_{\overline{GC}} + x_{SE}$$

wherein the variables $y_{\overline{RC}}$, $y_{\overline{CG}} \geq 0$ are entered to absorb any deficiencies which occur when the total debits to cash, arising from sales, are inadequate to cover the cost of merchandise sold, $x_{SG} + x_{SR}$, and the additional debit arising from the rental $x_{EC} = \$4.50$.

Now we assume that management imposes the following *preemptive*[33] priorities on inventory replenishment: First, replace all "Goods" inventory to the maximum possible extent. Second, with any remaining funds restore the "Raw Materials" inventory, so far as possible. Finally, and even more urgently, do not draw the cash account down below its initial \$30 balance. In other words, this condition, which overrides the other two, is intended to mean that even inventory drawdowns are to be permitted, if necessary, to cover operating deficits and, in any event, only actual net cash realized from operations may be used to restore inventory.

To render these latter conditions more precisely, we first replace the expressions (11.4) by

$$(13.3) \qquad \begin{aligned} 0 &= -x_{SG} & +x_{GC} & +y_{\overline{GC}} \\ 0 &= & -x_{SR} & +x_{RC} & +y_{\overline{RC}} \end{aligned}$$

wherein positive values of $y_{\overline{GC}}$ or $y_{\overline{RC}}$ correspond to deficiencies in replacing inventories, which are allowed to occur, if necessary, in order to conserve cash.

Inserting the constraints (13.1) through (13.3) in place of their corresponds in (12) and imposing non-negativity requirements on the ranges of admissible values, we can now complete the proposed L.P. formulation by means of a minimizing objective stated in terms of the following functional — *viz.*,

$$(14) \qquad \text{Minimize } M_1 y_{\overline{RC}} + M_2 y_{\overline{GC}} .$$

The coefficients of $y_{\overline{RC}}$ and $y_{\overline{GC}}$ are not numerically specified. They are defined by $M_2 \rangle\rangle\rangle M_1$ where "$\rangle\rangle\rangle$" is intended to mean that no positive

---

[33] This term is borrowed from the literature on queuing (waiting line) analysis in operations research.

number $k > 0$, however large, can produce $kM_1 > M_2$. Thus, $M_2 \rangle\rangle\rangle M_1$ and $M_1 \rangle\rangle\rangle k$, where k is any positive number whatsoever, accords M_2 and M_1 the status of "relative infinites."[34]

The way in which this formulation impounds the indicated preemptive priorities on inventory maintenance may, perhaps, be given a clearer operational significance by discussing how the solution routines of L.P. could proceed, in principle, to utilize these M_1 and M_2 coefficients. Because the objective is minimization, they could first attempt to make $y_{GC}^- \geq 0$ as small as the constraints allow. Then, without allowing any increase in y_{GC}^-,[35] these routines would drive y_{RC}^- to its smallest value, and so on.

The adjusted constraints for (12) are arranged so that $y_{GC}^- = 0$ is attainable, provided the variable $y_{RC}^- \geq 0$ is assigned non-zero values. Because of the indicated preemptive priorities (impounded in $M_2 \rangle\rangle\rangle M_1$) this will always be done irrespective of the increases in y_{RC}^- values that are needed to bring $y_{GC}^- = 0$ about. After $y_{GC}^- = 0$ has been attained, the minimization process then determines $y_{RC}^- = \$1.00$ as the smallest net depletion in Raw Material inventory which the constraints permit, sacrificing any of the x variable values, as required, to bring this about.

By relaxing the constraints in one way or another it would be possible, of course, to effect a still smaller net depletion. Alternatively, the constraints could be tightened by stipulating maximum amounts of net inventory depletion by, for example, introducing extra inequalities on some of the other variables. This is to say, of course, that the even more urgent cash requirements are incorporated in the constraints so that, at least in the present case,[36] even the dominating preemptions associated with M_2 and M_1 for the inventory depletion terms are not allowed to prevail against the requirement for maintaining the opening cash balance.

By tightening or loosening the constraints, or by undertaking suitable further alterations in the model, it is possible to accord different degrees of reflection to managerial requirements. This can all be done in a highly flexible manner although, of course, an approach via constraint alterations will almost necessarily entail a mathematical analysis to establish that the essential properties are, indeed, present in the model. If particular accounts or relations between accounts deserve it, the model can even be arranged to produce contradictions (nonsolvability) as a means of vividly directing managerial attention to danger spots before any operations are undertaken. It is worth noting that even such nonsolution-possibility needs can make managerial sense, under indicated circumstances. These are readily accommodated by L.P. methods that will even order (or arrange) the relative amounts of contradiction (deviations from solution values) which occur,

---

[34] See pp. 756–757 in [9] for a more precise characterization.
[35] Because, as the preceding discussion should make clear, any increase in y_{GC}^-, however small it might be, would necessarily drastically worsen the already achieved solutions.
[36] I.e., with the data given in (12).

at best, when multiple accounts and stipulations must simultaneously be accorded such an "urgent-immediate-management-review" status.[37]

Extending the Spread Sheet

All of these points may now be drawn together and sharpened by spread sheeting the solution for x_{EC} = $4.50 in order to show how the results of the L.P. model might be employed in accounting applications to production and financial budgeting. In order to do this in a convenient way it is first desirable to extend the ordinary spread sheet in certain respects. Thus, as in Table 4, certain extra rows and columns are adjoined to the format that was employed in Table 3. (See the new rows and columns which appear outside the heavy lined portion of Table 4.) These are labelled "Beginning Balance" and "Ending Balance" and employed according to conventions that will now be described.

Consider, first, the Beginning Balance row and column. These are treated in a manner that is analogous to the way a set of books is ordinarily closed. The entries in the Beginning Balance column represent the net amounts of Cash, Goods and Raw Materials carried forward from the preceding period. Similarly, the $50 balance for Net Worth is carried forward by the entry shown in the Beginning Balance row.

Discussion of the Ending Balance row and column is best delayed until after the results of the L.P. solution are entered within the heavy lined portion of Table 4. Because, by assumption, all transactions are effected on a

TABLE 4

Spread Sheet Extension

Credits / Debits	Beginning	Cash	Goods	Raw Materials	Net Worth	Sales	Ending Balance	Total
Beginning Balance					50.00			50.00
Cash	30.00					10.25		40.25
Goods	10.00	3.00						13.00
Raw Materials	10.00	2.75						12.75
Net Worth		4.50					49.00	53.50
Sales			3.00	3.75	3.50			10.25
Ending Balance		30.00	10.00	9.00				49.00
Total	50.00	40.25	13.00	12.75	53.50	10.25	49.00	228.75

[37] *Vide* Chapter VI in [9].

cash basis, the solution of (10) is also the solution in this case. Thus, after first adjusting the constraints in (12) to accord with (13.1)–(13.3), a substitution of $x_1 = 2$, $x_2 = 3$ can be made to generate the following entries in Table 4. Credits to cash are effected to replace Goods and Raw Materials inventories in the respective amounts of $3.00 and $2.75 and, in addition, the $4.50 entry shown in the Cash column represents the debit to Net Worth for facilities rental during the period. Turning to the Cash row, it is seen that the $10.25 entry originates from a credit to the Sales column. Finally, two debits of $3.00 and $3.75 are entered in the Sales row to reflect the cost of merchandise sold from Goods and Raw Materials inventories.

The $3.50 entry that is also shown in the Sales row is the entry that closes the nominal account, profit and loss, into Net Worth at the end of this period. This closing is, in fact, obtained by calculating the difference between total sales and cost of merchandise sold and effecting the indicated entry in a manner which brings the total debits and credits to Sales into balance.

At this point we total the debits to all *asset* accounts only. These amounts are then transferred to the foot of the corresponding account column. The difference between each such transferred amount and the total of the credit entries in each such column is next obtained. The result is then entered in the Ending Balance row. Notice, for instance, that the total of all credits in the Cash column is $10.25. Total debits to Cash amounted to $40.25, as shown by the relevant row total, and the Ending Balance (this difference) is therefore $30.00. This is the same as the Beginning Balance so that, via the constraints, a breakeven level on Cash account was achieved in accordance with the stated policies of management. Also, the dominant priority assigned to M_2 succeeded in achieving breakeven on Goods by bringing this account's Beginning and Ending Balances to equality. The result on the Raw Materials inventory is a drawdown of $y_{RC}^- = \$1.00$ as is verified by observing that the $10.00 Beginning Balance in this account is reduced to the $9.00 figure shown under the Materials column in the Ending Balance row.

To finish this discussion we observe that all credit balance accounts are treated in a fashion that is analogous to the previous treatment of debit balance accounts, except that the column footings are first obtained and then transferred into the corresponding account as a row total. Thus, the $53.50 figure was first obtained by totaling the Net Worth column and then transferring this same amount to the Net Worth row. The one transaction in this row appears as a $4.50 credit to Cash and so the entry for Net Worth in the Ending Balance column appears as $49.00 = $53.50 − $4.50.[38]

---

[38] It is not the case, of course, that the indicated row-column adjunctions represents the only way (or even the best way) of completing the spread sheet in this manner. Entries along the diagonal of cells stretching from the upper left to the lower right hand portion of Table 3 could also be used but this would require recourse to discussions of the suitable ways in which the resulting double counts could be eliminated. Therefore to avoid any further lengthening of the present discussion, we will not examine this or other possibilities and simply refer the reader to [45.1] where another possibility is discussed in terms of balanced-margin tables of so-called Paciolo-Stevinus type.

Reading from the Ending Balance rows and columns we now readily perceive that the end-of-the-period balance sheet will appear as follows:

Balance Sheet
End of Period Two

Cash......................	$30	Net Worth..................	$50*
Goods.....................	10	Less: Deficit for Period.......	(1)
Raw Materials	9		
Total....................	$49		$49

* From Beginning Balance row.

Next, the following operating statement is also obtained:

Operating Statement
For Period Two

Sales..		$10.25
Less: Cost of Mdse. Sold:		
Goods...	$3.00	
Raw Materials...................................	3.75	
Total..		6.75
Gross Margin...		$3.50
Deduct: Rent on Facilities....................................		4.50
Profit or Loss, Carried to Net Worth...........................		($1.00)

Then, to round out the roster of this firm's financial statements (as projected by the indicated solution), we exhibit the following version of a funds-flow analysis (recast as a Cash Flow):

Statement of Sources and Uses of Cash
For Period Two

Sources:		
Gross Sales.....................................	$10.25	
Working Capital (Raw Materials Inventory)...........	1.00	
Total Sources....................................		$11.25
Applications:		
Goods inventory.........................	$3.00	
Raw Materials Inventory..................	2.75	
Total to Inventory...............................	$5.75	
Equipment Rental...............................	4.50	
Reduction in Net Worth..........................	1.00	
Total Applications.................................		$11.25

In the first case, then, the accounting device of a spread sheet (when suitably extended) can be used to systematize the results of a L.P. solution in order to generate all of the statements that are ordinarily used for the financial aspects of budgetary planning. Of course, there is no need for a cash budget in this example since, by assumption, neither accruals, like depreciation, nor credit transactions are involved. But it is also obvious that the cash budget can always be derived, when needed, either from the spread sheet or, in the usual manner, by an adjusted flow of funds analysis.

The production planning budgets are also present, in principle, by virtue of the machine constraints that were incorporated in (12). Neither labor nor other raw materials, union or supplier restrictions (e.g., lead times on delivery) are present in this example, but the model can evidently be extended in these directions whenever there is a need to do so. Similar remarks also apply when extensions to the marketing aspects of budgetary planning need to be considered and, indeed, suitable allowances for lead times and other aspects of transportation and distribution can be effected whenever the value of such extensions warrants the complications and elaborations that might thereby be entailed in the model's structure. [39]

Conclusion

By means of very simple examples, the preceding sections have endeavored to show how L.P. might be joined with accounting in order to produce a coordinated budgetary planning model. This is, of course, only an "in principle" illustration and it should not be interpreted to mean that a literal translation and extension of this particular model should be undertaken in every conceivable circumstance. [40] Further research, especially on the network aspects of these accounting models, will probably be necessary in order to devise suitable artifacts that will avoid unwieldiness and achieve the efficiency that will undoubtedly be needed when actual applications to large-scale management problems are essayed. However, considerable progress has been made (and is being made) on the uses of L.P. in other areas — e.g., production scheduling — and there does not appear to be any obvious reason why similar kinds of research should not be equally successful when oriented in the direction of accounting. In fact, the incidence (network) models of L.P. have been the most successful of all so-called "model types"

---

[39] See the reports [29] and [36] for examples which effect some of the indicated extensions to production, marketing and distribution budgets.

[40] The models (12) ff. can also be simplified, of course, by suitable mathematical manipulations. This was not done because (a) the methods for effecting such simplifications are fairly evident and (b) the objective was, rather, to secure a full display of all pertinent accounting details.

in producing especially efficient solution methods[41] and simplifying arti-facts.[42] And this, of course, was one of the reasons that the model (12) was oriented so that its double-entry accounting aspects could be brought into a network analogy in the sharpest possible manner.

It is also worth observing that mathematical research[43] has established that every L.P. model carries along with it another problem, called its dual. These mathematically established duality relations can also be used to ef-fect still further simplifications. Furthermore, the standard methods of L.P. automatically,[44] and without extra effort, supply solutions to both the model and its dual. This has proved to be especially useful in supplying guides whereby top management can evaluate the implications of its various policies as these are reflected by the constraints that are thereby imposed on subordinates.[45] Thus, still another feature of the budgetary coordination that can be secured from this quarter is brought into view by reference to the top- and down-the-line information guides that are simultaneously ob-tained when L.P. methods are employed that simultaneously solve both an original problem and its dual.[46]

We now briefly examine some of the possible relations between mathe-matics and accounting. First we observe that, from a purely technical standpoint, the trial balance is the most fundamental of all accounting documents. It is, in fact, "the chart of accounts with the relevant entries exhibited on its face."[47] But the extended spread sheet that we have just exhibited is only an alternate way of drawing up a trial balance and so it, too, achieves this same fundamental status.

Next we observe that, from a mathematical standpoint, any spread sheet is simply a matrix.[48] Linear programming also rests heavily on the mathe-matical theory of matrices and so the spread sheet idea provides a very

---

[41] The so-called "transportation models" of L.P. are probably the best known members of this class of model types. See Chapters II and XIV in [9].

[42] The critical path scheduling techniques (of J. L. Kelley) which are discussed in [8] may provide a good enough illustration of such artifacts.

[43] Conducted by D. Gale, H. W. Kuhn and A. W. Tucker, under the auspices of the U. S. Office of Naval Research, and published as Chapter XIX in [41]. (This is the same volume in which G. B. Dantzig's fundamental paper on the simplex method of solving L.P. problems was also first published after it had been developed, at an earlier date, while Dr. Dantzig was employed, on the staff of M. K. Wood, in the Comptroller's office of the U. S. Department of the Air Force.)

[44] E.g., the simplex method of G. B. Dantzig.

[45] See [10] and [71] for discussions of dual solutions that are relevant to the present context.

[46] See [36] for examples of the kinds of "managerial accounting" statements that can be prepared for higher level executives who are thereby enabled to determine the "oppor-tunity cost" implications of altering financial policies, plant conditions, contract re-quirements, etc.

[47] We are indebted to Professor N. C. Churchill for giving effect to our thoughts in this manner.

[48] We should also perhaps note that matrix mathematics provides a very natural language when dealing with electronic computers. Indeed, our colleague, G. L. Thompson, has remarked to us that this fact alone will tend to weigh very heavily in biasing future elec-tronic computer applications to accounting in this direction.

natural bridge between mathematics and accounting.[49] This does not necessarily mean, of course, that either L.P. or the theory of matrices will be the only mathematics that could prove useful in accounting. This has not been true in the past and the future is not likely to prove more confining than past history has already suggested on those occasions when accounting and mathematics have been joined together.

There is, of course, a past tradition of association between mathematical developments and management practices. Werner Sombart, for example, the great German historian, virtually dates the origin of capitalist (industrial) development from the translation and extension of the Hindu-Arabic number system as published (in the *Liber Abacci*) by the Italian mathematician Leonardo Pisano[50] in 1202. This mathematical theory, which was thereby made available for use in western commercial enterprises, almost certainly constituted a necessary precondition for the development of accounting in its many modern aspects.[51]

The first clear and systematic exposition of double-entry accounting (at least for the modern Western world) was published in a tract on mathematics[52] — Fra Luca Paciolo's *Suma de Arithmetica, Geometria, Proportione, et Proportionalita*[53] — and it is possible that historical research will yet reveal that the development of accounting was rather closely attended by the work of other mathematicians.[54] Writings by Fibonacci and Paciolo

---

[49] For another example of the application of matrix ideas to accounting problems see [12].

[50] Better known as Fibonacci in the literature of modern mathematics. See [66].

[51] *Vide*, Sombart, in the source cited in footnote 1, *supra*, where (cf. pp. 129 ff.) he strongly emphasizes that Pisano (also called Leonardo da Pisa) in fact provided the basis for "an exact science of commercial calculation." See also G. E. M. de Ste. Croix, "Greek and Roman Accounting," pp. 62 ff. in [44.2].

[52] The divisions of Paciolo's book are given by R. Emmett Taylor, in [44.4], p. 179, as follows:

1. Arithmetic and Algebra   4. Money and Exchange
2. Their Use in Trade Reckoning   5. Pure and Especially Applied Geometry.
3. Book-keeping

See also, *loc. cit.* p. 180 for Paciolo's recognition of his debt to Leonardo da Pisa.

[53] An English translation of Paciolo's treatise on bookkeeping may be found in *Introduction to Contemporary Civilization in the West* (New York: Columbia University Press, 1946) as adapted from [11]. D. Rosenblatt has, in this connection, also called our attention to another important (but less widely known) book by Paciolo, called *De Divina Proportione*, which was illustrated by Leonardo da Vinci. (No English translation of this appears to be available but the *Quellenschriften für Kuntsgeschichte und Kunsttechnik des Mittelalters und der Neuzeit* provides a German accompaniment to the original in *Fra Luca Pacioli DIVINA PROPORTIONE*, Constantin Winterberg, Wien, 1889. See also Sarton [59] pp. 222, 230 and 236.)

[54] Standard American writings on accounting history have not always been even wholly aware of the issues raised by European historians of capitalism with respect to the roles they have assigned to accounting and related developments — e.g., Hindu-Arabic arithmetic — in achieving a widespread rationalistic view towards business capital along with an ability to reckon and control the processes of capital accumulation. See, e.g., Littleton [43]. It is also true, of course, that these historians did not always pay adequate attention to the developments in American accounting. Sombart, for example, relies heavily on Leo Gomberg's *La Science de la comptabilité et son système scientifique* and also his *Histoire Critique de la Théorie des Comptes*. One reason is, perhaps, that Gomberg, by reasoning

already occupy a position of prominence and the somewhat later work by Simon Stevin[55] appears to be achieving a greater degree of recognition.[56] There are other mathematicians whose work might have influenced — or been influenced by[57] — accounting and managerial developments (and problems).[58] But this would not be the place to dilate at length on this topic even if the evidence were at hand. We can, instead, close with the following statement by Arthur Cayley, 19th century mathematician, and one of the founders of modern matrix algebra:[59]

"Bookkeeping is one of the two perfect sciences."

Perhaps Cayley meant that, at bottom, the two are only one. In any event, from a mathematical standpoint, the notions of optimality, equilibrium, breakeven and linearity are all closely related to one another.[60] So are the concepts of matrices and double-entry principles.

Bibliography

1. ANTON, HECTOR R.: "Activity Analysis of the Firm: A Theoretical Approach to Accounting (Systems) Development," *Liiketaloudellinen Aikakauskirja* (*The Journal of Business Economics*), IV, 1961, pp. 290–305.

2. BARIDON, FELIX E.: "Profit and Loss Budget by Volume," *NAA Bulletin*, Sec. 1, Nov., 1960, pp. 83–89.

3. BERGE, C.: *The Theory of Graphs and Its Applications* (New York: John Wiley and Sons, Inc., 1962).

---

from accounting considerations only, had already achieved an explicit recognition of the fact that the double-entry principle carried with it a splitting apart of ownership and control which, only at a later date, was formulated by the American lawyer-economist, A. A. Berle.

[55] Cf., e.g., 0. ten Have in [44.5].

[56] This statement is drawn from Sarton [59], p. 254, in his discussion of Stevin's *Livre de compte de prince à la manière d'Italie.* . . . The references in [65] were called to our attention by D. Rosenblatt and pp. 1–24 of [65.1] contain an excellent sketch of Stevin's life and work.

[57] *Vide*, pp. 9–11 in [42].

[58] Allowance should perhaps also be made for negative as well as positive influence. See, for instance, the reference on p. 65 in [44.2], to the *Arte dei Cambi*, the guild regulations of 1299 which forbade the use of Arabic-Hindu numerals in the accounts of Florentine bankers. See also [66], p. 105. Another vivid example of delayed effects, and missed opportunities, is supplied by Charles Babbage, the British mathematician, whose early work on computing machines has now aroused a new interest in his other work on management. See, e.g., [26], or, for an extended treatment, see [33].

[59] From A. C. Littleton, [43]. See also [6], Volume VIII, p. XXIV in Biography, where it is noted that "Financial matters and accounts interested him [Cayley]; and only a few months before his death he published a brief pamphlet on book-keeping by double entry, which he had been known to declare one of the two perfect sciences. He could not resist some reference to the subject in his Presidential Address; making the remark that the notion of a negative magnitude 'is used in a very refined manner in book-keeping by double entry'."

[60] *Vide* the references to Cronhelm's and Jocet's equations on pp. 311 ff. in [44].

4. BRUMMET, R. L.: *Overhead Costing* (Ann Arbor: University of Michigan, 1957).
5. BURCHARD, JOSEPH R.: "A Critical Look at the Marginal Graph Technique," *NAA Bulletin*, May, 1961.
6. CAYLEY, ARTHUR: *The Collected Mathematical Papers of Arthur Cayley*, (Cambridge: University Press, 1895) Vols. I–XIII plus index volume.
7. ——,: *The Principles of Book-keeping by Double Entry* (Cambridge: University Press, 1907); available from Cambridge University Press Warehouse.
8. CHARNES, A. AND W. W. COOPER: "A Network Interpretation and a Directed Sub-Dual Algorithm for Critical Path Scheduling," *Journal of Industrial Engineering.* **XIII,** No. 4, July-August, 1962, pp. 213–219.
9. —— AND ——: *Management Models and Industrial Applications of Linear Programming* (New York: John Wiley and Sons, Inc., 1961).
10. ——, —— AND M. H. MILLER: "Application of Linear Programming to Financial Budgeting and the Costing of Funds," *Journal of Business,* **XXXII,** No. 1, Jan., 1959.
11. CRIVELLI, PIETRO: *An Original Translation of the Treatise on Double-Entry Book-Keeping by Frater Lucas Pacioli.* Published by the Institute of Book-Keepers, Ltd.; 133, Moorgate, London, E.C.2, 1924.
12. CYERT, R. M., JUSTIN DAVIDSON, AND G. L. THOMPSON: "Estimation of the Allowance for Doubtful Accounts by Markov Chains," *Management Science,* April, 1962.
13. DEAN, JOEL: "Cost Structure of Enterprises and Break-Even Charts," *American Economic Review Supplement,* Vol. 38, 1948, pp. 153–164.
14. ——: "Managerial Economics," William Grant Ireson and Eugene L. Grant, eds., *Handbook of Industrial Engineering and Management* (Englewood Cliffs, N. J.: Prentice-Hall, Inc., 1955).
15. ——: "Methods and Potentialities of Break-Even Analysis," *The Australian Accountant,* **XXI,** Nos. 10 and 11, Oct. and Nov., 1951, reproduced in [64].
16. D'EPENOUX: "Sur un Problème de Production et de Stockage dans l'Aléatoire," *Revue Française de Recherche Opérationnelle,* 4ᵉ Annee 1ᵉʳ trimestre, 1960, Numero 14, pp. 3–17.
17. DE GHELLINCK, GUY: "Application de la Théorie des Graphes Matrices de Markov et Programmes Dynamiques," *Cahiers du Centre de Recherche Opérationnelle,* 3, No. 1, 1961, pp. 5–35.
18. ——: "Aspects de la Notion de Dualité en Théorie des Graphes," *Cahiers du Centre de Recherche Opérationnelle,* 3, No. 2, 1961, pp. 94–123.
19. ——: "Les Problèmes de Décisions Séquentielles," *Cahiers du Centre d'Etudes de Recherche Opérationnelle,* No. 2, 1960, pp. 161–179.
20. DE ROOVER, R.: "Aux Origines d'une Technique Intellectuelle: La Formation et l'Expansion de la Comptabilité à partie double," *Annales d'Histoire Economique et Sociale,* Vol. IX, No. 44–45, 1937.
21. DEVINE, CARL T.: "Boundaries and Potentials of Reporting on Profit-Volume Relationships," *NAA Bulletin,* Sec. 1, Jan., 1961, pp. 5–14.
22. EASTWOOD, R. PARKER: "The Break-Even Chart as a Tool for Managerial Control," in *Practical Uses of Break-Even and Budget Controls,* Production Series No. 186 (New York 18, American Management Association, 330 W. 42nd St., 1949).

23. EDWARDS, R. S.: *A Survey of French Contributions to the Study of Cost Accounting During the* 19*th Century*, Publication No. 1 of the Accounting Research Association (London: Gee and Co., 1937).

24. ECKHOLDT, JOHN L.: "Using the Break Even Chart in Product-Line Decisions," *NAA Bulletin*, July, 1960, pp. 43–50.

25. GARDNER, FRED V.: *Profit Management and Control* (New York: McGraw-Hill Book Co., Inc., 1955) especially Section II, Chapters 12–27.

26. GARNER, S. PAUL: "Historical Development of Cost Accounting," *The Accounting Review*, XXII, No. 4, Oct., 1947, pp. 385–389.

27. ———: "Has Cost Accounting Come of Age?," *NA(C)A Bulletin*, XXIII, No. 3, Nov., 1951, pp. 287–292.

28. ———: *Evolution of Cost Accounting to 1925* (Alabama: University of Alabama Press, 1954).

29. GASSNER, L. M., E. B. MAGEE AND E. R. MAURER: "Linear Programming as a Method for the Analysis of the Break-Even Point of Sales Volume." Ditto, Term project for the course, Advanced Business and Engineering Economics, at the Graduate School of Industrial Administration. (Pittsburgh: Carnegie Institute of Technology, May, 1955.)

30. GEIJSBEEK-MOLENAAR, L. B.: *Ancient Double Entry Bookkeeping* (Denver, Colorado, 1914).

31. HACHIGIAN, JACK: "Some Further Results on Functions of Markov Processes," Ph.D. Thesis (Bloomington: Indiana University Department of Mathematics, June, 1961).

32. HATFIELD, HENRY RAND: "An Historical Defense of Book-keeping," *Journal of Accountancy*, 37 (April, 1924), pp. 241–253, reprinted in W. T. Baxter, ed., *Studies in Accounting* (London: 1950).

33. HOAGLAND, JOHN: "Charles Babbage — His Life and Works in the Historical Evolution of Management Concepts," Ph.D. Dissertation (Columbus: Ohio State University, 1946).

34. HOWARD, R.: *Dynamic Programming and Markov Processes* (New York: McGraw-Hill Book Co., Inc., 1960).

35. IJIRI, YUJI: *An Application of Input-Output Analysis to Some Problems in Cost Accounting*, Unpublished Term Paper (Minneapolis: University of Minnesota, 1960).

36. ———, F. LEVY AND R. LYON: "A Linear Programming Model for Budgeting and Financial Planning." *Journal of Accounting Research*, Vol. 1, No. 2 (Autumn, 1963), pp. 198–212.

37. JAEDICKE, ROBERT K.: "Improving B-E Analysis by Linear Programming Techniques," *NAA Bulletin*, Sec. 1, March, 1961, pp. 5–12.

38. ———: "Some Notes on Product-Combination Decisions," *The Accounting Review*, 33, No. 4, Oct., 1958, pp. 596–601.

39. JODKA, JOHN: "PERT — A Recent Control Concept," *NAA Bulletin*, Sec.1, Jan., 1962, pp. 81–86.

40. KOHLER, ERIC L.: *A Dictionary for Accountants* (Englewood Cliffs, N. J., Prentice-Hall, Inc., 1952).

41. KOOPMANS, T. C., ed.: *Activity Analysis of Production and Allocation* (New York: John Wiley and Sons, Inc., 1951).

42. LEONTIEF, W. W.: *The Structure of the American Economy*, 1919-1939 (New York: Oxford University Press, 1951).

43. LITTLETON, A. C.: *Accounting Evolution to 1900* (New York: American Institute Publishing Co., 1933).

44. —— AND B. S. YAMEY, eds.: *Studies in the History of Accounting* (Homewood, Ill., Richard D. Irwin, Inc., 1956).
   (44.1) YAMEY, B. S.: "Introduction."
   (44.2) DE STE. CROIX, G. E. M.: "Greek and Roman Accounting."
   (44.3) DE ROOVER, RAYMOND: "The Development of Accounting Prior to Luca Pacioli According to the Account-books of Medieval Merchants."
   (44.4) TAYLOR, R. EMMETT: "Luca Pacioli."
   (44.5) TEN HAVE, O.: "Simon Stevin of Bruges."

45. MACHOL, R. E., ed.: *Information and Decision Processes* (New York: McGraw-Hill Book Co., Inc., 1960).
   (45.1) ROSENBLATT, D.: "On Some Aspects of Models of Complex Behavioral Systems."
   (45.2) ROSENBLATT, M.: "An Aggregation Problem for Markov Chains."

46. MATTESSICH, RICHARD: "Budgeting Models and System Simulation," *Accounting Review*, July, 1961, pp. 384–397.

47. ——: "Towards a General and Axiomatic Foundation of Accountancy, with an Introduction to the Matrix Formulation of Accounting Systems," *Accounting Research*, Oct., 1957, pp. 328–355.

48. MAY, P. A.: "Profit Polygraph for Product Mix Analysis," *NA(C)A Bulletin*, Nov. 1955.

49. PATRICK, A. W.: "Some Observations on the Break-Even Chart," *The Accounting Review*, 33, No. 4 (Oct., 1958), pp. 573–580.

50. PERAGALLO, EDWARD: *Origin and Evolution of Double Entry Bookkeeping* (New York: American Institute Publishing Co., 1938).

51. PIGMAN, NATHANIEL M., JR.: "Simplified Financial Research — An Example in Profit Maximization," *NAA Bulletin*, Sec. 2, Jan., 1962, pp. 87–92.

52. PYE, M. L.: "How to Determine Break-Even Points with Simple Algebraic Formulas," *Journal of Accountancy*, August, 1948, pp. 133–137.

53. RANKIN, BAYARD: "The Concept of Enchainment," Ph.D. Thesis (Cambridge, Mass.: Massachusetts Institute of Technology Department of Mathematics, 1961).

54. RAUTENSTRAUCH, W. AND R. VILLERS: *The Economics of Industrial Management* (New York: Funk and Wagnalls Company, 1949).

55. RICHARDS, ALLEN B.: "Input-Output Accounting for Business," *The Accounting Review*, XXXV, July, 1960, pp. 429–436.

56. ROSENBLATT, D.: "On Aggregation and Consolidation in Finite Substochastic Systems, I, II, III, IV," Abstracts, *Annals of Mathematical Statistics*, 28, No. 4 (Dec., 1957), pp. 1060–1061.

57. ——: "On Aggregation and Consolidation in Linear Systems," Technical Report C, Office of Naval Research Contract Nonr-1180(00), NR-047-012 (Washington, The American University Department of Statistics, August, 1956). ASTIA Ref. No.: AD-117-944.

58. ROSENBLATT, M.: *Random Processes* (New York: Oxford University Press, 1962).

59. SARTON, GEORGE: Six Wings, *Men of Science in the Renaissance* (Bloomington: Indiana University Press, 1957).

60. SHILLINGLAW, GORDON: "Problems in Divisional Profit Measurement," *NAA Bulletin*, Sec. 1, March, 1961, pp. 33–43.

61. SMITH, D. E.: *A Source Book in Mathematics*, (Dover, 1959).

62. ———: *History of Mathematics* (New York: Dover Publications, Inc., 1951).

63. SMITH, JOHN H.: "The Use of Simultaneous Equations in Business Problems," *The Journal of Business*, University of Chicago, XI, No. 2, April, 1938, pp. 188–198.

64. SOLOMONS, DAVID, ed.: *Studies in Costing* (London: Sweet and Maxwell, Ltd., 1952).

65. STEVIN, SIMON: *The Principal Works of Simon Stevin:*
  I. *Mechanics*, edited by a committee of the Royal Netherlands Academy of Sciences; translation by Miss C. Dikshoorn, under editorial direction of E. J. Dijksterhuis (Deventer, Holland, Jan de Lange, 1955).
  II. A. and B, *Mathematics*, D. J. Struik, ed. (Amsterdam: C. V. Swets and Zeitlinger, 1958).

66. STRUIK, D. J.: *A Concise History of Mathematics*, 2nd ed. (New York: Dover Publications, Inc., 1948).

67. TAYLOR, R. EMMETT: *No Royal Road: Luca Pacioli and His Times* (Chapel Hill: University of North Carolina Press, 1942).

68. TSE, JOHN Y. D.: *Profit Planning through Volume Cost Analysis* (New York: The Macmillan Co., 1960).

69. VANCAMP, H. K.: "The Use of the Product Profit and Loss Budget for Marginal Sales Decisions," *NAA Bulletin*, Sec. 1, Nov., 1960, pp. 5–16.

70. VICKERS, DOUGLAS: "On the Economics of Break-Even," *The Accounting Review*, 35, No. 3, July, 1960, pp. 405–412.

71. WEINGARTNER, H. M.: *Mathematical Programming and the Analysis of Capital Budgeting Problems* (Englewood Cliffs, N. J.: Prentice-Hall, Inc., 1963).

72. WHINSTON, A.: *Price Coordination in Decentralized Systems*, Ph.D. thesis (Pittsburgh: Carnegie Institute of Technology, 1962.)

73. WILLSON, JAMES D.: "Practical Applications of Cost-Volume-Profit Analysis," *NAA Bulletin*, Sec. 1, Vol. 41, No. 7, March, 1960, pp. 5–18.

74. WOLFE, P. AND G. B. DANTZIG: "Linear Programming in a Markov Chain," *Operations Research* 10, No. 5, Sept.–Oct., 1962, pp. 702–710.

Supplemental
Readings
to Part Four

G. L. Battista and G. R. Crowningshield, "Cost Behavior and Breakeven Analysis — A Different Approach," *Management Accounting,* Vol. 48, No. 2 (October, 1966), pp. 3–15.

Breakeven analysis based on historical cost data can be misleading because perfect control must be assumed.

Réjean Brault, "Utility of the Classical Break-Even Chart: A Critique," *Cost and Management,* Vol. 43, No. 3 (March–April, 1969), pp. 24–27.

For those not using direct costing, a chart is presented that will show the operating results of both manufacturing and sales functions.

Claude S. Colantoni, Rene P. Manes, and Andrew Whinston, "Programming, Profit Rates and Pricing Decisions," *The Accounting Review,* Vol. XLIV, No. 3 (July, 1969), pp. 467–481.

Linear programming models for perfect competition and monopoly, as well as a full-cost pricing linear programming model for price fixers, are explained.

W. M. Harper, "Cost Profiles," *Accountancy,* Vol. LXXX (July, 1969), pp. 524–527.

Prediction of future costs and activity levels is one of management accounting's contribution to decision-making process.

Robert K. Jaedicke and Alexander A. Robichek, "Cost-Volume-Profit Analysis Under Conditions of Uncertainty," *The Accounting Review,* Vol. 39, No. 4 (October, 1964), pp. 917–926.

The effects of uncertainty on cost-volume-profit analysis are considered.

David O. Jenkins, "Cost-Volume-Profit Analysis," *Management Services,* Vol. 7, No. 2 (March–April, 1970), pp. 55–57.

A basic equation to provide proper data for cost-volume-profit analysis in any size organization is used.

Rene Manes, "A New Dimension to Breakeven Analysis," *Journal of Accounting Research,* Vol. 4, No. 1 (Spring, 1966), pp. 87–100.

Costs of capital are added to breakeven analysis.

Carl L. Moore, "An Extension of Break-Even Analysis," *Management Accounting,* Vol. 50, No. 9 (May, 1969), pp. 55–58.

Breakeven analysis is extended to revenue requirements and funds flows.

Donald L. Raun, "Volume-Cost-Analysis — The Multiple Regression Analysis Approach," *Management Accounting,* Vol. 48, No. 4 (December, 1966), pp. 53–55.

Multiple regression and curvilinear techniques are applied to volume-cost analysis.

Robert M. Soldofsky, "Accountants' vs. Economists' Concept of Break-Even Analysis," *NAA Bulletin,* Vol. XLI, No. 4 (December, 1959), pp. 5–18.

Eleven differences between the cost curves used in breakeven analysis and those used in economic analysis are discussed. Relationships between output, revenue, costs, and profits are emphasized.

David Solomons, "Breakeven Analysis Under Absorption Costing," *The Accounting Review,* Vol. XLIII, No. 3 (July, 1968), pp. 447–452.

This article clarifies assumptions underlying the classical breakeven chart, and adapts the breakeven chart to a situation in which absorption costing is being used.

Horace C. Walton, "Profit Control and Measurement Through Statistical Correlation," *The Controller,* Vol. XXVII, No. 9 (September, 1959), pp. 410–411, 430–431.

A method is described that permits prediction of profit-volume behavior from average cost data. Further use of statistical analysis provides confidence limits from "profit standard".

Herbert J. Weiser, "Break-even Analysis: A Re-evaluation," *Management Accounting,* Vol. 50, No. 6 (February, 1969), pp. 36–41.

Breakeven analysis is presented as an extension of marginal analysis.

Additional

Bibliography

to Part Four

Lester Ageloff, "Economic and Accounting Concepts in Break-Even Analysis," *The New York Certified Public Accountant*, Vol. XXIV, No. 1 (January, 1954), pp. 13–23.

Raymond W. Andrews, "Why Not Use the Break-Even Chart More Freely?" *NAA Bulletin*, Vol. XXXVIII, No. 6 (February, 1957), pp. 777–782.

Sterling K. Atkinson, "Short and Long-Range Considerations in Cost Analyses," *NA(C)A Bulletin*, Vol. XXXVIII, No. 3 (November, 1956), pp. 343–352.

K. C. Banerjee, "Cost, Price, Profit and Volume Reactions," *Accounting Research*, Vol. 5, No. 4 (October, 1954), pp. 343–362.

Raymond J. Barber, Jr., "When Does Part of a Business Break-Even?" *NA(C)A Bulletin*, Vol. XXXII, No. 9 (May, 1951), pp. 1040–1047.

Norman D. Berman, "Profit Analysis Practices in an Oil Refinery Company," *NAA Bulletin*, Vol. XLII, No. 11 (July, 1961), pp. 63–68.

Ronald Brenneck, "Break-Even Charts Reflective Learning," *NAA Bulletin*, Vol. XL, No. 10 (June, 1959), p. 34.

Richard W. Conway, "Breaking Out of the Limitations of Break-Even Analysis," *NA(C)A Bulletin*, Vol. XXXVIII, No. 10 (June, 1957), pp. 1265–1272.

E. G. Cox, "Diagnosing Some Cost-Volume Profit Relationships," *NAA Bulletin*, Vol. XXXIX, No. 8 (April, 1958), pp. 15–25.

Louis S. Drake, "Effect of Product Mix Changes on Profit Variance," *NAA Bulletin*, Vol. XLIII, No. 2 (October, 1961), pp. 61–70.

Francis W. Fehr, "Some Points to Watch in Studying the Fluctuation of Cost with Volume," *NAA Bulletin*, Vol. XLI, No. 7 (March, 1960), pp. 67–76.

William L. Ferrara, "Breakeven for Individual Products, Plants, and Sales Territories," *Management Services*, Vol. 1, No. 3 (July-August, 1964) pp. 38–47.

Fred V. Gardner, "Break-Even Point Control for Higher Profits," *Harvard Business Review*, Vol. 32, No. 5 (September-October, 1954), pp. 123–130.

R. A. Gordon, "Short-Period Price Determination in Theory and Practice," *The American Economic Review*, Vol. XXXVIII, No. 3 (June, 1948), pp. 265–288.

Paul E. Green and S. Reed Calhoun, "An Environmental Framework for Break-Even Analysis for Planning," *NAA Bulletin*, Vol. XXXIX, No. 7 (March, 1958), pp. 45–51.

James B. Hobbs, "Volume-Mix-Price/Cost Budget Variance Analysis: A Proper Approach," *The Accounting Review*, Vol. XXXIX, No. 4 (October, 1964), pp. 905–913.

Robert K. Jaedicke and Alexander A. Robichek, "Cost-Volume-Profit Analysis Under Conditions of Uncertainty," *The Accounting Review*, Vol. XXXIX, No. 4 (October, 1964), pp. 917–926.

John A. Kempster, "Break-Even Analysis — Common Ground for the Economist and the Cost Accountant," *NA(C)A Bulletin*, Vol. XXX, No. 12 (February, 1949), pp. 711–720.

Paul R. McClenon, "Cost Finding Through Multiple Correlation Analysis," *The Accounting Review*, Vol. XXXVIII, No. 3 (July, 1963), pp. 540–547.

A. W. Patrick, "Some Observations on the Break-Even Chart," *The Accounting Review*, Vol. XXXIII, No. 4 (October, 1958), pp. 573–580.

Donald L. Raun, "The Limitations of Profit Graphs, Breakeven Analysis and Budgets," *The Accounting Review*, Vol. XXXIX, No. 4 (October, 1964), pp. 927–935.

Sidney M. Robbins, "Emphasizing the Marginal Factor in Break-Even Analysis," *NAA Bulletin*, Vol. XLIII, No. 2 (October, 1961), pp. 53–60.

Leland G. Spencer, "The Profitgraph — Technique and Applications," *NA(C)A Bulletin*, Vol. XXXVIII, No. 4 (December, 1956), pp. 493–507.

Howard F. Stettler, "Break-Even Analysis: Its Uses and Misuses," *The Accounting Review*, Vol. XXXVII, No. 3 (July, 1962), pp. 460–463.

Spencer A. Tucker, "A System of Managerial Control Using 'Live' Ratios and Control Charts," *NAA Bulletin*, Vol. XLIII, No. 12 (August, 1962), pp. 5–24.

William J. Vatter, "Toward A Generalized Break-Even Formula," *NAA Bulletin*, Vol. 43, No. 4 (December, 1961), pp. 5–10.

Charles P. Voller, "Developing the Profit Planning Procedure," *NAA Bulletin*, Vol. XLII, No. 3 (November, 1960), pp. 31–40.

Wilbert C. Wehn, "Break-Even Points That Mean More in Profit Control," *The Controller*, Vol. XXVII, No. 7 (July, 1959), pp. 311 ff.

Julius Wiener, "Separation of Fixed and Variable Costs," *The Accounting Review*, Vol. XXXV, No. 4 (October, 1960), pp. 686–690.

Rolfe Wyer, "Replacing the Myth of Fixed and Variable Costs," *NA(C)A Bulletin*, Vol. XXXVIII, No. 3 (November, 1956), pp. 353–361.

PART FIVE

Motivation, Performance, and Evaluation:
Standards and Variance Analysis

A major part of cost and managerial accounting is concerned with the accumulation of costs and their identification with either the period or the inventory produced. Costs of direct materials, direct labor, and factory overhead (or burden) normally represent costs which are attached to inventoriable product — goods-in-process, finished goods — and ultimately to cost of goods sold. Their accumulation and assignment is a central part of the technique of cost accounting, especially for income determination, but also and in an important sense for motivation and measurement of performance and for evaluation of that performance.

Product costing is generally done either on a job-order, process, or project cost basis. For purposes of motivation, targets for performance need to be predetermined. For performance evaluation and cost control, these targets or standards serve as a basis for comparison of actual to expected performance. Integral to planning, decision-making, and the design of control models and systems is the setting of standards by operations research, engineering, economics, and other estimates; "variances" are derived from comparison of actual costs to standard costs, or by reference to other imputed measures. Performance is evaluated and control exercised by analyzing significant exceptions.

Standards may be set with different objectives in mind, and they often may be linked to an expected behavioral assumption. Zeff, in the first article, traces the development of standard cost accounting and discusses the general problem of whether the two objectives of cost control and income determination may be met by the one tool — standard "cost book-keeping". In so doing he raises critical philosophical issues relevant to types of standards and variances, as well as to financial statement requirements.

346

An important adjunct of standard cost accounting and the analysis of variances is the use of flexible budgets. Solomons discusses the use of these with particular reference to the analysis of overhead variances — the one area in which he finds significant variety of treatments. In this article he thoroughly discusses the two- and three-variance methods, following the usual dichotomy of controllable and volume variances. An assessment as to what an effective system should achieve is given, and finally some suggestions are made for improving flexible budgets with the end of further improving the analyses of overhead variances.

The increasing sophistication of the methodology of variance analysis is reflected in much of contemporary literature and practice. Models have been developed to determine optimum sequence for examining causes for variances, and methods for applying cost-effectiveness tests to the process of variance analysis have been advanced. Dopuch, Birnberg, and Demski illustrate one extension of variance analysis beyond conventional process and performance control to an evaluation of the performance of decision models. "The essential difference between process control and model control," they aver, "lies in the type of response management should make to an observed variance." This article stresses the uncertainties which attend model construction and identification of decision variables, and the relevance of observed system behavior to the determination of variance. A major point of this article is that the standard cost system can be extended (by the method described in the article) so that it can monitor both performance and decision process. "This monitoring is achieved by structuring the control system around the formal decision models used by the firm."

Horngren, in the final article of Part Five, supports the thesis of the preceding article by suggesting that accounting systems will best tie in with decisions regarding capacity utilization if a reporting system is defined with respect to a specific, well-defined decision model. To analyze capacity utilization, Horngren suggests that a measure of "lost contribution margin" be developed. This article discriminates between long-range and short-range factors, and clearly distinguishes between measurement and valuation. A strong argument is advanced for the use of multi-dimensional measures.

21 *The difference between standard and actual cost — variances and treatment — is the center of this article. The question is raised whether standards should be reported in the financial accounts and reports; that is, are variances inventoriable items. In the process, the author discusses briefly the historical emergence of standard cost, different kinds of standards, and the usefulness of standard costs for control.*

A brief survey of the literature on the main point is given. He concludes that theoretically standard costs should not be included in the statements, but that they often are in practice. The rationale given for the practice of inclusion is that increased attention is often given by management to variances reported, thereby effecting better control; and, that in complicated processes actual costs are often impossible to compute.

Standard Costs in Financial Statements — Theory and Practice*

Stephen A. Zeff

Standard costs were first used intensively in American industry shortly after the first world war when the absence of government-supported demand precipitated a slump in business activity. In order to survive, businesses had to tighten their cost belts. A more rigorous attention to costs was axiomatic. At about the same time, in 1919, a group of some 100 engineers and accountants founded the National Association of Cost Accountants. The N.A.C.A. (now N.A.A.) provided the needed forum for the discussion of cost matters. Thus, both standard costs and the N.A.A. became important to American industry at

* *From* NAA Bulletin, *Vol. XL, No. 8 (April, 1959), pp. 5–16. Reprinted by permission of the publisher.*

the same time. It is also true that the subject of standard costs has been one of the most frequently-debated issues in publications and annual meetings of the association. Much has been written in the *Bulletin* and other publications about the control value of standard costs.

Most writers on the subject of standard costs for control purposes assume without apparent question that standard costs are proper raw materials for bookkeeping entries and, more importantly, financial statements. A casual reader in this area would likely infer from the seeming unanimity among cost accounting writers that it is generally agreed among financial accountants as well that this is proper practice. This inference will inevitably lead the reader to draw a more fundamental conclusion: that standard costs are proper costs for the valuation of assets[1] and, conjointly, the determination of net income.

Are these sound inferences? If they are not, may the use of standard costs in the books and financial statements[2] nevertheless be justified? These two lines of inquiry deserve critical investigation. It is, therefore, the purpose of this paper to enlarge upon these problems in order that the use of standard costs in the financial statements may be accepted or rejected.

In order to answer the first question — the soundness of the two inferences — attention will be centered primarily on the theoretical plane of argument. Consideration of practical and expedient lines of argument will also be introduced. This is not to say that practical matters are of no importance; it is intended only to isolate as well as possible, and so study, the theoretical aspects. The second question, on the other hand, will involve only a discussion of practical matters.

Theoretical Side — Some Contrasting Views

An important goal of cost accounting is cost control. The chief aim of financial accounting is income determination. In themselves, these goals do not conflict. Both goals imply the use of one common tool: cost bookkeeping. To the financial accountant, cost bookkeeping is one phase of the record-keeping process which ultimately leads to the preparation of financial statements. To the cost accountant, cost bookkeeping may consist of the formalization of information which is useful for cost control. An essential requisite of effective cost control is some norm against which management can measure the results of actual operations. The norm is identified as a

---

[1] This paper restricts the scope of discussion to inventories, which is the asset category most affected by the booking of standard costs. Another category would be fixed assets manufactured by the user.

[2] As will be pointed out later, the real problem consists of the recognition of standard costs in *financial statements*. The mere booking is not important, for period-end adjusting entries can erase the effects of during-the-year book entries. Hereinafter, "booking" will also imply recognition in the financial statements.

standard or, more appropriately, a standard cost.[3] Variances between standard costs and actual costs are analyzed as to cause in order that future operations might approach or meet the standards. Cost accountants have learned, moreover, that at least two advantages may be realized by using standard costs in cost bookkeeping:

1. *Bookkeeping costs can be reduced* — Since the "life" of a standard cost is much longer than that of an actual cost (the latter is different for each job or process run), entries can be made without constantly re-computing costs.

2. *Executives will take standard costs and variances more seriously* — If cost control is to have any teeth, executives must give full support to the reduction of variances between standard costs and actual costs. It has been found that executives will be more responsive to cost reduction if the standard costs, and thus the variances, are entered in the accounts.[4]

To be sure, cost accountants have also presented arguments of philosophical as well as practical value as to why standard costs should be booked. These arguments are more profitably revealed at a later stage in the discussion.

Changes in bookkeeping procedures necessarily attract the attention of financial accountants, for the bookkeeping entries are the starting points along the road toward the preparation of financial statements. Because Advantage 2, above, implies that the standard costs should be carried into the statements, the financial accountant is inescapably involved in the standard cost problem: in the books or not? If all the cost accountant wished were bookkeeping entries based on standard costs without their recognition in the statements, the financial accountant could employ the expedient of adjusting entries to rid the accounts of the extraneous (standard cost) data. But here cost accounting has intruded upon financial accounting, and one side must give in. There is no compromise on principles.

In order to understand more fully the position of financial accounting, it is desirable to examine the related view of the nature of income determination. The income statement is the meeting place for the revenue and expense of a given fiscal period. Total revenue represents revenue attributable to operations of the period, expressed in actual dollars — dollars agreed upon by the seller

---

[3] "The term 'standard cost' is a grievous misnomer. Whatever may be the true character of the things called by that name, they are certainly not 'costs'." John B. Canning, *The Economics of Accountancy*, Ronald Press, 1929, p. 271, n. 8. A standard cost is certainly not an economic cost. For the sake of convenience, however, it will be referred to as "standard cost" in this paper. See also Cyril F. Gamber, "The Relationship Between Standard and Actual Costs," *NA(C)A Bulletin*, April 1, 1946, p. 674.

[4] Henry W. Maynard, "The Accounting Technique for Standard Costs," *NA(C)A Bulletin*, February 15, 1927, p. 562. Advantage 2 is of much lesser significance today than in 1927, when Maynard wrote. It may be updated by substituting "statements" for "accounts." It should also be noted that cost accountants have described standard costs as the only *true* costs. See *infra*, note 24.

and buyers. The expenses, though they cannot always be unquestionably identified with the revenue of a certain period, are ideally also expressed in actual dollars[5] — dollars agreed upon by the buyer and sellers. The difference between total revenue and total expense is either net income or net loss for the fiscal period. Although the financial accountant must concede that this matching process is not perfect, i.e., it is usually impossible to "pin" each item of expense on a certain item of revenue, he can, nonetheless, maintain that the netted figure is homogeneous. Everything is expressed in actual, or bargained, dollars.

Because the consumption of non-cash assets is a significant determinant of net income (via costs), it is important to proper income determination that assets be valued in harmony with the cost theory. Although in the last few decades such expediencies as "cost or market, whichever is lower," for inventories and marketable securities, and recognition of appreciation of fixed assets[6] have been evidenced, the fundamental principle of "actual cost" prevails. It is noteworthy that the deviations have not been accepted by many leading writers in financial accounting.[7]

Different Kinds of Standard Costs

In order to get down to the basic argument, it is first necessary to examine the kinds of standard costs, for different kinds will have different effects on the financial statement. Two major classifications of standard costs are basic and current. Basic standards are those which are not changed unless there are important alterations in the nature or sequence of manufacturing operations. Current standards are those which undergo periodic revision in order to reflect changes in methods and prices. Basic standards are, therefore, useful for long-run analyses of variances, while current standards are more suited to short-run analyses. There seems to be general agreement among cost accountants that, if standard costs are to be booked, they must be current.[8] After a short period of time has elapsed, basic standards are no longer realistic in

[5] It is to be noted, however, that there is strong support for some deviations from actual cost. See the next paragraph and note 7, *infra*.

[6] Whether the carrying value of fixed assets should be written up to current prices depends on the nature of the price rise. A change in price level might justify accounting recognition thereof if precautions are taken to identify clearly the character of the write-up. But the accounting recognition of changes in price *structure*, as contrasted with the price *level*, is not to be condoned generally.

[7] Objections to the upward revision of fixed asset account balances are numerous. The more widely-accepted "cost or market, whichever is lower," is frowned upon by Henry Rand Hatfield, *Accounting: Its Principles and Problems*, D. Appleton & Company, 1927, p. 99; Perry Mason, see his dissent in *Restatement and Revision of Accounting Research Bulletins*, American Institute of Accountants, 1953, p. 35; and W. A. Paton and A. C. Littleton, *An Introduction to Corporate Accounting Standards*, American Accounting Association, 1940, p. 81.

[8] Walter B. McFarland, "The Basic Theory of Standard Costs," *Accounting Review*, June, 1939, p. 152 and Gamber, *op. cit.*, p. 677.

view of technological and price-level changes. Thus, if financial statements are to reflect reality at all, basic standards are of no value for them.

In addition, current and basic standard costs may be set at different levels. Standard costs may reflect expected actual costs, average-capacity costs, practical-capacity or ideal costs. Expected actual costs resemble budgeted figures in that an attempt is made to forecast the results of future operations. Because expected actual costs anticipate and allow for inefficiencies and waste, they are not very useful standard costs for control purposes. Average-capacity costs, or standard costs at average capacity, are intended to level out seasonal and cyclical fluctuations. Standard costs under this plan are set at attainable levels. Practical-capacity costs represent activity at a theoretical maximum, reduced by unavoidable delays. As such, they provide an attainable and rigorous standard for control purposes. Ideal standard costs are the costs at theoretical capacity of the plant. As such, they are unattainable, for they do not allow for inefficiencies of any sort.

Standard costs help facilitate cost control by focusing attention on operational inefficiencies. For cost control purposes, therefore, standard costs must be substantially or completely free of inefficiencies which the computation of variances should uncover. Standard costs are consequently most useful for cost control purposes when they are "tight," or when inefficiences have been "squeezed out" of them. In terms of the levels enumerated above, standard costs for control purposes might best be structured on the practical-capacity idea in order to emphasize the deviations from the "efficient" norm.

The Basic Issue: A Conflict of Interests

Thus far, standard costs have been shown to be best for day-to-day cost control if they are current and tight. Are those characteristics consistent with those which financial accountants ascribe to costs for financial statement purposes? This question will be answered from the standpoints of pure financial accounting theory and financial accounting theory as interpreted by practitioners.

In terms of pure financial accounting theory, the answer is clearly "no." There is no substitute for actual costs. Ideally, the income statement is composed solely of actual revenues and actual costs.[9] The case for actual costs may be expressed in this fashion. An income statement purports to show the results of actual operations. Revenue is an actual sum evidenced by sales tickets. It would be inconsistent to charge against this revenue an expense total which assumes some efficiency "ideal," i.e., any efficiency standard other than the actually-achieved efficiency. If expenses are represented by an amount

---

[9] In effect this means that variances from standard costs may be reported as expense in the period during which the merchandise to which they pertain is sold. The argument here is against showing the variances as expense in the period when the related production operations take place. That is, variances are inventoriable costs.

which *would* have been incurred in accordance with a prescribed efficiency standard, it follows that revenue should be stated at an "ideal" volume multiplied by an "ideal" sales price. Then the income statement would resemble a whole budget, rather than half-results and half-budget. Is the income statement to be an operations summary or a restatement of a kind of budget? Is the object of financial accounting to arrive at an efficient net income? The answer to this last question is "no."

As regards "financial accounting theory as interpreted by practitioners," it is useful first to discuss the "current" and "basic" characteristics separately. Financial accountants would agree with cost accountants that, as between current and basic costs, the former are certainly preferable. Underlying the financial accounting principles of actual cost is the desire to be as up-to-date with present realities as is possible. Current standard costs follow the same guide.

If we ignore the materials usage variance, the following interesting analysis can be made with respect to raw materials inventory. "First-in, first-out" enthusiasts who also appreciate the conservatism of "cost or market, whichever is lower," would welcome current standard costs. In periods of falling prices, standard cost — because of time lags between adjustment to new, lower prices — will be somewhat higher than actual cost. As a result, the ending inventory at standard cost will appear in the accounts, before adjustment to market, at an amount somewhat above actual cost. There is no problem here, for the adjustment to market will eliminate the disparity. But in periods of rising prices, the standard costs will be somewhat lower, due to time lags between upward adjustments, than actual costs. Thus, the ending inventory will appear in the accounts at an amount somewhat below actual cost! Market price will be higher and no adjustment will take place. The latter instance illustrates how standard costs can contribute to the conservatism so cherished by many financial accountants.[10]

"Last-in, first-out" proponents, because of the above reasons, would also prefer current standard costs when prices are rising. For, in this instance, ending inventory cost at standard — somewhat lower than actual cost because of time lags between adjustments — will increase the cost of goods sold and thereby produce a more conservative profit.

In periods of either sustained rising or falling prices, average cost proponents will find smaller differences between standard cost and actual cost than is true in the instances above. (The magnitude of the difference between standard cost and actual cost has not been discussed above, for it is the subject of the next section.)

As to tight standard costs, these underscore the fact that standard costs represent conditions as they should be or, in the past tense, as they should have been. Financial accounting wants costs as they were. It would not be out of the question, however, for financial accountants to accept standard costs if the

---

[10] This is not to condone conservatism for the sake of conservatism. It must be remembered that the attempt is made here to reconcile standard costs with generally-practiced accounting, i.e., financial accounting theory together with generally accepted deviations therefrom, or "financial accounting theory as interpreted by practitioners."

differences between standard costs and actual costs were small (immaterial). But are the differences small?

To meet the wishes of practicing financial accountants, standard costs should be set at a level somewhere between expected actual and average-capacity costs, defined above. In this way, the standard costs would approach actual costs. But herein lies the basic disharmony between standard costs for control purposes and standard costs for financial reporting purposes. Cost control needs tight standards and financial accounting would want realistic standards. Both ends cannot be served by the same standards. Standard costs are inevitably either a poor cost control device or a poor income determination (inventory valuation) procedure. But this apparently hopeless conflict does not shut the door entirely on some use of standard costs for financial accounting purposes. However, before this exception is introduced and examined, it is well to gain perspective by observing what some leading accounting writers think on this controversy.

Philosophies of Leading Writers

Paton and Littleton in their monograph, *An Introduction to Corporate Accounting Standards*, write, "no substantial objection can be offered to the computation of standard costs and the compilation of these costs in any helpful manner, provided the periodic income statement, as finally presented, is based upon actual costs rather than upon hypothetical charges."[11] This view reflects pure financial accounting theory.

In his fourth edition (1927), Montgomery makes this statement: "For inventory purposes 'standard' costs should not be used without thoroughly testing the cost procedure to see that such costs are reasonable and may properly be considered actual."[12] But two editions and 13 years later, he explains his position differently: all variances save idle capacity should be apportioned to the ending inventory. In defense of this position, Montgomery states: "With respect to the manufacturing overhead application, it is now recognized that the cost of production should bear depreciation in respect of only those facilities which are considered necessary to current operations."[13] The effect of this apportionment is to convert standard costs to actual costs, in the aggregate. Morton Backer writes:

> Unless the effect on inventories is relatively insignificant, the variances from standard should be apportioned between cost of goods sold, work in process and completed but unsold inventories in a manner similar to the suggested treatment for over- or under-absorbed overhead.[14]

[11] *Op. cit.*, p. 121.
[12] Robert H. Montgomery, *Auditing Theory and Practice*, Ronald Press, 1927, p. 160.
[13] Robert H. Montgomery, *Auditing Theory and Practice*, Ronald Press, 1940, p. 163. What about the depreciation element in other fixed overhead variances?
[14] "Determination and Measurement of Business Income by Accountants" in Morton Backer, editor, *Handbook of Modern Accounting Theory*, Prentice-Hall, 1955, p. 233.

The American Institute of Certified Public Accountants, in its "restatement" bulletin, carefully identifies standard costs as "approximate" costs, as follows:

Standard costs are acceptable if adjusted at reasonable intervals to reflect current conditions so that at the balance-sheet date standard costs reasonably approximate costs computed under one of the recognized bases. In such cases descriptive language should be used which will express this relationship, as, for instance, 'approximate costs determined on the first-in, first-out basis,' or, if it is desired to mention standard costs, 'at standard costs, approximating average costs.' [15]

It should be noted, furthermore, that standard costs are not a "recognized base."

The views of two prominent cost accountants are also of interest. Blocker suggests that each variance from standard be first analyzed before the financial accountant makes a decision regarding its disposition. With material and labor variances, he states that the portion of the variance which was beyond the control of management be prorated between the inventory and profit and loss accounts. The controllable portion should be sent directly to profit and loss. In the case of overhead variances, a different treatment is proposed. Blocker maintains that variances which are due to seasonal fluctuations should be deferred until they are offset by future fluctuations. If the variances represent inefficiences or savings from the standard, they should be sent to profit and loss. Variances due to improperly-prepared standards should be prorated between inventories and profit and loss. [16] This procedure seems simple and clearcut "on paper" but it is seriously doubted that such fine distinctions can be made in practice. Nickerson recommends, however, that overhead should be carried to the inventories at standard cost, whereas materials and labor should best be shown at actual costs. This treatment presents a "clearer picture of operations, as well as conservative valuation. . . ." [17]

Montgomery's view is preferred by this writer. Materials, direct labor, and variable overhead are functions of activity. The presence of these costs, in all but extreme cases, supports the presumption that goods are being turned out. Marginal costs are the reflection of marginal product. As such, these costs should be identified with the net product which has caused their incurrence.

[15] *Op. cit.*, p. 30, n. 3.
[16] John G. Blocker, "Mismatching of Costs and Revenues," in William E. Thomas, editor, *Readings in Cost Accounting, Budgeting, and Control*, South-Western Publishing Co., 1955, pp. 252–53.
[17] Clarence B. Nickerson, "Application of the Cost or Market Rule to a Woolen Company" in the *Control and Valuation of Inventories*, National Association of Cost Accountants, 1941, p. 217. Nickerson's proposal probably extends beyond the woolen industry, for he writes, "Though the practices of this woolen company serve as a specific example, many of the matters considered are equally applicable to other manufacturing enterprises." *Ibid.*, p. 209.

The activity variance, or cost of idle capacity, stands for the cost of fixed plant facilities which were *not* utilized in the turning out of products.

It is as though a company owned two factories, and one was used at 100 per cent of capacity and the other was not used at all. The fact that one factory, or one segment of fixed plant facilities, was not used, does not change the cost required to turn out the products which were manufactured elsewhere. The cost of idle capacity is clearly a waste of fixed facilities which, during the fiscal period, were not a part of the company's productive assets. If these facilities are truly fixed, i.e., the length of their aggregate lives is a function of *time*, not *use*, that portion of their cost identified with this fiscal period (depreciation, insurance, taxes) is a loss in this period and, in no sense, is this cost identifiable with future periods by way of inventories. As was said above, the fixed plant facilities were unproductive assets for 100 per cent of the time; their cost is, therefore, a 100 per cent loss chargeable to the operations of the current period.

The other fixed overhead variances represent, for the most part, inefficiencies associated with fixed plant facilities which were used. Although the line of distinction is not so clear here as it was above, it seems best to identify these variances with the product, because they are due to efficiencies or inefficiencies in using the facilities. The facilities were used for the turning out of the products; therefore, the products should bear the actual cost of using these facilities. Similarly, loss of materials due to theft or destruction should be charged to the current period's operations. In general, production costs are inventoriable unless they expired without having a proximate relation to the turning out of the product.

In summary, "financial accounting as interpreted by practitioners" should observe actual cost as far as practicable,[18] except that the inventory cost should be reduced by the costs which expired "outside" of the productive process.

The Practical Side

Although the above recommendation lends most support to actual costs, it is not uncommon to find companies which value inventories at standard cost. This suggests that there must be one or more practical justifications, as opposed to the theoretical objections, for using standard costs for inventory valuation. The remaining discussion will present evidence that standard costs are being employed for inventory valuation today and attempt to infer the justifications which prompt this practice.

That the A.I.C.P.A. has taken a position on the treatment of standard costs for inventory purposes is testimony that standard costs are often used in

---

[18] Whether the use of actual costs is practicable is usually the controlling factor in deciding if they will be relied upon. This matter is the subject of the next section of this article, "The Practical Side."

financial statements.[19]   Both the Finney-Miller and Karrenbrock-Simons intermediate textbooks report that expected actual, normal, and ideal standard costs are frequently used for inventory pricing.[20] A 1947 N.A.C.A question-naire survey revealed that, of 65 companies which used standard costs and treated all of the different material and labor variances alike in the accounts, 54 firms closed these variances to cost of goods sold. Of 127 companies which used predetermined overhead rates, approximately eighty per cent closed both under- and over-absorbed overhead variances to cost of goods sold.[21] This evidence indicates apparent widespread usage of standard costs for inventories valuation, but why is this done? Although no one seems to have shown that the standard costs which are today being used for inventories are also being used for cost control, it is likely that this is true.

Two reasons which were given by companies which closed material and labor variances to cost of goods sold were:

1. "Variances represent costs of waste and inefficiency and, as such, should be excluded from cost of goods manufactured.

2. "Standard costs give more conservative inventory valuations since they eliminate the effects of excess prices and inefficiencies from inventories."[22]

One important reason, given above, cites the increased managerial attention shown to cost control when standard costs, and thus variances, appear in the statements.[23]

There are probably two additional, and more pressing, reasons, however, why standard costs are used in financial statements today:

1. In many plants, actual costs are too difficult (sometimes impossible) and costly to gather. The use of standard costs simplifies and, therefore, introduces economies in the cost-gathering and cost-bookkeeping processes.

2. Cost accountants have "sold" managements on the control value of standard costs and have also been successful, as suggested above, in convincing managements that standard costs are "real" costs and thus

[19] "Restatement," *loc. cit.*

[20] H. A. Finney and Herbert E. Miller, *Principles of Accounting: Intermediate*, Prentice-Hall, 1958, pp. 229–30. Wilbert E. Karrenbrock and Harry Simons, *Intermediate Accounting*, South-Western Publishing Co., 1958, comprehensive volume, pp. 247–48.

[21] "Cost Included in Inventories," National Association of Cost Accountants, Research Series No. 10, Section 3, *NA(C)A Bulletin*, August 15, 1947, pp. 1598 and 1601.

[22] *Ibid.*, p. 1599. The first reason assumes, as has been implied, that the cost of goods manufactured is to be stated at efficient cost, not actual cost. This assumption has already been discussed.

[23] Note 4, *supra.* Mention was also made earlier of lower bookkeeping costs to be derived from using standard costs.

should be booked.[24] When auditors are confronted, at the end of the fiscal period, with standard costs and variances instead of actual costs, they have but two choices: to accept them or to try to prorate the variances between inventories and cost of goods sold, which some have done. But there are often difficulties in finding satisfactory bases of apportionment.

The foregoing reasons appear to be the most cogent justifications for the prevailing standard cost accounting practices.

A General Conclusion

It should be clear that standard costs are found in financial statements today as a result of practical necessities, and not theoretical blessing. The use of standard costs in financial statements is one of the many areas in which accounting practice diverges from the accounting theory. Although the use of standard costs in financial statements is apparently desirable from a practical standpoint, accounting writers should, nevertheless, be careful not to infer therefrom, or allow their readers to infer therefrom, that such practice is consistent with good financial accounting theory.

[24] In this connection, some accountants have attacked the very foundation of actual costs. A British accountant contends that actual costs contain certain "inevitable inaccuracies" and are "mathematical abstractions." "The best that can be said about an 'actual cost', " he writes, "is that it is an arithmetical exactitude, being the average of a number of unspecified variations." K. W. Bevan, "The Accounting Processes of Standard Costing," *The Accountant*, April 10, 1948, p. 282.

Arguing that, if six public accountants were to draw up financial statements for one business, each set of statements would differ from the rest in some respects (which is certainly true), another accountant recommends standard costs as the only exit from the actual cost dilemma. He states, "Many overlook the point that, in determining this so-called actual cost, arbitrary divisions of overhead have been made and arbitrary divisions of joint costs and by-product costs have been used. No method has ever been devised to measure the actual cost of the product of a modern industrial plant." In proposing standard costs as the only solution, he concludes that "Costs of production should reflect the average cost under normal conditions." Howard E. Cooper, "Some Controversial Phases of Standard Cost," *NA(C)A Bulletin*, September 15, 1933, pp. 84 and 87.

These writers have some good points, but more basic to the whole argument presented by these and other accountants is: Do bookkeeping entries *determine* profits or do they *reflect* profits? It is conceded that the *correct* actual costs are often not calculable. This fact should not lead accountants to abandon all concepts of actual cost, however. What is more, the arguments above over-emphasize the portion of actual costs which is found by "averaging" and "arbitrary apportionment." Direct labor and direct materials can be found unequivocally for jobs in the absence of joint cost problems. Overhead per job needs to be estimated, of course, but the degree of error is not so large as that suggested by Cooper and others.

*2*2*Conventional systems for analyzing overhead variances are the two- or three-variance type. The con-
trollable/non-controllable dichotomy utilized by two-variance procedure
does not distinguish between the spending and efficiency elements of the
controllable variance. The "efficiency" variance of the three-variance
system is but a difference between two hypothetical absorbed expenses.
Budget allowances for overhead do not recognize the relationships
between overhead and variables other than output level, but they should.*

*In the example given, four-variance analysis is accomplished by
relating budget, efficiency, volume capacity, and volume efficiency
variances to a flexible budget which is functionally related to both
output and man-hours.*

Flexible Budgets and
the Analysis of
Overhead Variances*

David Solomons

Standard costing has become so generally accepted as a useful accounting
technique in industry that it is unusual to find any of its methods called in
question. Yet, while the analysis of variances between actual and standard
direct costs — direct materials and direct labor — has given rise to no important differences of theory or practice among writers and practitioners, the same
cannot be said of the analysis of overhead variances. Indeed, an examination

* *From* Management International, *1961–1, pp. 84–93. Reprinted by permission of the
publisher.*

of the literature of the subject over the last thirty years shows an extraordinary variety of treatments.[1] It would surely be in the best interests of management if some agreement could be reached about the most effective method of analysing overhead variances for general application.

In this paper I shall set myself three objectives. The first is to compare the two principal systems of overhead variance analysis in common use. I shall attempt to do this by the use of a diagrammatic method of representing variances which I have written about previously.[2] From the comparison of the two-variance and three-variance systems, an assessment of what an effective system should achieve is then made. Finally a suggestion is made for an improvement in the flexible budget, leading to a corresponding improvement in the analysis of overhead variances.

The Conventional Analysis of Overhead Variances

The conventional analysis of overhead variances is illustrated in Diagram 1.[3] Diagram 1 (a) shows the analysis of variance into two parts, a controllable variance, as it is usually called, and a volume variance. In the situation illustrated, the actual man-hours worked fell seriously short of the man-hours budgetted, and the actual efficiency of the work done was also substantially below 100 per cent, so that the output produced (expressed in standard hours) was less than it should have been in the man-hours actually worked. These three quantities, budgetted hours, actual hours and achieved standard hours (i.e., actual output) are represented by the three vertical lines. Budgetted fixed overheads are represented by the horizontal line B.F.O. and on top of this the variable expenses budgetted for varying levels of output are superimposed, to give the line B.T.O. representing budgetted total overheads. This line stands for the flexible budget, and shows at each level of activity the total overhead expenditure allowed by the budget. While this line is shown as a straight line in the diagram, the analysis would in no way be jeopardized, and would almost certainly gain in realism, if the budget line were shown as curved instead of straight, or even as rising in discontinuous jumps.

The standard overhead rate is computed by dividing the total overhead budget allowance appropriate to the budgetted level of activity by the number of man-hours to be worked. This gives the standard hourly rate of overheads,

---

[1] Reference may be made to *The Cost Accountants' Handbook*, ed. Theodore Lang (Ronald Press, 1944) pp. 78–95, for a review of a number of methods developed prior to 1945. The second (1960) edition of this publication (now called *The Accountants' Cost Handbook* edited by Robert Dickey) does not find much to add (see Chapter 17, pp. 28–31).

[2] "A Diagrammatic Representation of Standard Cost Variances," by David Solomons: *Accounting Research*, Vol. 2, No. 1 (January, 1951), pp. 46–51. In "The Mathematics of Variance Analysis-II," *Accounting Research*, Vol. 4, No. 4 (October, 1953), pp. 329–350, Mr. Gilbert Amerman uses a similar method to analyse overhead variances. While the results of his analysis are similar to mine, he does not form any judgment about the relative merits of existing systems, nor does he make any proposals for their improvement.

[3] See page 109.

and is represented by a straight line joining the point S (the point where the budget expense line B.T.O. cuts the "budget hours" vertical) to the origin. This line cannot be anything but straight, since the standard rate, once fixed, cannot vary during the period, whatever fluctuations of output or expenditure may occur. Only when there is a revision of standards will the standard overhead rate change.

It is important to make a clear distinction between the budgetary data in the diagram and the information about actual results. To enable this distinction to be kept in mind, budget data is represented by broken lines and "actual" data by unbroken lines. The actual expenditure on overheads during the period under examination is shown by the horizontal line passing through the point A.

With the two-variance system, the flexible budget allowance is regarded as being set by the level of output achieved, and in Diagram 1 (a) it is represented by the point B′, allowed expense, the point at which the vertical for actual output cuts the flexible budget line. The excess of actual expense over allowed expense, represented by the vertical distance AB′, is the controllable variance, the excess expenditure (in this case) for which the departmental officials and foreman can be held responsible. The difference between the allowed expense and the overheads absorbed into actual production at the standard overhead rate — the absorbed expense — is the non-controllable or volume variance. It represents the fixed overheads which are left unabsorbed because production (expressed in standard hours) fell short of budgetted production. As can be seen from the diagram, if output had been as budgetted, the volume variance would have been nil. If output had been zero, then the volume variance would have been equal to — it would in fact have consisted of — the total fixed overheads. The diagram makes it quite clear that there would be no volume variance if there were no fixed costs. It can further be seen that if the achieved standard hours were to exceed the budgetted hours, either because of intensive use of capacity or because of high productivity per hour, then the standard overhead recovery line would have crossed and be above the budget line, and the volume variance would be favorable, i.e., it would represent an over-absorption of fixed costs.

Substituting figures for the diagram,[4] suppose that the budget for the month calls for 2000 standard hours of output in 2000 man-hours. At this level of activity, budgetted expenses are $1000 fixed expense and $1000 variable expense for the month. At the end of the month, it is found that only 1800 man-hours were worked and only 1600 standard hours were produced, while actual overhead expenditure was $2150.

---

[4] In the diagrams, the variances have been exaggerated to make the demonstrations more effective. The diagrams are therefore not drawn on a scale corresponding to the numerical illustrations. It need hardly be pointed out that the method of analysis used is equally applicable, whether any or all of the variances are favorable or unfavorable.

Diagram 1 (a)

Conventional Two-Variance Analysis of Overheads

Diagram 1 (b)

Conventional Three-Variance Analysis of Overheads

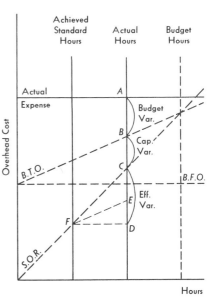

Diagram 2 (a)

Conventional Three-Variance Analysis of Overheads

Diagram 2 (b)

Four-Variance Analysis of Overheads (All expenses assumed to vary with hours worked)

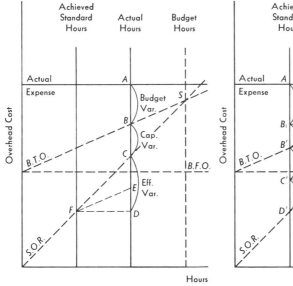
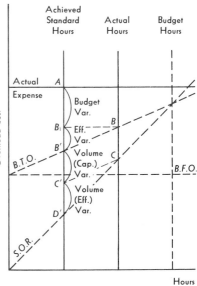

Then we have:

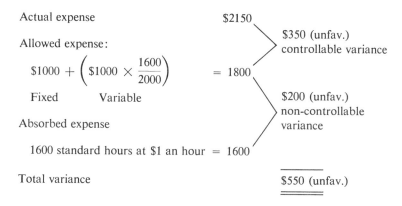

Actual expense	$2150	
Allowed expense:		$350 (unfav.) controllable variance
$1000 + \left($1000 \times \dfrac{1600}{2000}\right) = 1800$		
Fixed Variable		$200 (unfav.) non-controllable variance
Absorbed expense		
1600 standard hours at $1 an hour = 1600		
Total variance		$550 (unfav.)

Turning to Diagram 1 (b), we have an illustration of the conventional three-variance system. The data is the same as in Diagram 1 (a), and the notation is almost the same. As can be seen from the diagram, with this system the budget allowance for overheads is determined by reference to the actual man-hours worked, at point B.

The three variances can now be identified. The vertical distance AB, the excess of actual overheads over the budget allowance, represents the budget variance. This variance will usually be in part a price variance, due to differences between the standard and actual prices of overhead services or indirect materials, and in part a spending variance, due to divergences between actual and budget expenditures unrelated to price variations. There is no technical difficulty whatever in making this division between the price element and the "spending" element in the budget variance, for all that needs to be done is to have all overhead services, indirect materials and indirect labor priced at both actual and standard prices, in the same way as is done for direct materials and direct labor. But in practice it is not often thought worthwhile to go to these lengths.

The vertical distance BC is the capacity variance. As can be seen, it is the difference between the budget allowance for the hours actually worked, and the cost which would have been absorbed, at the standard overhead rate, if every hour worked had been 100 per cent effective in producing output. This latter amount, the actual hours worked evaluated at the standard overhead rate per hour, which we might appropriately call the time-absorbed expense, is represented by point C. Like the volume variance of Diagram 1 (a), the capacity variance can be seen to be equal to the full fixed costs when output is zero, falling to a nil variance when actual hours are equal to budget hours, and then reversing its sign and becoming a favorable variance when actual hours exceed budget hours.

The third member of the trinity is the efficiency variance. This is the vertical distance CD. The point D is merely a projection on to the "actual hours" vertical of the point F, which represents the standard cost recovered or absorbed by actual output. It will be seen that the efficiency variance, so measured, is the difference between the standard overhead cost absorbed by actual output and what we have called the time-absorbed expense — the standard overhead cost which would have been absorbed if the actual hours worked had been fully effective in producing output.

Using the same figures as previously, the total variance of $550 is the same as before; its analysis, however, would look like this:

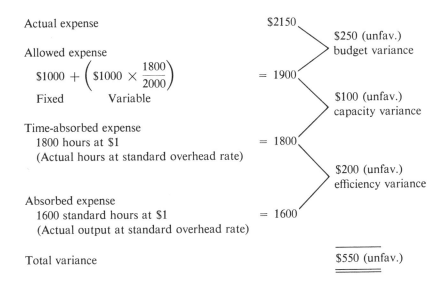

Actual expense — $2150

$250 (unfav.) budget variance

Allowed expense

$$\$1000 + \left(\$1000 \times \frac{1800}{2000}\right) = 1900$$

Fixed   Variable

$100 (unfav.) capacity variance

Time-absorbed expense
1800 hours at $1   = 1800
(Actual hours at standard overhead rate)

$200 (unfav.) efficiency variance

Absorbed expense
1600 standard hours at $1   = 1600
(Actual output at standard overhead rate)

Total variance $550 (unfav.)

As may be supposed, the two methods of variance analysis just explained are not unrelated to each other. The controllable variance of the two-variance method is equal to the budget variance plus part of the efficiency variance of the other method — a part equal to the difference between the budget allowance for actual hours and the budget allowance for achieved standard hours, represented on Diagram 1 (a) by the vertical distance B_1B'. The same quantity is shown on Diagram 1 (b) as the vertical distance ED, a part of the efficiency variance. The position of E is determined by drawing a straight line from F, the absorbed expense, parallel to the flexible budget line until it cuts the "actual hours" vertical. The slope of EF represents the variable overhead rate per hour, and ED therefore represents the extra variable cost incurred because it took more actual hours to get the output achieved than it would have done had efficiency been 100 per cent. Since Diagrams 1 (a) and 1 (b) are basically identical, it is easy to prove that ED is equal to B_1B', since the triangles FED and BB_1B' are congruent.

This relationship is significant in any assessment of the relative merits of the two systems. The chief defect of the two-variance system is that it does not distinguish between the "spending" element and the "efficiency" element of the controllable variance; it does not, that is to say, distinguish between excessive expenditure due to loose control of spending or price increases and excessive expenditure arising from man-hours wasted through inefficiency.[5] The three-variance system, on the other hand, does yield a separate efficiency variance, but it does so in a very questionable manner; for the efficiency variance, as conventionally determined, does not represent the true extra cost which results from inefficiency or the cost saving which results from high efficiency, but rather the difference between two hypothetical figures of "absorbed" expense.

Another criticism, which can be levelled at both methods, is that the budget allowance for overheads, as set by the flexible budget, is regarded as a function of a single variable. All expenses are regarded as varying, if they vary at all, either with the number of man-hours worked (as in the three-variance system) or with the level of output produced (as in the two-variance system), whereas the facts of cost behavior clearly make any such simple assumption unrealistic. Realism demands that we recognise at least three types of expense:

1. those that vary with the volume of output, e.g. manufacturing supplies, certain costs of materials handling and maintenance of equipment, royalties, inspection costs.[6]
2. those that vary with the number of man-hours worked, e.g. welfare expenditure, supervision, heating and lighting.
3. those that vary only with the length of the period, and not with the amount of work done or the output obtained, e.g. rent, fire insurance.

This points to the need to make the flexible budget flexible in more than one direction, taking each expense separately and making appropriate adjustments to the original budget figures in the light of what is known, at the end of the period, about the number of man-hours worked and the level of output achieved.[7]

Recognition of the fact that at least two independent variables control the level of overheads suggest that many more variables could be introduced into the function, bringing greater realism but also, unfortunately, greater complexity. For the more or less routine purpose of expenditure control with which we are now concerned, it is doubtful whether the greater complexity would be worthwhile.

---

[5] What is said here in terms of unfavorable variances of course applies, *mutatis mutandis*, to cost savings which give rise to favorable variances.

[6] The assertion of a functional relationship between cost and volume or cost and any other independent variable does not imply that the relationship is necessarily a simple one, and certainly not that it is one of direct proportionality. This point will be emphasised again below.

[7] Prof. W. J. Vatter gave a pointer in the same direction some years ago: "Rate of activity is often (and I think wrongly) taken as output or capacity or some related concept. Costs for planning and control purposes are related to decisions. Decisions have to do with inputs, not output. It would be better to talk and think about break-even charts, budgets, and other planning devices in terms of the input factors which must be controlled, rather than the output bases on which we can write up our post-mortems." (NA(C)A Conference Proceedings, August 1954, p. 1700.) I would rather say that we have to have regard to both inputs and outputs.

An Improved Method of Overhead Variance Analysis — Four Variances

The shortcomings of the conventional methods of variance analysis which were pointed out above can be met, while retaining their virtues, by recognising at least four separate variances, viz:

1. A budget variance. This is, as normally, the difference between actual expenditure on overheads and the allowance set by the flexible budget; but by making the flexible budget more flexible, as has already been suggested, the budget variance can be made much more meaningful than it commonly is. The flexible budget must be made to register the allowance for overheads appropriate to the actual number of hours worked *and* the actual level of output achieved.

   Nothing that is said here precludes more detailed analysis of the budget variance such as, for instance, the separation of the effects of price and quantity variations, although nothing more will be said about such further analysis. Again, it may be presumed that in practice the budget variance will be examined item by item rather than in terms of total overhead or of broad categories of overhead, as is done here.

2. A true efficiency variance — true, because it really measures the gain or loss in overhead expenditure attributable to variations away from the level of efficiency stipulated in the budget. One of the figures necessary in this calculation is the flexible budget allowance just mentioned. The other figure, which can easily be derived from the flexible budget, is the budget allowance appropriate to the production of the achieved output in the standard number of man-hours, as distinct from the actual number of man-hours. Clearly, those expenses which vary with output and not with working time (and also, of course, those which are fixed in relation to both) will be unaffected by excess man-hours or savings in man-hours as compared with the standard time required to produce the actual output. Such expenses are determined by the actual output, not by the time it takes to produce it. The expenses linked to man-hours, on the other hand, will be directly affected by excesses or savings in man-hours. It is these expenses, and these alone, which should enter into the overhead efficiency variance, which now becomes the difference between the flexible budget allowance for the actual output obtained in the actual man-hours worked and the budget allowance which would have been set if the actual output had been obtained in the standard number of man-hours. [8, 9]

[8] The standard number of man-hours is not to be confused with budgetted man-hours. The standard man-hours are arrived at by multiplying actual output by the standard time per unit of output. Budget man-hours are the result of multiplying budgetted output by the standard time per unit of output.

[9] This definition of the efficiency variance corresponds in effect to that used by Lang, McFarland & Schiff (*Cost Accounting*, 1953, p. 376), except that they do not recognise the distinction drawn above between output-variable and time-variable expenses. The same may be said of Matz, Curry and Frank (*Cost Accounting*, 2nd Edition, 1957, p. 581).

3. A volume (capacity) variance. This is one part of the unabsorbed (or over-absorbed) fixed costs — the part attributable to the loss or gain in output resulting from the difference between the budgetted number of man-hours and the actual man-hours worked.

4. A volume (efficiency) variance, being the remaining part of the unabsorbed or over-absorbed fixed costs. This part is attributable to the difference between actual output and the output which would have been obtainable from the actual number of man-hours worked if these had all been worked at standard efficiency.

It is not difficult to see that this system combines the advantages of the two-variance and the three-variance systems, without their shortcomings. All we need to do is to build into the system a capacity to distinguish between the two types of variable expense just discussed — the time-variable expenses, as they might be called, and the output variable expenses. This is not a difficult thing to do. The method is perhaps best explained by means of an illustration, using the same basic data as in the earlier illustrations but making the further assumptions that (1) the original overhead budget allowance of $1000 for variable expenses is divisible into $600 for output-variable items and $400 for the time-variables, while (2) the actual expenditure of $2150 is made up of $1050 in fixed expenses, $675 in output-variables and $425 in time-variable items.

Using this data, we can see from the table below how the variances would be arrived at.[10]

Column (1) of the table sets out the original budget figures, classified under types of expense, and based on a plan to produce 2000 standard hours of output in 2000 man-hours. The actual expenditure for the period, as ascertained at the end of the period, and following the same classification of expenses, is shown in column (2). Column (3) shows how the original budget is adjusted to take account of the actual time worked and the actual output produced in that time. Fixed expenses call for no adjustment. The expenses which vary with output are reduced to 1600/2000 of the original budget figure, and the expenses which vary with man-hours worked are reduced to 1800/2000 of the original budget. The total adjusted budget for the actual output in the actual time is therefore $1840. Column (4) shows what the budget allowance would have been if the actual output had been produced in the standard time. Fixed expenses and those that vary with output would have been as shown in column (3) but the allowance for expenses varying with time has to be reduced to only 1600/2000 of the original budget. The total adjusted budget for the actual output in the standard time is therefore

---

[10] In this illustration, the variable expenses (of both types) are regarded as being *proportionately* variable with man-hours or output. As was noted above in connection with Diagram 1 it is not really necessary to make any such simple assumption. The variations might be continuous but disproportional, or they might be discontinuous. In either case, the flexible budget would be embodied in a table, only a little more complex than the kind commonly used at present, and the figures could be read off quite simply.

Type of expense	Original over-head budget for 2000 standard hours of output obtained in 2000 man-hours	Actual overhead expenditure for period	Expense allowance for actual output (1600 standard hours) in actual time (1800 man-hours)	Expense allowance for actual output (1600 standard hours) in standard time (1600 man-hours)	Absorbed expense (1600 standard hours at standard rate of $1)
	(1)	(2)	(3)	(4)	(5)
Fixed	$1000	$1050	$1000	$1000	
Output-variable	600	675	480	480	$1600
Time-variable	400	425	360	320	
	$2000	$2150	$1840	$1800	$1600

$310
Budget
Variance
(unfav.)

$40
Efficiency
Variance
(unfav.)

$200
Volume
Variance
(unfav.)

$1800. Finally, column (5) shows the absorbed overheads as $1600, i.e. 1600 standard hours of output at the standard rate of $1 per hour.

The determination of the budget and efficiency variances from the table is sufficiently obvious to need no comment. The budget variance of $310 is the excess of col. (2) over col. (3) and the efficiency variance of $40 is the excess of col. (3) over col. (4). The treatment of the volume variance of $200 is not so obvious, however, and calls for explanation.

There is really only one difference between col. (4) and col. (5), and that is in the fixed expenses. In col. (4) only the fixed expenses are unchanged from the original budget in col. (1). The other types of expense have shrunk to 1600/2000 of the original figures. In col. (5), *all* the figures, in effect, have shrunk to 1600/2000 of the original budget. The difference between col. (4) and col. (5), therefore, consists of the 400/2000 of $1000, or $200, by which the fixed expenses have failed to shrink with the shortfall of output below the quantity originally budgetted, and this $200 is the volume variance. But we can go further than this. Using the *fixed* overhead rate of $1000/2000 or $0.50 per standard hour, we can say that $0.50 × (2000 − 1800) or $100 of fixed expenses remain unabsorbed because less capacity was used than was expected, and that $0.50 × (1800 − 1600) or a further $100 are left unabsorbed because the capacity that was used was used with less than standard efficiency. Thus the volume variance of $200 can be split into a volume (capacity) variance of $100 and a volume (efficiency) variance of a further $100.

Diagrammatic Representation of the Revised System

As overheads now have to be regarded as a function of two independent variables — man-hours *and* output — instead of one — man-hours *or* output — this system cannot be represented on a simple two-dimensional diagram. But it may be illuminating to compare it diagrammatically in a partial way with the conventional systems, and this can be done if we concentrate our attention on those costs which are fixed and those which vary with the number of man-hours worked, ignoring those costs which vary with output. By so doing, we can represent the system on a two-dimensional diagram.

Diagram 2 (a) merely repeats Diagram 1 (b), to facilitate comparison between the three-variance system there shown and the four-variance system represented in Diagram 2 (b). The underlying data are again the same as before, so that all the lines have the same slope as in the previous diagram, and the actual overhead expenditure for the period is the same as before also.

Since in Diagram 2 (b) we are dealing only with expenses which are fixed or which vary with the man-hours worked, the flexible budget allowance for the period is indicated by the point B, where the budget line is cut by the "actual hours" vertical. Point B is projected across to the left to give B_1, and the vertical distance AB is the budget variance. It is, of course, equal to AB, the budget variance in Diagram 2 (a).

The second of the four variances in Diagram 2 (b) is the efficiency variance. This is the vertical distance B_1B'; for B_1 (equal to B) is the budget expense allowance for the man-hours actually worked, and B' is the allowance for the hours which the output achieved ought to have taken. B_1B' is therefore the cost increment resulting from wasted hours,[11] and is truly an efficiency variance. As already noted when we were discussing Diagram 1 above, B_1B' in Diagram 2 (b) is equal to ED, a part of the efficiency variance in Diagram 2 (a).

The distance $B'C'$ is the volume (capacity) variance. It is, by construction, equal to BC, since the point C' is determined by the intersection of the "achieved standard hours" vertical with a line through C drawn parallel to the budget line, so that $B'BCC'$ is a parallelogram, the opposite sides of which are equal. $B'C'$, because it is equal to BC on Diagram 2 (b), is also equal to BC on Diagram 2 (a). It represents the fixed overheads which are unabsorbed by reason of the fact that the actual man-hours worked fell short of the budgetted hours by reference to which the standard overhead rate was fixed.

The fourth variance is the volume (efficiency) variance. It is the balance of the unabsorbed fixed costs, the portion which is unabsorbed because the actual output (which can alone really absorb costs) fell short of the output which the actual man-hours worked would have achieved if the standard level of efficiency had been maintained. It is represented by the vertical distance $C'D'$.

[11] See footnote on page 112.

23 *This trail-breaking article extends variance analysis beyond conventional process and performance control to an evaluation of performance of decision models. Not only is a change required in the types of variances which should be calculated and in the methods of assessing their significance, but there are essential differences in management response to observed variances. Random deviations should evoke no response; deviations reflecting a change in the process should.*

Effective control systems can be accomplished if they are designed around the formal decision models used by the firm, if specific control limits are established for critical variances, and if the system distinguishes between random deviations and those caused by process change.

Procedures for monitoring the decision process are described, with discussions focusing on measurement of random fluctuations, sensitivity analysis, inventory, allocation, and capital budgeting models, and on the problem of jointness.

An Extension of Standard
Cost Variance Analysis*

Nicholas Dopuch, Jacob G. Birnberg, and Joel Demski

Previous efforts to improve the usefulness of standard cost variance analysis have tended to focus on one of two related problems. Proposals have been offered that had as their objective either an improvement in the types of variances the accountant should calculate or in his methods for analyzing the significance of observed variances. An early paper by Solomons[1] and a more recent one by Samuels[2] reflect proposals of the first type.

* From The Accounting Review, *Vol. XLII, No. 3 (July, 1967), pp. 526–536. Reprinted by permission of the editor.*

[1] David Solomons, "Standard Costing Needs Better Variances," *N.A.A. Bulletin,* December 1961, p. 39.

[2] J. M. Samuels, "Opportunity Costing: An Application of Mathematical Programming," *Journal of Accounting Research,* Autumn 1965, pp. 182–91; we would also classify the following efforts in this same class: R. S. Gynther, "Improving Separation of Fixed and Variable Expenses," *N.A.A. Bulletin,* June 1963, pp. 29–38; and R. B. Troxel, "Variable Budgets Through Correlation Analysis: A Simplified Approach," *N.A.A. Bulletin,* February 1965, pp. 48–55.

The application of statistical models in setting control limits is illustrative of the second type of proposal.

Significantly, these previous efforts have concentrated on the control of processes and individual performances. Our purpose in this paper is to demonstrate how similar types of analyses may be applied to a second level of control — the control of the application and performance of formal decision models. As we will illustrate later, a systematic control of formal decision models will require changes in both the types of variances the accountant should calculate and in his methods for assessing the significance of these variances.[3]

The essential difference between process control and model control lies in the type of response management should make to an observed variance. The appropriate response by management depends upon the expected source of the deviation. In this respect, we note that when management implements a particular decision model, it is uncertain about (a) the appropriateness of the model relative to the specification of the decision problem, (b) the estimates of the decision variables which are critical to the implementation of the model, and (c) after the model is in operation, whether the actions specified by the model are being performed within the prescribed limits.

An observed variance from expected performances may reflect any one of the following conditions:[4]

Type 1 Deviation: The deviation resulted from the random aspect of the process being controlled. Assuming the deviation is not statistically significant, no response by management is necessary.

Type 2 Deviation: The deviation resulted from a temporary or permanent change in the process. Further investigation is required to determine whether:

a. The deviation is temporary in the sense that performance levels can be adjusted in the next period. This is the general definition of a controllable deviation.

b. The deviation resulted from a permanent change in the process. If this is established, management must review the decision process in order to assess the effect of the deviation on the decisions it has adopted and/or the decision model being implemented. The deviation is noncontrollable, but, nevertheless, a response may be required.

Traditionally, standard cost systems have concentrated on the analysis of type 1 and type 2-a deviations. These systems have not been designed to indicate when and if type 2-b deviations are critical to the decision process. These type 2-b deviations are central to the control of decision models.

---

[3] This relationship is also noted in Z. S. Zannetos, "Standard Costs as a First Step to Probabilistic Control: A Theoretical Justification, an Extension and Implications," THE ACCOUNTING REVIEW, April 1964, pp. 296–304.

[4] We are ignoring measurement errors per se, i.e., deviations arising from imperfect methods of measurement.

An effective control over decision models can be accomplished if the following rules are observed. First, the control system should be designed around the formal decision models used by the firm. The form of the model indicates the critical decision variables for which variances need to be calculated. Second, specific control limits should be established for these critical variances. These control limits can be built into the system to signal when and if changes in the estimates of the critical variables call for different decisions. Finally, the system should provide some mechanism for distinguishing between type 1 and 2 deviations since type 1 deviations are not significant to the decision process.

In the remainder of the paper we will describe procedures for monitoring the decision process. We will also comment on the basic problems in designing control systems that can monitor both performances and the decision process. As a first step, however, we wish to discuss further the relationship between type 1 and type 2 deviations.

The Measurement of Random Fluctuations

If a process being controlled can be described by $y_i = x_i + e_i$, where:

y_i = the observed level of performance in the ith period,

x_i = the level at which the stationary process is operating in the ith period, and

e_i = the random fluctuations occurring in the ith period,

then we desire a control system that can distinguish between fluctuations in y_i due to e_i and those due to a change in the x_i. This is essentially a problem in statistical analysis, for it is assumed that the random fluctuations can be identified by reference to the probability distribution of the y_i. A statistical analysis of deviations is preliminary to the control of decision models since management should respond to a deviation only if it represents a change in the estimates of the decision variables. Therefore, an effective control system depends first of all upon the efficiency with which we can eliminate the effect of type 1 (random) deviations.

In general, we are more confident in the analysis if we can work with a known distribution of the y_i. Bierman, Fouraker, and Jaedicke illustrate the procedures which can be followed whenever we can use an explicit prior distribution of the y_i to set control limits.[5] If the nature of the distribution is not known, we must fall back on a proposal by Zannetos which consists of using Chebyshev's inequality as the basis for setting the control

[5] H. Bierman, J. L. E. Fouraker, and R. K. Jaedicke, "A Use of Probability and Statistics in Performance Evaluation," THE ACCOUNTING REVIEW, July 1961, pp. 416–17.

limits.[6] This inequality can be applied regardless of the nature of the distribution of the y_i, but the analysis will be less efficient than one derived from a known distribution. Chebyshev's inequality represents the lower limit in the efficiency of our statements about the distribution. For example, if the distribution of the y_i can be described by the normal curve, 95% of the observations can be expected to fall within two standard deviations about the mean. An observation outside of this interval could be accepted as a signal of a change in the x_i because it has such a low probability of occurrence. However, the application of Chebyshev's inequality would only justify the expectation that at least 75% of the observations will fall within two standard deviations of the mean of the distribution.

The importance of an efficient method for analyzing type 2 deviations[7] follows from the nature of the final decision to investigate an observed deviation. The final decision to investigate must balance three factors: the probability that the deviation represents a non-random event, the costs of making the investigation, and the benefits expected from the investigation. Bierman, Fouraker, and Jaedicke illustrate the construction of a decision chart, given different estimates of these factors. A critical variable in the construction of the chart is the expected benefits from investigation. Thus, "we have to determine C (costs) and L (benefits) to compute the critical probability."[8] In another work, Bierman constructs the chart on the assumption that adjustments in performance levels are the benefits which will result from the investigation.[9] In effect, he has linked the statistical analysis to the investigation of type 2-a deviations.

However, recall that a deviation may be statistically significant but still non-controllable, i.e., it may represent a permanent change in a decision variable. Under these conditions, an investigation into the nature of the

---

[6] The Chebyshev inequality states the lower and upper bounds of the probabilities, P, that the difference between the observed value, X, and the mean, μ_x, is a certain distance, c, times the standard deviation, σ_x. Thus, as Zannetos shows:

$$P(|x - \mu_x|) \leq c\sigma_x \geq 1 - \frac{1}{c^2}$$

and

$$P(|x - \mu_x|) \geq c\sigma_x \leq 1 - \frac{1}{c^2}.$$

Zannetos, op. cit., p. 298.

[7] This includes related aspects of statistical analysis; e.g. see Paul R. McClenon, "Cost Finding Through Multiple Correlation Analysis," THE ACCOUNTING REVIEW, July 1963, pp. 540–47, and A. J. Duncan, "The Economic Design of X Charts Used to Maintain Current Control of a Process," *Journal of the American Statistical Association,* June 1956, pp. 228–242.

[8] See his *Topics in Cost Accounting and Decisions* (McGraw-Hill Book Company, 1963), p. 22. Actually it is possible to solve for a critical "L" if values of the other parameters are given. However, even in this case, we will have to have some means of assessing the likely value of "L", given actual observations.

[9] Loc. cit.

deviation can produce benefits only from changes in the firm's decisions or in the models it is employing. We now want to illustrate how the significance of these type 2-b deviations can be measured.

Sensitivity Analysis and Control Systems

A firm should adjust its decisions in response to permanent changes in the estimates of decision variables if the magnitude of change in a single estimate or in a group of estimates has significant effect on the firm's optimal decisions. A significant effect is measured by the positive difference between the opportunity costs incurred by the firm if it does not respond to the change and any organizational costs incurred if it does respond to the change. The difference between the two costs is the net benefit from a response to a permanent change in the estimate of a decision variable.

The extent of the opportunity costs incurred by the firm will depend on the sensitivity of the firm's decision model(s) to observed deviations. Therefore, the procedures necessary to determine the significance of type 2-b deviations consist mainly of the techniques for evaluating the sensitivity of the firm's decision models to assumed changes in the estimates of decision variables.

Our illustrations of these techniques will be quite similar to those found in the field of operations research. For many years an extensive use has been made of sensitivity analysis as a basis for improving the planning phase of a model's implementation. We see no reason why the same techniques cannot also be used in the control of these models. For obvious reasons, sensitivity analysis is meaningful only in the implementation of formal decision models. Our discussion is developed around two specific decision models — an inventory model and a resource allocation model. Later, we will comment on the difficulty of using sensitivity analysis to control less formal models, e.g., capital budgeting models.

Inventory Models and the Control System

An earlier proposal linking the control system to an inventory model was made by Gordon.[10] However, he was concerned only with the improvement in the evaluation of type 2-a or performance deviations. We will use the general form of the EOQ model as the basis for illustrating the evaluation of the inventory decisions. The following definitions apply to the model.[11]

[10] M. J. Gordon, "Toward a Theory of Responsibility Accounting Systems," *N.A.A. Bulletin,* December 1963, pp. 8–9.
[11] These symbols and the derivations of the optimal order quantities are based upon those found in C. W. Churchman, R. L. Ackoff, and E. L. Arnoff, *Introduction to Operations Research* (John Wiley and Sons, Inc., 1957), pp. 205–206.

C_p = cost of purchasing (per order)
C_s = cost of storage (per time period)
C_o = cost of stock-outs (per time period)
D = total demand for inventory during time period T
q = the amount of inventory to be ordered per order placed (q^* represents the optimal order quantity)
D/q = the number of orders placed during time period T.
t_s = the length of time required for the inventory to go from a level of q to the receipt of the next order, or

$$t_s = \frac{T}{D/q} = \frac{T \cdot q}{D}.$$

Exhibit 1 represents the sequence of inventory cycles.

EXHIBIT I

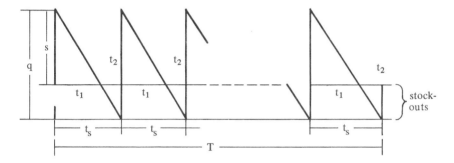

The total expected cost during time period T is:

$$T.C. = \left(\frac{s}{2} C_s t_1 + \frac{q-s}{2} C_o t_2 + C_p\right) \frac{D}{q}.$$

That is, Total Cost = (storage costs during time period t_1 + stock-out costs during time period t_2 + purchase order costs) times the number of orders, D/q. After some simplifying substitutions, the total cost equation can be differentiated with respect to s and q to obtain:[12]

$$q^* = \sqrt{\frac{2DC_p}{C_s T}} \cdot \sqrt{\frac{C_s + C_o}{C_o}}$$

$$s^* = \sqrt{\frac{2DC_p}{C_s T}} \cdot \sqrt{\frac{C_o}{C_s + C_o}}.$$

As the cost of stock-outs, C_o, becomes infinitely large, the expressions:

$$\sqrt{\frac{C_s + C_o}{C_o}} \quad \text{and} \quad \sqrt{\frac{C_o}{C_s + C_o}}$$

approach unity, and we have the EOQ model.

[12] Ibid., pp. 224–25.

Assume then that a firm faces a demand (D) of 3,600 units a year, that its purchase costs are $10 per order, that its storage costs are 20 cents per month per unit, and that its stock-out costs are an estimated 45 cents per unit per month. The inventory policies would be based on the following:

$$q^* = \sqrt{\frac{2C_pD}{C_sT}} \cdot \sqrt{\frac{C_s + C_o}{C_o}}$$

$$= 173\sqrt{\frac{.20 + .45}{.45}}$$

$$= 173(1.20)$$

$$\approx 208 \text{ units.}$$

$$s^* = \sqrt{\frac{2C_pD}{C_sT}} \cdot \sqrt{\frac{C_o}{C_s + C_o}}$$

$$= 173\sqrt{\frac{.45}{.20 + .45}}$$

$$= 173(.832)$$

$$\approx 143 \text{ units.}$$

This results in the following set of policies: order 208 units; allow back-orders of 65 units per cycle (i.e., stock-outs of 65 units will be permitted); and carry a maximum of 143 units (after back-orders are filled).

The total cost for this set of inventory policies can be determined by the equation:

$$T.C. = \sqrt{2DC_sTC_p} \cdot \sqrt{\frac{C_o}{C_s + C_o}}$$

$$= 415(.832)$$

$$= \$345^{13}$$

If we assume that a control system has been designed to include these standard inventory costs of C_p, C_s, and C_o, this model can serve as the basis for assessing the significance of any deviations from these standards.

Consider the effect of a 50 per cent deviation in the actual purchase order costs (C_p). If we substituted the new cost, C_p', into our equations and resolved for $q^{*\prime}$ and $s^{*\prime}$, $T.C.'$ would be $423. Thus, the 50 per cent change has caused an increase in costs of $78 ($423 - 345$). This is the change in the *yearly costs* of this new set of inventory policies.

Notice, however, that if the firm did not change its inventory policies in response to the new purchase order costs, the total purchase cost deviation for the year would be $(5)(17.3) = \$86.5$. The total yearly costs

---

[13] Specifically, this set of policies results in approximately 17.3 orders; if we assume a rate of usage of 10 units per day, the total stock-out time will be approximately 114 days or 3.8 months. This will produce a total cost of approximately $54. The average units on hand, 72 units, will be held for about 8.2 months. This will cost the firm approximately $118. Add the purchase order costs of $173 and the total is $345.

would be $345 + $86 = $431. Thus, the firm gains only $8 per year by changing its set of policies. This net benefit from change-over would have to be compared to any costs of change-over before the firm could determine its appropriate response.

A similar analysis may be performed assuming 50 per cent increases in storage costs (C_s) and stock-out costs (C_o). The effect of a 50 per cent change in storage costs is as follows: (1) order 183 units (19.6) orders; (2) stock a maximum of 109 units; and (3) permit stock-outs of 74 units. The new total cost, $T.C.'$, would be $394. However, if the firm did not shift its policies, its total cost would increase by $59 to a total of $404. Hence, the net benefit of a shift is only $10. A 50 per cent increase in stock-out costs would also result in a net benefit from shifting of only $10. That is, $T.C.'$ would equal $366, but if the firm did not alter its policies, its inventory costs would increase only to $376.

We do not want to leave the impression that this inventory model will always be more sensitive to storage costs and stock-out costs than to purchase-order costs. Our results are partially dependent upon the original values we assigned to the three cost inputs. The general form of the equations for determining changes in total costs for different changes in each of the standards is given in the appendix . . .

We can conceive of a control system for a firm which incorporates a . . . set of graphs for its inventory costs. The significance of deviations from any one of the three inventory standards could be determined by referring to the effect of the change on the total costs of the inventory system. In this manner, the benefit of shifting to a new solution could be measured by comparing the total costs if the inventory policies are altered to the opportunity costs of not changing the firm's decisions.

Certainly, there are some practical problems involved in trying to design such a control system. Our analysis considered the effect on only one change at a time. Some multiple changes have been analyzed in the literature,[14] and it is conceivable that a firm could construct graphs based upon multiple changes in its standards. But these would have to be based upon management's a priori judgment as to which set of multiple changes is likely to occur. We also found it practical to examine these issues relative to a rather simple kind of inventory model. The control system would have to be based upon whatever inventory model the firm uses.[15] Finally, we assumed that the firm can and would be willing to measure storage,

[14] See Eliezer Naddor, *Inventory Systems* (John Wiley and Sons, Inc., 1966), pp. 52–53 and 68.
[15] We know of no survey which indicates the kinds of models firms do employ. However, in one informal study, the following was noted: "Since the companies chosen for interviews were largely those that had demonstrated an interest in modern methods of inventory management, it must be concluded that the actual use of these techniques is less frequent than the literature on this subject might lead one to believe." National Association of Accountants, "Techniques in Inventory Management," *N.A.A. Research Report No. 40* (1964), p. 2.

purchase-order, and stock-out costs. Regarding the latter, Hadley and Whitin have said that the general procedure is "for someone to make a guess as to what they are."[16]

Allocation Models and the Control System

In terms of the present discussion we view the allocation problem as consisting of the determination of the best use to be made of the capital equipment available to the firm. For a single product firm, the decision variables are the various prices obtained for different output levels, the different combinations and types of inputs which can produce various output levels, and their input prices. A sensitivity analysis for a single-product firm would follow a procedure suggested by Zannetos. Specifically, he states:[17]

> Whenever prices change, or at the latest, whenever price variances appear, the system will be instructed to develop the new price ratios and search for the proper input-mix solution that is *stored*. If as a result of the comparison between the suggested and existing methods of operations input substitutions are dictated, the system will signal the need for such a change and also provide all the necessary details for its implementation.

We will extend this notion to a multi-product firm. The methods we will use and the issues we will raise will be similar to those discussed in the previous section. For illustration, we have selected a simple linear programming problem.

Consider a firm which produces two products, x_1 and x_2; the products pass through two facilities, b_1 and b_2, which have fixed capacities of 1.0 (million) and .9 (million) hours respectively.

Product x_1 requires 8/10 hour of resource b_1 and 5/10 hour of b_2; similarly, x_2 requires 5/10 hour of b_1 and one hour of b_2. Each unit of x_1 contributes (revenues − variable costs) $960 and each unit of x_2 contributes $875. The entire problem can be expressed as:

$$\text{Max. } z = 960x_1 + 875x_2$$

Subject to

$$8/10x_1 + 5/10x_2 \leq 1.0$$
$$5/10x_1 + 1x_2 \leq .9$$
$$x_1, x_2 \geq 0.$$

We can convert these inequalities into equations by using the variables x_3 and x_4, which represent unused capacity of b_1 and b_2 respectively. The initial and final solutions (I and II respectively) to this problem are indicated below in simplex tableau form, in Exhibit 2.

[16] G. Hadley and T. M. Whitin, *Analysis of Inventory Systems* (Prentice-Hall, Inc., 1963), p. 420.

[17] Z. S. Zannetos, op. cit., p. 303.

EXHIBIT 2

x_J			x_1	x_2	x_3	x_4	
C_J			960	875	0	0	
x_B	C_B	b_1					
x_3	0	1.00	8/10	5/10	1	0	
x_4	0	.90	5/10	1	0	1	
$z, z_J - C_J$		0	-960	-875	0	0	I
x_1	960	1.00	1	0	20/11	$-10/11$	II
x_2	875	.400	0	1	$-10/11$	16/11	
$z, z_J - C_J$		1310	0	0	950	400	

The sensitivity of this solution to changes in input or output prices can be assessed if we refer to the imputed values of the scarce resources. In the second tableau above, these prices are located in the z, $z_j - c_j$ row under the slack-variable columns; i.e., the values are \$950 and \$450 respectively.

The criterion followed in the simplex method is that if a negative value appears in the $z_j - c_j$ row, then the solution is not optimal. Therefore, we must determine changes in the contribution margins of C_1 and C_2 which will alter the solution shown in the second tableau.

Looking back at Tableau II, we note that the value 950 is obtained by multiplying 960 (20/11) and adding the result to 875 ($-10/11$). Similarly, the value 400 is the sum of 960 ($-10/11$) + 875 (16/11). Let us consider the effect of an increase in C_1 which we will denote as C_1'.

In the x_3 column, C_1 has the positive coefficient 20/11. Therefore, an increase in C_1 will have a positive effect on the $z_3 - c_3$ value. However, a sufficient increase in the C_1 will change $z_4 - c_4$ to a negative value since C_1 has the negative coefficient of ($-10/11$) in column x_4. We can determine this critical value of C_1' by solving the equation:

$$C_1'(-10/11) + 875(16/11) = 0$$
$$C_1' = 16/10(875)$$
$$= 1400.$$

Thus, an increase of 440 is a critical upper limit for C_1 since any additional increase will change the optimal solution.

If we apply the same analysis to an increase in C_2, the critical limit is an increase of 1045. Alternatively, a decrease in C_1 to 437.50 will cause x_3 to replace x_1 in the solution, and a decrease in C_2 to 600 will cause x_4 to replace x_2.

Hence, the upper and lower limits for C_1 are $437.50 \leq C_1 \leq 1400$, and those for C_2 are $600 \leq C_2 \leq 1920$, provided the changes in C_1 and C_2 are completely independent. If both contribution margins changed at the same time, the limits we calculated would not be valid. However, it is possible to analyze multiple changes provided that we specify which contribution margins are to be changed.

Since the contribution margins summarize both revenue and variable cost changes, these limits are sufficient to analyze changes in output prices, input prices, and to some extent changes in the technical coefficients of producing the different units of output. There are techniques for analyzing other changes as well, but we will not illustrate these.[18]

As in the previous section, a calculation of these limits represents only the first step in the analysis. A change in the solution to the linear programming problem might be indicated, but the firm would still not wish to alter its output combination of $1.0x_1$ and $.4x_2$. For example, suppose C_1 drops to $435 per unit. This would result in a change in the optimal solution as follows: $x_2 = .900$ and $x_3 = .550$; $x_1 = x_4 = 0$. Total contribution margin would be: $.900 (875) + .550 (0) = 787.50$. However, if the firm did not alter its solution and continued to produce $1.0x_1$ and $.4x_2$, its total contribution would be: $1.0 (435 = C_1') + .400 (875) = 775$. If there are organizational costs in making a solution shift, this decrease in C_1 would not be sufficient to warrant a change to the optimal solution.

It is obvious that the use of sensitivity analysis to establish limits for type 2-b deviations is much more difficult in terms of the allocation decisions of a firm. In the inventory analysis, we had to consider only three variables. However, linear programming models may involve hundreds of products of output. We cannot establish whether it is practical to control large programs unless we examine the properties of a firm's allocation model in its actual setting. More will be said about this later.

We should also stress another implication of the linking of the control system to a linear programming model. The sensitivity analysis we employed implies a different set of "variances" than the price and quantity variances normally calculated by the accountant. It is conceivable that some of the critical deviations illustrated in a sensitivity analysis will supplement, and perhaps even circumvent, the traditional standard cost variances. Indeed, the imputed values of the scarce resources have been used by Samuels to develop a different kind of capacity variance.[19]

Type 2-a and Type 2-b Deviations and the Jointness Problem

Thus far we have discussed the groupings of type 2-a and type 2-b deviations separately. However, the measurement of a particular financial variance may serve as an index of both sources of deviations. For example,

[18] For example, see S. I. Gass, *Linear Programming* (McGraw-Hill Book Company, 1964).
[19] J. Samuels, op. cit.

a price deviation could indicate either inefficient purchasing policies or a change in the prices quoted to the firm. Suppose the deviation is significant in terms of some decision of the firm. The decision should be changed only if a change in prices has taken place and this change is expected to hold for at least another decision cycle. We know of no formal method for distinguishing between sources of deviations. Yet, the benefits from investigating a deviation cannot be measured unless the source is ascertained in advance.

The solution to this problem may require a less formal methodology. We would not expect both types of deviations to have the same critical limits of significance. As one possibility, the limits for type 2-a deviations might be considerably tighter than those for type 2-b deviations. Any deviation which fell in this narrower band would be considered a type 2-a deviation. If the deviation is large enough to be significant in terms of both sets of responses, further investigation would be necessary. The firm might still wish to establish the same priority regardless, i.e., always investigate for type 2-a causes first.

Capital Budgeting Models and the Control System

Although a more complete discussion would result from a consideration of the sensitivity of capital budgeting models, we believe that, in general, it is impractical to design control systems around specific capital budgeting decisions. The decision to acquire long-lived assets is presumably made on the expectation that the net receipts generated by the utilization of the asset have a present value equal to or greater than the expenditure involved. In many instances the favorable decision implies that the firm will also commit itself to a sequence of operating and future capital budgeting decisions.

Regarding the first stage of the control problem, it is unlikely that management would be able to develop a probability distribution around the set of expected receipts which could be used to separate type 1 from other types of deviations. The uniqueness of capital budgeting decisions prevents a firm from developing a history of cash flows which could be used as a basis for predicting future cash flows. An alternative approach would be to apply a Bayesian analysis to the decision problem. However, an acceptable theory linking Bayesian analysis and capital budgeting remains to be developed.

We can also expect to encounter some major problems in trying to measure whether the expectations of specific capital budgeting decisions are being realized. The results of any capital budgeting decision become interwoven with the current operations of the firm. Consequently, it would be almost impossible to determine when and if a change in decision variables required new decisions. A more practical procedure is merely to control the current operations of the firm and let the significant deviations noted in this procedure signal the need to review capital budgeting decisions.

The Evaluation of Decision-Models

We have purposefully avoided any explicit references to an investigation of the appropriateness of the decision models used by the firm. We do not know of any formal analysis which can be employed to determine which of several available decision models is the appropriate one for the firm. The efficiency of different decision models can be evaluated only by comparing the effects of using alternative models to solve the same kind of problem. The motivation for making these comparisons develops primarily out of management's dissatisfaction with the results of the models implemented. Unsatisfactory results are reflected initially in excessive amounts of error in the estimates of the decision variables. Therefore, a control system may provide an index of the efficiency of the firm's decision models by accumulating a history of the magnitude and frequency of type 2-b deviations.

Conclusions

Our main conclusion is that the method of analysis we have described permits an extension of the standard cost system so that the system can monitor both performances and the decision process. This monitoring is achieved by structuring the control system around the formal decision models used by the firm. We recognize that there are some practical problems in implementing this type of analysis. Many of these are speculative, however, since the degree to which it will be practical to control decision models will vary from firm to firm. We know of only one accounting study aimed at describing the problems inherent in designing a control system around the linear programming model of a firm.[20] Similar studies might be conducted in the area of inventory models.

The use of formal decision models within a firm can be expected to increase as computers yield solutions to more sophisticated models. The firm's control system must be expanded to encompass these new models as they are adopted by the firm.

---

[20] Indeed, this study was initiated on the assumption that an analytical approach is not yet feasible. See Joel Demski, "Accounting for Capacity Utilization: An Opportunity Cost Approach," Ph.D. dissertation, University of Chicago, Graduate School of Business, 1967. For an example of how an analytical approach might be used in studying this problem see Yuji Ijiri, *Management Goals and Accounting for Control* (Chicago: Rand McNally and Company, 1965), especially Chapter VI.

Appendix

Changes in: $\qquad$ $T.C. = (2DC_sTC_p)^{1/2}\left(\dfrac{C_o}{C_s + C_o}\right)^{1/2}$.

A. Change in C_p to $C.P.'$

$$T.C.' = (2DC_sTC_p')^{1/2}\left(\frac{C_o}{C_s + C_o}\right)^{1/2}$$

$T.C.' - T.C.$

$$= \left[(2DC_sTC_p')^{1/2}\left(\frac{C_o}{C_s + C_o}\right)^{1/2} - (2DC_sTC_p)^{1/2}\left(\frac{C_o}{C_s + C_o}\right)^{1/2}\right]$$

$$= \left(\frac{C_o}{C_s + C_o}\right)^{1/2} [(2DC_sTC_p')^{1/2} - (2DC_sTC_p)^{1/2}]$$

$$= \left(\frac{C_o}{C_s + C_o}\right)^{1/2} (2DC_sT)^{1/2} [(C_p')^{1/2} - (C_p)^{1/2}]$$

B. Changes in C_s to C_s'

$$T.C.' = (2DC_s'TC_p)^{1/2}\left(\frac{C_o}{C_s' + C_o}\right)^{1/2}$$

$T.C.' - T.C.$

$$= \left[(2DC_s'TC_p)^{1/2}\left(\frac{C_o}{C_s' + C_o}\right)^{1/2} - (2DC_sTC_p)^{1/2}\left(\frac{C_o}{C_s + C_o}\right)^{1/2}\right]$$

$$= (2DTC_p)^{1/2}\left[(C_s')^{1/2}\left(\frac{C_o}{C_s' + C_o}\right)^{1/2} - (C_s)^{1/2}\left(\frac{C_o}{C_s + C_o}\right)^{1/2}\right]$$

$$= (2DTC_p)^{1/2}\left[\left(\frac{C_s'C_o}{C_s' + C_o}\right)^{1/2} - \left(\frac{C_sC_o}{C_s + C_o}\right)^{1/2}\right]$$

C. Change in C_o to C_o'

$$T.C.' = (2DC_sTC_p)^{1/2}\left(\frac{C_o'}{C_s + C_o'}\right)^{1/2}$$

$T.C.' - T.C.$

$$= \left[(2DC_sTC_p)^{1/2}\left(\frac{C_o'}{C_s + C_o'}\right)^{1/2} - (2DC_sTC_p)^{1/2}\left(\frac{C_o}{C_s + C_o}\right)^{1/2}\right]$$

$$= (2DC_sTC_p)^{1/2}\left[\left(\frac{C_o'}{C_s + C_o'}\right)^{1/2} - \left(\frac{C_o}{C_s + C_o}\right)^{1/2}\right]$$

2 4 *Maximization of current net income depends on the proper utilization of acquired capacity.* But the traditional accounting measure of capacity utilization, the volume variance, is based on historical cost and is "little more than a bookkeeping bridge between the control and product costing purposes of the cost accounting system." The unit fixed historical cost measure may be a useful device for looking backward to evaluate past capital budgeting decisions, but it has little relevance for planning and control. A better, forward-looking measure is the "lost contribution margin."

To measure "lost contribution margin," a framework involving practical capacity, master budgeted sales, scheduled and actual production is suggested. Variances computed, in physical terms, are expected idle capacity, total volume, marketing, and production. These variances are transformed by a dollar unit contribution margin factor into a total lost contribution margin — which represents an approximation of opportunity cost.

In the manner of the previous article (Dopuch, Birnberg and Demski), the author suggests that accounting systems will best tie in with decisions regarding capacity utilization if a reporting system is defined with regard to a specific, well-defined decision model.

A Contribution Margin Approach to the Analysis of Capacity Utilization*

Charles T. Horngren

The analysis of variances is one of the major topics in our cost accounting courses. The volume (capacity) variance, which supposedly gauges the utilization of capacity, probably gets the prize as the most

* *From* The Accounting Review, *Vol. XLII, No. 2 (April, 1967), pp. 254–264. Reprinted by permission of the editor.*

baffling measure[1] that is produced by variance analysis. What does it mean? Why should we compute it? This article develops a conceptual framework that may prove better than traditional volume variance analysis because it (1) distinguishes long-range and short-range factors, (2) demonstrates the weaknesses of existing practices, (3) sharply pinpoints responsibility in relation to the purposes of short-range planning and control and separates the role of physical measures of capacity[2] from the role of valuation of that capacity, and (4) indicates how a contribution-margin or opportunity-cost approach to valuation is superior to a unitized historical-cost approach.

Long-Range and Short-Range Factors

TWO ASPECTS OF CAPACITY: ACQUISITION AND UTILIZATION

Organizations assemble human and physical resources that provide the capacity to produce and sell. These commitments often require heavy expenditures that affect performance over long spans of time. The implications for managers are two-fold. First, careful planning is obviously crucial to the wise acquisition of fixed resources. Second, the acquired capacity should be properly utilized if current net income[3] is to be maximized.

Many fixed costs result from capital budgeting decisions, reached after studying the expected impact of these expenditures on operations over a number of years. The choice of a capacity size may be influenced by a

---

[1] Don T. Decoster, "Measurement of the Idle-Capacity Variance," ACCOUNTING REVIEW (April, 1966), pp. 297–302, discusses the "disparity that exists within accounting literature in quantifying the idle-capacity variance."

[2] A thorough study of capacity would include a rigorous operational definition of the word "capacity." This is not attempted here because such a definition is subordinate to the major purpose of this article. See Research Report 39, *Accounting for Costs of Capacity* (New York: National Association of Accountants, 1963), pp. 10–11. On page 10, Report 39 observes: "Capacity planning requires definition and measurement of capacity in a manner relevant to questions which arise in the planning process. This problem has two aspects. First, it is necessary to specify capacity in terms of how much the company should be prepared to make and to sell. Second, the capacity of specific facilities available or to be acquired must be determined. . . . A variety of alternative combinations of capacity and operating patterns is usually possible." There are many other difficulties of definition that are not being dealt with exhaustively in this article. *Variable cost, fixed cost,* and *contribution margin* are examples of concepts that raise difficult but not insurmountable practical problems of definition and measurement. Contribution margin is defined here as the excess of revenue over all variable costs of manufacturing and non-manufacturing.

[3] The focus here will be on the maximization of current net income, although long-run effects and other goals could be incorporated by extending the analysis. The expected inter-play of current net income and future net income obviously affects current decisions (e.g., pricing) even though these effects are seldom explicitly quantified.

combination of two major factors, each involving trade-off decisions and each heavily dependent on long-range forecasts of demand, material costs, and labor costs:

1. Provision for seasonal and cyclical *fluctuations* in demand. The trade-off is between (a) additional costs of physical capacity versus (b) the costs of stock-outs and/or the carrying costs of safety stocks of such magnitude as to compensate for seasonal and cyclical variations, the costs of overtime premium, sub-contracting, and so on.

2. Provision for upward *trends* in demand. The trade-off is between (a) the costs of constructing too much capacity for initial needs versus (b) the later extra costs of satisfying demand by alternative means. For example, should a factory designed to make color television tubes be 100,000, 150,000, or 200,000-tube level?

ACQUISITION OF CAPACITY AND FOLLOW-UP

Suppose that management decided to build a factory that can produce 200,000 units yearly. Also suppose that the expected demand used to justify the size of the factory was a long-run average of 160,000 units for five to ten years. The larger factory was built because management decided that this was the most economical way to provide for seasonal, cyclical, and trend factors that may result in a demand at a peak rate of 200,000 units per year (practical capacity) during certain times.

A follow-up or audit of planning decisions is needed to see how well actual utilization harmonizes with the activity levels used in the plan that authorized the acquisition of the facilities. The follow-up helps evaluate the accuracy of management's past long-range planning decisions and should improve the quality of similar decisions in the future. The pertinent base for comparison is a particular year's activity level used in the capital budget that authorized the acquisition of facilities. Comparison should be done on a project-by-project basis to see whether the predictions in the capital budgeting schedules are being fulfilled. Such comparisons need not be integrated in the over-all information system on a routine basis.

Normal activity, 160,000 units in our example, is the rate of activity needed to meet average sales demand over a period long enough to encompass seasonal and cyclical fluctuations; it is the average volume level used as a basis for long-range plans. In our example, a comparison of currently budgeted sales or actual sales with the 160,000-unit normal activity might be suggested as the best basis for auditing and assessing the impact of long-range planning decisions. However, normal activity is an average that has little or no significance with respect to a follow-up for a particular year.

Moreover, normal activity should not be a reference point for judging current performance (i.e., the volume variance so often computed using historical costs). This is an example of misusing a long-range average measure for a short-range particular purpose. The acquisition of facilities and other fixed resources requires a planning and control horizon of many years — a horizon that fluctuates because various resources are often obtained piecemeal or on a project-by-project basis. In contrast, our concern here is with the planning and control of current operations; we shall see that the notion of normal activity has no bearing on this problem.

Weakness of Existing Practices

UNITIZING HISTORICAL COSTS

How do accountants actually apply dollar measures to the utilization of capacity? They "unitize" historical fixed manufacturing costs and use the resultant unit rate to measure a volume variance (and to cost products). In our example, suppose that manufacturing costs are $131,200 per year. The accountant would relate this cost to the number of units to get a predetermined unit cost. He might select from several possible rates. Let us consider two:

Alternative A — Use practical capacity as a base:

$$\text{Unit cost} = \frac{\text{Total Fixed Manufacturing Costs}}{\text{Practical Capacity in Units}} = \frac{\$131,200}{200,000 \text{ units}} = \$.656 \text{ per unit}$$

Alternative B — Use budgeted sales as a base:

$$\text{Unit cost} = \frac{\text{Total Fixed Manufacturing Costs}}{\text{Budgeted Sales in Units}} = \frac{\$131,200}{164,000 \text{ units}} = \$.80 \text{ per unit}$$

He would use one or the other of these unit costs for costing product and for measuring volume variances.

There are numerous drawbacks to using a historical-cost approach for management planning and control. Historical costs have no particular bearing on the management problem of obtaining desired current utilization of existing capacity. For instance, let us compare the dollar results of using the above two historical unit costs:

Alternative A — Use a historical cost unitized at $.656 per unit:

Practical capacity 200,000 units; fixed costs to account for $131,200

Actual production and sales, 140,000 units at $.656 . 91,840

Volume variance, 60,000 units × $.656 .... $ 39,360

Alternative B — Use a historical cost unitized at $.80 per unit:

Master budget* sales of 164,000 units; fixed cost to account for	$131,200
Actual production and sales, 140,000 units at $.80 .	112,000
Volume variance, 24,000 × $.80	$ 19,200

Effect of Numerator and Denominator

Note that the fixed cost rate as traditionally computed depends on a numerator of historical manufacturing costs only. Fixed selling and administrative costs, which often can be huge, are not incorporated in the volume variance or in the cost of the product.

The unit cost is also affected by the denominator selected. Practical capacity as a denominator results in one unit cost, while master budgeted sales as a denominator results in another unit cost. The choice of the denominator thus affects the amount of the variances (and, incidentally, computed product costs). In our example, the volume variance is either $39,360 or $19,200, depending on whether practical capacity or master budgeted sales is selected as the denominator. Such variety in quantification is difficult to justify and explain.

Characteristics of the Volume Variance Based on Historical Costs

Most cost accounting systems simultaneously try to (1) accumulate costs for planning and control and (2) apply costs to product for inventory valuation and income determination. The approach to (1) and (2) for variable costs usually entails the use of unit costs for direct material, direct labor, and the variable manufacturing overhead. No volume variances arise because the total variable costs incurred are equal to the total variable costs applied to product. However, analytical troubles begin when the same approach is attempted with fixed costs.

A volume variance arises because of the conflict between accounting for control (via budgets) and accounting for product costing (via unit costing rates for applying overhead to product). The development of a product-costing rate results in an artificial transformation. Traditionally, for product-costing purposes, all costs rank abreast; no distinctions between cost behavior patterns are appropriate. Thus, the fixed cost is accounted for in product costing *as if it were a variable cost.* A volume variance appears whenever the activity level actually encountered fails to coincide with the

---

* "Master budget" is used here to designate the overall, comprehensive financial and operating plans for the year.

original activity level used as a denominator in the computation of a product-costing rate.

In a sense, the volume variance based on historical costs is little more than a bookkeeping bridge between the control and product costing purposes of the cost accounting system. It is difficult to see how such a variance could have been invented solely for purposes of current planning and control, our major concern here. Fixed costs and variable costs have different frames of reference, timing, and control features. Fixed costs simply are not divisible like variable costs. Fixed costs usually come in big masses, and they are related to providing big chunks of sales or production capacity rather than to the production of a single unit of product. To use parallel analytical devices (e.g., variances, unit costs) for costs with unlike patterns of behavior is illogical and is a reflection of the product-costing purpose's immense influence on cost accounting systems.

EFFICIENCY VARIANCES AND FIXED COSTS

Consider another example of the attempts to analyze variable costs and fixed costs in a parallel manner. Students of cost accounting are familiar with the usual way of computing efficiency variances for variable costs such as direct material, direct labor, and variable overhead:

$$\begin{matrix} \text{Variable cost} \\ \text{efficiency} \\ \text{variance} \end{matrix} = \left(\begin{matrix} \text{Actual hours of input} \\ \text{minus} \\ \text{Standard hours allowed} \\ \text{for units produced} \end{matrix} \right) \times \text{Hourly rate}$$

The same approach is commonly taken to the computation of an efficiency variance for fixed overhead:

$$\begin{matrix} \text{Fixed} \\ \text{overhead} \\ \text{efficiency} \\ \text{variance} \end{matrix} = \left(\begin{matrix} \text{Actual hours of input} \\ \text{minus} \\ \text{Standard hours allowed} \\ \text{for units produced} \end{matrix} \right) \begin{matrix} \text{Hourly fixed} \\ \times \ \text{overhead} \\ \text{rate} \end{matrix}$$

But the resulting variance should be distinguished sharply from the efficiency variances for material, labor, and variable overhead, because efficient usage of these three factors can affect total actual cost incurrence, whereas short-run fixed overhead cost incurrence is not affected by efficiency. Moreover, the managers responsible for inefficiency will be aware of its existence through reports on variable costs control; so there is little additional management information to be gained from expressing ineffective utilization of fixed factory overhead factors in historical dollar terms.

LACK OF ECONOMIC SIGNIFICANCE

The unit fixed historical cost measure has little direct economic significance for current planning and control. It is conceptually inferior to the lost contribution margin per unit notion, which will be examined in a later section. Unlike variable costs, total fixed costs do not change as volume fluctuates. Fixed cost incurrence often entails lump-sum outlays based on a pattern of expected recoupment. But ineffective utilization of existing facilities has no bearing on the amount of fixed costs currently incurred. The economic effects of the inability to reach target volume levels are directly measured by lost contribution margins, even though these often are approximations. The historical cost approach to current planning and control fails to emphasize the useful distinction between *fixed cost incurrence,* on the one hand, and the objective of *maximizing the total contribution margin,* on the other hand. These are separable management problems, and the utilization of existing capacity is more closely related to the latter. This

EXHIBIT 1
Summary Framework for Analyzing Utilization of Capacity

Time of Computation and Use			
When the master budget is prepared	P = Practical Capacity M = Master budgeted sales	200,000 164,000	36,000 units expected idle capacity variance (1)
At the end of the period, when results are being evaluated	M = Master budgeted sales S = Scheduled production (sales orders received) A = Actual production (and sales)	164,000 148,000 140,000	16,000 units, marketing variance (2a) 8,000 units, production variance (2b) — 24,000 units volume variance (2)

(1) $P-M$ = Expected idle capacity variance, a measure of the anticipated idle capacity.

(2) $M-A$ = Volume variance, the difference between master budgeted sales and actual sales. (Note that this is the same as the volume variance that is traditionally computed — provided that master budgeted sales, and not practical capacity or "normal or average" sales, is used as a basis for the computation.)

(2a) $M-S$ = Marketing variance, a measure of the failure of the sales force to get orders equal to the current sales forecast in the master budget.

(2b) $S-A$ = Production variance, a measure of the failure of the production departments to adhere to production schedules.

historical cost approach may possibly be useful in looking backward for an evaluation of past capital budgeting decisions. But the contribution margin approach is more useful in looking forward for current planning and control.

Short-Range Planning and Control[4]

MEASURING ACTIVITY

What information about capacity can help management in planning and controlling operations? The analytical framework in Exhibit 1, expressed in physical terms only, should be useful.

$P = Practical\ capacity\ or\ practical\ attainable\ capacity$ is the maximum level at which the plant or department can realistically operate efficiently, 200,000 units in our example. When an organization has provided a given amount of practical capacity, little can be done in day-to-day operations to affect the total level of the associated fixed costs. The practical capacity acts as a constraint on subsequent performance. Practical capacity is ideal production capability less allowances for unavoidable operating interruptions such as repair time, waiting time (down time) because of machine set-ups, and operator personal time. N.A.A. *Research Report No. 39* describes one company's approach:

> . . . practical attainable *hourly* capacity is developed by one company. Daily, monthly, and annual capacity is determined by multiplying the number of working hours in these periods by the practical attainable hourly capacity. Additional allowances are made for events which occur during a day, month, or year, but not hourly. For example, an allowance may be required for cleaning up equipment at the end of each day and for model change-over time once a year. Industry practice and current management policy determines the number of shifts, number of hours worked per week, holidays, reserve capacity provided for contingencies, and other allowances entering into the number of working hours per period. It may be noted that this company measures annual practical attainable capacity both with and without use of premium wage time. Thus management knows how much additional production can be obtained by use of premium wage rate time.[5]

$M = Master\ budgeted\ sales$ is that volume of activity employed in formulating the master budget for the period. In this example, it represents

---

[4] Many of the notions in this and the next section originally appeared in Charles T. Horngren, *Accounting for Management Control: An Introduction,* (Englewood Cliffs, N.J.: Prentice-Hall, Inc., 1965), Chapter 10. However, a number of changes and embellishments have been incorporated in the present paper.

[5] Op. cit., p. 22.

management's best single estimate[6] of expected sales for the period, 164,000 units.

$S = Scheduled\ production$ is that volume of sales orders received and assigned for production in the immediate current period[7], 148,000 units in this case. This may not agree with the master budgeted sales because the marketing department may eventually fail to sell the budgeted number of 164,000.

$A = Actual\ production$ (*and sales delivered to customers*) is self-explanatory, 140,000 units in this case.

For clarity, the framework in Exhibit 1 simplifies matters by making the following assumptions:

a. There are no changes in inventory levels; that is, all units currently produced are currently sold.

b. The single product, single department case is examined here. The same fundamental analysis is applicable (but not without difficulty) in more complex cases on a product-by-product, department-by-department basis.[8]

EXPECTED IDLE CAPACITY VARIANCE

The expected idle capacity variance (*P-M*) should be computed when the original master budget is prepared. Management may then (a) obtain a specific measure of anticipated idle capacity early enough (b) to adjust plans in light of possible uses for the expected idle capacity. This may be a give-and-take process, in which the initial master budget is altered (for example, prices may be changed) in light of the initial expected idle capacity.

---

[6] The use of probabilities in estimating sales and in the analysis of variances is germane but is not discussed here. For examples, see Robert K. Jaedicke and Alexander A. Robichek, "Cost-Volume-Profit Analysis Under Conditions of Uncertainty," THE ACCOUNTING REVIEW, October 1964, pp. 917–926; and Harold Bierman, Jr., Lawrence E. Fouraker, and Robert K. Jaedicke, "A Use of Probability and Statistics in Performance Evaluation," THE ACCOUNTING REVIEW, July 1962, pp. 409–417.

[7] For simplicity we shall assume throughout the subsequent discussion that all orders received are immediately scheduled and that production should occur immediately upon being scheduled; in other words, there are no lags between orders, schedules, and expected production. In this way, we will not have to bother with some messy technical adjustments in the analysis of variances caused by, say, an order being booked in November, scheduled in February, and produced in April. These adjustments may be difficult to construct in a particular company, and they impede practical application of these ideas.

[8] The linear programming model, using dual evaluators, will help management decide which combination of products will be most profitable when a given capacity must be utilized for their production or sale. When the primal solution shows the optimal production mix, the dual evaluators (shadow prices) of the constraining factors are the opportunity costs of their marginal products.

The responsibility for such a variance may be partially attributable to the sales department for inability to penetrate all possible market potential and partially attributable to the managers who may have wisely or foolishly over-built facilities to meet future demand. Other possible explanations may include general economic conditions or particular competitive circumstances.[9] The point is that the alternatives available under current planning and control are constrained by the past decisions which provided the present facilities. Current plans should concentrate on the optimum utilization of given facilities.

Note the difference in timing and in the frame of reference for evaluating different decisions. Practical capacity becomes important in the course of preparing the master budget. At the end of the period, however, the master budgeted sales is the key to the evaluation of results.

N.A.A. *Research Report No. 39* (p. 24) advocates evaluating performance by comparing practical capacity with scheduled production because it "measures the additional output that could be attained without incurring additional capacity costs." Advocates of practical capacity as a basis for the evaluation of performance rightly maintain that management should be regularly aware of all idle facilities. However, when do they need this information? The critical time is probably at the master budget planning stage, not the evaluation of performance stage. The master budgeted sales is the relevant base for analysis at the latter stage. The point is developed more fully below.

TOTAL VOLUME VARIANCE

The measurement system may be designed to follow up on various versions of capacity, each serving a different purpose. To continue our example, production for the current year was 140,000 units, although current production schedules called for 148,000 units. What measures would help management in the evaluation of current results? Variances should help pinpoint responsibility. Exhibit 1 shows a total volume variance (*M-A*), the overall difference between budgeted sales and actual sales. In turn, this volume variance is subdivided into marketing variance (*M-S*) which, to the extent that it can be assigned, is usually the responsibility of

[9] Conceivably, this variance could be sub-divided into two parts: (1) the difference between practical capacity and the activity level used for that particular year in a past capital budget; (2) the difference between the latter and the master budget. These subdivisions might help the evaluation of long range planning, particularly when excess facilities were deliberately acquired.

In this context, where excess capacity is deliberately acquired, the opportunity costs of bearing this capacity could be regularly compared to the costs of its elimination (e.g., overtime premium, second shift premium, sub-contracting, etc.). Then management could choose whether to eliminate the capacity through disposition or lease.

the sales manager, and the production variance $(S-A)$, which is usually the responsibility of the production manager.

Marketing Variance $(M-S)$. The 16,000-unit deviation from the master budgeted sales (164,000 units less 148,000 units scheduled) is a measure that is primarily traceable, at least initially, to the sales arm of the organization. This *marketing variance* should be computed on a routine basis because it integrates the master budget with the results and helps explain the differences between original expectations and results. "Results," as far as the marketing department is concerned, consists of getting sales orders. That is why scheduled production (sales orders received) rather than actual production (sales delivered to customers) is used as the measure of results. Possible explanations of the variance include ineffective advertising or sales promotion, unexpected changes in economic or competitive conditions, poor estimates, and an understaffed or inefficient sales force.

The master budgeted sales, rather than practical capacity, is more germane to the evaluation of current results. Managers, particularly the sales executives, will feel much more obligated to reach the master budgeted sales, which should have been conscientiously set in relation to the optimum opportunities for sales in the current period. To have any meaning, marketing variance must at least crudely reflect the existence of a bona fide opportunity to sell. Consequently, on the operating firing line the marketing variance is much more meaningful than a variance related to practical capacity. For example, a practical capacity variance could be computed by subtracting scheduled production from practical capacity in Exhibit 1. But this would blend two unlike items: the marketing variance plus the expected idle capacity variance.

Production Variance $(S-A)$. The production manager has two major responsibilities: to maximize efficiency and to meet production schedules.

The efficiency is monitored with the aid of standards and budgets for the variable cost factors, while the ability to meet production schedules is metered by some quantification of the difference between scheduled production and actual production.

The attainment of production schedules is a mutual effort by the producing departments and the production planning and control department. Common reasons for failure to meet schedules include poor direction of operations by factory supervisors; operating inefficiencies caused by untrained workmen, faulty machines, or inferior raw material; lack of material or parts; and careless scheduling by production planners. These reasons may be lumped together as possible explanations for a production variance.

Failure to meet a schedule would result in an unfavorable production variance. This is the most commonly encountered situation. However, it may happen that actual production exceeds scheduled production. In such a case, technically the variance would be favorable. But all unusual variances are supposed to be investigated, and the findings may or may not substantiate a favorable label in the layman's sense of the word. That is, sometimes unwanted excess production occurs because of misunderstandings of production schedules.

A common explanation for the bulk of the production variance is labor inefficiency, that is, inability to meet currently attainable standards. To pursue the example further, assume that the standard time allowance per unit is one direct labor hour, and that 148,000 actual direct labor hours were used but labor inefficiencies resulted in the production of only 140,000 good units. In such a case, the entire production variance may be attributable to inefficient labor rather than faulty scheduling or some other reason.

However, favorable or unfavorable variances in labor performance may not be necessarily related to the production variance. Departures from schedule could be caused by machine breakdowns, material shortages, poor production planning, or some other reason. Conversely, a manager can adhere to production schedules, but still produce the units inefficiently.

Expressing Variances in Dollars Rather than in Physical Measures

LIMITATIONS AND USES OF MONETARY MEASURES

Supposedly, once a certain capacity is provided, the addition of one unit of product to sales will increase net income by the unit contribution margin. The fixed costs in the short run will be unaffected by changes in volume, so failure to utilize capacity fully represents a lost opportunity to increase net income by the contribution margin associated with the unsold capacity.

So far, we have deliberately avoided expressing variances in dollar terms for two reasons. First, it is often unnecessary and confusing to express control measures in dollars when the operating personnel being judged think in physical terms only. The general guide is to express a measure in terms best understood by the individuals affected. The object is to help managers operate effectively and efficiently. If this can be achieved without converting data into dollar terms, so much the better. Second, the approximation of opportunity costs, which are the pertinent dollar measures, is hampered by many practical difficulties. For instance, a uniform unit contribution margin is often assumed. In many cases, of course, the increases in unit volume may be attained only by reducing unit prices or by accepting orders that would entail extraordinary incremental costs. In these instances, the dollar measure of the variance would have to be adjusted accordingly. The main objective is to approximate the probable impact on current net income of the best alternative uses of available capacity.

USING CONTRIBUTION MARGINS AS APPROXIMATIONS OF
OPPORTUNITY COSTS

What is the best way to measure the cost of unutilized capacity? The
total fixed costs will be the same regardless of whether production is
140,000 or 164,000 units. Therefore, from a short-run total operating cost
viewpoint, unutilized capacity will not affect costs as they are ordinarily
recorded by accountants. However, from an economic viewpoint, there
may be an opportunity cost as measured by the contribution margins foregone by failure to utilize capacity. This opportunity cost may be zero,
particularly if the sales force has done everything possible to market the
products and if there is no alternate use for the otherwise idle facilities. An
example of alternate use would be doing sub-contracting work for some
other manufacturer. However, to demonstrate the general idea, assume
that uniform unit contribution margins per unit can be validly used.

In our example, assume a sales price of $10.00 less unit variable costs
of $8.00, or $2.00 unit contribution margin. Exhibit 2 expresses the variances in dollar terms.

Contribution margins as an approximation of the opportunity cost notion
may be especially pertinent when the master budget sales forecast is hover-
ing near practical capacity. For example, production could be master
budgeted *and* scheduled at the practical capacity level of 200,000 units, but,
say, inefficiencies result in only 194,000 units being produced. The economic impact of this production variance is best measured by the lost
contribution margin per unit times the difference between the 200,000 and
the 194,000 good units produced ($2.00 × 6,000 units = $12,000 lost
contribution margin).

HELPING THE BUDGETARY PROCESS

The variances described above can also be useful in evaluating and
revising the budget as the year unfolds. Even if the variances were not used
to evaluate marketing and production management, they still could be
useful to the budgetary process because they stress careful estimation in
the first place — emphasizing consideration of alternative opportunities
before the master budget is adopted. Interim follow-up could prompt a
revised master budget,[10] as is now done in practice. That is, although the
illustration used a year as a time span for analysis, the same approach is
applicable to monthly or quarterly periods.

---

[10] This is akin to changing the optimal mix in linear programming in light of
changes in constraints, prices, etc.

EXHIBIT 2

Analysis of Volume Variance Using Contribution Margins

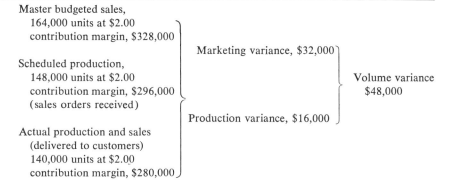

Master budgeted sales,
164,000 units at $2.00
contribution margin, $328,000

Marketing variance, $32,000

Scheduled production,
148,000 units at $2.00
contribution margin, $296,000
(sales orders received)

Volume variance
$48,000

Production variance, $16,000

Actual production and sales
(delivered to customers)
140,000 units at $2.00
contribution margin, $280,000

Somewhere in the reporting scheme, management will probably want an explanation of why the target net income is not achieved. The above analysis dovetails well with the income statement. Assume that total fixed costs are $200,000. A summary analysis follows:

	Master Budget 164,000 units	Actual Results 140,000 units	Variance
Sales at $10.00	$1,640,000	$1,400,000	
Variable costs at $8.00	1,312,000	1,120,000	
Contribution margin at $2.00	$ 328,000	$ 280,000	$48,000U
Fixed costs	200,000	200,000	
Net Income	$ 128,000	$ 80,000	$48,000U*

* EXPLANATION OF VARIANCE: Failure to reach volume level originally budgeted resulted in inability to obtain the contribution margin originally budgeted:

Marketing variance:
Sales department failed to obtain enough orders (164,000 units budgeted − 148,000 units scheduled for production) × $2.00 .... $32,000
Production variance:
Production departments failed to meet production schedules (148,000 units scheduled − 140,000 units produced and sold) × $2.00 16,000
Total volume variance, which in this case wholly explains the difference in net income $48,000

THE OPPORTUNITY COST APPROACH

The illustrations in this paper highlight the essence of the problem of assessing how well capacity is being utilized. However, the use here of the lost contribution margin, a single product, and a single constraint over-simplifies the real world difficulties of trying to obtain variances which are the best available measures of opportunity costs. Most companies have many products and many constraints. Interactions are manifold:

> "Alfred Marshall asked the question, which blade of scissors does the cutting? If you analyze one blade at a time, you will never find out how a scissors cuts a piece of paper. There is interaction between two blades, which is the crucial element for cutting.
>
> Many kinds of business and government phenomena that we observe can not be analyzed effectively one variable at a time. If you can analyze effectively one variable at a time, that is, by all odds, the means to use. But the crux of systems analysis is the application of the situation when you cannot explain the behavior of the system by looking at it one variable at a time — even if you exhaust all the variables, which may be many millions."[11]

How can an accounting system be designed that will tie in best with the decisions regarding the utilization of capacity? A logical first step is to try to formulate a reporting system that dovetails with a specific, well-defined decision model. Demski has developed what he calls an ex post model, based on the linear programming model, which envelopes shifts in the original master budget. It "compares what a firm actually accomplished during some planning period with what it deems on the basis of hindsight it should have accomplished — where accomplishments are measured in terms of the objective function in the firm's planning model. It is an opportunity cost approach in the sense that what a firm actually accomplished during some planning period is compared with what it should have accomplished by the ex post optimum program."[12] He ably demonstrated the feasibility of his model by applying it to the operations of an oil refinery. His approach was truly an opportunity cost approach because it considered the simultaneous changes in all relevant variables (mutatis mutandis) rather than one variable at a time (ceteris paribus). It produced variances that signaled the existence of opportunities and their exact sources and effects, as near as could be determined. The existence of well-defined decision models, such as linear programming, inventory, and queuing models, enhances the likelihood of implementing an ex post opportunity cost approach in practice.

---

[11] Comments by W. W. Cooper in Thomas J. Burns (ed.), *The Use of Accounting Data in Decision-Making* (unpublished, The Ohio State University, 1966), p. 228.

[12] Joel S. Demski, *Variance Analysis: An Opportunity Cost Approach with a Linear Programming Application,* unpublished Ph.D. dissertation, University of Chicago, 1966. Also, see J. M. Samuels, "Opportunity Costing: An Application of Mathematical Programming," *Journal of Accounting Research,* Autumn 1965, pp. 182–191.

Summary

Distinctions between long-range and short-range factors and between hierarchies of responsibility in an organization help to develop a conceptual framework for analyzing the utilization of capacity.

For purposes of current planning and control, physical measures of capacity should suffice in many instances, at least at lower levels of the organization. If dollar measures are sought, opportunity costs, even if they have to be crudely approximated via unit contribution margins, are superior to historical costs for measuring the effect on net income of the utilization of existing facilities.

Lost contribution margins directly measure the effects of volume on profits. Therefore, they are a better basis for the computation of volume variances than historical fixed costs, which unitize total costs that are not affected by current fluctuations in volume. The volume variance based on historical fixed costs has little, if any, economic significance for current planning and control.

The development in many firms of more sophisticated management control systems, which often are linked with formal, well-defined decision models, will facilitate attempts to produce variances that better approximate opportunity costs.

Supplemental
Readings
to Part Five

Max Block, "Practical Cost Controls — How They Can Help Management Improve Profits," *The New York Certified Public Accountant,* Vol. XXV, No. 6 (June, 1956), pp. 343–357.

Cost controls are needed to promote efficient utilization of resources. Pre-determined as well as historical costs are necessary. Cost reports should contain monetary and non-monetary information.

Henry L. Clayton, "Setting Standards and Evaluating Performance," *Cost and Management,* Vol. 39, No. 5 (May, 1965), pp. 195–203.

Essentials of installing and evaluating a standard cost system are stipulated.

Nikolai G. Chumachenko, "Once Again: The Volume-Mix-Price/Cost Budget Variance Analysis," *The Accounting Review,* Vol. XLIII, No. 4 (October, 1968), pp. 753–762.

Methods of variance analysis used in the U.S.A. and in the U.S.S.R. are compared.

Joel S. Demski, "An Accounting System Structured on a Linear Programming Model," *The Accounting Review,* Vol. XLII, No. 4 (October, 1967), pp. 701–712.

Description and implications of a pilot application of linear programming to the structure of an accounting control system are presented.

——, "Analyzing the Effectiveness of the Traditional Standard Cost Variance Model," *Management Accounting,* Vol. 49, No. 2 (October, 1967), pp. 9–19.

A comparison is made of information provided by the standard cost variance model with that required by management, with an operational extension.

——, "Optimizing the Search for Cost Deviation Sources," *Management Science,* Vol. 16, No. 8 (April, 1970), pp. B-486–B-494.

A model to determine the optimum sequence in which to examine the various possible causes of cost variances is developed.

——, "Predictive Ability of Alternative Performance Measurement Models," *Journal of Accounting Research,* Vol. 7, No. 1 (Spring, 1969), pp. 96–115.

Predictive ability is a surrogate to assess direct costing, absorption costing, and an *ex post* optimum model.

F. C. dePaula, "Commitment Accounting for Contract Profit Control," *Accountancy,* (November, 1965), pp. 1037–1040.

Commitment accounting deals with comparison of anticipated completion costs and profits with original estimates.

Raymond G. Drake, "Improved Control through Flexible Budgeting in the Retail Trade," *The Canadian Chartered Accountant,* Vol. 91, No. 6 (December, 1967), pp. 429–434.

Flexible budgeting techniques used in industry can be applied also to retail business.

Richard M. Duvall, "Rules for Investigating Cost Variances," *Management Science,* Vol. 13, No. 10 (June, 1967), pp. B-631–B-641.

Costs of determining the reasons for variances may be treated as part of the decision to analyze variances or not.

T. R. Dyckman, "The Investigation of Cost Variances," *Journal of Accounting Research,* Vol. 7, No. 2 (Autumn, 1969), pp. 215–244.

Means for making the cost-deviation investigation decision incorporate both the cost of investigation and the expected savings are developed.

Werner Frank and Rene Manes, "A Standard Cost Application of Matrix Algebra," *The Accounting Review,* Vol. XLII, No. 3 (July, 1967), pp. 516–525.

An illustration of a matrix algebra application to calculating standard prime cost variances is presented.

W. M. Harper, "Managerial Economic Control — IV: Profit Variance Analysis," *Accountancy,* Vol. LXXIX (August, 1968), pp. 536–540.

Overhead expenditure variances, marginal cost variances, and contribution variances are discussed.

————, "Managerial Economic Control — V: The Objection to Conventional Variance Analysis," *Accountancy,* Vol. LXXIX (November, 1968), pp. 796–799.

Fixed overhead variances have no control value.

C. R. Hasseldine, "Mix and Yield Variances," *The Accounting Review,* Vol. XLII, No. 3 (July, 1967), pp. 497–515.

Mix and yield variances are expressed in simple mathematical and graphic terms, and validity of the measures obtained is discussed.

Donald A. Juers, "Statistical Significance of Accounting Variances," *Management Accounting,* Vol. 49, No. 2 (October, 1967), pp. 20–25.

Statistical methods to determine the importance of a variance are described.

Fred M. Kirby, "Variance Analysis — The 'Step-through' Method," *Management Services,* Vol. 7, No. 2 (March–April, 1970), pp. 51–54.

The "step-through" method of eliminating the problem of sub-variances not being equal to the total variance is introduced.

Bernard J. Kravitz, "The Standard Cost Review," *Management Controls,* Vol. 15, No. 11 (November, 1968), pp. 253–255.

An examination is made of the frequency with which standard costs should be revised, and of the form the review should take.

Baruch Lev, "An Information Theory Analysis of Budget Variances," *The Accounting Review,* Vol. XLIV, No. 4 (October, 1969), pp. 704–710.

Concepts of information theory are used to supplement quality control techniques in analyzing variances of nonrepetitive operations.

F. S. Luh, "Controlled Cost: An Operational Concept and Statistical Approach to Standard Costing," *The Accounting Review,* Vol. XLIII, No. 1 (January, 1968), pp. 123–132.

A refinement of standard cost (controlled cost) using statistical techniques to evaluate operating efficiency and degree of control is proposed.

Rene P. Manes, "The Expense of Expected Idle Capacity," *Management Accounting,* Vol. 50, No. 7 (March, 1969), pp. 37–41.

A method of considering the cost of idle capacity as a period cost, removing it from the volume variance, is proposed.

Raymond E. Miles and Roger C. Vergin, "Behavioral Properties of Variance Controls," *California Management Review,* Vol. VIII, No. 3 (Spring, 1966), pp. 57–65.

Existing control theories and techniques offer a starting point for constructing a behaviorally sound and technically effective approach to control design.

R. W. Partridge, "Let's Do Right By Variance Analysis," *Cost and Management,* Vol. 40, No. 11 (December, 1966), pp. 491–498.

Models which describe the behavior of the joint variance and illustrate its importance are presented.

Yasuo Yoshida, "Cost Control in Product Feasibility Decisions," *NAA Bulletin,* Vol. XLII, No. 6 (February, 1961), pp. 27–38.

A case study is used to relate overhead cost behavior to dollar sales, unit volume of manufacturing, product development, and budgetary decisions. Performance variances are illustrated.

Zenon S. Zannetos, "Toward a Functional Accounting System: Accounting Variances and Statistical Variance Analysis," *Industrial Management Review,* Vol. 7, No. 2 (Spring, 1966), pp. 71–82.

The output of standard accounting systems can be used for statistical analyses of variances. Results of statistical analyses of functional managerial accounting systems are presented.

————, "On the Mathematics of Variance Analysis," *The Accounting Review,* Vol. XXXVIII, No. 3 (July, 1963), pp. 528–533.

A simple mathematical approach to two- and three-variance overhead analysis, supplemented by a geometrical appendix, is presented. The significance of variances is discussed.

Additional

Bibliography

to Part Five

Gilbert Amerman, "The Mathematics of Variance Analysis — The Theory of *N* Variance System," *Accounting Research*, Vols. 4, 4, and 5, Nos. 3, 4, and 1 (July, 1953, October, 1953, and January, 1954), pp. 258–269, 329–350, and 56–79.

Frank V. Bianchini and Thomas J. Cotter, "Profit Planning, Performance Reporting, Variation Analysis," *Financial Executive*, Vol. XXXI, No. 11 (November, 1963), pp. 37 ff.

Harold Bierman, Jr., Lawrence E. Fouraker, and Robert K. Jaedicke, "A Use of Problems and Statistics in Performance Evaluation," *The Accounting Review*, Vol. XXXVI, No. 3 (July, 1961), pp. 409–417.

George B. Cleveland, "Getting Down to Causes on the Labor Variance," *NA(C)A Bulletin*, Vol. XXXVII, No. 1 (September, 1955), pp. 82–86.

Mel Cook, "Five Ways of Discrediting Standard Costs — And the Lessons They Teach," *NAA Bulletin*, Vol. XL, No. 12 (August, 1959), pp. 29–34.

Ben R. Copeland, "Analyzing Burden Variance for Profit Planning and Control," *Management Services*, Vol. 2, No. 1 (January–February, 1965), pp. 34–41.

Thomas G. Cullinan, "Why We Use Standard Costs — Pointers and Reminders," *NA(C)A Bulletin*, Vol. XXXVII, No. 7 (March, 1956), pp. 892–897.

William L. Ferrara, "Controlling Production Overhead," *The Controller*, Vol. XXX, No. 3 (March, 1962), pp. 130 ff.

Jordan L. Golding, "Pinning Down Causes of Variation in Labor Unit Costs," *NAA Bulletin*, Vol. XXXIX, No. 2 (October, 1957), pp. 65–70.

Myron J. Gordon, "LIFO and Standard Costs," *Accounting Research*, Vol. 5, No. 3 (July, 1954), pp. 203–214.

Harold B. Guilfoyle, "Measuring Production Efficiency," *The Canadian Chartered Accountant*, Vol. 85, No. 1 (July, 1964), pp. 25–28.

Alex L. Hart, "Using Probability Theory for Economy in Cost Control," *NAA Bulletin*, Vol. XXXVIII, No. 2 (October, 1956), pp. 257–263.

Louis B. Kahn and Waino W. Suojanen, "Two Simple Measures of Productivity From Accounting Data," *NAA Bulletin*, Vol. XLVI, No. 5 (January, 1965), pp. 17–23.

Felix P. Kollaritsch and Norman E. Dittrich, "Standard Sales Prices and Their Variances," *Management Services*, Vol. 1, No. 4 (September–October, 1964), pp. 30–36.

Daniel Lipsky, "The Dimensional Principle in the Analysis of Variance," *NAA Bulletin*, Vol. XLII, No. 1 (September, 1960), pp. 5–18.

Robert A. Markell, "Standards Revision Tells the Story of Trends," *NA(C)A Bulletin*, Vol. XXXVI, No. 9 (May, 1955), pp. 1131–1137.

A. W. Patrick, "A Proposal for Determining the Significance of Variations from Standard," *The Accounting Review*, Vol. XXXII, No. 4 (October, 1957), pp. 587–592.

Charles M. Reinherr, "Profit Fluctuations Caused by Standard Cost Variances," *NAA Bulletin*, Vol. XLII, No. 3 (November, 1960), pp. 23–30.

Vincent J. Shroad, Jr., "Control of Labor Costs Through the Use of Learning Curves," *NAA Bulletin*, Vol. XLVI, No. 2 (October, 1964), pp. 15–22.

Robert L. Shultis, "Applying PERT to Standard Cost Revisions," *NAA Bulletin*, Vol. XLIV, No. 1 (September, 1962), pp. 35–43.

David Solomons, "A Diagrammatic Representation of Standard Cost Variances," *Accounting Research*, Vol. 2, No. 1 (January, 1951), pp. 46–51.

———, "Standard Costing Needs Better Variances," *NAA Bulletin*, Vol. XLIII, No. 4 (December, 1961), pp. 29–39.

Lawrence L. Vance, "The Fundamental Logic of Primary Variance Analysis," *The New York Certified Public Accountant*, Vol. XX, No. 3 (March, 1950), pp. 139–144.

John V. van Pelt III, "Factors Affecting Intelligent Use of Variances," *NA(C)A Bulletin*, Vol. XXXVI, No. 7 (March, 1955), pp. 904–910.

Charles Weber, "The Mathematics of Variance Analysis," *The Accounting Review*, Vol. XXXVIII, No. 3 (July, 1963), pp. 534–539.

Winston R. Willmert, "Repaired or Rebuilt — It Has to Be Accounted For," *NAA Bulletin*, Vol. XLI, No. 5 (January, 1960), pp. 11–20.

PART SIX

Motivation, Performance, and Evaluation:
Responsibility Accounting and Direct Costing

C onsiderable controversy exists about the proper handling of overhead costs. Direct costing advocates recommend that only direct costs (direct labor, direct materials, and variable overhead) should enter into product costs; and that fixed overhead should always be allocated to periodic profit and loss. Full, or absorption, costing on the other hand follows the conventional practice of including also the fixed overhead costs as part of the cost of the inventory. The crux of the problem for income determination, of course, is in the stability of manufacturing volume over time, or more precisely in the relation of capacity to production.

For short-run pricing and cost control, however, there is more general agreement about the usefulness of direct costing. Thus pricing in highly competitive situations requires that only direct costs be covered, while in the long-run all costs must be covered. Direct costing also has the advantage of focusing on the more controllable costs, and so makes for easier control of responsibility centers.

Netten summarizes the managerial information needs which contributed to the development of the concept of responsibility accounting, and he offers a lucid description of several dimensions of the concept. He outlines a system of responsibility accounting, and he gives the requisite conditions for, and the difficulties of, application. Additionally, he predicates the integration of accounting and other information systems of the firm with managerial responsibility for effective control.

Parker, in his article, looks more specifically into cost analysis, control, and internal reporting. He also lays the groundwork for later emphasis on contribution theory. Amerman subjects both direct and absorption costing to a rigorous mathematical analysis. Through these means he is able to test each method under various situations and to develop pertinent observations about the effects on income determination.

405

Ijiri, Jaedicke, and Livingstone investigate analytically the impact of various inventory costing methods on the pattern of profit differences. By example, the authors show that the inventory costing method is important, and they also illustrate the error present in the conventional generalizations contrasting full and direct cost profit. Extensive mathematical analysis is offered, and a summary is provided for those who do not wish to concern themselves with the detailed analysis.

25 *"Responsibility accounting" is another of the concepts developed to serve the burgeoning needs of management for better information. Although the principle is simple — classify information on enterprise activities by responsible manager — the application often is intricate and time-consuming.*

Areas of responsibility for organizational activities — and associated revenues and expenses, receipts and expenditures — must be defined. New informational needs of managers at all levels must be ascertained. Standards and other measures of performance must be developed, and appropriate data collection procedures devised.

Implementation of the responsibility accounting concept may involve integration of the accounting system with other (non-monetary) information systems, to avoid duplication of effort and to insure system effectiveness.

Responsibility Accounting
for Better Management*

E. W. Netten

In the biblical "Parable of the Talents," a businessman who was going abroad entrusted part of his capital to each of three servants. Two invested their money and doubled it, but the third was afraid of the risks and buried his. When the businessman returned he was pleased with the first two men and promoted them, but berated the third for not earning a profit and cast him into the place of wailing and gnashing of teeth.

Control and communication techniques being what they were in those days the businessman had no means of telling, while he was away, how good a job his men were doing. Nowadays, one might say that he lacked a system

* From The Canadian Chartered Accountant, *Vol. 83, No. 3 (September, 1963), pp. 164–168. Reprinted by permission of the publisher.*

of responsibility accounting. Nevertheless, circumstances not too dissimilar to these ancient ones exist in many enterprises today.

Need for Better Information

The impetus for development of responsibility accounting and the growing use of it by progressive enterprises, large and small, sprang from several sources. Chief among them were:

- Increased complexity of business operations. Witness the pace of technological and market changes, of diversification, mergers, and the lengthened time span between investment decisions and profit results.
- Management decentralization to grapple with this complexity and to provide a more flexible and dynamic organization structure.
- The importance of raising productivity and of tight cost control in the current competitive situation.
- Recognition of the vital role of planning and control in successful management.
- Realization that the means — the techniques and the information — available to management to exercise its planning and control functions were far from good.

These factors put heavy pressure on the accountant to reorient his work toward management's requirements. Responsibility accounting evolved in response.

What Is Responsibility Accounting?

Responsibility accounting classifies accounting and statistical information on an enterprise's activities according to the managers responsible for them. So many varied techniques are practised now under the name of responsibility accounting that really it is synonymous with management accounting. It ties accounting, reporting and budgeting to management organization and responsibilities. The techniques apply to enterprises big and small, centralized or decentralized, business, non-profit, or governmental. Information is reported, with comparisons to budgets or other standards, in the detail and at the time each manager requires it for effective planning, decision-making and control. In sum, it provides the right information to the right people at the right time.

The underlying principles are simple — deceptively so — yet their application to a specific enterprise can be intricate and time-consuming. The areas involved are:

- The determination of responsibility for each activity carried on in the enterprise and the assigning of each item of income, expense and other expenditure accordingly.
- The definition of the kind and amount of data each manager needs and the reflection of them in the account and statistical classifications.

- The use of management reports to convey the data to those who will use it, at the time they want it.
- Planning and budgeting practices made fully compatible with the reports.
- The setting up of measures of performance to be incorporated in the reports and budgets.
- Devising accounting and statistical procedures to gather and process the required data.

What Responsibility Accounting Is Not

Responsibility accounting can never be a substitute for good management. It is simply a tool, and a tool is inert until it is used. Some systems that are otherwise sound never get off the ground because the managers do not really understand them nor put them to good use.

Nor is it an accounting technique that stands or falls on the accountant's use of it. It is an integral part of the management process and the accountant's role is a technical and supporting one. This points up the great importance of careful attention to the human relations aspects; there should be full management participation in designing it and a clear understanding of its aims and uses. Unless the operating people enthusiastically support responsibility accounting and make it work, even the best-conceived system will fail.

Organization and Responsibility

Responsibility accounting is founded upon the organization structure. It must be tailor-made to the particular enterprise's distribution of responsibility and authority amongst its managers. There can be no packaged approach.

One of the more difficult tasks is the assignment of responsibility for each activity and for each corresponding item of expense, income, capital expenditure and, sometimes, asset investment. Organization charts and manuals, policy directives and similar documents provide leads but the managers concerned must participate actively if realistic assignments are to be made. Typically, there come to light many instances of fuzzy organization lines, misunderstanding of who is responsible for certain activities, overlapping of duties, authority not commensurate with responsibility, and expenses for which no one seems to be responsible. Sound organization principles must be followed if responsibility accounting is to work. Often it proves necessary to 'put the house in order' before proceeding further.

Strict Assignment of Items

Since all activities are the responsibility of someone in the enterprise, all items of income, operating costs, other expenses and capital expenditures are the responsibility of some manager. None should be left unassigned. Each expenditure should be assigned to the manager (whose unit is called a "responsibility unit") who has the authority to incur it and is therefore in the best position to control it. In most cases this will be the manager who 'spends the money' — that is, supervises the work force concerned, originates or approves personnel changes, and requisitions for materials and purchases. Expenditures should be charged to the lowest management level to which these can be directly assigned, closest to the point of action. Similarly, income controllable by a manager should be credited to his unit.

As a corollary, a manager is charged only with expenditures over which he can exercise a significant degree of direct control. Prorations and arbitrary allocations necessary for costing products or services have no place in short-term control reports. Assignment to a responsibility unit of expenses over which it has no control, if and when needed to ascertain the full cost of a department, operation or product, should be built up and reported separately.

How far down within the organization should responsibility accounting go? This depends, naturally, on the extent of delegation of authority and assignment of responsibility. Customarily, reports are provided down to the first-line supervisory level. A shop foreman, for example, is likely to be in the best position to control in the short run the efficiency of shop operations and labour and material usage, and he should receive reports on his performance in doing so.

The difference between responsibility accounting and an accounting system aligned only to product costing and inventory valuation should now be evident. For product costing, all expenses associated with a given production department may be charged directly or by proration to that department for distribution to the products processed. It is concerned with the disposition of costs. Responsibility accounting on the other hand is concerned with the origin of costs. Direct labour and material might, for example, be charged to several foremen; indirect labour and supplies to the department head; maintenance labour and materials to the maintenance superintendent; fire insurance to the treasurer; and building depreciation to the general manager.

Information Requirements

No hard and fast rules can be laid down for determining the accounting and statistical information that managers need. Our ability to produce vast amounts of raw figures mechanically or electronically has outstripped our ability to select those figures that are meaningful for planning and control. The problem is not more information but the right information. The managers concerned should play a predominant role in choosing the information to be reported to them. This is so even though most managers find it exceedingly difficult to pinpoint just what figures they want, how often they want them, and the format.

Responsibility accounting can be used with any chart of accounts simply by adding the classification by responsibility unit. Often, however, the account classification is revamped to suit new needs stemming from responsibility accounting.

Redrawing the Chart

Most conventional charts of accounts emphasize the natural classification of expenses — the numerous types of wages, salaries, materials, facilities and outside services for which funds are spent. This can be thought of as 'input' to the responsibility unit. Such charts may be inadequate because they do not distinguish the various major functions (types of work performed or 'output') in each responsibility unit and so do not provide costs of work done that can be related to the volume of the work. Therefore the chart frequently is redrawn to accumulate costs (and income if applicable) for each major function that can be compared to figures on the volume of work done, and thereby to measure performance. The natural classification, which details the resources used to carry out each function, is retained but assumes a secondary position in the chart.

Since the chart of accounts must serve many purposes a rather large number of kinds of groupings may have to be built into it. Depending on the nature of the enterprise it may be desirable to distinguish direct and indirect costs, variable, semivariable, managed and fixed costs and administrative and operating costs. Special data for planning and controlling cash, financial position, inventories, purchases and manpower will undoubtedly be needed. Beyond the basic chart of accounts, other classifications are necessary to gather detailed data such as sales by customer, salesman or distribution channel; costs by product; capital expenditures by project; and maintenance costs by facility.

Costs and Volume Matched

Due consideration should be given to the gathering of physical statistics in addition to or in place of dollar information in the accounts. Statistics on volume of work done must be in a form that can be matched with the corresponding costs in the accounts. Information expressed in man hours, units of material usage, yields, machine speeds, facilities-utilization percentages or output per man hour often is simpler and quicker to prepare, eliminates the effect of price or wage rate fluctuations and may be more easily understood. Dollars may be the only common denominator but it is possible to overemphasize them.

Expense information is expensive information. One must guard against overelaboration. To report a large amount of detail each month to each responsibility unit may increase accounting costs out of proportion to the value of the data and may overwhelm the unfortunate manager who receives a mass of indigestible figures. In most responsibility units a few operating factors, in physical or dollar terms or ratios, can be identified and reported upon. It is best to define functions and natural expense classes rather broadly, and to refine them later if really necessary. Only figures that are significant to each type of responsibility unit should be recorded separately. It is not desirable, for example, to impose a rigid natural expense classification to be applied to all units.

Responsibility Reporting

After the nature of the information required is known, thought must be given to how often it is to be reported, the amount of detail to be presented, and the format. Reports for control purposes may be produced monthly, weekly, daily or even hourly. At successively higher levels in the organizational chain, less and less time is devoted to control and more and more to planning. Foremen and first line supervisors may need considerable detail and frequent reports, often expressed in physical terms such as work performed, labour hours, materials used and machine efficiency. Reports to senior management are not so frequent, are in condensed form summarizing the results of lower levels, and are mainly expressed in dollars.

Control is centered on monthly reports, often called "responsibility reports," prepared by the accounting function for each responsibility unit. The report to each unit shows its expenses, income and capital expenditures in the detail appearing in the account classification (or some condensation of this), statistics such as volume of work, costs per unit and perhaps man-hour data and number of employees.

In selecting the contents of these reports the criterion should be: is the information important enough that action may be based on it? Care should be exercised not to clutter up the reports with reams of data when a few strategic figures will do. Each report runs to one or two pages on the average and should be released as quickly after the month end as is feasible.

Reports from Other Units

Each manager who has other units reporting to him receives a monthly summary listing the expenses, income and capital expenditures of each of these units, with pertinent statistics. He receives also a report on the activities retained under his own personal control, in the same fashion as other responsibility units do.

Since absolute figures alone are of little value, comparisons with budgets or other standards should always appear in the form of variations between actual and the standards. The variation data focus attention on items requiring action and conserve time by permitting 'management by exception.' Because the reports are aligned to the organization chart and the totals on each report appear in the detail on the report to the next higher level, it is easy to trace variations at any level back to their roots. Thus the reports achieve their prime purpose; they enable and stimulate control action. These monthly reports should show figures for the current month and the period (year or quarter) to date. The cumulative position and trends shown by to-date figures may at times be of greater significance than the month's results. Comparisons with the previous year can safely be omitted since the purpose is to control performance to standards rather than to raise questions already thrashed out when the standards were set.

Narrative Commentaries

Narrative commentaries should be prepared to explain important variations from standards and state the remedial action taken or to be taken. These commentaries come from two sources. The accounting function provides to the responsibility unit affected, details of the composition of a variation, but only the unit itself can explain the underlying cause. For example, the accountant might trace a material-usage variation to a certain chemical in a particular process, but the unit concerned must proffer the explanation that impurities due to careless storage caused it. Desirably, the head of each responsibility unit should furnish a narrative commentary to his superior, with a copy to the accounting function, so that the latter can prepare an over-all summary for senior management.

Many other types of control reports are used in managing special activities, such as cash, inventory levels and working capital. Reports may be prepared quarterly or as required for planning, pricing or special studies; these may cut across organizational lines and contain data analyzed by account, product, territory or facility, instead of by responsibility.

Care in laying out the format of reports will be amply repaid. They should be simple, attractive and couched in terms understood by the recipients. Presentation can be in the form of statements, graphs, charts or tables, although machine processing may force a uniform format for reports turned out in volume.

Responsibility Budgeting

The planning and control cycle calls for setting objectives, developing plans to meet them, expressing the plans in figures through budgets, gathering information, preparing reports and taking corrective action. Planning and budgeting practices are a field unto themselves and will not be discussed in detail here.

Effective responsibility accounting may require more sophisticated budgets than were previously used. Each manager receiving a responsibility report should prepare or at least participate in preparing his budget since he will be held accountable for achieving it.

Since the budgets provide the means for comparing plans with actual results, the form and content of the budgets must be fully compatible with the regular control reports. For example, the account and statistical classes should be the same for both and the budget must be broken down into time periods corresponding to the periods covered by the reports. The budgets and reports are in fact two sides of the same coin.

Based on Careful Plans

Management by exception depends on a realistic budget; without a good budget there is no point in trying to use it as a yardstick. The budget must be based on carefully set objectives and operating plans, not, as someone aptly put it, on "past history eloquently defended."

Fixed budgets, flexible budgets and profit planning can all be readily incorporated into an over-all system of responsibility accounting.

Fixed budgets offer a medium for over-all planning and expression of objectives. Sometimes responsibility reports include comparisons only with fixed budgets. This is adequate if the volume of activity can be predicted accurately or if volume changes take place slowly. Where it is hard to predetermine volume and changes happen quickly — and this is typical of a manufacturing concern — fixed budgets should be supplemented by flexible budgets or standard costs. If a manager cannot control the volume of his work, it can be positively misleading to compare results at one activity level with a budget predicated on another level.

Some planning and control systems tend to emphasize the reports and relegate budgets to a supporting role of providing the yardsticks for the reports. The shoe should really be on the other foot. Preparation of carefully thought out plans that are then used as a guide to action will usually produce more benefits than the same amount of effort devoted to accounting for and reporting of actual results.

Performance Measurement

It has been said that "to measure is to control." That is an oversimplification, but without some yardstick — a budget or other standard — real control cannot be exercised. Control may be defined, indeed, as taking the action necessary to make actual results conform to a predetermined standard.

Budgets provide the principal standard for measuring performance. Other standards can also be applied in certain areas, such as standard costs, engineered physical standards, manning tables, sales quotas and share of market.

To date, responsibility accounting has concentrated on concrete financial and statistical data. Some key measures of management performance are intangible and hard to set. This would include such important determinants of organizational health as industry leadership, product creation, manager development and employee, customer, supplier and community relationships. Measurements here are in their infancy but some progress is being made in developing specific and objective standards for them.

Accounting and Data Processing

Revisions in systems and procedures are needed to collect, process and summarize the data to be reported. Information classifications and application of codes to source documents have already been discussed. Data processing equipment is by no means essential but the job of sorting and summarizing large amounts of basic data in several ways, quickly and correctly, lends itself to mechanization in medium- and large-scale enterprises.

To produce reports promptly calls for careful planning, rigid scheduling of close-off dates and the intelligent use of estimates. At times, though, the speedy release of reports becomes a fetish achieved only by great effort not warranted by the value of the action that can be taken by having the reports so quickly. Nor is a high level of accuracy always justified. Many decisions can be based just as effectively on approximations worked up in a fraction of the time taken to prepare absolutely accurate figures.

Clear Audit Trails

Clear audit trails from the reports back to the source documents must be provided to facilitate the analysis of budget variations and of actual results. Audit trail listings of the documents supporting each account may be furnished to the responsibility units concerned, but preferably should be retained in the accounting department for reference.

Control information need not emanate from the accounting department. It may, especially if it is needed hourly or daily, be more cheaply and quickly prepared in the operating department where the work is done. Duplication and overlap must be avoided, however. Many operating units have their complement of bootleg bookkeepers who produce reports that the accounting department was unable or unwilling to provide in the past. Such reports tend to linger on when replaced by responsibility reports and may be a costly drain on clerical time.

New Ways to Serve

Responsibility accounting opens up new ways for the accountant to provide valuable services to his enterprise and to take his place on the management team. Enterprise after enterprise has adopted it and has found that it brought very worthwhile benefits through more realistic planning, greater profit consciousness, clearer definition of organizational responsibilities, closer control and better management decisions.

Absorption costing emphasizes the distinction between production costs and all other costs, stressing inventory valuation and profit determination, while direct costing distinguishes fixed from variable costs and is primarily interested in cost analysis.

Actual overhead costs, predetermined and standard burden rates, and flexible budgets — all have been landmarks of progress in the effort to generate more useful management information.

Cost information plays a motivational role, and therefore management accounting relies heavily on knowledge from other disciplines: economics, business administration, industrial engineering, and psychology. Direct costing, in particular, is rooted in economics.

The close relationship between usefulness and accounting principles offers hope of universal acceptance of direct costing; increasing automation militates against the realization of this hope. The controversy is sterile, for both types of analysis are needed — but for different purposes.

Perspectives on Direct Costing*

John R. E. Parker

Direct costing is a relatively recent development that has become the subject of widespread interest among accountants and businessmen. Within the past few years, much has been written and said concerning the advantages and disadvantages of direct costing. Opinion, however, as to its practicability is still widely varied. At one extreme are those who regard direct costing as "the next forward step in the evolutionary development of costing (and) given time, it will become the conventional method of cost accounting."[1]

---

* From The Canadian Chartered Accountant, *Vol. 78, No. 3 (March, 1961), pp. 225-232.* Reprinted by permission of the publisher.

[1] R. P. Marple, "Direct Costing and the Uses of Cost Data," *Accounting Review,* XXX (July, 1955) p. 436.

At the opposite extreme there are those who take the stand that "if accounting theory and practice is so 'flabby' that the direct costing theory becomes acceptable for reporting purposes, the progress of the last 500 years will be 'gone by the boards' ".[2] Since direct costing has not yet been fully evaluated by the accounting profession, it can be concluded that majority opinion is probably, as yet, uncommitted.

Nature of Direct Costing

In spite of numerous papers on the subject, there is still uncertainty as to the meaning and implications of direct costing. The Canadian Institute of Chartered Accountants' publication "Accounting Terminology" defines direct costing as "an application of marginal analysis to cost accounting, in which attention is directed to the direct, or variable, costs of production, with the spread between sales and direct costs of a product or department viewed as a contribution to joint and fixed costs and profits".[3] Essentially, direct costing is a concept under which only prime costs and variable overhead are treated as product costs, thus leaving all other manufacturing costs to be treated as period costs.

In comparison with conventional or absorption costing, direct costing requires a redesigning of the income statement, as well as certain underlying accounting records, in a way that reflects cost-volume-profit relationships and thus facilitates management decision-making. The basic characteristic of direct costing is the segregation of expenses into fixed and variable components. In practice, absorption costing is often supplemented by a segregation of expenses which, although separate from the books of account, provides information pertaining to cost-volume-profit relationships. The point to be emphasized is that under direct costing the segregation of expenses is incorporated into the recording phase of the accounting process and subsequently becomes the basis for reporting costs. It follows, therefore, that the consequences of any segregation of expenses tend to become more far-reaching under direct costing.

Direct material and direct labour are both considered to be variable costs; that is, they vary in total dollar amount directly and proportionately with the volume of production. Accordingly, with regard to the accounting treatment of direct material and direct labour, both methods, direct costing and absorption costing, are identical. The residual part of the cost of manufacturing, frequently referred to as manufacturing overhead, consists of a large number of different kinds of expense. These expenses react in differing ways to changes in the volume of production. In relation to volume, manufacturing

---

[2] J. D. Edwards, "This New Costing Concept — Direct Costing?" *Accounting Review*, XXXIII (October, 1958) p. 567.

[3] Canadian Institute of Chartered Accountants, "Accounting Terminology," Toronto, 1957, p. 25.

overhead is frequently classified into two distinct categories: fixed and variable. It is the accounting treatment of the fixed portion of manufacturing overhead that is the essence of the distinction between direct costing and absorption costing.

It may be stated, in general terms, that absorption costing emphasizes the distinction between production costs and all other costs, whereas direct costing emphasizes the distinction between fixed and variable costs. Furthermore, absorption costing tends to stress inventory valuation and, as a result thereof, profit determination, whereas direct costing is primarily interested in cost analysis.

Mainly Historical

Although recognition of the need for cost accounting dates back to the early stages of the evolution of the accounting process, its development received a major impetus from the Industrial Revolution. In more recent times, the years subsequent to the end of World War I are regarded as the most fertile period in the development of cost accounting. In concluding his book "Evolution of Cost Accounting to 1925," S. Paul Garner makes the following observation: "Cost theories and techniques have evolved as a product of their industrial environment, and their rapid development has been necessitated by the continually increasing complexity of manufacturing processes."[4]

Initially cost accounting dealt almost exclusively with costs for use in inventory valuation and profit determination. Even today these aspects of cost accounting are extremely important. However, as a result of the increasing growth and complexity of modern business, cost analysis and control have become the predominant justification for many cost accounting procedures. In modern practice cost accounting is expected to provide information which will be put to a variety of uses by management. While the variety of information thus derived is useful in the control of costs, the essence of control is action. Responsibility for cost control is distributed through various levels of organizational structure. The part played by cost information is basically that of initiating action on the part of those responsible. The point to be emphasized is that cost information, by itself, is of very little use unless it is used properly. Cost accounting is not an end in itself, but merely a means to an end.

Writing in the *N.A.C.A. Bulletin* of January 15, 1936, Jonathan N. Harris presented what is recognized as the first published description of direct costing. Prior to writing this article, Harris, as controller of Dewey and Almy Chemical Company, had played a leading part in the conversion of his company's accounting records to the direct costing method as of January 1, 1934. Although Harris is recognized as the first person to publish an article

---

[4] S. P. Garner, "Evolution of Cost Accounting to 1925." University of Alabama Press, 1954, p. 416.

on the subject, Dewey and Almy Chemical Company was not the first company to use direct costing methods. N.A.C.A. Research Series No. 23, entitled "Direct Costing," indicates that the budget director of one company had installed a cost system in 1908 which provided for separate accumulation of fixed and variable costs in order that marginal cost data would be available for pricing.[5]

In part, at least, the development of direct costing reflects a shift in accounting emphasis from the traditional balance sheet point of view. Increased interest has been shown in income determination to such an extent that, in many instances, the balance sheet point of view is regarded as being subordinate to profit and loss considerations. In retrospect, income tax considerations have played an important part in bringing about this shift in emphasis.

Influence of Management Accounting

A closely related trend that is also exerting its influence upon the development of direct costing is the attention being given to what is termed management accounting. In 1958, the Committee on Management Accounting of the American Accounting Association defined management accounting as "the application of appropriate techniques and concepts in processing the historical and projected economic data of an entity to assist management in establishing a plan for reasonable economic objectives and in the making of rational decisions with a view toward achieving these objectives." The committee stated further that management accounting "includes methods and concepts necessary for effective planning, for choosing between alternative business actions, and for control through the evaluation and interpretation of performance. Its study involves consideration of ways in which accounting information may be accumulated, synthesized, analyzed and presented in relation to specific problems, decisions, and day-to-day tasks of business management."[6]

In broadening its horizons in the direction of management accounting, the accounting profession is, to a considerable extent, relying on knowledge from the fields of economics, business administration, industrial engineering, and psychology. Direct costing is an example of an accounting development that is largely based on knowledge from the field of economics. While it is perhaps more accurate to say that direct costing is among the relatively recent developments that have brought about the current interest in management accounting, it seems obvious that as interest in management accounting increases, it will further the development of direct costing. Logically, developments in management accounting should interact favourably with the development of direct costing and vice versa.

[5] National Association of Cost Accountants, Research Series No. 23, Direct Costing, New York, 1953, p. 1081.
[6] American Accounting Association, "Report of Committee on Management Accounting," *Accounting Review*, XXXIV (April, 1959) p. 210.

Conventional Procedure Inadequate

The more specific developments that eventually culminated in the direct costing concept encompass various aspects in the evolution of conventional costing and, in particular, reflect the alleged inadequacies inherent in the conventional procedures. In discussing these inadequacies, Gilbert Amerman suggests that "two major objections to the use of the conventional absorption cost income statement are (1) it does not distinguish between profits resulting only from sales and those resulting from inventory changes, and (2) it is difficult to understand and analyze because it mixes costs which are variable with volume on a short-term basis with those which are variable with volume only on a long-term basis".[7] In addition, the use of direct costing eliminates the allocation of fixed costs and thus overcomes one of the most criticized aspects of absorption costing. Paton and Littleton have said: "Cost allocation at best is loaded with assumption and, in many cases, highly arbitrary methods of apportionment are employed in practice. Certainly it is wise not to take the results of the usual process of internal cost computation too seriously."[8]

The failure of absorption costing to distinguish clearly between fixed and variable costs creates difficulties long recognized by accountants. Since some costs do not increase proportionately with the volume of goods sold, profits in theory tend to increase out of proportion as volume exceeds the point where the fixed costs have been recovered from sales revenue. For the same reason, profits tend to decline more rapidly than sales revenue when sales volume declines. Attempts to have the actual volume of production absorb the total actual manufacturing overhead delay the determination of unit costs since the overhead applicable to a unit of product cannot be determined until the end of the accounting period. Moreover, since unit fixed costs vary inversely with volume, the resulting product costs, under absorption costing, also tend to vary inversely with the volume produced during the period. These difficulties result from the fact that sales volume, and hence the volume of production, is dependent upon conditions that, to a large extent, are beyond the control of management.

Overhead Rates

A significant improvement took place with the introduction of predetermined overhead rates based on normal capacity. Although they are rarely shown as such, predetermined overhead rates actually consist of two parts:

---

[7] Gilbert Amerman, "Facts about Direct Costing for Profit Determination," *Accounting Research*, V (April, 1954) p. 161.

[8] W. A. Paton, and A. C. Littleton, "Corporate Accounting Standards," Chicago, American Accounting Association, 1940, p. 120.

a rate that charges actual variable costs included in overhead, and a rate that distributes fixed costs, usually on the basis of normal capacity. The predetermination of overhead rates eliminates the delay previously encountered in developing product costs. Basing these rates on normal capacity results in the fixed portion of overhead being absorbed by the plant utilization necessary to meet average product demand over the period of a business cycle. Except under unique circumstances, this method results in an over-or-under absorption of overhead in relation to the actual manufacturing expense incurred.

Moreover, the use of predetermined overhead rates based on normal capacity tends to result in the emergence of troublesome volume variances. Generally speaking, under-absorbed overhead is regarded as the cost attributable to idle capacity, while over-absorption indicates that current production has been charged with overhead in excess of that actually incurred. Depending upon the causes of the over-or-under-absorbed overhead, it is disposed of by a write-off to cost of sales, or by a write-off to profit and loss, or by proration to inventories and cost of sales. Over the years the use of predetermined overhead rates has become so widespread that accountants generally think of actual cost as meaning actual material, actual labour and normal overhead.[9]

In N.A.C.A. Research Series No. 23 the above concept of actual cost is described as follows: "While very useful where this type of product cost was appropriate (for long-range pricing as an example) and where normal volume could be satisfactorily established, it was not helpful in determining how individual costs or groups of costs could be expected to vary with short-period volume fluctuations. The reason for this was that the normal volume concept was intended to help the accountant determine product costs for the one production volume chosen as normal."[10]

With the advent of the scientific management movement came the idea of setting standards of performance and of comparing the actual time taken to perform the work with the predetermined standards. Inevitably these ideas led to the development of standard costing. At about the same time flexible budgets were developed for the purpose of controlling costs, particularly those costs included in manufacturing overhead. The flexible budget, with or without standard costing, represents a refinement which indicates the costs that are justified by the actual volume of production achieved. There is a substantial change required to move from acceptance of flexible budgets to the utilization of direct costing for inventory valuation and internal reporting purposes. However, with minor modifications, the expense classification used in developing the flexible budget can become the basis for direct costing.

[9] R. I. Dickey (ed.), "Accountants' Cost Handbook" second edition, New York, Ronald Press, 1960, p. 16-24.

[10] National Association of Cost Accountants, *op. cit.*, p. 7.

Underlying Theory

Although the usefulness of direct costing is generally recognized for purposes of internal reporting, the method is still considered unacceptable for external reports. The explanation for the existence of such an anomaly lies in part with the long tradition associated with absorption costing, and in part with the generally recognized view that the same standards need not apply to both internal and external reports. It has been suggested by one writer that this situation "is perhaps the best example of a confusion between what is desirable cost information for certain purposes of management and what is acceptable cost bookkeeping."[11]

Generally accepted principles of accounting state that period costs should be recognized in the income account in the period in which they are incurred. Only those costs which are a function of output should be deferred and matched against future revenue by means of the inventory account. It is largely on this basis that direct costing claims soundness in theory.

Direct costing assumes that the fixed costs are not really costs of production, but are actually only stand-by costs which facilitate production, and which must be incurred regardless of the volume of production. The fixed costs are regarded by the proponents of direct costing as a constant quantity incurred during a period of time. When that period of time has expired, the fixed costs incurred expire with it. Furthermore, it is claimed that the subsequent accounting period will incur its own fixed costs; therefore, it is irrational to defer in the inventory account any portion of the previous period's fixed costs.

Jonathan N. Harris states that inventory costs should include "the delivered purchase cost of raw materials, and packages used, direct labour costs and direct production expenses, all of which items were incurred only because the goods were produced." Mr. Harris further states that "the fixed factory expenses, on the other hand, do not have any real relation to production as such . . . They go on substantially unabated when the wheels slow down or become idle."[12]

Counter Argument

The counter argument contends that the purpose of incurring manufacturing overhead is the production of goods. The fixed costs are as necessary as the variable costs in the accomplishment of this purpose. Accordingly, failure to include the fixed costs in inventory valuation prevents a proper matching of costs and revenue.

[11] H. F. Taggart, "Cost Accounting versus Cost Bookkeeping." *Accounting Review*, XXVI (April, 1951) p. 144.
[12] J. N. Harris, "The Case Against Administrative Expenses in Inventory," *Journal of Accountancy* LXXXII (July, 1946), p. 34.

The Committee on Accounting and Auditing Research of the Canadian Institute of Chartered Accountants states in Bulletin No. 5: "In the case of inventories of goods in process and finished goods, cost will include the laid-down cost of material plus the cost of direct labour applied to the product and ordinarily the applicable share of overhead expense properly chargeable to production." The committee further states: "In some cases, fixed overhead is excluded where its inclusion would distort the profit for the year by reason of fluctuating volume of production."[13]

It seems quite apparent from the foregoing that generally accepted principles of accounting ordinarily require that fixed manufacturing overhead be treated as a product cost. It is also apparent that two different concepts of inventory valuation are involved. It is difficult to see how two methods of inventory valuation, one of which omits a large portion of the cost included in the other, could ever both be recognized as being in conformity with generally accepted principles of accounting.

The test that should be applied in determining whether an item of cost should be treated as a period charge is not whether the nature of the cost is fixed regardless of fluctuating volume, but whether the item represents an expenditure from which only the current period will benefit. The concept of future benefit is widely accepted by accountants in explaining the nature of an asset. Referring to asset expiration, the American Accounting Association's Committee on Concepts and Standards Underlying Corporate Financial Statements states: "Expired costs are those having no discernible benefit to future operations."[14] If it is possible to reason from the foregoing that assets ordinarily represent expenditures whose reincurrence in the short run is unnecessary, then it might be possible to justify the treatment of fixed costs that is followed under direct costing.

Contribution Theory

Attempts have been made to justify direct costing on the basis of the so-called "contribution theory." Under this theory it is suggested that each sales dollar consists of two parts: a reimbursement of out-of-pocket costs, and the balance of the sales dollar which is viewed as a contribution to the coverage of fixed costs and profits. The economists' concept of the margin, as applied to this problem, establishes that profit does not accrue on a unit basis. No profit, regardless of price, is realized until the fixed costs are recovered, and then profit accrues in a manner not revealed by the margin between selling price and full unit costs, fixed and variable. After the fixed

---

[13] Committee on Accounting and Auditing Research, Bulletin No. 5. "The Meaning of the Term 'Cost' as Used in Inventory Valuation," Toronto, Canadian Institute of Chartered Accountants, 1950, p. 2.

[14] American Accounting Association, "Accounting and Reporting Standards for Corporate Financial Statements, 1957 Revision." *Accounting Review*, XXXII (October, 1957), p. 541.

costs have been recovered, the sale of an additional unit of product at a given price results in a corresponding addition to total revenue which, in the final analysis, contributes to net profit an amount equal to the difference between this price and the unit's variable cost.

Generally speaking, accounting is regarded as being utilitarian by nature. Thus, accounting principles are closely related to how accountants do their work in practice. In discussing various definitions of the word "principle," the American Institute of Certified Public Accountants' Committee on Terminology states as follows:

> Initially, accounting postulates are derived from experience and reason; after postulates so derived have proved useful, they become accepted as principles of accounting. When this acceptance is sufficiently widespread, they become part of the 'generally accepted accounting principles' which constitute for accountants the canons of their art.[15]

It is this close relationship between usefulness and accounting principles that offers the strongest likelihood of the ultimate acceptance of direct costing within the framework of generally accepted principles of accounting.

On the other hand, the increasing incidence of guaranteed annual wage plans and the development of automation loom as a serious threat to the acceptance of direct costing. The effect of these factors is to divert the major portion of direct labour and variable overhead into the category of fixed costs. Assuming the maximum development of these factors, it is possible to foresee a time when direct material would constitute the only variable item of manufacturing cost. Under such circumstances, the theoretical soundness of direct costing is questionable. The distinction between the assumed circumstances of the foregoing and those actually encountered in current practice is really only one of degree. As long as there is a considerable body of variable costs, direct costing appears to be sound, even in theory. However, if any substantial portion of the variable costs is eliminated, the method tends to lose its otherwise apparent soundness. In part, the confusion and controversy associated with direct costing results from failure to logically reason the method through to its inevitable conclusion.

Conclusion

Accounting is aptly referred to as the "language of business" and, as such, fulfills an important staff function in business management. With the increasing growth and complexity of modern business, an increasing amount of cost information is necessary to guide management in making decisions. The truth of the matter is that both direct and absorption cost data are

---

[15] Committee on Terminology, Bulletin No. 1, Review and Resume, New York, American Institute of Certified Public Accountants, 1953, p. 11.

required. Accordingly, the controversy between direct costing and absorption costing should center on which method provides a more satisfactory basis for recording and reporting costs. It is necessary to appraise carefully the comparative usefulness of the data supplied by each method. Whichever method is chosen, it should then become the basis for recording and reporting costs, while the data from the other method that is required by management should be developed by supplementary records and analysis. The fact that direct costing lacks general acceptability is important; however, it is always possible to convert the income statement to absorption costing for purposes of external reporting. Thus, it is almost possible to have one's cake and eat it too.

27 *This article, written in the early stages of the direct costing "controversy," places absorption costing and direct costing under the microscope of rigorous mathematical analysis to demonstrate the basic relationship between the two methods.*

The author demonstrates that general statements about the relative effect of either method on reported profits are invalid, and that direct costing simplifies greatly the technique of break-even analysis.

Facts About Direct Costing for Profit Determination*

Gilbert Amerman

Absorption Costing and Direct Costing

INTRODUCTION

The income statement prepared by the orthodox method of absorption costing has a number of disadvantages, among which are the following:

1. It does not distinguish between profits resulting only from sales and the increments to these profits resulting from fixed cost components of inventory change — using the word "profits" in the conventional (absorption cost) sense of the term.

2. It is difficult to understand because it mixes units throughout the income statement: costs which are variable with volume on a short-term basis are mixed with costs which are variable with volume only on a long-term basis. The equation relating incurred cost to cost of goods

* *From* Accounting Research, *Vol. 5, No. 2 (April 1954), pp. 154–166. Reprinted by permission of the publisher.*

sold includes components of fixed as well as variable costs, and so do all the subsequent income statement relationships used to arrive at net profit. This introduces almost at the outset a third variable (volume) into these figures in addition to the variables of price and quantity, with differing possibilities for handling this third variable. In other words, conventional income statements mix units when such mixture is not practically necessary, a procedure that inevitably leads to trouble.

3. It does not localise the errors due to allocating fixed costs to products and those due to estimating standard volume. This is one of the results of mixing units.

4. If any form of burden standard is used, burden volume variance must be included to arrive at profit. Resolution of incurred burden into absorbed and unabsorbed components should be an optional supplementary analysis.

The confusion in units has been expressed by the Research Committee of the National Association of (Cost) Accountants as follows:

> Those who use direct costing design an income statement in which costs are deducted from sales income in the order of their variability with volume. In this statement, sales income, direct costs, and marginal income are all expressed in product units. These units are therefore homogeneous and comparable. At the second step in the statement, total period costs are deducted from total marginal income for the period to obtain net operating profit. In this section of the statement, figures are expressed as dollars per unit of time, and again units are homogeneous. In contrast, the absorption costing income statement mixes costs measured in product units and in time units. The result is that income margins shown in the statement do not show clearly the impact of either variable or fixed costs. In the direct cost statement, marginal income measures the results of management's current decisions affecting sales volume while the net profit measures the effectiveness of long-range policies in balancing productive capacity with sales income. [1]

These shortcomings of the conventional income statement have made many accountants realise that there is something wrong and the problem has given rise to the "direct costers," a school of accountants advocating not only a reclassification of costs in terms of variability, but also a different concept of profit — one which subtracts variable costs of goods sold from income to arrive at profit as is done under the conventional method, but subtracts the fixed costs *incurred* during the period instead of subtracting the fixed cost of goods *sold* as in the conventional method. The profits arrived at by the two methods for any accounting period thus differ by the fixed cost component of the inventory difference for the period in question. [2]

[1] *Direct Costing* — NA(C)A Research Series No. 23, April, 1953, page 1119.
[2] It is assumed that the cost of usage of the fixed assets as represented by the depreciation is included in the fixed components of inventory cost.

Numerous articles on the subject of direct costing for profit determination have appeared in accounting literature, most of which advocated either the use of a direct cost income statement arriving at direct cost profit, or the retention of the conventional statement and conventional profit concept without reclassification of costs.

Strange to relate, little or no attention appears to have been given to the fact that the four objections noted above may be overcome and the two types of units in question segregated by arranging the income statement to arrive at the direct cost profit advocated by the direct costers and adding thereto an increment measuring the effect of the change in fixed cost components of inventory variation. This would eliminate the basic difficulty of mixture of units, without changing the conventional concept of profits.

Most publications on the subject have discussed the pros and cons of the two methods of profit determination at great length with endless assertions and opinions, and reams of illustrative figures. At this point, it appears that a statement of some of the facts about direct costing and the proof of these facts might be in order. Accordingly, the purpose of this paper is to state and prove facts, and so far as possible to refrain from expressing opinions.

The work on which this paper is based was carried on in connection with the NA(C)A research study referred to above and contains the proof for some of the statements made therein.

THE BASIC RELATIONSHIP

Comparison of profit results obtained from a direct cost plan with those obtained from the orthodox absorption cost plan may readily be made by analysis and the difference between them determined. However, some assumptions must be made to eliminate the effect of extraneous variables. These are:

1. A single product, a constant mix of products, or the use of consistent units to measure both production and sales.
2. Fixed costs, unit selling prices, and unit variable costs remain constant.
3. A predetermined fixed cost rate is assumed, so that beginning and ending inventories may be extended at the same unit cost, and over- or under-absorbed fixed costs are assumed to be period costs.
4. If work in process inventories are zero or constant, production may be measured by finished units. Otherwise, equivalent production may be used.

Nomenclature is as follows:

Constants

c_v = unit variable manufacturing cost in $

C_F = total fixed manufacturing cost in $

C_A = total s & a costs (all fixed) in \$
s = unit selling price in \$
H = standard volume in physical units

Variables
y = units manufactured in physical units
x = units sold in physical units
S = total sales in \$
P = total profit in \$
I_B = beginning inventory in \$
I_E = ending inventory in \$

Under absorption costing:
Cost of goods sold = $yc_v + C_F + I_B - I_E$
and total cost = $yc_v + C_F + I_B - I_E + C_A$
and $P = sx - yc_v - C_F - C_A - (I_B - I_E)$

But $I_B - I_E = (x - y)\left(c_v + \dfrac{C_F}{n}\right) = x\dfrac{C_F}{n} - y\dfrac{C_F}{n} + xc_v - yc_v$

since c_v and C_F are constants

$$\underbrace{\therefore P = sx - yc_v - C_F - C_A}_{\substack{\text{Cost of Goods}\\\text{Manufactured}}} \qquad \underbrace{-x\dfrac{C_F}{n} + y\dfrac{C_F}{n} - xc_v + yc_v}_{\text{Inventory Difference}}$$

Since unit variable costs are constant, the costs of goods manufactured is not dependent on an inventory difference.

Regrouping and cancelling yc_v:

$$P = sx - C_F - C_A - xc_v - x\dfrac{C_F}{n} + y\dfrac{C_F}{n}$$

Note that the yc_v terms would not cancel if c_v were not constant:

$$\text{Or } P = \underbrace{sx - (c_vx + C_F + C_A)}_{A} + \underbrace{\dfrac{C_F}{n}(y - x)}_{B} \tag{1}$$

The direct costers advocate determining profit by the equation $P = sx - c_vx - C_F - C_A$. It is thus seen that equation (1), which is the absorption cost profit equation, consists of two parts: (A) the direct cost profit, and (B) the absorption cost increment. It thus constitutes an exact statement of profits as determined by the two methods and the difference between them. Accordingly, it segregates the variable and fixed components of cost.

From the above equation (1), it may be immediately inferred that:

1. The absorption cost profit is equal to the direct cost profit increased by the fixed cost component of the inventory increase or decreased by the fixed cost component of the inventory decrease.

2. Direct cost profit is a linear function of sales only, since P and x are the only variables in the direct cost part of the equation.
3. If $y = x$ (production equals sales), the absorption cost equation reduces to the direct cost equation, and the two profits are identical.
4. If $y > x$ (production greater than sales), absorption cost profit is higher than direct cost profit by the standard fixed cost rate times the difference.
5. If $x > y$ (sales greater than production), absorption cost profit is less than direct cost profit by the standard fixed cost rate times the difference.

The reader is reminded that the accuracy of the above statement is subject to the assumptions stated, which exclude the effect of extraneous variables.

APPLICATIONS OF THE BASIC RELATIONSHIP

Additional facts about direct costs for profit determination may be obtained very readily from the basic relationship described above. The facts demonstrated have been selected primarily for their utility, although confusion in the literature was the determining factor in one case. On the basis of the assumptions previously noted, the following facts may be proved:

(1) If production is constant ($y = k$), profit is a linear function of sales only, for both absorption and direct costing:

(*A*) *Absorption Costing*

$$P = sx - c_v x - C_F - C_A + \frac{C_F}{n} y - \frac{C_F}{n} x \qquad \text{(Equation (1) for}$$
$$= x\left(s - c_v - \frac{C_F}{n}\right) - C_F - C_A + \frac{C_F}{n} y \qquad \text{Absorption Costing)}$$

Since the above is in the form $y = ax + b$, it follows that profit is a linear function of sales only under absoprtion costing.

(*B*) *Direct Costing*

$$P = sx - c_v x - C_F - C_A \qquad \text{(Equation (1) for Direct Costing)}$$
$$= x(s - c_v) - C_F - C_A$$

Again, the equation is in the form of $y = ax + b$, and again profit is a linear function of sales only.

(2) If sales are constant ($x = k$), profit is a linear function of production only when absorption costing is used, and profit is constant when direct costing is used.

(*A*) *Absorption Costing*

$$P = sx - c_v x - C_F - C_A + \frac{C_F}{n} y - \frac{C_F}{n} x \qquad \text{(Equation (1) for}$$
$$= \frac{C_F}{n} y + \left(sx - c_v x - C_F - C_A - \frac{C_F}{n} x\right) \qquad \text{Absorption Costing)}$$

Since the equation is in the form $y = ax + b$, profit is a linear function of production only.

(B) *Direct Costing*

$$P = sx - c_v x - C_F - C_A \qquad \text{(Equation (1) for Direct Costing)}$$

Since all terms on the right-hand side of the equation are constant, profit is constant.

(3) If sales are constant, the difference in profit during any two time intervals equals the difference in burden absorption for the two intervals:

Let $O_1 = $ the over-absorbed burden for the first time interval and $O_2 = $ the over-absorbed burden for the second.

$$O_1 = \frac{C_F}{n} (y_1 - n) \text{ and } O_2 = \frac{C_F}{n} (y_2 - n)$$

$$O_2 - O_1 = \frac{C_F}{n} (y_2 - n - y_1 + n) = \frac{C_F}{n} (y_2 - y_1)$$

$$P_1 = K + \frac{C_F}{n} y_1 \text{ and } P_2 = K + \frac{C_F}{n} y_2 \text{ since sales are constant}$$

$$\therefore P_2 - P_1 = \frac{C_F}{n} (y_2 - y_1)$$

$$\therefore P_2 - P_1 = O_2 - O_1$$

(4) The difference between the two methods of cost determination for any time interval equals the over-absorbed burden for the time interval in question if, and only if, sales for the period equal the standard volume for the period — in other words, when the amount sold out of inventory is equal to the difference between standard volume and actual production for the period:

$$O = \frac{C_F}{n} (y - n) \text{ and the difference between the two methods (absorp-}$$

tion cost increment$) = \dfrac{C_F}{n} (y - x)$

Assume that the over-absorbed burden equals the absorption cost increment. Then:

$$\frac{C_F}{n} (y - n) = \frac{C_F}{n} (y - x)$$

or $y - n = y - x$

or $n = x$

$\therefore$ The proposition stated is true only for the specific condition noted.

(5) If an enterprise makes profits continuously, the ratio of the cumulative difference between the two methods of cost determination to the cumulative profit by either method approaches zero as time approaches infinity.

Let $P_D = $ cumulative direct cost profit

and $P_A = $ absorption cost profit

Let $t \to \infty$

Then the absorption cost increment, $\frac{C_F}{n}$ $(y - x)$, approaches a finite limit set by storage capacity, financial limitations, etc.

And P_D and P_A both approach infinity since x approaches infinity.

$$\therefore \frac{\frac{C_F}{n}(y - x)}{P_D} \to 0$$

$$\text{and } \frac{\frac{C_F}{n}(y - x)}{P_A} \to 0$$

In the above examples, the slopes and intercepts may be readily determined for functions in the form $y = ax + b$, since a is the slope of the straight line and b is the y intercept.

These are simple relationships readily derived from the basic relationship expressing both direct and absorption cost profits as functions of the pertinent variables. The basic relationship is a simple tool that permits the testing of many propositions about direct and absorption costs. However, the reader is cautioned against the use of the tool without carefully noting the assumptions previously listed in connection with it.

RELATIVE RATES OF CHANGE IN PROFITS — DIRECT VERSUS ABSORPTION COSTING

Does the use of absorption costing, as opposed to direct costing, tend to level profits? Some interesting assertions on this point have been made in the literature. On the basis of the assumptions previously noted, the facts are as follows:

Case 1 — Sales and production both constant

The basis equation indicates that direct cost and absorption cost profits are both constant (although generally not equal) under these conditions. Therefore, neither method tends to level profits as opposed to the other.

Case 2 — Sales constant — production continuously variable

The direct cost profit is constant, since it is a function of sales only, but the absorption cost profit is continuously variable, since the absorption cost increment is a function of $(y - x)$. Therefore, the use of direct costing tends to level profits as opposed to absorption costing.

Case 3 — Production constant — sales continuously variable

To analyse this case, it is necessary to get the slope of the line representing the direct and absorption cost profits as functions of sales. This may be done very readily from the respective equations as follows:

For direct cost profit

$$P = sx - c_v x - C_F - C_A$$
$$= \frac{x(s - c_v)}{\text{Slope}} - \frac{(C_F + C_A)}{\text{Intercept}}$$

For absorption cost profit

$$P = sx - c_v x - C_F - C_A + \frac{C_F}{n} y - \frac{C_F}{n} x$$
$$= \frac{x\left(s - c_v x - \dfrac{C_F}{n}\right)}{\text{Slope}} - \frac{C_F - C_A + \dfrac{C_F}{n} y}{\text{Intercept}}$$

It will be noted that the slope of the direct cost profit line is $s - c_v$, while the slope of the absorption cost profit line is $s - c_v - \dfrac{C_F}{n}$. Since $\dfrac{C_F}{n}$ is always positive, the slope of the absorption cost profit line is always algebraically less than the slope of the direct cost profit line.

Case 3(1), where $s - c_v > 0$ (there is a direct cost profit)

As long as $\dfrac{C_F}{n}$ is not greater than $2(s - c_v)$, the slope of the absorption cost line has an absolute value less than the slope of the direct cost profit line, which means that the direct cost profit is more variable than the absorption cost profit.

Case 3(2), where $s - c_v = 0$ (break-even on a direct cost basis)

The slope of the direct cost profit line $= 0$, while that of the absorption cost profit line is negative, which means that the absorption cost profit is more variable than the direct cost profit.

Case 3(3), where $s - c_v < 0$ (there is a direct cost loss)

The absolute value of the slope of the absorption cost profit line is greater than the slope of the direct cost profit line, which means that absorption cost profit is more variable than direct cost profit.

For Case 3, the direct cost profit is more variable than the absorption cost profit under conditions normally met with in business, but the exceptions noted above should be kept in mind.

Case 4 — Production and sales both vary continuously and independently of each other

Whether the absorption cost increment is in or out of phase with the direct cost profit is indeterminate, and thus the absorption cost profit may be more or less variable than the direct cost profit, or may show no difference in variability.

The above facts show that generalisations with respect to the levelling of profits are dependent on the specific circumstances assumed.

CONCLUSIONS

Two major objections to the use of the conventional absorption cost income statement are (1) it does not distinguish between profits resulting only from sales and those resulting from inventory changes, and (2) it is difficult to understand and analyse because it mixes costs which are variable with volume on a short-term basis with those which are variable with volume only on a long-term basis. The first difficulty is the result of the second more fundamental objection.

These objections may be overcome by (1) abandoning the present concept of profits and reporting it as the difference between income and the sum of variable cost of goods sold plus total fixed costs incurred, or (2) retaining the present concept of profits but reclassifying the income statement in such a way that the direct cost profit is first computed and the absorption cost increment constituting the fixed cost component of inventory difference thereafter added.

The present study has demonstrated the basic relationship between the two methods and proved some facts arising from this relationship. It also offers a tool for the determination of additional facts.

It has also demonstrated that the use of one concept of profit as opposed to the other does not necessarily level profits. This depends on the circumstances.

It is hoped that the presentation and proof of basic facts will afford a more substantial basis for thinking in connection with the direct cost plan of accounting.

Direct Costing and Break-even Points

EFFECT ON CONVENTIONAL ANALYSIS

If direct costs are used for profit determination in the sense that the direct cost profit is the final profit, break-even computations are greatly simplified, since the fixed components of inventory differences need not be taken into account.

It has been shown on pages 154 and 155 that if we assume a single product or constant mix of products, constant fixed costs, constant unit selling prices, constant unit variable costs, a predetermined burden rate, and over- or under-absorbed burden a period cost, the profit under absorption costing is given by:

$$P = sx - (c_v x + C_F + C_A) + \frac{C_F}{n}(y - x)$$

and the profit under direct costing is given by:

$$P = sx - (c_v x + C_F + C_A)$$

the difference between the two profits (absorption cost increment) being:

$$\frac{C_F}{n} (y - x)$$

Under absorption costing, the graphical representation of profit is complicated by the fact that profit is a function of two variables, y and x. Accordingly the relationship may be expressed graphically by (1) a plane on a three-dimensional plot or (2) a family of straight lines, each one of which represents profit as a linear function of sales for a given assumed value of $y - x$, thus reducing the variables from three to two for each such line. In practice, this dilemma is frequently avoided by an assumption about inventory change that permits the use of a single straight line.

Under direct costing, graphical representation is simple, since inspection of the profit equation shows that profit as a function of sales may be represented by a single straight line with a slope of $s - c_v$ and a y intercept of $-C_F - C_A$.

Graphical representation of costs and profits by a family of straight lines and by a single straight line is illustrated on Diagram 1, which is based on the following table of values:

$$c_v = 5$$
$$C_F = 20$$
$$C_A = 10$$
$$s = 12$$
$$n = 10$$

$$
\begin{aligned}
P &= sx - (c_v x + C_F + C_A) + \frac{C_F}{n} (y - x) \\
&= \underbrace{12x}_{\text{Sales}} - \underbrace{(5x + 20 + 10)}_{\text{Direct Costs}} + \underbrace{2(y - x)}_{\substack{\text{Absorption} \\ \text{Cost} \\ \text{Increment}}}
\end{aligned}
$$

If $y - x = 3$, $P = 12x - (5x + 30) + 6 = 7x - 24$ for absorption costing.

If $y - x = 6$, $P = 12x - (5x + 30) + 12 = 7x - 18$ for absorption costing.

For both of the above cases, the direct cost profit is given by:

$$P = 12x - (5x + 30) = 7x - 30$$

DIAGRAM 1

Break-even Analysis

Family of Curves for $y - x = 0$, 3 and 6
Showing Sales, Direct Costs, Absorption Costs, and Profit on Both Bases

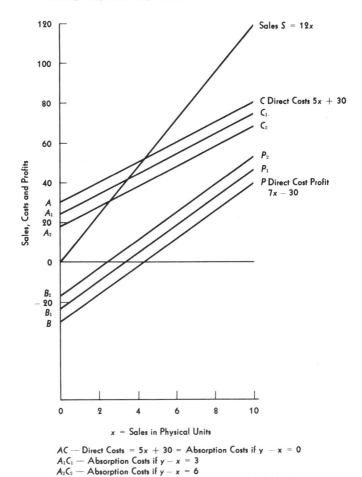

x = Sales in Physical Units

AC — Direct Costs = $5x + 30$ = Absorption Costs if $y - x = 0$
A_1C_1 — Absorption Costs if $y - x = 3$
A_2C_2 — Absorption Costs if $y - x = 6$
BP — Direct Cost Profit = $7x - 30$ = Absorption Cost Profit if $y - x = 0$
B_1P_1 — Absorption Cost Profit if $y - x = 3$
B_2P_2 — Absorption Cost Profit if $y - x = 6$

Table of values for the construction of Diagram 1 follows:

				Direct Cost Profit	Absorption Cost Increment	Absorption Cost		Absorption Cost Profit	
x	y	$y-x$	$12x$	$5x+30$	$7x-30$	$2(y-x)$	$5x+24$	$5x+18$	$7x-24$	$7x-18$
10	10	0	120	80	40	0				
7	10	3	84	65	19	6	59		25	
4	7	3	48	50	−2	6	44		4	
4	10	6	48	50	−2	12		38		10
10	16	6	120	80	40	12		68		52

Inspection of the chart indicates that there are three cost lines, one for each of the three assumed values for $y - x$, and thus three break-even points if absorption costs are used, and a single cost line and thus a single break-even point if direct costs are used. When production and sales are equal, the absorption cost line coincides with the direct cost line. Also, there are three profit lines, one for each of the three assumed values of $y - x$ if absorption costs are used, and a single profit line if direct costs are used. Similarly, when production and sales are equal, the absorption cost profit line coincides with the direct cost profit line.

EFFECT ON BREAK-EVEN LINE

It has been noted that under absorption costing, profit as a function of production and sales entails consideration of three variables, and may be represented as a plane with three-dimensional co-ordinates. However, if profit is zero, the number of variables is reduced to two and the relationship between production and sales may be represented by a straight line, every point on which satisfies the break-even requirement. This may be proved from the profit equation for absorption costing as follows:

$$P = sx - c_v x - C_F - C_A + \frac{C_F}{n}(y - x) = 0$$

$$= x\left(s - c_v - \frac{C_F}{n}\right) + y\frac{C_F}{n} - C_F - C_A = 0$$

$$\text{or } y = \frac{-\left[s - c_v - \dfrac{C_F}{n}\right]x}{\dfrac{C_F}{n}} + \frac{C_F + C_A}{\dfrac{C_F}{n}}$$

The last equation proves that the relationship between y and x under break-even conditions is represented by a straight line with a slope equal to the coefficient of x and a y intercept equal to $\dfrac{C_F + C_A}{\dfrac{C_F}{n}}$. Use of this relationship makes it possible to determine quickly the sales volume needed to break even at a given level of production or the production volume needed to break even at a given level of sales under absorption costing. This is illustrated in Diagram 2, which is computed from the following figures:

$$s = 10, c_v = 5, C_F = 20, C_A = 10, n = 10$$

Substituting these figures in the profit equation when $P = 0$ and simplifying, we get:

$$y = 15 - 1.5x$$

Setting up a table of values for x and y, assuming values for x and solving for y:

x	y
0	15
5	7.5
10	0
6	6

This is the table from which Diagram 2 is constructed.

If it be required to determine the break-even point when production and sales are equal, this may be done by substituting y for x in the equation $y = 15 - 1.5x$, from which we get $y = x = 6$. Similarly, any other relationship between x and y would make it possible to represent the break-even condition by a point on the break-even line.

The interpretation of the graph follows:

(1) Point P is the break-even point when production equals sales, one of the conditions under which the break-even condition may be represented by a point under absorption costing.

(2) The y intercept $(0, 15)$ shows that it is possible to break even at zero sales under absorption costing by producing 15 units, since the over-absorbed burden is equal to the selling and administrative costs. $(5 \times 2 = 10)$. This is, of course, contingent on the previously stated assumption that the over-absorbed burden is a period credit.

(3) The x intercept $(10, 0)$ shows that it is possible to break even at zero production under absorption costing by selling 10 units since gross profits at standard equals under absorbed burden plus selling and administrative costs $(3 \times 10 = 20 + 10)$.

(4) Every point on the straight line satisfies the condition $P = 0$ and thus gives a relationship between y and x at which the company will break even under absorption costing.

If direct costing is used, profit is a function of sales only and the relationship between profit and sales may be represented by a line using two dimensional co-ordinates, as has been previously noted. However, if profit is zero, there is one and only one point on this line which satisfies the break-even

DIAGRAM 2

The Break-even Line for Absorption Costing and Break-even Point for Direct Costing

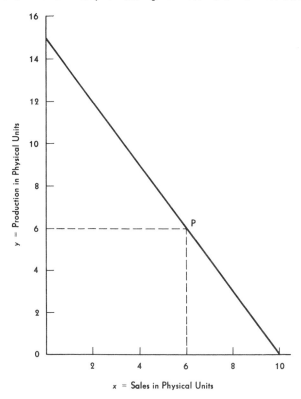

x = Sales in Physical Units

y = Production in Physical Units

requirements. This may be proved from the profit equation for direct costing as follows:

$$P = sx - c_v x - C_F - C_A = 0$$
$$= x(s - c_v) - (C_F + C_A)$$
$$\text{and } x = \frac{C_F + C_A}{s - c_v}$$

The last expression gives the break-even point.
Using the figures previously assumed:

$$x = \frac{20 + 10}{10 - 5} = 6$$

The point *P* on the chart is thus the break-even point under absorption costing when production and sales are equal, and it is also the break-even point under direct costing regardless of the relationship between production and sales.

The discussion on the break-even line illustrates the reduction of the line which is needed under absorption costing to a point under direct costing. If only direct costing is considered, the break-even line would not be applicable, and the break-even point would be the point on the direct-cost profit line shown in Diagram 1 at which profit is zero. Using the illustrative figures on pages 161 and 164, the direct profit is $7x - 30$, and the break-even point for this example is therefore $x = \dfrac{30}{7}$.

The reader is reminded that this analysis is subject to the assumptions noted on pages 153 and 154.

CONCLUSIONS

Break-even analysis is greatly simplified when direct costing is used as compared with absorption costing. Under direct costing, profit is a function of one other variable — sales — and the condition that profit is zero determines the amount of sales needed to satisfy this requirement, with the result that the break-even condition is a point on the profit line.

However, under absorption costing, profit is a function of two other variables — sales and production — and the requirement that profit is zero merely reduces the total number of variables to two, the relation between which may be represented by a straight line. An additional assumption or relationship is then needed to determine the amount of sales required to break even and thus reduce the break-even condition to a single point on the line.

2 8 *This article investigates analytically the impact of various inventory costing methods on the pattern of profit differences. Relative merits of various accounting methods are not considered, but the thorough discussion should aid management in choosing among methods.*

Conclusions reached far beyond — and correct — the usual simple generalizations about the influence of various inventory costing procedures on profit.

Techniques of sensitivity analysis expose relevant behavioral implications which need further study.

The Effect of Inventory Costing Methods on Full and Direct Costing*

Yuji Ijiri, Robert K. Jaedicke and John L. Livingstone†

I

Since about 1950, the controversy over full vs. direct costing has generated a voluminous literature[1] largely aimed at the relative merits of each (1) for external financial reporting purposes or (2) for internal use in

* From The Journal of Accounting Research, *Vol. 3, No. 1 (Spring, 1965), pp. 63–74. Reprinted by permission of the editor.*

† This study was supported, in part, by funds made available by the Ford Foundation to the Graduate School of Business, Stanford University, and, in part, by a Ford Foundation Doctoral Fellowship. However, the conclusions, opinions and other statements are those of the authors and are not necessarily those of the Ford Foundation. The authors wish to thank Charles T. Horngren, Gordon Shillinglaw and Carl L. Nelson for their detailed comments and suggestions on an earlier draft of this paper.

[1] See the extensive bibliography in Cecil Gillespie, *Standard and Direct Costing* (Englewood Cliffs: Prentice-Hall, Inc., 1962), pp. 141–43.

441

management planning and control.[2] The arguments rest on the assumption that each method produces different results; obviously if each method produced exactly the same results then controversy is idle.

The analyses to date have largely ignored the effect of the inventory *costing method*. A typical discussion of the generalized conditions which create differences between direct and full cost profit is: "When production exceeds sales (i.e., in-process and finished inventories increasing), absorption costing shows a higher profit than does direct costing. When sales exceed production (i.e., in-process and finished inventories decreasing), absorption costing shows a lower profit than does direct costing."[3]

This quotation emphasizes the relationship between production and sales *quantity* as the important variable. Although often correct, it is not universally valid. Under both the *FIFO* and the average inventory methods, it is possible for inventory quantity to increase and for direct cost and full cost profit to *be the same* or for direct cost profit *to exceed* full cost profit. Conversely, it is possible under FIFO or average cost for inventory quantity to decrease with direct cost showing a lower profit than full cost, contrary to the usual generalizations.

The difference in profit between full and direct cost profit is attributable to the amount of fixed cost charged to inventory; this amount is affected not only by the quantities produced but by the inventory costing method employed. It is the effect of the inventory costing method which is largely overlooked.

To illustrate, assume the following:

	1963	*1964*
Fixed Manufacturing Costs	$50,000	$50,000
Ending Inventory Quantity	5,000 units	10,000 units
Production Quantity	50,000 units	100,000 units
Sales	(Not relevant)	95,000 units

Under FIFO, the 1964 beginning inventory fixed cost would be $5,000 (i.e., ($50,000/50,000) × 5,000 units). The fixed cost in the 1964 ending inventory under FIFO would also be $5,000, calculated as ($50,000/100,000) × 10,000 units = $5,000. Hence, the two cost methods, direct and full cost, will give the *same* profit since the fixed cost portions of the beginning and the ending inventory are the same, even though inventory

---

[2] See James M. Fremgen, "The Direct Costing Controversy — An Identification of the Issues," *The Accounting Review*, January, 1964, pp. 43–51, for an excellent discussion of the issues concerning external reporting; and Charles T. Horngren, *Cost Accounting, A Managerial Emphasis* (Englewood Cliffs: Prentice-Hall, Inc., 1962), pp. 346–354, for an excellent discussion of the relative merits of the two methods for internal use.

[3] N.A.A. Research Report No. 23, "Direct Costing," *N.A.(C.)A. Bulletin,* April, 1953, page 1116.

quantity has increased (i.e., production exceeds sales). As will be shown later, this will happen under FIFO anytime the inventory quantity is increased proportionately with production quantity.

Assume, now, that 1964 is unchanged, but that production in 1963 was 100,000 units instead of 50,000. Then the 1964 beginning inventory (fixed cost portion) would have been only $2,500 while the 1964 ending inventory (fixed cost portion) would have been $5,000. In this case, full cost profit would be greater than direct cost profit by $2,500.

Alternatively, if production in 1963 had been 25,000 units, the fixed cost in the 1964 beginning inventory would have been $10,000 while the comparable amount in the 1964 ending inventory would be $5,000. In this case, direct cost profit is greater than full cost profit by $5,000. As the above examples show, three different results are possible and yet, *in each case, production quantity exceeded sales quantity during 1964.*

The main purpose of this paper (Part II) is to investigate analytically the differences between full and direct cost profit so far as the impact of inventory costing method is concerned. The above example shows that the inventory costing method is important in determining the pattern of profit differences. This example also illustrates the error in the usual generalizations regarding the difference between full and direct cost profit. However, having pointed out that the usual analysis is incomplete, it is necessary to investigate the effect of inventory costing methods on full and direct costing and to derive the generalized conditions which can be used to predict the pattern of profit differences. This investigation is carried out in the spirit that a more precise and complete statement of the difference between full and direct costing will aid in the choice between the two methods for any given purpose. We do not discuss the relative merits of these accounting methods; we believe, however, that a precise statement of the difference clarifies the error in the generalization.

Often, intuition is sufficient to detect incorrect generalizations. Here, to isolate the pertinent variables in the inventory costing method and in order to *analyse* the effect of each critical variable, we feel it necessary to employ simple algebra. For the reader who does not wish to follow this detail, a summary of the results appears in Table 1 at the end of Part II, and there is a nonmathematical synopsis in the *Summary and Conclusions* (Part V).

*II. Inventory Costing Methods and the Difference Between
Full and Direct Cost Profits*

As mentioned, the differences in profit and inventory cost under full and direct cost are caused by the difference between the fixed costs that are included in the beginning inventory and those included in the ending inventory. To show this, let us denote profit under full costing by *PF*, profit under direct costing by *PD*, the variable cost portion of beginning and ending inventory by *BV* and *EV*, respectively, and the fixed cost portion of beginning and ending inventory by *BN* and *EN*, respectively (*N* for non-variable). Then, under direct costing, inventory cost is given by *BV* and *EV*, whereas under full costing inventory cost is given by *BV* + *BN* and *EV* + *EN*.

Consider now a profit figure *PK* that is calculated by setting both beginning inventory cost and ending inventory cost equal to zero. Then, this profit *PK* must be the same for both full and direct costing, since only the inventory values are affected by the two cost methods. Using the profit *PK*, the profit calculation under full cost and direct cost can be stated in the following way:

(1) $$PF = PK + (EV + EN) - (BV + BN),$$
(2) $$PD = PK + EV - BV.$$

From these equations, the following relationship can be derived:

(3) $$PF - PD = EN - BN.$$

EN is calculated differently under different methods of inventory costing, e.g., average cost, FIFO, LIFO, etc. Under average cost, for example, the sum of *BN* and the fixed cost portion of current period's manufacturing cost, denoted by *MN*, is allocated to ending inventory according to the ratio of physical ending inventory quantity (denoted by *w*) to the sum of *w* and the current period's sales quantity (denoted by *s*). That is, under (periodic) average cost

(4) $$EN = \frac{w}{w + s} (BN + MN),$$

hence, substituting (4) into (3), we have:

$$
\begin{aligned}
(5) \quad PF - PD &= \frac{w}{w + s} (BN + MN) - BN, \\
&= \frac{w}{w + s} MN - \frac{s}{w + s} BN, \\
&= \frac{w(MN) - s(BN)}{w + s} = \frac{ws}{w + s} \left[\frac{MN}{s} - \frac{BN}{w} \right].
\end{aligned}
$$

From expression (5): the difference between full and direct cost profit (*PF* − *PD*) depends on the relative size of *w*(*MN*) compared with *s*(*BN*), or equivalently, on the relative size of *MN/s* compared with *BN/w*. To say that *PF* will be greater than *PD* when *w* is greater than the beginning inventory quantity is an oversimplified and possibly erroneous statement under average cost. If *w* is greater than the beginning inventory quantity, but *MN/s* is less than *BN/w*, then direct cost profit, *PD*, will be greater than full cost profit, *PF*.

Note also that the relationship between full and direct cost profit in time period *t* depends on *w* and *s* for period *t* − 1. This is because of the *BN* term. The beginning inventory (fixed cost portion), *BN*, for period *t* is the ending inventory, *EN*, for period *t* − 1. *EN* for period *t* − 1 depends on

w and s for period $t - 1$. Hence, the difference between full and direct cost profit for the current year is dependent on the relationship between sales quantity and ending inventory quantity for the previous period, $t - 1$, and hence for all previous periods.

Rather than analyse the average cost case further, let us turn to the more interesting cases of *FIFO* and *LIFO*. Under *FIFO*, the results will depend on whether the sales quantity for the period is greater or less than the beginning inventory quantity. In the analysis which follows, it is assumed that sales are greater than or equal to the beginning inventory. The reasonableness of this assumption seems clear; however, for the value of completeness, the case of $s \leq w^-$ (the inventory quantity at the beginning of the period will be denoted by a "$-$" used as a superscript) is discussed in footnote 4.

Under *FIFO*, if $s \geqq w^-$, the total amount of fixed cost in the beginning inventory, *BN*, is charged to cost of sales for the period and *EN*, the fixed cost in the ending inventory, is determined by the total fixed manufacturing cost for the period, *MN*, and the ratio of w (the quantity in the ending inventory) to q (the quantity produced during the period). That is,

$$(6) \qquad EN = \frac{w}{q} MN.$$

Using equation (3) and substituting (6) for *EN*, the difference between full and direct cost profit is:

$$(7) \qquad PF - PD = \frac{w}{q} MN - BN = w\left(\frac{MN}{q} - \frac{BN}{w}\right).$$

Therefore, $PF - PD$ depends on the relative size of MN/q and BN/w. (Remember that under average cost it was MN/s and BN/w.) If $w > w^-$, but $(MN/q) < (BN/w)$, the direct cost profit, *PD*, will be greater than full cost profit, *PF*, contrary to the generalizations cited above.

The above result which holds under the condition that $s \geq w^-$ can be extended if we accept the following two reasonable assumptions, namely, (a) in the previous period sales, s^-, were at least as great as the beginning inventory quantity in the previous period, w^{--}, i.e., $s^- \geq w^{--}$, and (b) the fixed manufacturing cost is the same for both periods, i.e., $MN = MN^-$. Then, the fixed cost portion of the beginning inventory, *BN*, can be expressed as a proportion of the fixed manufacturing cost as follows:

$$(8) \qquad BN = \frac{w^-}{q^-} MN^-,$$

which is, of course, analogous to (6).

Substituting equation (8) for the *BN* term in equation (7), we have:

$$(9) \qquad PF - PD = \frac{w}{q} MN - \frac{w^-}{q^-} MN^-.$$

Now, using the second assumption that fixed manufacturing cost is the same from one period to the next (i.e., $MN = MN^-$), the sign of the difference,

$PF - PD$, is not determined by q and s as usually stated but, rather, by the sign of $(w/q) - (w^-/q^-)$. That is, under *FIFO*, the difference between full and direct cost profit for the current period depends upon production quantity and ending inventory quantity for the previous period $(t - 1)$ as well as the same quantities for period t, the current period, provided that sales quantity is at least as great as beginning inventory quantity in both periods and that the fixed manufacturing cost is the same for both periods.[4]

[4] The above analysis assumes that sales quantity for period t is greater than the beginning inventory. The case where this assumption does not hold would seem to be very unusual. However, to show the significance of the assumption, this case will be analysed.

If $s \leqq w^-$, then EN consists of MN and a portion of BN that is determined by the ratio of $w^- s$ to w^-. Recall that in the case where a $s \geqq w^-$, the fixed portion of the ending inventory, EN, is based on MN only. However, where $s \leqq w^-$, a portion of the fixed cost in the beginning inventory (BN) is carried forward into EN. This amount is determined by the proportion of the beginning inventory quantity which remains unsold, or $(w^- - s)/w^-$. Hence,

$$(1)' \qquad\qquad EN = MN + \frac{w^- - s}{w^-} BN.$$

Recall that,

$$(2)' \qquad\qquad PF - PD = EN - BN.$$

Then by substitution,

$$(3)' \qquad\qquad PF - PD = MN + \frac{w^- - s}{w^-} BN - BN.$$

By combining terms, we have,

$$(4)' \qquad\qquad PF - PD = MN - \frac{s}{w^-} BN = s \left(\frac{MN}{s} - \frac{BN}{w^-} \right).$$

Thus, when $s \leqq w^-$, the sign of $PF - PD$ is determined by the sign of $(MN/s) - (BN/w^-)$. (Again compare this with the result under average cost where the sign of $PF - PD$ is determined by the sign of $(MN/s) - (BN/w)$.)

As in the case of $s \geqq w^-$, if we make the same two assumptions, i.e., $s^- \geqq w^- -$ and $MN = MN^-$, the above result can be developed further as follows. Recall, now, from equation (8) that if sales quantity in the previous year is greater than or equal to the beginning inventory.

$$BN = \frac{w^-}{q^-} MN^-.$$

By substitution $(4)'$, can be rewritten as follows:

$$(5)' \qquad\qquad PF - PD = MN - \frac{s}{w^-} \left(\frac{w^-}{q^-} MN^- \right).$$

By canceling w^-:

$$(6)' \qquad\qquad PF - PD = MN - \frac{s}{q^-} MN^-.$$

Hence, in the case where $s \leqq w^-$, but $s^- \geqq w^- -$ and $MN = MN^-$, the sign of the difference between full and direct cost profit is determined by the sign of $q^- - s$. The full cost profit will be greater than the direct cost profit if $s < q^-$ and less than if $s > q^-$.

If, however, in the previous period the sales quantity was also less than the beginning inventory quantity, then $PF - PD$ is related not only with MN in the current period and the previous period but also MN for earlier periods.

LIFO and Standard Cost. The results under the *LIFO* and under the standard cost methods of inventory costing are much simpler than those under *FIFO* and the average cost methods. Also, the results under the *LIFO* and the standard cost methods of inventory costing are much more in accord with the usual statements on the differences between direct and full cost profits.

Under (periodic) *LIFO*, if $s \le q$, then

$$(10) \qquad EN = \frac{q - s}{q} MN + BN,$$

and by using (3),

$$PF - PD = \frac{q - s}{q} MN + BN - BN,$$

$$(11) \qquad = \frac{q - s}{q} MN,$$

$$= \frac{w - w^-}{q} MN,$$

since

$$(12) \qquad w = w^- + q - s$$

and

$$(13) \qquad q - s = w - w^-.$$

If, on the other hand, $s \ge q$, then

$$(14) \qquad EN = \frac{w}{w^-} BN,$$

and by using (3),

$$(15) \qquad PF - PD = \frac{w}{w^-} BN - BN,$$

$$= \frac{w - w^-}{w^-} BN.$$

From the above analysis [equation (11)] it can be seen that if the ending inventory is greater than the beginning inventory quantity (i.e., $q > s$), then full cost will *always* give a greater profit than direct cost — a conclusion which agrees with the usual statements. If, on the other hand, the ending inventory quantity is less than the beginning inventory quantity (i.e., $q < s$ or $w < w^-$), then direct cost profit will always be greater than full cost profit, as shown by equation (15).

Finally, under a standard cost method, the results are similar to those under *LIFO*.[5] Let us denote by α the fixed inventory cost per unit and use

---

[5] See Gilbert Amerman, "Facts About Direct Costing for Profit Determination," *Accounting Research,* Vol. 5, April, 1954, pp. 154–66, for a mathematical treatment of the difference between full costing and direct costing. In his analysis, Amerman assumes that inventory is valued at standard cost. He does not, however, cover the FIFO, LIFO, or average cost cases.

the superscript * to denote the standard or budgeted figure. Then, since the standard fixed cost per unit, α^*, is used in calculating the inventory cost under full costing, we have:

(16) $$EN = \alpha^* w,$$

and

(17) $$BN = \alpha^{-*} w^-.$$

Then from equation (3),

(18) $$PF - PD = \alpha^* w - \alpha^{-*} w^-.$$

If the standard cost does not change from one period to the next, that is, $\alpha^* = \alpha^{-*}$, then (18) is reduced to:

(19) $$PF - PD = \alpha^* (w - w^-).$$

In this case, the usual generalizations about direct costing and full costing apply. That is, if inventory quantity is increasing, i.e., production exceeds sales), then $w > w^-$ and $PF > PD$. If sales exceeds production, then $w^- > w$ and $PD > PF$.

Table 1 summarizes the expression for $PF - PD$ under various inventory costing methods.

III. Full Cost vs. Direct Cost — Differences in Profit Variance Patterns

For external reporting purposes, the pattern of differences between direct and full cost (absolute) profit is important and useful. This is because absolute profit is normally the basis for external reporting. For management control, however, it is usually the variance of the reported profit from some pre-established profit budget which is reported. Hence, for many internal uses, the pattern of differences in the profit *variance* rather than the pattern of differences in *absolute* profit is the critical factor. There may be vast differences in absolute profits as reported by the two cost methods and yet there may be little or no difference in the variance patterns. The factors which cause differences in profit variance are not the same as those which cause differences in the pattern of absolute profits. In this part of the paper the variables which are important in accounting for differences in the pattern of profit variances are analysed.

The deviation from a profit budget or the profit variances under full costing and direct costing (denoted by VF and VD, respectively) are given by the following equations, where * denotes the budgeted quantities.

(20) $$VF = PF - PF^*,$$

(21) $$VD = PD - PD^*.$$

TABLE 1

Differences in Full and Direct Cost Profit

Inventory Costing Methods	$PF - PD$
Average	$\dfrac{ws}{w + s}\left(\dfrac{MN}{s} - \dfrac{BN}{w}\right)$
FIFO with $s \geq w^-$	$w\left(\dfrac{MN}{q} - \dfrac{BN}{w}\right)$
FIFO with $s \leq w^-$	$s\left(\dfrac{MN}{s} - \dfrac{BN}{w^-}\right)$
LIFO with $s \leq q$	$(w - w^-)\dfrac{MN}{q}$
LIFO with $s \geq q$	$(w - w^-)\dfrac{BN}{w^-}$
Standard	$\alpha^*(w - w^-)$

For those who have not read Part II, the notation used in Table I is:

PF = profit under full costing.
PD = profit under direct cost.
MN = the fixed cost portion of the current period's manufacturing cost.
BN = the fixed cost portion of beginning inventory.
w = ending inventory quantity.
w^- = beginning inventory quantity.
s = current period's quantity sold.
q = the quantity produced in the current period.
α^* = standard fixed cost per unit.
(Note) If $s = w^-$ then $w = q$ by equation (12), hence the above two expressions for FIFO are the same. If $s = q$, then $w = w^-$ by equation (12), hence the above two expressions for LIFO are the same.

By using equation (3) we have,

$$(22) \qquad VF - VD = (PF - PF^*) - (PD - PD^*)$$
$$= (PF - PD) - (PF^* - PD^*).$$

The first term, $PF - PD$, has been analysed in Part II under various inventory costing methods. Therefore, the second term is the only one which now needs to be explained. By applying the same process as in equations (1) through (3) for $PF^* - PD^*$, we have,

$$(23) \qquad PF^* - PD^* = EN^* - BN^*.$$

However, as observed in (15) and (16), $EN^* - BN^*$ may be expressed as

$$(24) \qquad EN^* - BN^* = \alpha^* w^* - \alpha^{-*} w^{-*}.$$

If the same standard cost per unit is used for both beginning and ending inventory, we have

$$(25) \qquad \alpha^{-*} = \alpha^*,$$

hence

(26) $$EN^* - BN^* = \alpha^*(w^* - w^{-*}).$$

From this we can see that

(27) $$VF - VD < PF - PD \text{ if } w^* > w^{-*},$$
$$VF - VD = PF - PD \text{ if } w^* = w^{-*},$$
$$VF - VD > PF - PD \text{ if } w^* < w^{-*}.$$

Namely, when there is no change in the unit standard cost, (a) the difference in profit variances under full and direct costing will be smaller than the difference in absolute profits, i.e., $PF - PD$) under the two costing methods if the budgeted inventory quantity is greater at the end of the period than at the beginning of the period, (b) the difference in profit variance will be exactly equal to the difference in absolute profits if the budgeted inventory quantity is the same at the end as at the beginning, and (c) the difference in profit variances will be greater than the difference in absolute profits if the budgeted inventory quantity is smaller at the end of the period than at the beginning.

IV. A Sensitivity Analysis

In Part II, we explained that the condition $w > w^-$ does not always imply $PF > PD$, as is usually stated. In addition we can make the following observation that holds regardless of inventory costing methods. Take any combination of figures for the beginning inventory quantity, w^-; sales quantity, s; production quantity, q; the beginning inventory fixed costs, BN; and the manufacturing fixed costs, MN; and calculate $PF - PD$ according to any of the four given inventory costing methods. Then increase production quantity by k units (k being any positive number) or decrease sales quantity by k units, holding all other factors constant. In either case, the ending inventory quantity, w, is increased by k units. Then, recalculate $PF - PD$ for the second case. We will show that $PF - PD$ for the second case is always greater than $PF - PD$ for the first case *regardless of the inventory costing method;* an increase in production or a decrease in sales always makes $PF - PD$ greater than before, making full cost profit larger or direct cost profit smaller or both.[6]

This statement clearly holds for the standard cost method since, from (19), $PF - PD$ is given by $\alpha^*(w - w^-)$ and obviously $PF - PD$ is increased whenever w is increased, holding w^- *and* α^* constant. It also holds for the *LIFO* method with $s \leq q$ in which case $PF - PD$ is given by

(11) $$PF - PD = \frac{q - s}{q} MN = MN - \frac{s}{q} MN.$$

---

[6] There is one exception to this rule which will be discussed later.

Since an increase in q or a decrease in s always makes $(s/q)MN$ smaller, it always makes $PF - PD$ greater. Under the *LIFO* method with $s \geq q$, $PF - PD$ is given by

$$\text{(15)} \qquad PF - PD = \frac{w - w^-}{w-} BN = \frac{w}{w-} BN - BN,$$

from which it is clear that the above statement also holds for this case. It holds for the average method, too, for from (5) we have

$$PF - PD = \frac{w}{w + s} MN - \frac{s}{w + s} BN$$

$$\text{(5)} \qquad = \frac{w + s - s}{w + s} MN - \frac{s}{w + s} BN$$

$$= MN - \frac{s}{w + s} (MN + BN)$$

$$= MN - \frac{s}{w- + q} (MN + BN),$$

since from (12),

$$\text{(28)} \qquad w + s = w^- + q.$$

From this, it is clear that an increase in q or a decrease in s makes

$$\frac{s}{w- + q} (MN + BN)$$

smaller and hence $PF - PD$ larger.

Finally, under the *FIFO* method with $s \geq w^-$, $PF - PD$ is given by

$$\text{(7)} \qquad PF - PD = \frac{w}{q} MN - BN = \frac{w^- - s}{q} MN + MN - BN,$$

hence an increase in q or a decrease in s increases $PF - PD$. On the other hand, under the *FIFO* method with $s \leq w^-$, $PF - PD$ is given (in footnote 4) by

$$\text{(6)}' \qquad PF - PD = MN - \frac{s}{w-} BN,$$

hence a decrease in s certainly increases $PF - PD$, but an increase in q does not change the value of $PF - PD$. This is the only exception to the above rule.

Thus the rule may be stated precisely as follows: if q is increased, holding w^-, s, MN, and BN constant, or if s is decreased, holding w^-, q, MN, and BN constant, then $PF - PD$ is always increased unless q is increased under the *FIFO* method with $s \leq w^-$ in which case $PF - PD$ remains unchanged. This rule may seem to be obvious at first sight since EN seems to be increased whenever w is increased. However, this is not necessarily true as shown by the example using *FIFO*. The unit fixed inventory cost, α, may be decreased as w increases and so an increase in w may not imply an increase in EN which is equal to αw. The above analysis clarifies this point.

V. Summary and Conclusions

Part II analysed the differences in profit under full and direct costing in relation to four methods of inventory costing — average cost, *FIFO*, *LIFO*, and standard cost. As noted, the critical factors that determine whether the full or the direct cost method yields greater profits vary according to the inventory costing methods. This analysis is summarized in Table 1, at the end of Part II. From Table 1 we can see that the usual generalizations about full and direct costing hold only under the *LIFO* and the standard cost methods of inventory costing. Under the *FIFO* and the average cost methods of inventory costing, the results are more complex than those considered by the usual generalizations which therefore do not apply. Table 1 shows the correct generalizations for these cases.

Part III focused attention on the management side of the problem and noted that the difference in profit variance (i.e., actual minus budgeted profit) under full and direct costing is less than (equal to, or greater than) the difference in absolute profits under full and direct costing if the budgeted inventory quantity at the end is greater than (equal to, or less than) the budgeted inventory quantity at the beginning.

In Part IV it was shown that, regardless of the inventory costing method, an increase in ending inventory quantity will always increase the difference between full cost profit and direct cost profit by increasing the former or decreasing the latter or both.[7] It is, therefore, clear that there is always more pressure to build up inventory under full than under direct costing if the manager prefers to show more, rather than less, profit. This objective can always be achieved under full costing by increasing the ending inventory quantity to a higher level. The behavioral implication of such a pressure toward inventory build-up needs to be studied empirically.[8]

[7] The one exception to this rule is discussed at the end of Part IV. Note that we are *not* saying whether full cost profit is actually greater or less than direct cost profit, unlike the statements cited in the introduction.

[8] See, for example, William Bruns, *A Stimulation Study of Alternative Methods of Inventory Valuation*, unpublished Ph.D. dissertation, University of California, Berkeley, 1962; Charles P. Bonini, *Simulation of Information and Decision System in the Firm*, Prentice-Hall, Inc. Englewood Cliffs, N.J., 1963; Thomas R. Dyckman, "The Effects of Alternative Accounting Techniques on Certain Management Decisions," *Journal of Accounting Research*, Vol. 2, No. 1, Spring 1964; and Yuji Ijiri, Robert K. Jaedicke and Kenneth E. Knight, "The Effect of Accounting Reporting Alternatives on Management Control," Working Paper No. 18, Graduate School of Business, Stanford University, 1964, for recent efforts to explore and analyse the behavioral effects of different accounting methods.

Supplemental
Readings
to Part Six

Donald S. Brightly, "A Statistical Tool for the Cost Accountant," *Management Services,* Vol. 2, No. 5 (September-October, 1965), pp. 13–17.

Statistical tools for the management accountant to use in analyzing fixed and variable costs are presented.

E. J. Broster, "The Dynamics of Marginal Costing," *The Accountant,* Vol. 162, No. 4971 (March 26, 1970), pp. 451–454.

The advantages of using marginal costing are explained.

Leonard A. Doyle, "Overhead Accounting Comes Full Circle," *NA(C)A Bulletin,* Vol. XXXV, No. 12 (August, 1954) pp. 1575–1585.

A brief history of the development of overhead accounting is given. Recent developments are portrayed as a return to simplicity rather than a refinement.

William L. Ferrara, "Responsibility Reporting vs. Direct Costing — Is There A Conflict?," *Management Accounting,* Vol. 48, No. 10 (June, 1967), pp. 43–54.

This paper states a series of hypotheses that such a conflict is imaginary.

Myron J. Gordon, "Cost Allocations and the Design of Accounting Systems for Control," *The Accounting Review,* Vol. XXVI, No. 2 (April, 1951), pp. 209–220.

Accounting systems can be used to control or to provide direct solutions to problems. Costing prime costs to centers directly (not direct costing) is advocated, as is control through use of current standards.

Richard J. L. Herson and Ronald S. Hertz, "Direct Costing in Pricing: A Critical Reappraisal," *Management Services,* Vol. 5, No. 2 (March-April, 1968), pp. 35–44.

Direct costing is dangerous for pricing decisions — full costing is better for the long run.

William L. Leffler, "Shadow Pricing," *Data and Control Systems,* (July, 1966), pp. 26–29.

Shadow pricing is presented as a theory of marginal costing derived from mathematical programming.

Raymond P. Marple, "Management Accounting Is Coming of Age," *Management Accounting,* Vol. 48, No. 11 (July, 1967), pp. 3–16.

Management accounting will have come of age when full responsibility accounting, complete direct costing, and contribution reporting systems are adopted.

Robert D. Miller and Terry L. Robinson, "Performance Reports Based on Direct Costing: A Case Study," *Management Accounting,* Vol. 51, No. 10 (April, 1970), pp. 43–47.

The value of direct cost reporting for evaluation and measurement is illustrated.

Rolf E. Rogers, "How Good Are Financial Performance Control Systems?", *Systems and Procedures Journal,* Vol. 18, No. 1 (January-February, 1967), pp. 17–20.

Advantages and disadvantages of a responsibility accounting system in terms of organizational and managerial aspects are reviewed.

Wilmer Wright, "Use of Standard Direct Costing," *Management Accounting,* Vol. 48, No. 5 (January, 1967), pp. 39–46.

Standard direct costing is compared with simple direct costing, and the benefits of using a standard direct costing system are illustrated.

Additional
Bibliography
to Part Six

George F. Armstrong, "Performance Information Through Responsibility Accounting," *NAA Bulletin*, Vol. XLI, No. 7 (March, 1960), pp. 89–93.

William E. Arnstein, "Direct Costing Approaches to Management Decisions," *The New York Certified Public Accountant*, Vol. XXIX, No. 9 (September, 1959), pp. 651–661.

George J. Benston, "The Role of the Firm's Accounting System for Motivation," *The Accounting Review*, Vol. XXXVII, No. 2 (April, 1963), pp. 347–354.

Robert Beyer, "Is Direct Costing the Answer?" *The Journal of Accountancy*, Vol. 99, No. 4 (April, 1955), pp. 45–49.

——, "Profitability Accounting: The Challenge and the Opportunity," *The Journal of Accountancy*, Vol. 117, No. 6 (June, 1964), pp. 33–36.

Harold Bierman, Jr., "A Way of Using Direct Costing in Financial Reporting," *NAA Bulletin*, Vol. XLI, No. 3 (November, 1959), pp. 13–20.

Albert J. Bows, Jr., "Broadening the Approach to Management Reporting," *The Arthur Andersen Chronicle*, Vol. 22, No. 2 (April, 1962), pp. 7–25.

John J. Brausch, "Direct Costing: Progress or Folly?" *The Journal of Accountancy*, Vol. 112, No. 2 (August, 1961), pp. 52–60.

R. Lee Brummet, "Direct Costing — Its Weaknesses and Strengths," *NAA Bulletin*, Vol. XLIII, No. 7 (March, 1962), pp. 61–68.

——, "Direct Costing — Should It Be A Controversial Issue?" *The Accounting Review*, Vol. XXX, No. 3 (July, 1955), pp. 439–443.

Charles F. Caufield, "A Favorable Appraisal of Direct Costing," *NAA Bulletin*, Vol. XL, No. 4 (December, 1958), pp. 15–25.

Peter M. Chinminatto, "Is Direct Costing the Answer to Better Management Accounting?" *NA(C)A Bulletin*, Vol. XXXVII, No. 6 (February, 1956) pp. 699–712.

Gerald R. Crowningshield and George L. Battista, "Fixing Responsibility Through Profit and Loss Analysis," *NAA Bulletin*, Vol. XLIII, No. 4 (December, 1961), pp. 11–27.

Robert J. Donachie, "Converting To and Using Direct Costing," *NAA Bulletin*, Vol. XL, No. 7 (March, 1959), pp. 19–30.

Thomas S. Dudick, "Direct Costing — 'Handle With Care', " *The Journal of Accountancy*, Vol. 114, No. 4 (October, 1962), pp. 45–52.

——, "Is Direct Costing the Answer?" *The New York Certified Public Accountant*, Vol. XXXIII, No. 12 (December, 1963), pp. 857–862.

James S. Earley, "Recent Developments in Cost Accounting and the Marginal Analysis," *The Journal of Political Economy*, Vol. 63, No. 3 (June, 1955), pp. 227–242.

James Don Edwards, "This New Costing Concept — Direct Costing?" *The Accounting Review*, Vol. XXXIII, No. 4 (October, 1958), pp. 561–567.

William L. Ferrara, "The Contribution Approach," *NAA Bulletin*, Vol. XLVI, No. 4 (December, 1964), pp. 19–29.

———, "Direct Costing: Are Direct Costs Relevant Costs?" *The Journal of Accountancy*, Vol. 112, No. 2 (August, 1961), pp. 61–62.

———, "Responsibility Accounting — A Basic Control Concept," *NAA Bulletin*, Vol. XLVI, No. 1 (September, 1964), pp. 11–22.

Philip E. Fess and William L. Ferrara, "The Period Cost Concept for Income Measurement — Can It Be Defended?" *The Accounting Review*, Vol. XXXVI, No. 4 (October, 1961), pp. 598–602.

James M. Fremgen, "Variable Costing for External Reporting — A Reconsideration," *The Accounting Review*, Vol. XXXVII, No. 1 (January, 1962), pp. 76–81.

George Gibbs, "New Cost Accounting Concepts," *The Accounting Review*, Vol. XXXIII, No. 1 (January, 1958), pp. 96–101.

Samuel R. Hepworth, "Direct Costing — The Case Against," *The Accounting Review*, Vol. XXIX, No. 1 (January, 1954), pp. 94–99.

Robert W. Hirschman, "Direct Costing and the Law," *The Accounting Review*, Vol. XL, No. 1 (January, 1965), pp. 176–183.

Charles T. Horngren and George H. Sorter, " 'Direct' Costing for External Reporting," *The Accounting Review*, Vol. XXXVI, No. 1 (January, 1961), pp. 84–93.

Charles E. Johnson, "Inventory Valuation — The Accountant's Achilles Heel," *The Accounting Review*, Vol. XXIX, No. 1 (January, 1954), pp. 15–26.

R. Kendall Jones, "Why Not Capacity Costing?" *NAA Bulletin*, Vol. XXXIX, No. 3 (November, 1957), pp. 13–21.

Louis H. Jordan, "A Discussion of the Usefulness and Theory of Direct Costing," *NAA Bulletin*, Vol. XLIII, No. 7 (March, 1962), pp. 53–60.

Martin N. Kellogg, "Fundamentals of Responsibility Accounting," *NAA Bulletin*, Vol. XLIII, No. 8 (April, 1962), pp. 5–16.

Patrick S. Kemp, "Accounting Data for Planning, Motivation, and Control," *The Accounting Review*, Vol. XXXVII, No. 1 (January, 1962), pp. 44–50.

J. R. Kiessling, "Profit Planning and Responsibility Accounting," *Financial Executive*, Vol. XXXI, No. 7 (July, 1963), pp. 13–15.

Ray E. Longenecker, "Converting to Direct Costing," *NAA Bulletin*, Vol. XLIII, No. 12 (August, 1962), pp. 25–37.

Winfield I. McNeill, "Groping Through the Accounting Maze," *The Controller*, Vol. XXX, No. 12 (December, 1962), pp. 610–615.

Raymond P. Marple, "Direct Costing and the Uses of Cost Data," *The Accounting Review*, Vol. XXX, No. 3 (July, 1955), pp. 430–438.

Henry K. Moffitt, "Controlling Indirect Costs of Research and Development," *The Controller*, Vol. XXX, No. 10 (October, 1962), pp. 486–491.

Morton F. Moss and Wilber C. Haseman, "Some Comments on the Application of Direct Costing to Decision Making," *The Accounting Review*, Vol. XXXII, No. 2 (April, 1957), pp. 184–193.

Oswald Neilsen, "Direct Costing — The Case 'For', " *The Accounting Review*, Vol. XXIX, No. 1 (January, 1954), pp. 89–93.

A. W. Patrick, "Direct Versus Absorption Costing," *The Controller*, Vol. XXIX, No. 4 (April, 1961), pp. 167–173.

Edward J. Phillippe, "Reports Which Give Effect To Responsibility Accounting," *NAA Bulletin*, Vol. XLI, No. 3 (November, 1959), pp. 89–93.

Jack M. Pompan, "Direct and Absorption Costing in One System," *NAA Bulletin*, Vol. XL, No. 7 (March, 1959), pp. 5–18.

Charles Reitell, "Direct Costing Opens the Door to Profit Planning," *NAA Bulletin*, Vol. XXXIX, No. 8 (April, 1958), pp. 5–14.

Kenneth R. Rickey, "Direct Costing — An Aid in Contract Profit Planning and Control," *NAA Bulletin*, Vol. XLIII, No. 3 (November, 1961), pp. 43-48.

Ralph W. Sauber, "Management Appraises Direct Costing — A Play," *NA(C)A Bulletin*, Vol. XXXVII, No. 4 (December, 1955), pp. 459–472.

Michael Schiff, "Reporting for More Profitable Product Management," *The Journal of Accountancy*, Vol. 115, No. 5 (May, 1963), pp. 65–70.

—— and Joseph Schirger, "Incremental Analysis and Opportunity Costs," *Management Services*, Vol. 1, No. 3 (July-August, 1964), pp. 13–17.

Robert E. Seiler, "Improvements in External Reporting by Use of Direct Costing," *The Accounting Review*, Vol. XXXIV, No. 1 (January, 1959), pp. 59–66.

George J. Tasso, "Responsibility Accounting," *The New York Certified Public Accountant*, Vol. XXXII, No. 12 (December, 1962), pp. 809-817.

Donald J. Wait, "The Use of Responsibility Reporting in the Control of Costs," *Cost and Management*, Vol. XXXV, No. 11 (December, 1961), pp. 483–90, 492.

Robert B. Wetnight, "Direct Costing Passes the 'Future Benefit' Test," *NAA Bulletin*, Vol. XXXIX, No. 12 (August, 1958), pp. 83–84.

Wilmer R. Wright, "Direct Costs Are Better for Pricing," *NAA Bulletin*, Vol. XLI, No. 8 (April, 1960,) pp. 17–26.

——, "Why Direct Costing is Rapidly Gaining Acceptance," *The Journal of Accountancy*, Vol. 114, No. 1 (July, 1962), pp. 40–46.

PART SEVEN

Motivation, Performance, and Evaluation: Decentralization, Internal Transaction Pricing, and Cost Allocation

There are two primary schools of thought relative to costs and pricing. Essentially, one holds that price is independent of cost except in long-run equilibrium. The firm then reacts to given price situations (market), and adjusts its cost to operate within the given price schedule. This is the essence of the cost-minimization goal. The other school holds that in imperfect markets the individual firm controls its price to a considerable extent; and further, that its price is directly related to its cost. Price has to be set to cover cost plus a reasonable profit.

A major and recurring problem area in accounting is the determination of internal prices for purposes of both profit measurement and control. This problem has been accentuated by the growth of multi-product, multi-division firms, by a major merger movement, and by significant decentralization of corporate management's authority. The problem, of course, is that any intra-company price scheme cannot truly be a "free" price mechanism in the competitive market sense. At the same time these "shadow" prices may have to serve many purposes and thus be constrained by conflicting objectives. Even if the goal of measuring department efficiency solely through the profit medium is stipulated, there are usually inter-departmental conflicts in the price settings.

Shillinglaw describes an accounting theory of divisional income measurement based on five postulates. From these he develops a set of eight measurement standards that support the objectives of divisional income measurement and he discusses them in some detail. Shillinglaw's article is complementary to Greer's, which follows, and approaches an integrated theory.

Greer's brief note succinctly identifies and discusses the kernel of the transfer pricing problem in a manner which clearly identifies the issues involved. His view is pragmatic, and he cites examples from industry. He devotes most, but not all, of his attention to the transfer price side of the story. Major means of establishing transfer prices (cost, market, and negotiation) are discussed; their advantages and disadvantages are illustrated; and implications of their use for divisional and top managers are cited. Although despairing of any real solution, Greer offers a seemingly viable compromise.

Livingstone deals at a methodological level with a related problem of inter-divisional cost allocation. The matrix cost allocation model is but a special case of input-output analysis, he argues; and he presents the input-output model as a superior tool for allocating costs and for planning and control. The concepts presented in this article are based on Leontief's input-output model, and are well illustrated with examples and adequate discussions. Special attention is paid to the problem of expressing variables in physical as well as monetary terms, and to the use of the model to analyze incremental and opportunity costs. As is the case with most models, certain simplifying assumptions have been made. But these are clearly identified and do not impair the soundness of the concept presented.

In the last article of this book, Onsi underscores the problem originally exposed by Greer — no single approach to transfer pricing will suffice, because the transfer-price problem is inherently insoluble. Onsi recognizes, however, that increasing decentralization in decision making renders the problem even more important and acute.

Onsi proposes a new transfer price system based on the opportunity cost concept, taking into consideration many of the behavioral problems that attend pricing transfer against divisions and evaluating divisional performance on a "profit center" basis. This article examines a variety of solutions and their permutations, and concludes that a system based on opportunity cost, with central administrative subsidy "in the form of motivation cost" reduces the level of conflict in a transfer pricing system.

29

An accounting theory that will provide valid standards for divisional income is based on five postulates as to the nature of the firm: (1) the firm is expected to yield income, (2) a division is a semi-independent unit, (3) divisional management has as its prime goal company income, *(4) divisions are going-concerns, (5) divisional management has at least partial control over resources that determine division income.*

These postulates lead to a set of measurement standards that require that divisional income be determined objectively, be independent of performance in other divisions, co-variable with the division's contribution to company profit, and strictly comparable with income objectives of the current period, deviations from budget being restricted to those currently controllable by divisional management.

The main emphasis is that divisional income (defined as profit contribution) should reflect divisional management performance. Warnings are given about unsound intra-company transfer-pricing and unsound allocations of common costs.

Toward a Theory of Divisional Income Measurement*

Gordon Shillinglaw

Accounting theory traditionally has been restricted to the twin problems of valuation and income measurement for an economic entity, usually the private business firm, with emphasis on an institutionally determined accounting period, usually one year. There is no reason, however, why theory cannot or should not be extended to cover any aspect of accounting. Indeed,

* From The Accounting Review, *Vol. XXXVII, No. 2 (April, 1962), pp. 208–216. Reprinted by permission of the editor.*

theory has been applied to accounting for governmental units and non-profit organizations and there is evidence of increasing interest in these branches of accounting. Two gaps in accounting theory remain relatively untouched, however: (1) interim measurements of enterprise income for public reporting, and (2) internal income measurement for segments of the enterprise, segments that correspond to major organizational subdivisions of the corporate entity. This paper is directed to the second of these neglected areas, the measurement of divisional income.[1] More specifically, the object of this paper is to take the first steps toward a theory of divisional income determination, employing a structure similar to that used for the theory of enterprise annual financial reporting.

The Need for a Theory

Why is such a theory needed? To answer this question, it is perhaps wise to consider briefly why it has been necessary to construct a theory for enterprise accounting. The reason is not hard to find. Enterprise financial statements are prepared primarily for the information and guidance of outsiders, many of whom have in the past or may in the future invest in the enterprise. Lacking access to the company's internal records, the outsider needs some way of learning and defining what the published statements purport to show; he also wants assurance that measurement rules consistent with these definitions have been followed. Theory is designed to supply the first of these; it also provides the auditor with a basis for satisfying the outsider on the second count, through the mechanism of the independent audit and the auditor's certificate. In addition, the accountant himself needs a theory for another reason, to furnish him with directives as to what is to be measured and how to measure it.

In divisional income determination the purpose of theory is certainly not to provide the basis for annual auditors' certificates. There is no distant public that needs this kind of periodic reassurance that the rules of the game are being followed. Rather the objective of theory is to provide a basis for designing the measurement systems in the first place, and then for revising them as conditions change. Without a theory, this is likely to be a haphazard process, yielding systems notable mainly for their lack of consistency, the measurements of income clouded in ambiguity. Furthermore, without a good theory divisional income measurements are more likely to mislead than to inform.

---

[1] Throughout, the term "division" will be used to refer to a major organizational subdivision of a company although it may take the legal form of an incorporated subsidiary or bear some other name such as "department," "product-business," or "profit center." The wholly-owned subsidiary is of course a special case, but the objectives of measurement are the same and these, as this paper will try to demonstrate, govern the establishment of measurement principles. The partially-owned subsidiary is, for external reporting, subject to enterprise accounting standards; for internal reporting, it should be treated in the same manner as other divisions.

Elements of Divisional Accounting Theory

The elements of an accounting theory for divisional income determination, and indeed of any accounting theory, are:

1. A set of basic concepts and definitions.
2. A set of postulates, or axioms, including a statement of the assumed objectives of the divisional units.
3. A set of objectives of accounting measurement, derived by deductive reasoning from the postulates.
4. A set of measurement standards or principles that, if followed, will produce division financial statements that meet the measurement objectives. These standards provide a basis for testing the acceptability of proposed rules of measurement.

Most of the concepts and definitions to be used in the theory are part of the professional vocabulary and need not be repeated here. A few of the more important concepts will be spelled out as the argument proceeds, but in the main this paper will be concerned with outlining a tentative set of postulates, measurement objectives and measurement standards. Specific rules of measurement will not be discussed, except to illustrate how a particular standard might be applied.

Basic Postulates

As used in accounting, the term "postulate" means a statement that is assumed to be true for purposes of theory construction. The theory, therefore, is valid only if the postulate is true. In scientific disciplines, the truth of a set of postulates may be inferred from comparisons of observed data with those predicted with the aid of the theory based on the set of postulates, but in accounting, the validity of the postulates must be tested by other means. The purpose of accounting theory is to provide a basis for generating data and not for predicting the consequences of specified actions, predictions that can be compared with actual results.

The theory of divisional income measurement proposed in this paper is based on the following set of postulates:

Postulate 1: The firm is expected to yield income for the suppliers of long-term capital funds.

Postulate 2: The division is an organizational segment of the firm, operated by division management as a semi-independent company, its independence of action subject only to the restrictions imposed by general company policies.[2]

---

[2] It should be noted that this postulate is often invalid in that many divisions lack the requisite degree of independence. Most functional divisions (e.g., manufacturing) fall into this category.

Postulate 3: The management of the division is expected to employ the re-sources of the division in such a way as to produce income for the company.

Postulate 4: The division is a going concern which is expected to continue operations for an indefinite period of time that is long relative to the length of a single accounting period.

Postulate 5: Division management has at least partial control over some, but not all, of the elements that determine the amount of income generated by the division's operations.

Some of these postulates are largely definitional and may be acceptable without further proof; others, the third postulate in particular, are advanced here without empirical proof, even though an empirical test would be pos-sible. Supplying such proof would be a worthwhile research project, but in this paper the validity of the postulates will be unquestioned. At the same time, it should be recognized that this is not the only set of postulates that might be advanced. If there is reason to believe that another set of postulates is truer or more universal, then a theory could and should be constructed on that alternate basis. For example, the going concern postulate might be replaced by one stating that each division is at all times regarded as an active candidate for liquidation, which would lead to an entirely different set of measurement objectives and standards from those that follow from accept-ance of the going concern postulate.

Measurement Objectives

Given these postulates, the next step is to determine the appropriate meas-urement objectives. The objective of any measurement, of course, is utility. As Kircher has said, the only useful measure of performance is one that indicates progress toward the goals of the recipient of the measure.[3] These goals are indicated by the nature and objectives of the business unit, in the present instance the corporate division. Once these fundamentals have been established, preferably by empirical research but by assumption if need be, then and only then is it possible to proceed with the next step, the identifica-tion of the objectives of measurement.

The nature and objectives of the division are embodied in the first four postulates. First, the company as a whole is assumed to have an income objective. Second, the division is a segment of the company, operating in many respects as an independent business unit, with the company as its primary and in most cases the only supplier of ownership capital, and formed with an income objective. Third, the managers of any business unit are al-ways accountable to the suppliers of capital and in particular to the suppliers of ownership capital, in this case to company management. In view of the

---

[3] Paul Kircher, "Theory and Research in Management Accounting," *The Accounting Review*, Vol. XXXVI, No. 1 (January, 1961), pp. 43–49.

postulated income objective, this accountability must be regarded as primarily accountability as to the amount of *income* produced. Therefore, the primary measurement objective is to provide both company and division management with a basis for evaluation of division management's use of company resources to produce *income*. Measurements of wealth enter in only insofar as they have a bearing on the effectiveness of division management's utilization of resources in producing income.

The goal, therefore, is to provide a measure of income produced by division *management*. There is a second measurement objective, however: to provide top management with a measure of the profitability of the *resources* invested in the division. This also follows from the postulate that management expects resources to be utilized to produce income. If divisional income is inadequate to meet management's objectives and efforts to increase income are unavailing, then presumably resources will be diverted to other uses. It follows that top management needs some means of identifying unprofitable resource utilization for guidance in these future resource allocation decisions. The second income measurement objective, therefore, is to provide such a guide, an index of the level and trend of divisional resource profitability.

Unfortunately, it is not possible to satisfy this second objective precisely without abandoning one of the other basic postulates. The period income of the division can never be measured in absolute terms as long as the going concern postulate is accepted. Common costs and revenue interdependence among divisions create problems that can never be solved uniquely in the going concern. Only if the going concern assumption is dropped does the notion of absolute divisional income have operational meaning. Then the measurement objective becomes the determination of the income that would have been lost had the division been liquidated. This can be measured, or at least estimated, uniquely, but only by introducing drastic changes in accounting procedures. For example, it would be necessary to credit more than one division for *all* the revenue from a given sale if the sale would have been lost if *either* division had not been in existence.

To put this another way, abandonment of the going concern postulate means that each division must be regarded continuously as a candidate for liquidation. To accomplish this, its wealth must be defined to include all those resources, and only those resources, that could be set free by liquidation, and this wealth must be measured at liquidation prices. Division revenue becomes company revenue that would have been forfeited by liquidation, and division expense becomes company outlays that could have been avoided by liquidation, adjusted for any changes in net asset liquidation values during the period.

Fortunately, acceptance of the going concern postulate not only makes it impossible to measure division income uniquely — it also makes it unnecessary. If the division is regarded as a going concern, then liquidation is not an active possibility. And with liquidation not a recognized alternative, evaluation of the desirability of discontinuing the division's activities is not a proper measurement objective. The problem, therefore, is to devise income measures consistent with the going concern postulate that will be adequate to serve the objective of providing a rough measure of resource profitability, recognizing that absolute accuracy can never be achieved.

Measurement Standards

With these objectives as a guide, it is now possible to specify a set of accounting standards or principles that must be met by a system of divisional income measurement. The following eight measurement standards should be both necessary and sufficient to complete the theory presented in this paper:

1. Objectivity
2. Co-variability
3. Independence
4. Comparability
5. Controllability
6. Service potential expiration
7. Realization
8. Revenue-expense matching

Objectivity

First, the standard of objectivity: This pillar of enterprise accounting is no less essential in divisional accounting. Divisional income measurements are to be used by management in appraising managerial performance. The measurements, therefore, must be free from personal bias. This is all that objectivity means — it neither requires nor rejects the historical cost basis of valuation. Neither does the objectivity standard necessarily presume verifiability to the extent necessary in enterprise reporting. Verifiability merely means the ability to determine the true facts about a transaction.[4] When there is room for dispute as to the truth, more than one interpretation may be objective, and for this reason in enterprise accounting it is often necessary to postulate that one interpretation is verifiable to the exclusion of others. For example, the postulate of a constant value of money means that price index adjustments are not verifiable even though they may be objective. In divisional accounting, in contrast, there is no need to specify the minimum degree of verifiability that will be acceptable. If a given procedure is objective, and meets the other measurement standards as well, then it can be regarded as adequately verifiable.

---

[4] For example, see William A. Paton and A. C. Littleton, *An Introduction to Corporate Accounting Standards* (Urbana, Ill.: American Accounting Association, 1940), p. 20.

Co-Variability

The standard of co-variability requires that the income measured for the division respond in direction and if possible in amount to changes in the division's contribution to real company income. Division income is unimportant in itself; its importance stems from its relationship to overall company income. This follows from the third basic postulate, that division management is expected to utilize a portion of the company's resources to generate income for the *company*. Top management is not interested in spurious income, produced by inappropriate accounting procedures or conventions. If the management of a division has taken actions that have increased company income, the division's income statement should reflect this increase.

This standard is most likely to be violated by unsound intracompany transfer prices or allocations of costs common to two or more divisions, but it is an important test to apply to other income-determining elements as well. It should be noted that although division profit contribution as a measure of divisional income is wholly consistent with the standard of co-variability, the standard does not require that divisional income be defined in terms of contribution. The division income figure must, however, reflect *changes* in the division's profit contribution and the safest way to accomplish this may be to accept a profit contribution definition of income.

Independence

Closely related to the standard of co-variability is the standard of independence. The second postulate states that each division is to be operated as a semi-independent unit. Its independence, however, is both contrived and restricted, and the artificial nature of the independence should be clearly recognized in income measurement. To accomplish this, each division's reported income should be independent of performance in other divisions. This follows primarily from the managerial performance measurement objective, an unstated postulate being that the effects of actions that are not subject to an executive's control are irrelevant in evaluating his performance. Variations in executive performance in other divisions are controllable, if at all, only by the management of those divisions. Therefore, such variations should be excluded from the measure of divisional income.

It should be acknowledged immediately that neither the firm nor the division is independent of its environment, and any attempt to eliminate all the effects of interdependence would lead to a sterile income measure. For example, one division's income may be influenced by reductions in the sales volume of the divisions that are its internal customers. If the division were a completely independent company it would experience a similar effect, however, and it is not proposed that the results of this kind of interdependence be eliminated. Instead, the measurement standard of independence refers to the elimination of effects that result solely from the fact that the division operates within a larger company framework and that its independence in its relationships with other units of the company is synthetic and incomplete. To illustrate, this standard is violated by any cost redistribution procedure that permits sales volume in one division to influence the amount of administrative expense to be assigned to another division.

Comparability

Fourth, the measure of divisional income must be comparable in all respects with the income objective that is to serve as the bench mark for appraisal. This standard has no immediate counterpart in enterprise accounting, although it might be argued that the latter embodies an implicit comparability standard in the standard of universality.

In enterprise financial reporting, the income objective is typically multi-valued, a value being supplied, often implicitly, by each investor. Furthermore, it is by no means certain how each investor would measure income if he had unlimited access to company data. For this reason the accounting profession has supplied a basic definition of income to be used universally for all companies. Each investor then must either phrase his income objective in comparable terms or must make whatever adjustments to reported income he deems appropriate to render it comparable with the statement of his objective.

In divisional accounting, in contrast, the income objective is expressed explicitly by a specified group of recipients. The standard of universality in defining income is unimportant and unnecessary. Income can be defined in any way that makes for a sensible and useful definition of the income objective. This flexibility is most disturbing to those who seek a universal definition of divisional income, but it is unavoidable. The truth is that no single definition of income follows from the basic postulates. Only by introducing additional postulates, such as constancy of purchasing power or the homogeneity of costs, is it possible to derive a unique definition of income.[5]

Just what does the standard of comparability require, then? First, for management performance appraisal the income *objective* should be stated explicitly and should be agreed upon beforehand as a reasonably attainable goal, given the expected environmental conditions of the period; in other

[5] Paton and Littleton, for example, denied the validity in enterprise reporting of any but a net income definition, based on the postulate that costs are homogeneous, differing only in the difficulty of assignment. *Op. cit.*, pp. 67–69. Similar reasoning presumably was behind the conclusion in the 1957 revision of the concepts and standards statement that "the omission [from product cost] of any element of manufacturing cost is not acceptable." American Accounting Association, "Accounting and Reporting Standards for Corporate Financial Statements — 1957 Revision," *The Accounting Review*, Vol. XXXII, No. 4 (October, 1957), p. 539.

words, it should be budgeted income rather than a uniform company-wide percentage return-on-investment objective. This conclusion is inescapable so long as divisional income is to be used as a basis for appraisal of division management. Appraisal of personal performance requires the measurement of differences between attainable objectives and achievements; if the objectives are not attainable, then the differences are not valid measures of performance.[6]

Second, for meeting the objective of providing a rough measure of *resource* profitability the income objective should consider the amount of resources committed to a division; company-wide, minimum acceptable return-on-investment ratios provide one means of accomplishing this. This does not necessarily mean, however, that divisional income must be net income, after deducting charges for a share of noncontrollable common expenses, as well as expenses traceable to the division but not controllable by division management. Although there is little objection to making such deductions from divisional income so long as they do not reduce the comparability of reported and budgeted income for management appraisal, these allocations are in fact unnecessary. Instead of reducing reported income, it is sufficient to inflate the return-on-investment objective by an equivalent amount to allow for unallocated or unreported expenses. A similar adjustment can also be made to allow for undistributed investments. Such adjustments can be quite crude because they are to be used only in preliminary evaluation of resource profitability; examination of any apparent problem areas will require more careful analysis based on different postulates. All that is required is that the periodic income measurements and the income objectives be stated in comparable terms.

Controllability

Closely allied with the independence and comparability standards is the standard of controllability. Division management should be charged for the use of all those resources over which it has control, and any variances between the income objective and income achieved should result from factors that are at least partially subject to division management's control. This is based on the fifth postulate, that division management has only partial control over the division's destiny and no control at all over some of the income-determining elements. Given that income measures are to be used in management appraisal, then the influences of any noncontrollable elements should be eliminated from reported income or else neutralized in the appraisal of income. For example, if materials purchasing is not under the

---

[6] This is based on an unstated postulate that performance standards that are unattainably high will provide an unfair basis for personal appraisal. This assumption should be distinguished clearly from the assumption that unduly tight standards do not stimulate performance, an assumption that is neither used nor rejected in this paper.

control of the operating divisions, then purchase price variances should not be shown on the divisional income statements that are used in management appraisal. Observance of the independence standard will insure comparability in this regard in most instances, but if noncontrollable variances are allowed to appear they should at least be neutralized by means of equivalent adjustments of the income objective.

Although this standard requires that divisional income reflect all controllable resource consumption, it does not mean that the division should not be charged for any consumption of resources, whether controllable or not. In fact, for the appraisal of resource profitability, the more complete the statement of resource use the better. For managerial appraisal, however, the fifth standard requires only that controllable elements be reported and that noncontrollable variances be eliminated; it is possible to record other income-determining elements in divisional accounts and then either to suppress such elements in managerial performance reports or to neutralize any variances arising from these elements, as suggested above.

Expiration of Service Potentials

The three final standards are more familiar. The sixth standard is the standard of service potential expiration. A useful and valid carry-over from enterprise accounting, this standard requires that expenses be measured in terms of the expiration of service potential. Once again this is derivable from the basic postulates. Division management is entrusted with certain resources. These resources may be tangible or intangible, but in any event they may without further proof be regarded as repositories of given quantities of potential services which may decline or expire with use or age. Inasmuch as division management is answerable for its use of the division's resources, it follows that any service potential that expires as a result of the use of these resources should be deducted from the division's revenues.

It should be noticed once again that this standard does not state how service potential should be measured. If historical outlay cost satisfies all the other standards in a particular case, then decline in service potential should be, or at least can be, measured in terms of historical cost. But if one of the standards, such as the standard of controllability, is violated by historical cost measurements, then some other measure such as standard cost should be substituted.

Nothing in this should be interpreted as implying that depreciation on long-life assets must be charged against division revenues. In measuring resource profitability such charges presumably should be made. For management performance reports, on the other hand, it is well to recognize that depreciation is seldom controllable in any significant sense and a comparison of actual with budgeted depreciation adds little, if anything, to the evaluation of the performance of division management. Control over division management's exercise of its limited authority to make capital expenditures can be achieved better by other means, such as required pre-outlay justification procedures and routine performance audits. Whenever resource utilization meets the controllability standard, however, the expense charge should reflect the expiration of service potential in whatever terms are most appropriate to the particular situation.

Revenue Realization

The next standard is the realization standard, or realization criterion, which states that divisional revenue should be recognized at that moment when realization is deemed to take place. But what is "realization?" A useful statement of the concept is the following: Realization occurs at that point in the transfer of an asset or a service to a party outside the division (*including another division of the same company*) when the amount of cash or its equivalent ultimately obtainable from the transfer becomes predictable with an acceptably high degree of accuracy.

Although the concept is not customarily described in these exact terms, this definition not only fits practice very well but also makes sense. The postulate that management's performance is to be appraised in part on the basis of its reported income leads to the conclusion that income should be recognized when the results of management's efforts are statistically determinable at an acceptable level of probability. Myers would phrase this differently, as a recognition of revenue at the time of the "critical event" in the process of asset transfers, but the result is essentially the same.[7]

Revenue-Expense Matching

Finally, there is the standard of revenue-expense matching. Expenses of a given period must include the monetary equivalent of those service potentials consumed *specifically* to produce the revenues of that period, provided that such expense recognition does not violate any of the other measurement standards. This also follows from the evaluation objective in that income will be an inappropriate measure of performance if some service potentials consumed to produce current revenues have been charged off in prior periods or are deferred to future periods. This standard does not, however, preclude charges to expense covering service potentials that have expired during the period but that have had neither a direct connection with current revenues nor have created a significant benefit for future periods. Whether and how individual divisions are to be charged for such additional items will depend

---

[7] John H. Myers, "The Critical Event and Recognition of Net Profit," *The Accounting Review*, Vol. XXXIV, No. 4 (October, 1959), pp. 528–32.

on the objective of measurement and on whether the charges meet the standards of controllability, comparability and independence. Inventory obsolescence, for example, is likely to be a valid charge against division management, even though it results not from use but from non-use of resources. As such, it should be shown on the management performance report and on the division resource profitability statement. For other expiring service potentials that do not meet the controllability test, however, the only justification for charging the division is to meet the resource profitability measurement objective.

Conclusions

To summarize briefly, there is a need for an accounting theory that will provide valid standards for measures of divisional income. Such a theory needs to be based on postulates as to the nature of the firm and of the division and their objectives. These postulates should be tested empirically, if possible. The postulates that I have proposed lead to a set of standards which, briefly stated, require that divisional income be determined objectively, be independent of performance in other divisions, co-variable with the division's contribution to company profit, and strictly comparable with income objectives attainable in the current period, deviations from budget being restricted to those currently controllable by division management. Such income measures may be supplemented, but not replaced, by measures giving rough approximations to the profitability of the division's resources, but the main emphasis should be on division income as a reflection of *management* performance.

Objections undoubtedly will be raised that this paper has not explored such questions as the use of variable costing, the validity of the profit contribution definition of income or the appropriateness of various methods of dealing with price level fluctuations. It will even be objected that income measurement standards that do not include a unique definition of income present a contradiction in terms. The second of these objections can only be answered with the observation that for management appraisal it is not important that all companies measure divisional income in the same terms; what is important is that performance be appraised in terms that make sense in each individual case.

In reply to the other objection, that this paper has overlooked many important topics, it must be observed that measurement rules are subordinate to measurement standards, and in internal accounting the use of replacement cost or of variable costing are questions of measurement rules rather than of standards. If standards can be agreed upon, the validity of measurement rules can be tested, but in the absence of standards the discussion of rules must necessarily take place in a vacuum.

30 *Divisional profit calculation is useful when divisions are relatively independent of one another, but less so when they are closely interrelated. Arbitrary standards and allocations, as noted before, tend to become meaningless for evaluation and guidance of divisional managers. The company, not divisional, profit is the major goal.*

The transfer-price problem is inherently insoluble; one approach will not serve all purposes so advantages and limitations of each must be understood. The main transfer-price criteria are (1) cost, (2) market, (3) negotiation.

Cost has the advantage of integrity and convenience, but lacks utility for evaluation, planning, and motivation. Market is satisfactory when market alternatives are available, but these are difficult to obtain and determine realistically. An unbiased referee may be required. Negotiation may be realistic if viable alternatives to inter-divisional trading are possible, but often leads to divisional rivalries and bitterness as well as misallocation of managerial time. An alternative cost-market compromise is offered.

Divisional Profit
Calculation — Notes on the
"Transfer Price" Problem*

Howard C. Greer

Management of complex industrial enterprises often involves efforts to calculate profits and return on investment for each of a number of product divisions. Such calculations are believed to be useful in evaluating performance, planning future investments, and maximizing overall results.

* *From* NAA Bulletin, *Vol. XLIII, No. 11 (July, 1962), pp. 5–12. Reprinted by permission of the publisher.*

Where the several divisions are completely independent of one another, such measurements serve an important purpose. Where the divisions are closely interrelated, producing substantial quantities of goods for one another, the case is much less clear. When the stated results are heavily influenced by the prices at which goods are transferred from one division to another, weaknesses and defects in the transfer-price mechanism frequently invalidate the conclusions which the divisional profit figures might seem to suggest.

In such cases, the figures may not merely fail to motivate the right management decisions, they may actively encourage the wrong ones. This danger is not just the accidental result of unsound philosophy or careless application, it is inherent in the nature of the accounting process involved. In essence, the divisional profit calculation is based on the presumption that the results of two closely interrelated processes can be separated and independently evaluated. In the realities of a complex business activity, this just isn't so.

Through use of arbitrary standards and procedures, interdivisional profit allocations are possible, and for certain purposes (later noted) these are plainly indispensable. If, however, they are permitted to become the yardsticks for evaluating performance by division managers, and the motivating force in the decisions and efforts of those managers, they may lead not to better returns for the entire company but to the exact opposite.

The meat-packing industry provides a classic example of interrelated divisional operations, in which products of most departments may be either (a) sold in their existing semi-finished state, or (b) transferred to some other department for further processing — with most companies convinced that results for each department can be (must be) separately evaluated for all management purposes. A quarter-century of intensive study of this problem by the writer has led to the conclusion that (1) there is no satisfactory basis for such evaluations, (2) the use of such data as may be developed, at the department manager level, leads to wrong decisions as often as to right ones.

The reasons are quite simple. If a manager is to be judged by the reported profitableness of his division, pressure is on him to do two things:

1. Take whatever steps seem indicated to maximize the profits of his division, regardless of their effect on other divisions, or on the company as a whole.
2. Apply himself to manipulating the profit-measurement procedures to his individual advantage, at the expense of other division heads less concerned or less influential.

It may be properly said, of course, that the division manager should be "broad enough" in his outlook to put company advantage ahead of division advantage but, if that is expected of him, it is unjust and ineffective to set up a measure of performance which has precisely the opposite bias.

While interdivision overhead allocations (possibly involving such elements as research, administration, advertising, public relations, etc.) are often a subject of controversy, they are normally minor influences on divisional profits.

The crux of the problem usually is the establishment of interdivisional transfer prices, and that becomes the focus of the attention of all concerned. Factors and alternatives involved are sketched in the following sections.

The three principal bases for establishing interdepartment transfer prices may be designated briefly as (1) cost, (2) market, (3) negotiation. Each may be judged: first, in terms of the mechanics of its application; and second, in terms of its usefulness for purposes of (a) performance evaluation, (b) investment planning, and (c) managerial motivation.

Cost Basis

The term, as here used, embraces all transfer prices in which cost to the producing department is the primary determinant of the charge to the receiving department. The cost figure adopted may be "standard" or "actual," overall or incremental, "full-apportioned" or "direct charge" only, etc. It may well include an allowance for "profit" (return on investment), or any other arbitrary factor deemed appropriate.

The outstanding advantage of this criterion is its integrity, its understandability, and its convenience. The "cost" (or "cost-plus") figure employed may be a pure accounting convention, but once the principle is established the calculations can be made precisely and easily, and all concerned can readily apprehend just what has been done and just what it signifies.

The obvious weakness of the method is its almost complete lack of utility in the fields of evaluation, planning, and motivation. Each primary and intermediate processing department is "guaranteed" the recovery of its cost (or cost plus profit) on each product transferred to another department — no less, no more. If, in the producing department, costs are high (poor location, poor facilities, poor management), it suffers no penalty — the burden is passed on to the receiving department. If, in the producing department, costs are low (fortunate position, efficient operation) it derives no advantage — the saving is ultimately reflected in the profit of the department doing the final processing and selling.

Furthermore, the assigned "cost" may be heavily influenced by varying conditions within the producing department — e.g., the current and changing "product mix" in that department. If Product A is made for outside sale and Product B for transfer to another department (same facilities employed), fluctuating quantities of Product A sold to others may affect the costs chargeable to Product B, in turn distorting the results of departments receiving that product, through wholly unrelated operating factors.

Worse yet, if there are several joint-products, or by-products, involved in the calculations, the philosophy of inter-product cost assignment may become a controlling, if entirely irrelevant, determinant of transfer prices. How much of the combined cost of joint products A, B, C, D, and E should be assigned to Product B, when input, output, yield, raw material cost, available sales prices, and facility usage are continually fluctuating in a radical and unpredictable manner? As long as reference is made solely to supposed "costs," the problem becomes insoluble, except in terms so arbitrary as to become managerially meaningless.

Consider the stated result as a motivating influence. Assume that alternative available processes will increase or decrease the relative yield of Product B from the raw materials and facilities available. If large returns are currently obtainable on outside sales or other joint products, the pressure is toward reduction of output of Product B, no matter how badly it may be needed by a receiving department, which may employ it even more profitably. Conversely, if other products are losing money, while B returns a satisfying "cost-plus" price, the influence is toward pushing receiving departments into accepting more of the product — even expanding their own facilities to utilize it. Thus, overall company policy may become infected with purely divisional influences, with a resulting confusion of objectives, arising from circumstances both fortuitous and transitory.

The unrealistic and illusory nature of reports and decisions, reflecting assumed "cost" elements only, eventually pushes almost every enterprise affected into complete or partial use of one of the other available transfer price bases, of which so-called "market" pricing clearly has the greatest theoretical justification.

Market Basis

The theory of this measurement procedure is that transfers should be priced at whatever would be realized or paid in an "arm's-length" transaction occurring in an "open market." This is to say that each producing department should charge, and each receiving department should pay, a price which the product would command if sold to, or bought from, outside customers or suppliers.

From the philosophical viewpoint, this procedure almost fully satisfies the requirements of evaluation, planning, and motivation. Granted the premise — that there is a free, open, and virtually limitless market for the product, at an established, known price — the appropriateness of the measure is virtually unchallengeable. Each division becomes, in effect, a business of its own, with completely free choice as to selling outlets and purchase sources. Its achievements, its potentials, and its administration are well measured and guided by reports made on this basis.

Unhappily, the applicability of the method is severely limited by the absence of dependable market price quotations on a majority of industrial products. An item may be unique, or at least peculiar, and trading may be quite restricted, mostly on a contract or sale-by-sale price basis. Actual transactions, even if published, do not necessarily establish a dependable "open market" value.

Furthermore, the quantities involved may radically alter the apparent position. The fact that 100 x units sold yesterday at a certain price does not insure that 100,000 x units can be sold (or bought) tomorrow at an identical figure. Major expansion (or contraction) of a market supply may lead to much lower (or higher) prices. Quotations are often "nominal" even when available; they may reflect the "last previous sale" of some months ago, or a contract which could not be renewed under present conditions.

Moreover, reported price quotations are (regrettably) not always free from purposeful manipulation. Distress sales, at cheap prices, may be cloaked with the anonymity of "private terms." A propped-up price, at an artificially high level, may reflect only a price agreed on between affiliated enterprises. A well regularized set of transactions may involve a price schedule that would not apply to a "spot" sale, or the erratic occasional dumping or grabbing of a quantity outside the limits of normal marketing conditions.

When prices change, what weight should be given to the old and the new price, as applied to transfers occurring at about the time of the change? What recognition should be given to quantity discounts, area and trade channel differentials, transportation and delivery allowances, service factors, etc.? And if, (as often happens), what one must accept to make a sale differs from what one must pay to effect a purchase, should the figure selected for bookkeeping purposes be one which will benefit the producing or the receiving department?

These and many other questions are difficult to resolve in a manner which all concerned will recognize as "fair." Sometimes the decision is left wholly to an impartial referee, with the parties stripped of any influence on the outcome. The alternative may be a requirement that the department heads concerned shall "agree" on what constitutes a "fair" price. This automatically transfers the subject into the realm of "negotiation" — the third of the suggested bases for transfer pricing, discussed in the following section.

Negotiated Basis

There is often a feeling that "trading," between the division managers concerned, will establish a more realistic price than is likely to be arrived at by reference to a cost-plus formula or a published market price. Each manager is presumed to understand the economics of his own situation and the importance of "making a trade" at some specific price. If free to offer the same buying or selling opportunity to outsiders, he can bargain intelligently for his output or his requirements, closing the deal (internal) or accepting an alternative (external) as conditions warrant.

The trouble with this appealing alternative is that it diverts the efforts of key personnel from activities promoting company welfare to those affecting divisional results only. Where the price in question is a major determinant of divisional results, the bargaining may be protracted and bitter. Some managers, pressured by unfavorable influences in their outside dealings, attempt to bolster their position by out-trading their fellow-executives in other divisions. Some become experts in persuasion and cajolery (to say nothing of deceit and bribery) as a means of achieving their profit objectives.

This sort of activity is not merely a time-waster and dissension-breeder; it may lead also to confusing top management as to the facts of a situation. A complaisant or inattentive manager in one department may accept an artificially high or low price on an item which is of minor importance to him, thereby inflating the results of another department in which the item is a major factor. From such misstatement, top management may derive a completely false impression as to managerial performance and profit opportunities. Result, at worst, may be expanded capital investment in facilities unlikely to yield a genuine return under normal competitive conditions.

Conclusion — and a Proposal

Reference was made earlier to the writer's long experience with this problem in an industry which has probably studied it more intensively than any other. This experience was partly as an accounting and marketing expert for the industry trade association (having intimate contact with top management in every major company), and partly as general manager of one of the larger companies (having responsibility for establishing policies, procedures, and controls within that company). The net result of years of study and experimentation in this field was a painful and grudging recognition of the fact that he could neither (a) evolve a method which served the desired purposes in his own company, nor (b) discover such a method which was giving satisfaction in any other. This provides some excuse for a conclusion that the problem is inherently insoluble.

This does not mean, however, that the practice of assigning transfer prices to interdivision product movements can be abandoned. Some value must be placed on each element of input and output, or the whole structure of intra-department analysis and control will fall to pieces. It is merely necessary to recognize that no available transfer-price scheme is likely to serve all possible purposes equally well, and that the results of any method employed must be interpreted with a clear conception of its limitations (as a device for performance evaluation, policy determination, and managerial motivation).

The writer's considered judgment is that a method will be most useful if it has these characteristics: (a) is uniform, consistent and invariable, (b) utilizes only specific criteria, objectively determined and impartially applied, (c) can be easily administered with a minimum of delay, research, and negotiation. It is his further opinion that review and interpretation of the resulting computations should be restricted to those who are, by training, experience, and position (1) fully cognizant of the precise and limited significance of the data, and (2) solely responsible for company-wide (not divisional) achievements.

This means abandonment of the demonstrably fallacious idea that in an integrated, multi-product, sequential-processing enterprise, the activities of any segment can be either evaluated or motivated by its calculated individual *profitableness.* The division exists not to earn a profit of its own, but to contribute to the profit of the entire business. The manager should be stimulated to make, not the most for himself, but the most for the company. Saying that he will be judged on his individual results, but must also take a "broad view" of company-wide needs and interests, involves a contradiction in both terms and objectives. To paraphrase: What's good for General Motors *isn't* necessarily good for the country, and no purpose is served by ignoring the fact.

The preferable course would seem to be: (a) let judgments on profitableness be made, and implemented, exclusively by top management (with aid from experts in analysis and interpretation); (b) develop other criteria for evaluating and motivating divisional management performance.

The latter is by no means difficult. The division manager may be encouraged to concentrate on such problems as improving volume, maximizing yields, minimizing costs, utilizing facilities to best advantage, evaluating capital investment programs in terms of their potential additions to company-wide return on investment, etc. When his responsibilities include developing and maintaining sales to outsiders, his results naturally must be measured *in part* by the profitableness of such business, if its contribution can be successfully segregated from that arising from production for (or purchases from) other company divisions.

Use of a cost (or cost-plus) valuation on transferred output may best serve to remove (or at least normalize) the influence of interdivision production from profit calculations of a producing unit (though a market or market-related price must necessarily be employed for by-products which cannot be independently costed). On the other hand, assessing all previously accumulated "other-division" costs to a receiving unit on transferred *input* may so penalize (or inflate) its results as to give a false impression of its real profit contributions and potentialities.

A partial solution, in some instances, might be found in a combination procedure, under which (a) the producing unit is credited with cost (plus) or market, whichever is *higher,* and (b) the receiving unit is charged with cost (plus) or market, whichever is *lower.* The difference (if determinable) is then identifiable as the cost *to the company* of compelling two divisions to do business with each other, instead of utilizing independent outlets or sources. Such a figure could be studied and interpreted by top management, for purposes of company-wide policy decisions, without infecting divisional results evaluation or interdivision political relationships.

This is no cure-all, and it is not applicable in all situations. It does, however, permit each manager to state his own results on a basis which puts them in the most favorable light, leaving appraisal of their validity, from an overall viewpoint, where such appraisal belongs, as a function of top management. The essential is to free divisional managers of what are not divisional responsibilities.

How useful this method would be in practice, the writer is unable to say with any great confidence (never saw it tried). It might work well in some cases and not in others (would depend on circumstances). It appears, however, to be well worth trying out in any enterprise where the problem is major and the difficulty acute.

It should be fairly simple to develop measurements of this type, through statistical calculations collateral to the basic accounting records, and to expose them to a selected executive group, with carefully prepared explanations and interpretations. If initial reactions are favorable, the method might next be applied, experimentally, to one or more selected operations, in areas where the greatest uncertainty, controversy, and dissatisfaction exist. Outcome of the experiment might well suggest whether such a plan, or some adaptation or modification of it, might lead to better operations and/or sounder policy-making procedures.

Whatever the program, it should be developed with due regard for the following conclusions, each well-supported by both reason and experience:

1. Data most useful for motivation purposes are commonly least suited for pragmatic analysis and realistic forecasting, and vice versa (e.g., sales quotas established as goals for selling achievements are seldom acceptable as the foundation of dependable production or financial budgets).

2. Conclusions and decisions stemming from reports on "results" should be reached only by those well-schooled in the correct interpretation of the figures and responsible only for the results of the business as a whole (not just some one of its parts).

Establishment of a practical and productive transfer-price policy will depend on full recognition of these inescapable realities of business experience.

31 *Input-output analysis is presented as a general model, of which the matrix model is a special case, for handling interactive cost allocation problems. From unit variable and fixed costs computed for varying output volumes, breakeven analyses, flexible budgets, and overhead absorption rates can be computed for each division and for the system as a whole.*

The author illustrates and discusses the basic input-output model, its application to planning and to an analysis of incremental and opportunity costs. He also suggests that the input-output technique can be as valuable for intrafirm analysis as it has been for inter-industry and interfirm economic analysis.

Input-Output Analysis for Cost Accounting, Planning and Control*

John Leslie Livingstone†

Several articles in the recent accounting literature have dealt with the allocation of costs among interacting departments in an organization.[1] The term "interacting departments" is used here to describe departments which both make and receive allocations of costs to and from other departments. An example would be a service department which supports several operating departments and which in turn receives support from other service departments.

The articles cited make use of simultaneous linear equation systems and linear algebra to handle the interactive cost allocation problems. The purpose of this paper is to present some more powerful extensions of these

* *From* The Accounting Review, *Vol. XLIV, No. 1 (January, 1969), pp. 48–64.* *Reprinted by permission of the editor.*

† The author wishes to express appreciation to Gerald L. Salamon, doctoral candidate at The Ohio State University, for helpful comments on this paper.

[1] Thomas H. Williams and Charles H. Griffin, "Matrix Theory and Cost Allocation," THE ACCOUNTING REVIEW (July 1964), pp. 671–78. Neil Churchill, "Linear Algebra and Cost Allocations: Some Examples," THE ACCOUNTING REVIEW (October 1964), pp. 894–904. Rene P. Manes, "Comment on Matrix Theory and Cost Allocation," THE ACCOUNTING REVIEW (Teachers' Clinic) (July 1965), pp. 640–43.

techniques and to show their uses for planning and decision-making. This will be done through input-output analysis. It will be shown that input-output analysis is a general model, of which the matrix cost allocation model is a special case.

Matrix Cost Allocation

To show the link between matrix cost allocation and input-output analysis it is convenient to borrow the example used by Williams and Griffin.[2] This example is based on five interacting service departments and three operating departments, and is summarized as follows:

Cost Allocation Percentage

	Allocations from Service Departments				
	1	*2*	*3*	*4*	*5*
To Service Departments					
1	0	0	5	10	20
2	0	0	10	5	20
3	10	10	0	5	20
4	5	0	10	0	20
5	10	10	5	0	0
To Operating Departments					
A	25	80	20	0	10
B	25	0	30	40	5
C	25	0	20	40	5
Total	100%	100%	100%	100%	100%

Direct costs of each department, before any allocations are:

Service Departments
1	$ 8,000
2	$ 12,000
3	$ 6,000
4	$ 11,000
5	$ 13,000

Operating Departments
A	$120,000
B	$200,000
C	$ 80,000

[2] Williams and Griffin, *op. cit.,* p. 675.

The following system of simultaneous equations is formed:

$$
\begin{aligned}
(1) \quad & X_1 && - .05X_3 - .10X_4, - .20X_5 = 8{,}000 \\
(2) \quad & && X_2, - .10X_3 - .05X_4, - .20X_5 = 12{,}000 \\
(3) \quad & -.10X_1 - .10X_2 + X_3 - .05X_4 - .20X_5 = 6{,}000 \\
(4) \quad & -.05X_1 && - .10X_3 + X_4 - .20X_5 = 11{,}000 \\
(5) \quad & -.10X_1 - .10X_2 - .05X_3 && + X_5 = 13{,}000
\end{aligned}
$$

Where X_i is the redistributed cost of the ith service department after receiving cost allocations from the other service departments. In matrix form these equations are expressed as $Ax = b$, where A is the matrix of cost allocation percentages, x is the vector of redistributed service department costs with elements $X_1, X_2, \cdots, X_5$, and b is the vector of service departments' direct costs.

The system is solved for x by premultiplying $Ax = b$ by the inverse of A, so that $x = A^{-1}b$. The result is:

$$
x = \begin{bmatrix} X_1 \\ X_2 \\ X_3 \\ X_4 \\ X_5 \end{bmatrix} = \begin{bmatrix} 13{,}657.46 \\ 17{,}503.59 \\ 13{,}290.64 \\ 16{,}368.06 \\ 16{,}780.64 \end{bmatrix}
$$

By summing equations (1) through (5) we get:

$$.75X_1 + .80X_2 + .70X_3 + .80X_4 + .20X_5 = \$50{,}000$$

so that a total of $50,000 (which is the total of service department direct costs, ΣB_i) is allocated to the operating departments.

The X_i are now distributed to operating departments, by using the matrix of percentages of service department costs allocable to operating departments to premultiply the x vector, as follows:

$$
\begin{bmatrix} .25 & .80 & .20 & 0 & .10 \\ .25 & 0 & .30 & .40 & .05 \\ .25 & 0 & .20 & .40 & .05 \end{bmatrix} \begin{bmatrix} 13{,}657.46 \\ 17{,}503.59 \\ 13{,}290.64 \\ 16{,}368.06 \\ 16{,}780.64 \end{bmatrix} = \begin{bmatrix} 21{,}755 \\ 14{,}787 \\ 13{,}458 \end{bmatrix}
$$

which, subject to some small rounding errors, gives the allocation to the three operating departments of the $50,000 of service department costs.

To the vector of redistributed service department costs we add the vector of direct costs of operating departments and arrive at the total costs — both allocated and direct — of operating departments, as follows:

$$
\begin{bmatrix} 21{,}755 \\ 14{,}787 \\ 13{,}458 \end{bmatrix} + \begin{bmatrix} 120{,}000 \\ 200{,}000 \\ 80{,}000 \end{bmatrix} = \begin{bmatrix} 141{,}755 \\ 214{,}787 \\ 93{,}458 \end{bmatrix}
$$

We now recast the same example in terms of input-output analysis and show the same result achieved in a single matrix multiplication instead of the three sets of matrix operations used above.

Input-output Representation

Input-output analysis summarizes transactions between all possible economic units involved, in a square matrix. For this reason we express our example in such a manner (in the table below), adding zeros to indicate the absence of cost flows from operating to service departments.

		Allocations from Departments							
		1	*2*	*3*	*4*	*5*	*A*	*B*	*C*
	(1)	0	0	.05	.10	.20	0	0	0
	(2)	0	0	.10	.05	.20	0	0	0
	(3)	.10	.10	0	.05	.20	0	0	0
	(4)	.05	0	.10	0	.20	0	0	0
To Departments	(5)	.10	.10	.05	0	0	0	0	0
	(A)	.25	.80	.20	0	.10	0	0	0
	(B)	.25	0	.30	.40	.05	0	0	0
	(C)	.25	0	.20	.40	.05	0	0	0

We refer to the above matrix as A^* and, as before, we use the vectors x (now 8 by 1, to include all departments — both service and operating) and b (also now 8 by 1).

In our matrix formulation of equations 1 through 5 earlier, the matrix A actually consisted of the service department reciprocal cost allocation percentages subtracted from an identity matrix of the same dimensions. This is seen in equations 1 through 5 by the unity coefficients along the main diagonal and negative or zero coefficients elsewhere.

We now formalize this procedure and define:

$$A = I - A^*.$$

The input-output conditions[3] for clearing all costs out of service departments into operating departments are:[4]

$$Ax = b.$$

---

[3] See R. G. D. Allen *Mathematical Economics* (Macmillan, 1963), p. 483. Our formulation is of an open (rather than closed) system.

[4] Readers can, of course, verify from our example that this equation holds.

Since we are given b and want to find x, we have:

$$x = A^{-1}b$$

and the reader who makes this computation will find that:

$$x = \begin{bmatrix} 13,658 \\ 17,503 \\ 13,290 \\ 16,368 \\ 16,780 \\ 141,755 \\ 214,787 \\ 93,458 \end{bmatrix}$$

which is the same result that we previously obtained in three steps of matrix operations.

In our example so far we have made no distinction between fixed and variable costs. Suppose that certain service departments have both fixed and variable costs. In particular, let us assume that the direct costs of departments 1 and 4 include fixed costs of $2,000 and $5,000, respectively. We can separate the fixed cost allocations by redefining the b vector for fixed costs only as:

$$b^t = [2,000 \quad 0 \quad 0 \quad 5,000 \quad 0 \quad 0 \quad 0 \quad 0]$$

and recomputing x, which we rename x'. Then:

$$x' = A^{-1}b = \begin{bmatrix} 2,624 \\ 393 \\ 631 \\ 5,261 \\ 333 \\ 1,130 \\ 2,967 \\ 2,903 \end{bmatrix}$$

Now the last three elements of b total $7,000 and represent the fixed cost portion of the aggregate costs of operating departments. It is vitally important that the fixed cost portion be separated, otherwise the model automatically unitizes fixed costs as in absorption costing but does not allow for under- or overabsorption when activity levels change. Of course, the first five elements of b represent fixed cost components of service departments' total costs. By subtracting x' from x the variable costs of each department can be found.

With this information, unit fixed and variable costs can be computed by dividing these respective costs for each department by its unit output.

From these unit variable costs, and unit fixed costs computed for varying volumes of output, there can be developed breakeven analyses, flexible budgets and absorption rates for overhead for each department and the system as a whole.

In the above example we were given *b*, the vector of direct cost inputs, and solved for *x*, the output vector. Usually the input-output model is used for the opposite purpose. Given the output vector, it is sought to determine the inputs required. The model is briefly described below, after which we will again apply it to our example — this time as a planning technique to compute resource requirements from an expected level of outputs.

The Basic Input-Output Model

The input-output model, which is due to Leontief,[5] analyzes transactions between economic activities, where an activity may represent an industry, a firm, or — as in our case — a single department or cost center. It is assumed that there is only one primary input (usually labor) and only one output for each activity. There are *n* activities and *n* output commodities, each of which may comprise a final product or an intermediate product serving as input for other activities. Production takes place through processes with fixed technological yields of constant proportionality. There is only one process used with no substitution in each activity. The use of only one process does not necessarily imply that alternative processes are non-existent. It may be that an activity has a production function that includes alternative processes, each with constant technological yields, and then elects a single, perhaps optimal, process for use. In this case the process selected is preferred only for a given set of prices.

The basis of the input-output model is a matrix of transactions (presently assumed to be in monetary terms), with a row and a column for each activity. The transactions matrix can be summarized as:

$$
\begin{array}{c}
n \text{ rows} \\
\\
1 \text{ row}
\end{array}
\left[
\begin{array}{c|c|c}
V_{rc} & v_r & V_r \\
\hline
e_c & 0 & W
\end{array}
\right]
$$

$$
\begin{array}{ccc}
n & 1 & \text{total} \\
\text{columns} & \text{column} & \text{column}
\end{array}
$$

The amounts V_{rc} (with $r,c = 1,2,\cdots, n$) are the monetary values of output of the *r*th activity used as input by the *c*th activity. The rows thus represent distribution of the output of each activity, while the columns

[5] Wasily W. Leontief, *The Structure of American Economy, 1919–39*, second edition (Oxford University Press, 1951). A very good, concise description of the model is given in Richard Mattessich, *Accounting and Analytical Methods* (Richard D. Irwin, Inc., 1964), pp. 295–311.

represent sources of the inputs of activities. The n dimensional vector, v_r, shows the final demand for each commodity (or the "bill of goods") and V_r (n by 1) is the total output column so that:

(1) $$V_r = v_r + \sum_c v_{rc}, \quad r = 1, 2, \cdots, n.$$

The n dimensional row vector e_c represents the costs of the primary input (say labor) to the activities, with a total of W, and thus:

(2) $$W = \sum_c e_c$$

Fixed technological coefficients are assumed:

(3) $$a_{rc} = v_{rc}/V_c \quad r, c = 1, 2, \cdots, n$$

which are the $(n + 1)$ elements of each column, respectively, divided by their sum, V_c, which is:

(4) $$V_c = e_c + \sum_r v_{rc}.$$

These give an input coefficient matrix:

(5) $$A^* = [a_{rc}], \quad \text{of order } n \text{ by } n$$

and a technology matrix:

(6) $$A = I - A^* = \begin{bmatrix} 1 & -a_{12} & \cdots & -a_{1n} \\ -a_{21} & 1 & \cdots & -a_{2n} \\ \hline -a_{n1} & -a_{n2} & \cdots & 1 \end{bmatrix}.$$

The solution to the system, expressing the condition that all output is exactly distributed over uses (both final and intermediate) is:

(7) $$AV_r = v_r.$$

Note that equation (7) does not directly give us e_c which can be derived as follows: Given v_r, final demand, we compute V_r, total output, and then calculate e_c. From (7) we compute V_r,

(8) $$V_r = A^{-1}v_r.$$

Since all output is exactly distributed over uses, total inputs equal total output for each activity, i.e.,

(9) $$V_r = V_c \quad \text{for all } r = c$$

in other words, the row total for any activity equals its column total.

Now consider any column, with subscript $c = 0$. We can rewrite (3) as:

(10) $$a_{r0} = v_{r0}/V_0$$

and sum both sides over rows:

(11) $$\sum_r a_{r0} = \sum_r v_{r0}/V_0.$$

Similarly, (4) can be rewritten as:

(12) $$V_0 = e_0 + \sum_r v_{r0}.$$

Then, we divide (12) by V_0 and obtain:

(13) $$1 = e_0/V_0 + \sum_r v_{r0}/V_0$$

and substitute from (11) into (13):

(14) $$1 = e_0/V_0 + \sum_r a_{r0}$$

which can be rearranged into:

(15) $$e_0 = V_0\left(1 - \sum_r a_{r0}\right).$$

Since V_0 is known to us from (8) and (9), and $\Sigma_r a_{r0}$ is given, e_0 can be computed from (15). Having set up the basic input-output model, we now

TABLE 1

Inputs

		1	2	3	4	5
	(1)			1,366	683	1,366
	(2)			1,750		1,750
	(3)	655	1,329		1,329	665
	(4)	1,637	818	818		
Outputs	(5)	3,356	3,356	3,356	3,356	
	(A)					.
	(B)					
	(C)					
	e_c	8,000	12,000	6,000	11,000	13,000
Total	(V_c)	13,658	17,503	13,290	16,368	16,781

		A	B	C	v_r	Total (V_r)
	(1)	3,415	3,414	3,414		13,658
	(2)	14,003				17,503
	(3)	2,658	3,986	2,658		13,290
	(4)		6,548	6,547		16,368
Outputs	(5)	1,679	839	839		16,781
	(A)				141,755	141,755
	(B)				214,787	214,787
	(C)				93,458	93,458
	e_c	120,000	200,000	80,000		450,000
Total	(V_c)	141,755	214,787	93,458	450,000	977,600

apply it to our example as a planning technique to compute requirements for primary inputs from a given level of outputs.

Input-Output Applied To Planning

Input-output applications normally proceed by gathering the data for the transactions matrix and then computing the technological coefficients from these data. We will follow this procedure, using the same example as before. The dollar transactions matrix in canonical (or standard) form is shown in Table 1.

The transactions matrix in Table 1 requires some explanation. Note that it differs in form from the cost allocation model where outputs were stated in columns and inputs along rows as shown above. The standard transactions matrix is the transpose of that arrangement, with outputs stated rowwise and inputs columnwise. The vector V_r

$$V_r = \begin{bmatrix} 13,658 \\ 17,503 \\ \vdots \\ 93,458 \end{bmatrix}, \quad 8 \text{ by } 1.$$

is seen to be identical with the vector x which we computed previously in the one-step procedure for cost allocation. Note that the vector V_c of column totals is simply the transpose of the V_r vector, so that the row and column totals for any activity are equal.

The V_r vector of final demand shows the output of operating departments which, as expected, totals \$450,000 and equals the scalar, W, which is the total value of primary inputs (the elements of the e_c vector). It is worth pointing out that the overall total of the table, namely \$977,600, amounts to twice the total of primary inputs (\$450,000) or final demand, plus the sum of interactivity transfers (\$77,600), i.e.:

$$2(450,000) + 13,658 + 17,503 + 13,290 + 16,368 + 16,781 = 977,600.$$

Thus the table adds to the aggregate value of all transactions of all activities in the system. The familiar macro-economic quantities of gross national product, national income, consumption and so on that are used in national income accounting have their analogies at the micro level of our system of activities.

Payments to primary factors, or gross system product at factor prices, is \$450,000 — the sum of the e_c row, which is also gross system income, or total consumption — the sum of the v_r column. This is the fundamental identity of the product and expenditure sides in national (or here, system) income accounting. Interactivity transactions would, of course, be excluded as double-counting since they do not represent any value added. Thus, input-output analysis can be regarded generally as a double-entry accounting technique for recording and analyzing transactions between activities in an economic system.

Finally, in explanation of Table 1, it remains to show the derivation of the v_{rc}, i.e., the amounts in the upper left hand part of the transactions matrix. These are obtained by applying the cost allocation percentages previously given to the total redistributed cost of each service department. For instance, of service department #2's total redistributed costs of $17,503, 10% (or $1,750) each is allocated to departments 3 and 5 and the remaining 80% (or $14,003) to operating department A. We now calculate the a_{rc} to obtain A^*. Applying (3) to column 1 of the transactions matrix we have:

$$
\begin{aligned}
V_1 &= 13,658 \\
a_{31} = v_{31}/V_1 &= 665/13,658 = 0.0487 \\
a_{41} = v_{41}/V_1 &= 1,637/13,658 = 0.1199 \\
a_{51} = v_{51}/V_1 &= 3,356/13,658 = 0.2457 \\
e_1/V_1 &= = 8,000/13,658 = \underline{0.5857} \\
& \text{Total} = \overline{\underline{1.0000}}
\end{aligned}
$$

The remaining columns are treated in the same way to compute A^* and then A, which is:

$$
\begin{bmatrix}
1 & & -.1028 & -.0417 & -.0814 & -.0241 & -.0159 & -.0365 \\
 & 1 & -.1317 & & -.1043 & -.0988 & & \\
-.0487 & -.0759 & 1 & -.0812 & -.0396 & -.0188 & -.0186 & -.0284 \\
-.1199 & -.0467 & -.0616 & 1 & & & -.0305 & -.0701 \\
-.2457 & -.1918 & -.2525 & -.2050 & 1 & -.0118 & -.0039 & -.0090 \\
 & & & & & 1 & & \\
 & & & & & & 1 & \\
 & & & & & & & 1
\end{bmatrix}
$$

and

$$
A^{-1} =
\begin{bmatrix}
1.0386 & .0319 & .1391 & .0737 & .0934 & .0319 & .0217 & .0471 \\
.0424 & 1.0378 & .1734 & .0402 & .1186 & .1082 & .0056 & .0094 \\
.0767 & .0947 & 1.0410 & .0995 & .0573 & .0314 & .0238 & .0394 \\
.1312 & .0581 & .0889 & 1.0169 & .0203 & .0108 & .0348 & .0786 \\
.3096 & .2427 & .3485 & .2594 & 1.0643 & .0506 & .0235 & .0403 \\
 & & & & & 1 & & \\
 & & & & & & 1 & \\
 & & & & & & & 1
\end{bmatrix}
$$

Now, for any given final demand vector v_r we can compute e_c, the primary input resource requirements. For instance, consider a final demand one-tenth as large as before, so that:

$$v_r = \begin{bmatrix} 0 \\ 0 \\ 0 \\ 0 \\ 0 \\ 14,176 \\ 21,479 \\ 9,346 \end{bmatrix}$$

Then, from (8),

$$V_r = A^{-1}v_r = \begin{bmatrix} 1,359 \\ 1,742 \\ 1,326 \\ 1,636 \\ 1,668 \\ 14,176 \\ 21,479 \\ 9,346 \end{bmatrix}$$

Note that rounding error impairs the accuracy of the computation. We know from Table 1 that the elements of V_r should be (to the nearest dollar) 1,366, 1,750 and so on rather than the 1,359, 1,742, etc., above. This is due to the use of only four decimal places in setting up the A^* matrix, a nearest-dollar v_r vector, and use of a single-precision computer routine for the inversion of A.[6] The inaccuracy is of the order of one-half of one per cent. Users wishing superior accuracy may be well advised to resort to double-precision routines.[7]

Having determined V_r, the next step is to compute e_c, the primary input resource requirements. We use expression (15), which can be expressed in matrix form as:

(16) $$e_c = V_r^T Z$$

where Z is a matrix with elements

$$\left(1 - \sum_r a_{r0}\right)$$

---

[6] Inversion was done using the General Electric Time-Sharing Service and one of its library routines called MATRIX***. Even though this program requires a redundant (for this purpose) matrix multiplication, its run time was 7 seconds. This run time (inefficiently used) for an 8 by 8 matrix inversion, is interesting to compare with the 10 seconds reported by Manes (*op. cit.*, p. 641) for a 5 by 5 matrix, which resulted in a loss of one-third of one per cent average accuracy.

[7] See Manes, *op. cit.*, p. 641, for a report on the use of a double-precision routine.

on the main diagonal and zeros elsewhere:

$$
Z = \begin{bmatrix}
\left(1 - \sum_r a_{r1}\right) & 0 & \cdots & \cdots & 0 \\
0 & \left(1 - \sum_r a_{r2}\right) & \cdots & \cdots & 0 \\
\hline
0 & 0 & & \left(1 - \sum_r a_{rn}\right)
\end{bmatrix}.
$$

In our example we have: [8]

$$
Z = \begin{bmatrix}
.5857 & 0 & 0 & 0 & 0 & 0 & 0 & 0 \\
0 & .6856 & 0 & 0 & 0 & 0 & 0 & 0 \\
0 & 0 & .4514 & 0 & 0 & 0 & 0 & 0 \\
0 & 0 & 0 & .6721 & 0 & 0 & 0 & 0 \\
0 & 0 & 0 & 0 & .7747 & 0 & 0 & 0 \\
0 & 0 & 0 & 0 & 0 & .8465 & 0 & 0 \\
0 & 0 & 0 & 0 & 0 & 0 & .9311 & 0 \\
0 & 0 & 0 & 0 & 0 & 0 & 0 & .8560
\end{bmatrix}
$$

and using V_r corrected for rounding error,

$$e_c = [800 \quad 1{,}200 \quad 600 \quad 1{,}100 \quad 1{,}300 \quad 12{,}000 \quad 20{,}000 \quad 8{,}000],$$

which we can see from Table 1 is correct, being one-tenth of the primary input requirements in the table.

Expression (16) can be generalized and used to find any desired row of the dollar transactions matrix. The Z matrix applied to find e_c can be subscripted e. A Z matrix, Z_r, can be formulated to find any row r as follows:

$$
Z_r = \begin{bmatrix}
a_{r1} & 0 & \cdots & 0 \\
0 & a_{r2} & \cdots & 0 \\
\hline
0 & 0 & \cdots & a_{rn}
\end{bmatrix},
$$

and then (16) in general form becomes:

(17) $$r = V_r^T Z_r.$$

For instance let $r = 2$. Then:

$$Z_{33} = .1317, \quad Z_{55} = .1043 \quad \text{and} \quad Z_{66} = .0988$$

with all other $Z_{ij} = 0$, and:

$$\text{row } 2 = V_r^T Z_2 = [0 \quad 0 \quad 175 \quad 0 \quad 175 \quad 1400 \quad 0 \quad 0]$$

which, it is seen from Table 1, is correct.

---

[8] Note that the $\left(1 - \sum_r a_{r0}\right)$ can be obtained by summing the columns of the A matrix.

To summarize, it has been shown how any vector of expected final demand can be translated into the required vector of primary inputs. In addition, we have shown how to derive the associated interactivity transactions. Once the A^{-1} and Z matrices have been computed, so long as the mix of services is constant, they can be used again and again for any values of expected final demand, and the computational load of evaluating the effects of various final demand vectors is quite light. Therefore, the technique has advantages for planning and resource allocation purposes, and also for ensuring proper coordination of input and output requirements. In fact, it conforms to the normal budgeting procedure of commencing with expected sales and then working back to determine production and other budgets consistent with the sales forecast. However, in the standard budget procedure this internal consistency is not assured as it is in input-output analysis — where the output of any activity is consistent with the demands, both final and from other activities, for its product.

The illustration above is only the most obvious application of input-output analysis for planning. Before proceeding to more sophisticated levels, however, it is necessary to examine the model in greater detail.

Physical Coefficients and the Numeraire

The transactions matrix has so far been dealt with in terms of dollars. It can, however, be broken down into physical quantities and unit costs or prices which enables more precise planning use. The effects of price and quantity changes can then be separated in similar fashion to standard cost variance analysis.

Let there be n activities plus a final demand vector and a vector of primary inputs. Let x_{rc} be the physical amount of the output quantity X_r of the rth activity used by the cth activity. Then the physical transactions matrix is composed of elements x_{rc} and sums across rows to the vector X_r of total physical output. Let f_c be the vector of primary input quantities (say labor hours), summing to Y for all activities. Thus, the physical transactions matrix is:

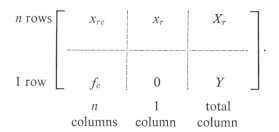

Fixed physical coefficients, t_{rc}, are assumed:[9]

(18) $$t_{rc} = x_{rc}/X_r, \text{ for all } r = c = 1, 2, \ldots, n.$$

The t_{rc} comprise an input coefficient matrix, T^*, and a technology matrix $T = I - T^*$ which is n by n in dimension. The T matrix can be expanded by adding a bottom row of labor input coefficients, $-d_c$, where:

(19) $$d_c = f_c/X_r, \text{ for all } c = r.$$

Finally we need two vectors of prices: p is the row vector of unit commodity prices, and w is the row vector of labor cost per unit of output, and both are n-dimensional.

The system takes as given T, x, and w. For all output to be exactly distributed over final and intermediate uses, the conditions are:

(20) $$TX_r = x_r$$

(21) $$pT = w.$$

Note from (21) that the prices, p, are dependent on unit labor costs, w, just as in a standard cost system amounts transferred to work-in-process and finished goods depend on standard material, labor and overhead unit costs. In other words, output prices are determined by cost-based primary input prices, as is generally the case in accounting. In addition we can compute Y, total labor hours, and S, total labor costs (which equals system gross income or aggregate final demand), as follows:

(22) $$\begin{aligned} Y &= d_c X_r \\ &= d_c T^{-1} x_r, \quad \text{substituting from (20)} \end{aligned}$$

and:

(23) $$\begin{aligned} S &= p x_r \\ &= w X_r \\ &= w T^{-1} x_r, \quad \text{substituting from (20).} \end{aligned}$$

As mentioned before, prices of outputs are cost-determined by the w vector of labor unit costs (or — more generally — unit costs of whatever the primary input happens to be, say computer time for that matter). Since specification of w determines p, w can be called the numeraire vector, or common denominator for assigning value. Thus, w serves the same purpose as a set of standard costs, which are also exogenous, or given, in an accounting system.

---

[9] These are analogous to physical standards for material and labor usage in a standard cost system.

Although perhaps theoretically less acceptable, it should be noted that there is no mathematical reason for w to be given. If p is given, equation (21) is then:

$$(24) \qquad v_{rc} = p_r x_{rc}$$

recalling that the v_{rc} are the dollar elements of the dollar transactions matrix and the x_{rc} are the elements of the physical transactions matrix. From (3) we have the dollar technological coefficients, a_{rc}:

$$(25) \qquad \begin{aligned} a_{rc} &= v_{rc}/V_c \\ &= P_r x_{rc}/V_c \\ &= (p_r/p_c) t_{rc} \end{aligned}$$
$$\text{since for any } c = r, \ P_c X_r = V_c.$$

Thus the relationship between a_{rc} and t_{rc} is determined by the ratio of the respective row and column unit prices. Then, given v_{rc}, the system can be solved as shown previously.

Up to now, we have followed the usual input-output approach of determining primary inputs given final demand, i.e., the last column vector of the transactions matrix is treated as exogenous (or given) and it is desired to find the last row vector (of primary inputs). However, any column vector and any row vector of the transactions matrix can be made exogenous, say the ith row and the jth column. Then the technical matrix A is reduced, by elimination of the ith row and jth column, to order $(n-1)$, and the vector V_r of total output also becomes $(n-1)$ dimensional by elimination of the ith row. Expression (7) may then be generalized to:

$$(26) \qquad AV_r = v$$

where v_j is the given column vector of inputs to the jth activity.[10]

Analysis of Incremental and Opportunity Costs

In order to illustrate the analysis in terms of physical inputs and outputs, a new example is required. This is as follows:

		Process Inputs			Final Demand x_r	Total Output X_r
		1	2	3		
	(1) (lbs.)	0	14	30	36	80
Process Outputs	(2) (gals.)	4	0	48	18	70
	(3) (cu. ft.)	16	28	0	56	100
	Labor (hrs.)	20	98	72	0	190

[10] Allen, *op. cit.*, pp. 486–488.

Using (18) we compute the t_{rc}, for instance:

$$t_{21} = 4/80 = .05, \qquad t_{31} = 16/80 = .20.$$
$$t_{12} = 14/70 = .20, \qquad t_{32} = 28/70 = .40.$$

and then the technology matrix, T:

$$T = \begin{bmatrix} 1 & -.20 & -.30 \\ -.05 & 1 & -.48 \\ -.20 & -.40 & 1 \end{bmatrix}.$$

Computation of the inverse results in:

$$T^{-1} = \begin{bmatrix} 1.13356 & .448934 & .555556 \\ .204826 & 1.31874 & .694444 \\ .308642 & .617284 & 1.38889 \end{bmatrix}.$$

From (20) we have:

(27) $$X_r = T^{-1}x_r = \begin{bmatrix} 80 \\ 70 \\ 100 \end{bmatrix},$$

which agrees with the transactions matrix above.

We now consider what it takes to produce one pound of final output from process 1. This is best shown by setting final demand accordingly, i.e.:

$$x_r = \begin{bmatrix} 1 \\ 0 \\ 0 \end{bmatrix}.$$

Then:

$$X_r = T^{-1}x_r = \begin{bmatrix} 1.13356 \\ .204826 \\ .308642 \end{bmatrix},$$

which is simply the first column of T^{-1}. Thus, the columns of T^{-1} show the total production required to end up with a single unit of output from each activity. For instance, to produce one gallon from process 2 requires 0.448934 pounds from process 1, 1.31874 gallons from process 2 and 0.617284 cubic feet from process 3.

Note that 1.31874 gallons from process 2 are needed as intermediate output, since this process requires inputs from processes 1 and 3 — both of which in turn, require inputs from process 2. Note also that the T matrix does not give this information. It shows inputs of 0.20 pounds from process 1 and 0.40 cubic feet from process 3 to produce 1 gallon from process 2. However, these are simply the direct or "first round" inputs and not the total additions to production after allowing for indirect effects through the system. The cumulative results, after all the feedback effects have worked themselves out, are therefore shown in the T^{-1} matrix. In other words, the analysis is not *ceteris paribus* but *mutatis mutandis*.[11]

By use of the T^{-1} matrix *mutatis mutandis* physical standards become available, relating the work loads of the respective process to the demands imposed by exogenous activities.[12] These standards are useful tools in planning for the logistics of changes in the future levels of activities, in budgeting for processes, activities and products, and in appraising performance for control purposes.

We now introduce monetary values to the system. It is convenient to take as given the price vector p, rather than the more usual step of determining p from a given w, the unit wage cost. Let:

$$p = [5 \quad 10 \quad 15]$$

with elements representing the dollar cost per pound, gallon and cubic foot, respectively, of the output of each process.[13] Then, from (21):

(28) $$w = pT = [1.5 \quad 3 \quad 8.7].$$

Using (19) we compute the labor input coefficients:

(29) $$\begin{aligned} d_c &= [20/80 \quad 98/70 \quad 72/100] \\ &= [0.25 \quad 1.4 \quad 0.72] \end{aligned}$$

and from (22) we set Y, total labor hours:

(30) $$Y = d_c X_r = 190$$

which is also verified as correct from the transactions matrix. Finally, from (23), S, total labor cost is:

(31) $$S = wX_r = \$1,200.$$

Now the dollar transactions matrix can be completed:

		Process Inputs			Final Demand	Total Output
		1	2	3	v_r	V_r
Outputs	(1)	0	70	150	180	400
	(2)	40	0	480	180	700
	(3)	240	420	0	840	1,500
	e_c	120	210	870	0	1,200
Total	V_c	400	700	1,500	1,200	3,800

[11] For further discussion and illustration of *mutatis mutandis* vs. *ceteris paribus* approaches see Yuji Ijiri, Ferdinand K. Levy and R. C. Lyon, "A Linear Programming Model for Budgeting and Financial Planning," *Journal of Accounting Research* (Autumn 1963), pp. 208–210.

[12] For discussion of the dependent nature of service departments on the volume demands of other activities, and for exposition of budgeting and control techniques with respect to non-interactive departments, see Gordon Shillinglaw. *Cost Accounting,* revised edition (Richard D. Irwin, Inc., 1967), pp. 481–494.

[13] Given the direct linear proportionality of cost and volume in the system, p and w represent both average and incremental unit costs.

The v_{rc} were computed as in (24), by multiplying the x_{rc} by their unit prices and similarly for the v_r and V_r vectors. The labor costs, e_c, were inserted as balancing figures,[14] which sum to $1,200 as shown in (31) above.

We now consider the effects of changes in prices. Suppose that a wage rate increase takes place in process 1. Previously, as shown in the physical and dollar transactions matrices, 20 hours of labor cost $120 giving an average wage rate of $6 an hour. Say that this average now becomes $10 an hour.

From (29) we computed the labor input coefficient[15] for process 1, d_1:

$$d_1 = 0.25$$

and multiplied d_1 by the wage rate to calculate w, the vector of labor cost per unit of output. Previously W_1 (the first element of w) was 0.25 times $6 or 1.5. Now, with an average wage rate of $10 an hour:

$$W_1 = 0.25(\$10) = 2.5$$

and

$$w = [2.5 \quad 3 \quad 8.7].^{16}$$

From (23) we compute S, total labor costs:

$$S = wX_r$$
$$= \$1,280$$

which have increased from the previous $1,200 in the dollar transactions matrix. The increase of $80 is, of course, the 20 hours in process 1 multiplied by the rise of $4 an hour in the wage rate. This can be computed directly by using the change in w, which we designate w'. Then:

$$w' = [1 \quad 0 \quad 0]$$

and

$$w'X_r = \$80 = S$$

which is the increment to the total wage bill.

From the new value of w a revised dollar transactions matrix can be derived. First, from (21),

(32) $\qquad p = wT^{-1} = [6.13356 \quad 10.448934 \quad 15.555556].$

By multiplying the x_{rc}, the x_r and the X_r by these new unit prices, the revised dollar transactions matrix is found to be:

[14] They could be directly derived by multiplying each W_r (elements of w) with the corresponding X_r element, for instance $W_1 = 1.5$, $X_1 = 80$ and $e_1 = W_1 X_1 = 1.5(80) = \$120$.

[15] Representing the hours of labor required to produce one unit of output in that process.

[16] Note, by comparison with (28), that remaining elements of w are unchanged.

		Process Inputs			Final Demand v_r	Total Output V_r
		1	*2*	*3*		
	(1)	0	85.87	184.01	220.81	490.69
Outputs	(2)	41.79	0	501.55	188.08	731.42
	(3)	248.90	435.55	0	871.11	1,555.56
	e_c	200.00	210.00	870.00	0	1,280.00
Total	V_c	490.69	731.42	1,555.56	1,280.00	4,057.67

A comparison with the previous dollar transactions matrix shows that while total wages increased by $80, total output increased by $90.69 in process 1, $31.42 in process 2, and $55.56 in process 3, amounting to $177.67 altogether. This illustrates the multiplier (or amplification) effect in the interactive system. It can be more directly analyzed by again taking the incremental approach with respect to p, where we use p' to designate the change or difference between the old and revised p vectors.

From (32):

(33) $\qquad p' = w'T^{-1} = [1.13356 \quad .448934 \quad .555556].$

Using p' to multiply the x_{rc}, x_r and X_r we can compute the changes in the dollar transactions matrix. These changes are, of course, the increments resulting in each input-output element of each process in the dollar transactions matrix due to the change in wage rate in process 1. Thus, for each increment in the cost of primary inputs, there is a complementary set of process opportunity costs arising in the interactive system.

It is worth glancing back at (33) and noting that the elements of p' are identical to the first row of T^{-1}. The reason for this is as follows: labor costs in process 1 went up by $4 an hour. Since 4 pounds of output are produced per hour in process 1, the increase in labor costs per pound, is $1. In other words, $W_1' = 1$ as we previously found.

Now the first row of T^{-1} shows the inputs in pounds, from process 1 required to produce one unit of output in each process. Equivalently, this row shows the increase in cost per unit of each process from a $1 per pound increase in the costs of process 1. Therefore, given the strict linear proportionality of the system, we can generalize that the ith row of T^{-1} shows the unit opportunity cost in each process per $1 increment in the unit cost of the ith process. Thus by using (33), the effects on the system of any labor rate change in any process can easily and speedily be computed. Where labor rates vary in more than one process, the effects of individual changes can be computed separately if desired and then in the aggregate.

It should be emphasized that this analysis of cost changes and their effects was made without any need to adjust the T matrix. Any adjustments to T would, of course, have required the computation of a new inverse, T^{-1}, to be used in the analysis. This is an advantage of basing the system on physical relationships and explicit independent price vectors, rather than using monetary values as the original basis.[17] If the system had been built from scratch on a dollar transactions matrix, any change in wage rates (or in any other prices) would have altered the input-output coefficients and thus required computation of a new inverse.

Note that we refer to a change in the unit cost of a primary input as an incremental cost, and to its effect on the costs of the system as the associated opportunity cost. It was also shown that the interactive nature of the system amplified the incremental cost into a larger cost[18] — which we termed opportunity cost. This is a true opportunity cost since it reflects the total sacrifice associated with the wage rate increase on a *mutatis mutandis* (rather than a *ceteris paribus*) basis. In other words, it takes into account the effects on every other activity resulting from the single change in wage rate, as opposed to the more usual approach of assuming that only one or a few effects are considered, while all others are treated as constant.

Expanding the Transactions Matrix

The analysis can be extended to take into account factors not yet considered. For instance, the notion of beginning and ending inventories has not explicitly been considered. Implicitly, however, there has been an unstated inventory assumption made in the following sense. Given a system of interacting activities, many or most of which use each other's outputs as inputs, it seems very unlikely that the system could start up or continue to operate without inventories. In the absence of inventories the situation may be likened to attempting to produce a chicken without an egg or vice versa.[19]

Extension of the system can be accomplished to include inventories and other factors by expanding the transactions matrix. Instead of a single

[17] For a more general and complete discussion of separating physical measurement and monetary valuation in accounting see Yuji Ijiri, "Physical Measures and Multi-Dimensional Accounting," in *Research in Accounting Measurement,* R. K. Jaedicke, Y. Ijiri and O. Nielsen, editors (American Accounting Association, 1966), pp. 150–164.

[18] In our example, for instance, incremental cost of the wage rate increase in process 1 was $80, while the cost of total output went up by $177.67.

[19] It is possible for activities to use their own output as input. Usually self-consumption is offset against output. For the opposite approach see Yuji Ijiri, "An Application of Input-Output Analysis to Some Problems in Cost Accounting," *Management Accounting,* (April 1968), pp. 60–61.

vector for final demand it is possible to have a series of column vectors such as the following, one for each component of final demand:

Additions to Inventory	*Outputs Sold Outside Without Further Processing*	*Outputs for Use Elsewhere in Firm*	*Sales to Customer Classes A, B · · · N*

Similarly, the vector of primary inputs can be expanded into a series of row vectors such as:

Inventory Depletion
Direct Outside Purchases
Depreciation Allowances
Materials
Labor
Variable Overhead
Fixed Overhead
Profit Margin

Thus, the expanded transactions matrix (in either physical or money terms) now consists of multiple vectors of final demand and of primary input components, in addition to the sector which states the input-output flows between processes or activities.[20] The latter sector is normally termed the processing sector.

For the purposes of performing any computations it is necessary to collapse the multiple vectors of final demand and primary input components into single vectors by addition. Then the computation is carried out as previously shown. However, after computation the computed vector (usually that of primary inputs) can be disaggregated again into its components, so that an expanded transactions matrix is made available. The disaggregation may be done by using previously established ratios between various components (such as proportionalities between materials, labor, variable overhead and profit) and/or use of constraints (such as a limit to the quantities of beginning inventory available, or a constant amount as in the case of fixed costs). A component such as inputs purchased direct from outside may serve as a slack, to provide for demands in excess of available inventory quantities.

With respect to lump sum constant items such as fixed costs and possibly depreciation and profit (unless treated as factors directly varying with output volume) the cautions previously noted must be observed. Also, it should be remembered that the transactions matrix is required to meet a symmetry condition: that total inputs match total outputs. Thus, primary

---

[20] An example of a transactions matrix expanded to include ending inventories, overhead, and profit, appears in Shawki M. Farag, "A Planning Model for the Divisionalized Enterprise," THE ACCOUNTING REVIEW, (April 1968), pp. 317–318.

input components, such as depreciation and profit for example, must have their theoretical output complements — such as "Outputs Used Elsewhere in the Firm" (perhaps in capital investment) and "Sales," respectively. Of course, the dollar totals of aggregate final demand and primary inputs must be the same.

Conclusions

As in the case of every model, input-output analysis is conditioned on strict assumptions. These were previously described, but will be briefly noted below. The would-be user is cautioned to ensure that the assumptions are met by the situation in which the model is hoped to be applied. Three critical assumptions may be summarized as follows.

(a) *One standard output for each activity:* it is required that each activity produce a single, standardized output. If individual activities were to vary their commodities produced, we would not be able to specify the fixed input-output coefficients needed to form the technology matrix. If there are joint or by-products it is necessary for them to be produced in constant combination, so that a fixed ratio exists between the quantities of each product of a process and thus this combination can be specified as a standardized single output. Also, the same commodity should not be produced by two or more processes, since this creates alternative rather than unique input-output coefficients.

(b) *Fixed input-output coefficients:* it is not permissible for the proportions among inputs used in a process to be varied. If such input substitutions are allowable it again becomes impossible to specify fixed input-output coefficients from which to derive the technology matrix.

(c) *A linear homogenous production function:* this requires the relations between inputs and outputs not only to be linear, which follows from (b) above, but also to be homogenous. The mathematical condition for linear homogeneity is:[21]

$$f(kx_1 \quad kx_2 \quad \cdots, \quad kx_n) = kf(x_1, \quad x_2, \quad \cdots, \quad x_n).$$

For instance the function $y = a_1x_1 + a_2x_2$ meets this condition since:

$$a_1kx_1 + a_2kx_2 = k(a_1x_1 + a_2x_2).$$

However, the function $y = c + a_1x_1 + a_2x_2$ does not since:

$$c + a_1kx_1 + a_2kx_2 \neq k(c + a_1x_1 + a_2x_2).$$

[21] See Allen *op. cit.*, p. 335.

In the model, each column of the technological matrix represents a process in the firm's production function. If any process is not linear homogenous due to the presence of a constant term, a different input-output coefficient would be needed for each value of the x_1 (i.e., for every possible volume of operation the technological yield would vary). Therefore, once again, we would not have fixed input-output coefficients for the technology matrix.

Subject to the assumptions outlined above, input-output analysis may usefully be applied as shown in this paper. There seems to be no reason why it cannot be as valuable a technique for intrafirm as it has been for interfirm and interindustry economic analysis.

32 *Increasing decentralization of decision-making and creation of profit centers makes the transfer pricing problem acute. Existing accounting and economic solutions are seriously deficient. In this article, a new transfer pricing system based on the concept of opportunity cost is advocated.*

The economic transfer pricing system is examined, under both the "simple maximizer" and "cooperative" cases. Behavioral problems are exposed, and suggested refinements are offered. A set of solutions involving the opportunity cost concept then is offered, with consideration given to the need for certain policy decisions at the corporate level. The use of "motivation costs" to resolve residual areas of conflict which persist in a few special cases is one of this article's significant new ideas.

A Transfer Pricing System Based on Opportunity Cost*

Mohamed Onsi

With decentralization of decision-making and creation of profit centers in multi-product organizations, the transfer pricing system becomes an acute problem. To arrive at an optimal solution, or at an approximation to it, both accounting and economic thought have recommended certain solutions.[1] However, some of the suggested solutions have shortcomings that cannot be ignored or assumed to be insignificant. The problem is material when the performance of a divisional manager is measured based on profit, and incentive compensation is so determined.

In this paper, the economic foundation of a transfer pricing system and its limitations will be briefly presented. A new transfer pricing system is

---

* *From* The Accounting Review, *Vol. XLV, No. 3 (July, 1970), pp. 535–543. Reprinted by permission of the editor.*

[1] See: David Solomons, *Divisional Performance* (Financial Executives Research Foundation, 1965), pp. 212–228, and Jack Hirshleifer, "Internal Pricing and Decentralized Decisions," in *Management Controls*, ed. by C. P. Bonini, R. K. Jaedicke and H. M. Wagner (McGraw-Hill, 1964), pp. 27–37.

suggested, based on an opportunity cost concept. The advantages of this approach, compared to others, will be discussed.

The Economic Transfer Pricing System

When there is a market price for intermediate goods, they are transferred according to such a price, assuming that the goods transferred are produced in a competitive market where the supplying center cannot influence the sales price in the open market by its own output decision. Pricing intermediate goods according to market price has the advantage of motivating the supplying center to reduce its cost as much as possible and emphasize innovation and research and development, since it will be to its advantage.

However, if there is no market price for the intermediate goods, then the volume which Profit Center A should produce and that which Profit Center B should demand, ideally, is at that level where the MC_A is equal to the NMR_B. Operationally, however, the profit center manager, in this case, may behave according to one of two possibilities: (1) as *a simple maximizer* of his own profit, or (2) as a *cooperator* who is concerned with maximizing total joint profits.

THE SIMPLE MAXIMIZER CASE

If the selling profit center (A) is in a monopolistic position, he will keep the price of the intermediate goods at P_2 (Exhibit 1) and will produce at a level equal to that demanded, OBd_2; that is, the volume where the buying center equates its own $NMR_B = P_2$. The profit area of Center A lies between the P_2 line and his MC_A line. This area is larger than his profit if he accepts lowering the price to P^*, where $MC_A = NMR_B$ and corresponds to the ideal volume X. On the other hand, if the buying profit center (B) is in a monopsonistic position, it will force the selling center (A) to set the price at P_1 and produce a volume OAS_1, where it equates its own $MC_A = P_1$. This results in a maximization of profit for center B, as shown in the area between the NMR_B line and P_1. This profit area is larger than that of a transfer price set at P^*. The total profit of both centers, however, is smaller than the joint profit that can be achieved if both centers set the transfer price at P^*.

THE COOPERATIVE CASE

In this second case, in which the profit center manager is a *cooperator* concerned with maximizing total joint profits; the volume produced will be optimal from the corporate point of view. Total profit will be a maximum

EXHIBIT 1
Transfer Price is Equal to $MC_A = NMR_B$

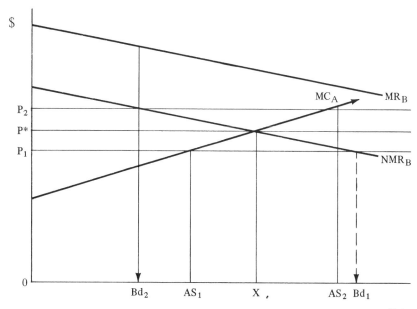

and larger than that under the first case, but the distribution of such profits is not clear-cut (see Exhibit 2 [on the following page]).

If Profit Centers A and B are conceived to maximize their combined profits, the volume of transferred goods is the quantity OX^*, for which $MC_A = NMR_B$, and the ideal price is P^*. However, in such a situation where the buyer is obliged to buy from within, there is no guarantee that the price is going to be P^*, even if they are cooperative. The transfer price, in other words, is indeterminate, i.e., between P_1 and P_2. That is to say, the transfer price can be negotiated somewhere between ANR_B and AC_A (e.g., the average net revenue for Center B and the average cost of Center A for the volume OX^*).

If the transfer price is negotiated at P_1 for the optimal volume OX^*, Center A receives zero profits and Center B receives the total joint profit. If the transfer price is negotiated at P_2, Center A will receive the total joint profit and Center B receives zero. So, operationally, the negotiated transfer price is in a range with P_2 as an upper limit and P_1 as a lower limit, and the actual transfer price somewhere in between. This negotiated transfer price is set after reaching the optimal product volume and not before.

To overcome such a limitation, it is believed that the budget committee should be in a position to receive the necessary information from each profit center, establish the volume which maximizes corporate profit (OX^*), and

EXHIBIT 2
The Paretian Optima Solution

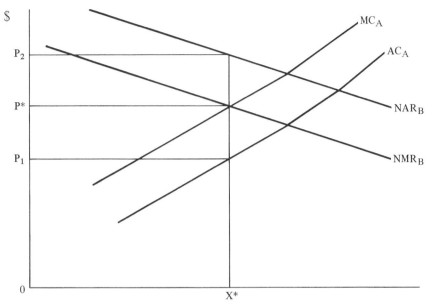

set the price at *P**. The accounting practice of pricing the transfer goods as equal to variable costs, approximating marginal costs, is felt to yield such an optimal volume. However, imposing a transfer price does not guarantee an optimal solution. The reason is that the selling profit center knows the rules of the game and, as a result, it adjusts its level of accuracy in estimating variable costs according to its belief in the accuracy of other centers' estimations. This managerial response is feasible especially when the selling profit center is not given the option to produce another product that is more profitable.

Another weakness in the economic transfer system is its failure to provide incentive for a center manager to reduce his *MC* below the determined level ($MC_A = NMR_B$). Suppose that the transfer price of intermediate goods is \$8.00/unit.[2] If the supplying profit center discovers a new method for producing such goods at \$7.00/unit, should this be the new price for transferred goods according to the $MC_A = NMR_B$? If the answer is yes, there is no motivation or reward for the innovating supplying profit center,

---

[2] Remember that we are assuming, in the entire discussion, no cost interdependence, i.e., MC_A is independent from the MC_B. If the marginal cost of (A) (which is *P**) depends also on the volume of output of the final product (B), through common cost savings, the level of over-all marginal costs of the final product B for the organization is not equal to the sum of MC_A & MC_B. The analysis in such a case will be different.

since the receiving profit center will reap all the profit increment, while the supplying center breaks even. Should the transfer price remain at $8.00/ unit, the receiving profit center will find no incentive to remix its production or increase its output to take advantage of the relatively cheaper input prices. As a solution to this problem, it is suggested, violating the main principle of $MC_A = NMR_B$, that the supplying profit center should charge $8.00/unit for additional units over that budgeted volume. Another solution is that the supplying center will negotiate a lump sum grant or subsidy from the receiving center as a condition for continuous cost reduction and innovation.[3] While this is a deviation from the theoretical principle (e.g., P is determined having $MC = MR$), its purposes are motivationally oriented.

Another operational difficulty stems from the assumption that there are no constraints (physical or monetary) on the resources available for each profit center in producing the volume OX^* that is optimal based on $MC = MR$. This assumption is not realistic, because each profit center has certain constraints, either manpower, capacity, etc. If these constraints are not explicitly dealt with in the system, the theoretical solution is no longer a pragmatic one.

To solve these problems, a new approach to solving the transfer price problem based on an opportunity cost concept is needed. Opportunity cost is used here with cost accounting derived surrogates. This approach takes into consideration in arriving at the optimal solution the physical and financial constraints that exist at divisional levels and at the top corporate level. While the transfer price under this system is determined based on the decomposition principle, the final suggested price is not necessarily equal to it as we will show later. Since we will not discuss the mathematical operational steps of solving a case using the decomposition principle, a bibliography at the end of this article is a representative reference for this purpose. In addition, we will show how this approach, with some motivational factors, can induce a profit center manager to act in the right direction and lessens his reason to manipulate cost estimates. This approach works as follows.

Transfer Price and Opportunity Cost

If Profit Center (A) transfers a part of its goods to Profit Center (B), and there is an outside market price, the transferred goods are priced equal to the market price, which represents the opportunity cost of not selling to outsiders.

If there is no market price, the transferred goods still should be priced equal to the opportunity cost of diverting divisional (A) resources into

[3] Jack Hirshleifer, "On the Economics of Transfer Pricing," *Journal of Business* (July 1956), pp. 172–184.

producing such goods, instead of producing another kind of goods that has an outside market. In developing the framework of this system, two cases will be differentiated.

I. Profit Center (A) transfers product X_1, that has no outside market price, to Profit Center (B). However, Profit Center (A) also produces X_2, which has a known market price.[4]

In this case, the price of the transferred product X_1 is equal to the opportunity cost or the shadow price of resources utilized in its production instead of being used to produce X_2. The following example is written in a linear programming model:

$$\text{Max } \pi = C_1X_1 + C_2X_2 = ?X_1 + 8X_2$$

subject to:

$$\text{Process I} \quad 3X_1 + 6X_2 \leq 60$$
$$\text{Process II} \quad 2X_1 + 4X_2 \leq 40$$
$$X_1, X_2 \geq 0$$

Since the market price of product X_1 is unknown, we will first *a priori* assume that Profit Center A will maximize its profit by producing only X_2. The optimal solution is to produce 10 units of X_2, yielding a contribution margin of $80.00 and shadow price of $W_1 = \frac{8}{10}$ and $W_2 = \frac{8}{10}$. No idle capacity is available.

If Profit Center A is to produce X_1, it will divert a portion of its resources devoted to producing X_2 to produce X_1. For example, to reduce X_2 by 1 unit, it will increase X_1 by 2 units. Such a substitution rate will maintain the total contribution margin ($80.00) at the same level. This means that if Profit Center A is to produce (X_1), it should charge Profit Center B $7.00/unit in order to maintain its profitability intact. The $4.00/unit represents the opportunity cost of profit foregone by not producing X_2, calculated as follows:

$$C_1 = a_{11}W_1 + a_{12}W_2$$
$$= \left(3 \times \frac{8}{10}\right) + \left(2 \times \frac{8}{10}\right)$$
$$= \frac{24}{10} + \frac{16}{10} = \frac{40}{10} = \$4.00$$

Sales price = Variable costs + Contribution margin = 3.00 + 4.00 = $7.00

[4] This is assuming that X_2 has a free competitive market, and that the organization will be able to sell all it produces of X_2. If this assumption is released, the analysis still can be applied, although it gets complicated.

If the preceding example had resulted in idle capacity with the optimal solution, it would create motivational problems that the operating manager of Profit Center A may find difficult to ignore. For example, assume that the preceding example is the same, except for a change of the coefficient a_{22}.

$$\text{Max} = CX_1 + C_2X_2$$
$$?X_1 + 8X_2$$
$$\text{subject to:} \quad 3X_1 + 6X_2 \leq 60$$
$$2X_1 + 3X_2 \leq 40$$
$$X_1, \quad X_2 \geq 0$$

The solution is to produce 10 units of X_2, with a contribution margin of $80.00. However, process II has an idle capacity of 10 hours and, accordingly, $W_2 = 0$. Process I has dual evaluator of $W_1 = 1\frac{1}{3}$. The substitution rate is still 2 units of X_1 for 1 unit of X_2, requiring X_1 to be priced at $7.00/unit. However, if Profit Center A is being asked to completely divert its resources into producing X_1, it will produce 20 units of X_1, yielding the same contribution margin of $80.00. There is no idle capacity in process II, however. The center manager will hardly accept the utilization of all of his center's resources and still receive the same contribution margin. Theoretically, this is explainable on the grounds that the idle capacity of a slack variable is considered cost-free, assuming that such idle capacity cannot be leased, rented, or have its utilization deferred to next year without a reduction in its value. If these conditions are not met, the opportunity cost concept will require that the transfer price of X_1 be more than $7.00/unit to account for such additional profit foregone. If this is not accounted for, the manager of Profit Center A may believe that top corporate policy favors Profit Center B, because it does not reward his profit foregone.

The previous example also raises a crucial problem operationally. The shadow price value of W_1 and W_2 depends on the contribution margin of X_2 per unit and its required [A] coefficients. If the CM is high, the values of the dual evaluators will be high, and vice versa, assuming that the [A]'s are the same. If it happens that X_2 is the most profitable product for Center A, the transfer price for X_1 will be so high that Profit Center B may not be able to pay. The opposite may also be possible, leaving Profit Center A at a disadvantage. While such operational problems have long-run implications for policy planning, in the short-run it is a situation to reckon with! A suggested solution is that the corporate level may use dual pricing for motivating reasons, since its total profit is still optimal because the volume of both centers is determined by the system.

It is not advisable to obtain the optimal solution for Profit Center A first, and then that of Profit Center B.[5] This procedure usually leads to dis-

---

[5] This is due to the fact that Profit Center A acts as a simple maximizer, and, as such, forces Center B to behave in the same way, leading to suboptimization. See the example illustrated above.

economies or a suboptimal solution for the company as a whole. To overcome such a difficulty, a solution for the combined efforts of both centers has to be obtained. If such an optimal solution, company-wise, put Profit Center A at a disadvantage, the system should provide a motivational solution to induce and maintain the divisional manager's motivation in the right direction, or at least minimize the chance of moving in the wrong motivational direction. Motivation costs (the difference between the center's maximization figure and that resulting from the corporate optimal solution) should be credited to Center A's profitability plan. If this is not done, conflict between the division's goal and that of the corporation moves into full gear, especially when the reward system is based on each center's profit. These points are illustrated in the following example:

Profit Center A	*Profit Center B*
Max $C_1 X_1 + C_2 X_2$	$C_3 Y_1 + C_4 Y_2$
$? X_1 + 8 X_2$	$(10 - C_1 X_1) Y_1 + 5 Y_2$

subject to:

$3X_1 + 6X_2 \leq 60$	$4Y_1 + 5Y_2 \leq 28$
$2X_1 + 4X_2 \leq 40$	$3Y_1 + 2Y_2 \leq 14$
$X_1, X_2 \geq 0$	$Y_1, Y_2 \geq 0$

To solve this problem, maximizing profit from a corporate point of view, assume that the variable cost of X_1 is \$3.00/unit, and that one unit of X_1 is needed to produce one unit of Y_1. This makes the net contribution margin of $Y_1 = \$7.00$/unit.

A linear programming model based on decomposition is as follows:[6]

$$
\begin{aligned}
\text{Max } \pi(X, Y) = 0X_1 + 8X_2 + 7X_1 + 5Y_2 & \\
-X_1 \qquad\qquad + Y_1 \qquad\quad & \leq 0 \\
3X_1 + 6X_2 \qquad\qquad\qquad & \leq 60 \\
2X_1 + 4X_2 \qquad\qquad\qquad & \leq 40 \\
4Y_1 + 5Y_2 & \leq 28 \\
3Y_1 + 2Y_2 & \leq 14 \\
X_1 \qquad X_2, \quad Y_1, \quad Y_2 & \geq 0.
\end{aligned}
\right] \text{Master Budget}
$$

The mathematical solution of such a case is illustrated in Exhibit 3, where the feasible plans and optimal one are shown.[7] The slack variables

---

[6] See: George Dantzig and Philip Wolf, "Decomposition Principles for Linear Programming," *Operations Research* (FEBRUARY 1960); and George Dantzig, *Linear Programming and Extensions* (Princeton University Press 1963); Chapters 22–24.

[7] No top corporate constraints are assumed. If any exist, the problem can still be solved, using the decomposition principle. The operating costs of each center are assumed to be independent of the level of activity of the other center and linear. Also, any additional sales of Y's will not reduce the external demand for X_2. These two conditions are called technological independence and demand independence consecutively. However, there is a demand interdependence for Y_1 and X_1; the demand of X_1 is derived from that of Y_1. If the demand for X_2 and Y_2 is interrelated, the problem still can be solved, although it gets complicated.

EXHIBIT 3
Different Operating Profitability Plans

	Plan I			Plan II			Plan III	
Production	Center (A)	Center (B)	Production	Center (A)	Center (B)	Production	Center (A)	Center (B)
Y_2 = 5 units		$25.00	Y_2 = 1 units		$ 5.00	Y_2 = 4		$20.00
Y_1 = 0 units		0	Y_1 = 4 units		28.00	Y_1 = 2		14.00
X_1 = 0 units			X_1 = 4 units	0		X_1 = 2		
X_2 = 10 units	$80.00		X_2 = 8 units	$64.00		X_2 = 9	$72.00	
S_1 = 0 hours			S_1 = 0 hrs.			S_1 = 0		
S_2 = 0 hours			S_2 = 0 hrs.			S_2 = 0		
S_3 = 3 hours			S_3 = 7 hrs.			S_3 = 0		
S_4 = 4 hours			S_4 = 0 hrs.			S_4 = 0		
Divisional Profit	$80.00	$25.00	Divisional Profit	$64.00	$33.00	Divisional Profit	$72.00	$34.00
Corporate Profit	$105.00		Corporate Profit	$97.00		Corporate Profit	$106.00	

(S_1, S_2, S_3, S_4) corresponding to each plan are also shown, indicating any idle capacity in the corresponding process of each profit center.

For the corporation as a whole, plan III is optimal. However, if we look at the solution from the point of view of each profit center, do we reach the same conclusion?

From the Profit Center B's point of view, plan III is optimal. From Profit Center A's point of view, it is not, since plan I is its optimal program. Would the manager of Profit Center A accept plan III, knowing what this means for his incentive compensation at the end of the year? Will the rate of return on his divisional investment reflect a fair measure of his performance if he accepts plan III?

What is the source of the problem and how should it be solved? The problem arises from the fact that the intermediate good X_1 is priced equal to its marginal (variable) costs. No contribution margin is given to Profit Center A, meaning that Profit Center B has captured all the gains yielded from this process itself, without sharing it with Profit Center A. This reflects unfair treatment. Accounting literature argues for the distribution of the joint profit of $7.00/unit of (X_1, Y_1) between both centers, either through bargaining or by means of an equalization rate based on the ratio of production cost in both centers related to (X_1, Y_1). This accounting solution, as seen in this example, leads to suboptimization.[8] If a fair and equitable distribtuion is to be followed, Profit Center A should be given the profit foregone as a result of producing X_1. This means that the operating budget of Center A, if plan III is adopted, should be increased by $8.00 as motivation costs. Profit Center B's additional contribution, as a result of further processing X_1 to Y_1, is $1.00. This is the additional gain the company obtained by encouraging the production of (X_1, Y_1). If the corporate level does not adhere to such an opportunity cost approach, budgetary conflict arises between the profit center managers and the corporate level.

The previous solution in general, however, raises two important implications:

1. If product X_2 is highly profitable, the opportunity cost of producing X_1 is high. If product Y_1, which uses X_1 as input, is not so profitable as to afford paying such opportunity costs, the company as a whole will be better off by not producing Y_1. However, if product Y_1 should be produced in order to meet a contract commitment, or as a result of a policy decision, this decision is a top corporate decision and not a center one. The profit (or loss) consequence of such a decision should be isolated. Center A should not be penalized by a decision not of its own.

---

[8] If Center A charges B a sales price of $8.00/unit of X_1, using the accounting equalization method, Center B finds it in its best interest not to buy X_1 and not to produce Y_1. Center B will produce 5 units of Y_2 and yield CM of $25.00, and Center A will then produce 10 units of X_2 yielding CM of $80.00. The total of $105.00 (equal to plan I) is a suboptimization case.

2. If product X_2 is not highly profitable, the opportunity cost of producing X_1 will be less, and Profit Center B may be in an advantageous position. Profit Center A should not blame Profit Center B for this condition. Profit Center A would be well advised, if the demand for X_2 is decreasing and profitability is declining, to shift its resources to a new product. In the short run, however, Profit Center A should not ask Profit Center B to subsidize its operation and increase its profits.

These two implications do not necessarily require that the top corporate level use motivation costs in profitability planning, as in the case above.

II. *Profit Center A produces both product X_1 and product X_2 for Profit Center B, and there are no market prices for either product.*

In this case, Profit Center A, in reality, is not a profit center. It will function the same if it is treated as a cost center,[9] or is joined with Profit Center B to compose one large profit center. The latter may require a change in the organization's structure, which may be justifiable to minimize the undesirable motivational consequence of a system based on "games" if the price of suboptimization is too high for the company to bear!

Summary

Under the assumption $MC_A = NMR_B$, the supplying profit center is not motivated to change the relative use of various factors of production in response to changes in factor prices, since these favorable effects will pass over to the buying profit center. In addition, the profit center selling the final product will be motivated either to manipulate its sales by delaying them to next year, if this year is especially profitable, or to increase its production inventory level so that a part of its overhead will be capitalized, leading to an increase of its profit if it is originally unfavorable. This will affect the production of intermediate goods. To prevent this, the corporate level watches the inventory level and asks for an explanation if it exceeds a certain level. Another solution is that the buying division commits itself to acquire a certain volume. These methods are partial solutions to the problem.

We have shown that using variable costs, approximating marginal costs, to price transfer goods has several limitations since this approach ignores several strategic factors. Also, we have shown that using the accounting equalization method leads to suboptimization and that any solution to a transfer pricing system cannot ignore the motivational conflict that is pertinent. We have used "motivation costs" to reduce the level of conflict

---

[9] If it is treated as a cost center, it will have a zero marginal contribution which a budgetary system should accept. Its performance can be evaluated in terms of cost control and volume attainment.

due to the transfer pricing system. As a result, arriving at an optimal solution based on oppotrunity costs from the company's point of view, accepted by profit centers, is feasible.

References on the Decomposition Principle

1. A. Charnes, and W. W. Cooper, *Management Models and Industrial Application of Linear Programming,* Vol. I, II (John Wiley & Sons, 1961).
2. G. B. Dantzig, *Linear Programming and Extensions* (1963).
3. —— and P. Wolfe, "The Decomposition Principle for Linear Programs," *Operations Research,* Vol. 8 (1960), pp. 101–111.
4. Warren E. Walker, "A Method for Obtaining the Optimal Dual Solution to a Linear Program Using the Dantzig-Wolfe Decomposition," *Operations Research* (March-April 1969), pp. 368–370.
5. Adi Ben-Israel and Philip D. Roberts, "A Decomposition Method for Interval Linear Programing," *Management Science* (January 1970), pp. 374–387.
6. David P. Rutenberg, "Generalized Networks, Generalized Upper Bounding and Decomposition for the Convex Simplex Method," *Management Science* (January 1970), pp. 338–401.
7. William J. Baumol and Tibor Fabin, "Decomposition Pricing for Decentralization and External Economics," *Management Science* (September 1964), pp. 1–32.
8. Jerome E. Hass, "Transfer Pricing in a Decentralized Firm," *Management Science* (February 1968), pp. 310–331.
9. C. S. Colantoni, R. P. Manes and A. Whinston, "Programming, Profit Rates and Pricing Decisions," *The Accounting Review* (July 1969), pp. 467–481.
10. Andrew Whinston, "Pricing Guides in Decentralized Organization," *New Perspective in Organizational Research,* edited by W. W. Cooper, et al., (John Wiley and Sons, 1964), pp. 405–448.
11. Edwin V. W. Zschau, *A Primal Decomposition Algorithm for Linear Programming,* Ph.D. Thesis (Graduate School of Business, Stanford University, December 1966).

Supplemental Readings to Part Seven

Lloyd Amey, "On Opportunity Costs and Decision Making," *Accountancy,* Vol. LXXIX (July, 1968), pp. 442–451.
Opportunity costs are explained in light of the types of decisions for which they are relevant.

Jacob G. Birnberg, Louis R. Pondy, and C. Lee Davis, "Effect of Three Voting Rules on Resource Allocation Decisions," *Management Science,* Vol. 16, No. 6 (February, 1970), pp. B-356–B-372.
The effect of the voting rule adopted by a capital budgeting committee on the allocation of resources among divisions is discussed.

James Bulloch and Richard M. Duvall, "Adjusting Rate of Return and Present Value for Price-Level Changes," *The Accounting Review,* Vol. XL, No. 3 (July, 1965), pp. 569–573.
Modifications in rate of return and present value calculations which must be made to account for price-level changes are presented.

David E. Cook, "Inter-Unit Pricing and Your New Pricing Expert: The IRS," *Management Accounting,* Vol. 51, No. 2 (August, 1969), pp. 9–11.
Regulations set up by the Internal Revenue Service regarding transfer prices are reviewed.

Doris M. Cook, "The Effect of Frequency of Feedback on Attitudes and Performance," *Journal of Accounting Research,* Vol. 5, Supplement (1967), pp. 213–224.
The results of an experiment relating feedback and performance are reported.

Joel Dean, "An Approach to Internal Profit Measurement," *NAA Bulletin,* Vol. XXXIX, No. 7 (March, 1958), pp. 5–12.
Internal profit measurement has different objectives than external profit reporting, so the same measurement methods should not be used. Divisional managers require specific performance criteria, but measurement of results should not prejudge evaluation.

John Dearden, "The Case Against ROI Control," *Harvard Business Review,* Vol. 47, No. 3 (May–June, 1969), pp. 124–135.
The reasons that Return on Investment creates conflict and is of limited use in evaluating division performance are explored.

John Dearden and Bruce D. Henderson, "New System for Divisional Control," *Harvard Business Review,* Vol. 44, No. 5 (September–October, 1966), pp. 144–160.

An evaluation system based on contribution and managed-cost budgets is advocated.

Don T. DeCoster, Victor Powers, and George I. Prater, "Accounting Information and Capacity Utilization," *Cost and Management,* Vol. 42, No. 10 (November, 1968), pp. 10–16.
  Failures of traditional accounting approaches to the measurement of plant capacity are illustrated, and an effective approach is suggested.

Joel S. Demski, "Decision — Performance Control," *The Accounting Review,* Vol. XLIV, No. 4 (October, 1969), pp. 669–679.
  A broader view of the decision process, including the interaction between planning and control, is described.

Shawki M. Farag, "A Planning Model for the Divisionalized Enterprise," *The Accounting Review,* Vol. XLIII, No. 2 (April, 1968), pp. 312–320.
  A micro input-output model which can be used for planning the activities of divisionalized enterprises is constructed.

Gerald A. Feltham, "Some Quantitative Approaches to Planning for Multiproduct Production Systems," *The Accounting Review,* Vol. XLV, No. 1 (January, 1970), pp. 11–26.
  A way to use linear algebra and linear programming in planning, estimation, and normative prediction in a multiproduct system is illustrated.

Frederick D. Finney, "Pricing Interdivisional Transfers," *Management Accounting,* Vol. 48, No. 3 (November, 1966), pp. 10–18.
  Pricing transfers of raw materials, goods-in-process, and finished goods in an inter-plant setting is discussed at length.

John Friedman, "A Conceptual Model for the Analysis of Planning Behavior," *Administrative Science Quarterly,* Vol. 12, No. 2 (September, 1967), pp. 225–252.
  A model for the analysis of the planning process itself is presented.

William L. Furlong and Leon H. Robertson, "Matching Management Decisions and Results," *Management Accounting,* Vol. 49, No. 12 (August, 1968), pp. 3–10.
  Management's current performance should be judged by its ability to maintain the proper level of "domino" costs.

Trevor E. Gambling, "A Technological Model for Use in Input-Output Analysis and Cost Accounting," *Management Accounting,* Vol. 50, No. 4 (December, 1968), pp. 33–38.
  Accounting aspects of technological models are considered.

Billy E. Goetz, "Transfer Prices: An Exercise in Relevancy and Goal Congruence," *The Accounting Review,* Vol. XLII, No. 3 (July, 1967), pp. 435–440.
  Using incremental costs as transfer prices is the unique way to achieve congruence of goals.

W. M. Harper, "Managerial Economic Control-III: The Concept of Control Profit," *Accountancy,* Vol. LXXIX (June, 1968), pp. 415–417.
  Control profit and its use to evaluate results is explained.

Jerome E. Hass, "Transfer Pricing in a Decentralized Firm," *Management Science,* Vol. 14, No. 6 (February, 1968), pp. B-310–B-331.

A transfer pricing concept is applied via a decomposition algorithm for quadratic programming.

Yuji Ijiri, "An Application of Input-Output Analysis to Some Problems in Cost Accounting," *Management Accounting,* Vol. 49, No. 8 (April, 1968), pp. 49–61.

Useful data can be derived when input-output analysis is applied to cost data.

David H. Li, "Interdivisional Transfer Planning," *Management Accounting,* Vol. 46, No. 10 (June, 1965), pp. 51–54.

Discussing transfer prices without knowing the number of units transferred usually yields undesirable results.

Thomas A. Mahoney and William Weitzel, "Managerial Models of Organizational Effectiveness," *Administrative Science Quarterly,* Vol. 14, No. 3 (September, 1969), pp. 357–364.

Differences between research and development and general business models of organizational effectiveness are discussed.

Walter F. O'Connor, "Intercompany Pricing In Foreign Operations," *Management Controls,* Vol. 13, No. 7 (July, 1966), pp. 144–149.

Transfer pricing policies of a domestic corporation and a foreign subsidiary are discussed.

A.G. Piper, "Internal Trading," *Accountancy* (October, 1969), pp. 733–736.

Results of a survey to discover the basis used for pricing transfers between the operating units of an organization are reported.

Alfred Rappaport, "A Capital Budgeting Approach to Divisional Planning and Control," *Financial Executive,* Vol. 36, No. 10 (October, 1968), pp. 47–63.

The suggestion is made that "discounted cash flow" is the most reasonable measure of capital productivity, and that a "time-adjusted rate of return" should be determined for a division's long-range cash forecast, to replace return on investment as a measure of performance.

Fred H. Ruff, "Planning for Profit," *Financial Executive,* Vol. 37, No. 7 (July, 1969), pp. 31–50.

If the goal of an enterprise is to "maximize profits", contribution reporting and direct costing provide the way to achieve this goal by planning for profits.

R. C. Skinner, "Return on Capital Employed as a Measure of Efficiency," *Accountancy,* Vol. LXXVI (June, 1965), pp. 530–533.

Return on capital is defined and used as a measure of performance.

Henri Theil, "How to Worry About Increased Expenditures," *The Accounting Review,* Vol. XLIV, No. 1 (January, 1969), pp. 27–37.

Ways to analyze differences between budgeted performance and actual performance using information theoretic concepts are explored.

R. F. Tuckett, "Combined Cost and Linear Programming Models of Industrial Complexes," *Operational Research Quarterly,* Vol. 20, No. 2 (June, 1969), pp. 223–236.

This paper proposes a general combined cost/LP model usable either for costing or planning.

Herbert J. Weiser, "The Impact of Accounting Controls on Performance Motivation," *The New York C.P.A.*, Vol. 38, No. 3 (March, 1968), pp. 191–201.

In establishing accounting controls, one should consider their significance as stimulants of motivational efforts as well as devices for evaluation.

James T. Wormley, "Ensuring the Profit Contribution of a Corporate Data Processing Department," *Management Accounting*, Vol. 48, No. 5 (January, 1967), pp. 3–12.

Transfer pricing policies which can be used by an EDP department are explored.

Additional

Bibliography

to Part Seven

Charles B. Allen, "Distribution of National and Divisional Overheads," *NA(C)A Bulletin*, Vol. XXXVIII, No. 10 (June, 1957), pp. 1237–1249.

———, "Price Analysis for Recommendations to Management," *NAA Bulletin*, Vol. XLI, No. 11 (July, 1960), pp. 71–80.

Robert G. Allyn, "Some Economic and Accounting Observations on the Utility of Costs for Pricing," *NAA Bulletin*, Vol. XL, No. 11 (July, 1959), pp. 5–10.

Dermot Barrett, "Centralization and Decentralization," *The Canadian Chartered Accountant*, Vol. 78, No. 5 (May, 1961), pp. 445–450.

Harold Bierman, Jr., "Pricing Intracompany Transfer," *The Accounting Review*, Vol. XXXIV, No. 3 (July, 1959), pp. 429–432.

Robert W. Boyd, "Transfer Prices and Profitability Measurement," *The Controller*, Vol. XXIX, No. 2 (February, 1961), pp. 88–89.

Paul W. Cook, "New Techniques for Intracompany Pricing," *Harvard Business Review*, Vol. 35, No. 4 (July–August, 1957), pp. 74–80.

Joel Dean, "Cost Forecasting and Price Policy," *Journal of Marketing*, Vol. 13, No. 3 (January, 1949), pp. 279–288.

———, "Decentralization and Intra-Company Pricing," *Harvard Business Review*, Vol. 33, No. 4 (July–August, 1955), pp. 65–74.

———, "Profit Performance Measurement of Division Managers," *The Controller*, Vol. XXXV, No. 9 (September, 1957), p. 423 ff.

John Dearden, "Interdivisional Pricing," *Harvard Business Review*, Vol. XXXVIII, No. 1 (January–February, 1960), pp. 117–125.

———, "Problem in Decentralized Profit Responsibility," *Harvard Business Review*, Vol. XXXVIII, No. 3 (May–June, 1960), pp. 79–86.

Nicholas Dopuch and David F. Drake, "Accounting Implications of a Mathematical Programming Approach to the Transfer Price Problem," *Journal of Accounting Research*, Vol. 2, No. 1 (Spring, 1964), pp. 10–24.

Wilford J. Eiteman, "Price Determination — Business Practice vs. Economic Theory," *Michigan Business Report* No. 16, 1949.

I. Wayne Keller, "Pricing for Return on Capital Employed," *NAA Bulletin*, Vol. XXXVIII, No. 5 (January, 1957), pp. 635–646.

S. Laimon, "Cost Analysis and Pricing Policies," *Cost and Management*, Vol. XXXV, No. 8 (September, 1961), pp. 360–375.

E. A. G. Robinson, "The Pricing of Manufactured Products," *The Economic Journal*, Vol. 60, No. 240 (December, 1950), pp. 771–780.

Lester J. Schneider, "Calculating Price Determining Factors — A Procedure," *NAA Bulletin*, Vol. XLIII, No. 4 (December, 1961), pp. 83–88.

Gordon Shillinglaw, "Divisionalization, Decentralization — And Return on Investment," *NAA Bulletin*, Vol. XLI, No. 4 (December, 1959), pp. 19–33.

Gordon Shillinglaw, "Problems in Divisional Profit Measurement," *NAA Bulletin*, Vol. XLII, No. 7 (March, 1961), pp. 33–43.

Herbert A. Simon, "Organizing for Controllership: Centralization and Decentralization," *The Controller*, Vol. XXIII, No. 1 (January, 1955), pp. 11–13.

Raymond Villers, "Control and Freedom in a Decentralized Company," *Harvard Business Review*, Vol. 32, No. 2 (March–April, 1954), pp. 89–96.